Computerized Accounting with
QuickBooks® Online
2021 Update

GAYLE WILLIAMS
Sacramento City College

JENNIFER JOHNSON
The University of Texas at Dallas

Cambridge
BUSINESS PUBLISHERS

To my son, Marcus, who has inspired me and encouraged me and remains my biggest fan.
—Gayle Williams

To my husband, Brad, who helps me stay balanced.
—Jennifer Johnson

Cambridge Business Publishers

COMPUTERIZED ACCOUNTING WITH QUICKBOOKS ONLINE 2021 Update, by Gayle Williams and Jennifer Johnson

ISBN 978-1-61853-430-9

Bookstores & Faculty: to order this book, contact the company via email customerservice@cambridgepub.com or call 800-619-6473.

Students: to order this book, please visit the book's website and order directly online.

Printed in the United States of America.
10 9 8 7 6 5 4 3 2 1

About the Authors

Gayle Williams is an Adjunct Professor of Accounting at Sacramento City College, where she teaches financial accounting courses. She received a BA in Comparative Literature and an MBA with a concentration in Accounting from the University of Washington. Professor Williams is licensed as a CPA in Washington and California and has worked in public accounting, with Voldal Wartelle & Co, P.S and Moss Adams LLP, and in private industry.

Jennifer Johnson is a Senior Lecturer at the University of Texas at Dallas where she teaches accounting information systems courses and related software courses, cost accounting, and seminars in Excel. She is a CPA licensed in the state of Texas. In 2017 she was named as an Outstanding Accounting Educator by the Texas Society of CPAs. Prior to joining UT Dallas in 2009, Professor Johnson spent time in both public accounting and industry as an auditor with PwC, an Assistant Controller at a regional financial services firm, and a Finance Manager at Dr Pepper Snapple Group. Professor Johnson holds both a BBA and MS in Accounting from Texas A&M University. Jennifer is a Certified QuickBooks User and is on the Board of Directors for the Dallas CPA Society and the Texas Society of CPAs. Professor Johnson has a passion for using systems and accounting to communicate the language of business.

Preface

Welcome to *Computerized Accounting with QuickBooks Online*. We wrote this book to give students an introduction to QuickBooks Online that focuses not only on the software mechanics, but also on the basic accounting concepts that underlie all accounting systems.

This book is not meant to be a user manual. It is our intention that students will come away from this book with an understanding that it is their knowledge of the principles of accounting, not their data-entry skills, that is needed to be successful in business.

TARGET AUDIENCE

This book is primarily intended for use in undergraduate accounting programs, although it could be used in business or computer information programs as well. It is expected that students taking this course have already successfully completed a course in financial accounting and have a firm understanding of the basic principles of accounting.

ACCESS TO QUICKBOOKS ONLINE PLUS

Intuit, the developer of QuickBooks Online Plus, provides students with a free one-year software subscription. Students should refer to the insert at the front of the book, which contains instructions on obtaining their software license and accessing the complimentary cloud-based software. With QuickBooks Online, students use their Internet browser to use the software—no installation required—and it can be used on any device with Internet access. Browsers supported by Intuit are: Google Chrome, Mozilla Firefox, Microsoft Edge, and Safari 11 or newer. (A high-speed Internet connection is recommended, such as DSL or cable modem. For more information go to https://quickbooks.intuit.com/learn-support/en-us/install-or-update-products/system-requirements-for-quickbooks-online-accountant-and/00/188943.)

NEW TO THIS EDITION

- Section Six—Cognitive Technologies, Data Analysis, and QBO—has been revised and updated. The section now includes a chapter on big data, artificial intelligence, and cognitive technologies and one on data analysis and visualization.
- A new appendix, Keyboard Shortcuts in QBO, has been added to Chapter 1.
- A new appendix, FIFO Layers in QBO, has been added to Chapter 7.
- Math Revealed! and Salish Software Solutions homework companies have both been updated with new transaction dates. Math Revealed! has also been updated with new transaction amounts.
- Chapter road maps of tasks and transactions are now available to instructors.
- The book has been updated for changes to QBO software.

OUTSTANDING FEATURES OF THIS BOOK

Structure

The book is designed in such a way that the accounting concepts, as well as the software mechanics, get more complex with each section. Other books focus primarily on software data entry. This book allows the students to see why events are recorded the way they are in a computerized accounting system while refreshing students' knowledge of accounting concepts and reinforcing the accounting and journal entries behind transactions.

- *Section One—Introduction*
  - Chapter 1 introduces students to the basic structure of QuickBooks Online Plus (QBO).
  - Chapter 2 discusses the process of creating company files in QBO.

- *Section Two—Service Companies*
  - The section introduction includes suggestions for finding errors in QBO.
  - Chapters 3, 4, and 5 cover basic transactions in the sales, purchase, and end-of-month cycles of a service company.

- *Section Three—Merchandising Companies*
  - The section introduction includes a description of internal controls in QBO.
  - Chapters 6, 7, and 8 cover more advanced transactions including those found in the sales, purchase, and end-of-month cycles of a merchandising company.

- *Section Four—Beyond the Basics*
  - Chapter 9 covers budgeting, segment reporting, and automated entries.
  - Chapter 10 covers tracking and billing for time and expenses.
  - Chapter 11 covers a number of special tools in QBO such as saving customized reports, customizing forms, managing attachments, exporting to Excel, and uploading receipts.

- *Section Five—Paying Employees*
  - Chapter 12 covers basic payroll functions.

- *Section Six—Cognitive Technologies, Data Analysis, and QBO*
  - Chapter 13 covers big data, artificial intelligence, cognitive technologies, and QBO.
  - Chapter 14 covers data analysis and data visualization.

Clear Writing

The book is written clearly to aid student understanding of difficult concepts. Clear explanations of why certain procedures are used in QBO are supported by relevant examples and relatable end-of-chapter assignments, serving to bridge the gap between computerized accounting concepts and real-world application.

Real-World Scenarios

Most computerized accounting textbooks on the market approach the teaching of Quick-Books in a prescriptive manner, going through the procedures of the software while overlooking how an accountant would actually utilize the software in the real world. The book takes a practical approach and shows the student how the software is used in a business environment. In addition to the standard financial reports, students are exposed to job, segment, and variance reports.

Unique Pedagogy

The book's four-color format facilitates student understanding and draws attention to the key concepts and pedagogy. Ample screenshots provide students realistic snapshots of what they will see when working in the software. A host of pedagogical elements serve as helpful illustrations, providing additional context and further concept reinforcement.

HINT Boxes

HINT boxes appear throughout to provide helpful quick tips and tricks for working more efficiently in QBO.

 HINT: For access to the full list of customers when you're in a specific customer record, click the three parallel lines to the left of the customer name (top left corner in Figure 3.14). A sidebar will open. This can be a handy feature when a user is making changes to multiple customer records. New customers can also be added on the sidebar.

WARNING Boxes

WARNING boxes highlight common technical pitfalls to avoid.

 WARNING: Do not select **Finish Now** in the dropdown menu if you haven't finished the reconciliation (the **difference** isn't zero). QBO will give you a warning if you try but if you persist, it will allow you to "reconcile" without actually reconciling. That would leave what my former accounting professors would call a "dangling" credit or debit. Of course QBO won't actually allow you to create an unbalanced transaction so it will either debit (or credit) an account called **Reconciliation Discrepancies** for the **Difference** amount. You'd then have to fix that later.

BEHIND THE SCENES Boxes

BEHIND THE SCENES boxes provide additional context in support of the accounting that is going on inside the computer.

 BEHIND THE SCENES QuickBooks Online uses the original check date to record a voided check. This can create problems if financial reports have already been distributed for that accounting period. For example, let's say a $100 check was written in December to pay for some travel expenses. In the December income statement, net income would, of course, be decreased by the $100 travel expense. Now let's say that the $100 check was lost so a new check was issued and the original check was voided in QBO in February. The replacement check would have a February date but the original check would be voided by QBO as of the original December check date. If you then prepared a new December income statement, net income would automatically be $100 higher than it was before due to the voided check. On the other hand, February's net income would be reduced by the $100 December travel expense. The expense is now reported in the wrong accounting period. If the amounts are significant or if tax reports have already been filed, journal entries should be made to correct the balances.

QuickChecks

When students are learning accounting application software, it's natural for them to focus on the software mechanics and forget that they're taking an accounting course. To help put some of their focus back on accounting, students are periodically asked a question related to material covered in the chapter. The questions are intended to remind them, either directly or indirectly, of underlying accounting concepts. The answers are included at the end of each chapter.

Why aren't purchase orders and estimates accounting transactions? (Answer at end of chapter.)	**Quick**Check **1-2**

Key Terms

Appearing in red, bold font in the first instance, key terms are defined for the student in the margins of the text for a quick refresher. A comprehensive glossary is included in the back of the book.

Bad debt expense The expense stemming from the inability of a business to collect an amount previously recorded as receivable. It is normally classified as a selling or administrative expense.

Allowance method An accounting procedure whereby the amount of bad debts expense is estimated and recorded in the period in which the related credit sales occur.

Recording Uncollectible Accounts

Unfortunately, companies don't always collect the balances owed to them by their customers. Merchandisers will often try to get the product back when the customer defaults but, depending on the type and value of the products sold, that may not be feasible or even possible.

If the company has exhausted all reasonable collection methods, the invoice must be written off. Deleting or voiding the invoice in QBO would not be good accounting. The company did make the sale and should show the revenue. They should also report that uncollectible sales (recorded as **bad debt expenses**) are a real cost of selling on credit.

There are two methods for accounting for uncollectible accounts: the **allowance method** and the **direct write-off method**. Only the allowance method is acceptable under generally accepted accounting principles.

Allowance Method Refresher

Under the allowance method, an estimate of the amount of uncollectible receivables is

Practice Exercises

Practice Exercises are included at the end of sections in the first eleven chapters. The exercises provide students an immediate opportunity to practice the material they just learned and prepare them for completing the chapter assignments. The exercises use the QBO test drive company, a fictional company called Craig's Landscaping and Design set up by Intuit.

The Practice Exercises can be done in class, with the instructor, or can be done by the students, on their own, as part of the lab component of a face-to-face course or in online courses. Check figures are included with the exercises to reassure students that they are recording the transactions accurately.

Set up a new credit term for Craig's Design and Landscaping. (Craig's is considering offering an early payment discount to some of its customers.) 1. Click the ⚙ on the icon bar. 2. Click **All Lists** in the **LISTS** column. 3. Click **Terms**. 4. Click **New**. 5. Enter "Net 45" as the **Name**. 6. Click **due in fixed number of days** and enter "45" in the **days** field. 7. Click **Save**. 8. Click **Dashboard**.	**PRACTICE** EXERCISE 3.4

End-of-Chapter Material

End-of-chapter review material includes:

- Chapter shortcuts.
- Chapter review with **matching of terms** to definitions and **multiple choice questions** related to chapter content.
- Essay questions focused on issues faced by accounting and information systems managers, related to chapter content.
- A choice of two end-of-chapter assignments featuring fictional companies that move from selling services exclusively in the early chapters to selling both services and products in the later chapters.

The assignments include transaction and end-of-assignment check numbers for students. This allows them to focus on the process and reduces student frustration.

Appendices

There are a number of additional topics that are helpful to students as they master QBO, and these have been included as end-of-chapter and end-of-book appendices. Instructors may wish to cover these topics in class or have students go over them on their own time. End-of-chapter appendices on special topics include:

Appendix	Title	Description
Appendix 1A	Keyboard Shortcuts in QBO	Provides a list of keyboard shortcuts available in QBO
Appendix 2A	Setting Up a Google Gmail Account	Instructions for opening a separate Gmail account used in registering the student's company file
Appendix 4A	Reporting 1099 Vendor Activity	Covers 1099 setup and reporting tools available in QBO
Appendix 5A	Getting It Right	Suggestions to help students find errors in the month-end financial statements, mirroring what accountants in industry might look at before publishing financial statements
Appendix 5B	Understanding the Reconciliation Report	Provides a review of temporary and permanent differences and covers the sections in QBO's reconciliation report
Appendix 5C	Fixing Reconciliation Errors	Includes instructions for manually "undoing" a reconciliation
Appendix 7A	FIFO Layers in QBO	Covers FIFO valuation of inventory in QBO
Appendix 8A	Direct Downloading of Bank Transactions into QBO and Setting Bank Rules	Covers QBO features allowing the download of banking and credit card activity
Appendix 9A	Creating and Managing Tags	Covers new QBO transaction "tagging" feature
Appendix 10A	Working With Estimates	Covers creating and managing customer estimates

Students often have a difficult time seeing any similarities between computerized accounting systems and the more manual systems they saw in their introductory financial accounting classes (the journal entries, T-accounts, and general ledgers). To help students connect the two, **Appendix A (Is Computerized Accounting Really the Same as Manual Accounting?)** is an accounting refresher that compares manual and computerized accounting and provides examples of how journal entries, journals, T-accounts, and trial balances show up in QBO. It also covers cash versus accrual accounting.

Appendix	Title	Description
Appendix A	Is Computerized Accounting Really the Same as Manual Accounting?	Comparison of manual and computerized accounting
Appendix B	Account Types and Common Transaction Types Used in QBO	A summary of account types and transaction types in QuickBooks Online
Appendix C	Common Options Available on Various Forms	Common options available on various toolbars in QuickBooks Online

Certiport-Mapped

The book has been mapped to the 10 domains that comprise the exam objectives for the QuickBooks Certified User Exam. A map correlating the chapter content to the Certiport domains is available to students on the book's website so they can streamline their exam preparation. A practice exam question bank is included in myBusinessCourse.

What Is the QuickBooks Certified User Exam?

The Intuit® QuickBooks Certification exam is an online exam that is proctored at Certiport Authorized Testing Centers. The certification program validates QuickBooks accounting skills while providing students with credentials that demonstrate real-world abilities to prospective employers. Once passed, test takers receive an official digital certificate representing their skills in QuickBooks.

TECHNOLOGY THAT IMPROVES LEARNING AND COMPLEMENTS FACULTY INSTRUCTION

BusinessCourse is an online learning and assessment program intended to complement textbook and faculty instruction. Access to **myBusinessCourse** (MBC) is included with the purchase of a new textbook and can also be purchased separately.

MBC is ideal for faculty seeking opportunities to augment their course with an online component. MBC is also a turnkey solution for online courses. Following are some of the features of MBC.

Increase Student Readiness

- **Auto-graded question banks** comprised of practice exercises and assignment questions related to the end-of-chapter content provide immediate feedback to students. Assignments available in MBC are denoted by the (MBC).

- **Test Bank** questions can be incorporated into your assignments for additional quizzing and tests.

- **Instructor gradebook** with immediate grade results

- **eLecture videos** created and narrated by the author provide extra coverage of essential topics and procedures (see the *For Students* section below for the full list of videos). eLecture videos available in MBC are denoted by the ◉.

95% of students who used MBC, responded that MBC helped them learn accounting.*

Make Instruction Needs-Based

- Identify where your students are struggling and customize your instruction to address their needs.

---

* These statistics are based on the results of two surveys in which 2,330 students participated.

- Gauge how your entire class or individual students are performing by viewing the easy-to-use gradebook.
- Ensure your students are getting the additional reinforcement and direction they need between class meetings.

Provide Instruction and Practice 24/7

- Assign homework from your textbook and have MBC grade it for you automatically. Assignments with the MBC logo in the margin are available in my BusinessCourse.
- With the author-created eLecture videos, your students can revisit accounting topics as often as they like or until they master the topic. Topics with the logo next to it in the margin are available as an eLecture video in myBusinessCourse.
- Offer students multiple homework attempts giving them valuable practice finding and fixing accounting errors.

86% of students said they would encourage their professor to continue using MBC in future terms.*

Integrate with LMS

myBusinessCourse integrates with many learning management systems, including **Canvas**, **Blackboard**, **Moodle**, **D2L**, **Schoology**, and **Sakai**. Your gradebooks sync automatically.

Supplement Package

For Instructors

- **Solutions Manual** files prepared by the authors contain solutions to all the assignment material.
- **PowerPoint** presentations illustrate chapter concepts and outline key elements with corresponding screenshots for each chapter.
- **Test Bank** questions written by the authors include true/false, dropdown selection, drag and drop, matching, and multiple-choice questions for each chapter.
- **Chapter Outlines** with student and instructor versions. Teaching notes included on instructor version.
- **Extra credit** project suggestions including solutions. One business memo project, one "find and fix" project, and two financial analysis projects (one for each homework company).
- A **Midterm** and **Final Exam** are provided with solution files. The exams are designed to test students' understanding of the fundamentals of accounting and the mechanics of QBO. The exams can be completed in a two-hour class session using the test drive company available in QBO.
- myBusinessCourse: An online learning and assessment program intended to complement your textbook and classroom instruction (see previous section for more details). Access to myBusinessCourse is included with the purchase of a new textbook and can also be purchased separately. Detailed diagnostic tools assess class and individual performance. myBusinessCourse is ideal for online courses or traditional face-to-face courses for which you want to offer students more resources to succeed.
- **Website:** All instructor materials are accessible via the book's website (password protected) along with other useful links and marketing information. www.cambridgepub.com.

---

* These statistics are based on the results of two surveys in which 2,330 students participated.

For Students

- Access to QuickBooks Online software with purchase of each new copy of the book.
- myBusinessCourse: An online learning and assessment program intended to complement your textbook and faculty instruction (see previous section for more details). This easy-to-use program grades assignments automatically and provides you with additional help when your instructor is not available. Access is included with new copies of this textbook (look for the page containing the access code towards the front of the book).
- **Over 55 eLecture Presentations** created and narrated by the authors and available in myBusinessCourse cover essential topics and procedures in QuickBooks Online. Look for the ⬛ logo in the margins.

  - Moving around in QuickBooks Online
  - Adding, Editing, and Deleting Accounts
  - Customizing QBO (multiple)
  - Setting Up Company Files
  - Setting Up Customers
  - Recording Sales Transactions (multiple)
  - Managing Sales Taxes
  - Managing Vendors
  - Recording Purchase Transactions (multiple)
  - Managing Employees
  - Recording Payroll Transactions
  - Tracking and Billing for Time in QBO (multiple)
  - Managing Product and Service Items (multiple)
  - Reconciling Bank and Credit Card Accounts (multiple)
  - Making Adjusting Journal Entries
  - Setting up Recurring Transactions
  - Customizing Reports
  - Segment tracking
  - Setting Up Budgets
  - Creating Custom Forms
  - Hints for Finding Errors (multiple)

- **Check Figures** are included for assignments, allowing students to focus on the process and reduce frustration.
- **Website:** Student supplements and instructor supplements can be accessed from the book's website.

ACKNOWLEDGMENTS

We would like to thank the following people for their assistance and support.

Thank you also to the following computer accounting faculty from across the country who provided review feedback on the book:

Sara Adams, *Southern Oregon University*

Dave Alldredge, *Salt Lake Community College*

Rick Andrews, *Sinclair Community College*

Ulises Arcos-Castrejon, *North Shore Community College*

Felicia Baldwin, *Richard J. Daley College*

Patricia Ball, *Massasoit Community College*

Sara Barritt, *Northeast Community College*

Erik Bell, *Los Positas College*

Brenda Bindschatel, *Green River Community College*

James Bird, *Ohio State University*

Sean Bliley, *Edinboro University of Pennsylvania*

Bryan Bouchard, *Southern New Hampshire University*

Lisa Briggs, *Columbus State Community College*

Marilyn Brooks-Lewis, *Warren County Community College*

Regina Butts, *Fort Valley State University*

Karlencia Calvin, *Baton Rouge Community College*

Amy Cesario, *Point Park University*

Amy Chataginer, *Mississippi Gulf Coast Community College*

Jay Chittal, *College of Lake County*

Russell Ciokiewicz, *Brenau University*

Howard Clampman, *Bronx Community College*

Jay Cohen, *Oakton Community College*

Renee Crawford, *Saint Anselm College*

Dana Cummings, *Lower Columbia College*

Patricia Davis, *Keystone College*

Susan Davis, *Green River College*

Wanda DeLeo, *College of Coastal Georgia*

Suryakant Desai, *Cedar Valley College*

Anne Diamond, *Sierra College*

Donna Dixon, *Grossmont College*

Doris Donovan, *Dodge City Community College*

Carol Dutchover, *Eastern New Mexico University, Roswell*

Pennie Eddy, *Lanier Technical College*

Jen Emerson, *Cincinnati State*

Keith Engler, *Richland College*

Rena Galloway, *State Fair Community College*

Marianina Godinho, *Cosumnes River College*

Patricia Goedl, *University of Cincinnati*

Victoria Hall, *University of Indianapolis*

James Halstead, *Neosho County Community College*

Becky Hancock, *El Paso Community College*

Merrily Hoffman, *San Jacinto College*

Janet Hosmer, *Blue Ridge Community College*

Nancy Howard, *Mt. Hood Community College*

Paul Jaijairam, *Bronx Community College*

Yan Jin, *Dominican University California*

Bill Jefferson, *Metropolitan Community College*

Ked Kederian, *Azusa Pacific University*

Ethan Kinory, *Rutgers The State University of New Jersey, Camden*

Angela Kirkendall, *South Puget Sound Community College*

Becky Knickel, *Brookhaven College*

Harold Krul, *Baker College*

Christopher Kwak, *De Anza College*

Amber Lamadrid, *Mt. Hood Community College*

Mark Law, *Bloomsburg University*

Theresa Laws-Dahl, *Madison College*

Miriam Lefkowitz, *Brooklyn College*

Heather Lynch, *Northeast Iowa Community College*

DeAnna Martin, *Santiago Canyon College*

Kristy McAuliffe, *San Jacinto College*

Molly McFadden-May, *Tulsa Community College*

Paul McLester, *Florida State College at Jacksonville*

Allen Montgomery, *Bridge Valley Community & Technical College*

Sheila Muller, *Northern Essex Community College*

Carolyn Nelson, *Coffeyville Community College*

Brian Newman, *Macomb Community College*

Joseph Nicassio, *Westmoreland Community College*

Jeffrey Niccum, *Spokane Falls Community College*

Lisa Novak, *Mott Community College*

Joanne Orabone, *Community College of Rhode Island*

Denice Pardee, *Arapahoe Community College*

Paige Paulsen, *Salt Lake Community College*

Margaret Pond, *Front Range Community College*

Mark Quinlan, *Madison College*

Kristen Quinn, *Northern Essex Community College*

Michelle Randall, *Schoolcraft College*

Arwyna Randall-Gay, *Vernon College*

Napoleon Raymundo, *Citrus College*

Robin Reilly, *American River College*

Steven Rice, *Northwestern Michigan College*

Cecile Roberti, *Community College of Rhode Island*

Jennifer Robinson, *Trident Technical College*

Stephanie Anne Rowe, *Sacramento City College*

Dasha Russell, *Missouri State University West Plains*

Joanne Salas, *Olympic College*

Perry Sellers, *Lone Star College*

Sherrie Slom, *Hillsborough Community College*

Dave Sobotka, *Monterey Peninsula College*

Kortney Song, *Estrella Mountain Community College*

Stephanie Swaim, *North Lake College*

Jay Thibodeaux, *Austin Community College*

Christine VanNamee, *Mohawk Valley Community College*

Vasseliki Vervilos, *American River College*

Lori Yecoshenko, *Lake Superior College*

Melissa Youngman, *National Technical Institute for the Deaf*

Additionally, we would like to thank the following student who provided feedback on the text:

Qianchang Liang, *Sacramento City College*

We would also like to thank George Werthman, Jocelyn Mousel, Marnee Fieldman, Jill Sternard, Dana Zieman, Lorraine Gleeson, Debbie McQuade, Terry McQuade, and everyone at Cambridge Business Publishers for their encouragement, guidance, and dedication to this book.

Finally, thank you to the instructors and students using this book.

Gayle Williams & Jennifer Johnson
March 2021

Brief Table of Contents

Contents

Section Two

Service Companies   *3-1*

❸ Sales Activity (Service Company)   *3-5*

4 Purchasing Activity (Service Company) *4-1*

7 Purchasing Activity (Merchandising Company) *7-1*

8   End-of-Period and Other Activity (Merchandising Company)   *8-1*

Section Four
Beyond the Basics   *9-1*

9   Management Tools   *9-3*

⑩ Project Tracking and Billing for Time and Expenses   *10-1*

⑪ Additional Tools   *11-1*

QuickBooks

SECTION ONE

Introduction

Before we go any further, let's be clear about two facts.

First, "computerized accounting" uses the same accounting principles and processes you're learning in your financial accounting courses.

- **Assets = Liabilities + Equity.**

- **Debits** are on the left; **credits** are on the right.

- Transactions are recorded through journal entries.

- Assets, liabilities, and equity accounts are reported on the balance sheet; revenue and expense accounts are reported on the income statement.

The advantage of using accounting software is that certain processes are automated, which makes the job of the accountant a little easier. For example, in QuickBooks Online (the software that you'll be using in this class), when you prepare an invoice for a customer:

- A journal entry will automatically be created,

- the entry will automatically be posted to the general ledger,

- and the balance sheet and income statement will automatically be adjusted to reflect the new account balances.

The second fact you should be clear about is this: a computer application only knows as much accounting as has been programmed into it. For example:

- QuickBooks Online (QBO) is programmed to know that an account that's been identified by the user as an asset should appear on the balance sheet. What QBO doesn't know is whether the account identified by the user as an asset IS actually an asset.

Assets The economic resources of a business that can be expressed in money terms.

Liabilities The obligations or debts that a business must pay in money or services at some time in the future as a consequence of past transactions or events.

Equity The residual interest in the assets of a business after all liabilities have been paid off; it is equal to a firm's net assets, or total assets less total liabilities.

Debit An entry on the left side (or in the debit column) of an account.

Credit An entry on the right side (or in the credit column) of an account.

- QuickBooks Online (QBO) is also programmed to know that a journal entry must balance (the sum of the debits must equal the sum of the credits) and it will not allow you to create an unbalanced entry. However, it doesn't know whether the specific accounts you just debited and credited in an adjusting journal entry are the appropriate accounts.

It's important that you remember these two facts as you're going through this book. The software is not the accountant; you are. You are the one who ultimately controls the accuracy of the financial data. You are the one who is ultimately responsible for providing meaningful information to users of the financial reports.

SECTION OVERVIEW

Chapter 1 covers:

- Getting in and out of QuickBooks Online (QBO)

- The general organization of QBO

- Customizing and navigating QBO

- Reporting using QBO

Chapter 2 covers setting up and customizing QBO company files.

1

Introduction to QuickBooks Online (QBO)

Objectives

After completing Chapter 1, you should be able to:

1. Recognize the various versions of Intuit's QuickBooks series.

2. Log into the test drive version of QuickBooks Online.

3. Use the various access tools in QuickBooks Online.

4. Open common transactions forms.

5. Use the Search function.

6. Demonstrate an understanding of the various lists in QuickBooks Online.

7. Recognize various account types and detail types used in QuickBooks Online.

8. Create, edit, and delete accounts in the chart of accounts.

9. Create and modify reports.

10. Use keyboard shortcuts in QBO (Appendix 1A).

A LITTLE BACKGROUND

There are many, many different accounting software applications available for purchase. They range in price from under $1,000 to well over $1,000,000. In this book, we're going to look at QuickBooks Online Plus, an application developed and marketed by Intuit.

Intuit Inc. creates accounting software solutions for consumers and professionals. Intuit first came out with desktop accounting software for small businesses (QuickBooks) in 1992. QuickBooks Pro, a more robust software application, was released in 2002. Intuit currently offers four primary desktop versions of QuickBooks.

Table 1.1

QuickBooks Desktop versions

Version	Basic Features	Number of Simultaneous Users Allowed
Pro Plus	Full accounting software system. Users can: ✓ Download bank transactions ✓ Import credit card receipts ✓ Manage invoices and accounts receivable ✓ Manage bills and accounts payable ✓ Track time ✓ Track inventory ✓ Track revenues and costs by project ✓ Create budgets ✓ Track business segments ✓ Run reports	3
Premier Plus	Includes all features in Pro. In addition, users can: ✓ Create and manage sales orders ✓ Create forecasts	5
Premier—Accountant	Includes all features in Premier. In addition, software includes special tools for accountants with multiple clients including the ability to batch enter and delete transactions.	3
Enterprise 21.0	Includes all features in Premier. In addition, users can: ✓ Track inventory by bin location ✓ Use FIFO or average cost for valuing inventory ✓ Factor in freight and duty charges when determining product costs ✓ Develop sophisticated price rules	40
Desktop for Mac	Similar in functionality to Premier but built for macOS	3

Payroll is an add-on feature available in all versions of QuickBooks Desktop.

The software for desktop versions is loaded on to your computer (either downloaded from Intuit's website or loaded using a disk). QuickBooks Desktop company files can be networked but each user must have the software loaded on his or her computer.

Intuit introduced QuickBooks Online in 2001. The software was completely rebuilt in 2013. There are currently five primary versions of QuickBooks Online.

Table 1.2

QuickBooks Online versions

Version	Basic Features	Number of Users Allowed
Self-Employed	Basic accounting software for freelancers. Users can: ✓ Bill customers ✓ Track income and expenses ✓ Download banking and credit card transactions ✓ Import receipts ✓ Run basic reports	1

(continued)

(continued from previous page)

Version	Basic Features	Number of Users Allowed
Simple Start	Includes all the features of Self-Employed. In addition, users can: ✓ Send estimates ✓ Track sales tax ✓ Manage 1099 vendors	1
Essentials	Includes all the features of Simple Start. In addition, users can: ✓ Enter vendor bills for payment later ✓ Track time ✓ Limit access by user	3
Plus	Includes all the features of Essentials. In addition, users can: ✓ Create purchase orders ✓ Track inventory ✓ Track revenue and costs by project ✓ Create budgets ✓ Categorize income and expenses by class and/or location	5
Advanced	Includes all the features of Plus. In addition, users can: ✓ Create smart reports using Fathom (a financial analysis tool) ✓ Backup and restore data ✓ Receive premium technical support from Intuit	25

Payroll is an add-on feature available to users of any of the QuickBooks Online products. There is also a QuickBooks Online Advanced Accountant version that includes additional features for those users who are working with multiple clients.

QuickBooks Online is a cloud-based system. This means that the software and the accounting data of all customers is stored (hosted) on a web server by Intuit. Users can access the software from any computer with Internet access. Although Intuit does back up company data, backups are not currently accessible to users in versions other than QuickBooks Online Advanced.

There are a variety of apps developed by other companies that work with QuickBooks Online. Although we will not be using any apps in this course, those of you who are interested can check them out at https://apps.intuit.com.

QuickBooks Online is a subscription service. Users pay a monthly fee based on the version of QuickBooks Online being used. The annual cost of QuickBooks Online Plus (the software you will be using) is normally just under $1,000 per year, not including payroll. Fortunately, Intuit provides a free one-year subscription to QuickBooks Online Plus to students. You will be using your subscription to complete your homework assignments. Directions for obtaining your subscription license and setting up your homework company are included in Chapter 2.

In this textbook, the terms QuickBooks Online and QBO are used interchangeably to refer to the QuickBooks Online Plus version you will be using.

QUICKBOOKS ONLINE

QBO is a **powerful** tool for small businesses.

- It is flexible (can be used by most small businesses).

- It is intuitive (easy to understand).

- It is accessible from any desktop computer with an Internet connection.
  - Supported browsers for QBO include Google Chrome, Internet Explorer, Microsoft Edge, Mozilla Firefox, and Safari. Google Chrome is the browser recommended by Intuit for use with QBO.

> **HINT:** There may be times when a particular feature in QBO cannot be activated or is not working as you expected. Simply changing browsers may resolve the issue.

- It is accessible (through the QBO mobile app) from most smartphones and tablets.
- It is updated and improved regularly and automatically.

As noted in the Section One Introduction, these are some of the things that QBO automatically knows:

- It knows that behind every transaction is a **journal entry** and that each journal entry must balance. You will not be allowed to enter an unbalanced journal entry.
- It knows that accounts identified as assets, liabilities, or equity appear on the **balance sheet** and accounts identified as income or expense accounts appear on the profit and loss statement (QBO's name for the **income statement**).

These are some of the things that QBO **doesn't** automatically know (so make sure you DO know):

- It doesn't know whether the account you just set up as an asset really does represent a resource owned or controlled by the company that is expected to provide future benefit.
- It doesn't know whether the amounts on the invoice you just created represent income the company has already earned or income that will be earned in the future.
- It doesn't know whether there are salaries that employees have earned but haven't been paid for.
- Etc., etc.

Journal entry An entry of accounting information into a journal (a tabular record in which business transactions are analyzed in debit and credit terms and recorded in chronological order).

Balance sheet A financial statement showing a business's assets, liabilities, and stockholders' equity as of a specific date.

Income statement A financial statement reporting a business's sales revenue and expenses for a given period of time.

BEFORE WE GO ANY FURTHER

Writing about QBO is a little like trying to throw a dart at a moving target. By the time the book gets written, the software has changed! So, fair warning: The information and screenshots in this book are based on QuickBooks Online Plus as it existed at the beginning of 2021. There will likely be changes to the software during the class term. Changes may appear in your classmate's or your instructor's software before they appear in yours. Information will be provided to instructors as new features roll out. Information will also be posted in Student Ancillaries (https://cambridgepub.com/book/qbo2021). If your screen looks different from a screenshot in the book, and you don't see anything in Ancillaries, talk to your instructor.

Continuous updating, of course, is one of the benefits of QBO. Corrections can be made and new features can be added without users needing to download and install a new release. Given the popularity of cloud computing, Intuit is choosing to put a great deal of energy into developing its online accounting software products and that benefits all users.

WHERE TO GO FOR HELP

Although QBO is a very intuitive program, there are a lot of "places to go and things to see" and that can be intimidating. It's easy to forget what was covered in a previous chapter. Most of the time, you'll be able to find the answer by using the index for this book. If you can't, here are some options:

* Use the Help feature in QBO.
    * Help is accessed by clicking the **Help** icon in the icon bar at the top of the screen.

Figure 1.1

Help icon

> **WARNING: QBO changes often and information on the internet (even from the QuickBooks Community) may be out-of-date. Make sure you check the date the information was created or updated.**

* Ask for help from your instructor, from a student assistant (if there is one), or from your fellow students (if they're willing and you're not taking a test!).
* Check the textbook ancillaries at https://cambridgepub.com/book/qbo2021 for information about recent changes to the software.
* If you have a technical question (not an accounting question), check out the Education Support site specially created by Intuit for students (www.intuit.com/partners/education-program).

PRACTICE

Throughout this textbook, you will practice the steps necessary to record transactions and use the various tools available in QBO using an imaginary company set up by Intuit to allow users to test drive the software. The test drive company (sample company), Craig's Design and Landscaping Services, provides landscaping services for individuals and small businesses.

Your homework will be done in a separate company file. The homework company will be introduced in Chapter 2.

Practice Exercises using Craig's Design and Landscaping will be located at the end of each section. Read through each section **before** you attempt the exercises. The explanations and screenshots provided in each section are meant to help you complete the Practice Exercises and your assignments.

Some Practice Exercises will include an instruction to **make a note** of certain information. Your instructor may ask you questions about the Practice Exercises in graded quizzes so it's a good idea to have a notebook handy where you can write down this information.

Accessing the Test Drive Company

To access the practice company file, you'll need to enter https://qbo.intuit.com/redir/testdrive as the URL in your browser.

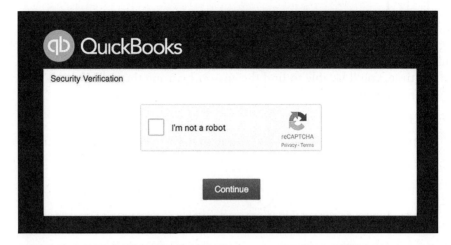

In the first screen, you'll be asked to check **I'm not a robot** before clicking **Continue**.

You may get a message denying access because of privacy settings related to cookies. The message looks something like this:

You must enable cookies in order to continue.

Firefox 3.x for Windows

1. Choose Tools > Options > Privacy.
2. Select the "Accept cookies from sites" checkbox.
3. Click OK.

Internet Explorer 6.x/7.x/8.x for Windows

1. Choose Tools > Internet Options > Privacy > Advanced.
2. If "Override automatic cookie handling" is selected, then make sure "Always allow session cookies" is also selected.
3. Click OK.

Safari 3.x/4.x for Mac

1. Choose Safari > Preferences > Security.
2. In the Accept cookies section, click Always.
3. Close the Security window.

After enabling cookies, choose View > Refresh/Reload to refresh your browser.

Most of the time, refreshing the browser, reentering the URL for the test drive company, and checking the **I'm not a robot** box will allow you to access the program. If you continue to get the message, you will need to adjust your browser's security settings before you can move forward.

 HINT: To enable cookies in Chrome, click Settings on the Chrome menu. Select Privacy and Security and click Site Settings. Click Cookies and site data and toggle Allow sites to save and read cookie data.

Occasionally, QBO will ask you to identify pictures containing specific content (mountains, trains, etc.) after you've checked the **I'm not a robot** box. These are security measures so try to be patient.

The screen (the **Dashboard** screen) will look something like this when your identity as a human and not a robot has been confirmed!

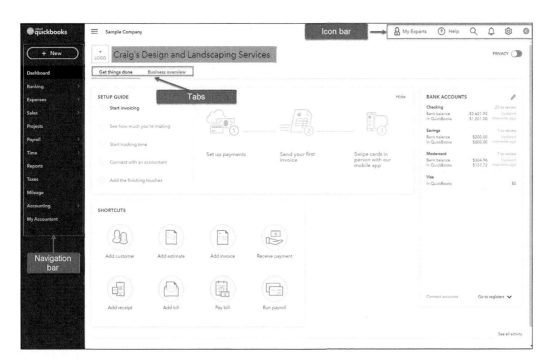

Figure 1.4

The Dashboard (home page)

HINT: As of early 2021, Intuit was considering a change to the **Get things done** tab. Your screen may look more like this:

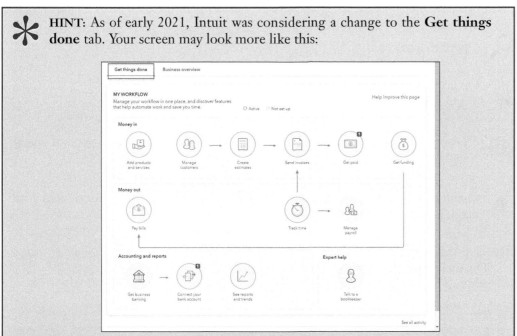

WARNING: Whenever you close out of the test drive website (or whenever you're automatically logged out for lack of activity), <u>nothing you previously entered will be saved</u>. The next time you access the site, the Intuit-developed transactions will stay the same in name and amount, but the dates will most likely differ. The Practice Exercises have been developed with that in mind.

To save yourself time and minimize frustration, complete each Practice Exercise in one study session. If you log off in the middle of a Practice Exercise, you will need to start the exercise over from the beginning when you return.

MOVING AROUND IN QUICKBOOKS ONLINE

Accessing Tools

You can access lists, forms, reports, and anything else you might need from a variety of locations in QBO.

Icon Bar

The icon bar is located at the top of the **Dashboard** screen. The icon bar looks something like this:

Each icon on the icon bar has a purpose:

My Experts — Opens to a link for users looking to find an accounting professional or to add their accountant to their file. This will appear in your homework company. It does not appear in the test drive company.

Help — Opens a Help screen.

Opens to a search tool.

Opens to notifications from Intuit.
- A red dot next to the bell indicates a new notification.

Opens to a menu where company preferences can be set and other general operational tools can be accessed.

Opens to a sign out link. In your homework company, the first letter of your first name will appear here.

The icon you'll be accessing most often is the ⚙ icon.
    The menu accessed through the ⚙ icon looks like this:

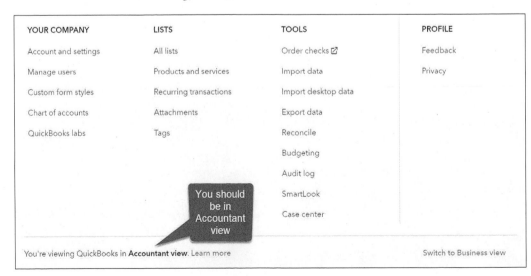

This menu is sometimes called the **Company** menu. The options here primarily relate to setting up and managing the overall structure of the company file.

 HINT: Intuit has been working on simplifying some of the terms and forms in QBO for non-accountant users. Those simplifications are included in the **Business view** version. All of the terms and screenshots in this book are from the **Accountant view**.

Navigation Bar

The navigation bar is located at the far left of the screen. The navigation bar looks something like this:

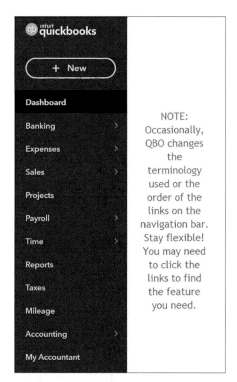

NOTE: Occasionally, QBO changes the terminology used or the order of the links on the navigation bar. Stay flexible! You may need to click the links to find the feature you need.

Figure 1.7

The navigation bar

The **+ New** button opens the following menu:

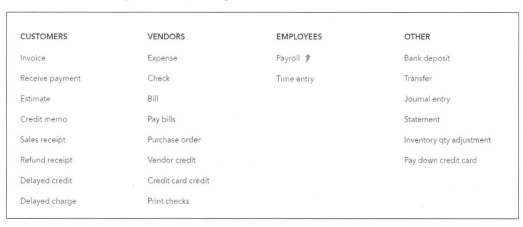

CUSTOMERS	VENDORS	EMPLOYEES	OTHER
Invoice	Expense	Payroll 🖈	Bank deposit
Receive payment	Check	Time entry	Transfer
Estimate	Bill		Journal entry
Credit memo	Pay bills		Statement
Sales receipt	Purchase order		Inventory qty adjustment
Refund receipt	Vendor credit		Pay down credit card
Delayed credit	Credit card credit		
Delayed charge	Print checks		

Figure 1.8

Transaction menu

This menu is sometimes referred to as the **Create** menu. All of the forms needed to record transactions in QBO can be accessed through this screen.

If you hover your mouse over some of the links in the navigation bar, subsections of the link will be displayed. These are often referred to as **drawers**. The **drawer** display for **Banking** looks like this:

Figure 1.9

Drawers in the Banking link on the navigation bar

If you click **Banking** on the navigation bar, the **drawers** will show up as tabs in a new window. QBO defaults to the first tab.

Figure 1.10

Tabs in Banking

Users who download banking transactions directly into QBO, verify and accept those transactions on the **Banking** tab. Bank activities are covered in Appendix 8A.

The **App Transactions** tab includes links to certain external applications that work with QBO. For example, an app that allows users to track purchases made on Amazon Business is available on that screen.

On the **Rules** tab, users can identify accounts and names to be used with transactions downloaded directly from the bank that meet certain conditions. **Bank rules** are covered in Appendix 8A.

On the **Receipts** tab, users can manage uploaded vendor bills and receipts. Uploading **receipts** is covered in Chapter 11.

Tags can be used to categorize information in QBO. They are similar to the hashtags used on various social network platforms. **Tags** are not directly related to general ledger accounts or various segment reporting features in QBO. **Tags** are covered in more detail in Appendix 9A.

The **drawer** display for the **Sales** link on the navigation bar looks like this:

Figure 1.11

Drawers in the Sales link on the navigation bar

The **Overview** tab includes shortcut links to various sales forms. Links to activate features related to online customer payments are also included on this tab.

The **All Sales** tab includes a list of **all** sales related transactions: sales on account, cash sales, credit memos, and payments. New sales transactions can be initiated in this tab. The **Invoices** tab includes a list of recent invoices and their status (**due**, **overdue**, or **paid**). New invoices can be created on this tab.

Setting up features to handle online customer payments by credit card or bank transfer is done on the **Payment Links** tab. The **Customers** tab includes a list of all current customers. Customers can be added or edited in the tab. The **Products and Services** tab includes a list of all products held for sale and all services performed by the company. Products and services can be added and edited in the tab.

Clicking **Expenses** on the navigation bar opens a screen with two tabs. In the **Expenses** tab, all purchase related transactions are listed. New purchase transactions can be initiated in this tab. The **Vendors** tab includes a list of all current vendors. Vendors can be added or edited in the tab.

Clicking **Projects** on the navigation bar opens the Project Center. Project tracking, useful to companies who perform multiple jobs for a single customer, is covered in Chapter 10.

Clicking **Payroll** on the navigation bar opens a screen with an **Employees** tab for managing employees, a **Contractors** tab for managing independent contractors, and a **Workers' Comp** tab which includes links to Intuit insurance partners. The **Workers' Comp** tab would not appear for users in states that do not require that insurance.

Clicking **Time** on the navigation bar opens a screen with two tabs. Setting up time tracking is done on the **Overview** tab. Entering time is done on the **Time Entries** tab.

Clicking **Reports** on the navigation bar opens a screen with three tabs. The **Standard** tab includes various reports developed by Intuit, by category. Reports that have been customized by users are included on the **Custom Reports** tab. More sophisticated report packages developed by Intuit are included on the **Management Reports** tab. **Management reports** are covered in Chapter 11. Figure 1.12 shows a partial list of the **standard** report categories.

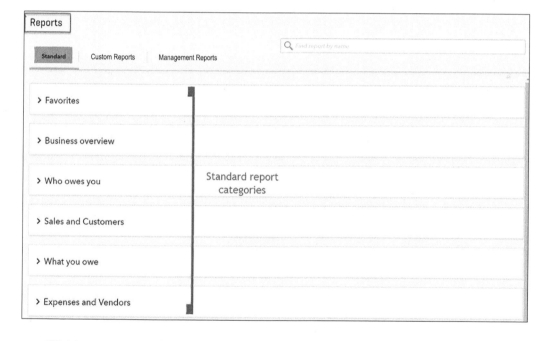

Figure 1.12

Standard report window

Clicking **Taxes** on the navigation bar will open windows for sales taxes and payroll taxes, if those features are activated in a company file. In the test drive company, only sales tax features are available.

Business miles tracking can be done through the **Mileage** link on the navigation bar. Mileage tracking will not be covered in this course.

Clicking **Accounting** on the navigation bar gives users quick access to the chart of accounts and to account reconciliation windows.

Users can give their outside accountant access to their company file by clicking **My Accountant** on the navigation bar.

The navigation bar can be closed by clicking the triple lines at the far left edge of the icon bar, right above the navigation bar. Re-clicking the triple lines will reopen the navigation bar.

Figure 1.13

Tool to open or close the navigation bar.

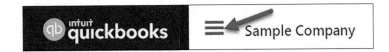

Display Area of the Dashboard

There are two tabs on the QBO **Dashboard**.

Figure 1.14

Get things done tab on the Dashboard

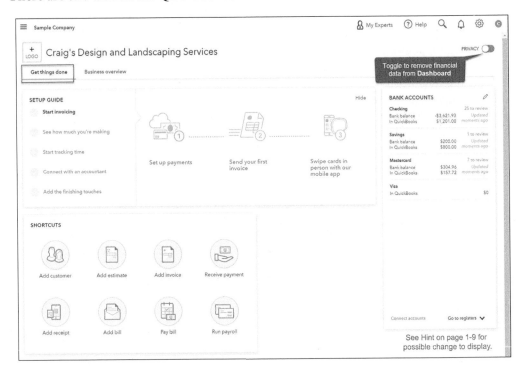

Shortcuts (links) to commonly used forms are included on the **Get things done** tab. Cash balances are also displayed. If users don't want financial information to be visible, they can toggle the **Privacy** button in the top right corner of the display area.

Figure 1.15

Business overview tab on the Dashboard

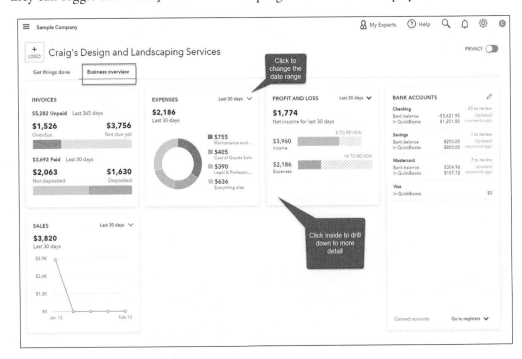

Additional financial information is included on the **Business overview** tab.

The data is generally displayed graphically (charts and graphs). Clicking some, but not all, of the amounts allows you to drill down to more detail.

As discussed earlier, Intuit is constantly improving QBO in response to user needs and requests. The **Dashboard** page is one area that tends to change fairly frequently so if your screen doesn't look exactly like the screenshots above, don't be alarmed.

Forms

Transactions are recorded in "forms" in QBO.

To open the **check** form, click **+ New** on the navigation bar.

The transaction menu will appear.

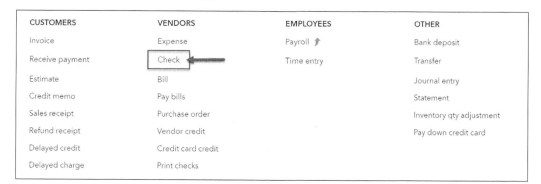

Figure 1.16

Access to the Check form

Click **Check.** You are now in a new window.

Figure 1.17

Check form

All transaction forms will have a **Save and close** or **Save and new** button that is used to save a transaction and automatically exit the window. (In Figure 1.17 the dropdown menu has been clicked so that both options are displayed.) If you want to close the form without saving, simply click the **X** at the top right of the window or the **Cancel** button in the lower left corner. Other **Save** options are available on some of the sales and purchase forms.

Options for voiding or deleting transactions, copying transactions, and reviewing transaction history are available through the black bar at the bottom of each form. The specific options available will depend on the type of transaction and whether the transaction is being created or is being edited.

You can also access forms from other links on the navigation bar. To open a customer invoice, click **Sales** on the navigation bar.

Figure 1.18

Sales link on the navigation bar

Click **All Sales** to open the list of sales transactions.

Figure 1.19

All Sales window

Click **New Transaction** and select **Invoice**. The screen will look something like this:

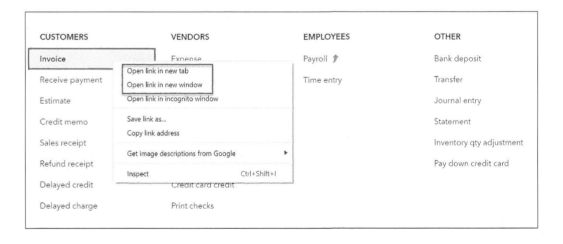

Figure 1.20

Invoice form

Multiple Open Screens

Most of the time, a user will only need one screen open at a time. Sometimes, though, it's convenient to have multiple screens open.

If you want to have a form open in a new tab or in a new window, simply right-click the form in the **+ New** menu and select the preferred option.

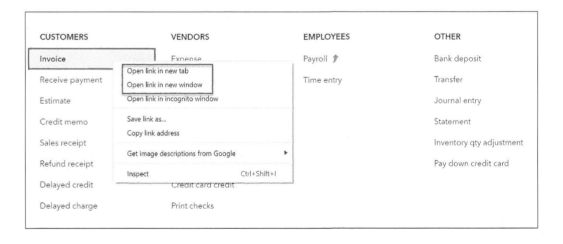

Figure 1.21

Tool for opening forms in a new tab or new window

You can also right-click links in the navigation bar to have those screens open in a new tab or a new window.

Finding Transactions

You can find transactions and details about transactions in QBO in various ways:

- You can "drill down" (double-click) on a specific transaction in a report to see the transaction details.

- You can re-sort lists by name, amount, date, or account by clicking the title of the column you want to use as the sort criterion.

- You can find recent transactions of a certain type using the **clock** icon that appears in the top left corner on various forms.

  - The **clock** icon looks like this:

Figure 1.22

Clock icon

For example, if you opened a check form in QBO and clicked the **clock** icon, you would see the most recent check transactions:

Figure 1.23

Recent transactions displayed using the clock icon

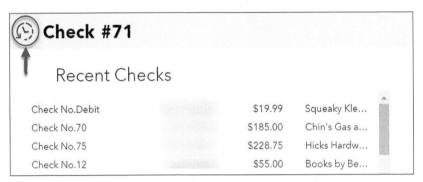

- You can use the **Search** feature to look for transactions using one or more filters.

The **Search** tool has the most flexibility. The **Search** tool is accessed by clicking the **magnifying glass** in the icon bar.

Figure 1.24

Icon bar access to search feature

The screen will look something like this:

Figure 1.25

Basic search window

On this screen, you can enter a single detail about a transaction. Press **Enter** on your keyboard to open the form that matches your search.

Clicking **Advanced Search** under the list of recent transactions opens a new window:

Figure 1.26

Filter fields in advanced search

The first dropdown menu allows you to narrow the search. You can search detailed lines in all transactions or you can narrow the search to specific types of transactions. A partial list of options is shown here:

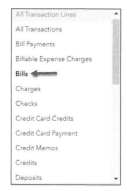

Figure 1.27

Options to narrow a search

The next dropdown menu will change depending on what transaction you filtered initially. If **Bills** was selected, the set of filtering options would show as:

Figure 1.28

Options to further filter a search

If **Vendor** was selected, you would be able to enter details about your search in the next two fields.

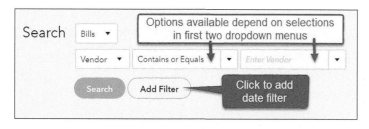

Figure 1.29

Options for filtering by name

Clicking **Add Filter** allows users to add a date filter to their search.

Figure 1.30

Option to filter by date

Clicking **Apply** completes the search.

If a search for **Bills** received from Cal Telephone during the prior six months was selected, the screen would look something like this:

Figure 1.31

Results of advanced search

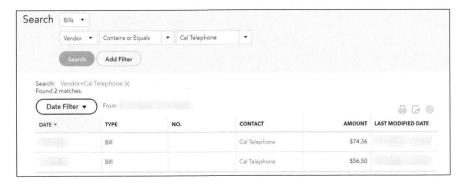

> **HINT:** Remember, your QBO file may have different dates than the screenshots that appear in this book.

PRACTICE

EXERCISE

1.1

MBC

Access forms using the navigation bar and use the Search tool in Craig's Design and Landscaping to locate specific transactions.

1. To access a form using the navigation bar:

   a. Click **+ New** on the navigation bar.

   b. Click **Receive Payment**.

   c. **Make a note** of the account displayed in the **Deposit to** field.

      i. Remember, **make a note** instructions may be used by your instructor to make sure you completed the exercises. It would be a good idea to keep a notebook handy.

   d. Close the **Receive Payment** window by clicking the **X** (upper right corner of the window).

2. To search using the **Search** feature:

   a. Click the **magnifying glass** on the icon bar.

   b. Click **Advanced Search**.

   c. Open the first (top) dropdown menu and select **Bills** as the filter.

   d. In the next set of fields, select **Vendor**, **Contains or Equals**, and **Norton Lumber and Building Materials**.

   e. Click **Search**.

(continued)

(continued from previous page)

 f. Click the $205.00 in the **AMOUNT** field to open the vendor bill.

 g. **Make a note** of the descriptions for the two items purchased from Norton Lumber.

 h. Close the window by clicking the **X** in the upper right corner of the window.

ORGANIZATION OF QUICKBOOKS ONLINE

The Importance of "Lists"

QBO uses lists as part of the organizational structure of the software so it's important that you have a good understanding of the types and uses of the various lists.

Chart of Accounts

The primary list in QBO is the **chart of accounts**. An **account type** and a **detail type** must be selected for each **account** used by an organization.

 The **account** and **detail type** chosen will determine:

- the financial statement on which an account will appear.
- where on that statement the account will be displayed.
- which QBO features are available for that account.

QBO prepares **classified balance sheets** and **multi-step income statements**. There are lots of groupings and subtotals in those statements (as you might remember from your previous classes). To provide the necessary flexibility, QBO uses an expanded list of **account types**. Here's a list of financial statement account classifications and the corresponding **account types** used by QBO:

Financial Accounting Classifications				
Assets	**Liabilities**	**Equity**	**Revenues**	**Expenses**
QuickBooks Online Account Types				
Bank	Accounts payable (A/P)	Equity	Income	Cost of Goods Sold
Accounts receivable (A/R)	Credit card		Other income	Expenses
Other Current Assets	Other Current Liabilities			Other expense
Fixed Assets	Long Term Liabilities			
Other Assets				

Account A record of the additions, deductions, and balances of individual assets, liabilities, stockholders' equity, dividends, revenues, and expenses.

Classified balance sheet A balance sheet in which items are classified into subgroups to facilitate financial analysis and management decision making.

Multi-step income statement An income statement in which one or more intermediate performance measures, such as gross profit on sales, are derived before the continuing income is reported.

You can have many different accounts with the same **account type** in your chart of accounts.

 Here are some examples of the way **account type** determines placement in a financial statement: Let's say you are going to set up an account called Petty Cash. You would want to set the account up as type **Bank** so that it shows up at the top of the balance sheet along with any checking or savings accounts the company has. (Checking and savings accounts would also be set up with the account type **Bank**.) A Salaries Payable account would be set up as type **Other Current Liabilities**. That way it shows up on the balance sheet as a current liability along with accounts like Interest Payable and Payroll Taxes Payable.

 Here are some examples of the way **account type** is associated with various features in QBO: If an account were set up as an **Accounts receivable (A/R)** type, you would be able to use that account when preparing customer invoices. You would also be able to pull an accounts receivable aging report for that account. You would not be able to do either of those things with an account set up as an **Other Current Assets** type. You will learn more about these features as you go through the textbook. For now, just be aware that selecting the appropriate **account type** is important for a variety of reasons.

Detail types are subsets of each **account type**. The options available for **account** and **detail types** are defined by QBO and cannot be modified. Although it should be easy for you to determine the correct **account type**, it can be difficult to find an appropriate **detail type**. If you don't find an exact match, select the available **detail type** that most closely matches the account you're setting up.

> **!** **WARNING:** As you work through your homework assignments, you'll find that QBO occasionally adds an account to your chart of accounts without warning. This might happen if you add a new feature or if you initiate certain types of transactions. Make sure you closely follow the directions in your assignment to ensure that you're using the proper accounts.

Adding, Editing, or Inactivating Accounts

Figure 1.32

Icon bar access to chart of accounts link

To add, edit, or inactivate accounts, click ⚙ on the icon bar.

The screen will look something like this:

Figure 1.33

Link to chart of accounts

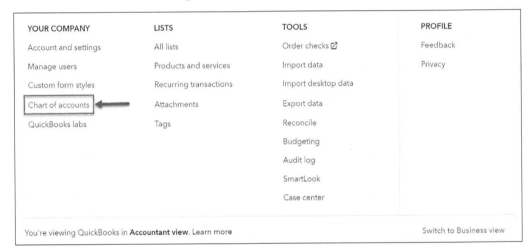

YOUR COMPANY	LISTS	TOOLS	PROFILE
Account and settings	All lists	Order checks ☑	Feedback
Manage users	Products and services	Import data	Privacy
Custom form styles	Recurring transactions	Import desktop data	
Chart of accounts	Attachments	Export data	
QuickBooks labs	Tags	Reconcile	
		Budgeting	
		Audit log	
		SmartLook	
		Case center	

You're viewing QuickBooks in **Accountant view**. Learn more   Switch to Business view

Click **Chart of Accounts**.

Figure 1.34

Welcome page for chart of accounts

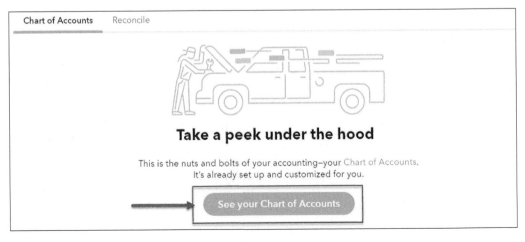

Chart of Accounts   Reconcile

Take a peek under the hood

This is the nuts and bolts of your accounting–your Chart of Accounts. It's already set up and customized for you.

See your Chart of Accounts

Click **See your Chart of Accounts.**

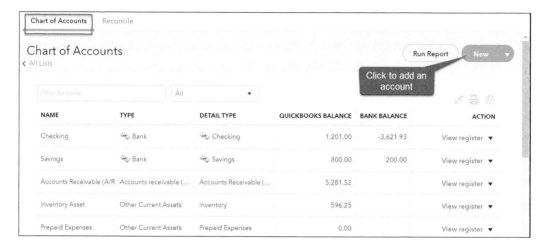

Figure 1.35
Chart of accounts list

 HINT: The Bank Balance column displays the current bank (or credit card) balance for those users downloading transactions directly from financial institutions. You can ignore those balances.

Adding an Account

Click **New** in the account list window to open the **Account** window.

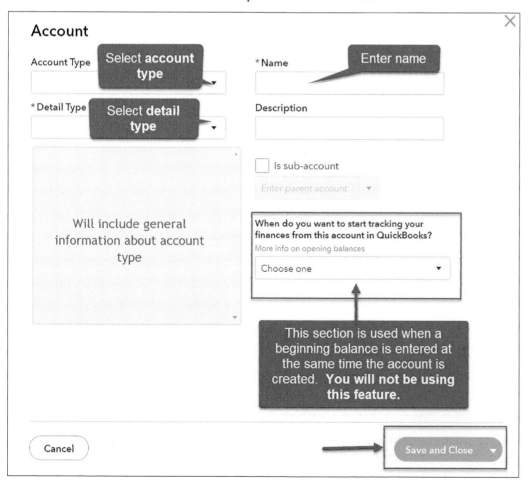

Figure 1.36
Account set up screen

The appropriate **account type** is selected first.

Figure 1.37

Detail type dropdown
menu example

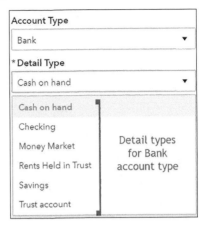

The available **Detail Types** will appear after the **Account Type** is selected. Most categories will have a number of available **Detail Types** to choose from.

You then enter a **Name** for the account. You should enter a name that accurately describes the account. The **Name** is what will appear on the financial statements.

The **Description** field can be used when users want to include additional detail about the account.

For certain balance sheet accounts, users can select a date when transactions are first tracked in the account. QBO will then ask for the balance in the account as of that date. You will not be entering beginning balances in this way.

To group similar accounts together for presentation purposes, you can create a **parent account** and then identify other accounts as **sub-accounts** of the parent. In the chart of accounts list, sub-accounts appear as follows: Parent account name: Sub-account name. Sub-accounts must have the same **account type** as the parent account.

The window for a new Repair & Maintenance account might look something like this if it's set up as a sub-account of Automobile:

Figure 1.38

Example of completed
account setup

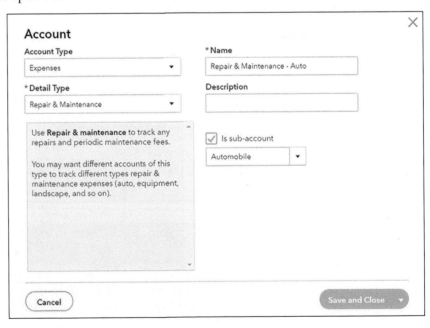

You can use account numbers in QBO. To include an account number, you need to elect that as a preference. Setting that preference will be covered in Chapter 2. You will be using account numbers in your homework assignments.

Editing an Account

To edit an account in the chart of accounts list, open the dropdown menu in the **ACTION** column of the account you wish to edit.

Figure 1.39

Access to account editing

Click **Edit** to open the **Account** window.

You can change the account's name, number (if applicable), **account type**, or **detail type**. You can also make it a **sub-account**.

Inactivating an Account

To remove an account from the chart of accounts list, follow the procedures listed above for editing an account but instead of clicking **Edit**, click **Make inactive**. (See Figure 1.39.)

If you click **Make inactive** on an account with activity, QBO will make the account inactive but the data is not deleted. An inactive account is not available in new transactions but the account would appear in any financial reports covering the period the account was used. Reactivating accounts is covered in Chapter 8.

Also in Chapter 8, we will cover how to manage accounts that are no longer useful but can't be deleted.

> True or False? QBO will allow you to create an account with the name Salaries Payable with an Expenses account type. (Answer at end of chapter.)

QuickCheck
1-1

Work with Craig's Design and Landscaping's chart of accounts.

(Craig needs an account to track airfare to conferences and wants to change some existing accounts.)

1. Click ⚙ in the icon bar.

2. Click **Chart of Accounts**.

   a. If you get a screen that says "Take a peek under the hood," click **See your Chart of Accounts**.

3. To add a new account:

   a. Click **New**.

   b. Select **Expenses** as the **account type**.

   c. Select **Travel** as the **detail type**.

   d. Type in "Airfare" as the **name**.

   e. Check **Is sub-account** and select Travel.

   f. Click **Save and Close**.

4. To edit an account:

   a. Select **Edit** in the **ACTION** column dropdown menu for the **Travel Meals** account.

(continued)

PRACTICE

EXERCISE

1.2

(continued from previous page)

     b.   Change the **detail type** to **Travel.**

     c.   Change the **name** to "Hotel and meals."

     d.   Click **Is sub-account** and select Travel.

     e.   Click **Yes** if asked about changing the detail type.

     f.   Click **Save and Close.**

5. To inactivate an account:

     a.   Select **Make inactive** in the **ACTION** column dropdown menu for **Other Portfolio Income** account.

     b.   Click **Yes** when prompted.

6. Make a note of the number of sub-accounts under **Legal & Professional Fees.**

7. Click **Dashboard** to exit the chart of accounts list.

Other Lists in QuickBooks Online

There are a number of other lists used in QBO.

The **Products and Services** list contains sales and purchase (if applicable) information about every product sold or service provided by the organization. The individual items on the list are used when billing customers and when purchasing inventory in QBO. **Services** will be covered in Chapter 3 and **products** will be covered in Chapter 6.

There are lists of customers, vendors, and employees. Other lists represent options that might be used. For example, there is a list of payment terms that can be used for entering credit terms offered to customers or entering credit terms set by vendors.

These (and other) lists will be covered in more detail in later chapters but, just for practice, we'll look at editing **products** and **services** here.

Editing a Product or Service Item

Click ⚙ on the icon bar.

Figure 1.40

Icon bar access to products and services center link

The screen will look something like this:

Figure 1.41

Link to products and services center

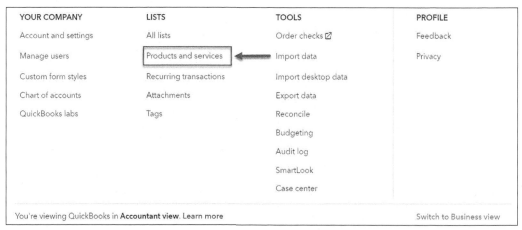

Click **Products and Services** to open the products and services list.

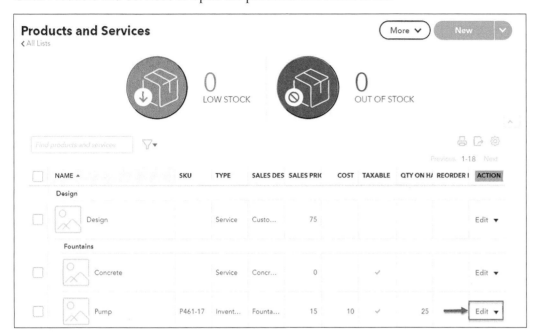

Figure 1.42

Products and services
list

Click **Edit** in the **ACTION** column for Pump. The Edit screen looks like this:

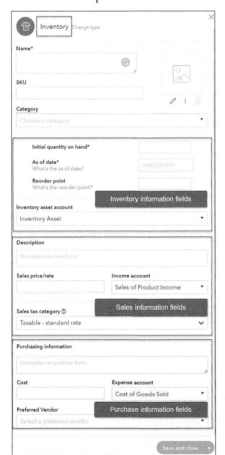

Figure 1.43

Inventory item record

Because pumps are products purchased for resale, the screen includes sales, purchase, and inventory tracking information. Any of this information can be changed using the Edit feature. Service items require less detail.

PRACTICE
EXERCISE
1.3

Homework
MBC

Work with Craig's Design and Landscaping product and service items.

(Craig wants to change the price charged for Design services.)

1. Click ⚙ in the icon bar.

2. Click **Products and Services**.

3. To edit an item:

   a. Select **Edit** in the **ACTION** column for **Design**.

   b. Change the **Name** to "Custom Design."

   c. Change the **Sales price/rate** to "$80."

   d. Click **Save and close**.

4. **Make a note** of the cost listed for **Rock Fountain** in the **Products and Services** list.

5. **Make a note** of the sales price listed for **Pest Control** in the **Products and Services** list.

6. Click **Dashboard** to exit the list.

Journal A tabular record in which business transactions are analyzed in debit and credit terms and recorded in chronological order.

General ledger An accounting record with enough flexibility so that any type of business transaction may be recorded in it; a diary of a business's accounting transactions.

Subsidiary ledger A ledger that provides detailed information about an account balance.

Trial balance A list of the account titles in the general ledger, their respective debit or credit balances, and the totals of the debit and credit balances.

TRANSACTIONS IN QUICKBOOKS ONLINE

In a manual accounting system, the mechanics of accounting work something like this:

✓ Documentation (for transactions) is received from outside sources or prepared internally.

✓ Details from the documents are recorded in **journals**.

✓ Journal entries are posted (transferred) to the **general ledger** and, as appropriate, to **subsidiary ledgers**.

✓ A **trial balance** is prepared.

✓ Financial statements are prepared from the trial balance and subsidiary ledger reports are prepared from the subsidiary ledgers.

In QBO, the mechanics work like this:

✓ Certain documents (invoices and checks, for example) are prepared directly in QBO using specific forms.

✓ Documents received from outside sources (vendor invoices for example) are entered into QBO using other forms.

✓ That's all the user has to do (other than making those pesky adjusting journal entries!).

> **BEHIND THE SCENES** The journal entries related to transactions are automatically created by QBO and posted to the general ledger when the form is completed (saved). Subsidiary ledgers, trial balances, and financial statements are also automatically updated every time a transaction is entered.

There is a journal entry behind every completed form in QBO EXCEPT (there are always exceptions, right?):

- Purchase orders (not **accounting transactions**)

- Estimates (not accounting transactions)

- Timesheets

- **Delayed charges** and **delayed credits**

  - These transactions are unique to QBO and are covered in Chapter 6.

> **BEHIND THE SCENES** Timesheets are, strictly speaking, accounting transactions. (A liability is created as soon as employees work.) Wages are only recorded in QBO, however, when payroll checks are created or when general journal entries are made by the user to recognize earned but unpaid salaries.

> Why aren't purchase orders and estimates accounting transactions? (Answer at end of chapter.)

Accounting transaction An economic event that requires accounting recognition; an event that effects any of the elements of the accounting equation—assets, liabilities, or stockholders' equity.

QuickCheck
1-2

Each form is identified as a specific **transaction type** in QBO. Knowing the various types allows you to easily find transactions or modify reports.

There are many **transaction types**. Here are a **few** of them (see Appendix B for a list of other types):

- **Sales receipt** (cash sales)

- **Invoice** (sales on account)

- **Payment** (collections from customer for sales on account)

- **Check** (payments by check NOT including payments on account or payroll checks)

- **Bill** (purchases from vendors on account)

- **Bill payment (Check)** (payments by check to vendors for purchases on account)

- **Journal entry** (adjusting entries)

Transaction type names in QBO are **very** specific.

In business, we might "bill" a customer OR we might receive a "bill" from a vendor. In QBO, we **invoice** customers and we record **bills** from vendors that we will be paying at a later date. You cannot enter a sale to a customer, on account, using a **bill**.

In business, we write "checks" to pay for something on the spot. We write "checks" to pay the phone bill we recorded in the general ledger last month. We also write "checks" to pay our employees. In QBO there are three different **transaction types** for those activities. **Check** is the **transaction type** used when we pay for something on the spot. Checks written to vendors to pay account balances are **bill payment transaction types**. **Paycheck** is the **transaction type** for employee payroll checks.

> **BEHIND THE SCENES** You will be using various sales and purchase forms to enter transactions in QBO. You **could** enter these transactions as journal entries. However, it's important to use the appropriate form for a number of reasons.
>
> 1. Forms (**transaction types**) are connected to subsidiary ledgers in QBO. Not all ledgers can be updated using journal entries.
> 2. Companies often need to provide documentation to customers and vendors. QBO forms can be printed out or emailed.

REPORTING

There are lots of reports already set up in QBO. You'll be using many of those reports during the class term.

Reports are accessed by clicking **Reports** on the navigation bar. The screen will look something like this:

Figure 1.44

Report Center

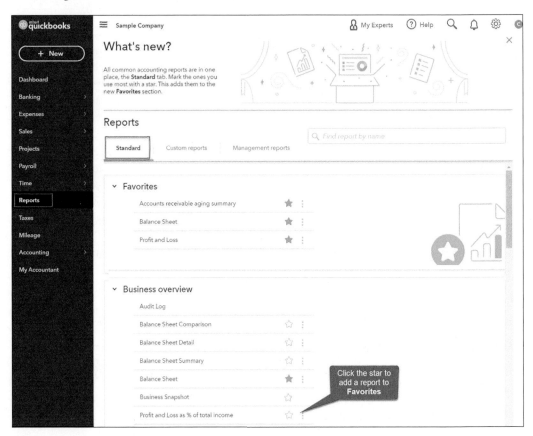

The **Standard** tab includes the reports already set up in QBO. Figure 1.44 is a partial view of the **Standard** tab in the **Reports** window.

Reports on this tab are grouped by category. Some reports are included in multiple categories. The categories are:

Favorites—the most popular reports from all the categories. Reports can be added to or deleted from this list by clicking the star next to the report name. Reports added to **Favorites** will still be listed in the original category.

Business Overview—the typical accounting reports created at the end of each accounting period

Who Owes You—reports related to accounts receivable

Sales and Customers—reports related to sales and customer activity

What You Owe—reports related to accounts payable

Expenses and Vendors—reports related to purchase and vendor activity

Sales Tax—reports related to state and local sales taxes

Employees—reports related to employees and time tracking

For My Accountant—common accounting reports created at the end of each accounting period plus fairly detailed reports of financial activity. Journal reports are included in this category.

Payroll—reports related to employees, compensation, and time tracking. Certain reports will only be listed here if payroll is activated in QBO.

The **Management Reports** tab includes three report packages developed by Intuit.

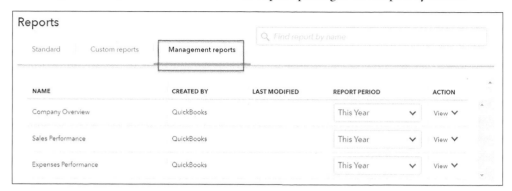

Figure 1.45

Management Reports tab in report center

Management Reports are covered in Chapter 11.

Reports customized and saved by users are included on the **Custom Reports** tab.

Customizing Reports

Most reports in QBO can be customized and you'll likely need to be able to customize reports to complete your homework assignments.

There are many ways you can customize reports:

- You can add or delete the types of information that appear on the report and/or the order in which the information is presented.
- You can specify which transactions are included in the report.
- You can modify the appearance of the reports (fonts, titles, etc.).

Simple Report Modification

Certain report modifications can easily be made on the face of most report screens.

For an example, click **Reports** on the navigation bar. On the **Standard** tab, click **Journal** report in the **For My Accountant** section.

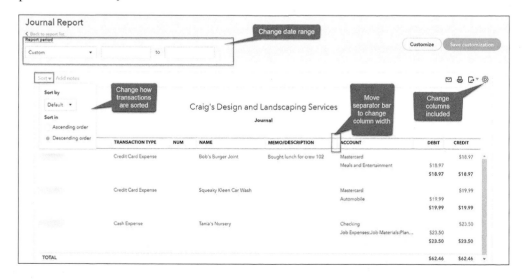

Figure 1.46

Simple report modification options on a Journal report

On the **Journal** report shown in Figure 1.46, simple modifications could include:

- Changing the date range of the report.
- Changing how the data in the report is sorted (under **Sort**).

- Changing the column widths (done by clicking the separator bar just to the right of the column name and dragging left to decrease the width and dragging right to increase the width).

Other reports, the Profit and Loss statement for example, have many more modifications that can easily be made on the face of the report screen.

Reports can be created with differing levels of detail for different users. For example, a creditor might need less detail on an income statement than an owner. If there are sub-accounts set up for income or expense accounts, the income statement can easily be modified to:

- Show all sub-accounts with subtotals by parent account.

- Show only parent accounts.

QBO calls changing this level of detail **expanding** or **collapsing** a report. This option, when available, is included on the face of the report screen.

When a report is initially opened, the report will show all detail. A **profit and loss** report, for example, would appear something like this if **All Dates** was selected as the **Report period**.

Figure 1.47

Expanded profit and loss report

	TOTAL
▾ Income	
Design income	2,250.00
Discounts given	-89.50
▾ Landscaping Services	1,477.50
▾ Job Materials	
Fountains and Garden Lighting	2,246.50
Plants and Soil	2,351.97
Sprinklers and Drip Systems	138.00
Total Job Materials	4,736.47
▾ Labor	
Installation	250.00
Maintenance and Repair	50.00
Total Labor	300.00
Total Landscaping Services	6,513.97
Pest Control Services	110.00
Sales of Product Income	912.75
Services	503.55
Total Income	$10,200.77
▾ Cost of Goods Sold	
Cost of Goods Sold	405.00
Total Cost of Goods Sold	$405.00
GROSS PROFIT	$9,795.77
Total Maintenance and Repair	940.00
Meals and Entertainment	28.49
Office Expenses	18.08
Rent or Lease	900.00
▾ Utilities	
Gas and Electric	200.53
Telephone	130.86
Total Utilities	331.39
Total Expenses	$5,237.31
NET OPERATING INCOME	$4,558.46
▾ Other Expenses	
Miscellaneous	2,916.00
Total Other Expenses	$2,916.00
NET OTHER INCOME	$ -2,916.00
NET INCOME	$1,642.46

Craig's Design and Landscaping Services

Profit and Loss
All Dates

Click the **Collapse** button to include only parent accounts. The report would look something like this when **collapsed**:

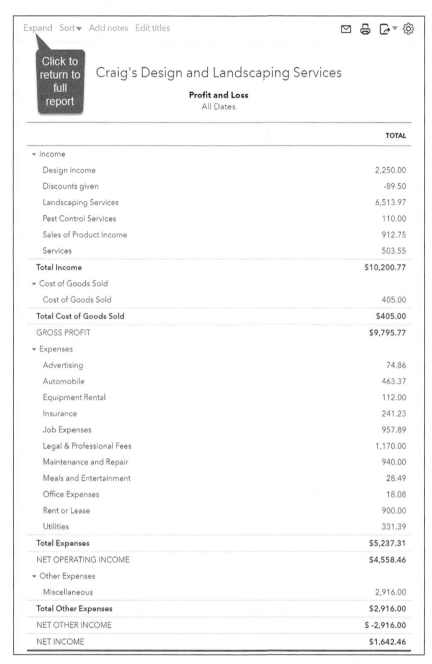

To return to the more detailed report, you would just need to click the **Expand** button.

Advanced Report Modification

Sometimes a company might want to limit the type of information included in a report or do more extensive modifications to the appearance of the report. For example, a company might want to limit a sales report to include only sales to certain customers. Or a company might want to show reports in whole dollars.

Modifying the type of information that is included in a report is done through a filtering process. Modifying the appearance of a report is done through a selection process. Both are done through a customization window.

To more extensively modify a **Journal** report, click **Customize** in the top right of the report screen.

Figure 1.49

Access to report customization window

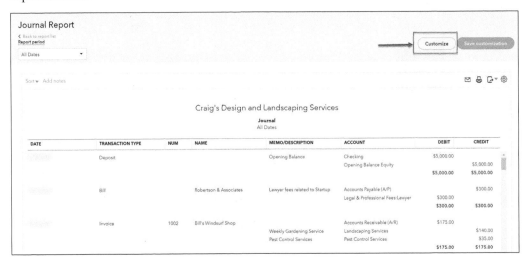

You'll see a window that looks something like this (different reports have different customization options so the screens will differ):

Figure 1.50

General section of report customization window

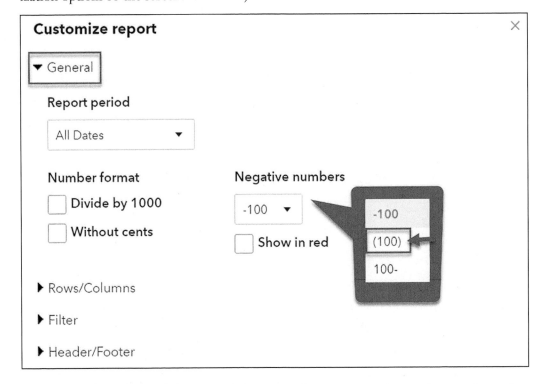

In the **General** section of the customization window, you can change dates and number formatting.

 HINT: The QBO default is to display negative numbers with a leading minus sign in reports. However, in financial reports, negative numbers are more commonly displayed using parentheses. To create more professional looking statements, the **negative numbers** formatting should be changed by customizing the report.

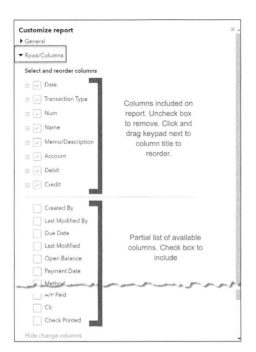

Figure 1.51

Example of Rows/
Columns section of
report customization

In the **Rows/Columns** section of the customization window, you can select, and reorder included fields by clicking **Change columns**.

Figure 1.52

Example of Filter
section of report
customization

In the **Filter** section of the customization window, you can filter the data that's included in the report. Figure 1.52 shows the filters available on a **Journal** report.

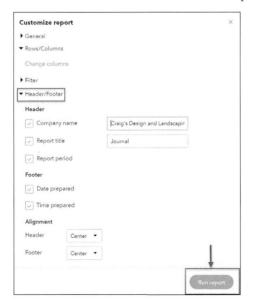

Figure 1.53

Example of Header/
Footer section of report
customization

Basic changes to report titles and footers are made in the **Headers/Footers** section of the customization window as shown in Figure 1.53.

Click **Run Report** in the bottom right corner of the customization window to apply the changes.

Figure 1.54

Link to save
customized report

Customized reports are saved to the **Custom Reports** tab of the report center by clicking **Save customization** on the report screen.

Figure 1.55

Saved report options

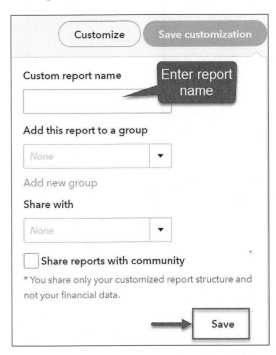

Reports can be saved in groups set up by the user. If there are multiple users of a company file, reports can be shared with some or all the other users. Report structures (no financial data) can be shared with the Intuit community.

Printing Reports

Reports can be printed, emailed, or exported (to Excel or PDF).

All of the options are accessible from the toolbar at the top of each report. The toolbar looks like this:

Figure 1.56

Report print and export
options

The first two links (for emailing or printing) take you first to a new window where page orientation (portrait or landscape) is selected. Final links for printing or emailing appear in the new window.

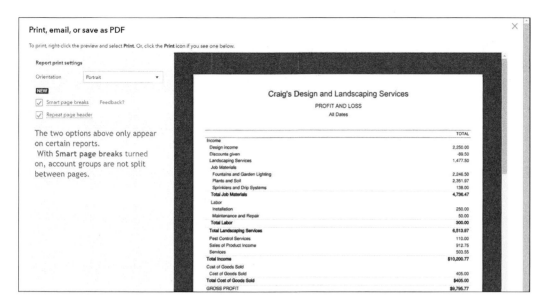

Print, email, or save as PDF

To print, right-click the preview and select **Print**. Or, click the **Print** icon if you see one below.

Report print settings

Orientation   Portrait   ▼

`NEW`
☑ Smart page breaks   Feedback?
☑ Repeat page header

The two options above only appear on certain reports. With **Smart page breaks** turned on, account groups are not split between pages.

Craig's Design and Landscaping Services
PROFIT AND LOSS
All Dates

	TOTAL
Income	
Design income	2,250.00
Discounts given	-89.50
Landscaping Services	1,477.50
Job Materials	
Fountains and Garden Lighting	2,246.50
Plants and Soil	2,351.97
Sprinklers and Drip Systems	138.00
Total Job Materials	4,736.47
Labor	
Installation	250.00
Maintenance and Repair	50.00
Total Labor	300.00
Total Landscaping Services	6,513.97
Pest Control Services	110.00
Sales of Product Income	912.75
Services	503.55
Total Income	$10,200.77
Cost of Goods Sold	
Cost of Goods Sold	405.00
Total Cost of Goods Sold	$405.00
GROSS PROFIT	$9,795.77

Figure 1.57

Print, email, or save as PDF options

The **Export** dropdown menu allows you to select **Export to Excel** or **Export to PDF**. Page orientation can be selected for an export to PDF but not for an export to Excel.

The options available by clicking ⚙ at the far right of the toolbar (Figure 1.56) vary depending on the report. For some reports, columns can be changed or reordered in the ⚙ window. In other reports, the only option included is to change the display density to compact.

Customize and print reports for Craig's Design and Landscaping.
(Craig's wants a hard copy of its chart of accounts and general journal.)

1. Modify and print a chart of accounts.
    a. Click **Reports** in the navigation bar.
    b. Scroll down to the **For My Accountant** section on the **Standard** tab.
    c. Click **Account List**.
    d. Click **Customize**.
    e. Click **Change columns** in the **Rows/Columns** section.
        i. Remove the checkmarks next to **Description** and **Balance**.
    f. Click **Run report**.
    g. Open the **Sort** dropdown menu.
    h. Select **Type** in the **Sort by** dropdown.
    i. Choose **Descending order** under **Sort in**.
    j. **Make a note** of the number of sub-accounts associated with **Maintenance and Repair**.
    k. Click the export link and select **Export to PDF**.
    l. Select **Portrait** as the orientation.
    m. Click **Save as PDF**.
    n   Save to your desktop, laptop, or USB drive.
        i. Close out of Adobe Acrobat if needed.

(continued)

**PRACTICE
EXERCISE
1.4**

Homework
MBC

(continued from previous page)

    o.   Click **Close** (bottom left corner of the report) to exit out of the report window.

    p.   Click **Back to report list** (top left corner of the window).

2. Modify a Journal report.

    a.   Click **Journal** in the **For My Accountant** section of **Reports**.

    b.   Click **Customize**.

    c.   In the **General** section, change **Report period** to **All Dates**.

    d.   Click **Change columns** in the **Rows/Columns** section.

        i.   Remove the checkmarks next to **Num, Memo/Description**.

    e.   Open the **Filter** section.

        i.   Check the **Transaction Type** field.

        ii.   In the dropdown menu, check **Bill**.

    f.   Open the **Header/Footer** section.

        i.   Change the **Report Title** to "Vendor Bills."

    g.   Click **Run report**.

    h.   Select **Date** in the **Sort** dropdown menu. Keep the **sort in** order as ascending.

    i.   **Make a note** of the total (dollars) in the **Debit** column.

3. Click **Dashboard** to exit out of **Reports**.

ANSWER TO
QuickCheck
1-1

> Yes. The user creates the account name and chooses the account type. Be careful that the account type you select is correct.

ANSWER TO
QuickCheck
1-2

> Purchase orders and estimates are not considered accounting transactions because the **accounting equation** does not change as a result of those transactions.

Accounting equation An expression of the equivalency of the economic resources and the claims upon those resources of a business, often stated as Assets = Liabilities + Stockholders' Equity.

CHAPTER SHORTCUTS

Open the test drive company

1. Open your browser
2. Enter https://qbo.intuit.com/redir/testdrive as the URL
3. Check "I'm not a robot" and, if asked, select the correct images displayed on the screen

Add an account

1. Click ⚙ on the icon bar
2. Click **Chart of Accounts**
3. Click **New**

Edit an account

1. Click ⚙ on the icon bar
2. Click **Chart of Accounts**
3. In the **ACTION** column of the account you want to edit, select **Edit** from the dropdown menu

Inactivate an account

1. Click ⚙ on the icon bar
2. Click **Chart of Accounts**
3. In the **ACTION** column of the account you want to inactivate, select **Make inactive** from the dropdown menu

CHAPTER REVIEW

Matching
Match the term or phrase (as used in QuickBooks Online) to its definition.

1. item	**5.**	icon bar
2. transaction type	**6.**	privacy
3. expand or collapse	**7.**	account type
4. account detail type	**8.**	navigation bar

MBC

Assignments with the MBC **are available in myBusinessCourse.**

_____ name given to a specific form

_____ toggle button used to remove all financial data from the display area of the Dashboard

_____ subset of account types

_____ specific type of customer or inventory charge

_____ modifying the level of detail included on a report

_____ set of links to the left of the display area of the Dashboard

_____ type associated with each account to identify where it should appear in the financial statements

_____ set of links on the bar above the display area of the Dashboard

Multiple Choice

1. QuickBooks Online can be accessed through _____.
  a. Safari
  b. Internet Explorer
  c. Google Chrome
  d. Any of the above

MBC

2. Which QBO **account type** should be selected when setting up the general ledger account "Buildings"? (Assume the buildings are used as the corporate headquarters.)
  a. Other asset
  b. Property, plant & equipment
  c. Asset
  d. Fixed Asset

MBC

3. **Invoice** forms can be accessed _____.
  a. in the **+ New** menu
  b. on the **Customers** tab of **Sales**
  c. on the **Get things done** tab of the **Dashboard**
  d. **Invoice** forms can be accessed in all of the above locations.

MBC

4. Which of the following statements is false?
  a. General ledger accounts can be added to QBO by users.
  b. You can have more than one account set up as an "Accounts receivable (A/R)" **account type** in QuickBooks Online.
  c. You cannot make an account of **account type** "Expenses" a sub-account of an account of **account type** "Cost of Goods Sold."
  d. The chart of accounts is considered a "list" in QBO.

MBC

5. In QBO, the **transaction type** for recording a sale on account is _____.

   a. Sale

   b. Sales receipt

   c. Bill

   d. Invoice

BEYOND THE CLICKS—THINKING LIKE A MANAGER

Accounting: Click **Reports** on the navigation bar and open the **Standard** tab. A balance sheet report, a profit and loss report, and an accounts receivable aging summary report are all, by default, included in the **Favorites** section. Look through the other report sections on that tab and pick three additional reports you would include as **Favorites** if you were the accounting manager for a large law firm. Explain why you picked those reports.

Information Systems: You're opening a small toy store. Identify three decisions about inventory you would need to make during your first year of operations. What type of information, if any, would you want or need to have available in your accounting information system to help you make each of those decisions?

ASSIGNMENT

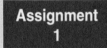

In this assignment you will be working in the test drive company, Craig's Design and Landscaping Services.

1. Click **Expenses** on the navigation bar.

   a. On the **Expenses** tab, determine the **Total** amount for

   i. Check No. 75, Hicks Hardware payee

   ii. Bill Payment (check) 6, PG&E payee

   b. On the **Vendors** tab,

   i. determine the total amount due to Brosnahan Insurance Agency

   ii. determine the email address for Computers by Jenni

2. Click **+ New** on the navigation bar, and select **Receive Payment**. Determine what must be selected in the first dropdown menu (top left):

   a. Date

   b. Customer name

   c. Vendor name

   d. Account name

3. Identify the appropriate financial statement classifications (asset, liability, equity, revenue, or expense) for the following QBO **account types**.

   a. Accounts receivable (A/R)

   b. Other Current Liabilities

   c. Cost of Goods Sold

   d. Bank

   e. Fixed Assets

4. Identify the appropriate QBO **account type** for the following general ledger accounts in a law firm.
   a. Prepaid expenses
   b. Interest payable
   c. Gain on sale of office equipment
   d. Office furniture
   e. Accumulated depreciation
   f. Inventory

5. What are the steps for opening multiple QBO windows in your browser?

6. Using the **Advanced search** function, determine how many transactions have occurred between Books by Bessie (a vendor) and Craig's Design and Landscaping Services.

7. Create a **Journal** report. Set the **report period** as **All Dates**. Filter the report to only include **Journal Entry transaction types**. What is the total in the debit column?

8. Would you be able to find the following through the navigation bar, the icon bar, or both?
   a. Balance sheet report
   b. Form for recording a cash sale
   c. Options for changing company preferences
   d. List of Products and Services

9. Create a **Profit and Loss** report for **All Dates**. Collapse the report and export the report to PDF.

10. Open the **+ New** menu. How many different types of vendor transactions (financial transactions) can be created in QBO?

APPENDIX 1A KEYBOARD SHORTCUTS IN QBO

There are many keyboard shortcuts available in QBO. These shortcuts work in Internet Explorer, Firefox, and Chrome. Most also work in Safari.

QBO Keyboard Shortcuts Available on the Dashboard or in Navigation Tab Windows

To take advantage of the shortcuts, press and hold Ctrl/control and Alt/option and then press one of the keys below. (Press and hold CMD and Alt first in Macs.)

Shortcut Key	Action
i	Opens an **Invoice** form
w	Opens a **Check** form
e	Opens an **Estimate** form
x	Opens an **Expense** form
r	Opens a **Receive payment** form
c	Opens the Customer center

(continued)

(continued from previous page)

Shortcut Key	Action
v	Opens the Vendor center
a	Opens the Chart of Accounts
f	Opens the Find screen
l	Opens the List screen
h	Opens the Help screen

QBO Keyboard Shortcuts Available in Forms

To take advantage of the shortcuts, press and hold Ctrl/control and Slt/option and then press one of the keys below. (Press and hold CMD and Alt first in Macs.)

Shortcut Key	Action
x or c	Exits the transaction
s	Saves the transaction and opens a new form
d	Saves the transaction and closes the window
m	Saves the transaction and opens an email dialog box (not available on all forms)
p	Opens print preview screen (not available on all forms)

Useful Shortcuts in Date Fields

Enter	Action
+ / –	Next day / Previous day
t	Today
w / k	First day of the week / Last day of the week
m / h	First day of the month / Last day of the month
y / r	First day of the year / Last day of the year

2

Setting Up Company Files

Objectives

After completing Chapter 2, you should be able to:

1. Set up a new company in QuickBooks Online.

2. Convert an existing company not currently using an Intuit product to QuickBooks Online.

3. Customize settings in company files.

4. Import Excel data into QuickBooks Online.

5. Set up a Gmail account (Appendix 2A).

INTRODUCTION

New company files can be created in QBO for:

- Newly formed companies.

- Existing companies that are converting from a manual system (or other accounting software system) to QBO.

- Existing companies that are converting from QuickBooks Desktop software to QBO. (Desktop conversions will not be covered in this textbook.)

In all of these cases, obtaining a clear understanding of business operations and the organization's informational needs is the best place to start. Some questions you might ask your client or yourself (if you're the owner or the accountant) include:

- Does the company currently sell or anticipate selling products, services, or both?
    - If products are currently being sold:
        - Does the company manufacture the products?
        - Is a product inventory maintained, or are products purchased to order?
        - Are products sold to consumers, to distributors, or to both?
    - Is the company responsible for collecting sales taxes from customers?

- Are there significant business segments within the company currently or expected in the future?

- Does the company have employees?

- Does the company have specific reporting needs (internal or external) currently, or does it expect to have such needs in the future?

There is a reason that "anticipated" operations are part of some of the questions. If you understand the direction of the company, you can design a system that will accommodate expected changes. For example, let's say you're opening a barbershop. You have some great ideas and expect that you will be able to open several more shops within the next year. When you have multiple shops, you're going to want to track operations by shop. QBO has features that can handle multiple locations.

If this is an existing company, management will need to decide the conversion date (start date). Although you can start recording transactions at any point in time, it is important to understand the implications of selecting various dates. For example, all federal and state payroll reporting is based on calendar quarters or calendar years, so companies often convert data as of the first day of a calendar quarter or calendar year.

As of early 2021, the fee for the QBO plan we will be using in this course (QBO Plus) was $70 per month. This fee covers all the basic recordkeeping functions other than payroll.

In this chapter, we're going to go over the basics of setting up new companies in QBO. We'll also cover setting up files for existing companies and we'll use data imported from Excel and CSV files to create the company file you'll be using for your homework assignments.

SETTING UP COMPANY FILES IN QBO

Setting Up Brand New Companies in QBO

The initial setup of a new company in QBO is very straightforward. To start, a user only needs an email address and some general information about the company and about which QBO features the user expects to use.

 WARNING: This section gives you a basic overview of a new company setup in QBO. The steps for setting up your homework company file are covered in the SETTING UP YOUR HOMEWORK COMPANY section later in this chapter. Make sure you follow those steps carefully.

Subscriptions to the various versions of QBO are purchased through the Intuit website: https://quickbooks.intuit.com/pricing/.

Once a QBO version is selected, users create an Intuit account and register for the software.

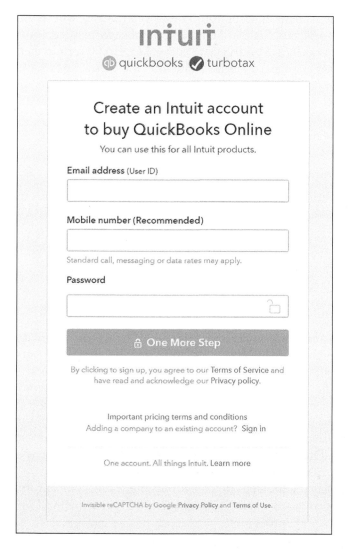

Figure 2.1
QBO sign up screen

Once they've registered, users are asked to enter the company name and answer a series of questions about their business. The answers are used by QBO to activate features in the software and develop a customized chart of accounts.

The questions cover:

- company business structure

- company industry

- expected business activities

- types of users that will be accessing the company file

Once all questions have been answered, the user clicks **All set** to create the new company file.

 HINT: Once the company file has been created, the new company's **Dashboard** will appear.

QBO automatically creates basic accounts and makes other certain selections based on the features selected as part of the setup. For example, QBO will assume the company uses accrual, not cash, as its basis of accounting. Inventory tracking will be turned on if **Manage your inventory** was selected. Standard date and number formatting conventions are automatically selected as well (MM/dd/yyyy for date; 123,456.00 for number).

If a company has just started business, the software is now ready for use. All users need to do is review and modify, if necessary, the settings, the chart of accounts, and the items created by QBO to match the needs of the company. Modifying settings is covered in the **CUSTOMIZING QUICKBOOKS ONLINE** section of this chapter. Modifying **accounts** and **product** and **service** items was covered in Chapter 1.

Converting Existing Companies to QBO

The initial setup outlined in the **Setting Up Brand New Companies in QBO** section of this chapter is also required for converting existing companies to QBO.

- Users register with an email address.

- Users enter the company name and describe the business industry.

- Users select the basic features needed.

- The users identify their role at the business.

Of course, if an existing company is converting to QBO, the current chart of accounts must be set up. Products and services, customers, vendors, and employees must also be entered. To make it easier, all of these lists can be imported into QBO.

To complete the conversion, account balances as of the conversion date must be entered. For some accounts, the balances can easily be entered using a journal entry. For other accounts, new users must decide how much detail to bring into QBO. For example, users can enter outstanding customer invoices individually or they can simply enter the full customer balance. The same is true for vendor balances. If the company sells products, the quantity and value of items on hand must be entered.

You will be practicing the steps for converting an existing company into QBO as you set up your homework company in the **SETTING UP YOUR HOMEWORK COMPANY FILE** section of this chapter.

CUSTOMIZING QUICKBOOKS ONLINE

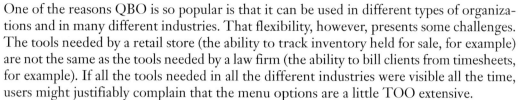

One of the reasons QBO is so popular is that it can be used in different types of organizations and in many different industries. That flexibility, however, presents some challenges. The tools needed by a retail store (the ability to track inventory held for sale, for example) are not the same as the tools needed by a law firm (the ability to bill clients from timesheets, for example). If all the tools needed in all the different industries were visible all the time, users might justifiably complain that the menu options are a little TOO extensive.

Optional tools and features are known as **settings** in QBO. When a company file is first created, choices between **settings** are made automatically. For example, it's assumed that all US companies use the accrual method of accounting, have January as the first month of the fiscal year, show dates in the MM/dd/yyyy format, and use commas and two decimals as the number format. Other **settings** are automatically activated (or deactivated) based on answers to questions posed in the file setup process. For example, if a user indicates that the company sells inventory, the inventory tracking feature is activated. If products or services are sold, preferred invoice terms are automatically set at Net 30.

Some of the initial **settings** may need to be changed to better meet the needs of the user. Users can customize the tools and features available in QBO:

* As part of the initial company setup.
  * Customizing settings as part of the initial setup will be covered in the **SETTING UP YOUR HOMEWORK COMPANY FILE** section of this chapter.
* By changing the **settings** in an existing company.

Editing Settings In a Company File

To change settings, click the ⚙ in the icon bar.

Figure 2.2

Icon bar

The screen will look something like this:

YOUR COMPANY	LISTS	TOOLS	PROFILE
Account and settings	All lists	Order checks ⧉	Feedback
Manage users	Products and services	Import data	Privacy
Custom form styles	Recurring transactions	Import desktop data	
Chart of accounts	Attachments	Export data	
QuickBooks labs	Tags	Reconcile	
		Budgeting	
		Audit log	
		SmartLook	
		Case center	

You're viewing QuickBooks in **Accountant view**. Learn more   Switch to Business view

Figure 2.3

Link to company settings

Click **Account and Settings** under the **Your Company** column.

Figure 2.4

Company tab of
Account and Settings

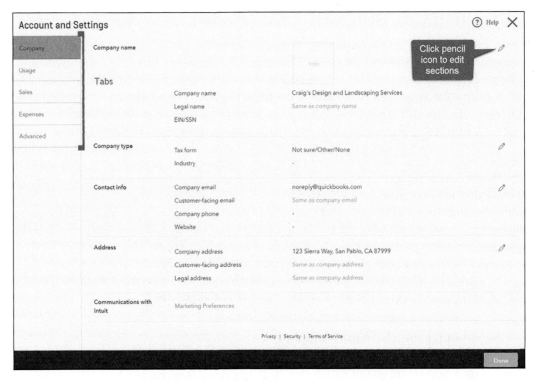

There are five tabs on the left side of the page in the test drive company file. (There are two additional tabs relating to user subscriptions in company files.) On each tab, various settings can be changed. On the **Company** tab, basic information about the company is entered (name, address, etc.). Changes are made on all tabs by clicking the **pencil** icon in the top right corner of the appropriate section.

Figure 2.5

Company tab of
Account and Settings

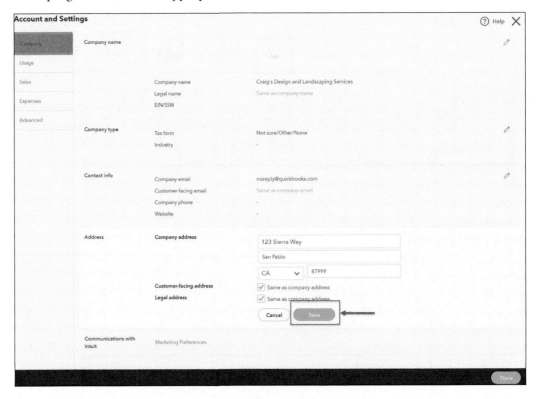

Clicking **Save** in the modified section saves the changes in the section (Clicking **Done** in the bottom right corner of the screen closes **Account and Settings**.)

On the **Sales** tab, changes can be made to sales form content and inventory tracking options.

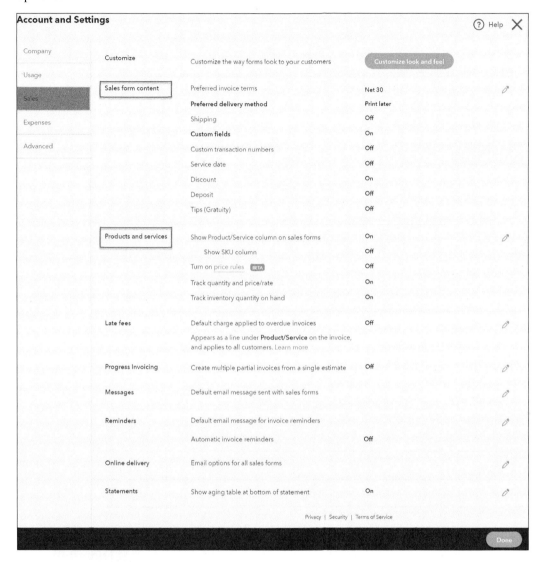

Figure 2.6

Sales tab of Account and Settings

On the **Expenses** tab, features such as purchase orders and expense tracking by customer can be turned on and off.

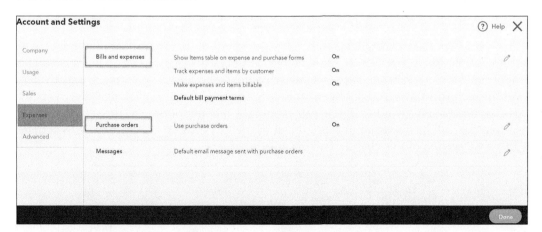

Figure 2.7

Expenses tab of Account and Settings

The **Advanced** tab includes options for choosing an accounting method, setting up accounts, and tracking by segment or project.

Figure 2.8

Advanced tab of
Account and Settings

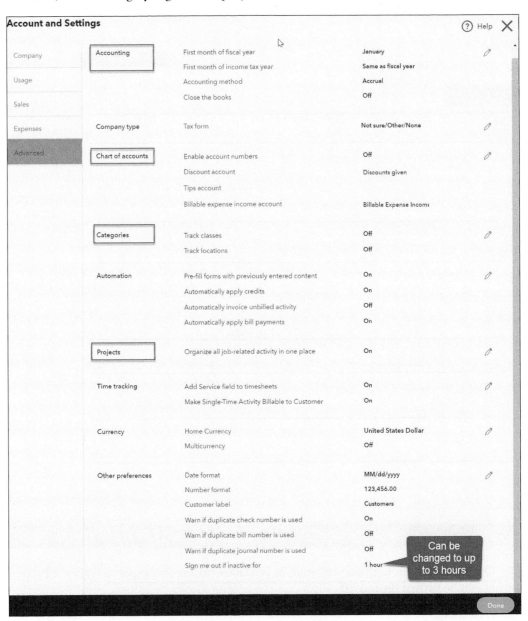

One setting that can be changed in the **Advanced** tab relates to the amount of user inactivity (in hours) that the software will allow before automatically signing off. This is especially important for you to change in the test drive company because all your work is lost whenever the company file is closed. When all changes have been made, clicking **Done** closes the **Account and Settings** window. Users can extend the amount of time to three hours.

Settings will be discussed in more detail in the **SETTING UP YOUR HOMEWORK COMPANY FILE** section of this chapter and in future chapters.

 WARNING: When you make changes in settings, the appearance of various forms will often change.

Customize QBO for Craig's Design and Landscaping.

(Craig's wants to increase the amount of allowed inactivity and set up a default message for invoices.)

PRACTICE

EXERCISE

2.1

MBC

1. Click the ⚙ on the icon bar.

2. Click **Account and Settings**.

3. Open the **Advanced** tab to change the amount of time of inactivity allowed.

    a. In the **Other preferences** section, click **Sign me out if inactive for**.

    b. Select **3 hours** on the dropdown menu.

    c. Click **Save**.

4. Open the **Sales** tab to set up a default message on sales forms.

    a. Click the **pencil** icon in the **Messages** section.

    b. Select **Invoices and other sales forms** from the **second** Sales Form dropdown menu (the one at the bottom of the **Messages** section).

    c. Change the message to "We appreciate your business."

    d. Click **Save**.

5. **Make a note of** the following:

    a. the company address on the **Company** tab.

    b. the **Preferred invoice terms** on the **Sales** tab.

    c. whether the **Purchase order** feature is activated on the **Expenses** tab.

    d. the **First month of fiscal year** on the **Advanced** tab

    e. the **Accounting method** selected on the **Advanced** tab.

6. Click **Done** (bottom right corner of screen) to exit the **Account and Settings** window.

SETTING UP YOUR HOMEWORK COMPANY FILE

eLectures

Your homework assignments will be done in the company file provided to you by Intuit. General information about the company assigned by your instructor is given to you at the end of this chapter (under Chapter Two Assignments). In this section, we'll go through the steps necessary to get your homework company file set up. The steps are the same no matter which homework company your instructor assigns (Math Revealed! or Salish Software Solutions).

> **BEHIND THE SCENES** You will be prompted by QBO to save transactions and setting changes as you go. You do not need to do a file save at the end of a session. Unlike your work in the test drive company, QBO automatically saves your work in your company file.

STEP 1—Read the background information for the homework company assigned by your instructor included at the end of the chapter.

Having a good understanding of the company you're setting up should help as you move through the process.

STEP 2—Obtain your license and open your company file.

Your instructor will direct Intuit to provide you with a one-year free license to QuickBooks Online Plus. Intuit Education will then email you an invitation to set up your homework file.

HINT: The email will likely be sent to the address on file for you at your school. Make sure that the email address is correct.

Email invitation to set up a company file

WARNING: Make sure you have enough time to complete Step 3 before you move forward. It could be difficult to get back into your QBO file if the initial setup process wasn't finished.

When you're ready, click **Accept Invitation**.

HINT: If you get an error message about the link not working, right-click the *Accept invitation* link, select *Copy link location*, open a new window in Incognito (private) mode, and paste the copied URL into the address bar. If that doesn't work, clear your cache and try again. If you're still having issues, contact your instructor.

Registration screen

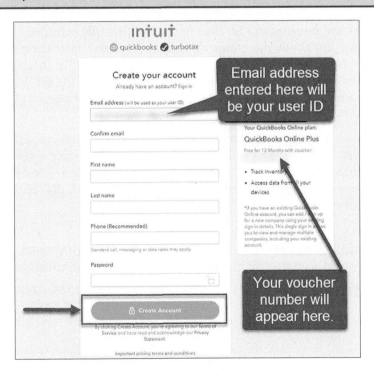

Create your Intuit account by entering an email address, your name, and creating a password. The email address (and the related password) will be used each time you log in to QBO.

> **HINT:** You can use your school email address, your own personal email address, or you can set up an email address specifically for this course. Setting up a separate email offers the most security. Instructions for setting up a Gmail account are provided in Appendix 2A if you want to use a unique email address.
>
> If you already have an Intuit account, simply sign in using the link under **Create your account** at the top of the screen.

Intuit accepts passwords that have the following characteristics:

1. It must be at least 8 characters long.

2. It must include both lowercase and uppercase letters.

3. It must include a number.

4. It must include a symbol.

Click **Create Account**.
You may see the following welcome message:

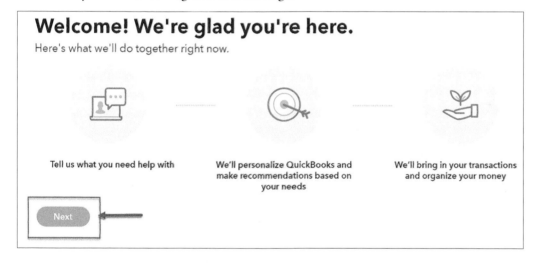

Figure 2.11

Welcome message

Click **Next**.

STEP 3—Answer the informational questions that appear in the next set of screens.

General information is entered in the first screens you'll see in QBO. The company name is entered, and its legal structure and business activities are identified. Intuit uses this information to activate various features so users can get started.

In early 2021, Intuit started to change the order and wording of the setup questions. The specific questions that appear in **your** homework company file setup may differ from those that appear for your fellow students or your instructor. The answers are the same regardless of the homework company assigned by your instructor. Your homework company should be set up as a Corporation; your role in the company is the Accountant; you will be entering all standard business transactions (including time tracking); you will not activate payroll in your homework company.

Table 2.1 shows the most common question wording and the answers that you should answer or select.

Table 2.1	Screen Heading	Answers
Company setup questions	What's your business name?	Your homework company name should be your name followed by the name of the homework company assigned by your instructor. For example, if your name were John Smith and your instructor assigned Math Revealed! as the homework company, you would enter *John Smith Math Revealed!* as your business name. Do **not** check the box next to **I use QuickBooks Desktop and want to bring in my data. TIP:** Check to make sure your instructor doesn't have special instructions for your company name.
	What's your role at the company? or Who works at this business?	Select the option that includes the word **Accountant**.
	Who helps run this business?	Select **Only the owner** or **I fly solo**.
	Link your accounts	Select **Skip for now** or **Manually add transactions**.
	What kind of business is this?	**Corporation** or **C-Corp**
	What does your business do? or What's your industry?	Enter *Professional services* in the field. From the displayed options, select **All other professional, scientific, and technical services**.
	How does your business make money?	Select **I sell services** and **I sell products**.
	What is everything you want to set up?	Select all options other than those related to paying employees, accepting online payments, and purchasing insurance.
	Ready for a free trial of QuickBooks Payroll?	Select **Maybe later**.

> ✱ **HINT:** If you need help with the setup questions, watch the *Setting Up Your Company File* video in myBusinessCourse or download the *Setting Up Your Company File* PDF on the Student Ancillaries tab at https://cambridgepub.com/book/qbo2021#ancillaries.

Click **Done** or **All set** on the final question screen.

Figure 2.12

Dashboard

You now have a company file!

You may see an offer for a 30-second tour. Click **Let's go** to take the tour or click the **X** in the top right corner of the box to skip it.

BEHIND THE SCENES Intuit automatically assigns a software license to each user when a company file is created. Your license number (called **Company ID**) can be found on the **Billing and Subscription** tab of **Account and Settings**.

STEP 4—Change the settings.

Now that you have a company file, it's time to change some of the settings.

 HINT: If you signed out or were logged out of QBO after setting up your new company, go to qbo.intuit.com to sign back in. You may be asked to add a company address before you can access the file. If so, enter "3835 Freeport Blvd, Sacramento, CA 95822."

Click the ⚙ on the icon bar.

Figure 2.13
Gear menu

YOUR COMPANY	LISTS	TOOLS	PROFILE
Account and settings	All lists	Order checks ☑	Feedback
Manage users	Products and services	Import data	Refer a friend
Custom form styles	Recurring transactions	Import desktop data	Privacy
Chart of accounts	Attachments	Export data	Switch company
QuickBooks labs	Tags	Reconcile	
		Budgeting	
		Audit log	
		SmartLook	
		Case center	

You're viewing QuickBooks in **Accountant view**. Learn more   Switch to Business view

---

! **WARNING:** If you inadvertently selected a role other than **Accountant** when answering the **What is your role?** question in Step 3, you will be in **Business view** and certain tools and features may not be available to you. Click **Switch to Accountant view** at the bottom of the ⚙ menu before moving forward.

Click **Account and settings**.

Figure 2.14

Company tab of
Account and Settings

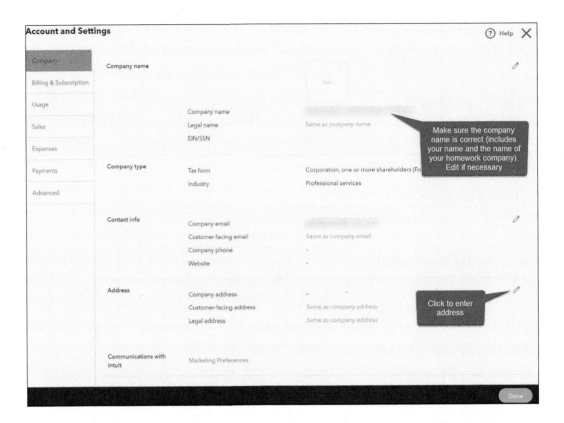

On the **Company** tab, make sure the **Company name** includes your name and the name
of the homework company. Edit the field if necessary.

Click the pencil icon in the **Address** section and enter "3835 Freeport Blvd, Sacramento, CA 95822." The same address is used for **customer-facing** and **legal** addresses in
both homework companies.

Click **Save**.

Click to open the **Sales** tab.

Many of the sales settings were automatically changed when you selected the services
needed. For example, when you checked **Manage your inventory** in the initial setup of your
company file (Step 3), QBO automatically made changes to the **Products and services** section.

Check to make sure the **Custom transaction numbers** setting is **On**. If not, click the
pencil icon in the **Sales form content** section and check the **Custom transaction numbers**
box. Click **Save**. Your screen should look something like this:

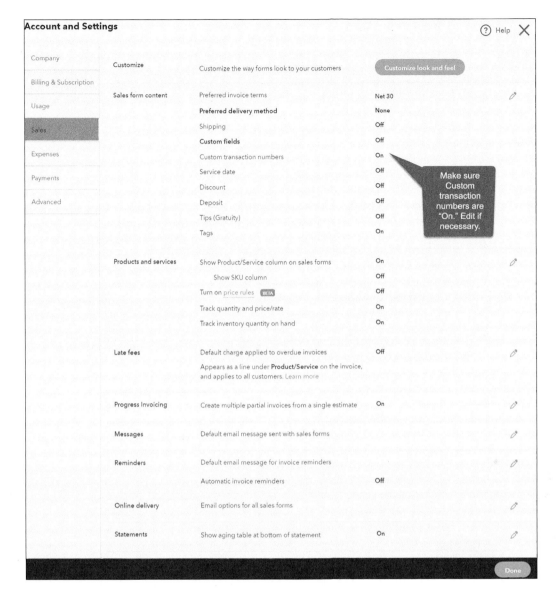

Figure 2.15

Completed Sales tab in Account and Settings

Click to open the **Expenses** tab.

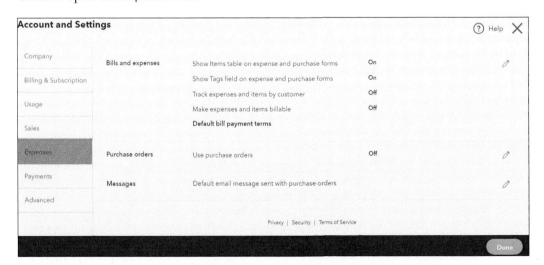

Figure 2.16

Expenses tab in Account and Settings

Features related to purchase transactions are included here.

No changes need to be made on the **Expenses** tab.

Since this is a real company file, not the test drive file, three additional tabs are included in **Account and Settings**. The **Billing & Subscription** tab gives information about your subscription. The **Usage** tab displays information about file size limits in QBO. The **Payments** tab provides links to additional services related to sales transactions. There are no settings to change on these tabs.

Click the **Advanced** tab. Click the pencil icon to open each section and make the following changes:

- **Company type**—If necessary select, **Corporation, one or more shareholders (Form 1120)** in the **Tax form** dropdown menu. Click **Save**.

- **Chart of accounts**—Toggle the box next to **Enable account numbers** to turn the feature on. Check the box next to **Show account numbers** and click **Save**.

- **Automation**—Toggle the box next to **Pre-fill forms with previously entered content** to turn the feature to **Off**. Click **Save**.

- **Other preferences**—Toggle the boxes next to **Warn if duplicate check/bill/journal number is used** to turn the warnings on. Click **Save**.

  - You may also want to extend the amount of time QBO remains open when you're not actively working on your assignments. If so, make the change in the dropdown menu next to **Sign me out if inactive for**.

The screen should look something like this when you've made the changes:

Figure 2.17

Completed Advanced tab of Account and Settings

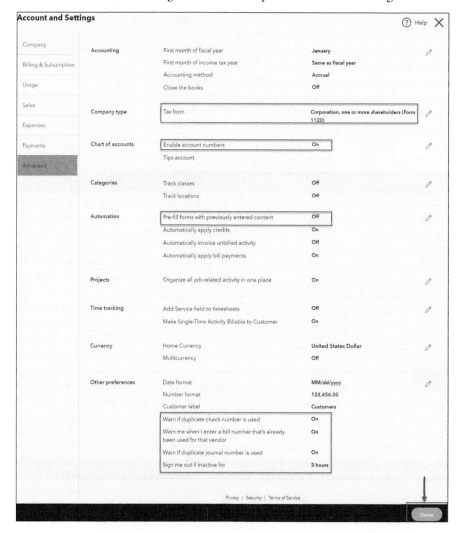

Click **Done** to exit **Account and Settings**. On the Dashboard, the full name of your home-work company should have replaced your email address.

STEP 5—Purge the chart of accounts.

QBO automatically created quite a few accounts for you when you set up your company in Step 3. Unfortunately, many of the accounts that were set up are not needed in your homework company and many of the accounts you will need were not created by QBO.

 HINT: To see the chart of accounts set up by QBO, click the ⚙ on the icon bar and click **Chart of accounts**. Click **See your Chart of Accounts**.

Instead of adding and deleting these accounts (which is a tedious process), you will be purging the chart of accounts QBO set up and importing your own accounts into the company file.

With QBO open, change the URL by replacing 'homepage' with 'purgecompany' and clicking Enter. The URL will look something like https://c26.qbo.intuit.com/app/purgecompany. (You may have different numbers after the c or you may have no c number.)

BEHIND THE SCENES Intuit rolls out QBO software updates in batches. The c-number at the front of the URL represents the batch (referred to as a **cluster**) for your homework company file. Your **cluster** number may differ from the numbers of your classmates and/or your instructor and you may see software updates before or after they do. Contact your professor with any questions.

The screen will look something like this:

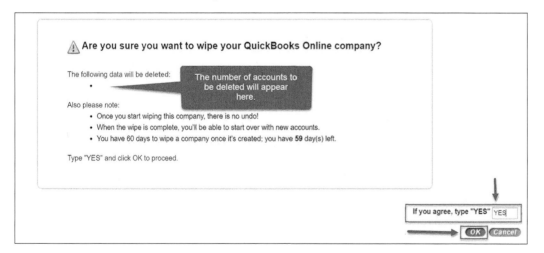

Figure 2.18

Purge warning message

Enter **YES** and click **OK**. The screen will look something like this:

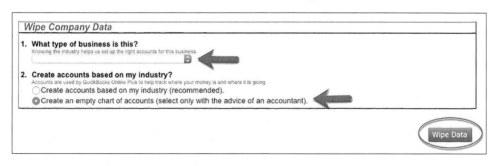

Figure 2.19

Final purge screen

If your instructor assigned Math Revealed!, select "Teachers, Tutors, Coaches" in the dropdown menu for the first question. (It's in the **Educational Services** section.) If your instructor assigned Salish Software Solutions, select "Other Consulting, Professional, and Technical Services." (It's in the **Consulting, Professional, and Technical Services** section.)

Select **Create an empty chart of accounts** to answer the second question.

 HINT: You may see the Figure 2.18 screen again (a smaller number of accounts will be listed). If so, click **Cancel** or **Dashboard** (on the navigation bar) to exit out of the screen.

Click **Wipe Data**. The chart of accounts has now been purged.

Click ⚙ on the icon bar and click **Chart of Accounts** in the **Your Company** column.

Click **See your Chart of Accounts**. The screen should look something like this:

Figure 2.20

Purged chart of accounts

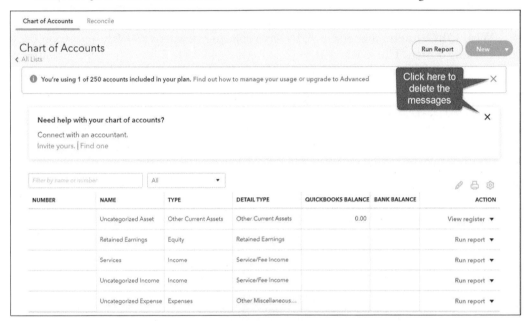

The accounts remaining in the chart of accounts are default accounts that can't be deleted.

 **BEHIND THE SCENES** The chart of accounts and all transactions are deleted when a company file is purged. All of the settings remain intact. Purging a company and importing data into a company can be done an unlimited number of times within the first 60 days of a new subscription.

You are now ready to start importing data. All of the files you will need for importing in the next five steps are available at https://cambridgepub.com/book/qbo2021#ancillaries. You may want to download them all to your desktop, hard drive, or to a USB drive before you move forward.

STEP 6—Import a new chart of accounts.

In QBO, click the ⚙ on the icon bar.

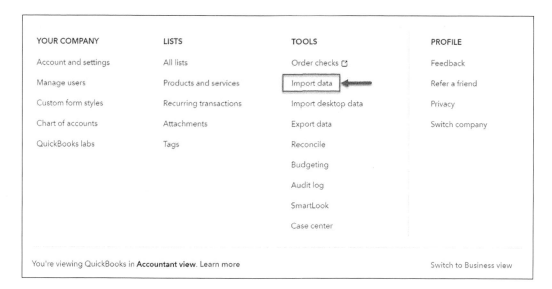

Figure 2.21

Access to import feature

Click **Import data.** The screen should look something like this:

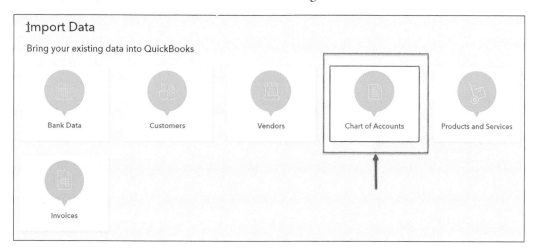

Figure 2.22

Import data selection

Click **Chart of Accounts.**

Figure 2.23

File selection screen for account import

Upload your **Chart of Accounts for Importing** .xlsx file into the **Select a CSV or Excel file to upload** field. The account selected may be barely visible in the field. As long as you can see it, you're fine.

Click **Next.**

The screen should look like this:

Figure 2.24

Mapped fields for account import

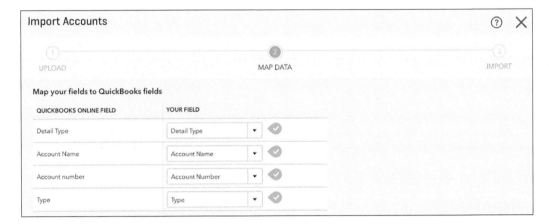

Click **Next**.

Figure 2.25

Accounts to be imported

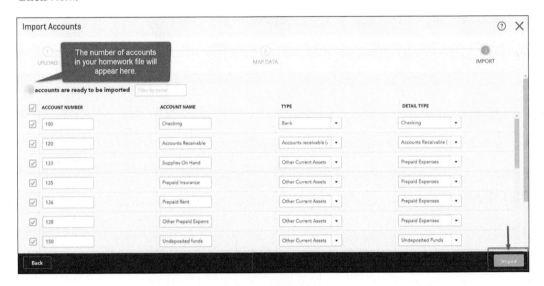

> HINT: Depending on which homework company your instructor has assigned, your window may show a different number of accounts ready to be imported.

Scroll down through the screen. Any problems will be highlighted in red. If you have inadvertently changed a field, refer to the Excel spreadsheet and make the correction.

> **!** WARNING: If the **Import** light is not bright green, there is a problem with the data. Click **Back** to see if you uploaded the correct file. QBO is very sensitive to issues in import files. If changes have inadvertently been made to the Excel file, you will not be able to import the accounts.

Click **Import**.

> **HINT:** You may see a message that some of the accounts can't be imported because they are duplicates. If so, simply remove them (uncheck the box next to those accounts) and proceed. You can make corrections later.

Click ⚙ on the icon bar. Click **Chart of Accounts** to see the new chart of accounts. It should include all of the accounts listed on the Excel spreadsheet.

There's still some work to do in the chart of accounts but first you need to import customers, vendors, and products and services. You will complete the work on the chart of accounts in your homework assignment for Chapter 2.

STEP 7—Import the products and services list. (This process will be similar to the import of the chart of accounts.)

In QBO, click the ⚙ on the icon bar. Click **Import Data**.

Click **Products and Services**.

Upload the **Products and Services List for Importing** .xlsx file into the **Select a CSV or Excel file to upload** field and click **Next**.

The screen should look like this:

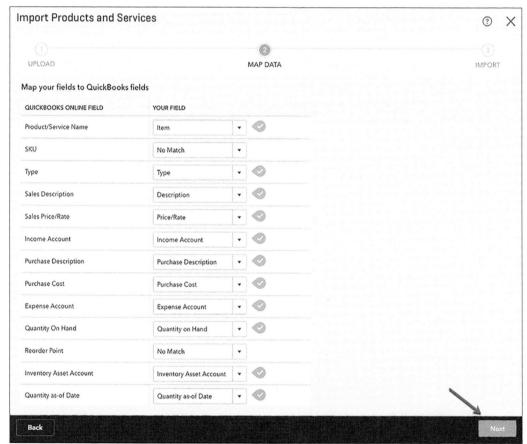

Figure 2.26

Mapped fields for products and services import

> **BEHIND THE SCENES** QBO automatically maps the fields on the Excel worksheet to the fields in the **Products and Services** in QBO. Not all data fields need to be completed with an upload.

Click **Next**.

The screen, without data included, would look something like this:

Figure 2.27

Products and Services
to be imported

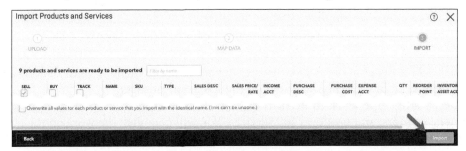

> ✱ **HINT:** Depending on which homework company your instructor has assigned, your window may show a different number of products and services ready to be imported.

All of the data from the Excel spreadsheet should show on your screen.

You will see red 0s in the **QTY** field in the first 3 rows of Math Revealed! and the first 4 rows of Salish Software Solutions. (These are **service** items so there is no quantity on hand.) Click each 0 to remove the red.

> ! **WARNING:** If the **Import** light is not bright green, there is a problem with the data. Click **Back** to see if you uploaded the correct file. QBO is very sensitive to issues in import files. If changes have inadvertently been made to the Excel file, you will not be able to import the accounts. Quantity fields in service items may be highlighted in red. Click the field to remove the highlight and proceed.

Click **Import**.

Click the ⚙ on the icon bar and click **Products and Services**. You should see all of the items from the Excel worksheet.

You MAY see the following message when you open the **Products and Services** list:

Figure 2.28

Category option
message

If you do, click **Ready to make your life easier?** (If you don't see the message, move on to Step 8. QBO has automatically activated the **Categories** feature in your file.)

Figure 2.29

Category activation

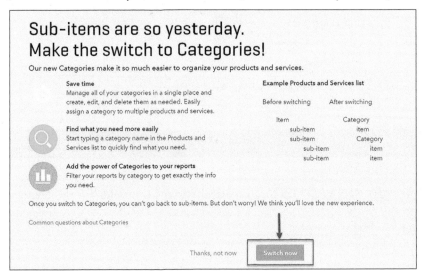

Click **Switch now**. This will activate the feature in your company file. **Categories** will be covered in more detail in Chapter 3.

STEP 8—Import customers. (This process will be similar to the import of products and services.)

In QBO, click the ⚙ on the icon bar. Click **Import Data**.

Click **Customers**.

Upload the **Customer List for Importing** .xlsx file into the **Select a CSV or Excel file to upload** field and click **Next**. The screen should look like this:

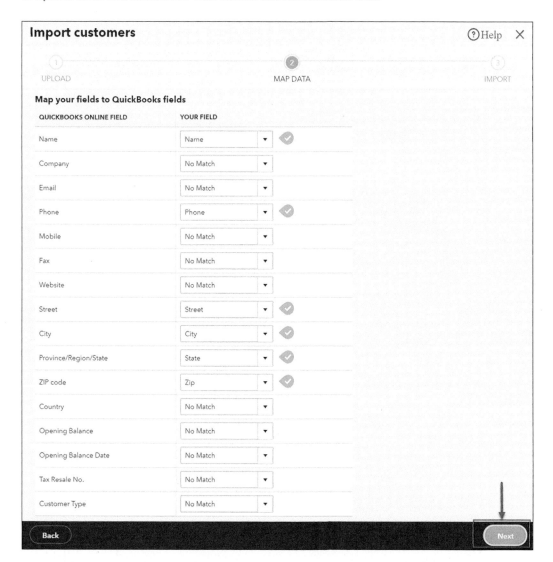

Figure 2.30

Mapped fields for customer import

> **BEHIND THE SCENES** QBO automatically maps the fields on the Excel worksheet to the fields in the **Customer List** in QBO. Not all fields need to be uploaded.

Click **Next**.

The screen, without data included, would look something like this:

Figure 2.31

Customers to be
imported

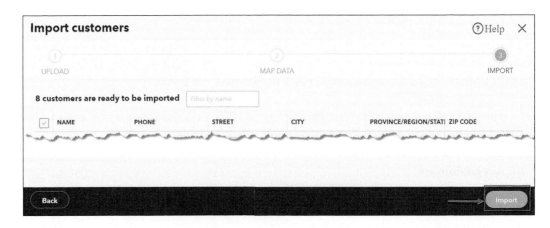

> **HINT:** Depending on which homework company your instructor has assigned,
> your window may show a different number of customers ready to be imported.

> **WARNING:** If the **Import** light is not bright green or if any of the fields
> are red, there is a problem with the data. Click **Back** to see if you up-
> loaded the correct file. QBO is very sensitive to issues in import files. If
> changes have inadvertently been made to the Excel file, you will not be
> able to import the accounts.

Click Import.

Click Sales on the navigation bar and select the Customers tab. The customer list should
include all of the customers included on the Excel spreadsheet.

STEP 9—Import vendors. (This process will be similar to the import of customers.)

In QBO, click the ⚙ on the icon bar. Click Import Data.

Click Vendors.

Upload the **Vendor List for Importing** .xlsx file into the Select a CSV or Excel file to
upload field and click Next. The screen should look like this:

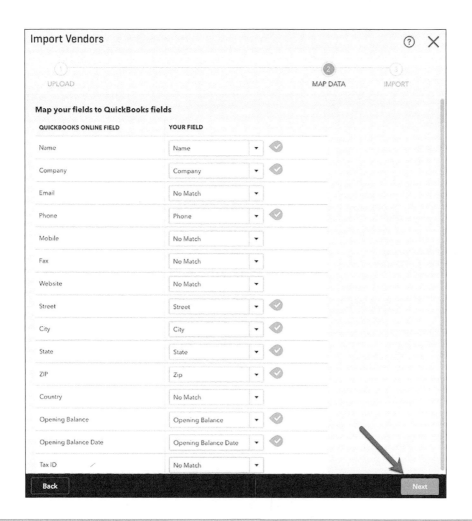

Figure 2.32
Mapped fields for
vendor import

BEHIND THE SCENES QBO automatically maps the fields on the Excel work-sheet to the fields in the **Vendor List** in QBO. Not all fields need to be uploaded.

Click **Next**.

The screen, not including data, should look like this:

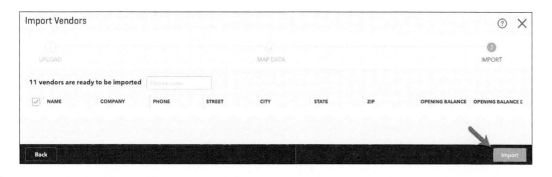

Figure 2.33
Vendors to be imported

HINT: Depending on which homework company your instructor has assigned, your window may show a different number of vendors ready to be imported.

> **!** **WARNING:** If the **Import** light is not bright green or if any of the fields are red, there is a problem with the data. Click **Back** to see if you uploaded the correct file. QBO is very sensitive to issues in import files. If changes have inadvertently been made to the Excel file, you will not be able to import the accounts.

Click **Import**.

Click **Expenses** on the navigation bar and select the **Vendors** tab. The vendor list should include all of the vendors and balances included on the Excel spreadsheet.

STEP 10—Import invoices.

In QBO, click the ⚙ on the icon bar. Click **Import Data**.

Click **Invoices**.

Figure 2.34

File selection screen for invoice import

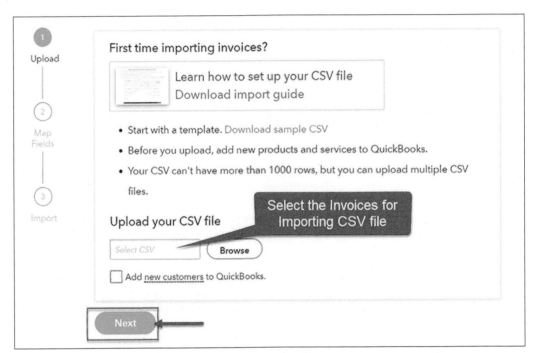

Upload the **Invoices for Importing** file into the **Upload your CSV file** field and click **Next**. The screen should look like this:

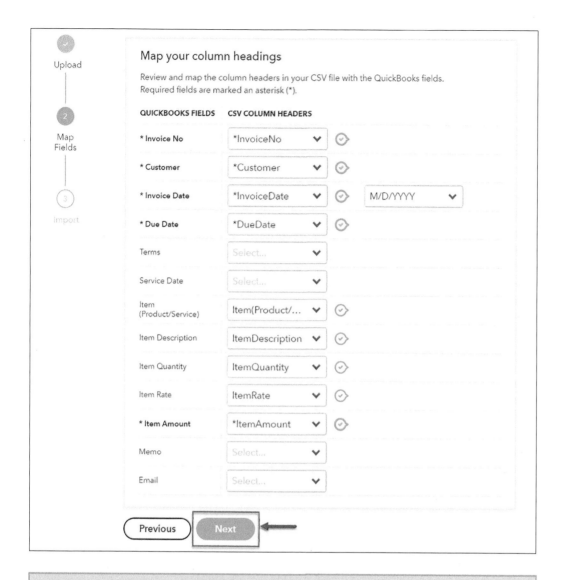

Figure 2.35

Mapped fields for
invoice import

BEHIND THE SCENES QBO automatically maps the fields in the CSV file to the
fields on invoices in QBO. Not all fields need to be uploaded.

Click **Next**.
   The screen should look like this:

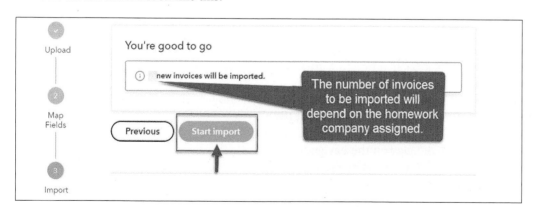

Figure 2.36

Link to start invoice
import

Click **Start Import**.

When the import is complete, the following screen will appear:

Figure 2.37

Invoice import results
screen

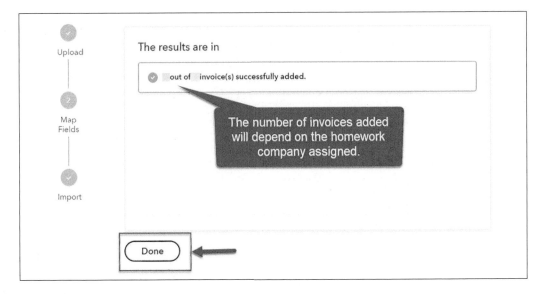

Click **Done**.

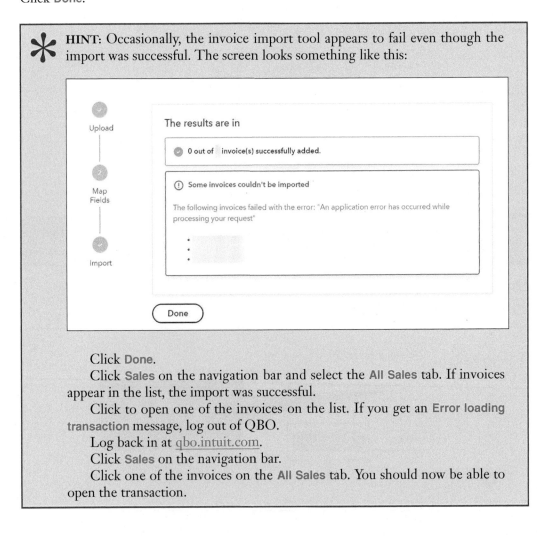

HINT: Occasionally, the invoice import tool appears to fail even though the import was successful. The screen looks something like this:

Click **Done**.

Click **Sales** on the navigation bar and select the **All Sales** tab. If invoices appear in the list, the import was successful.

Click to open one of the invoices on the list. If you get an **Error loading transaction** message, log out of QBO.

Log back in at qbo.intuit.com.

Click **Sales** on the navigation bar.

Click one of the invoices on the **All Sales** tab. You should now be able to open the transaction.

STEP 11—Check your balances.

This is still accounting so all the importing you just did should have resulted in a number of balanced journal entries, right? QBO creates entries for the accounts receivable, accounts payable, and inventory balances you imported using several different offset accounts. You will be adjusting those entries as part of your homework assignment for this chapter.

> **BEHIND THE SCENES** One of the accounts used by QBO when importing data is Opening balance equity, an equity account. This account is unique to QBO and is used as a tool for balancing entries. There is no equivalent to this account in financial accounting. Any balance in opening balance equity should be cleared before financial reports are prepared.

To make sure you've got a good start, click Reports on the navigation bar.

Click Balance Sheet in the Favorites section. Change the date to 12/31/21 (in both date fields).

Click Run report.

Your balance sheet should look like one of the following (depending on the homework company assigned by your instructor). If it doesn't, go back to Step 5, purge the data, and start the import process over.

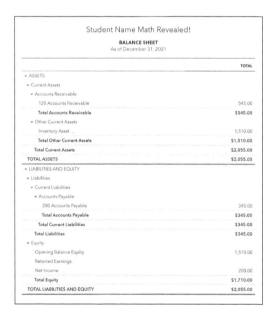

Figure 2.38

Starting balance sheets for company files

CHAPTER SHORTCUTS

Change settings
1. Click ⚙ on the icon bar
2. Click Account and Settings

Purge the chart of accounts
1. Open your company file
2. Enter http://qbo.intuit.com/app/purge-company as the URL
3. Type YES in the If you agree field

4. Click OK
5. Choose a business similar to your homework company in the What type of business is this? dropdown menu
6. Select Create an empty chart of accounts
7. Click Wipe Data

Import data

1. Click ⚙ on the icon bar
2. Click **Import Data**
3. Select the type of list to be imported
4. Upload the appropriate Excel or CSV file

Make a journal entry

1. Click ⊕ **New** on the navigation bar
2. Click **Journal Entry**

CHAPTER REVIEW

Matching

Assignments with the ᴹᴮᶜ are available in myBusinessCourse.

Match the term or phrase (as used in QuickBooks Online) to its definition.

1. Settings
2. Importing
3. Cluster number

4. License number
5. Purge
6. Opening balance equity

_____   the act of bringing external data into a company file

_____   default account used by QBO as part of the import process

_____   number used to identify a specific user of QBO

_____   removal of all data from a company file

_____   customizable features

_____   number used to identify batch for timing of software updates

Multiple Choice

1. Which of the following cannot be imported into QBO?
   a. Sales and expense settings
   b. Inventory balances
   c. Accounts receivable balances
   d. Accounts payable balances

2. Which of the following is not deleted when a company file is purged?
   a. Transactions
   b. Most general ledger accounts
   c. Company settings
   d. None of the listed answers are correct. Transactions, accounts, and settings are all deleted.

3. A company file _____.
   a. can be purged an unlimited number of times as long as the user's subscription is active
   b. can be purged an unlimited number of times within the first 60 days of a new subscription
   c. can be purged up to 60 times
   d. cannot be purged

4. Which account might be debited when a vendor list is imported? (Refer to the FINAL CONVERSION section of the assignment for help answering this question.)
   a. Interest expense
   b. Accounts payable
   c. Cost of goods sold
   d. Opening balance equity

5. Which account might be credited when a Product and Services list is imported?(Refer to the FINAL CONVERSION section of the assignment for help answering this question.)

    a. Inventory

    b. Cost of goods sold

    c. Accounts payable

    d. Opening balance equity

BEYOND THE CLICKS—THINKING LIKE A MANAGER

Accounting: You're opening a restaurant and want to be able to analyze operations on a monthly basis. You can only add 10 revenue and expense accounts to your general ledger. Which accounts would you choose and why?

Information Systems: What are the pros and cons of a company using a cloud based accounting software system like QuickBooks Online compared to a desktop accounting software system like QuickBooks Desktop?

ASSIGNMENTS

Background information: Martin Smith, a college student and good friend of yours, has always wanted to be an entrepreneur. He is very good in math, so, to test his entrepreneurship skills, he has decided to set up a small math tutoring company serving local high school students who struggle in their math courses. He set up the company, Math Revealed!, as a corporation in 2021. Martin is the only owner. He has not taken any distributions from the company since it opened.

The business has been successful so far. In fact, it's been so successful he has decided to work in his business full time now that he's graduated from college with a degree in mathematics.

He has decided to start using QuickBooks Online to keep track of his business transactions. He likes the convenience of being able to access his information over the Internet. You have agreed to act as his accountant while you're finishing your own academic program.

Martin currently has a number of regular customers that he tutors in Pre-Algebra, Algebra, and Geometry. His customers pay his fees by cash or check after each tutoring session but he does give terms of Net 15 to some of his customers. He has developed the following fee schedule:

Name	Description	Rate
Refresher	One-hour session	$ 60 per hour
Persistence program	Two one-hour sessions per week	$100 per week
Crisis program	Five one-hour sessions per week	$225 per week

The tutoring sessions usually take place at his students' homes but he recently signed a two-year lease on a small office above a local coffee shop. The rent is only $750 per month starting in January 2022. A security deposit of $500 was paid in December 2021.

The following equipment is owned by the company:

Description	Date placed in service	Cost	Life	Salvage Value
Computer	7/1/21	$3,000	36 months	$300
Printer	7/1/21	$ 240	24 months	$ 0
Graphing Calculators (3)	7/1/21	$ 300	36 months	$ 30

All equipment is depreciated using the straight-line method.

Assignment 2A

Math Revealed!

As of 12/31/21, Martin owed $2,500 to his father (Richard Smith) who initially helped him get started. Richard is charging him interest at a 6% annual rate. Martin has been paying interest only on a monthly basis. His last payment of interest only was on 12/31/21.

Over the next month or so, he plans to expand his business by selling a few products he believes will help his students. He has already purchased a few items:

Category	Description	Vendor	Quantity on Hand	Cost per Unit	Sales Price
Books and Tools					
	Geometry in Sports	Books Galore	20	18	25
	Solving Puzzles: Fun with Algebra	Books Galore	20	15	22
	Getting Ready for Calculus	Books Galore	20	20	28
	Geometry Kit	Math Shack	10	12	18
	Handheld Dry-Erase Boards	Math Shack	25	10	15
	Notebooks (pack of 5)	Paper Bag Depot	10	8	12

Final Conversion Work

The basic structure for Math Revealed! was set up in QBO as part of your work on pages 2-9 to 2-29 in this chapter. Now it's time to update all the account balances.

The values for Accounts Receivable, Accounts Payable, and Inventory were brought in when the invoices and the customer, vendor, and products and services lists were imported.

Click **Reports** on the navigation bar, click **Balance Sheet** in the **Favorites** section, and change the dates to 12/31/21 to 12/31/21.

Click **Run Report**. The report should look like this:

Figure 2.39

Student Name Math Revealed!

BALANCE SHEET
As of December 31, 2021

	TOTAL
▾ ASSETS	
▾ Current Assets	
▾ Accounts Receivable	
120 Accounts Receivable	545.00
Total Accounts Receivable	**$545.00**
▾ Other Current Assets	
Inventory Asset	1,510.00
Total Other Current Assets	**$1,510.00**
Total Current Assets	**$2,055.00**
TOTAL ASSETS	**$2,055.00**
▾ LIABILITIES AND EQUITY	
▾ Liabilities	
▾ Current Liabilities	
▾ Accounts Payable	
200 Accounts Payable	345.00
Total Accounts Payable	**$345.00**
Total Current Liabilities	**$345.00**
Total Liabilities	**$345.00**
▾ Equity	
Opening Balance Equity	1,510.00
Retained Earnings	
Net Income	200.00
Total Equity	**$1,710.00**
TOTAL LIABILITIES AND EQUITY	**$2,055.00**

The balances are correct for Accounts Receivable, Accounts Payable, and Inventory but notice the amounts for Opening Balance Equity ($1,510) and Net Income ($200). Opening Balance Equity is a default equity account credited by QBO when inventory is imported into the system. There is no business account called "opening balance equity."

Click the $1,510 balance to see the underlying transactions. The report should look something like this: [**TIP:** Your transactions may not appear in the same order.]

Figure 2.40

DATE	TRANSACTION TYPE	NUM	NAME	MEMO/DESCRIPTION	ACCOUNT	SPLIT	AMOUNT	BALANCE
▾ Inventory Asset								
12/31/2021	Inventory Starting Value	START		Notebook - Opening inventory a...	Inventory Asset	Opening Balance Equity	80.00	80.00
12/31/2021	Inventory Starting Value	START		Kit - Opening inventory and value	Inventory Asset	Opening Balance Equity	120.00	200.00
12/31/2021	Inventory Starting Value	START		Ready - Opening inventory and ...	Inventory Asset	Opening Balance Equity	400.00	600.00
12/31/2021	Inventory Starting Value	START		Puzzles - Opening inventory and ...	Inventory Asset	Opening Balance Equity	300.00	900.00
12/31/2021	Inventory Starting Value	START		Sports - Opening inventory and ...	Inventory Asset	Opening Balance Equity	360.00	1,260.00
12/31/2021	Inventory Starting Value	START		Dry-Erase - Opening inventory a...	Inventory Asset	Opening Balance Equity	250.00	1,510.00
Total for Inventory Asset							$1,510.00	
TOTAL							$1,510.00	

Student Name Math Revealed!
TRANSACTION REPORT
December 31, 2021

You can see that as part of the import of products and services list on hand, the Opening Balance Equity was credited when Inventory Asset was debited. You could click each line item to correct the entry. Instead, the entire balance will be adjusted as part of a journal entry created later in this assignment.

Click Dashboard to close the window.

Click Reports on the navigation bar and click Profit and Loss in the Favorites section. Change the dates to 12/1/21 to 12/31/21. (All of the data was imported with December dates.)

Click Run Report. The report should look something like this:

Figure 2.41

Student Name Math Revealed!

PROFIT AND LOSS
December 2021

	TOTAL
▾ Income	
Services	545.00
Total Income	$545.00
GROSS PROFIT	$545.00
Expenses	
Total Expenses	
NET OPERATING INCOME	$545.00
▾ Other Expenses	
700 Interest expense	345.00
Total Other Expenses	$345.00
NET OTHER INCOME	$ (345.00)
NET INCOME	$200.00

Click the $345 amount listed for **Interest Expense**. The report looks like this:

DATE	TRANSACTION TYPE	NUM	NAME	MEMO/DESCRIPTION	ACCOUNT	SPLIT	AMOUNT	BALANCE
▾ Interest expense								
12/16/2021	Bill		Paper Bag Depot	Opening Balance	700 Interest expense	200 Accounts Payable	80.00	80.00
12/20/2021	Bill		Kathy's Coffee	Opening Balance	700 Interest expense	200 Accounts Payable	25.00	105.00
12/27/2021	Bill		Math Shack	Opening Balance	700 Interest expense	200 Accounts Payable	240.00	345.00
Total for Interest expense							$345.00	
TOTAL							$345.00	

Student Name Math Revealed!
TRANSACTION REPORT
December 2021

Permanent account
An account used to prepare the balance sheet—that is, an asset, liability, or stockholders' equity account. Any balance in a permanent account at the end of an accounting period is carried forward to the following accounting period.

Unlike customer invoices, specific vendor bills cannot be imported to QBO. Instead the vendor balances were imported, along with the vendor address information, in Step 9 of the homework company setup.

As you can see, QBO debited **Interest Expense**, by default, to offset the credit to Accounts Payable recorded as part of the import of vendors. Since you will only be recording Math Revealed! activity starting January 1st, we won't take the time to correct these entries. Interest Expense, along with the revenue account, will be closed to Retained Earnings as part of the final journal entry.

The final step is to bring in the remaining **permanent account** balances as of December 31. There's more than one way to do this. The easiest way is to create a journal entry.

Click **+ New** on the navigation bar. The screen will look something like this:

+ New

CUSTOMERS	VENDORS	EMPLOYEES	OTHER
Invoice	Expense	Payroll 🔥	Bank deposit
Receive payment	Check	Single time activity	Transfer
Estimate	Bill	Weekly timesheet	Journal entry
Credit memo	Pay bills		Statement
Sales receipt	Purchase order		Inventory qty adjustment
Refund receipt	Vendor credit		Pay down credit card
Delayed credit	Credit card credit		
Delayed charge	Print checks		

Click **Journal Entry**. The screen should look something like this:

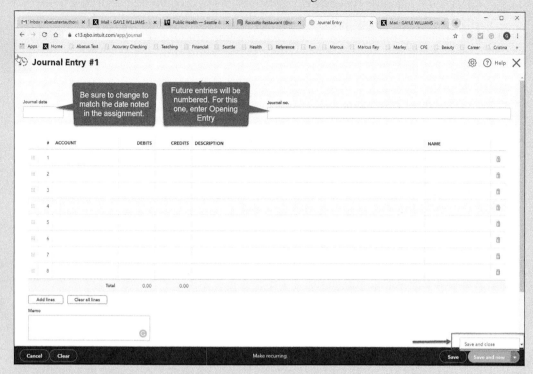

Figure 2.44

You'll be learning more about journal entries in Chapter 5. For now, the basics are all you need.

Change the **Journal date** to 12/31/21 and enter "Opening Entry" as the **Journal no.**

Enter the journal entry exactly as it appears below:

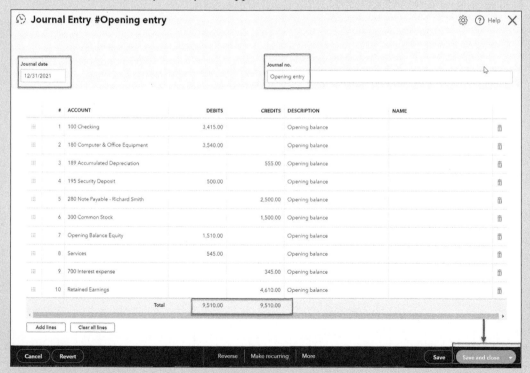

Figure 2.45

> **HINT:** You can directly enter the accounts (using account names or numbers) or you can use the dropdown menu. QBO will constantly try to "help" you by populating the debit or credit field with an amount that will balance the entry. Don't get distracted. Continue to enter the amounts as shown in the screenshot above.

Click **Save and close.**

Click **Reports** on the navigation bar. Click **Balance Sheet**. Change the dates to 12/31/21 to 12/31/21.

Click **Run report**. The report should look like this:

Figure 2.46

Student Name Math Revealed!

BALANCE SHEET
As of December 31, 2021

	TOTAL
▾ ASSETS	
▾ Current Assets	
▾ Bank Accounts	
100 Checking	3,415.00
Total Bank Accounts	**$3,415.00**
▾ Accounts Receivable	
120 Accounts Receivable	545.00
Total Accounts Receivable	**$545.00**
▾ Other Current Assets	
Inventory Asset	1,510.00
Total Other Current Assets	**$1,510.00**
Total Current Assets	**$5,470.00**
▾ Fixed Assets	
180 Computer & Office Equipment	3,540.00
189 Accumulated Depreciation	(555.00)
Total Fixed Assets	**$2,985.00**
▾ Other Assets	
195 Security Deposit	500.00
Total Other Assets	**$500.00**
TOTAL ASSETS	**$8,955.00**
▾ LIABILITIES AND EQUITY	
▾ Liabilities	
▾ Current Liabilities	
▾ Accounts Payable	
200 Accounts Payable	345.00
Total Accounts Payable	**$345.00**
Total Current Liabilities	**$345.00**
▾ Long-Term Liabilities	
280 Note Payable - Richard Smith	2,500.00
Total Long-Term Liabilities	**$2,500.00**
Total Liabilities	**$2,845.00**
▾ Equity	
300 Common Stock	1,500.00
Retained Earnings	4,610.00
Net Income	0.00
Total Equity	**$6,110.00**
TOTAL LIABILITIES AND EQUITY	**$8,955.00**

If it does, you're ready to start making some changes in the chart of accounts. If not, go back through the section and see where you went wrong. Although QBO is a fairly easy system to use for day-to-day operations, it can be tough to get everything set up.

Chart of Accounts Work

1/1/22

✓ You decide to change the name of the Services account to Tutoring Revenue. You use 400 as the account number. **TIP:** Click the ⚙ on the icon bar and select **Chart of accounts** to access the account list. Click Edit in the ACTION column for the Services account.

✓ You also notice that several accounts don't have account numbers. You edit the following accounts:

Account Name	New Account Number
Inventory Asset	130
Retained Earnings	350
Sales of Product Income	420
Cost of Goods Sold	500

✓ You review the chart of accounts. You see that Advertising expense isn't showing as a sub-account of Marketing Costs. You edit the account and make Advertising expense (Account 641) a sub-account of Marketing Costs (Account 640).

✓ You also decide to add an account called "Client relations expense" (Account 645). You make it a sub-account of Marketing Costs. **TIP:** This is an expenses account type. Use Entertainment as the detail type.

Suggested reports for Chapter 2 assignment

All reports can be found by clicking Reports on the navigation bar. All reports should be in portrait orientation. Customizing and exporting reports was covered in Chapter 1.

- Balance Sheet (in the Favorites section)
  - Report date should be December 31, 2021.
  - Customize the report as follows:
    - In the General section, select (100) in the Negative Numbers dropdown menu. This is a normal accounting convention for displaying negative numbers.
    - In the Rows/Columns section, select Non-zero for both rows and columns in the Show non-zero or activity only dropdown menu.
    - Consider saving the customized report to avoid having to make these formatting changes in future chapters.
  - Save as a PDF (export to PDF).

- Account List (in the For My Accountant section)
  - Customize the report so just the Account #, Account, and Type columns appear.
  - Save as PDF (export to PDF).
  - **TIP:** There will be a few accounts without account numbers. These are default accounts that you will not be using.
- Product/Service List (in the Sales and Customers section)
  - Customize the report so that the following columns appear (in this order):
    - Product/Service
    - Type
    - Description
    - Qty On Hand

○   Price

○   Income Account

○   Cost

○   Expense Account

■   Click **Run report**.

■   In the **Sort** dropdown menu on the report toolbar (left edge), select **TYPE** and click **ascending order**.

■   Save as a PDF (export to PDF).

Assignment 2B

Salish Software Solutions

Background information: Sally Hanson, a good friend of yours, double majored in Computer Science and Accounting in college. She worked for several years for a software company in Silicon Valley but the long hours started to take a toll on her personal life.

Last year she decided to open up her own company, Salish Software Solutions. Sally currently advises clients looking for new accounting software and assists them with software installation. She also provides training to client employees and occasionally troubleshoots software issues.

She has decided to start using QuickBooks Online to keep track of her business transactions. She likes the convenience of being able to access financial information over the Internet. You have agreed to act as her accountant while you're working on your accounting degree.

Sally has a number of clients that she is currently working with. She gives 15-day payment terms to her corporate clients but she asks for cash at time of service if she does work for individuals. She has developed the following fee schedule:

Name	Description	Rate
Select	Software selection	$500 flat fee
Set Up	Software installation	$ 75 per hour
Train	Software training	$ 50 per hour
Fix	File repair	$ 60 per hour

Sally rents office space from Alki Property Management for $600 per month.

The following furniture and equipment are owned by Salish:

Description	Date placed in service	Cost	Life	Salvage Value
Office furniture	6/1/21	$1,400	60 months	$200
Computer	7/1/21	$4,620	36 months	$300
Printer.	7/1/21	$ 900	24 months	$ 0

All equipment is depreciated using the straight-line method.

As of 12/31/21, she owed $3,500 to Dell Finance. The monthly payment on that loan is $150 including interest at 5%. Sally's last payment to Dell was 12/31/21.

Over the next month or so, Sally plans to expand her business by selling some of her favorite accounting and personal software products directly to her clients. She has already purchased the following items.

Item Name	Description	Vendor	Quantity on Hand	Cost per Unit	Sales Price
Easy1	Easy Does It	Abacus Shop	15	$100	$ 200
Retailer	Simply Retail	Simply Accounting	2	$400	$ 800
Contractor.	Simply Construction	Simply Accounting	2	$500	$1,000
Organizer	Organizer	Personal Software	20	$ 25	$ 50
Tracker	Investment Tracker	Personal Software	20	$ 20	$ 40

Final Conversion Work

Now that the basic structure has been set up in QBO as part of your work on pages 2-9 to 2-29 in this chapter, it's time to update the account balances.

The values for Accounts Receivable, Accounts Payable, and Inventory were brought in when the invoices and the customer, vendor, and products and services lists were imported. For example, QBO debited A/R for the balances due from customers included in the invoices list.

Click **Reports** on the navigation bar, click **Balance Sheet** in the **Favorites** section, and change the dates to 12/31/21 to 12/31/21.

Click **Run Report**. The report should look something like this:

Figure 2.47

Student Name Salish Software Solutions ✏

BALANCE SHEET
As of December 31, 2021

	TOTAL
▾ ASSETS	
▾ Current Assets	
▾ Accounts Receivable	
120 Accounts Receivable	1,420.00
Total Accounts Receivable	$1,420.00
▾ Other Current Assets	
Inventory Asset	4,200.00
Total Other Current Assets	$4,200.00
Total Current Assets	$5,620.00
TOTAL ASSETS	$5,620.00
▾ LIABILITIES AND EQUITY	
▾ Liabilities	
▾ Current Liabilities	
▾ Accounts Payable	
200 Accounts Payable	1,235.00
Total Accounts Payable	$1,235.00
Total Current Liabilities	$1,235.00
Total Liabilities	$1,235.00
▾ Equity	
Opening Balance Equity	4,200.00
Retained Earnings	
Net Income	185.00
Total Equity	$4,385.00
TOTAL LIABILITIES AND EQUITY	$5,620.00

The balances are correct for Accounts Receivable, Accounts Payable, and Inventory but notice the amounts for **Opening Balance Equity** ($4,200) and **Net Income** ($185). **Opening Balance Equity** is a default account credited by QBO when inventory is imported into the system. There is no business account called "opening balance equity."

Click the $4,200 balance to see the underlying transactions. The report should look something like this [**TIP:** Your transactions may not appear in the same order.]:

Student Name Salish Software Solutions ✎

Transaction Report

January - December 2021

DATE	TRANSACTION TYPE	NUM	NAME	MEMO/DESCRIPTION	ACCOUNT	SPLIT	AMOUNT	BALANCE
▾ Inventory Asset								
12/31/2021	Inventory Starting Value	START		Easy1 - Opening inventory and v...	Inventory Asset	Opening Balance Equity	1,500.00	1,500.00
12/31/2021	Inventory Starting Value	START		Contractor - Opening inventory ...	Inventory Asset	Opening Balance Equity	1,000.00	2,500.00
12/31/2021	Inventory Starting Value	START		Tracker - Opening inventory and...	Inventory Asset	Opening Balance Equity	400.00	2,900.00
12/31/2021	Inventory Starting Value	START		Organizer - Opening inventory a...	Inventory Asset	Opening Balance Equity	500.00	3,400.00
12/31/2021	Inventory Starting Value	START		Retailer - Opening inventory and...	Inventory Asset	Opening Balance Equity	800.00	4,200.00
Total for Inventory Asset							$4,200.00	
TOTAL							$4,200.00	

You can see that as part of the import of **products and services**, the Opening Balance Equity was credited when Inventory Asset was debited. You could click on each line item to correct the entry. Instead, the entire balance will be adjusted as part of a journal entry created later in this section.

Click **Dashboard** to close the window.

Click **Reports** on the navigation bar and click **Profit and Loss** in the **Favorites** section. Change the dates to 12/1/21 to 12/31/21. (All of the data was imported with December dates.)

Click **Run Report**. The report should look something like this:

Student Name Salish Software Solutions

PROFIT AND LOSS

December 2021

	TOTAL
▾ Income	
410 Troubleshooting	120.00
Services	1,300.00
Total Income	$1,420.00
GROSS PROFIT	$1,420.00
Expenses	
Total Expenses	
NET OPERATING INCOME	$1,420.00
▾ Other Expenses	
700 Interest expense	1,235.00
Total Other Expenses	$1,235.00
NET OTHER INCOME	$ (1,235.00)
NET INCOME	$185.00

Click the $1,235 amount listed for **Interest expense**. The report looks like this:

Student Name Salish Software Solutions

TRANSACTION REPORT

December 2021

DATE	TRANSACTION TYPE	NUM	NAME	MEMO/DESCRIPTION	ACCOUNT	SPLIT	AMOUNT	BALANCE
▾ Interest expense								
12/20/2021	Bill		Personal Software	Opening Balance	700 Interest expense	200 Accounts Payable	135.00	135.00
12/28/2021	Bill		Simply Accounting	Opening Balance	700 Interest expense	200 Accounts Payable	900.00	1,035.00
12/31/2021	Bill		Abacus Shop	Opening Balance	700 Interest expense	200 Accounts Payable	200.00	1,235.00
Total for Interest expense							$1,235.00	
TOTAL							$1,235.00	

Unlike customer invoices, specific vendor bills cannot be imported to QBO. Instead the vendor balances were imported, along with the vendor address information, in Step 9 of the homework company setup.

As you can see, QBO, by default, debited **Interest expense** to offset the credit to Accounts Payable recorded as part of the import of vendors. Since you will only be recording Salish Solutions activity starting January 1st, we won't take the time to correct these entries. Interest expense, along with the revenue accounts, will be closed to Retained Earnings as part of the final journal entry.

The final step is to bring in the remaining **permanent account** balances as of December 31. There's more than one way to do this. The easiest way is to create a journal entry.

Click **+ New** on the icon bar. The screen will look something like this:

Permanent account An account used to prepare the balance sheet—that is, an asset, liability, or stockholders' equity account. Any balance in a permanent account at the end of an accounting period is carried forward to the following accounting period.

Figure 2.51

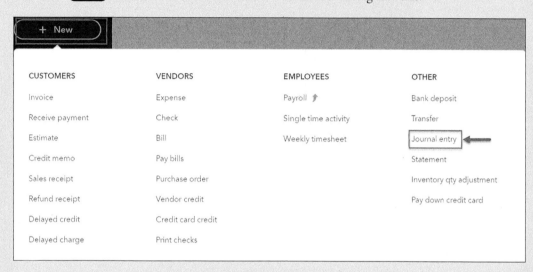

Click **Journal Entry**. The screen should look something like this:

Figure 2.52

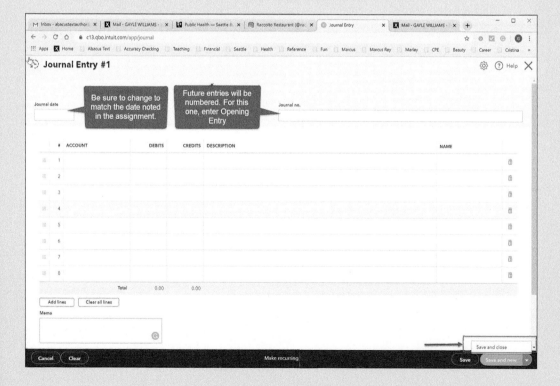

You'll be learning more about journal entries in Chapter 5. For now, the basics are all you need. Change the **Journal date** to 12/31/21 and enter "Opening Entry" as the **Journal no**. Enter the journal entry exactly as it appears below:

Figure 2.53

#	ACCOUNT	DEBITS	CREDITS	DESCRIPTION	NAME
1	100 Checking	10,500.00		Opening Balance	
2	180 Computer Equipment	5,520.00		Opening Balance	
3	182 Office Furniture & Equipment	1,400.00		Opening Balance	
4	189 Accumulated Depreciation		1,085.00	Opening Balance	
5	195 Security Deposit	1,000.00		Opening Balance	
6	280 Note Payable		3,500.00	Opening Balance	
7	300 Common Stock		2,000.00	Opening Balance	
8	Opening Balance Equity	4,200.00		Opening Balance	
9	Services	1,300.00		Opening Balance	
10	410 Troubleshooting	120.00		Opening Balance	
11	700 Interest expense		1,235.00	Opening Balance	
12	Retained Earnings		16,220.00	Opening Balance	
	Total	24,040.00	24,040.00		

HINT: You can directly enter the accounts (using account names or numbers) or you can use the dropdown menu. QBO will constantly try to "help" you by populating the debit or credit field with an amount that will balance the entry. Don't get distracted. Continue to enter the amounts as shown in the screenshot above.

Click **Save and close**.

Click **Reports** on the navigation bar. Click **Balance Sheet**. Change the dates to 12/31/21 to 12/31/21.

Click **Run report**. The report should look like this:

Figure 2.54

Student Name Salish Software Solutions

BALANCE SHEET
As of December 31, 2021

	TOTAL
▾ ASSETS	
▾ Current Assets	
▾ Bank Accounts	
100 Checking	10,500.00
Total Bank Accounts	$10,500.00
▾ Accounts Receivable	
120 Accounts Receivable	1,420.00
Total Accounts Receivable	$1,420.00
▾ Other Current Assets	
Inventory Asset	4,200.00
Total Other Current Assets	$4,200.00
Total Current Assets	$16,120.00
▾ Fixed Assets	
180 Computer Equipment	5,520.00
182 Office Furniture & Equipment	1,400.00
189 Accumulated Depreciation	(1,085.00)
Total Fixed Assets	$5,835.00
▾ Other Assets	
195 Security Deposit	1,000.00
Total Other Assets	$1,000.00
TOTAL ASSETS	$22,955.00
▾ LIABILITIES AND EQUITY	
▾ Liabilities	
▾ Current Liabilities	
▾ Accounts Payable	
200 Accounts Payable	1,235.00
Total Accounts Payable	$1,235.00
Total Current Liabilities	$1,235.00
▾ Long-Term Liabilities	
280 Note Payable	3,500.00
Total Long-Term Liabilities	$3,500.00
Total Liabilities	$4,735.00
▾ Equity	
300 Common Stock	2,000.00
Retained Earnings	16,220.00
Net Income	0.00
Total Equity	$18,220.00
TOTAL LIABILITIES AND EQUITY	$22,955.00

If it does, you're ready to start making some changes in the chart of accounts. If not, go back through the section and see where you went wrong. Although QBO is a fairly easy system to use for day-to-day operations, it can be tough to get everything set up.

Chart of Accounts Work

1/1/22

✓   You change the name of the **Services** account to Software Selection and Installation Revenue. You use 400 as the account number. [**TIP:** Click the ⚙ on the icon bar and select **Chart of Accounts** to access the account list.]

✓   You also notice that several accounts you'll be using don't have account numbers. You edit the accounts as follows:

Account Name	New Account Number
Inventory Asset	130
Retained Earnings	350
Sales of Product Income	420
Cost of Goods Sold	500

✓   You review the chart of accounts. You see that Advertising expense isn't showing as a sub-account of Marketing Costs. You edit the account and make Advertising expense (Account 631) a sub-account of Marketing Costs (Account 630).

✓   You also decide to add an account called "Client relations expense" (Account 635). You make it a sub-account of Marketing Costs. [**TIP:** This is an **expenses account type**. Use **Entertainment** as the **detail type**.]

Suggested reports for Chapter 2 assignment

All reports can be found by clicking **Reports** on the navigation bar. All reports should be in portrait orientation. Customizing and exporting reports was covered in Chapter 1.

- Balance Sheet (in the **Favorites** section)
  - Report date should be December 31, 2021.
  - Customize the report as follows:
    - In the **General** section, select **(100)** in the **Negative Numbers** dropdown menu. This is a normal accounting convention for displaying negative numbers.
    - In the **Rows/Columns** section, select **Non-zero** for both rows and columns in the **Show non-zero or activity only** dropdown menu.
    - **TIP:** Consider saving the customized report to avoid having to make these formatting changes in future chapters.
  - Save as a PDF (export to PDF).
- Account List (in the **For My Accountant** section)
  - Customize the report so just the Account #, Account, and Type columns appear.
  - Save as a PDF (export to PDF).
  - **TIP:** There will be a few accounts without account numbers. These are default accounts that you will not be using.
- Product/Service List (in the **Sales and Customers** section)
  - Customize the report so that only the following columns appear (in this order):
    - Product/Service
    - Type
    - Description
    - Qty On Hand
    - Price

- Income Account
  - Cost
  - Expense Account
- Click **Run report**.
- In the **Sort** dropdown menu on the report toolbar, select **Type** as the **Sort by** method and click **Ascending order**.
- Save as a PDF (export to PDF).

APPENDIX 2A SETTING UP YOUR GOOGLE GMAIL ACCOUNT

If This Is Your First Gmail Account

Open your Internet browser and enter https://accounts.google.com/signup as the URL. You should see the following screen.

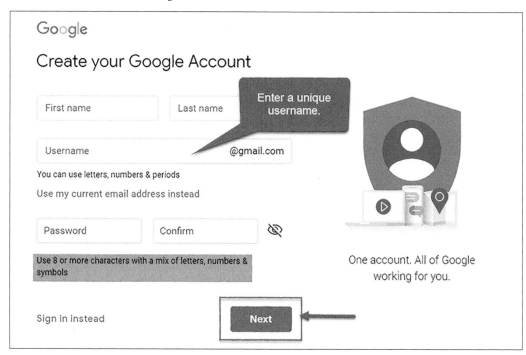

Figure 2A.1

Google account setup screen

You may want to use your own name followed by your homework company name or your accounting course number as your username.

The password you create should be unique. The password should have 8 or more characters (letters, numbers, and symbols). Click **Next**.

To increase your security, enter your phone number and an alternate email address. You are not required to provide that information but it can be helpful for keeping your account secure. You will be required to enter your birth date and gender.

Click **Next**.

You may be asked about using your phone number for various Google services. Click **Skip** or **I'm in**.

Google

Privacy and Terms

To create a Google Account, you'll need to agree to the Terms of Service below.
In addition, when you create an account, we process your information as described in our Privacy Policy, including these key points:

Data we process when you use Google

- When you set up a Google Account, we store information you give us like your name, email address, and telephone number.
- When you use Google services to do things like write a message in Gmail or comment on a YouTube video, we store the information you create.
- When you search for a restaurant on Google Maps or watch a video on YouTube, for example, we process information about that activity – including information like the video you watched, device IDs, IP addresses, cookie data, and location.
- We also process the kinds of information described above when you use apps or sites that use Google

You're in control of the data we collect & how it's used

Cancel   **I agree**

You will need to read and agree to Google's **Terms of Service**. Click **I agree** when you've completed your review.

If You Already Have a Gmail Account

It's probably best to set up a new Gmail account for use with your homework assignments but it's not required.

To set up a new Gmail account, open your Internet browser and enter www.google.com as the URL.

Figure 2A.4

Google sign in screen

Click your account icon at the top right corner of the page. The screen should look something like this:

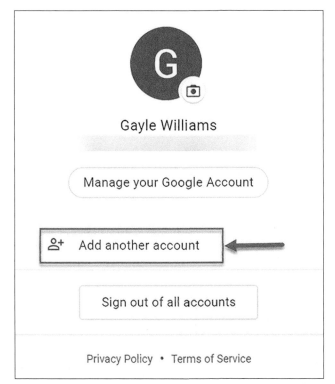

Figure 2A.5

Access to new Gmail account setup

Click **Add another account** to progress to the next screen.

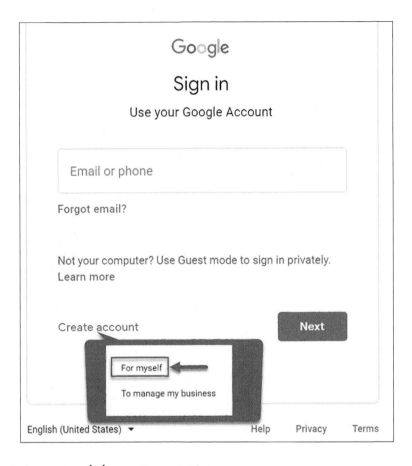

Click **Create account** and choose **For myself**.

> ✳ **HINT:** If you see a **Choose an account** screen instead of the one shown above, click **Use another account**, click **More options**, then click **Create account**.

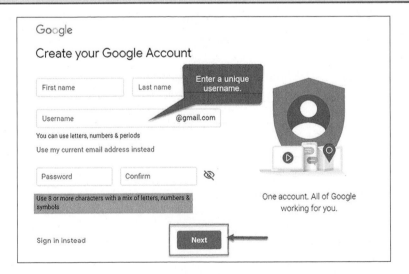

You may want to use your own name followed by your homework company name or your accounting course number as your username.

The password you create next should be unique. The password should have 8 or more characters (letters, numbers, and symbols). Click **Next**.

If you already have security features activated with Google, you will get a screen asking for your phone number. An activation code will be texted to you. You will need to enter the code to move forward.

Figure 2A.8

Security information for Google account

To increase your security, enter your phone number and an alternate email address. You are not required to provide that information but it can be helpful for keeping your account secure. You will be required to enter your birth date and gender.

Click **Next**.

You may be asked about using your phone number for various Google services. Once you've verified your number, click **Skip** or **Yes, I'm in**.

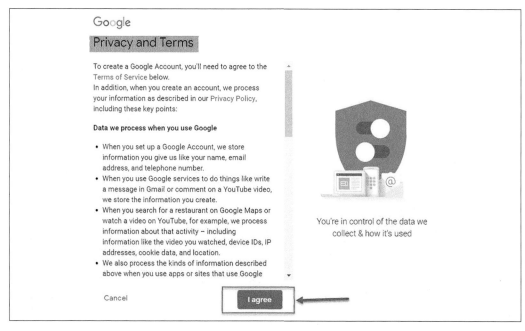

Figure 2A.9

Google account privacy and terms information

You will need to read and agree to Google's **Terms of Service**. Click **I agree** when you've completed your review.

QuickBooks

SECTION TWO

Service Companies

Businesses are frequently classified by primary source of revenue.

- Service companies earn revenue by charging a fee for services they perform.

- Merchandising companies earn revenue by buying products from one company and selling those products to consumers (or to distributors).

- Manufacturing companies earn revenue by making products and selling them to consumers (or to merchandisers).

In this textbook, we'll be looking at how QuickBooks Online can be used by service and merchandising companies.

> **BEHIND THE SCENES** Currently, the features needed for managing inventory in a manufacturing company are not available in QBO. There are, however, a few apps (add-on products) that can be purchased by manufacturing companies interested in using QBO.

We'll look at service companies first because the accounting for service companies is, in general, the least complex.

WHEN YOU MAKE MISTAKES

QBO is very forgiving. You can change, void, or delete most transactions pretty much at will.

Just remember, in a regular company transactions would not be changed or deleted if the transaction has been completed. (For example, the invoice has been sent out or a check has been sent to the vendor.) Why? Because the transaction has already occurred. (The customer has the invoice. The vendor has the check.) Instead, errors are corrected by creating a new transaction. (A credit memo or additional invoice is sent to the customer. A new check or a request for credit is sent to the vendor.) If the transaction has not been completed, it could be changed or voided. For example, if an invoice was created but not sent to the customer, it could be changed. If a check was printed but not mailed, it could be voided.

That being said, we're not in a real business so you will probably want to edit or delete transactions that you enter incorrectly in your homework assignments.

> **BEHIND THE SCENES** In QBO, deleted transactions don't appear on reports. Voided transactions do appear but with zero dollar amounts. (Keeping a record of voided transactions is a good internal control policy.)

There is one thing you need to know before you start changing or deleting transactions in QBO. Oftentimes, transactions are related. For example, you record a customer invoice. You record the customer payment of that invoice. You record the deposit of the customer payment. Those are three transactions that are linked in QBO.

Certain linked transactions cannot be changed. For instance, QBO will not allow you to change a customer payment that's already been deposited. You would need to delete the deposit of that check, make the change to the payment, and then re-record the deposit. If a linked transaction can be changed or deleted, QBO will give you a warning first.

Figure S3.1

Warning message when editing linked transactions

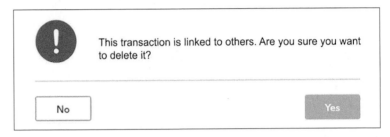

This transaction is linked to others. Are you sure you want to delete it?

No   Yes

Although QBO will allow you to make the change, related transactions will likely be affected. Make sure you consider the full impact of your changes.

Suggestions for Finding Mistakes

You will be given check figures to help you as you complete your homework assignments. If all your numbers agree to the check figures, you have a reasonably good chance of having completed the assignment correctly. (Agreeing to check figures is not a **guarantee** that all the entries are recorded correctly but it's certainly a comfort!)

What if you don't agree? Where do you start looking? Here are some suggestions.

- **CHECK DATES.** Entering an incorrect date is the single most common cause of student errors (and student headaches!). QBO enters default dates when you first open a form. It defaults to the current date when you start entering transactions during a work session. If you change the date on the first invoice, it will default to that new date when you enter the second invoice. If you open a new form, however, it will default back to the current date. Accounting is date driven, so your financial statements won't match the check figures if you enter a transaction in the wrong month. First thing to do? Pull a report of transactions dated BEFORE the first transaction date in the assignment (a journal) and then one of transactions dated AFTER the last transaction date of the assignment.

- **There are always two sides to every story.** This is **double-entry accounting** so if one account is wrong, then at least one other account is also wrong. It's hard to find errors in cash, accounts receivable, and accounts payable due to the sheer volume of transactions that affect these accounts. So, if your numbers don't match the check figures, see if you can find the other account(s) that is (are) also off. If you can find the error(s), you can fix all the affected accounts.

- **Debits on the left, credits on the right.** QBO gets the debit and credit part down really well when it comes to standard transactions (invoices, checks, etc.). However, when it comes to journal entries, QBO relies completely on you. It will debit (credit) whatever you tell it to debit (credit). We're all human. Sometimes we get our journal entries reversed. You can often fairly quickly spot those errors by looking at the balance sheet. Does Accumulated Depreciation show a debit balance? That's a problem. Look at supplies accounts, prepaid accounts, and accrued expense accounts and see if the balances look reasonable. Adjusting journal entries are frequently made to those accounts.

- **Math hints.** Errors can also be found, sometimes, by checking the difference between the check figure and your total. Is the number divisible by nine? You may have a transposition error (for example, you entered 18 instead of 81). All differences due to transposition errors are divisible by nine. Is the difference equal to the amount of a transaction? Maybe you forgot to enter it (or entered it on the wrong date). Is the difference equal to twice one of your transactions? You may have entered in a journal entry backwards (watch those debits and credits!).

Double-entry accounting A method of accounting that results in the recording of equal amounts of debits and credits.

Debit An entry on the left side (or in the debit column) of an account.

Credit An entry on the right side (or in the credit column) of an account.

SECTION OVERVIEW

Chapter 3 will cover the sales cycle in a service company.
Chapter 4 will cover the purchase cycle in a service company.
Chapter 5 will cover end-of-period accounting in a service company.

3

Sales Activity
(Service Company)

Objectives

After completing Chapter 3, you should be able to:

1. Set up standard sales settings.

2. Add and edit customers.

3. Add and edit **service** items.

4. Set up credit terms.

5. Record sales on account and cash sales.

6. Record customer payments on account.

7. Record deposits to bank.

8. Record and apply credit memos.

9. Record customer refunds.

10. Create and modify sales and receivables reports.

WHAT IS THE SALES CYCLE IN A SERVICE COMPANY?

The sales cycle in a service company normally follows these steps:

- Get the job (client).
- Provide the service.
- Bill for the service.
- Collect the fee.

Getting the job (or the client) is outside the accounting function, but the accounting system does need to maintain records related to the transactions with every customer.

At the very least, the following information must be maintained for each customer:

- Contact information
- Terms of payment
- Record of past transactions
- Record of any unpaid invoices

SETTING UP STANDARD SALES SETTINGS

Companies may have standard policies applicable to all customers. For example, a company might have standard credit (payment) terms. Some companies send out bills in batches. Invoices might be created when work is performed but instead of printing the invoice immediately, it is batched with other invoices and printed later.

Settings in QBO can be changed to reflect those policies.

Click the ⚙ in the icon bar. Click **Account and Settings**.

Click **Sales**. Click the **pencil** icon in the top right corner of the **Sales form content** section to open the section for editing. The window should look like this:

Figure 3.1

Sales tab of Account and Settings

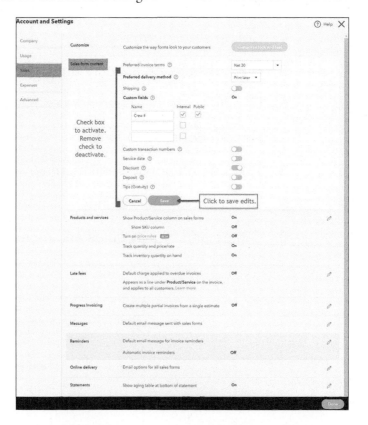

Settings are changed by checking or unchecking the boxes to turn features on or off. Features with multiple options use dropdown menus. To get more information about the feature, click the **?** next to the option.

The **Sales form content** section of the **Sales** tab would look like this for a company that:

● had standard payment terms of Net 10

● did not do batch processing

● had no custom fields

● gave discounts to customers on occasion

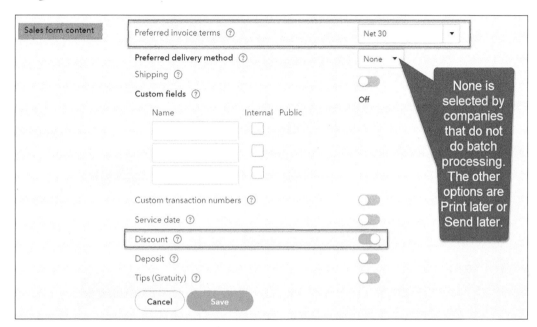

None is selected by companies that do not do batch processing. The other options are Print later or Send later.

Figure 3.2

Sales form content section of Account and Settings

Clicking **Save** updates the features.

Clicking **Done** in the bottom right corner of the window exits **Account and Settings**.

> **BEHIND THE SCENES** The settings selected are defaults. Many defaults can be changed when specific transactions are entered.

Make some changes to the sales settings for Craig's Design and Landscaping.

1. Change settings.

   a. Click the ⚙ on the icon bar.

   b. Click **Account and Settings**.

   c. Click **Sales**.

   d. Click **Preferred invoice terms**.

   e. **Make a note** of the various terms available in QBO.

   f. Select **Net 15** as the preferred terms.

   g. Click **Save**.

   h. Click **Done** to close the **settings** window.

PRACTICE EXERCISE 3.1

eLectures

MANAGING CUSTOMERS

Customers are managed in the Customer Center. The Customer Center is accessed through the **Sales** link on the navigation bar.

Select the **Customers drawer.**

The Customer Center screen looks something like this:

In the Customer Center, you can:

- access the new customer setup window.

- access forms necessary to record activity with existing customers.

- access existing customer data for editing.

Customer Center Display

Selected information about sales activity is highlighted in the **Money Bar** at the top of the Customer Center screen.

Click on any of the amounts to bring up a list of the transactions included in the total.

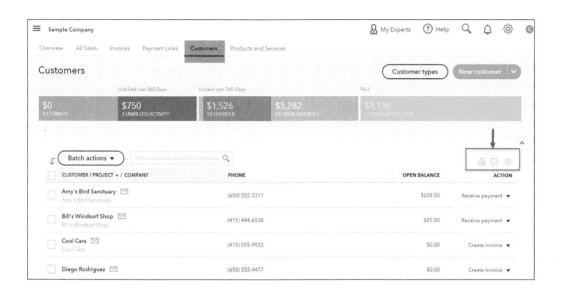

Figure 3.6

Icons on Customer
Center screen

Just above the list of customers are three small icons.

The **printer** icon (far left) allows users to print a list of all vendors. The list includes all customer information included on the screen.

Clicking the **export** icon (the middle icon) automatically downloads the list as an Excel file.

Clicking the third icon (the ⚙) allows users to customize the fields displayed in the Customer Center.

Display columns can include any of the following:

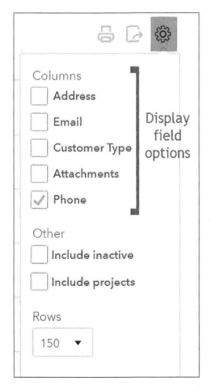

Figure 3.7

Column options for
Customer Center
screen

BEHIND THE SCENES Having the phone number and/or the email address displayed can be time-saving for accountants working directly with customers on a regular basis.

Adding a Customer

To add a new customer, open the Customer Center by clicking **Sales** in the navigation bar and selecting the **CUSTOMERS** tab.

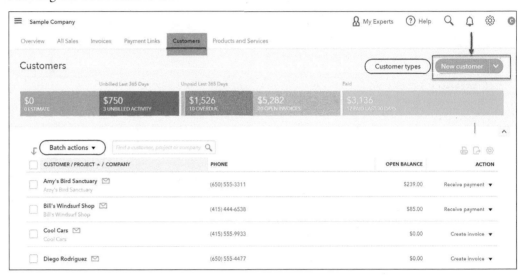

Click **New customer** to open the **Customer Information** window. It should look something like this:

The name entered in the **Company** field is the name used in any correspondence with businesses' customers (on invoices for example). If the customer was an individual, the name would be entered in the row above (**First name** and **Last name**, for example).

The **Display Name** is used as a customer identifier. It could be a number or a shortened version of the name. This is the primary name used to organize the customer list. It's also the name used in any search functions. The **Display Name** is used for internal purposes only and would not appear on customer correspondence. In the homework, you'll use the **Company** name as the **Display Name**.

HINT: **Display names** must be unique. An entity that is both a customer and a vendor can use the same **company name** but must have two different **display names**. One option would be to add a C (customer) or a V (vendor) to the end in the **display name** fields.

Phone and other contact information is entered in the top right section of the **Customer Information** window.

As you can see in Figure 3.9, there are seven tabs in the lower left section of the window. Billing and shipping addresses are included on the **Address** tab.

BEHIND THE SCENES If shipping and billing addresses differ, both must be entered. The shipping address generally determines the sales tax rate used. Sales taxes are covered in detail in Chapter 6.

The **Payment and billing** tab of the customer record looks something like this:

Figure 3.10

Payment and billing tab of Customer Information window

Default credit terms for the customer are noted on the **Payment and billing** tab. This is an important field. Payment terms need to be communicated to customers and payment status needs to be tracked by companies. Users can also indicate information about the customer's preferred payment method (check, cash, credit card, etc.). If the user normally prints or emails invoices in batches, that would be noted in the **Preferred delivery method** field. If batch processing is not appropriate, **None** would be selected in the field. These are all defaults. Terms and payment methods can be changed when a specific sales transaction is entered.

All customers are identified as taxable unless the user identifies the customer as tax exempt on the **Tax info** tab of the customer record.

Figure 3.11

Tax info tab for customer subject to tax

If **This customer is tax exempt** is checked, additional fields are displayed.

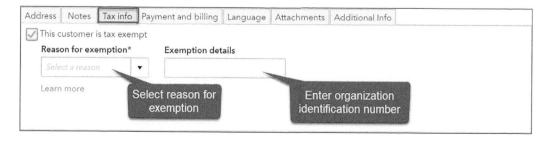

Figure 3.12

Tax info tab for tax exempt customer

The user must select the reason for the exemption and indicate the customer's business identification number, if applicable. Reasons for exemption listed in the dropdown menu include resale, government, education, charitable, etc. State tax laws identify which of those reasons are valid in a particular location.

 HINT: The screenshots in Figures 3.11 and 3.12 are similar to what you will see in your homework company file. The **Tax Info** tab of customers in the test drive company looks slightly different. The basic process is the same. All customers are considered taxable unless changed in the customer record.

Sales taxes will be covered in Chapter 6.

The **Notes** tab can be used for adding unique information about the customer.

If companies have documents that apply specifically to the customer, they can be uploaded to the **Attachments** tab. **Attachments** will be discussed in Chapter 11.

Companies can track customers by **type** on the **Additional Info** tab. **Customer types** are set up by the user. There are no default **types** set up in QBO.

On the **Language** tab, users can elect to send **invoices** to companies in a specific language. English is the default. Other options are French, Spanish, Italian, Chinese, and Portuguese. Only the basic field titles are translated. The language used in setting up item names and messages is used in the body of the **invoice**.

Viewing Customer Information

To view information about a specific customer, click the customer's name in the Customer Center. The **Customer Details** tab in the customer record would look something like this for Craig's customer, Cool Cars.

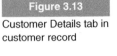

Customer Details tab in customer record

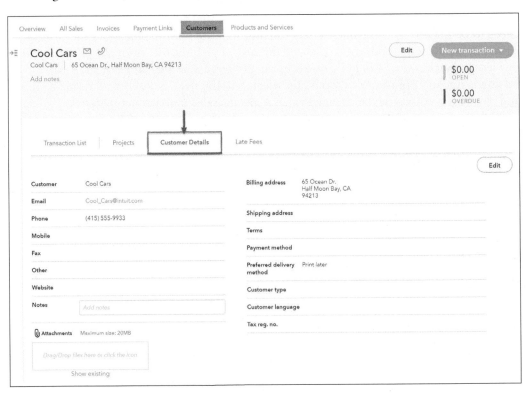

Basic information about the customer is included on the **Customer Details** tab.

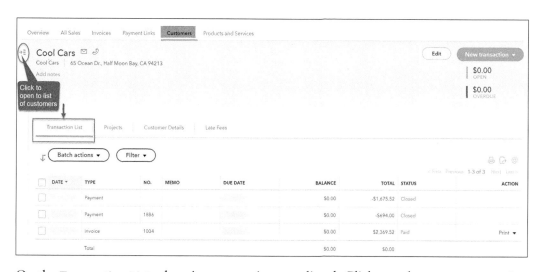

Figure 3.14

Transaction List tab in
customer record

On the **Transaction List** tab, prior transactions are listed. Click anywhere on a transaction row to open the appropriate form.

Projects can be set up for customers on the **Projects** tab. Projects will be covered in Chapter 10. We will not cover late fees (the final tab) in this course.

> **HINT:** For access to the full list of customers when you're in a specific customer record, click the three parallel lines to the left of the customer name (top left corner in Figure 3.14). A sidebar will open. This can be a handy feature when a user is making changes to multiple customer records. New customers can also be added on the sidebar.

Changing Customer Information

Customer information can be changed at any time. To edit an existing customer, open the Customer Center by selecting **Sales** on the navigation bar and opening the **Customers drawer**.

Click the name of the company you wish to edit.

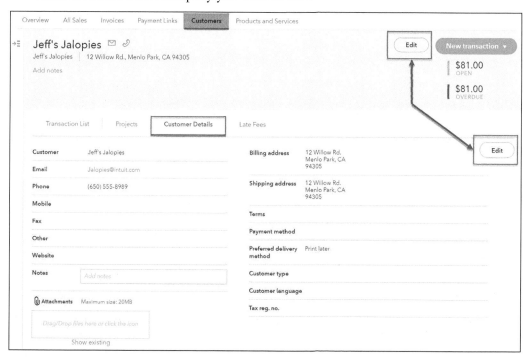

Figure 3.15

Customer record
window

Click the **Edit** link at the top of the screen or the **Edit** link on the **Customer Details** tab to open the **Customer information** window.

Figure 3.16

Customer information screen

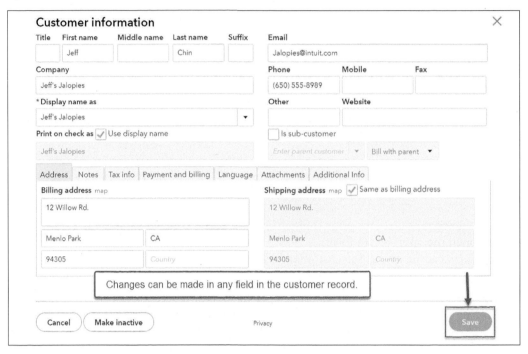

Make the desired changes and click **Save**.

Inactivating a Customer

Although customers cannot be deleted in QBO, customers with no open balance can be identified as inactive. Companies might inactivate customers that are no longer in business or that have not purchased products or services in the past year.

To inactivate a customer, open the Customer Center by clicking **Sales** in the navigation bar and selecting the **CUSTOMERS** tab.

Figure 3.17

Make inactive option on Action dropdown menu

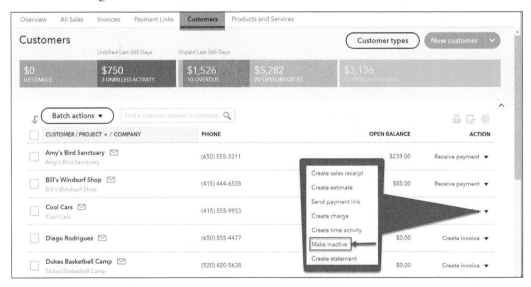

On the dropdown menu in the far-right column of the customer name, select **Make inactive**. This option would not be available on the dropdown menus for customers with open balances.

Customers can also be made inactive in the **Customer information** window.

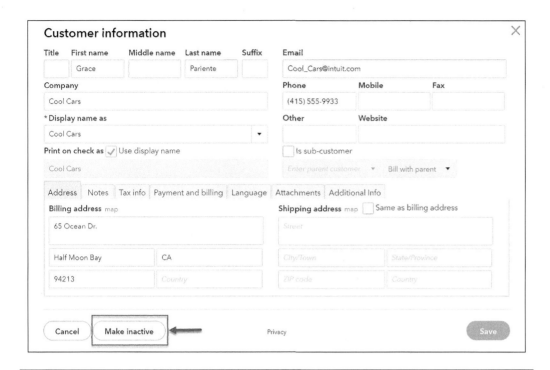

Figure 3.18

Make inactive option in customer record

HINT: If customers with open balances are inactivated in the customer record, a journal entry or credit memo is automatically created. Accounts receivable is credited and a revenue account is debited. Open balances should be cleared before customers are inactivated.

Inactive customers can't be used in transactions and aren't available in search functions, although they will show up on appropriate reports.

To reactivate a customer, all inactive customers must be visible in the Customer Center.

Figure 3.19

Option to include inactive customers in Customer Center display

Click the ⚙ icon right above the **ACTION** column in the Customer Center and check the **Include inactive** box to make inactive customers visible.

Figure 3.20

Option to reactivate customer

An option to reactivate the customer will now appear in the **ACTION** column next to the inactivated customer name.

> **BEHIND THE SCENES** Although the customer shows as "deleted" in Figure 3.20, the customer has been inactivated.

PRACTICE
EXERCISE 3.2

Add and edit customers for Craig's Design and Landscaping.
(Craig's gets a new client and receives an address change for an existing client.)

1. Click **Sales** (navigation bar).

2. Click the **CUSTOMERS** tab.

3. Click **New Customer** and set up Barrio Café as a new customer:

    a.   Enter "Barrio Cafe" in the **Company** field.

    b.   Tab to the **Phone** field and enter "415-199-2222."

    c.   Leave the checkmark next to **Use display name**.

    d.   In the **Billing Address** section:

        i.   Enter "1515 Oceanspray Drive; Sausalito, CA 94965."

    e.   Click the **Payment and billing** tab.

        i.   Select **Net 15** in the **Terms** dropdown menu.

        ii. Click **Save**.

4. Click **Sales** (navigation bar).

5. Click the **CUSTOMERS** tab.

6. Edit a customer. (Change the billing address for Jeff's Jalopies.)

    a.   Click the name **Jeff's Jalopies** in the Customer Center.

    b.   Click **Edit**.

    c.   In the **Billing Address** section change the street address to "4848 Dragrace Road."

    d.   Open the **Payment and billing** tab and select **Net 15** as the **Terms**.

    e.   **Make a note** of Jeff's last name.

    f.   Click **Save**.

    g.   Click **Dashboard**.

MANAGING SERVICE ITEMS

As you might recall from Chapter 1, there are various types of **product** and **service** items. In this chapter, we are concerned only with **service** items. **Service** items represent charges for the various services performed by a company as part of its regular operations and are used when entering sales transactions and when reporting sales activity.

The following information is included in the setup of a **service** item:

- The standard rate (price) to be charged to the client.

- The description that should appear on sales transaction forms.

- The income account that should be credited when the client is charged and debited when a credit memo is issued.

Each **service** item can be associated with only one income account but one income account can be associated with many items. This allows the company to keep considerable detail in subsidiary ledgers but keep the general ledger (and the financial statements) relatively simple. For example, a law firm might have one income account called Client Fees but could have separate service items to track the various types of fees (meetings, research, courtroom time, etc.).

Service items are set up through the Products and Services Center.

To access the center, click the ⚙ on the icon bar and select **Products and Services** under **Lists**. The screen should look something like this:

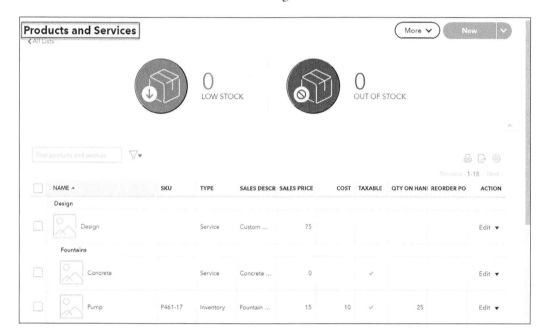

Figure 3.21

Products and Services Center

Organizing Products and Services

Products and **services** can be grouped into **categories** in QBO. Grouping items makes it easier for users to access (find) specific items when entering specific transactions. Grouping also makes it easier to create effective reports about company operations.

> **BEHIND THE SCENES** **Categories** are only used for organizing items. Assigning an item to a **category** does not determine the general ledger account debited or credited when the item is used in a transaction. See the Adding a Service Item section in this chapter for information about assigning general ledger accounts to items.

To set up **categories**, click the ⚙ on the icon bar and select **Products and Services** under **Lists**.

Figure 3.22

"More" options on Products and Services page

Select **Manage categories** on the **More** dropdown menu. The screen should look something like this:

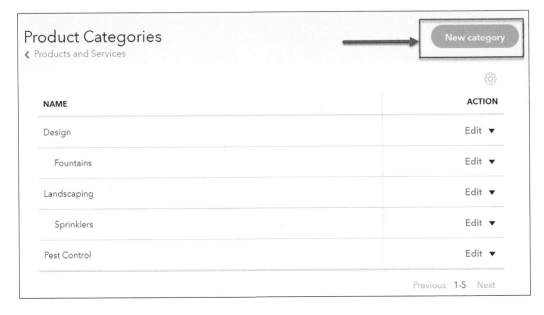

To add a new **category**, click **New category**. A sidebar will open:

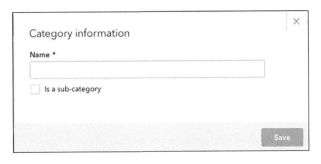

Enter a **category** name.

Users can group categories together by identifying **sub-categories**. Multiple **sub-categories** can be created for each parent **category**. Users can also create **sub-categories** of **sub-categories** (up to 4 levels).

> **BEHIND THE SCENES** On reports, the entire name (including the category and all sub-categories) will appear. This can be quite confusing to viewers of the report. In a small company, having only one level of sub-categories is probably the best practice.

Categories can be changed or deleted. Open the **Products and Services** list.

Select **Manage categories** on the **More** dropdown menu.

Figure 3.26

Options to edit or remove categories

Click **Edit** to change the name or **Remove** to delete the **category**. If you delete a **category**, any related **sub-categories** will be moved up one level. If a **parent category** is deleted, the items previously included in the **category** will be displayed as uncategorized.

To return to the **Products and Services** list, click the **back arrow** under **Product Categories**.

Adding a Service Item

To add a new **service** item, click the ⚙ on the icon bar and select **Products and Services** under **Lists**.

Figure 3.27

Access to new item sidebar

Click **New**. A sidebar will appear that looks like this:

Figure 3.28

New item sidebar

Click **Service** to open the **service** item setup window:

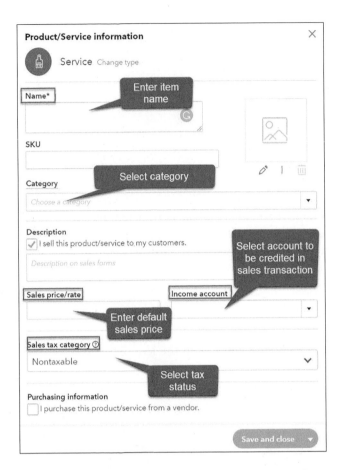

Figure 3.29

New service item
screen

An item **Name** must be entered and an **Income account** must be identified. The general
ledger account identified here is the account that will be credited when a sales transaction
is recorded. This account will be debited when the item is included on a customer credit
memo.

The following fields are also available:

- **SKU**—a SKU (stock keeping unit) is a product or service identification code assigned
  by the company.
  - A SKU is similar to the UPCs (Universal Product Codes) used by most retail-
    ers. Both are codes used for tracking purposes. The difference is that a SKU is
    unique to a particular company. UPCs are standardized for all businesses.

- **Category**—group assigned for tracking purposes

- **Description**—the default description that will appear on all sales forms

- **Sales price/rate**—the default selling price

Because most services are not taxable in most states, you would select **Nontaxable** in the
Sales tax category dropdown menu when creating a service item.

 HINT: The **Sales tax category** field (visible in Figure 3.29) is not included on
the item setup screen if sales tax is not activated. In your homework company,
you will activate sales tax as part of your homework in Chapter 6 so you will
not see it until then.

If a service may be performed by an outside vendor (an independent contractor for example), **I purchase this product/service from a vendor** should be checked. If the box is checked, the sidebar will expand to show the following:

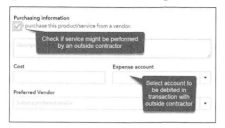

Figure 3.30

Purchasing information section of service item setup

Default descriptions and costs (rates) can be entered. The general ledger account to be debited when the purchase of the service is recorded is identified in the **Expense account** field.

Editing, Duplicating, and Inactivating Products and Services

To edit **products** and **services**, click the ⚙ on the icon bar and select **Products and Services**.

Figure 3.31

Access to item edit screen

Click **Edit** in the **ACTION** column of the appropriate item. You can edit the item name or description, the default rate, the general ledger account associated with the item, and any other fields. If you edit the general ledger account associated with an item that has already been used in a transaction, you will be asked if you want to update existing transactions (called historical transactions in QBO) in addition to changing the account for future transactions:

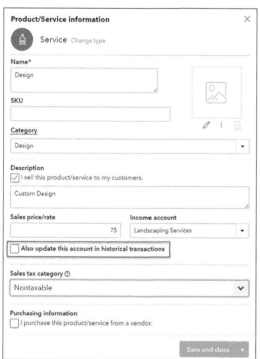

Figure 3.32

Option to update prior transactions when distribution account is changed

Items can also be duplicated.

Figure 3.33

Option to create a
duplicate item

A user might choose to duplicate an item instead of creating a new item from scratch to
save time. Only the name would need to be changed if all other selections (rates, categories,
etc.) were the same.

> **BEHIND THE SCENES** If the duplicated item **name** isn't changed by the user,
> QBO will save the new item using the original **name** and adding—**copy** at the end.
> For example, if the Deck Design item was duplicated and the **name** wasn't changed,
> the new item would be saved with the **name** Deck Design—copy.

Items can be made inactive but cannot be deleted. Historical activity would be retained for
an inactive item but you would no longer be able to use the item in future sales transactions.

Figure 3.34

Option to inactivate an
item

Inactive items can be reactivated. To display inactive items, select **inactive** in the **status** field
of the **Filter** dropdown menu (above the **NAME** column). A **Make active** option will then be
available in the **ACTION** column.

PRACTICE
EXERCISE
3.3

Homework
MBC

Add and edit items for Craig's Design and Landscaping.
(Craig's Design and Landscaping has decided to offer deck design and construction. It will start
by working only on residential projects but the company may later decide to expand its deck
business so it sets up a new category (Decks) with two sub-categories (Commercial and Residential). Because it will be designing and constructing decks, it sets up two service items (Deck
Design and Deck Construction). All deck income is to be tracked in the Other Income general
ledger account. It also needs to adjust the default rate for landscaping hours.)

1. Set up categories.

    a. Click the ⚙ icon and select **Products and Services** in the **LISTS** column.

    b. Click **Manage categories** in the **More** dropdown menu in the top right corner.

        i. Click **New category**.

        ii. Enter "Decks" as the name.

        iii. Click **Save**.

    c. Add another **category**.

        i. Click **New category**.

        ii. Enter "Commercial" as the name.

        iii. Check **Is a sub-category**.

(continued)

(continued from previous page)

  iv. Select **Decks** in the dropdown menu.

  v. Click **Save**.

 d. Add another **category**.

  i. Click **New category**.

  ii. Enter "Residential" as the name.

  iii. Check **Is a sub-category**.

  iv. Select **Decks** in the dropdown menu.

  v. Click **Save**.

 e. **Make a note** of the number of **parent categories** there are in the category list. (This would include the **parent category** you just set up.)

 f. **Make a note** of the name of the **sub-category** under **Landscaping**.

 g. Click the **back arrow** under **Product Categories** to return to **Products and Services**.

  i. You should now be in the **Products and Services** list window.

 h. Click **New**.

  i. Select **Service**.

  ii. Enter "Deck Design" as the **Name**.

  iii. Select **Decks:Residential** as the **Category**.

  iv. Enter "Deck design work" as the description.

  v. Enter "75" as the **Sales price/rate**.

  vi. Select **Design Income** as the **Income account**.

  vii. Select **Nontaxable** in the **Sales tax category** dropdown menu.

  viii. Click **Save and close**

 i. Click **New**.

  i. Select **Service**.

  ii. Enter "Deck Construction" as the **Name**.

  iii. Select **Decks:Residential** as the **Category**.

  iv. Enter "Deck construction work" as the description.

  v. Enter "40" as the **Sales price/rate**.

  vi. Select **Services** as the **Income account**.

  vii. Remove the check next to **Is taxable**.

  viii. Check **I purchase this product/service from a vendor**.

  ix. Enter "Assistance with deck construction" as the **description**.

  x. Enter "35" as the **Cost** and **Cost of Labor:Installation** as the **Expense account**.

  xi. Click **Save and close**.

 j. Click **Edit** in the **ACTION** column for **Hours**.

  i. Enter "50" as the **Sales price/rate**.

  ii. Click **Save and close**.

 k. **Make a note** of the default sales price set for **Installation** (a sub-category of **Landscaping**).

 l. Click **Dashboard** to exit the **Products and Services** list.

SETTING UP CREDIT TERMS

Companies that sell on account set up payment terms for their customers to let them know when payment is due and whether there's a discount if they pay early. A company can, of course, have different terms for different customers.

Required payment dates are usually based on the invoice date. Payment would be due a certain number of days after the date of the invoice. Payment terms of 10, 15, and 30 days are common choices.

Some companies set a particular day of the month as the payment due date. A common date is the last day of the month. An invoice dated January 3rd would be due on January 31st. An invoice dated January 23rd would also be due on the 31st. Companies that use a date driven payment term will usually give an extra month for invoices dated close to the payment date. For example, if the payment date were the last day of the month, an invoice dated January 29th would be due at the end of February instead of the end of January.

New credit terms can be created by clicking the ⚙ on the icon bar.

Figure 3.35

Access to Lists page

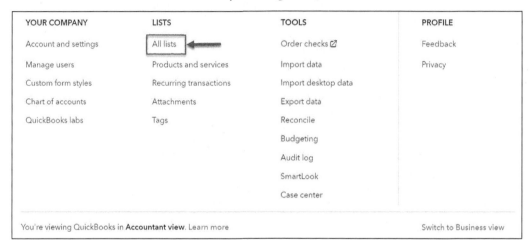

Click **All Lists.**

Figure 3.36

Lists page

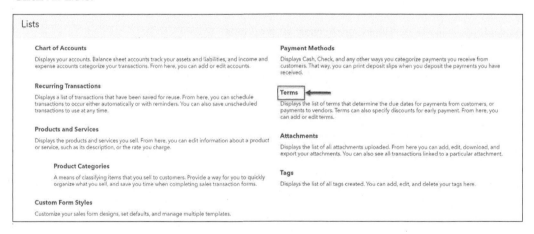

Click **Terms.**

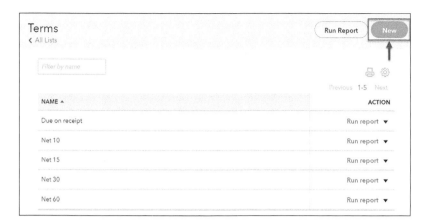

Figure 3.37

Terms list

Click **New.**

Figure 3.38

New credit term
window

A **Name** for the new term must be entered. Users can either create a new term that is based on the invoice date (**Due in fixed number of days**) or a term that is based on a particular day (**Due by certain day of the month**). The window would look something like Figure 3.39 if a user created a new term called EOM that required payment by the last day of the month unless the bill was issued during the last five days of the month.

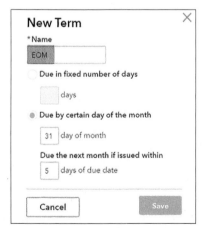

Figure 3.39

Example of new term
setup

At the time this book was written, credit terms with early payment discounts (e.g., 2% 10, net 30) can be created in QBO but there is no tracking or automatic calculation of those discounts built into the software. Options for recording early payment discounts taken by customers will be covered in Chapter 6.

Set up a new credit term for Craig's Design and Landscaping.

(Craig's is considering offering an early payment discount to some of its customers.)

1. Click the ⚙ on the icon bar.

2. Click **All Lists** in the **LISTS** column.

3. Click **Terms**.

4. Click **New**.

5. Enter "Net 45" as the **Name**.

6. Click **due in fixed number of days** and enter "45" in the **days** field.

7. Click **Save**.

8. Click **Dashboard**.

eLectures

RECORDING SALES REVENUE

In a manual accounting system:

- An invoice is created.

- The invoice is recorded in the sales journal if sales are made on account and in the cash receipts journal for cash sales.

- The journals are posted, in total, to the general ledger.

- Each transaction in the sales journal is posted to the appropriate customer's subsidiary ledger.

In QBO:

- A form is completed for each sale.

    - Each **transaction type** has its own form.

- When the form is saved, QBO automatically records the transaction in the sales journal and automatically posts the transaction to the general ledger and to the appropriate subsidiary ledger.

Because everything is done automatically the form must include all the relevant information needed.

- Who is the customer? (Customer name is needed for posting to the subsidiary ledger.)

- What are we charging them for? (What general ledger account should QBO credit?)

- Have they paid already or will they pay later? (What general ledger account should QBO debit?)

We've already got the customers and the **product** and **service** items set up so QBO knows which subsidiary ledger should be updated and which income accounts should be credited when the sales form is completed. But how does QBO know which account to debit in a sale? Should it be Cash or Accounts Receivable? QBO solves that problem by setting up two different forms (two separate **transaction types**).

BEHIND THE SCENES For processing purposes, QBO assigns certain default accounts for common transactions. For example, the default debit account for recording a sale on account is Accounts Receivable. The default credit account for recording a bill from a vendor is Accounts Payable. These accounts are automatically set up (categorized with the proper account type) by QBO. The user can change the name of the account but not the type.

Recording Sales on Account

The form (**transaction type**) used to record sales on account is the **Invoice**. The default debit account for **invoices** is Accounts Receivable (A/R).

 WARNING: Although multiple accounts can be set up in QBO using the account type Accounts Receivable (A/R), only one A/R account can be associated with sales transactions in the current version of QBO. If a company wanted to track accounts receivable in multiple accounts, it would need to be done through journal entries.

The credit account(s) in the journal entry underlying an invoice transaction will depend, of course, on the items included on the invoice. As explained earlier in this chapter, the general ledger account associated with a specific item is set up through the **Products and Services** list.

QBO provides many opportunities for users to record sales on account! The **invoice** form can be accessed:

- by clicking **+ New** on the navigation bar and selecting **Invoice** in the **CUSTOMERS** column.
- by clicking **Sales** on the navigation bar and selecting **Invoice** in the **New transaction** dropdown menu on the **All Sales** tab.
- by clicking **Sales** on the navigation bar and clicking **Create invoice** in the **SHORT-CUTS** section of the **Overview** tab.
- by clicking **Sales** on the navigation bar and selecting **New invoice** on the **Invoices** tab.
- by clicking **Sales** on the navigation bar, clicking the **Customer** tab, and selecting **Create invoice** in the **ACTION** column dropdown menu for the customer.

The **Invoice** form looks something like this:

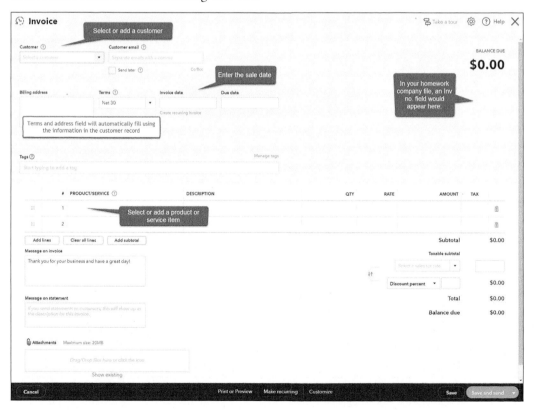

Figure 3.40

Invoice form

If custom transaction numbers are not activated, invoice numbers do not appear on the screen when an invoice is first created. Instead, an invoice (transaction) number is assigned by QBO when the invoice is saved.

> **BEHIND THE SCENES** Companies that want more control over invoice numbers can elect to create custom transaction numbers. To make that election, click the ⚙ icon (top right corner of the **invoice**). Check **Custom transaction numbers**. A new field (**Invoice no.**) will automatically appear on sales forms. The election can also be made in the **Sales form content** section of the **Sales** tab in **Account and Settings**. **Custom transaction numbers** were activated in your homework company file as part of the setup process. Once activated, custom transaction numbers will continue to be used on all sales forms going forward.

To complete an **invoice**, you must enter the customer name, the invoice date, the credit terms, and the items to be charged to the customer.

Credit terms are accessible through the dropdown menu in the **Terms** field.

Figure 3.41

Default credit terms in test drive company

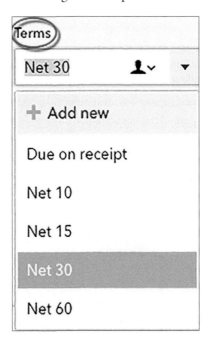

Setting up new credit terms was covered in the **SETTING UP CREDIT TERMS** section of this chapter. If needed, a new term can be created by clicking **Add new**.

If a default message has been set up in the **Sales** tab of **Account and Settings**, it will appear in the **Message on invoice** field. The message can be modified or deleted for a specific invoice.

> **HINT**: Documents related to the charges can be uploaded to QBO by clicking **Attachments** in the bottom left corner of the **invoice**. Documents related to the customer (price lists, contracts, etc.) that are not unique to the invoice would normally be uploaded to the **Customer Information** window. **Attachments** will be covered in more depth in Chapter 11.

To record an **invoice** click **Save and close** (or **Save and new** if you are recording multiple invoices) in the bottom right corner of the form. There are two other options for saving.

- **Save and send** emails the **invoice** to the customer.
- **Save and share link** emails a link to the customer for online payment. This is only available to companies that have linked bank accounts in QBO.

BEHIND THE SCENES Remember: As soon as you save a transaction, a journal entry is created and posted to the general ledger and the subsidiary ledgers and financial statements are updated.

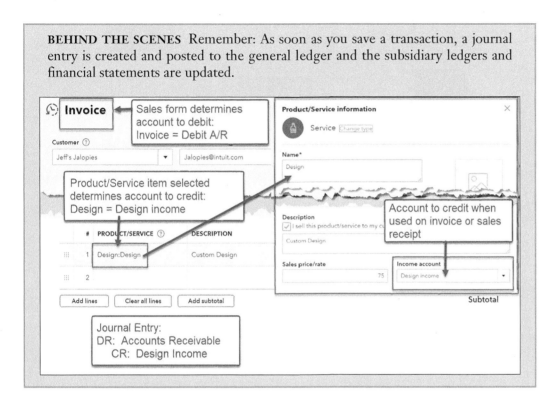

Recording Cash Sales

The **transaction type** (form) used to record cash sales is the **Sales Receipt**. The default debit account for **sales receipts** in the test-drive company is an asset account called Undeposited Funds. (The Undeposited Funds account is covered later in this chapter under the section **MAKING DEPOSITS**.) Users can also elect to record the debit directly to a **Bank** account. The credit accounts for **sales receipts** depend on the **product** and **service** items included in the sale.

The **Sales Receipt** form can be accessed in four ways:

- by clicking **+ New** on the navigation bar and selecting **Sales Receipt** in the **CUSTOMERS** column.
- by clicking **Sales** on the navigation bar and selecting **Sales Receipt** in the **New transaction** dropdown menu on the **All Sales** tab.
- by clicking **Sales** on the navigation bar and clicking **New sale** in the **SHORTCUTS** section of the **Overview** tab.
- by clicking **Sales** on the navigation bar, clicking the **Customer** tab, and selecting **Create Sales Receipt** in the **ACTION** column dropdown menu for the customer.

The form will look something like this:

Figure 3.42

Sales receipt form

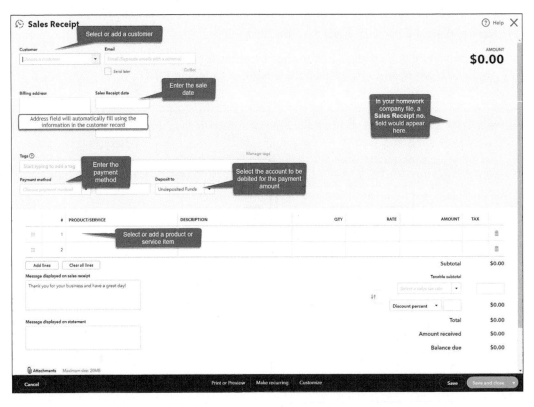

To complete a **sales receipt**, enter the customer name, the receipt date, and the items to be charged. You also select the **Payment method** (cash, check, or credit card).

If the customer is paying with a check, the customer's check number can be entered in the **Reference no.** field. For security reasons, full credit card numbers would normally not be included in the **Reference no.**

> ✳ **HINT:** If a company has a lot of walk-in customers and it doesn't want to track each cash customer's name, it can set up a "Cash Customer" or "Walk-in" customer. Click **Add new** in the **add a customer** dropdown menu, enter the name, and click **save**. The name will appear in the customer list but no additional detail will need to be added to the customer record unless any sales at the location are subject to sales tax. In that case, the physical address of the business would need to be added.

You can also add a customer message at the bottom of sales receipts or use the default message set up on the **Sales** tab in **Account and settings**.

Clicking **Save and close**, **Save and new** or **Save and send** records the transaction.

BEHIND THE SCENES Remember: As soon as you save a transaction, a journal entry is created and posted to the general ledger and the subsidiary ledgers and financial statements are updated.

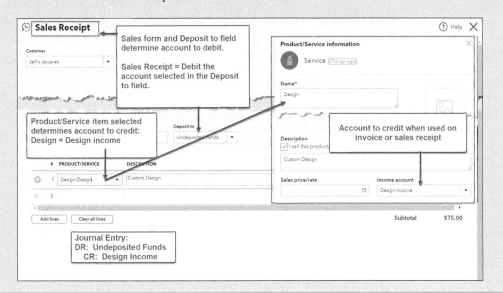

Record cash and credit sales for Craig's Design and Landscaping.

(Craig's Design and Landscaping prepares invoices for some work it did for Kookies by Kathy and Video Games by Dan. It also records the cash collected at time of service for some repair work it did for Red Rock Diner.)

1. Create invoices.

   a. Click **Sales** on the navigation bar.

   b. Select **Invoice** on the **New Transaction** dropdown menu of the **All Sales** tab.

   c. Invoice Kookies by Kathy for 3 hours of Design work.

      i.   Select **Kookies by Kathy** in the **Select a customer** field.

      ii. Select **Net 30** for the **Terms**.

      iii. Use the current date for the **Invoice date**.

      iv. Select **Design** as the Item in the **PRODUCT/SERVICE** field.

      v.   Enter "3" as the **QTY** (hours in this case).

      vi. The default rate of 75 should appear in the **RATE** field.

      vii. Total invoice balance should be $225.

      viii. Click **Save and new**.

   d. Invoice Video Games by Dan for some gardening and pest control work.

      i.   Select **Video Games by Dan** in the **Select a customer** field.

         1.   Ignore any charges that appear in a sidebar.

      ii. Select **Net 30** as the **Terms**.

      iii. Use the current date for the **Invoice date**.

      iv. Select **Gardening** in the **PRODUCT/SERVICE** field with a **QTY** of "5" and a **RATE** of "$30."

(continued)

PRACTICE
EXERCISE
3.5

Homework
MBC

(continued from previous page)

> v. On the second line select **Pest Control** as the **PRODUCT/SERVICE.** Enter "2" as the **QTY.** Leave the **RATE** at $35.
>
> vi. Total invoice balance should be $220.
>
> vii. Click **Save and close.**

2. Record a cash sale. (Red Rock Diner paid $180 (by check #6789) for some maintenance work.)

   a. Click **+ New** on the navigation bar.

   b. Select **Sales Receipt** in the **CUSTOMERS** column.

   c. Select **Red Rock Diner** in the **Choose a customer** field.

   d. Enter the current date for the **Sales Receipt date.**

   e. Select **Check** as the **Payment method.**

   f. Enter "6789" as the **Reference no.**

   g. Leave **Undeposited Funds** in the **Deposit to** field.

   h. Select **Maintenance & Repair** in the **PRODUCT/SERVICE** field.

   i. Enter a **QTY** of "3" and a **RATE** of "60."

   j. The total should be $180.

   k. Click **Save and close.**

3. **Make a note** of the accounts that were debited and credited for the sales receipt you created for Red Rock Diner. To do this, click **Sales** on the navigation bar and select the **All Sales drawer.** Locate and click the **Sales receipt** you just created for $180 to open it. Select **More** in the black bar menu at the bottom of the form. Select **Transaction Journal** to open the underlying journal entry.

QuickCheck
3-1

> What's the underlying journal entry for Invoice 1038 to Kookies by Kathy in Practice Exercise 3.5? (Answer at end of chapter.)

eLectures

RECORDING PAYMENTS FROM CUSTOMERS

Companies generally give customers or clients a number of payment options.

- Customers can pay with check, cash, or credit card at the time of service.
  - Recorded as **sales receipts** (covered earlier in this chapter).
- Customers can buy on account and pay later.
  - Recorded as **payments.**

Most companies that sell to individuals would generally only accept cash/check or major credit cards. An exception would be retail outlets that have their own credit cards. (Target and Lowe's are two examples.)

Most companies that sell to other companies sell primarily on account. It would simply be impractical for their customers to pay cash or have checks or credit cards ready whenever goods or services are delivered.

In a manual accounting system, customer payments are recorded through the Cash Receipts Journal. The journal is posted, in total, to the general ledger and each transaction is posted to the appropriate customer's subsidiary ledger (if paying on account). In QBO, all of the steps are done when the form recording the payment transaction is saved.

Payments on Account

Customer payments on account balances are recorded using the **Receive Payment** form (**Payment transaction type**).

To access the form, click ➕ New on the navigation bar. The window should look something like this:

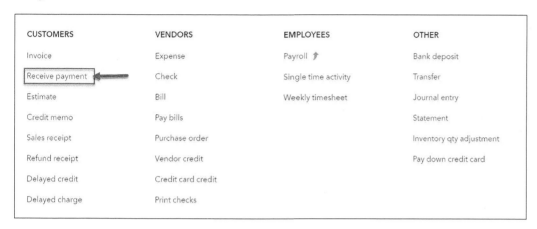

Figure 3.43

Access to customer payment form

Select **Receive Payment** in the **CUSTOMERS** column. The form would look something like this:

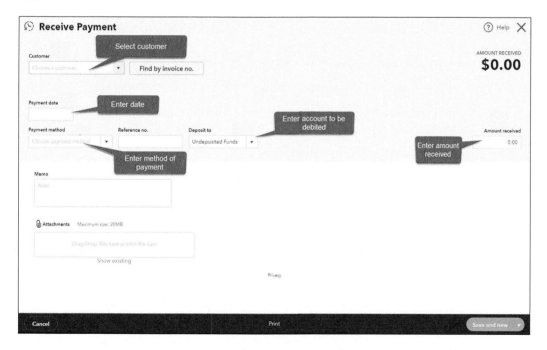

Figure 3.44

Customer payment form

To enter a customer payment, you need to know the customer name, the payment amount, the date received, and the payment method. If payment is made by check, the check number would normally be entered in the **Reference no.** field.

Once the customer is selected, all outstanding invoices from that customer will be displayed. The screen would look something like this:

Figure 3.45

Example of customer
payment screen

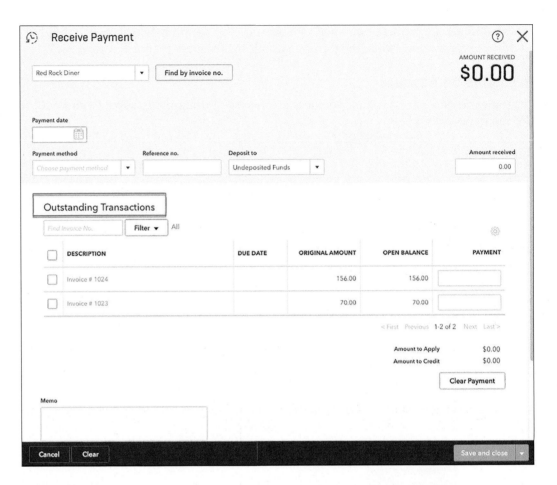

Figure 3.45

Example of customer payment screen

QBO will automatically apply payments for you in this order:

- It will be applied first to an invoice of the **exact** same dollar amount as the payment.

- If there's no exact match, QBO will apply the payment in due date order (oldest invoice first).

You can change how payments are applied if needed.

Full or partial payments can be entered. If a partial payment is received, you should make sure that the amount(s) entered in the **PAYMENT** field(s) agree(s) to the payment amount that should be applied to the specific invoice.

If a partial payment is entered, QBO will leave the unpaid balance for the invoice in Accounts Receivable.

If there are unapplied credits available to the customer, they will appear when the **Receive Payment** form is opened. The user has the option of applying the credit or leaving it as an open credit that would be available at a later date.

For example, the form to record a payment of $375 from a customer with an open credit memo would look something like this if the credit was applied.

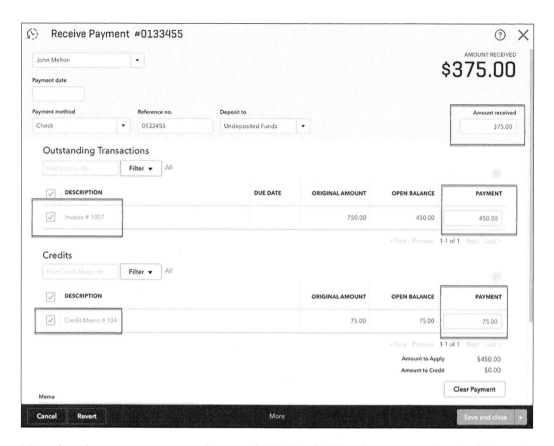

Figure 3.46

Example of customer payment net of credit memo

Note that the **Amount to Apply** shows as $450 (the $375 cash payment plus the $75 credit memo).

> **WARNING:** Once you enter the **Amount received**, QBO will automatically update the **PAYMENT** field to the net amount (the payment amount) instead of the full amount (the open balance). If this is not corrected, QBO will not properly clear the balance on the transaction.
>
> You may have to work with the fields a few times before the credit is applied correctly, but we've found that after entering the amount received, it usually works best to:
> - Uncheck the **credit memo box.**
> - Uncheck the **invoice box.**
> - Recheck the **invoice box.**
> - Recheck the **credit memo box.**
> - Enter the open balance ($450 in the example above) in the **invoice PAYMENT** field.
>
> (This sounds like a bit of magic, right?)

The default journal entry underlying a **payment** transaction in the test-drive company includes a debit to **Undeposited Funds** and a credit to Accounts Receivable. The **Undeposited Funds** account is discussed in the **MAKING DEPOSITS** section of this chapter.

Record customer payments on account for Craig's Design and Landscaping.
(Craig's Design and Landscaping received payments from two of its customers.)

1. Record customer payment in full. (Check #5865 for $160 received from Sushi by Katsuyuki in payment of invoices 1018 and 1019)

   a. Click **+ New** on the navigation bar.

   b. Click **Receive Payment** in the **CUSTOMERS** column.

   c. Select **Sushi by Katsuyuki** as the customer.

   d. Enter the current date as the **Payment date**.

   e. Select **Check** as the **Payment method**.

   f. Enter "5865" as the **Reference no.**

   g. Leave **Undeposited Funds** as the **Deposit to** account.

   h. Enter "$160" as the **Amount received**.

   i. Make sure that QBO automatically:

      i. placed a checkmark next to both **invoices** in the **Outstanding Transactions** section.

      ii. entered $80 in both **PAYMENT** fields.

   j. The total **Amount to Apply** should be $160.00.

   k. Click **Save and new**.

2. Record customer partial payment. (Check #6899 for $40 received from Bill's Windsurf Shop in partial payment of invoice 1027)

   a. Select **Bill's Windsurf Shop** as the customer.

   b. Enter the current date as the **Payment date**.

   c. Select **Check** as the **Payment method**.

   d. Enter "6899" as the **Reference no.**

   e. Leave **Undeposited Funds** as the **Deposit to** account.

   f. Enter "$40" as the **Amount** received.

   g. Make sure that QBO automatically:

      i. placed a checkmark next to Invoice #1027 under **Outstanding Transactions**.

      ii. entered $40 in the **PAYMENT** field.

   h. The total **Amount to Apply** should be $40.00.

   i. Click **Save and close**.

   j. **Make a note** of the outstanding balance owed by Bill's Windsurf Shop on Invoice 1027 after check #6899 was posted. **TIP:** Use the search features you learned in Chapter 1 to search for the invoice.

MAKING DEPOSITS

Before you learn how to record bank deposits, you need to understand how QBO handles cash receipts. As you know, there's a journal entry behind every sales receipt (cash sale) and every customer payment on account. Based on your knowledge of accounting, you would probably expect that the debit account for each of the transactions would be Cash, right? (Debit Cash, Credit Revenue for the cash sales and Debit Cash, Credit Accounts Receivable for the customer payments on account.)

Since QBO updates the general ledger automatically and immediately for every transaction, that would mean there would be a debit entry to the cash account for every check and cash payment received. Why is that a problem? Well, it's not if you're depositing every payment separately. But most companies group checks when they're making deposits. On the bank statement, the actual deposit amount is shown (not each check that makes up the deposit). It would be difficult (not impossible, but difficult) to reconcile the bank account every month if QBO didn't group the payments together to correspond to the actual deposit amount.

So, here's what QBO does. Instead of debiting Cash for every customer payment, an account called "Undeposited Funds" is debited. **Undeposited Funds** is an **Other Current Asset account type** (not a **Bank account type**). You can think of it as a temporary holding account.

When the actual deposit is later recorded, QBO credits **Undeposited Funds** and debits the **bank** (Checking) account for the total of the funds deposited. Now the entries in the Checking account agree (hopefully!) to the entries on the bank statement.

Deposits are recorded using the **Bank Deposit** form (the **transaction type** is **Deposit**). This form is accessed by clicking **+ New** on the navigation bar.

CUSTOMERS	VENDORS	EMPLOYEES	OTHER
Invoice	Expense	Payroll 🖈	Bank deposit
Receive payment	Check	Single time activity	Transfer
Estimate	Bill	Weekly timesheet	Journal entry
Credit memo	Pay bills		Statement
Sales receipt	Purchase order		Inventory qty adjustment
Refund receipt	Vendor credit		Pay down credit card
Delayed credit	Credit card credit		
Delayed charge	Print checks		

Figure 3.47

Access to deposit form

Click **Bank Deposit** in the **OTHER** column. The window will look something like this:

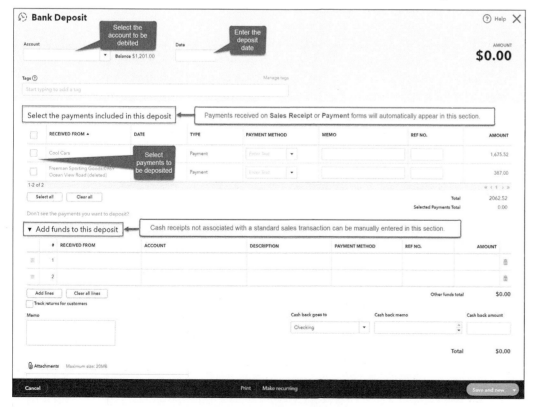

Figure 3.48

Example of deposit form

The first step is to select the appropriate bank account in the top left field and enter the deposit date. This tells QBO what account to debit.

Customer payments (receipts) that are being included in the day's bank deposit are selected by placing a checkmark next to the payor's name in the **Select the payments included in this deposit** section (the names are in the **RECEIVED FROM** column). You can select all the payments or just some of them. Any customer payments selected will create a credit to Undeposited Funds. The amount is debited to the cash (checking) account.

You can also add additional cash receipts directly into this form. For example, if a company received a tax refund, the amount would be entered in the **Add funds to this deposit** section in the lower half of the form. Cash received from lenders (loan processed) and owner contributions would also be entered in the **Add funds to this deposit** section. Additional cash receipts are covered in more detail in Chapter 8.

 HINT: When a customer is paying an account balance, the best practice is to enter it through the **Payment** form. Although QBO does allow direct entry of customer payments on account into the **Bank Deposit** form, the payment would then have to be linked to the appropriate invoice at a later date. This adds another step to the process.

The **cash back** fields at the bottom right corner of the window are used to record cash withdrawals taken directly from a deposit amount.

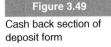

Figure 3.49

Cash back section of deposit form

This would rarely be done in a business organization.

Save and close records the transaction.

 HINT: If there are **no** undeposited receipts in the Undeposited Funds account, only the **Add funds to this deposit** section will appear when you open the **Bank Deposit** form.

PRACTICE
EXERCISE
3.7

Make a deposit for Craig's Design and Landscaping.

(Craig's Design and Landscaping deposits checks received from customers.)

1. Click **+New** on the navigation bar.

2. Click **Bank Deposit** in the **OTHER** column.

3. Select **Checking** as the account.

4. Enter the current date as the **Date**.

5. Check the boxes next to Cool Cars and Freeman Sporting Goods.

(continued)

(continued from previous page)

6. **Make a note** of the amount received from Cool Cars.

7. The **Selected Payments Total** should be $2,062.52.

8. Click **Save and close**.

RECORDING CUSTOMER CREDITS AND REFUNDS

Stuff happens! A client is mistakenly overbilled or maybe the work isn't done to the satisfaction of the client. In either case, a company will probably decide to either credit the customer's account by issuing a **credit memo** or issue a refund to the client.

If the client has unpaid invoices, the company will normally decide to credit the client's account using the **transaction type Credit Memo**. The credit account underlying a **credit memo** is Accounts Receivable (A/R). The debit account(s) underlying the transaction depend(s) on the **product** and **service** item(s) selected in the form.

Depending on the **settings** in the company file, **credit memos** are either:

• automatically applied by QBO or

• manually applied by the user.

Automatic application of **credit memos** is a **setting**. To change the **setting**, click the ⚙ on the icon bar. Click **Account and Settings** in the **Your Company** column.

On the **Advanced** tab, click the **pencil** icon in the **Automation** section.

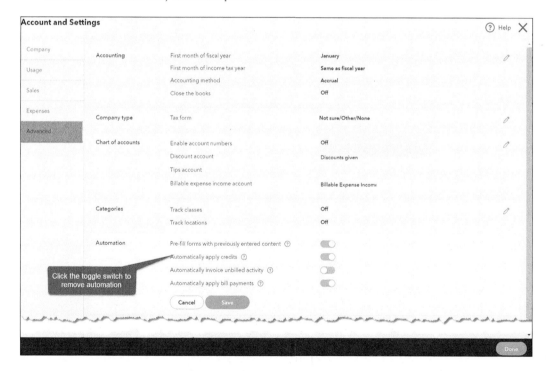

Figure 3.50

Automation section of the Advanced tab in Account and Settings

The toggle switch next to **Automatically apply credits** turns the feature on or off. If the switch is turned off, the user can manually select the specific **invoice** to be credited. Automatic application saves time; manual selection gives the user better control.

Creating Credit Memos with Automatic Application Set as the Preference

Click **+ New** on the navigation bar.

Figure 3.51

Access to credit memo form

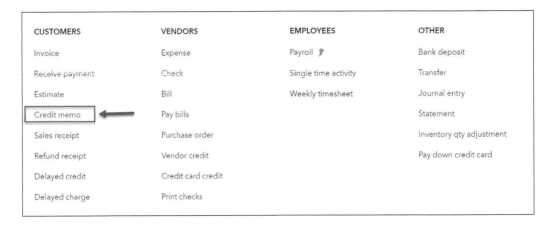

Click **Credit Memo**. The window will look something like this:

Figure 3.52

Credit memo form

The customer account to be credited must be selected. The credit memo date and number (if custom transaction numbers are being used) must be entered.

The item selected in the **PRODUCT/SERVICE** column represents the service (or product) for which the credit memo is being issued. For example, if the client is being issued a credit for two hours of gardening services, then the item associated with gardening would be selected.

QBO automatically credits specific invoices in this order:

- Oldest open invoice first.

- If the credit is greater than the oldest invoice, the balance is credited to the second oldest.

    - QBO will continue to apply any balances (in reverse chronological order) until the credit is fully applied.

- If the client has no open invoices, the credit will be automatically applied to the **next invoice** recorded.

A completed **credit memo** might look something like this after it was saved.

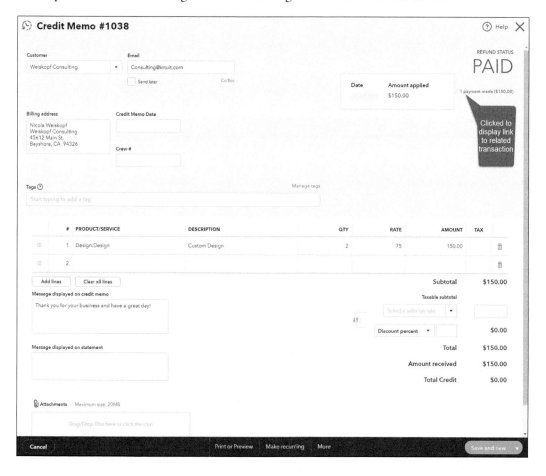

Figure 3.53

Example of a completed credit memo

QBO applied the credit by creating a customer **payment** transaction. The **payment** transaction can be viewed by clicking the link to the payment that appears directly under **PAID** in the top right corner of the form. The **payment** screen would look something like this:

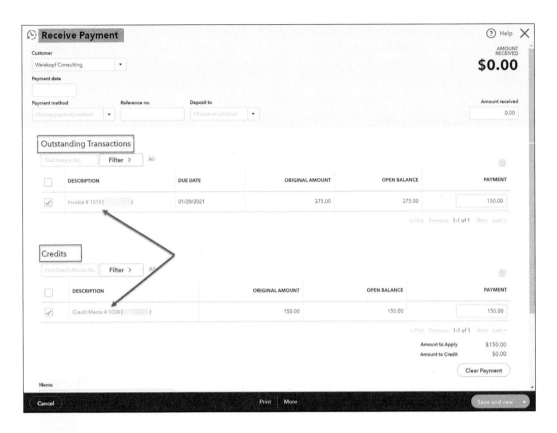

Figure 3.54

Example of automatic application of credit memo

Users could change the application of the **credit memo** in this window if there were other open **invoices** available.

Creating Credit Memos with Manual Application (Automatic Application Preference Turned Off)

The **credit memo** form is accessed by clicking **+ New** on the navigation bar and clicking **Credit Memo**.

The **credit memo** is completed as described in the above section, **Creating Credit Memos with Automatic Application Set as the Preference**.

Once saved, the **credit memo** will show with an **Unapplied** status in the customer's record.

Click **Sales** in the navigation bar. Click the customer name on the **CUSTOMERS** tab. The screen would look something like this:

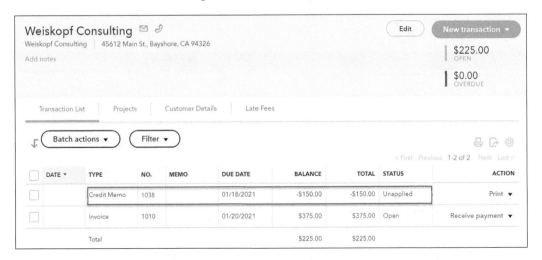

Figure 3.55

Customer transaction list screen

To apply the credit, from the customer record screen click **New Transaction** and select **Payment**.

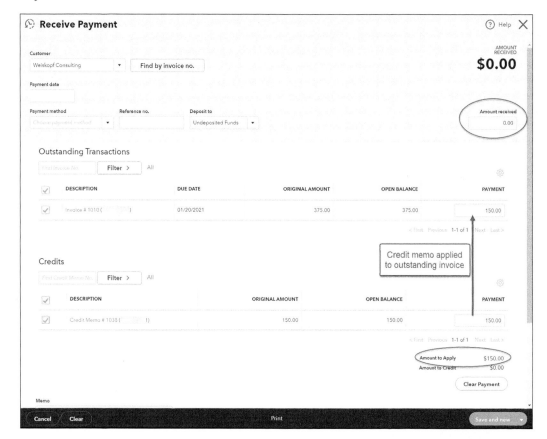

Figure 3.56

Example of manual application of credit memo

Place a checkmark in the box next to the **invoice** to be credited and enter the credit amount in the **PAYMENT** field. Place a checkmark in the box next to the **Credit Memo** to be applied. The **Amount received** should be 0.00. The **Amount to Apply** should equal the credit amount.

> **BEHIND THE SCENES** When a credit memo is created, with or without automatic application turned on, QBO creates the same basic journal entry (debit: income account of the product/service item selected, credit: accounts receivable). The total customer balance is also the same regardless of the method. However, with manual application, the credit memo is saved with a status of **unapplied** and the user determines when and to which specific invoice the credit is applied.

Some companies wait to receive a customer payment before applying available credit memos. This process was covered in the **Payments on Account** section of this chapter.

Issuing Refunds to Customers

Instead of issuing a credit memo, companies may choose to issue a refund directly to the client. This would most likely occur when the company wants to give a credit to a client with no open (unpaid) invoices.

Refunds to clients are entered as **transaction type Refund Receipt**. The underlying credit in the transaction is to the **Bank** account. The underlying debit depends on the **product** or **service** item selected in the form.

To access the form, click **+ New** on the navigation bar.

Figure 3.57

Access to Refund
Receipt form

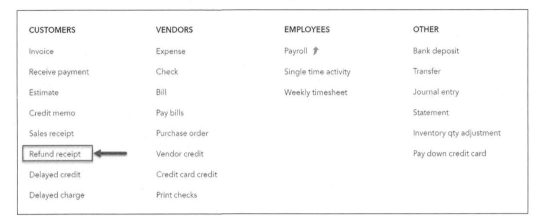

Select **Refund Receipt**. The form would look something like this:

Figure 3.58

Refund receipt form

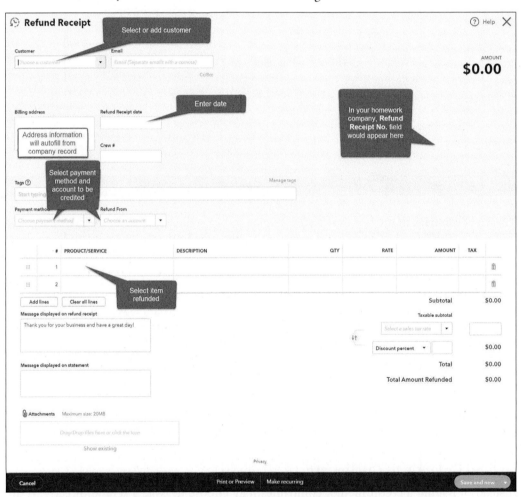

The form must include the customer name, the date of the refund, and items to be debited. The **Payment method** used (usually cash or check) and the bank account to be credited must be selected. If the refund is being made using a check, the **Check No.** field must be completed.

A completed **refund receipt** might look something like this if a check was issued for the refund:

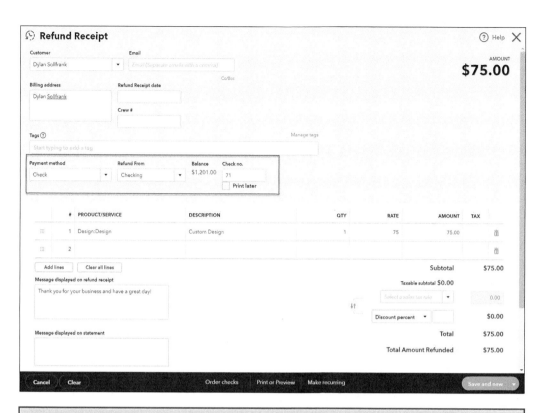

Figure 3.59

Example of completed
refund receipt

> ✳ **HINT:** The Check no. field and the bank balance appeared when the Checking
> account was selected in the Refund From dropdown menu.

The following message will appear after a **refund receipt** is saved:

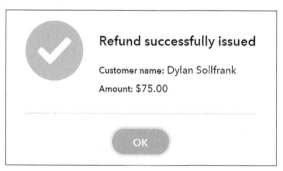

Figure 3.60

Refund receipt
message

Record a credit memo and a refund for Craig's Design and Landscaping.
(Amy's Bird Sanctuary complained about the amount of its recent bill. Craig's Design and
Landscaping decides to give Amy's Bird Sanctuary a $150 credit toward that invoice. Dylan
Sollfrank paid $337.50 for a custom landscape design. Dylan was happy with the design
but has decided to postpone the project. To maintain good client relations, Craig decides to
issue Dylan a $75 refund.)

1. Change settings to allow for manual application of credit memos and custom
   transaction numbers.

   a. Click the ⚙ in the icon bar.

   b. Click **Account and Settings**.

PRACTICE

EXERCISE
3.8

Homework
MBC

(continued)

(continued from previous page)

    c. Click **Advanced**.

    d. Click the **pencil** icon in the **Automation** section.

    e. Toggle **Automatically apply credits** to turn the feature off.

    f. Click **Save**.

    g. Click the **Sales** tab.

    h. Click the **pencil** icon in the **Sales form content** section.

    i. If necessary, toggle **Custom transaction numbers** box to turn the feature on.

    j. Click **Save**.

    k. Click **Done**.

2. Create a credit memo.

    a. Click **+ New** on the navigation bar.

    b. Click **Credit memo** in the **CUSTOMERS** column.

    c. Select **Amy's Bird Sanctuary** as the customer.

    d. Enter the current date as the **Credit Memo Date**.

    e. Enter CM1011 as the **Credit Memo no.**

    f. Select **Design:Design** as the **PRODUCT/SERVICE** and enter "2" as the **QTY**.

    g. The total credit amount should be $150.00.

    h. Click **Save and close**.

    i. **Make a note** of the open balance for Amy's Bird Sanctuary as displayed in the Customer Center.

3. Apply the credit.

    a. Click **Sales** in the navigation bar and select the **Customer** tab.

    b. Click **Amy's Bird Sanctuary**.

    c. Click **New transaction** and select **Payment**.

    d. Place checkmarks in the boxes next to Credit Memo #CM1011 and Invoice #1021.

    e. Click **Save and close**.

4. Record a refund.

    a. Click **+ New** on the navigation bar.

    b. Click **Refund receipt** in the **CUSTOMERS** column.

    c. Select **Dylan Sollfrank** as the customer.

    d. Enter the current date as the **Refund Receipt date**.

    e. Enter "1045" as the **Refund Receipt no.**

    f. Select **Check** as the **Payment method**.

    g. Select **Checking** in the **Refund From** field and enter "1002" as the **Check no.**

    h. Select **Design:Design** as the **PRODUCT/SERVICE** and enter "1" as the **QTY**.

    i. The **Total Amount Refunded** should be $75.00.

    j. Click **Save and close**.

    k. Click **OK**.

    l. Click **Dashboard**.

SALES AND CUSTOMER REPORTS

Sales and customer reports can be accessed through **Reports** on the navigation bar.

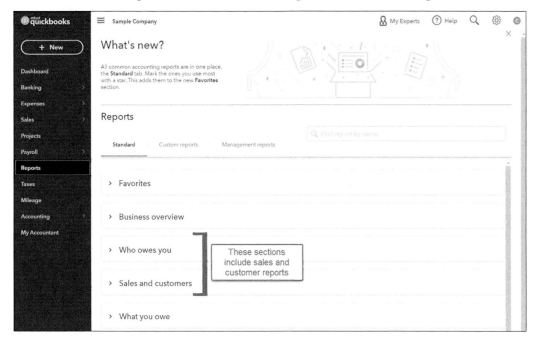

Figure 3.61

Sales and customer reports section

Most of the sales and customer reports are included in the **Who owes you** and **Sales and Customers** sections. Some of the most commonly used sales reports in service companies are highlighted in Figure 3.62:

Figure 3.62

Common sales reports for service companies

The **Who Owes You** group includes reports on uncollected invoices as seen in Figure 3.63:

Figure 3.63

Common customer
reports for service
companies

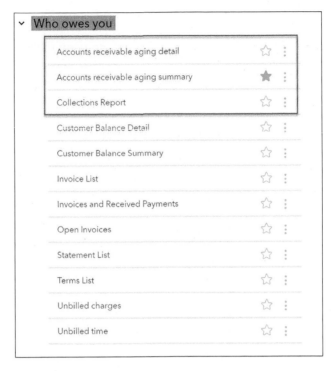

As discussed in Chapter 1, reports can be modified as needed. (Refer to the **REPORTING** section of Chapter 1 for a refresher on report modification.)

For example, the **AR Aging Summary** default report looks something like this:

Figure 3.64

A/R Aging Summary
report

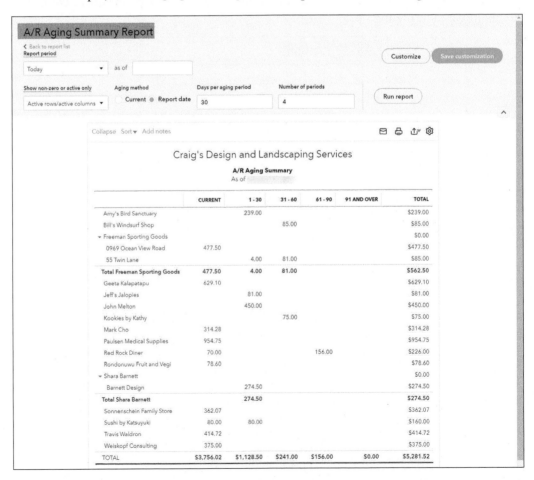

HINT: Your report will show different balances if you haven't logged out since completing Practice Exercise 3.8.

The same report modified to show eight 15-day aging periods would look something like this:

Figure 3.65

Customized A/R Aging Summary report

Prepare sales and receivable reports.

(Craig's Design and Landscaping needs an A/R aging and a revenue by type of service report.)

1. Prepare an accounts receivable aging report.

   a. Click **Reports**.

   b. Click **Accounts receivable aging summary** in the **Who owes you** section.

   c. Drill down (click) on the **TOTAL** column for Sonnenschein Family Store.

      i. **Make a note** of the invoice number for the $362.07 charge to Sonnenschein.

   d. Click **Dashboard**.

2. Prepare a sales report by service item.

   a. Click **Reports**.

   b. Click **Sales by Product/Service Detail** in the **Sales and Customers** section.

   c. Change **report period** to **All Dates**.

   d. Click **Customize**.

   e. Open the **Filter** dropdown section.

(continued)

PRACTICE EXERCISE 3.9

(continued from previous page)

   f.   Check **Product/Service** and select **Design:Design** and **Design:Lighting**.

   g.   Open the **Rows/Columns** section.

   h.   Click **Change columns**.

   i.   Check **Product/Service** to add the column to the report.

   j.   Uncheck Balance.

   k.   Click **Run Report**.

   l.   **Make a note** of the AMOUNT included in the report for **Design:Lighting**.

   m.   Click **Dashboard**.

SALES CYCLE SUMMARY

Let's summarize the sales steps we have learned and their related journal entries. First let's review the difference between a cash sale and a sale on account.

Cash sales are recorded on Sales receipts. The customer is buying something now and paying for it now.	Sales on account are recorded on Invoices. The customer is buying something now and will pay for it at a later date.
2-step process: 1. Create a Sales receipt for each sale. 2. Record a Deposit when receipts are deposited into the bank account.	3-step process: 1. Create an Invoice for each sale. 2. Receive payments from customers. 3. Record a Deposit when customer payments are deposited into the bank account.

Let's also review the basic sales journal entries that are created in service companies based on the above transactions.

Cash Sales—Journal Entry	Sales on Account—Journal Entry

• Journal entry underlying a Sales receipt
  – Dr: Undeposited Funds
  – Cr: Revenue
• Journal entry underlying a Deposit
  – Dr: Checking
  – Cr: Undeposited Funds
NOTE: Multiple payments can be grouped together
	• Journal entry underlying an Invoice
	  – Dr: A/R
	  – Cr: Revenue
	• Journal entry underlying a Payment from customer
	  – Dr: Undeposited Funds
	  – Cr: A/R
	• Journal entry underlying a Deposit
	  – Dr: Checking
	  – Cr: Undeposited Funds
	NOTE: Multiple payments can be grouped together

> ✳ **HINT:** Journal entries for sales of products (covered in Chapter 6) would include additional debits and credits to accounts such as Cost of Goods Sold, Inventory, and Sales Taxes Payable.

ANSWER TO
QuickCheck
3-1

Accounts receivable (A/R)	$225	
Design income		$225

CHAPTER SHORTCUTS

Add a customer
1. Click Sales on the navigation bar
2. Click the CUSTOMERS tab to open the Customer Center
3. Click New Customer

Edit a customer
1. Open Customer Center
2. Click customer name
3. Click Edit

Inactivate a customer
1. Open Customer Center
2. Open the dropdown menu in the ACTION column for the customer to be inactivated
3. Select Make inactive

Add service item
1. Click the ⚙ in the icon bar
2. Click Products and Services
3. Click New
4. Click Service

Edit item
1. Click the ⚙ in the icon bar
2. Click Products and Services
3. Click Edit in the ACTION column for the item to be edited

Inactivate an item
1. Click the ⚙ in the icon bar
2. Click Products and Services
3. Open the dropdown menu in the ACTION column for the item to be inactivated
4. Select Make inactive

Record cash sale
1. Click ⬤ + New on the navigation bar
2. Click Sales Receipt in the CUSTOMERS column

Record sale on account
1. Click ⬤ + New on the navigation bar
2. Click Invoice in the CUSTOMERS column

Record credit memo
1. Click ⬤ + New on the navigation bar
2. Click Credit Memo in the CUSTOMERS column

Record customer payments on account balances
1. Click ⬤ + New on the navigation bar
2. Click Record Payment in the CUSTOMERS column

Record deposits
1. Click ⬤ + New on the navigation bar
2. Click Bank Deposit in the OTHER column

CHAPTER REVIEW

Matching
Match the term or phrase (as used in QuickBooks Online) to its definition.

1. customer name
2. display name
3. sales receipt
4. invoice
5. deposit
6. credit memo
7. undeposited funds
8. payment

Assignments with the MBC are available in myBusinessCourse.

_____ transaction type used for recording cash sales

_____ specific customer identifier

_____ transaction type used to record bank deposit

_____ default general ledger account used to initially record cash received

_____ transaction type used for recording customer payments on account

_____ transaction type used to record sales on account

_____ transaction type used to record credit given to customer

_____ customer name appearing on invoices, sales receipts, or credit memos

Multiple Choice

1. A **service** item in QBO
   a. can be linked to more than one general ledger account.
   b. must be linked to one, and only one, general ledger account.
   c. can only be linked to an accounts receivable type account.
   d. can be, but doesn't need to be, linked to an account.

2. The general ledger account Undeposited Funds in QBO represents _____.
   a. all cash sales
   b. the balance in accounts receivable
   c. amount of cash, checks, or credit card payments received and recorded but not yet deposited
   d. None of the above

3. The account that is credited when a credit memo is completed in QBO must have the **account type** _____.
   a. Bank
   b. Accounts receivable
   c. Accounts payable
   d. Other current asset
   e. Other current liability

4. The default account Undeposited Funds has the **account type** _____.
   a. Bank
   b. Other current asset
   c. Other asset
   d. Other current liability
   e. Accounts receivable

5. There is an underlying journal entry behind every completed form listed below **except** _____.
   a. Invoice
   b. Credit memo
   c. Bank deposit
   d. Sales receipt
   e. None of the above answers is correct.

BEYOND THE CLICKS—THINKING LIKE A MANAGER

Accounting: What factors are important to consider when setting credit terms for your customers?

Information Systems: Customer payments are sometimes received one day and deposited into the company's bank one or two days later. What are some internal control processes that could be used to safeguard the payments until they are deposited?

ASSIGNMENTS

Background information: Martin Smith, a college student and good friend of yours, has always wanted to be an entrepreneur. He is very good in math, so, to test his entrepreneurship skills, he has decided to set up a small math tutoring company serving local high school students who struggle in their math courses. He set up the company, Math Revealed!, as a corporation in 2021. Martin is the only owner. He has not taken any distributions from the company since it opened.

The business has been successful so far. In fact, it's been so successful he has decided to work in his business full time now that he's graduated from college with a degree in mathematics.

He has decided to start using QuickBooks Online to keep track of his business transactions. He likes the convenience of being able to access his information over the Internet. You have agreed to act as his accountant while you're finishing your own academic program.

Martin currently has a number of regular customers that he tutors in Pre-Algebra, Algebra, and Geometry. His customers pay his fees by cash or check after each tutoring session but he does give terms of Net 15 to some of his customers. He has developed the following fee schedule:

Name	Description	Rate
Refresher	One-hour session	$ 60 per hour
Persistence program	Two one-hour sessions per week	$100 per week
Crisis program	Five one-hour sessions per week	$225 per week

The tutoring sessions usually take place at his students' homes but he recently signed a two-year lease on a small office above a local coffee shop. The rent is only $750 per month starting in January 2022. A security deposit of $500 was paid in December 2021.

The following equipment is owned by the company:

Description	Date placed in service	Cost	Life	Salvage Value
Computer	7/1/21	$3,000	36 months	$300
Printer	7/1/21	$ 240	24 months	$ 0
Graphing Calculators (3)	7/1/21	$ 300	36 months	$ 30

All equipment is depreciated using the straight-line method.

As of 12/31/21, Martin owed $2,500 to his father (Richard Smith) who initially helped him get started. Richard is charging him interest at a 6% annual rate. Martin has been paying interest only on a monthly basis. His last payment of interest only was on 12/31/21.

Over the next month or so, he plans to expand his business by selling a few products he believes will help his students. He has already purchased a few items:

Category	Description	Vendor	Quantity on Hand	Cost per Unit	Sales Price
Books and Tools					
	Geometry in Sports	Books Galore	20	18	25
	Solving Puzzles: Fun with Algebra	Books Galore	20	15	22
	Getting Ready for Calculus	Books Galore	20	20	28
	Geometry Kit	Math Shack	10	12	18
	Handheld Dry-Erase Boards	Math Shack	25	10	15
	Notebooks (pack of 5)	Paper Bag Depot	10	8	12

1/3/22

✓ You're ready to start recording some transactions for Martin but you know you have some setup work to do first.

✓ You organize the **products/services** list into **categories**.

• You click the ⚙ on the icon bar and select **Products and Services**.

Assignment 3A

Math Revealed!

- You select **Manage categories** on the **More** dropdown menu and you create three categories: Books and Tools, Tutoring, and Other. **TIP:** If you do not see **Manage categories**, be sure to return to Chapter 2 in **Step 8 Import Products and Services** to see how to activate categories. If the option to activate **categories** doesn't appear in the **Products and Services** list, try opening the company file in a different browser.
- You edit the **inventory** items (**Dry Erase, Sports, Puzzles, Ready, Kit**, and **Notebooks**) to link them to the **Books and Tools category**. You edit the **service** items (**Refresher, Persistence, Crisis**) to link them to the **Tutoring category**.
- You edit the default items created by QBO (**Hours** and **Services**) to include them in the **Other category**. **TIP:** If you do not have **Hours** and/or **Services** then skip this step. These items are auto-generated by QBO and may not always appear.

✓ You also set some credit terms and check on payment methods for Math Revealed!

- You click the ⚙ on the icon bar and select **All Lists**.
- You set up two new terms in the **Terms** list.
  - You name one term "Net 15." This will be the default terms for most customers. Customers will be expected to pay within 15 days of the invoice date if they don't pay at time of service.
  - You create a second term—"Net 30." You think Martin might decide to give some of his long-time customers a bit more time to pay.
- You click **Payment Methods** on the **All Lists** screen and make sure there are at least two methods available: Cash and Check.

✓ You also decide to set some preferences in **Account and Settings** that you think will be helpful.

- In the **Sales form content** section of the **Sales** tab:
  - You select **Net 15** as the **Preferred invoice terms**.
  - You choose **None** as the **Preferred delivery method** since you intend to print out invoices or receipts to customers when the services are completed.
  - **TIP: Custom transaction numbers** should have been turned **On** as part of the homework in Chapter 2. If you missed that, make sure you turn it on now.
- You want to control how credits are applied so you turn **Automatically apply credits off** in the **Automation** section of the **Advanced** tab in **Account and Settings**.

✓ Martin has let you know that he will be giving payment terms of Net 15 to all existing customers. You edit all existing customers to add the Net 15 payment terms.

TIPS: To speed up the process, use the sidebar described in the Hint on page 3-13.
Terms are added on the **Payment and billing** tab of the customer record.

1/7/22

✓ Martin gives you a check from a new customer for $120 for two **Refresher** tutoring sessions. The check, #56772, is dated 1/7.

- You set up the new customer.
  - The customer is Alonso Luna. You use Luna, Alonso as the **display name**.
  TIP: Enter the **display name** first. Then complete the **first name** and **last name** fields.

  4755 Hastings Road, Sacramento, CA 95822

  916-118-8111

  You set the payment terms at Net 15.
- You create a sales receipt (#SR-101) for the two tutoring sessions.
  - You make sure to use 150 Undeposited Funds as the **Deposit to** account. You'll be depositing checks in batches.

✓ Martin also gives you a list of all sessions held this past week. He did not collect payment for any of these sessions so you prepare invoices dated 1/7, with credit terms of Net 15, for the following customers:

- Debbie Han—**Crisis** $225, INV-1004
- Marcus Reymundo—**Refresher** $60, INV-1005
- Eliot Williams—**Persistence** $100, INV-1006

✓ Several customers have also set up tutoring sessions for the next few weeks. Now that Martin has decided to offer payment terms to his customers, you will be invoicing them in advance. All customers have Net 15 terms. You use 1/7/22 as the invoice date.

- Jon Savidge—Three weeks of the **Persistence** program, starting 1/10. $300, INV-1007
- Paul Richard—Two weeks of the **Crisis** program, starting 1/17. $450, INV-1008
  - Paul is totally focused on an upcoming Algebra exam. He intends to get an A.

1/11/22

✓ Martin is always looking for ways to expand his services. He decides to offer a walk-in tutoring clinic on January 15th. It will be open to all high school students. He's going to charge each student $20 for the afternoon. A couple of his college friends have agreed to help out.

- You set up the new **service** item you'll use to record Saturday's fees. Martin is calling the clinic "Mathmagic" so that's what you decide to name the item. You add the new item to the **Tutoring category**. You select Tutoring Revenue as the **Income account**. You use "Mathmagic Clinic" as the description.

1/12/22

✓ You receive two checks in the mail from customers. **TIP:** Make sure you use 150 Undeposited Funds for the **Deposit to** account for both.

- Check #189 from Kim Kowalski, dated 1/12, for $100 on INV-1002.
  - You give Kim a call and remind her that the total amount due was $200. She apologizes and promises to pay the balance before the end of the month.
- Check #2840 from Annie Wang, dated 1/12, for $225 in full payment of INV-1003.

✓ You deposit the checks received today with the check received last week. The total deposit is $445.

1/14/22

✓ Annie Wang's mother calls. She is so happy with the progress Annie is making in her Advanced Algebra course that she sets up appointments for the next four weeks (1/17/22–2/11/22) under the **Persistence** package. You invoice Annie $400, net 15. (INV-1009).

- You realize that some of the revenue just invoiced to Annie will not be earned until February. (The four weeks will be up on February 11th.) You decide to wait until the end of the month to make any necessary adjustments to the income statement. **TIP:** You'll do this as part of the homework for Chapter 5 so don't worry about it now.

1/15/22

✓ Thirty high school students show up for the Mathmagic Clinic. All of them pay cash ($600 in total). You create one **sales receipt** (SR-102) to record all the payments instead of creating a receipt for each student. You decide to create a "Drop-In" customer for this purpose.

- You click **Add new** in the customer name field. You enter "Drop-In" as the **Name**. You click **Details** to open the customer record window. You use 3835 Freeport Blvd, Sacramento, CA 95822 as the address.

TIP: Enter the number of students in the **QTY** field on the **Sales Receipt**.

✓ One of the students, Navi Patel, decides to also sign up for two **Refresher** sessions. She pays the $120 in cash. Martin schedules the service for 1/21 and 1/28.

- Since she may be an ongoing customer, you decide to set her up as a customer and prepare a separate receipt for the future tutoring sessions (SR-103).

- Navi's address is 2525 Fractal Drive, Sacramento, CA 95822. Her phone number is 916-121-8282. Credit terms (for future invoices) are Net 15. You use Patel, Navi as the **display name**.

1/19/22

✓ You receive the following checks in the morning mail all dated 1/19:

- $420 from Jon Savidge, check #3334, in payment of INV-1001 and INV-1007.
- $100 from Eliot Williams, check #8114 in payment of INV-1006.
- $225 from Debbie Han, check #4499 in payment of INV-1004.

✓ You deposit all checks and cash received since 1/12. The total deposit is $1,465.

1/21/22

✓ Martin gives you a list of the sessions for the past two weeks. (He's gotten a little behind on his paperwork and you remind him that his business needs cash to grow!)

- Some of the students paid for the sessions. You use 1/21 as the check date on the **sales receipts**.
  - Marley Roberts paid $200 for two weeks of **Persistence** with check #1701. (SR-104)
  - Alonso Luna paid $120 for two **Refresher** sessions with check #56792. (SR-105)

- Jon Savidge came in with four of his friends. All of them chose the **Crisis** package. Jon's father agreed to pay for all five of them. You bill Jon for $1,125. (INV-1010, net 30). Martin rewarded Jon's generosity by giving him longer terms!

✓ Martin lets you know that he closed the office on January 17th for Martin Luther King Day. As a result, Paul Richard missed one of his **Crisis** sessions. You create a **credit memo** (#CM-1008) for $45, dated 1/21. You use **Crisis** as the **PRODUCT/SERVICE** and change the **AMOUNT** to 45. You enter "Credit for missed session due to holiday" in the **Message displayed on credit memo** field. Since Paul has an outstanding invoice, you'll apply the credit when he pays the balance due. All other students scheduled make-up sessions and did not miss any tutoring.

✓ The father of one of Martin's Mathmagic students storms into the office right before closing. Gus Ranting is very upset that Math Revealed! did not get his consent before tutoring his son. Martin talks to the father and explains that the tutoring clinic was voluntary and that there was no pressure on any of the students to sign up for more sessions. Nonetheless, Martin agrees to refund the $20 and that seems to calm Gus down.

- You add Gus Ranting as a customer when you create **refund receipt** #RR-100. You enter Ranting, Gus as the **display name**. You don't enter any address information.
  - You issue the $20 refund from the Checking account. The Math Revealed! check number is 1100.
  - You use Mathmagic as the **PRODUCT/SERVICE**.

✓ You deposit the two checks received. The total deposit is $320.

1/24/22

✓ Martin gets a call from Teacher's College. Mr. Learn, the college president, has heard that Martin has developed some innovative techniques for helping students develop strong math skills. Mr. Learn asks Martin whether he's ever considered training other educators in his techniques. Martin is always up for new challenges and agrees to develop a workshop for the college for $3,000. Mr. Learn expects that there will be at least 50 math teachers from around the area in attendance. The workshop will be held February 12-13.

- You decide to set up a new income account called Workshop Revenue to track this new source of revenue. You select **Income** as the **account type** and **Service/Fee Income** as the **detail type**. You assign 405 as the account number.

- Martin thinks there may be opportunities for other types of workshops in the future so you decide to set up a new **category** named "Workshops." **TIP: Categories** are managed in **Products and Services**.

- You also create a new **service** item called "Educator Workshop."

  ○ You use "Tips for Teaching Math Workshop" as the item description and link the item to the Workshops **category**.

  ○ You enter a rate of "$3,000" as the default **sales price/rate** and select account 405 Workshops as the **Income account**.

- You also set up Teacher's College as a customer.

  ○ 21 Academy Avenue, Sacramento, CA 95822.

  ○ 916-443-3334.

  ○ Terms are Net 30.

✓ Teacher's College asks you to prepare an **invoice** for them now so that they can start processing the paperwork. You prepare INV-1011, dated 1/24, for the $3,000.

  ○ **TIP:** You will make an adjustment for unearned income as part of the homework for Chapter 5 so don't worry about it now.

1/27/22

✓ You receive two checks from customers.

- Check #7788090, dated 1/27, from Teacher's College for $3,000, in payment of INV-1011.

  ○ Martin was very surprised but very grateful for the prompt payment.

- Check #45678, dated 1/27 from Paul Richard for $405 in payment of INV-1008.

  ○ You apply CM-1008 to the balance when you enter the payment. **TIP:** This can be tricky. Before you close the transaction, make sure that the **PAYMENT** field for the **Invoice** shows the full amount (the original amount of the invoice), the **Amount received** is accurate, and the **Credit memo** box is checked. Review the **WARNING** on page 3-35 for more information.

- Martin was really impressed by Jon Savidge's father's willingness to pay for tutoring sessions for his son's friends. He decided to help out by crediting Jon's bill $125. You prepare a credit memo (CM-1010) and date it 1/27. **TIP:** The original invoice was for **Crisis** tutoring packages. The $125 is a small adjustment of the service cost.

1/28/22

✓ Martin gives a list of tutoring sessions held since 1/21.

- You prepare an invoice for:

  ○ Marley Roberts, one **Persistence** package $100, INV-1012, Net 15

- One student paid by check so you created a sales receipt for:

  ○ Eliot Williams, one **Persistence** package $100 (Check # 8144, SR-106)

✓ Martin lets you know that he won't be setting up any additional sessions for January 31. He's going to use that time to prepare the workshop for Teacher's College.

✓ You deposit all the checks received this week. The deposit totals $3,505.

Check numbers 1/31

Checking account balance:. $9,130
January Sales Revenue:. $6,830

Suggested reports for Chapter 3:

All reports should be in portrait orientation.

- Journal—1/01 through 1/31 transactions only **TIP:** The **Journal** report is in the **For my accountant** section of **Reports**.

- Sales by Product/Service Summary (January sales only)

  Customize (filter) the report to only show items in the Tutoring or Workshops **categories**.

- Accounts receivable aging summary dated 1/31
- Balance Sheet as of 1/31
- Profit and Loss for January
- Product/Service List (in the **Sales and Customers** section). Customize the report so that the following columns appear (in this order):
  - Product/Service
  - Type
  - Description
  - Qty On Hand
  - Price
  - Income Account
  - Cost
  - Expense Account

Assignment 3B

Salish Software Solutions

Background information: Sally Hanson, a good friend of yours, double majored in Computer Science and Accounting in college. She worked for several years for a software company in Silicon Valley but the long hours started to take a toll on her personal life.

Last year she decided to open up her own company, Salish Software Solutions. Sally currently advises clients looking for new accounting software and assists them with software installation. She also provides training to client employees and occasionally troubleshoots software issues.

She has decided to start using QuickBooks Online to keep track of her business transactions. She likes the convenience of being able to access financial information over the Internet. You have agreed to act as her accountant while you're working on your accounting degree.

Sally has a number of clients that she is currently working with. She gives 15-day payment terms to her corporate clients but she asks for cash at time of service if she does work for individuals. She has developed the following fee schedule:

Name	Description	Rate
Select	Software selection	$500 flat fee
Set Up	Software installation	$ 75 per hour
Train	Software training	$ 50 per hour
Fix	File repair	$ 60 per hour

Sally rents office space from Alki Property Management for $600 per month.

The following furniture and equipment are owned by Salish:

Description	Date placed in service	Cost	Life	Salvage Value
Office furniture	6/1/21	$1,400	60 months	$200
Computer	7/1/21	$4,620	36 months	$300
Printer.	7/1/21	$ 900	24 months	$ 0

All equipment is depreciated using the straight-line method.

As of 12/31/21, she owed $3,500 to Dell Finance. The monthly payment on that loan is $150 including interest at 5%. Sally's last payment to Dell was 12/31/21.

Over the next month or so, Sally plans to expand her business by selling some of her favorite accounting and personal software products directly to her clients. She has already purchased the following items.

Item Name	Description	Vendor	Quantity on Hand	Cost per Unit	Sales Price
Easy1	Easy Does It	Abacus Shop	15	$100	$ 200
Retailer	Simply Retail	Simply Accounting	2	$400	$ 800
Contractor	Simply Construction	Simply Accounting	2	$500	$1,000
Organizer	Organizer	Personal Software	20	$ 25	$ 50
Tracker	Investment Tracker	Personal Software	20	$ 20	$ 40

1/4/22

✓ You're excited for the chance to use your accounting knowledge in a real business and you want to get started with an organized QBO file.

✓ You take a look at the **product/services** list and decide to group items into **categories**.

- You click the ⚙ on the icon bar and choose **Products and Services**.

- You select **Manage categories** on the **More** dropdown menu and you create three **categories** (Consulting and Installation, Products, and Other). **TIP:** If you do not see **Manage categories**, be sure to return to Chapter 2 in **Step 8 Import Products and Services** to see how to activate categories. If the option to activate **categories** doesn't appear in the **Products and Services** list, try opening the company file in a different browser.

- You edit the **inventory** items (**Easy1**, **Retailer**, **Contractor**, **Organizer**, and **Tracker**) to include them in the **Products category**.

- You edit **service** items (**Select**, **Set Up**, **Train**, and **Fix**) to include them in the **Consulting and Installation category**.

- You edit the default items created by QBO (**Hours** and **Services**) to include them in the **Other category**. **TIP:** If you do not have **Hours** and/or **Services** then skip this step. These items are auto-generated by QBO and may not always appear.

✓ You also set up some credit terms and check on payment methods for Salish Software.

- You click the ⚙ on the icon bar and select **All Lists**.

- You set up two new terms in the **Terms** list.

  ○ You name one term Net 15. This will be the default terms for most customers.

  ○ You create a second term—Net 30. You think Sally might decide to give some of her larger customers a bit more time to pay.

- You click **Payment Methods** on the **All Lists** screen and make sure there are at least two methods available: Cash and Check.

✓ You ask Sally about the payment terms on her current customers. She says they all are expected to pay within 15 days. You edit the customer record for all existing customers to add the Net 15 payment terms. **TIP:** Terms are added on the **Payment and billing** tab of the customer record.

✓ You also decide to set some preferences in the **Sales** tab of **Account and Settings** that you think will be helpful.

- In the **Sales form content** section of the **Sales** tab:

  ○ You select **Net 15** as the **Preferred invoice terms**.

  ○ You choose **None** as the **Preferred delivery method** since you intend to print out invoices or receipts for customers when the services are completed.

  ○ **TIP: Custom transaction numbers** should have been turned **On** as part of the homework in Chapter 2. If you missed that, make sure you turn it on now.

- Since you want to control how credits are applied in QBO, you turn **Automatically apply credits** to **Off** in the **Automation** section of the **Advanced** tab in **Account and Settings**.

1/6/22

✓ Sally gives you a check from Dew Drop Inn for $180 for some work she did for the company today. There were some software issues. Sally spent three hours fixing the file. The check (#8134) is dated 1/6.

- You create a sales receipt (SR-101) for the three hours of file repair (**Fix**).
  - You make sure to use 150 Undeposited Funds as the **Deposit to** account. You'll be depositing checks in batches.

✓ Sally also gives you a list of all of her hours from the week. She did not collect payment from any of these customers so you prepare invoices dated 1/6, with credit terms of Net 15, as follows:

- Lou's Barber Shop—**Set Up**—10 hours ($750, INV-1006)
- Alki Deli—**Set Up**—8 hours ($600, INV-1007)
- Uptown Espresso—**Train** 5 hours ($250, INV-1008)

1/7/22

✓ Sally is always looking for ways to grow her business. She decides to offer a Software Workshop on January 20th. She will be offering tips on software selection and will be demonstrating some of the software products she expects to start selling in February. She's going to charge participants $75 for the afternoon. A couple of her college friends have agreed to help out with what she hopes is a large crowd. You decide to go ahead and set up the accounts and items you'll need to record the workshop revenue on the 20th.

- You decide to track the revenue from the workshop in a new **income** account (Workshop Revenue). Use 415 as the account number.
  - **TIP:** You can use **Service/Fee Income** as the **Detail Type**.
- You set up a new **category** called "Workshops and Seminars."
- You also set up a new **service** item. Sally is calling the workshop "Picking the Right Software" so you decide to name the item "Picks." You set it up in the Workshops and Seminars category.
  - You enter "Picking the Right Software Workshop" as the description and 75 as the **sales price/rate**.
  - You select 415 Workshop Revenue as the **income account**.

1/10/22

✓ You receive two checks in the mail. **TIP:** Make sure you use 150 Undeposited Funds as the **Deposit to** account for both.

- Check #1998 from Champion Law, dated 1/10, for $200 on INV-1003.
  - You call Lawrence (the accountant at the law firm) and remind him that the total amount due was $250. He apologizes and promises to pay the balance before the end of the month.
- Check #3751 from Lou's Barber Shop, dated 1/10, for $250 full payment of INV-1004.

✓ You deposit the checks received today with the check received last week. The total deposit is $630.

1/13/22

✓ The Operations Manager at Butter and Beans calls. The software Sally helped to select is ready for installation. The company would prefer to be billed for the entire cost in one invoice. Sally estimates that the **Set up** work will take 40 hours. (It's a complicated system to set up.) You invoice Butter and Beans for the $3,000 and give them 30-day terms as agreed to by Sally. (INV-1009).

- You realize that some of the revenue just invoiced to Butter and Beans may not be earned until February. You decide to wait until the end of the month to make any necessary adjustments to the income statement. **TIP:** You'll do this as part of the homework for Chapter 5 so don't worry about it now.

1/14/22

✓ Sally gives you a breakdown for her hours since 1/8. (She's gotten a little behind on her paperwork and you remind her that her business needs cash to grow!) You use 1/14 as the date for each transaction.

- Two of her customers paid her when she completed the work. You record both on **sales receipts**.

    Dew Drop Inn paid for 4 more hours of file repair (**Fix**) work with check #8144. ($240, SR-102)

    Lou's Barber Shop paid for 6 more hours of training (**Train**) with check #3767. ($300, SR-103)

- Sally also did software research work for a new client (Fabulous Fifties).

    You set them up as a new customer using the following information:

    > 834 Fashion Boulevard
    > Sacramento, CA 95822
    > 916-555-5555
    > Terms: Net 15

- You invoice Fabulous Fifties the $500 **Select** fee on INV-1010.

1/20/22

✓ Twenty people showed up for the "Picking the Right Software" workshop. All of them paid with cash ($1,500 in total), which was convenient but very surprising. You decide to create one sales receipt (SR-104) to record all the payments instead of creating a receipt for each participant.

- You enter "Cash Customer" as the customer in the **sales receipt** customer name field. You click **Add** and **Details** to open the customer record window. You use 3835 Freeport Blvd, Sacramento, CA 95822 as the address.

- **TIP:** On the **sales receipt** use 20 as the quantity sold.

✓ One of the participants, Leah Rasual, asks Sally to come to her home to do some troubleshooting on her personal computer. She's using QuickBooks to track the fees she gets from her singing engagements and she's having some issues. Since Sally hasn't worked with Leah before she asks for payment in advance for the first two hours. She pays the $120 by check (#241). Sally schedules the appointment with Leah for Friday 1/21.

- Since Leah may be an ongoing customer, you decide to set her up as a customer and prepare a separate **sales receipt** for the **Fix** work. (**Sales Receipt** SR-105).

- Use **Rasual, Leah** as the **display name** and enter her first and last name in the appropriate boxes. Leah's address is 3131 Tyson Avenue, Sacramento, CA 95822. Her phone number is 916-281-2086. Credit terms (for future invoices) are Net 15.

✓ With all that cash, you head straight to the bank and make a deposit. The total (including the checks received last week) is $2,160.

1/21/22

✓ Sally met with Leah Rasual and the work only took 2 hours. No additional billing is necessary.

✓ Sally lets you know that she made an error on the **Set Up** hours for Lou's Barber Shop included on INV-1006. She actually worked 8 hours not the 10 hours Lou's was billed for. You create a **credit memo** (#CM-1006) for $150, dated 1/21. Since Lou's has an outstanding invoice, you'll apply the credit when he pays the balance due.

- You enter "Sorry for the overbilling." in the **Message displayed on credit memo** box.

✓ You receive the following checks in the morning mail:

- $900 from Alki Deli, check #3334, in payment of INV-1001 and INV-1007.

- $50 from Champion Law, check #2001 for the remaining balance due on INV-1003.

- $500 from Butter and Beans, check #9191 in payment of INV-1002.

✓ One of the participants at Saturday's workshop (Marie Elle) stops by the office. She explains that she was only able to stay for the first 30 minutes of the workshop and would like to request a refund. She had to leave right after she got a call from her office letting her know that the pipes had burst in the warehouse basement. Sally agrees to refund the $75 **Picks** fee and promises to let her know about any future workshops.

- You add Marie Elle when you create **refund receipt** #RR-104. You save the name without adding any additional details to the customer record. You pay the refund out of your Checking Account. The Salish Software check number is 1100.

✓ You deposit the 3 checks. The total deposit is $1,450.

1/25/22

✓ Sally gets a call from Albus Software. Mr. Deposit, the CEO, has heard from several people that Sally does an exceptional job troubleshooting software problems. Mr. Deposit asks Sally whether she would be willing to share some tips and techniques with Albus' technical support staff. Sally thinks this might be an interesting project and agrees to develop a workshop for the company for $2,500. Mr. Deposit expects that there will be around 20 Albus employees in attendance. The workshop will be held in mid-February.

- You set up a new **service** item called "Tips." You include it in the **Workshops and Seminars category**.

  ○ You enter "Effective Troubleshooting" as the description and select 415 Workshop Fees as the **Income Account**.

  ○ You set the default **sales price/rate** as $2,500.

- You also set up Albus Software as a customer.

  ○ 11 Potter Road, Sacramento, CA 95822.

  ○ 916-443-3334.

  ○ Terms are Net 30.

✓ The accountant for Albus Software asks you to create an **invoice** for the workshop now so that they can start processing the paperwork. You prepare INV-1011, dated 1/25, for the $2,500.

- **TIP:** You won't earn the $2,500 until you present the workshop in February. You will make an adjustment for unearned income as part of the homework for Chapter 5 so don't worry about it now.

1/27/22

✓ Dew Drop Inn decided they need to install a new accounting software system after paying Sally for multiple hours spent trying to repair their current system. They asked Sally to help them select an appropriate program. She reviewed the company's needs this week and put together a proposal for them that spelled out her recommendation. You prepare the invoice for that service. (**Select**, $500, INV-1012, Net 15).

✓ Sally lets you know that she won't be doing any consulting during the last few days of January. She's going to use that time to prepare training materials for the Effective Troubleshooting workshop at Albus Software.

1/28/22

✓ You receive two checks from customers. Both checks are dated 1/28.

- Check #5333 from Uptown Espresso ($370) in payment of INV-1005 and INV-1008.

- Check #3790 from Lou's Barber Shop ($600) in full payment of INV-1006.

  ○ You apply CM-1006 to the balance when you enter the payment.

  ○ **TIP:** This can be tricky. Before you close the transaction, make sure that the **PAYMENT** field for the **Invoice** shows the full amount (the original amount of the invoice), the **Amount received** is accurate, and the **Credit memo** box is checked. Review the **WARNING** on page 3-35 for more information.

✓ You deposit both checks in the bank. The deposit should total $970.

Check numbers 1/31

> **Checking account balance:....$15,635**
> **January Sales Revenue:.......$10,215**

Reports to create for Chapter 3:

- Journal—1/01 through 1/31 **TIP:** The Journal report is in the For my accountant section of Reports.

- Accounts receivable aging summary dated 1/31

- Sales by Product/Service Summary (January sales only)
  - Customize (filter) the report to only show items in the Consulting and Installation and Workshops and Seminars categories.

- Balance Sheet as of 1/31

- Profit and Loss for January

- Product/Service List (in the Sales and Customers section). Customize the report so that the following columns appear (in this order):
  - Product/Service
  - Type
  - Description
  - Qty On Hand
  - Price
  - Income Account
  - Cost
  - Expense Account

Purchasing Activity
(Service Company)

WHAT IS THE PURCHASE CYCLE IN A SERVICE COMPANY?

The purchase cycle in a service company, like the sales cycle, is fairly straightforward. A company

- Incurs the cost.
- Receives a bill from the vendor.
- Pays the vendor.

Service companies can

- Pay at the time of purchase of goods or services.
- Pay later (buy "on account" or "on credit").

Before any purchases can be recorded in QuickBooks Online, a vendor must be set up.

MANAGING VENDORS

Vendors are managed in the Vendor Center.

 HINT: A vendor, in business, is an individual or company from whom a company purchases products or services. The phone company, the landlord, and the local newspaper are all vendors. In QBO, a **vendor** is set up for any individual (other than an employee) or company that the user expects to pay. Vendors might include owners, lenders, and tax authorities.

The Vendor Center is accessed through the **Expenses** link on the navigation bar.

Figure 4.1

Navigation bar

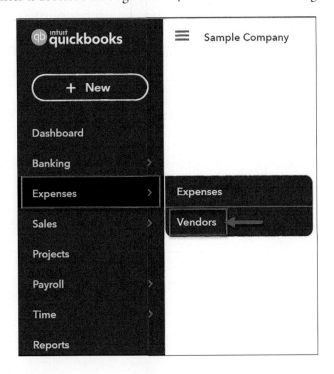

Select the **Vendors drawer**.
The Vendor Center looks something like this:

Figure 4.2

Vendor Center

In the Vendor Center, you can:

- Access the new vendor setup window.
- Access forms necessary to record activity with existing vendors.
- Access existing vendor data for editing.

Vendor Center Display

Selected information about vendor activity is highlighted in the **Money Bar** at the top of the Vendor Center screen.

Figure 4.3

Money Bar in Vendor Center

Clicking any of the amounts brings up a list of the transactions included in the total.

 HINT: The amount identified as **Paid** in your **Money Bar** may differ slightly.

Figure 4.4

Icons on Vendor Center screen

On the right side of the Vendor Center screen, just above the list of vendors, are three small icons.

The **printer** icon (far left) allows the user to print a list of all vendors. The list includes all vendor information currently displayed on the screen (including **OPEN BALANCE**).

Clicking the **export** icon (the middle icon) automatically downloads the list as an Excel file.

Clicking the third icon (the 🖫) allows users to customize the fields displayed in the Vendor Center.

Display columns can include any of the following:

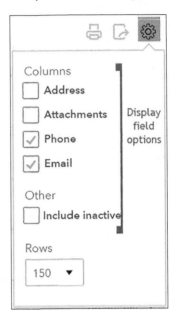

Adding a Vendor

To add a new vendor, open the Vendor Center by clicking **Expenses** in the navigation bar and clicking the **Vendors** tab.

Click **New Vendor** to open the **Vendor Information** window. It should look something like this:

Figure 4.7
Vendor record

Vendor Information

Title	First name	Middle name	Last name	Suffix

Company

Name used on forms and in correspondence

*Display name as

Name used as identifier in QBO   ▼

Print on check as ☑ Use display name

Address map

Street

City/Town   State/Province

ZIP code   Country

Notes

📎 **Attachments**   Maximum size: 20MB

Drag/Drop files here or click the icon

Email

Separate multiple emails with commas

Phone	Mobile	Fax

Other	Website

Cost rate (/hr)	Billing rate (/hr)

Terms

Enter Text   ▼

Opening balance   as of

                01/20/2021

Account no.

Appears in the memo of all payments

Business ID No. / Social Security No. ┐
                                        │ 1099 information
☐ Track payments for 1099   ┘

Default expense account

Choose Account   ▼

(Cancel) (Make inactive)   Privacy   (Save)

The name entered in the **Company** field is the name used in any correspondence with the vendor. This would normally be the business name used by the vendor. If the vendor is an individual, the name would be entered in the first row (in the **First name**, **Last name** fields).

The **Display Name** is used as a vendor identifier. It could be a number or a shortened version of the vendor name. This is the primary name used to organize the vendor list. It's also the name used in any search functions. The **Display Name** is used for internal purposes only. In this class, we'll use the **Company** name (or individual name) as the **Display Name**.

> **HINT:** **Display names** must be unique. An entity that is both a customer and a vendor can use the same **company name** but must have two different **display names**. One option would be to add a C (customer) or a V (vendor) to the end in the **display name** fields.

Contact information is entered in the majority of the fields in the **Vendor Information** window.

Other important fields include **Terms** (used to enter the vendor's payment terms) and **Account no.** (used to enter the account number assigned to the company by the vendor).

> **HINT:** You may need to scroll down to see it but a **Default expense account** can be selected for the vendor. That account will automatically be selected in purchase transactions with the vendor. It can be changed in the form, if necessary.

Documents can be attached to the vendor record for easy access by clicking **Attachments** in the bottom left corner of the screen. **Attachments** will be discussed further in Chapter 11.

Companies are required to report payments of more than $600 during the year to certain types of vendors to the Internal Revenue Service. Payments to independent contractors are reported on Form 1099-NEC. Payments to attorneys and landlords are reported on Form 1099-MISC.

Required tax information for 1099 vendors (including their federal tax identification number) is entered in the fields in the bottom right corner of the window. (Reporting payments to 1099 vendors is covered in the Appendix to this chapter.)

> **BEHIND THE SCENES** Using QBO, users can obtain 1099 information directly from vendors through email. The setup is done by clicking the **Payroll** tab on the navigation bar and selecting **Add a contractor** on the **Contractors** tab. Any vendor set up as a **Contractor** will appear in the Vendor Center.

Viewing Vendor Information

To view information about a specific vendor, click the vendor's name in the Vendor Center. The screen should look something like this:

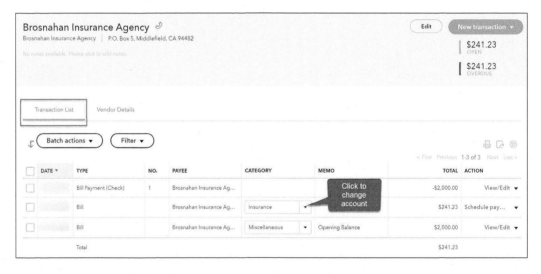

Prior transactions are listed on the **Transaction List** tab. Clicking any of the transactions listed will open the original form. Once in the form, details can be edited (dates, amounts, distribution accounts, etc.).

 HINT: Distribution accounts can also be changed directly on the **Transaction List** tab for **bill** transactions as long as the original transaction was not split into multiple accounts.

The **Vendor Details** tab screen would look something like this:

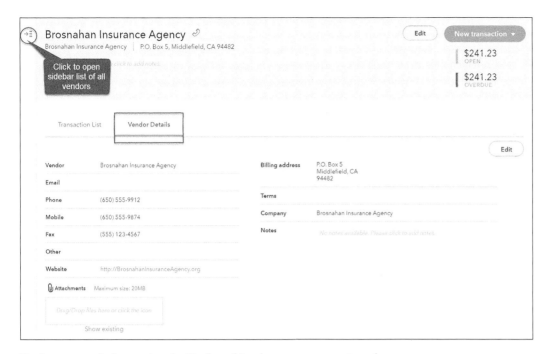

Figure 4.9

Vendor Details tab in vendor record

Basic contact information is displayed in the **Vendor Details** tab.

> **HINT:** For access to the full list of vendors when you're in a specific vendor record, click the three parallel lines to the left of the vendor name (top left corner in Figure 4.9). A sidebar will open.

Editing Vendor Information

Vendor information can be changed at any time. To edit an existing vendor, open the Vendor Center by clicking **Expenses** on the navigation bar and selecting the **Vendors** tab.

Click the name of the vendor you wish to edit and open the **Vendor Details** tab.

Figure 4.10

Access to edit vendor record

Click either **Edit** link to open the **Vendor Information** window. Make the desired changes and click **Save**.

Inactivating a Vendor

Vendors cannot be deleted in QBO.

Vendors with zero balances can, however, be inactivated. Most companies would choose to inactivate vendors they don't expect to use in the future to minimize the size of the vendor list.

To inactivate a vendor, open the Vendor Center.

Figure 4.11

Tool for inactivating vendor

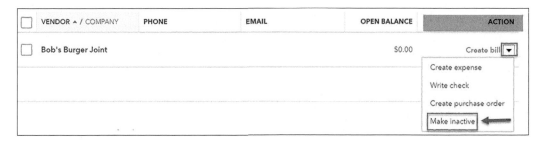

On the dropdown menu in the far right column of the vendor row, select **Make inactive**. This option wouldn't be available on the dropdown menu for vendors with open balances.

 HINT: Vendors can also be made inactive by clicking **Make inactive** in the vendor record. That option is visible on Figure 4.7. If vendors with open balances are inactivated in the vendor record, QBO will automatically create an entry (issue a **vendor credit** or a **journal entry**) to debit accounts payable and credit an **other expense** or **equity** account. Open balances should be cleared before vendors are inactivated.

Inactive vendors can't be used in transactions and aren't available in search functions, although they will show up on the appropriate reports.

To reactivate a vendor, inactive vendors must be visible in the Vendor Center.

Figure 4.12

Access to inactive vendors

Click the ⚙ icon right above the **ACTION** column in the Vendor Center to make inactive vendors visible.

Figure 4.13

Tool to reactivate an inactive vendor

An option to reactivate a vendor will now automatically appear in the **ACTION** column next to the vendor name.

> **BEHIND THE SCENES** Although the vendor shows as "deleted" in Figure 4.13 above, the vendor had been inactivated.

Set up and edit vendors for Craig's Design and Landscaping.
(Craig's Design adds two new vendors and edits an existing vendor's record.)

PRACTICE

EXERCISE

4.1

1. Enter a new vendor: Office Supplies Shop.

    a. Click **Expenses** in the navigation bar.

    b. Click the **Vendors** tab.

    c. Click **New Vendor** (top right of screen).

    d. Enter the following information on the left side of the **Vendor Information** window:

        i. Office Supplies Shop (**Company** and **Display Name** fields)

            2121 Capital Avenue

            West Sacramento, CA 95691

    e. Select **Net 30** in the **Terms** dropdown menu on the right side of the window.

    f. Click **Save**.

2. Enter a new 1099 vendor: Beverly Okimoto (accountant who may be hired as contract labor to assist with consulting work).

    a. Click **New Vendor** in the Vendor Center (top right of screen).

    b. Enter the following contact information:

        i. "Beverly" in the **First name** field and "Okimoto" in the **Last name** field

        ii. Use Beverly Okimoto as the **Display name**.

        iii. Enter address information:

            2525 Paradise Road

            Suite 2502

            Sacramento, CA 95822

    c. Select **Net 15** in the **Terms** dropdown menu.

    d. Check the box next to **Track payments for 1099** and enter "444-22-9898" in the **Business ID No.** field.

    e. Click **Save**.

3. Edit a vendor.

    a. Click **Computers by Jenni** in the Vendor Center.

    b. Click **Edit**.

    c. Change the **Mobile** number to "916-375-5511."

    d. Enter **Business ID No.** as "91-1112222."

    e. Check the box next to **Track payments for 1099**.

    f. **Make a note** of Jenni's last name.

    g. Click **Save**.

RECORDING PURCHASES

In a service company, most purchases are made "on account." It's just an easier, more efficient way to do business. There are times, however, when payment is made at the time of purchase (by cash/check or by credit card). As you can probably guess by now, QBO has a separate form for each alternative. The **transaction types** are:

● **Bill**—used for purchases on account.

● **Check**—used when payment is made with a check or with cash at the time of purchase or when the bill wasn't entered into QBO before payment was made.

    ■ A different transaction type (**Bill payment**) is used when **bills** previously entered in QBO are paid. **Bill payments** are covered in the **PAYING VENDOR BALANCES** section of this chapter.

● **Expense**—generally used when payment is made at the time of purchase with a credit card. Payments by check can also be entered in the **Expense** form but a check number field is not available in the form. Users would need to enter the check number in the **Ref no.** field.

> **BEHIND THE SCENES** QBO gives users many options for accomplishing the same task. As you continue to work with the software, you'll find yourself developing personal preferences. In your homework, you will only be using **Expense** transaction types for purchases with a credit card.

Automation in QBO

QBO allows users to automate a number of processes. This is a great tool for many small businesses. While you're learning QBO, however, it can create some confusion. This is especially true in the purchasing cycle. To turn off that automation, click the ⚙ on the icon bar.

Figure 4.14

Link to Account and Settings

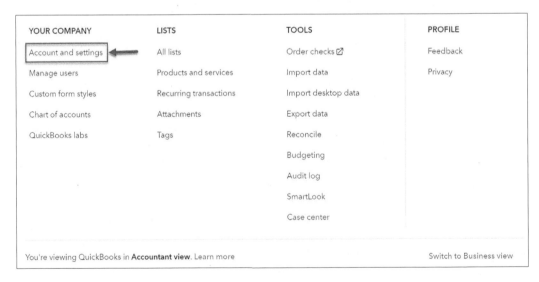

YOUR COMPANY	LISTS	TOOLS	PROFILE
Account and settings	All lists	Order checks ☒	Feedback
Manage users	Products and services	Import data	Privacy
Custom form styles	Recurring transactions	Import desktop data	
Chart of accounts	Attachments	Export data	
QuickBooks labs	Tags	Reconcile	
		Budgeting	
		Audit log	
		SmartLook	
		Case center	

You're viewing QuickBooks in **Accountant view**. Learn more   Switch to Business view

Click **Account and Settings**.

Open the **Advanced** tab and click the **pencil** icon in the **Automation** section.

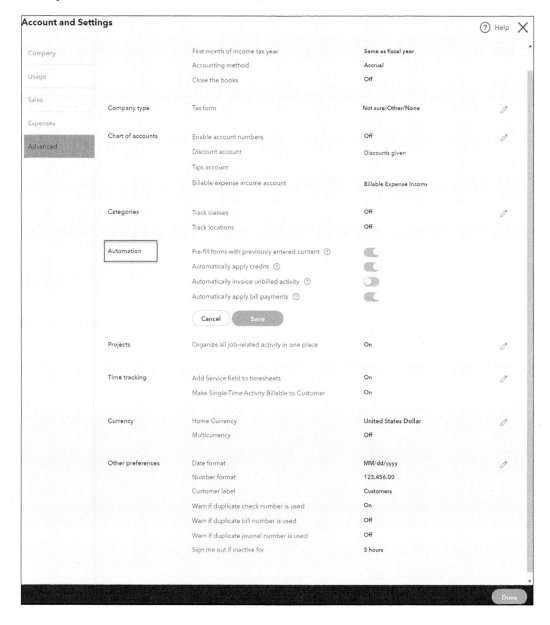

Figure 4.15

Automation section in Account and Settings

For maximum control, remove all automation features.

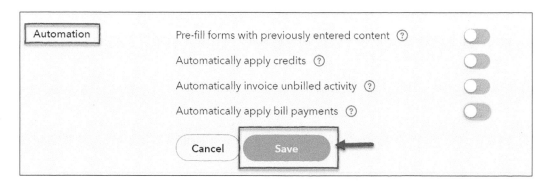

Figure 4.16

Example of Automation section in Account and Settings

Uncheck all automation fields. Click **Save**.
Click **Done** to exit **Account and Settings**.

> ✳ **HINT:** Since all of your transactions and settings will be deleted/cleared each time you log out or time out of QBO's test drive company, you would need to clear the automation functions each time you start a new work session. Settings in your assignment file will not change when you log out or time out of QBO.

Purchasing on Account

In a manual accounting system, a bill is received from the vendor. The bill is recorded in the purchases journal. The purchases journal is posted, in total, to the general ledger and each transaction in the purchases journal is posted to the appropriate vendor's subsidiary ledger.

In QBO, the form for entering a purchase on account is called a **bill**. (Remember, the vendor might call it an invoice but QBO calls it a **bill**. Only charges to customers are called invoices in QBO.) All accounts, ledgers, and statements are updated automatically when the **bill** is saved, so the form must include all relevant information needed.

That information includes:

- Who's the vendor? (This is needed for posting to the subsidiary ledger.)

- What are we buying? (What account should QBO debit?)

  ▪ The credit account for **bills** is Accounts payable.

- When do we have to pay for it? (What are the vendor's credit terms?)

> ❗ **WARNING: Although users can set up multiple accounts payable accounts in the chart of accounts, QBO is not currently designed to work with multiple A/P accounts. Bills are automatically credited to the default Accounts Payable (A/P) account set up by Intuit. If a user wanted to maintain more than one accounts payable account, journal entries could be used.**

There are many ways to access the **bill** form:

- by clicking on the navigation bar and selecting **Bill** in the Vendors column.

- by clicking **Expenses** on the navigation bar, clicking the **Expenses** drawer or tab, and selecting **Bill** in the **New transaction** dropdown menu

- by clicking **Expenses** on the navigation bar, clicking the **Vendors** drawer or tab, and selecting **Create bill** in the **Action** column dropdown menu for the vendor

- by clicking **Expenses** on the navigation bar, clicking the **Vendors** drawer or tab, clicking the vendor name, and selecting **Bill** in the **New transaction** dropdown menu

To open the **Bill** form, click **+ New** on the navigation bar. The **bill** form looks like this:

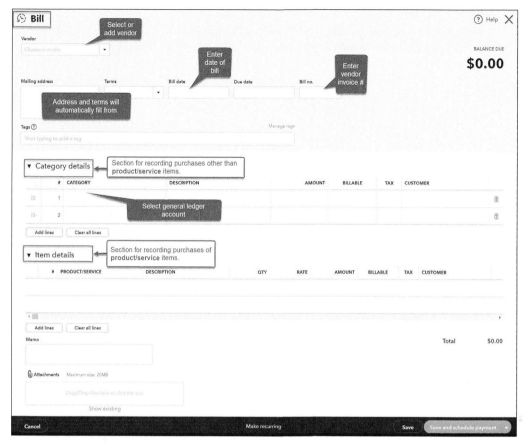

Figure 4.17
Bill form

To complete a **bill**, you must select a **Vendor**, enter the **Bill date**, and the **Bill no.** (vendor's reference number) in the top section of the form.

> **HINT**: If the vendor hasn't been previously entered, you can click **Add new** at the top of the **Choose a vendor** dropdown menu. Click **Details** to open the **Vendor Information** window and add contact information. If you don't need to enter details, simply enter the vendor name and click **Save**.

You also need to enter the vendor's credit terms. If you've already set up the credit terms for the vendor, these will show up automatically in the **Terms** field. If you haven't, you can select a term from the dropdown menu or create a new one by clicking **Add new** in the **Terms** dropdown menu. QBO can be used to keep track of any available early payment discounts so it's important to make sure the date and the terms are entered correctly.

> **BEHIND THE SCENES**   The same **terms** are used for both vendors and customers. You can see the full **Terms** list by selecting the ⚙ icon and selecting **All Lists** from the **List** menu.

Amounts and the accounts to be debited (the distribution accounts) are entered in the lower section of the form. As you can see in Figure 4.17, there are two sections on the bottom half of the form (**Category details** and **Item details**). Clicking the triangle just to the left of the name opens or closes the section.

Both sections are used to specify the account(s) to be debited.

- **Category details**
  - Used to record all purchases other than inventory. Most likely you would be debiting an asset or expense account in this section but you could debit any type of account.

- **Item details**
  - Used to record purchases of **product/service** items. The account debited depends on the **service** or **product** item selected. Inventory purchases will be covered in Chapter 7.

You can enter multiple accounts in the account distribution section of the form (under **Category Details**). You can even enter negative amounts, which would, of course, appear as credits in the underlying journal entry. A negative amount would be entered if, for example, the vendor gives you a discount and you decide to track discounts in a separate account. The sum of all the distributions must equal the total amount of the bill. (This is, after all, still accounting! The underlying journal entry must balance.)

QuickCheck
4-1

> What's the default credit account for a bill? (Answer at end of chapter.)

You can enter additional information about the nature of each charge in the **Description** field. You can also enter general information about the bill in the **Memo** field at the bottom left of the form. Anything included in either the **Description** or **Memo** fields will appear in **Journal** reports.

The bill itself or other documents related to the charge can be uploaded to QBO by clicking **Attachments** in the bottom left corner of the **bill**. Documents related to the vendor (price lists, contracts, etc.) that are not unique to the bill would normally be uploaded on the **Vendor Information** page. **Attachments** will be covered in greater depth in Chapter 11.

Click **Save and close** in the bottom right corner of the window to exit the form. Click **Save and new** to open a new blank **bill** form. **Save and schedule** is used to set up automatic payments. A company must have set up a bank connection in QBO in order to use the payment scheduling feature.

PRACTICE
EXERCISE
4.2

Enter bills for Craig's Design and Landscaping.
(Craig's Design enters several bills received in the mail.)

1. Click **+ New** on the navigation bar.

2. Click **Bill** in the **Vendors** column.

3. Enter the telephone bill for the current month. (The total bill was $285. $35 for the phone and a $250 charge for a repair.)

   a. Select **Cal Telephone** as the **Vendor**.

   b. Select **Net 30** for **Terms**.

   c. Enter the current date as the **Bill date**.

   d. Enter "118-1119" as the **Bill No.**

   e. In the **Category details** section, select **Telephone** as the **ACCOUNT** and enter "35" as the **AMOUNT**.

      i. **Make a note** of the parent account for **Telephone**.

(continued)

(continued from previous page)

f.   On the second line, select **Equipment repairs** as the **ACCOUNT** and enter "250" as the **AMOUNT**.

g.   Click **Save and new**.

4. Enter a $450 bill for an ad placed in the Business Weekly.

   a.   Select **Add new** in the **Choose a vendor** dropdown menu.

      i.   Click **+ Details**.

      ii.   Enter "Business Weekly" in the **Company** and **Display name as** fields.

      iii.   Click **Save**.

   b.   Select **Net 15** as the **Terms** in the **Bill** form.

   c.   Enter the current date as the **Date**.

   d.   Enter "121520" as the **Bill no.**

   e.   In the **Category details** section, select **Advertising** as the **ACCOUNT**.

   f.   Enter "Ad in the Weekly" in the **Memo** field.

   g.   Enter "450" as the **AMOUNT**.

   h.   Click **Save and new**.

5. Enter a $720 bill from Tania's Nursery for the purchase of a new lawn mower ($650) and 10 boxes of trash bags ($70).

   a.   Select **Tania's Nursery** as the **Vendor**.

   b.   Select **Net 15** for the **Terms**.

   c.   Enter the current date as the **Bill date**.

   d.   Enter "67-1313" as the **Bill no.**

   e.   The lawn mower is expected to last for more than one year so it should be recorded in a **fixed asset** account. In the **Category details** section, select **Add new** in the **CATEGORY** dropdown menu to set up a new account.

      i.   **Account Type—Fixed Assets**

      ii.   **Detail Type—Machinery & Equipment**

      iii.   **Name—Mowing equipment**

         •   Check **Track depreciation of this asset**. **TIP:** When this box is checked, QBO automatically creates two sub-accounts. One called "Original cost" and one called "Depreciation." Both sub-accounts have the **fixed assets account type**. This option would not be used by companies that do not create individual accumulated depreciation accounts for each property, plant, or equipment account.

      iv.   Click **Save and Close**.

   f.   Enter "$650" as the **AMOUNT** for the mower in the **category details** section of the **bill**.

   g.   The trash bags are expected to be used in the current month so the cost is debited to an **Expense account type**. Select **Supplies** as **Category** and use "$70" for the **AMOUNT**.

   h.   Click **Save and close**.

6. Review the accounts set up for the lawn mower.

   a.   Click the ⚙ on the icon bar.

(continued)

(continued from previous page)

   b. Click **Chart of Accounts.**

   c. Click **See your Chart of Accounts**, if necessary.

   d. **Make a note** of how many accounts have an account **Type** of **Fixed Assets.**

   e. Click **Dashboard** to close the window.

---

eLectures

Purchasing with Cash or Check

In a manual system, cash payments are recorded in the cash disbursements journal. The journal is recorded, in total, to the general ledger.

   In QBO, cash payments made at the time of purchase are entered through the form (**transaction type**) **Check. Checks** are also used to record a payment to a vendor when the vendor bill wasn't previously entered in QBO.

   You can easily access the form by clicking **+ New** on the navigation bar and clicking **Check** in the **Vendor** column. You can also access the **Check** form through **Expenses** on the navigation bar (on both the **Expenses** and **Vendor** tabs).

   The screen will look something like this:

Figure 4.18

Check form

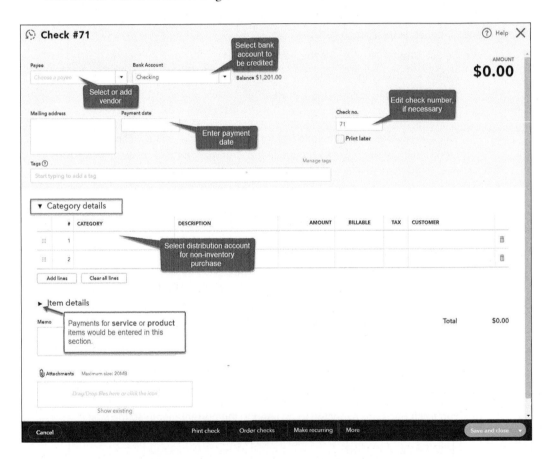

You need to select a vendor (**Payee**) and enter the **Payment date**. The **Check no.** will be automatically updated by QBO but you can change the number if necessary.

   The **Bank Account** you want to be credited for the check amount also needs to be selected. Users can track multiple bank accounts in QBO.

You'll notice the form has the same two distribution sections as the Bill form (Category details and Item details). Both sections are used for entering the general ledger accounts to be debited (or credited if a negative is entered) and the amounts.

> **BEHIND THE SCENES** Users can add information about the payment in the Description field and/or the Memo field. If the user prints the check from QBO, anything included in the Memo field will appear on the face of the check; anything included in the Description field will appear on the voucher copy of the check.

PRACTICE
EXERCISE
4.3

Enter checks for Craig's Design and Landscaping.

(Craig's Design pays its rent, makes a loan payment, and pays a retainer fee to a consultant.)

1. Record $900 rent payment for the current month.
   a. Click **+ New** on the navigation bar.
   b. Click **Check**.
   c. Select **Hall Properties** as the vendor.
   d. **Make a note** of the contact name for Hall Properties. **TIP:** The name is included in the **Mailing address** box.
   e. Leave **Checking** as the **Bank Account**.
   f. Enter the current date as the **Payment date**.
   g. Use "71" as the **Check no.**
   h. In the **Category details** section, select **Rent or Lease** as the **CATEGORY**.
   i. Enter "900" as the **AMOUNT**.
   j. Click **Save and new**.

2. Record a $120 check for the loan payment ($100 of principal; $20 of interest for the current month).
   a. Select **Fidelity** as the vendor.
   b. Leave **Checking** as the bank account.
   c. Enter the current date as the **Payment date**.
   d. Use "72" as the **Check no.**
   e. There are two distributions in the **Category details** section.
      i. On the first line, select **Notes Payable** as the **CATEGORY** and enter "100" as the **AMOUNT** (principal).
      ii. On the second line, select **Add new** in the **CATEGORY** field, choose **Other expense** as the **account type**, **Vehicle loan interest** as the **detail type**, and enter "Interest Expense" as the **Name**. Click **Save and close**.
      iii. Enter "20" as the **AMOUNT**.
      iv. The check total should be $120.
   f. Click **Save and new**.

3. Record check to Computers by Jenni for a retainer fee. (You're giving her an advance for future computer work.)
   a. Select **Computers by Jenni** as the vendor.
   b. Leave **Checking** as the bank account.

(continued)

(continued from previous page)

   c. Enter the current date as the **Payment date**.

   d. Use "73" as the **Check no.**

   e. In the **Category details** section, select **Prepaid Expenses** as the **CATEGORY**.

   f. Enter "400" as the **AMOUNT**.

   g. Click **Save and close**.

Voiding Checks

If a check is printed but contains an error and won't be distributed, it should be voided (not deleted) in QBO. This ensures that all check numbers are properly accounted for.

> **BEHIND THE SCENES** Information about **checks** that have been voided is retained in QBO (payee, check number, date, and distribution accounts). No information is retained for **deleted** checks.

The **check** form must be open before it can be voided. There are many ways to find a transaction in QBO. The **Search** feature is a good option.

Click the **magnifying glass** option on the icon bar.

The screen will look something like this:

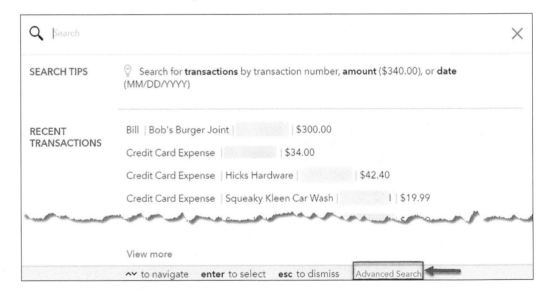

Click **Advanced Search**.

The first dropdown menu is primarily used to narrow the search to a specific transaction type although other options are available. The second dropdown menu is used to further narrow the search by specifying a date, amount, payee, etc. A search can be further narrowed to a range of dates by clicking **Add Filter**. Searching for all checks written to a specific vendor would return something like the following:

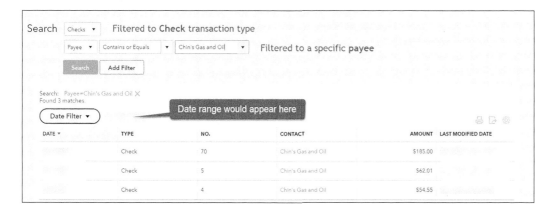

Figure 4.22

Advanced search for transactions with specific vendor

Click the check to be voided to open the **check** form.

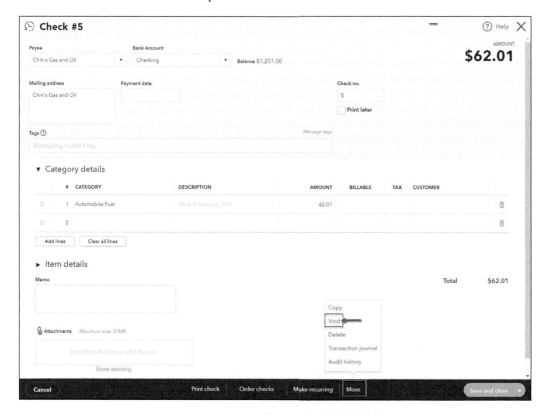

Figure 4.23

Tool for voiding check

Click **More** on the bottom bar of the **check** form and select **Void**.

You will have an opportunity to cancel the transaction before QBO completes the voiding process and will get an additional message when void is successful.

Voided checks do appear on journal reports (0.00 dollar amounts) and are accessible using the **Search** feature. A voided check would look something like this:

Figure 4.24

Example of voided check

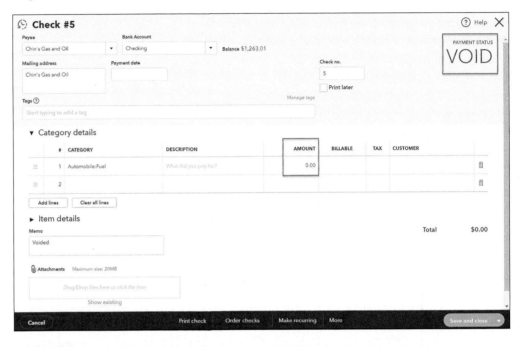

BEHIND THE SCENES QuickBooks Online uses the original check date to record a voided check. This can create problems if financial reports have already been distributed for that accounting period. For example, let's say a $100 check was written in December to pay for some travel expenses. In the December income statement, net income would, of course, be decreased by the $100 travel expense. Now let's say that the $100 check was lost so a new check was issued and the original check was voided in QBO in February. The replacement check would have a February date but the original check would be voided by QBO as of the original December check date. If you then prepared a new December income statement, net income would automatically be $100 higher than it was before due to the voided check. On the other hand, February's net income would be reduced by the $100 December travel expense. The expense is now reported in the wrong **accounting period**. If the amounts are significant or if tax reports have already been filed, journal entries should be made to correct the balances.

PRACTICE EXERCISE 4.4

Void a check for Craig's Design and Landscaping.
(Craig's Design voids a check prepared in error.)

1. Void the check to Books by Bessie. Craig used the company account instead of his own personal checkbook when he bought some books.

   a. Click the **magnifying glass** icon in the icon bar.

   b. Click **Advanced Search**.

   c. Select **Checks** in the first dropdown menu.

   d. Select **Books by Bessie** in the **Payee** dropdown menu (second dropdown menu).

   e. Click **Search**.

   f. Click check #12. The original check form should appear.

   g. **Make a note** of the amount of the check being voided.

(continued)

(continued from previous page)

    h.   Click **More** at the bottom of the screen.

    i.   Click **Void**.

    j.   Click **Yes** when asked about voiding the check.

    k.   Click **OK**.

Purchasing with a Credit Card

Some companies obtain corporate credit cards. Owners or employees who need to be able to purchase items when they're traveling are the typical users of these cards.

Although the seller might see a payment by credit card as the same as cash, the purchaser is really buying on credit. The company that issued the card is the creditor.

In QBO, credit cards are set up as a separate liability **account type (Credit Card)**. When individual credit card charges are entered, the amounts are credited to the credit card account and debited to the appropriate expense or asset account. This allows the user to track the details of all purchases.

When the credit card statement is received, the user reconciles the amounts recorded in QBO to the statement and processes the credit card bill for payment. (Credit card reconciliations are covered in Chapter 5.)

Before you can enter credit card charges, the general ledger account must be set up. This is done through the Chart of Accounts list. Remember, the account must be set up as a **Credit Card account type**.

Users would normally use the **Expense** form (**transaction type**) for entering credit card charges.

You can easily access the form by clicking **+ New** on the navigation bar and clicking **Expense** in the **Vendor** column. **Expense** forms can also be accessed through **Expenses** on the navigation bar (on both the **Expenses** and **Vendor** tabs).

The screen will look something like this:

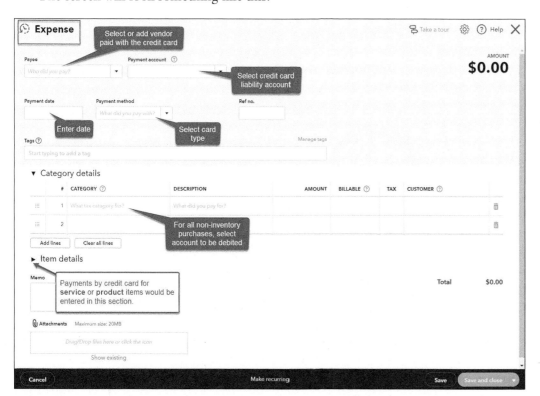

Figure 4.25

Expense form

The **Expense** form is similar to the **Bill** and **Check** forms. You need to enter the name of the business where the credit card was used and the date of the charge in the **Payee** field. Many companies will add the vendor name for credit card transactions but will not add much vendor detail (address, etc.).

> **BEHIND THE SCENES** Remember, you will be paying the entity that issued the card, not the business where you used the card. The business name is entered for informational purposes only.

The account credited (**credit card account type**) is selected in the **Bank/Credit account** field. The type of credit used can be selected in the **Payment method** dropdown menu.

Figure 4.26

Payment method list

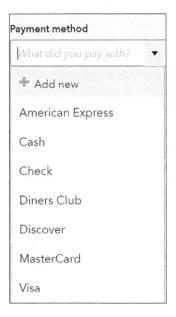

The accounts debited will be identified in the **Category details** section, the **Item details** section, or both.

Below is a summary of how the various transactions and journal entries occur for purchases made with a credit card.

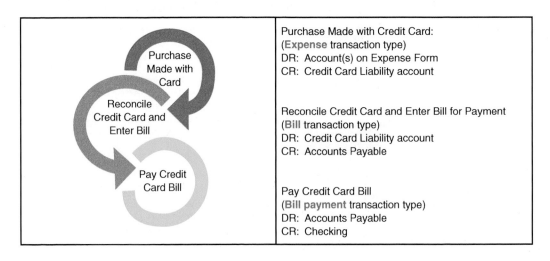

BEHIND THE SCENES Users can record payments on a credit card balance without reconciling the statement first.

CUSTOMERS	VENDORS	EMPLOYEES	OTHER
Invoice	Expense	Payroll 🗲	Bank deposit
Receive payment	Check	Time entry	Transfer
Estimate	Bill		Journal entry
Credit memo	Pay bills		Statement
Sales receipt	Purchase order		Inventory qty adjustment
Refund receipt	Vendor credit		Pay down credit card
Delayed credit	Credit card credit		
Delayed charge	Print checks		

Click **+ New** on the navigation bar and select **Pay down credit card**.

The credit card being paid and the bank account used to make the payment would need to be selected. A payment, by check, of $500 toward the Mastercard balance would look something like this:

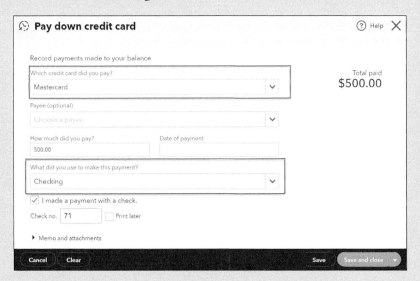

Pay down credit card   ⑦ Help ✕

Record payments made to your balance

Which credit card did you pay?   Total paid
Mastercard   ⌄   **$500.00**

Payee (optional)
Choose a payee   ⌄

How much did you pay?   Date of payment
500.00

What did you use to make this payment?
Checking   ⌄

☑ I made a payment with a check.

Check no. 71   ☐ Print later

▸ Memo and attachments

Cancel   Clear   Save   Save and close ⌄

Credit card payment is the form's **transaction type**.

Set up and use a credit card in Craig's Design and Landscaping.

(Craig's Design uses its corporate credit card to make several purchases.)

1. Set up a credit card account.
   a. Click the ⚙ on the icon bar.
   b. Click **Chart of Accounts**.
   c. Click **See your Chart of Accounts**, if necessary.
   d. Click **New**.
   e. Select **Credit Card** as the **Account Type**.

(continued)

PRACTICE
EXERCISE
4.5
Homework
MBC

(continued from previous page)

  f. Select **Credit Card** as the **Detail Type**.

  g. Enter "Global Credit Card" in the **Name** field.

  h. Click **Save and close**.

 2. To record a client lunch (paid with credit card):

  a. Click **＋New** on the navigation bar.

  b. Click **Expense**.

  c. Select **Add new** in the **Choose a payee** dropdown menu.

    i. Enter "Fancy Restaurant" as the **Name**.

    ii. Select **Vendor** as the **Type**.

    iii. Click **Save**.

  d. Select **Global Credit Card** as the **Payment account** to be credited.

  e. Enter the current date as **Payment date**.

  f. Select **MasterCard** as the **Payment method**.

  g. Leave **Ref. No.** blank.

  h. In the **Category details** section, select **Meals and Entertainment** as the **CATEGORY**.

  i. Enter "94.10" as the **AMOUNT**.

  j. Enter "Lunch with July Summers" in the **Memo** field.

  k. Click **Save** to record the transaction without leaving the form.

  l. Open the **Transaction journal** from the **More** menu bar at the bottom of the form.

  m. **Make a note** of the transaction type and the account that was credited.

  n. Press and hold Ctrl/Alt and click x (or CMD/Alt + x in a Mac) to return to the **Expense** form.

  o. Click **Save and close**.

PAYING VENDOR BALANCES

Eventually vendors must be paid! Most companies pay vendors in batches. A check run might be processed twice a month in a smaller company. Check runs would likely be processed more frequently in larger companies.

 In a manual system, checks are prepared and then entered in the cash disbursements journal. The totals of the journal are posted to the general ledger and each transaction is posted to the appropriate vendor's subsidiary ledger.

 In QBO, bill payment transactions are automatically posted to the general ledger and the vendor subsidiary ledger when the transaction is saved.

 Companies can pay bills using cash, checks, or credit cards. Paying vendor balances by check is the most common payment method in small- to medium-sized companies.

 There are two methods for recording payments of vendor balances in QBO. Payments to more than one vendor can be batch processed through the **Pay Bills** window. Payment of one or more **bills** to a single vendor can be processed through the Vendor Center. The **transaction type** under either method is **bill payment**.

Paying Multiple Vendor Bills

Click **+ New** on the navigation bar.

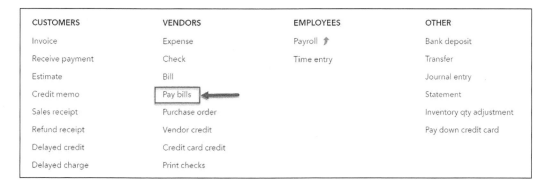

Figure 4.27

Access to bill payment screen

Click **Pay Bills** to open the **Pay Bills** window.

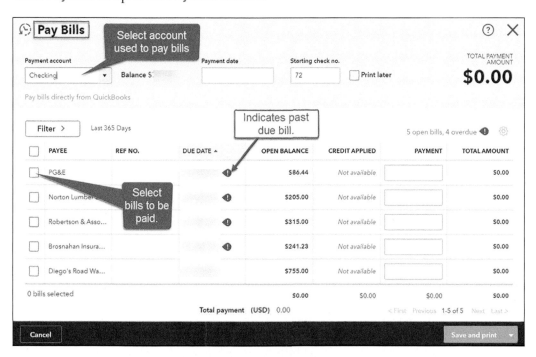

Figure 4.28

Bill payment screen

There is a lot to do on this screen so take your time!

You must identify the **Payment account** being used (checking, credit card, etc.) and the **Payment date**. If you choose to pay by check, QBO will display a **Starting check no.** That can be changed, if needed.

You can limit the number of items displayed by opening the **Filter** dropdown menu.

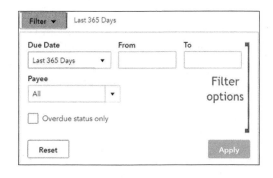

Figure 4.29

Filtering options in bill payment screen

Filtering is available by due date or by vendor (**payee**) name. For vendor names, your choice is limited, however, to either all vendors or one specific vendor.

Overdue bills are highlighted (with an exclamation point!) in the **DUE DATE** column. If there are any available credits, the amounts will be displayed in the **CREDIT APPLIED** field when the vendor is selected for payment. Vendor credits are covered in Chapter 7.

Bills to be paid are selected by checking the box to the left of the specific **bill**. If you want to see the details of a specific **bill**, double-click the **PAYEE** name to access the original **bill**.

The total amount to be paid is displayed on the screen. The balance remaining in the account used to pay the **bill** is also displayed. The window might look something like this if two bills were paid:

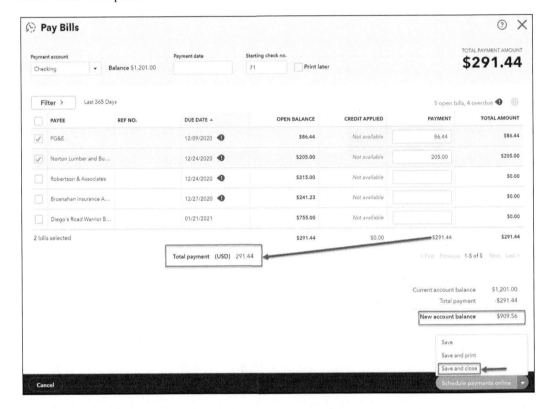

BEHIND THE SCENES If multiple bills from the same vendor have been selected for payment, QuickBooks Online will automatically combine the amounts and create a single check for that particular vendor.

Click **Save and close** to record the payments without printing physical checks. **Schedule payments online** is available to users who have connected a bank account to QBO.

BEHIND THE SCENES If **bill payments** are printed from QBO, the **Account no.** identified in the vendor record will appear on the face of the check. Information entered in the **Description** or **Memo** fields of the **bill** will not be printed.

Paying One or More Bills from a Single Vendor

Payment of one or more **bills** from a single vendor can be processed through the Vendor Center.

Click **Expenses** on the navigation bar.
Click the vendor name on the **Vendors** tab.

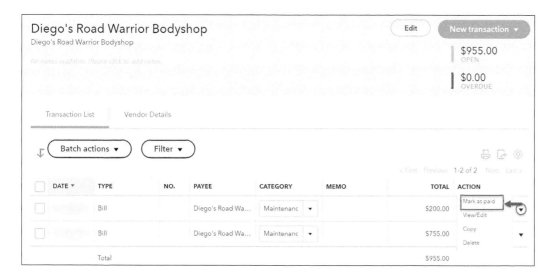

Figure 4.31

Action column in a transaction list

Click **Mark as paid** in the **ACTION** column for a bill to be paid.

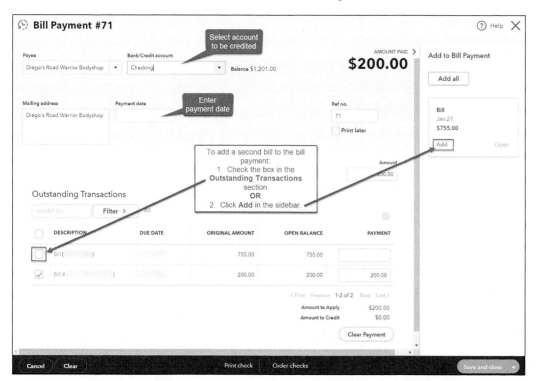

Figure 4.32

Example of a sidebar on a bill payment form

If multiple bills are outstanding for a vendor, a sidebar including the additional bills would automatically be displayed. Users could add some or all of the additional bills to the transaction by clicking **Add** in the sidebar or by checking the box in the far left column of the **Outstanding Transactions** section of the form.

QBO automatically creates a **Bill Payment** transaction. Partial payments can be recorded by changing the amount in the **PAYMENT** field.

PURCHASES CYCLE SUMMARY

Let's summarize the purchasing steps we have learned and their related journal entries. First let's review the difference between a purchase now (with a check or credit card) and a purchase on account.

If the company buys something now and pays for it now with a check or cash, the company uses a **Check**.	Purchases on account mean that you have purchased something or used a service and you will pay for it at a future date. You enter the **Bill** from the vendor (or an **Expense** if purchased using a credit card) to document the purchase and **Pay bills** at a later date.

1-step process:
  1. Write a **Check** for each purchase.
	2-step process
	  1. Enter each **Bill**.
	  2. **Pay bills** when due.

Let's also review the basic purchase and cash disbursement journal entries that are created based on the above transactions.

Purchase with cash or credit card—Journal Entry	Purchase on Account—Journal Entry

• Journal Entry to record **Check**
  – Dr: Asset/Expense/Inventory
  – Cr: Checking
	• Journal Entry to record **Bill** or **Expense**
	  – Dr: Asset/Expense/Inventory
	  – Cr: Accounts Payable (or Credit Card Payable)
	• Journal Entry to pay vendor or credit card company
	  – Dr: Accounts Payable
	  – Cr: Checking
	NOTE: This assumes the company pays its bills with checks.

PRACTICE
EXERCISE
4.6

Record payment of bills for Craig's Design and Landscaping.

(Craig's Design pays several vendor balances.)

1. Click **+ New** on the navigation bar.

2. Click **Pay Bills**.

3. **Make a note** of the balance due to **Robertson & Associates**.

4. Select **Checking** as the **Payment account** and the current date as the **Payment date**.

5. Leave the **Starting check no.** as 71.

   a. **TIP:** If you didn't log out after the last Practice Exercise, use 77 as the **Starting check no.**

6. Place a checkmark next to **Norton Lumber** and **Robertson & Associates**.

7. **Make a note** of the total amount paid.

8. Click **Save and close.**

> Assume you selected 5 bills to be paid in a single run. Three of the bills were to the same vendor. How many checks would QBO create? (Answer at end of chapter.)

QuickCheck
4-2

VENDOR REPORTS

Reports related to vendors and purchases can be accessed by clicking **Reports** on the navigation bar.

Common reports used by service companies are highlighted in Figure 4.33.

Figure 4.33

Standard vendor reports menu

Reports		
Find report by name		
Standard Custom reports Management reports		

˅ What you owe

- 1099 Contractor Balance Detail
- 1099 Contractor Balance Summary
- Accounts payable aging detail
- Accounts payable aging summary
- Bill Payment List
- Bills and Applied Payments
- Unpaid Bills
- Vendor Balance Detail
- Vendor Balance Summary

> Reports related primarily to unpaid bills.

˅ Expenses and vendors

- 1099 Transaction Detail Report
- Check Detail
- Expenses by Vendor Summary
- Open Purchase Order List
- Open Purchase Order Detail
- Purchases by Product/Service Detail
- Purchases by Vendor Detail
- Transaction List by Vendor
- Vendor Contact List

> Reports related primarily to purchases.

Prepare reports on payables for Craig's Design and Landscaping.
(Craig's Design needs an A/P Aging and wants a check register.)

1. Prepare an A/P Aging.

    a. Click **Reports**.

    b. Click **Accounts payable aging summary** in the **What You Owe** section.

    c. Change date to the current date and click **Run report**.

(continued)

PRACTICE
EXERCISE
4.7

(continued from previous page)

2. Prepare a check register.

    a. Click **Reports**.

    b. Click **Check Detail** in the **Expenses and Vendors** section.

    c. Change **Report period** to **All Dates**.

    d. Click **Customize**.

    e. Click **Rows/Columns**.

        i. Click **Change columns**, if necessary.

        ii. Remove the check next to **Clr**.

        iii. NOTE: Checks not marked as **Clr** are still outstanding (haven't cleared the bank).

    f. Click **Filter**.

        i. Check the box next to **Transaction Type**.

        ii. Select **Check** and **Bill Payment (Check)**.

    g. Click **Run report**.

    h. **Make a note** of the account debited in the journal entry underlying the check to Tony Rondonuwu. **Tip:** Click on the transaction in the report to open up the detail.

3. Click **Dashboard** to exit the window.

ANSWER TO
QuickCheck
4-1

> Accounts Payable (A/P)

ANSWER TO
QuickCheck
4-2

> Three checks would be created.

CHAPTER SHORTCUTS

Add a vendor

1. Click **Expenses** on the navigation bar
2. Click the **Vendors** tab to open the Vendor Center
3. Click **New Vendor**

Edit a vendor

1. Open Vendor Center
2. Click vendor name
3. Click **Edit**

Inactivate a vendor

1. Open Vendor Center
2. Open the dropdown menu in the **ACTION** column for the vendor to be inactivated
3. Select **Make inactive**

Record a check

1. Click **+ New** on the navigation bar
2. Click **Check** in the **Vendors** column

Record a credit card charge

1. Click **+ New** on the navigation bar
2. Click **Expense** in the **Vendors** column

Record payments to vendors on account balances

1. Click **+ New** on the navigation bar
2. Click **Pay Bills** in the **Vendors** column

Set up a new credit term

1. Click the ⚙ on the icon bar
2. Click **All Lists**
3. Click **Terms**

CHAPTER REVIEW

Matching

Match the term or phrase (as used in QuickBooks Online) to its definition.

1. Bill
2. 1099 vendor
3. Bill Payment
4. Display Name

5. Vendor
6. Net 15
7. Bill No.
8. Check

_____ transaction type used for recording invoices received from vendors

_____ vendor invoice number

_____ transaction type used to record payments to vendors on account

_____ individual or company from whom goods or services are purchased

_____ an individual or company that receives payments that must be reported to the IRS

_____ an example of a payment term

_____ transaction type used to record up-front payments to vendors

_____ vendor identifier

Multiple Choice

1. A purchase of a computer, on account, would be recorded in the _____ section of a **bill** in QBO.
   a. Item details
   b. Fixed assets
   c. Category details
   d. Computer Equipment

2. Vendors
   a. can be deleted as long as there are no outstanding amounts due to the vendor.
   b. can be deleted at any time.
   c. can be deleted if there has never been any activity with that vendor.
   d. cannot be deleted.

3. When a purchase made with a credit card is recorded in QBO,
   a. cash is credited.
   b. a liability account is credited (**Account Payable account type**).
   c. a liability account is credited (**Credit Card account type**).
   d. a liability account is credited (**Other Current Liability account type**).

4. Payments to vendors can be entered _____.
   a. using the **Check transaction type**
   b. using the **Bill Payment transaction type**
   c. using the **Expense transaction type**
   d. using **Check, Bill Payment**, or **Expense transaction types**

5. Which of the following statements is true?

    a. You can only have one account with an **account type** of **Accounts Payable** in QBO.

    b. You can have multiple accounts payable accounts for use in recording vendor bills and tracking vendor balances in QBO but they must each have a different name and they must all have an **Accounts Payable account type**.

    c. You can have multiple accounts payable accounts in QBO but only the default Accounts Payable account created by Intuit can be used when entering bills or bill payments.

    d. Vendor balances cannot be tracked in QBO.

BEYOND THE CLICKS—THINKING LIKE A MANAGER

Accounting: Your company uses the accrual method of accounting. List three types of purchase transactions you would want to review at the end of each month to determine if an accrual adjustment needs to be made. Explain your choices.

Information Systems: Many companies give credit cards to multiple employees in a business. List three good practices around the use of credit cards.

ASSIGNMENTS

Assignment 4A

Math Revealed!

Background information: Martin Smith, a college student and good friend of yours, has always wanted to be an entrepreneur. He is very good in math, so, to test his entrepreneurship skills, he has decided to set up a small math tutoring company serving local high school students who struggle in their math courses. He set up the company, Math Revealed!, as a corporation in 2021. Martin is the only owner. He has not taken any distributions from the company since it opened.

    The business has been successful so far. In fact, it's been so successful he has decided to work in his business full time now that he's graduated from college with a degree in mathematics.

    He has decided to start using QuickBooks Online to keep track of his business transactions. He likes the convenience of being able to access his information over the Internet. You have agreed to act as his accountant while you're finishing your own academic program.

    Martin currently has a number of regular customers that he tutors in Pre-Algebra, Algebra, and Geometry. His customers pay his fees by cash or check after each tutoring session but he does give terms of Net 15 to some of his customers. He has developed the following fee schedule:

Name	Description	Rate
Refresher	One-hour session	$ 60 per hour
Persistence program	Two one-hour sessions per week	$100 per week
Crisis program	Five one-hour sessions per week	$225 per week

The tutoring sessions usually take place at his students' homes but he recently signed a two-year lease on a small office above a local coffee shop. The rent is only $750 per month starting in January 2022. A security deposit of $500 was paid in December 2021.

    The following equipment is owned by the company:

Description	Date placed in service	Cost	Life	Salvage Value
Computer	7/1/21	$3,000	36 months	$300
Printer	7/1/21	$ 240	24 months	$ 0
Graphing Calculators (3)	7/1/21	$ 300	36 months	$ 30

All equipment is depreciated using the straight-line method.

As of 12/31/21, Martin owed $2,500 to his father (Richard Smith) who initially helped him get started. Richard is charging him interest at a 6% annual rate. Martin has been paying interest only on a monthly basis. His last payment of interest only was on 12/31/21.

Over the next month or so, he plans to expand his business by selling a few products he believes will help his students. He has already purchased a few items:

Category	Description	Vendor	Quantity on Hand	Cost per Unit	Sales Price
Books and Tools					
	Geometry in Sports	Books Galore	20	18	25
	Solving Puzzles: Fun with Algebra	Books Galore	20	15	22
	Getting Ready for Calculus	Books Galore	20	20	28
	Geometry Kit	Math Shack	10	12	18
	Handheld Dry-Erase Boards	Math Shack	25	10	15
	Notebooks (pack of 5)	Paper Bag Depot	10	8	12

1/3/22

✓ Since Martin is expanding his business, he decides to purchase a general liability insurance policy from Protector Insurance Company. The annual premium is $360. It covers the period 1/1–12/31/22. You write a check (#1101) to pay the full year premium amount. (You add Protector Insurance as a vendor without adding any detail information.) You will make an adjustment to recognize insurance expense for January at the end of the month. **TIP:** Enter the policy period in the description or memo field. This will help when you make the adjustment as part of Chapter 5's assignment.

✓ Martin is moving into his new space today. The furniture arrives in the morning. The total cost of the desk, large study table, and eight chairs Martin ordered from Frank's Furniture is $726. A bill, dated 1/3 (#ST8990) for the total amount, is included with the shipment. The terms are Net 30.

• You set up the new vendor:

  Frank's Furniture

  2174 Hardwood Street

  Sacramento, CA 95822

• You also set up a new account called Office Furniture (Account #185). You decide to record depreciation on all fixed assets in a single account so you don't check the **Track depreciation of this asset** box. **TIP:** The account should have a **Fixed Asset account type**; **Furniture & Fixtures detail type**.

• Martin expects the furniture to last four years.

✓ Martin also purchases two more computers and three more calculators since he's doing more tutoring at his new location. The equipment, purchased from Paper Bag Depot, costs $1,701 in total ($441 for the three calculators and $1,260 for the two computers). Martin expects the calculators and computers to last three years. Martin uses a new credit card to make the purchase.

• You set up the general ledger account for the new credit card first. You use Prime Visa Payable as the account name and 220 as the account number. **TIP:** Don't forget to select the appropriate **account type**. You do not need to answer the question about when you want to start tracking your finances in the account.

• You enter the credit card charge using 1/3 as the date. **TIP:** Use the **Expense** form to record credit card charges. Paper Bag Depot is the **payee**. Select the new credit card account as the **Payment account**. Leave the **Ref no.** blank. Set up VISA as a new **payment method**. Be sure to check the box indicating that "**This is a credit card.**"

- **TIP:** If a sidebar appears on the right-hand side asking you to add a bill to this expense, ignore it.

✓ You know you will have to pay the credit card company eventually so you go ahead and set them up as a vendor.

- Prime Visa Company
  55 Wall Street
  New York, NY 10005
  Terms: Net 15

✓ You pay January's rent ($750) with check #1102. The landlord is Pro Spaces.

1/5/22

✓ Martin purchases some graphing paper, lined paper, markers, and pencils from Math Shack for $201.07, on account (Vendor Invoice #3659). He is tracking all tutoring supplies as an asset. At the end of the month, he'll determine the value of the supplies on hand and you'll make any necessary adjustments. The terms are Net 15.

1/7/22

✓ Martin hands you the receipt for the $30 of gas he purchased at Cardinal Gas & Snacks using his VISA credit card and you enter the credit card expense in QBO.

- You save the new vendor without adding any additional vendor details.

✓ You take a look at the **Unpaid Bills** report in the **What You Owe** section of **Reports**. It looks like some of the bills were due last month! You know that can't be true so you look through the unpaid bill file. You correct the terms on each of the bills as follows:

- Kathy's Coffee ($25)—Net 15
- Math Shack ($240)—Net 15
- Paper Bag Depot ($80)—Net 30

TIP: Click on the appropriate bills in the **Unpaid Bills** report, enter the terms, and click **Save and close**. You don't need to update reference numbers or change account distributions.

✓ Since these are the normal terms for these three vendors, you also change the terms in the vendor records.

✓ While you're in the Vendor Center, you go ahead and add Net 30 terms to Sacramento Utilities, Books Galore, and Horizon Phone Inc. and Net 15 terms to Parent's Survival Weekly.

✓ You pay all bills due on or before 1/20/22 from the Checking account.

- **TIP:** There should be four bills totaling $546.07. Start with check #1103. (There will be three **checks**.)

1/10/22

✓ You use the credit card to purchase a few general supplies (hand sanitizer, hand towels, etc.) from Math Shack. The cost ($28.61) is insignificant so you decide to expense the entire amount to the Office supplies expense account.

1/12/22

✓ You receive two bills in the mail, which you record in QBO.

- One of the bills, dated 1/12, is from Sacramento Utilities. The January bill (#01-59974) total is $145.21. The bill is due in 30 days.
- The other bill is from Parent's Survival Weekly, a parenting magazine targeting parents with teenage children. Martin had placed an ad for the Mathmagic clinic in this week's issue. The total cost is $100 (vendor invoice #12213, dated 1/12). The payment terms are Net 15.

1/17/22

✓ Although the Mathmagic Clinic was a success overall, there was one small incident. One of the friends of Martin who helped with the tutoring tripped over the feet of one of the students and fell into the study table. She ended up with a gash on her left hand. She went to the 24 Hour Quick Stitch Clinic and had her hand bandaged up. Luckily, she didn't require any stitches. The cost of the visit was $220 and the clinic gave Martin a bill, dated 1/15 (#121521).

- The 24 Hour Quick Stitch Clinic's address is 7500 Medical Boulevard, Sacramento, CA 95822. The phone number is 916-222-9999. The terms are Net 10.
  - **TIP:** You'll need to set up a new term.
- You decide to expense the cost to Miscellaneous expense (Account 699).

1/19/22

✓ Martin asks you to contact Frank's Furniture and order some shelving for the new space. He wants a unit that includes open shelves and some drawers. You call and talk to the representative who gives you an estimate of $820. That sounds reasonable to you and you place the order. The furniture should arrive by the end of the month.

1/21/22

✓ Your friend Samantha Levin helped Martin out at the clinic last Saturday by checking students in and out. Martin doesn't expect to hire her as an employee, but if you pay her more than $600 during the year, you'll need to file a 1099 for her at year-end. You decide to get everything set up just in case she's paid over the threshold.

- You set up a new general ledger account. You decide to name the account "Contract labor" and use account #625. You make it a sub-account of Labor costs and you use **Cost of labor** as the **detail type**.
- You also set Samantha up as a vendor. Her address is 901 Angles Lane, Sacramento, CA 95822. Her phone number is 916-654-4321. Terms are Net 10.
  - You set her up as a 1099 vendor. Her social security number (**Business ID number**) is 222-33-6666.

✓ Samantha had agreed to a $25 per hour pay rate. She helped out for five hours so you write her a check (#1106) for $125.

1/25/22

✓ Martin hands you another gas receipt for $30. He purchased the gas at Cardinal Gas & Snacks using his credit card today. You record the charge in QBO.

✓ You pay all bills due on or before 2/5/22.
- **TIP:** There should be three bills totaling $1,046. Start with check #1107.

1/28/22

✓ Martin brings in coffee drinks from Kathy's Coffee as a treat for getting through the first month in the new space. He hands you the receipt for $8.75. (He used the credit card to buy the coffee.) You decide to charge the coffee to a new account called "Staff relations" (a labor cost). You use 628 as the account number. **TIP:** This should be a sub-account of Labor Costs. The Detail Type should be Other Business Expenses.

✓ The shelving unit is delivered and installed by Frank's Furniture. Martin is impressed by the quality of the product. The actual price is the $820 you were originally quoted. The invoice number is ST9998, dated 1/28, and the terms are Net 30.

✓ Martin has been working hard and asks you to write him a check for $2,000. (Use check #1110.)
- **TIP:** This is a corporation so a payment to Martin (other than salary or reimbursement) is a dividend, an equity account. Use 345 as the account number and "Dividends" as the account name. QBO doesn't have a **detail type** for dividends. Use **Partner Distributions** as a substitute.

Check numbers as of 1/31

> Checking account balance:. $4,302.93
> Accounts Payable:. . . . .$ 965.21
> Net income (January only):. $5,392.43

Suggested reports for Chapter 4:

All reports should be in portrait orientation.

- Journal—1/01 through 1/31.
  - Include only these transaction types: Check, Bill, Bill Payment (Check), Expense.
    TIP: You'll need to scroll down the list to find the Expense transaction type.

- Vendor Balance Detail (as of 1/31)

- Vendor Contact List

- Balance Sheet as of January 31

- Profit and loss statement (January only)

Assignment 4B

Salish Software Solutions

Background information: Sally Hanson, a good friend of yours, double majored in Computer Science and Accounting in college. She worked for several years for a software company in Silicon Valley but the long hours started to take a toll on her personal life.

Last year she decided to open up her own company, Salish Software Solutions. Sally currently advises clients looking for new accounting software and assists them with software installation. She also provides training to client employees and occasionally troubleshoots software issues.

She has decided to start using QuickBooks Online to keep track of her business transactions. She likes the convenience of being able to access financial information over the Internet. You have agreed to act as her accountant while you're working on your accounting degree.

Sally has a number of clients that she is currently working with. She gives 15-day payment terms to her corporate clients but she asks for cash at time of service if she does work for individuals. She has developed the following fee schedule:

Name	Description	Rate
Select	Software selection	$500 flat fee
Set Up	Software installation	$ 75 per hour
Train	Software training	$ 50 per hour
Fix	File repair	$ 60 per hour

Sally rents office space from Alki Property Management for $600 per month.

The following furniture and equipment are owned by Salish:

Description	Date placed in service	Cost	Life	Salvage Value
Office furniture	6/1/21	$1,400	60 months	$200
Computer	7/1/21	$4,620	36 months	$300
Printer.	7/1/21	$ 900	24 months	$ 0

All equipment is depreciated using the straight-line method.

As of 12/31/21, she owed $3,500 to Dell Finance. The monthly payment on that loan is $150 including interest at 5%. Sally's last payment to Dell was 12/31/21.

Over the next month or so, Sally plans to expand her business by selling some of her favorite accounting and personal software products directly to her clients. She has already purchased the following items.

Item Name	Description	Vendor	Quantity on Hand	Cost per Unit	Sales Price
Easy1	Easy Does It	Abacus Shop	15	$100	$ 200
Retailer	Simply Retail	Simply Accounting	2	$400	$ 800
Contractor	Simply Construction	Simply Accounting	2	$500	$1,000
Organizer	Organizer	Personal Software	20	$ 25	$ 50
Tracker	Investment Tracker	Personal Software	20	$ 20	$ 40

1/4/22

✓ You pay January's rent ($600) to Alki Property Management with check #1101.

✓ Sally recently decided to purchase business insurance from Albright Insurance Company. The policy was effective as of 1/1/22. You write a check (#1102) to pay the full year premium amount ($720).

  • You add Albright Insurance as a vendor without adding any detail information.

  • You will make an adjustment to recognize insurance expense for January at the end of the month. **TIP:** Enter the policy period in the description or memo field. This will help when you make the adjustment as part of Chapter 5's assignment.

✓ You notice that payment terms aren't set up for many of Salish's vendors. You change the vendor records as follows:

  • Abacus Shop—Net 15

  • Paper Bag Depot—Net 30

  • Personal Software—Net 30

  • Sacramento Light & Power—Net 30

  • Simply Accounting—Net 15

  • Western Phone Company—Net 30

1/5/22

✓ Sally receives the credit card she applied for last month.

  • You set up the general ledger account for the new credit card. You use Capital Three Visa Payable as the account name and 220 as the account number. (**HINT:** Don't forget to select the appropriate account type. You do not need to answer the question about when you want to start tracking your finances in the account.)

  • You also set up a new vendor for the card.

      Capital Three
      58 Wall Street
      New York, NY 10005
      Terms: Net 15

✓ Sally had completely run out of office supplies at the end of December so she uses her VISA card to purchase paper, pens, and file folders at Paper Bag Depot. You enter the credit card charge of $500 using the Expense form. You remember to select the new credit card account as the Payment account and you add VISA as a new Payment method. **TIP:** Be sure to select This is a credit card. You leave the Ref no. blank. You're not sure how long the supplies will last but you're sure they won't all be used in January. You will take an inventory to see how many supplies are on hand at the end of the month. **TIP:** You will do this in the homework for Chapter 5.

1/6/22

✓ You receive two bills in the mail, which you record in QBO.

  • One of the bills (#01-59974), dated 1/6, is from Sacramento Light & Power. The bill total is $95 and is due in 30 days. The bill is for January utilities.

  • The other bill (#8911-63) is from Western Phone Company for Sally's January cell phone service. The $108.95 bill, dated 1/6, has payment terms of Net 30.

1/7/22

✓ Sally purchases some new computer software today from Abacus Shop. The software costs $960 and will help Sally track her installation projects. She expects it to last 2 years (no salvage value). Abacus gives you a bill (#8944-11) with 15-day payment terms.

- You set up a new account called Computer Software (#184). You decide to record all depreciation in a single accumulated depreciation account, so you **don't** check the **Track depreciation of this asset** box. You'll record depreciation at the end of the month. **TIP:** The account should have a **Fixed Assets account type** and a **Fixed Asset Software detail type**.

1/11/22

✓ You take a look at the **Unpaid Bills** report in the **What You Owe** section of **Reports**. It looks like some of the bills were due last month! You know that can't be true so you look through the unpaid bill file. You correct the payment terms on each of the **bills** with a December date as follows:

- Abacus Shop—Net 15
- Personal Software—Net 30
- Simply Accounting—Net 15
- **TIP:** Click each invoice on the **Unpaid Bills** report to open the bill form. Enter the terms and save.

✓ You pay all bills due on or before January 20 from the Checking account using 1/11 as the payment date.

- There should be three bills totaling $1,235. Start with check 1103.

1/14/22

✓ You receive a bill from Entrepreneur, a local magazine targeting small business owners. Sally had placed an ad in January's magazine for the upcoming workshop. The total cost is $120 (vendor invoice #12213, dated 1/14). The payment terms are Net 10. **TIP:** You'll need to create a new payment term.

- Entrepreneur Magazine
  534 American River Drive
  Sacramento, CA 95822

✓ Sally asks you to order a large storage cabinet from Rikea. She needs to have a storage area for the inventory she plans to sell starting in February. You call and talk to a sales representative who gives you an estimate of $1,500. That sounds reasonable to you and you place the order. The expected arrival date is 1/28.

- You go ahead and set up the vendor anticipating the future bill.
- Rikea
  25 Bigbox Lane
  Sacramento, CA 95822
  Terms: Net 30

✓ Sally uses her credit card to pay for the space she rented at Hacker Spaces (a new vendor) for next week's workshop. You record the $300 charge. This is a new type of expense for Salish Software so you set up two new accounts.

- You add a parent account "Workshop Costs" with 660 as the account number and a sub-account "Space rental expense" (#661). You use **Other Miscellaneous Service Cost** as the **detail type** for each account. You charge the $300 to Account 661.

✓ Just before closing, you get a call from Hacker Spaces. They made a mistake on the fee. It should have been $600 for the space. You transfer the call to Sally and, although she's unhappy, she agrees to make another credit card payment. She did think the fee was almost too good to be true. You record the additional $300 charge. **TIP:** You should create two transactions for this since your credit card statement will reflect two $300 charges.

1/20/22

✓ Although the Picking the Right Software workshop was a great success overall, there was an unexpected additional expense. Sally ended up breaking one of Hacker Spaces' tables when she was trying to get the room set up. You write Hacker Spaces a check (#1106) for $200 to cover the cost of replacing the table.

  • You decide to expense the cost to Space rental expense.

✓ While you are writing the check to Hacker, you realize that there are two bills due soon. You pay all bills due on or before the end of January. You write two checks totaling $1,080 starting with check number 1107.

1/25/22

✓ Your friend Oscar Torres helped Sally out at the workshop last week. Sally doesn't expect to hire him as an employee, but you know that if you pay him more than $600 during the year, you'll need to file a 1099-NEC for him at the end of the year. You decide to get everything set up just in case he's paid over the threshold.

  • You set up a new general ledger account. You decide to name the account "Workshop helpers" with 665 as the account number. You make it a sub-account of Workshop Costs. You use **Cost of Labor** as the **detail type**.

  • You also set Oscar up as a vendor. His address is 901 Luna Drive, Sacramento, CA 95822. His phone number is 916-654-4321.

    ○ You set him up as a 1099 vendor. His social security number (**Business ID number**) is 222-33-4444.

    ○ You select Net 10 as the **terms**.

✓ Oscar had agreed to work for $20 per hour pay rate. He helped out for six hours so you write him a check (#1109) for $120.

✓ Sally has lunch with the IT director for Metro Markets, a large grocery chain. She is hoping to do some work for the company in the future. She uses her credit card to pay for the $110, very nice, lunch at The Blue Door (a new vendor). You record the charge to Client relations expense.

  • Nothing is decided at the lunch so you don't set up Metro Markets as a customer.

1/28/22

✓ The storage cabinets are delivered and installed by Rikea. The final price is the $1,500 you were originally quoted. The invoice number is RK65541, dated 1/28, and the terms are Net 30. You expect the cabinets to last for 5 years.

✓ Sally has been working hard and asks you for a $2,000 check. (Use check #1110.)

  • You set Sally Hanson up as a vendor first.
    14 Technology Drive
    Sacramento, CA 95822
    916-346-9258
    Net 10

  • **TIP:** This is a corporation so a payment to Sally (other than salary or reimbursement) is a dividend, an equity account. Use 345 as the account number and "Dividends" as the account name. QBO doesn't have a **detail type** for dividends. Use **Partner Distributions** as the detail type.

Check numbers as of 1/31

Checking account balance:. $9,680.00
Accounts Payable:. $1,703.95
Net income (January only):. $8,261.05

Suggested reports for Chapter 4:

All reports should be in portrait orientation; fit to one page wide

- Journal—1/01 through 1/31.
    - Include only these transaction types: Check, Bill, Bill Payment (Check), Expense.
- Vendor Balance Detail (as of 1/31)
- Vendor Contact List
- Profit and loss statement (January only)
- Balance Sheet as of January 31

APPENDIX 4A REPORTING 1099 VENDOR ACTIVITY

Companies are required to report certain types of payments of more than $600 during the year. Payments to independent contractors are reported on Form 1099-NEC to the Internal Revenue Service annually. Independent contractors are, in general, individuals who provide services to the general public through an independent business.

Payments to landlords and attorneys are reported on Form 1099-MISC.

As noted in the Adding a Vendor section of this chapter, 1099 vendors can be identified, along with the required tax information, in the Vendor Information window when a new vendor is created. Users can update 1099 information about existing vendors by clicking Vendors on the navigation bar, clicking the vendor name, and clicking Edit.

To prepare 1099s, click Expenses on the navigation bar and select the Vendors tab.

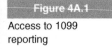

Figure 4A.1

Access to 1099 reporting

Click Prepare 1099s.

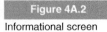

Figure 4A.2

Informational screen

Click Let's get started.

Figure 4A.3

Company information
screen

The address, tax identification number, and phone number of the company filing the 1099s
are reviewed and edited if necessary. Click **Next** after updating any information.

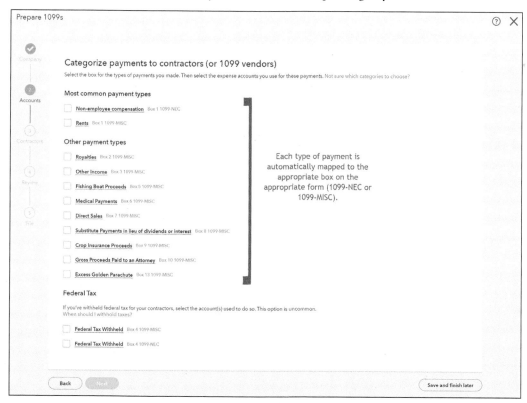

Figure 4A.4

Screen for mapping
general ledger
accounts to 1099-Misc
form

The types of 1099 payments made by the company (1099-NEC and 1099-MISC) are identified first. If any federal taxes have been withheld from any 1099 vendors, that is identified
as well.

For each payment type identified, the user is also required to indicate the account used to record the payments. The screen might look something like this for the test drive company.

Figure 4A.5

Example of completed
account mapping

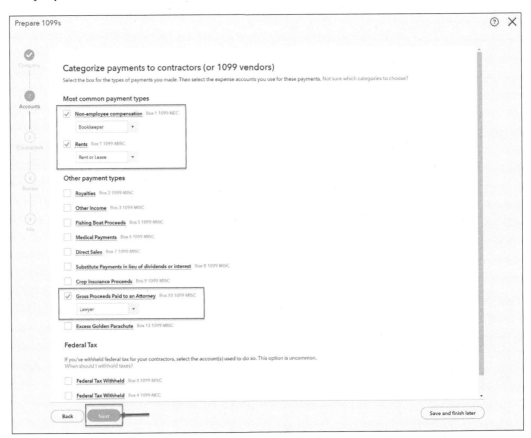

BEHIND THE SCENES "Bookkeeper" has been identified for **Box 1 1099-NEC** in Figure 4A.5. Note that wages paid to employees who perform bookkeeping functions would not be reported on **1099s**.

Click **Next** to review 1099 vendor details (address, tax identification number).

Figure 4A.6

1099 Vendor
information screen

Computers by Jenni and Robertson & Associates will not appear in your test drive company. Certain changes were made to the file for illustration purposes.

Edits can be made to vendor information on this screen. Any edits here will also update the vendor record.

Click **Next** to review vendors who were paid amounts over the IRS threshold during the calendar year.

Figure 4A.7
Review of 1099
amounts by vendor

BEHIND THE SCENES Any amounts paid to 1099 vendors using a credit card would not be included on 1099-MISC forms. Reporting credit card payments is the responsibility of the credit card company.

Click **Finish preparing 1099s** to review options for filing. Intuit provides filing services for a fee or users can prepare the forms independently.

End-of-Period Activity
(Service Company)

Objectives

After completing Chapter 5, you should be able to:

1. Reconcile bank and credit card accounts.

2. Make adjusting journal entries.

3. Create and modify financial statement reports.

4. Close an accounting period.

5. Find common errors (Appendix 5A).

6. Understand the reconciliation report (Appendix 5B).

7. Fix reconciliation errors (Appendix 5C).

BEFORE ISSUING FINANCIAL STATEMENTS

Sales, purchases, cash receipts, and cash payments make up the vast majority of transactions in a company. You've already learned how most of those standard transactions are entered in QBO and you've seen how QBO does a lot of the work related to posting and tracking those transactions for you. As we discussed in Chapter 1, though, the accuracy and the usefulness of all that data are still dependent on the operator(s) of QBO.

For most companies, the primary financial reports (such as the profit and loss statement and the balance sheet) are prepared monthly. It's at the end of the month, then, that the accountant needs to make sure that:

- All accounting transactions have been recorded.
- No accounting transactions have been duplicated.
- All accounting transactions have been recorded in the proper accounts at the appropriate amounts.
- All accounting transactions are recognized in the proper accounting period.

There is, unfortunately, no foolproof method for ensuring the accuracy of the financial statements. There are some tools though. They include:

- Reconciling account balances to external sources.
  - Cash accounts to bank statements.
  - Vendor payable balances to vendor statements.
  - Debt balances to lender reports.
- Reconciling account balances to internal sources.
  - Physical count of supplies on hand to supplies account balance.
  - Physical count of inventory to inventory account balance.
  - Timesheets for the last period of the month to salaries payable account if all salaries have not been paid as of the end of a period.
- Reviewing accounts for reasonableness.
  - Most account balances should reflect their **normal** balance (assets should have debit balances, **contra** assets should have credit balances, expenses should have debit balances, etc.).
  - Relationships between accounts should make sense. For example, payroll tax expense shouldn't be higher than salaries expense!
  - Account balances that are significantly higher or lower than the prior month should be investigated.

Normal balance The side (debit or credit) on which increases to the account are recorded.

Contra account An account with the opposite normal balance as other accounts of the same type.

As a result of all this reconciliation and review, we can virtually **guarantee** you that adjustments will need to be made! Without even thinking very hard, we know you can come up with a few examples.

They might include:

- Recording bank charges that you weren't aware of until you saw the bank statement.
- Adjusting the Supplies on Hand account to record supplies used during the period.
- Adjusting revenue accounts to ensure that all revenue reported is earned revenue and all earned revenue is recognized.
- Recording depreciation expense for the period.

- Accruing expenses that weren't recorded through the normal payable process (interest for example).

- Amortizing prepaid expenses for amounts expiring in the period (insurance for example).

RECONCILING BANK AND CREDIT CARD ACCOUNTS

Bank Reconciliations

QBO has an account reconciliation tool that can actually be used for any balance sheet account other than Accounts Receivable, Accounts Payable, Undeposited Funds, and Retained Earnings. That's a useful tool for companies that take advance deposits, for example. In this textbook, we'll only be using the tool for bank and credit card reconciliations.

To access the reconciliation tool, click the ⚙ on the icon bar.

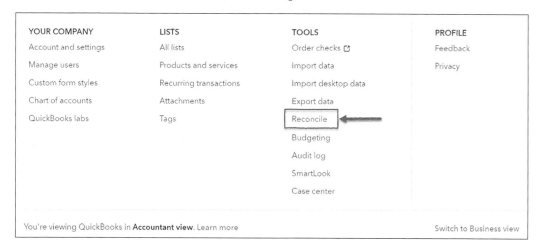

Figure 5.1

Access to reconciliation tool

Click **Reconcile**.

 HINT: You can also access the reconciliation tool by clicking **Accounting** on the navigation bar and selecting the **Reconcile** tab.

The first time you use the reconciliation function, you'll need to move through a few informational screens.

Figure 5.2

Link to reconciliation tool

Click **Get started**.

Click **Let's do it.**

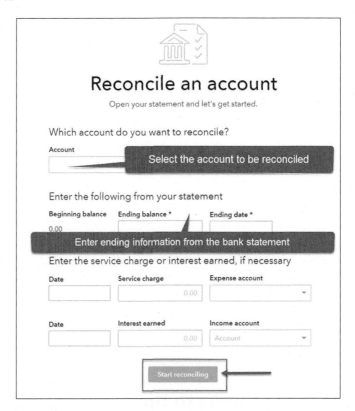

Select the account to be reconciled. In the test drive company, you will be limited to entering an **Ending balance** and **Ending date** in this window.

The date and balance fields **must** agree to the bank statement you're reconciling.

- The **Ending balance** would be the ending **bank** balance listed on the bank statement you're reconciling.

- The **Ending date** would be the ending date listed on the bank statement.

In your homework company file, you will also be able to enter bank charges or interest income amounts that appear on the bank statement. You can use the dropdown menus to select the general ledger account you want debited for service charges or credited for interest income. If you had already entered these transactions, you would leave the fields blank.

Click **Start reconciling**.

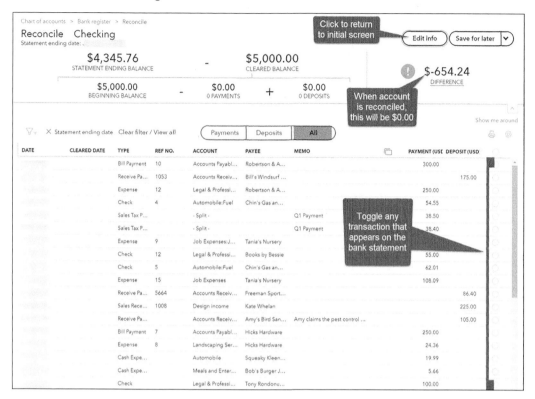

Figure 5.5

Account reconciliation screen

There are three tabs on the screen (**Payments**, **Deposits**, and **All**). Transactions in the account being reconciled that have **not** been cleared in a prior reconciliation are listed on the **All** tab.

 HINT: Transactions appearing in the reconciliation screens can be filtered using the funnel icon above the **DATE** column. Options include filtering by date, payee, and transaction type.

The **Payments** tab includes only those transactions (**checks**, **bill payments**, **transfers**, or **journal entries**) that credit the cash account. The **Deposits** tab includes the transactions (**deposits**, **transfers**, or **journal entries**) that debit the cash account.

BEHIND THE SCENES Take a look at the column titles on the right side of the **All** tab. These are set up from the bank's point of view. You'll notice that the far right column is titled **DEPOSIT**. A debit to cash to record a bank deposit on the company's books is a credit (liability) on the bank's books since they now owe you that amount. Although the column to the left of **DEPOSIT** is titled **PAYMENT**, any journal entries crediting the cash account would be listed here as well.

To reconcile the account, click the circle next to any transaction on this screen that also appears on the bank statement. These are the transactions that "cleared" the bank. Any unclicked transactions represent outstanding checks or deposits in transit.

 HINT: It's sometimes easier to use the **Payments** and **Deposits** tabs (instead of the **All** tab) when reconciling.

A few hints that might help with the reconciliation process:

- If you can't complete the reconciliation in one sitting, you can:
  - click the **Save for later** button in the top right corner of the screen. QBO will save all your work until you return to complete the reconciliation. When you open the **Reconcile** function again, QBO will ask if you want to **Resume reconciling** the account that was in process.
  - click the **Close without saving** button. The reconciliation process could then be restarted at a later date.
- Click **Edit Info** in the top right corner of the screen to make changes to the **Ending balance** or **Ending date**.
- You can leave the reconciliation window open and create (or edit) a transaction if you need to. QBO will automatically refresh the screen for any changes. To add a new transaction, click **+ New** on the navigation bar.
- If you click any of the listed transactions, the row will expand and you will be able to change data fields that are not grayed out. It will look something like this:

Figure 5.6

Expanded transaction on reconciliation screen

  - Click **Edit** to open the form and make more substantial changes.
- QBO automatically filters the list to only include those uncleared transactions dated prior to the statement ending date (the only transactions that **could** have cleared the bank assuming all transactions are dated correctly).
  - If you only want to display certain types of transactions, click the funnel above the far left column.
- You can change the sort order of either **Checks and Payments** or **Deposits and Other Credits** by clicking the column headings.

When you've reconciled the account, the **Difference** field in the top right section of the screen will equal zero and **Finish Now** will be the default option in the dropdown menu in the top right corner of the reconciliation screen.

> **!** **WARNING:** Do not select **Finish Now** in the dropdown menu if you haven't finished the reconciliation (the **difference** isn't zero). QBO will give you a warning if you try but if you persist, it will allow you to "reconcile" without actually reconciling. That would leave what my former accounting professors would call a "dangling" credit or debit. Of course QBO won't actually allow you to create an unbalanced transaction so it will either debit (or credit) an account called **Reconciliation Discrepancies** for the **Difference** amount. You'd then have to fix that later.

Once you've reconciled the account, the following screen will appear:

Figure 5.7

Message when reconciliation is complete

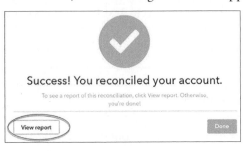

To view the reconciliation report immediately, click **View report**. The report includes lists (by type) of all cleared transactions and all uncleared transactions. Appendix 5B goes over the reconciliation report in detail.

Reconciliation reports are also accessible in the **For My Accountant** section of **Reports**.

Reconcile the bank account for Craig's Design and Landscaping.
(Craig's Design receives its bank statement. The ending balance is $4,345.76. There were no bank service charges included on the statement.)

1. Click the ⚙ on the icon bar.

2. Click **Reconcile**.

3. Click **Get started**.

4. Click **Let's do it**.

5. Select **Checking** as the **Account**.

6. Enter the current date as the **Ending Date** and "4,345.76" as the **Ending Balance**.

   a. Since you're working in the test drive company and dates in that company are constantly being updated, you need to enter the date you're actually doing the reconciliation.

7. Click **Start reconciling**.

8. Click the **Payments** tab and check the circles next to the first ten checks.

   a. The ten checks you're marking as cleared should start with a $300 check and end with a $250 check for a total of $1,245.64.

9. Click the **Deposits** tab and check the circles next to the first four deposits.

   a. The first deposit you check as cleared should be for $175. The last one should be for $105 for a total of $591.40.

10. **Difference** should be 0.00.

11. Click **Finish Now**.

12. Click **View reconciliation report**.

13. **Make a note** of the total for **Uncleared checks and payments**.

14. Click **Dashboard** to close the window.

PRACTICE
EXERCISE
5.1

Homework
MBC

Reviewing the Reconciliation Status of Transactions in the Register

In QBO, each account on the balance sheet has a **Register**. A **Register** is a listing of the activity in the account along with the **reconciliation status** of each item. As you reconcile items in the account, the reconciliation status of an account is updated. To open the **register** for the checking account:

- Click the ⚙ on the icon bar and select **Chart of Accounts**.

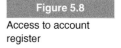

Figure 5.8

Access to account register

- Click **View Register** in the **ACTION** column for the Checking account.

Figure 5.9

Reconciliation status column in account register

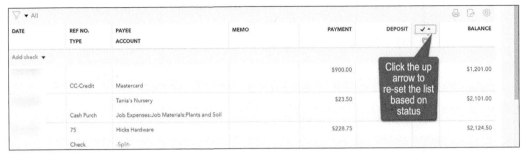

- The column to the left of the **BALANCE** column shows the reconciliation status of each transaction. The status field for every **bank** account transaction listed will either be **R**, **C**, or blank.
    - **R** means that the transaction has been reconciled. The reconciliation has been closed.
    - **C** means that the transaction has been identified as 'cleared' but the reconciliation is still open.
    - Blank means that the transaction is outstanding and has not yet been reconciled.

BEHIND THE SCENES Transactions that are downloaded directly from bank accounts are automatically assigned a C (cleared) status in the register.

Fixing Bank Reconciliation Errors

It can be quite difficult to correct a bank reconciliation. Best practice, by far, is to make sure the reconciliation is completed correctly before moving forward.

That being said, one option for correcting reconciliation errors is outlined in Appendix 5C.

✱ **HINT:** There is an "undo Reconciliation" feature available to users of the QBO Accountant edition of the software. You may want to check with your instructor to see if they might be able to assist you.

Credit Card Reconciliations

You learned in Chapter 4 how company credit cards are handled in QBO. A separate account is set up (**Credit Card account type**) and individual card transactions are posted to the account as they occur. There are a number of credit card forms (**transaction types**). One thing they all have in common though is that because they are not **bills** or **vendor credits** they do not show up in the **Pay Bills** screen. That's a good thing since companies would rarely pay individual credit card charges; they would, instead, pay the credit card statement balance or make a partial payment against the balance.

At some point, though, the balance of all credit card activity must be paid to the credit card company. QBO provides a few options.

- The statement balance can be paid after the reconciliation is complete.
- A partial payment can be made after the reconciliation is complete.
- A payment can be made against the credit card balance without reconciling the credit card by clicking **Pay down credit card** on the ➕ **New** menu.

The first two options are covered in this section. The third option was covered in the **Purchasing with a Credit Card** section of Chapter 4.

> **BEHIND THE SCENES** It's important to reconcile credit card account activity to the credit card statement because there aren't a lot of controls on credit cards. Whoever holds the card can generally use the card and companies need to make sure that all charges are legitimate. Companies would normally require employees with access to credit cards to submit original receipts for all purchases.

The process for reconciling a credit card account is very similar to the bank reconciliation process.

The reconciliation tool is easily accessed by clicking the ⚙ on the icon bar and choosing **Reconcile**.

In the **Reconcile an account** window, the credit card account should be selected.

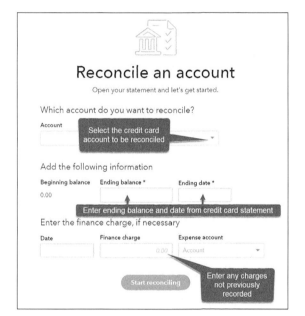

Figure 5.10

Initial data screen for credit card reconciliations

The dates and amounts entered on the initial screen are from the statement being reconciled. Interest or late fee charges can be entered in this window if they haven't been previously recorded.

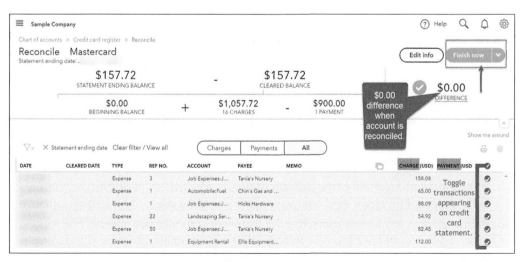

Figure 5.11

Credit card reconciliation screen

You will notice a change in column titles when reconciling a credit card compared to reconciling a bank account.

- The **PAYMENT** column is now **CHARGE**.
  - The **CHARGE** column includes the credit card **Expenses** that have been recorded.
- The **DEPOSIT** column is now **PAYMENT**.
  - The **PAYMENT** column includes payments made to the credit card company as well as any **Credit Card Credits**.

All displayed transactions that agree to items listed on the credit card statement should be checked (marked).

> **HINT:** If you discover that there's an error on one of the recorded **Charges** or **Payments** while you're in the reconciliation process, you can click the transaction to edit the form. You can also leave the reconciliation screen open while you create a new transaction. The new transaction will automatically appear in the reconciliation screen once it's saved.

Once the statement is reconciled, the following screen will appear:

Figure 5.12

Successful reconciliation message with payment options

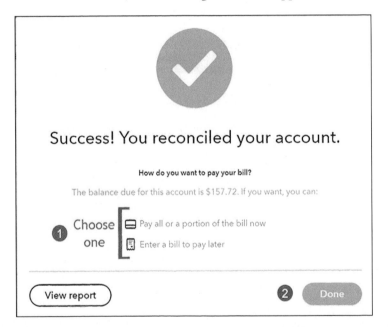

> **WARNING:** If you click **Done** on the screen in Figure 5.12 before selecting one of the two options, the credit card balance will remain in the credit card account. The amount would not be available in the **Pay Bills** screen. A **Bill** would have to be manually entered after the fact or the account would need to be re-reconciled.

Users have two options on this screen.

1. If the **Pay all or a portion of the bill now** option is selected, a **Check** form will automatically appear. The credit card company name would be selected in the payee field.
2. If **Enter a bill to pay later** is selected, a **Bill** form will automatically appear. The appropriate vendor would need to be selected. QBO will automatically enter the credit card liability account in the distribution section of the form (in the **Category details** section). The amount entered should be the total amount of the credit card bill.

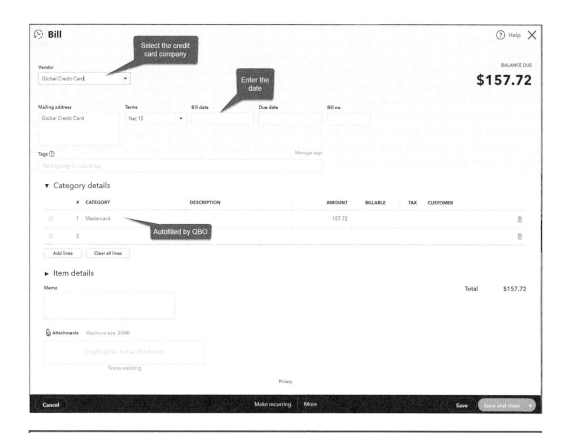

Figure 5.13

Bill for credit card statement balance

 HINT: Remember, credit cards are issued either by banks (VISA or Master-Card credit cards for example) or by companies (like Macy's or Union 76 credit cards). You will need to set up the company that issued the credit card as a vendor in QBO.

Once the **Bill** is completed and saved, it would appear on the **Pay Bills** screen and would be included in the Accounts Payable account.

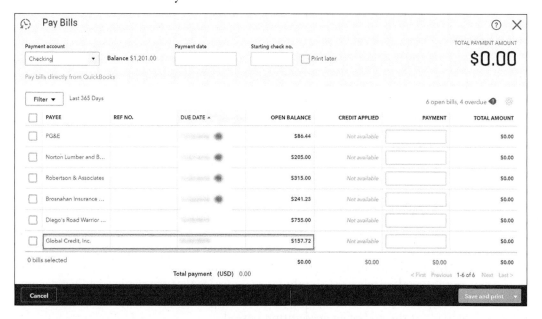

Figure 5.14

Bill payment screen including a credit card bill

What journal entry does QBO make if you select the **Enter a bill for payment later** option after reconciling a credit card?

QuickCheck
5-1

Reconcile Craig's Design and Landscaping's credit card statement.

(Craig's Design received its December statement from Global Credit. The ending statement balance is $157.72. There were no service charges.)

1. Click the ⚙ on the icon bar.

2. Click **Reconcile**.

    a. If you exited Craig's Design and Landscaping after the previous exercise, then do the following:

       i. Click **Reconcile an account**.

       ii. Click **Get started**.

3. Select **MasterCard** as the **Account**.

4. Enter the current date as the **Statement Ending Date** and "157.72" as the **Ending Balance**.

5. Click **Start reconciling**.

6. Check the circles next to all charge and all payment transactions. **TIP:** Checking the circle at the top of the far right column will mark all circles.

7. **Difference** should be 0.00.

8. **Make a note** of the amount of the transaction on the **Payments** tab.

9. Click **Finish Now**.

10. Select **Enter a bill to pay later**.

    a. Set up a vendor for the bank that issued the card.

       i. Click **+ Add New** in the **Vendor** dropdown menu.

       ii. Click **+ Details**.

       iii. Vendor name is "Global Credit, Inc." (**Company** and **Display** names)

          1000 Wall Street

          New York, NY 10000

       iv. **Terms** are **Net 15**.

       v. Click **Save**.

11. Enter "CC Stmt" as the **Bill No.**

12. Make sure **MasterCard** shows as the **CATEGORY** in the **Bill**.

13. Make sure "157.72" shows as the **AMOUNT**.

14. Click **Save and close** to return to the reconciliation screen.

15. Click **Done**.

16. Click **Dashboard** to close the window.

---

eLectures

Journal entry An entry of accounting information into a journal.

MAKING ADJUSTING JOURNAL ENTRIES

All transactions are recorded as journal entries, right? You only have to look at a **Journal** report in QBO to see that all the **Invoices**, **Checks**, **Bills**, **Bill Payments**, etc. are listed (and they're in journal entry form, too).

Adjusting **journal entries** are simply journal entries that are made to adjust account balances. Although they can be made at any time during an accounting period, the majority of them are made at the end of an accounting period.

In a manual system, adjusting journal entries are created in the general journal. The entries are then posted to the general ledger.

In QBO, adjusting journal entries are created in an electronic version of the general journal. They are posted automatically to the general ledger.

The form used to create an adjusting entry (**Journal Entry** transaction type) is accessed by clicking **+ New** on the navigation bar.

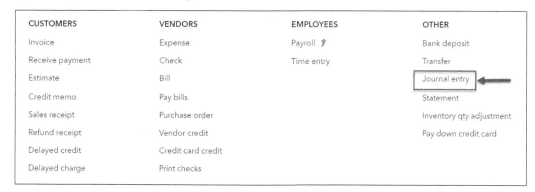

Figure 5.15

Link to journal entry form

Select **Journal Entry** in the **Other** column.

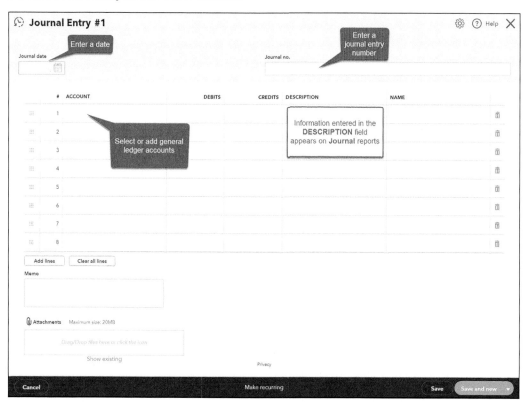

Figure 5.16

Journal entry form

To complete the form, you need to enter the date, the accounts (selected in the **ACCOUNT** field), and the amounts.

> **BEHIND THE SCENES** Although you **can** use the **Journal Entry** form to create entries in accounts receivable, accounts payable, and cash accounts, it's generally better to use the standard forms for transactions that affect those accounts. If you do make an adjusting journal entry to accounts receivable (or payable), you would need to enter the name of the customer (vendor) in the **NAME** field so that the subsidiary ledger is updated.

Here are some "good practice" points for working with adjusting entries:

- Include a brief description of the transaction in the **Description** field of the form.
  - It's easy to forget the source of an adjusting journal entry.
- Make one entry per type of adjustment. In other words, don't make one big entry with lots of different types of transactions on it. Companies should keep documentation to support adjusting journal entries and it's easier to match the entry to the documentation if you keep the entries simple.
- Journal entries are numbered in the **Journal no.** field. QBO will number these automatically or you can create your own numbering pattern such as Jan22.1, Jan22.2 to clearly identify the accounting period.

The mechanics of recording adjusting journal entries in QBO are very simple. To help with the hardest part (knowing what adjustments need to be made), here's a list of common monthly entries for service companies:

- Depreciation
- Accrual of:
  - Unpaid salaries
  - Interest or other charges for which a vendor bill has not yet been received
  - Unbilled revenue
- Expiration (consumption) of
  - Prepaid expenses
  - Supplies on hand
- Recognition of deferred revenue as earned

PRACTICE
EXERCISE
5.3

Record some adjusting journal entries for Craig's Design and Landscaping.
(Craig's Design records month-end adjustments for depreciation on the truck and prepaid rent.)

1. Click **+ New** on the navigation bar.

2. Click **Journal Entry** (in the **OTHER** column).

3. Record depreciation expense of $225 for the current month.

   a. Enter the current date as the **Date**. You can leave the **Journal no.** as 1.

   b. In the first row, select **Depreciation** (the one with the **Other Expense account type**) in the **ACCOUNT** field and enter "225" in the **DEBITS** column.

      i. Enter "Current month depreciation" in the **DESCRIPTION** field.

   c. In the second row, select **Depreciation** (the one listed as a **sub-account** of **Truck**) in the **ACCOUNT** field and enter "225" in the **CREDITS** column. **TIP:** This account has a **Fixed Assets account type**. This account would normally be named "Accumulated Depreciation."

      i. The **Description** field should have autofilled.

   d. Click **Save and new**.

4. Adjust for $450 of rent paid in advance. Craig expensed $900 to rent expense. Half that amount represented rent for the subsequent month.

(continued)

(continued from previous page)

    a. Enter the current date as the Date. Leave the Journal no. as 2.

    b. In the first row, select Prepaid Expenses in the ACCOUNT field and enter "450" in the DEBITS column.

        i. Enter "Rent paid in advance" in the DESCRIPTION field.

    c. In the second row, select Rent or Lease in the ACCOUNT field and enter "450" in the CREDITS column.

    d. Click Save and close.

PREPARING FINANCIAL STATEMENTS

As you know, there are four basic financial statements:

- **Balance sheet**
- Profit and loss statement (**Income statement**)
- Statement of retained earnings (or **Statement of stockholders' equity**)
- **Statement of cash flows**

You can prepare a balance sheet, profit and loss statement, and statement of cash flows automatically in QBO. In this course, we'll only be looking at the balance sheet and profit and loss statement.

> **HINT:** The purpose of start and end dates on a QBO balance sheet report is to provide users with access to all the activity in the listed accounts over the period of time selected in the date range. The amounts showing on the report will **always** represent the balance as of the last date of the identified date range (the balance sheet "as of" date). When you click (drill-down) on an account balance, a transaction report listing the activity over the date range will be displayed. Specific forms can be accessed by clicking any amount in the transaction report.

> **BEHIND THE SCENES** QBO's statement of cash flows can contain some inaccuracies. For example, activity in short-term loans is classified in the operating activity section instead of the financing activity section. Although it's still a useful tool for management, it's generally better to prepare the cash flow statement manually.

The financial statements are accessed by clicking Reports on the navigation bar. The most common reports are found in the Business Overview section.

Sidebar glossary:

Balance sheet A financial statement showing a business's assets, liabilities, and stockholders' equity as of a specific date.

Income statement A financial statement reporting a business's sales revenue and expenses for a given period of time.

Statement of stockholders' equity A financial statement presenting information regarding the events that cause a change in stockholders' equity during a period. The statement presents the beginning balance, additions to, deductions from, and the ending balance of stockholders' equity for the period.

Statement of cash flows A financial statement showing a firm's cash inflows and cash outflows for a specific period, classified into operating, investing, and financing activity categories.

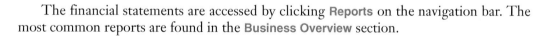
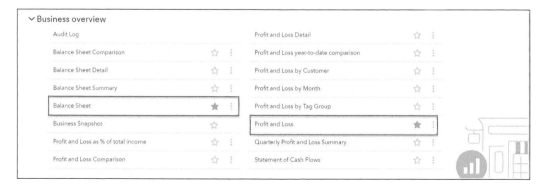

Figure 5.17

Business Overview section of Reports

> **BEHIND THE SCENES** The **Business Snapshot** report included in the **Business Overview** section is a great report for owners and managers. It includes six focus boxes.
> - Pie chart of income accounts during any selected period
> - Pie chart of expense accounts during any selected period
> - Bar chart comparing current and prior period revenues
> - Bar chart comparing current and prior period expenses
> - List of customer balances
> - List of vendor balances

Statements can be prepared on the accrual or the cash basis. QBO allows for a number of simple modifications to be made on the face of reports.

Figure 5.18

Modification options on face of balance sheet report

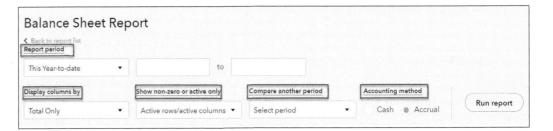

The modification bar for a **Balance Sheet** report is shown in Figure 5.18. In the **Display columns by** field, the **Balance Sheet** report can be modified to show balances by month, by quarter, even by customer (Figure 5.19).

Figure 5.19

Column display options for balance sheet report

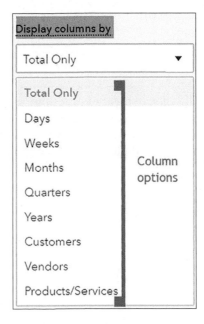

Accounts displayed can be limited to accounts with activity (**Active**) or to accounts with balances (**Non-zero**) in the **Show non-zero or active only** modification dropdown. Activity options can be used for rows or columns (Figure 5.20).

Figure 5.20

Account display options
for balance sheet
report

Comparative statements can be created using the **Compare another period** options (Figure 5.21).

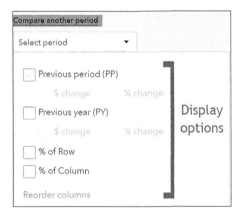

Figure 5.21

Comparative statement
options for balance
sheet report

Other modifications can be made by clicking **Customize** in the top right corner of the report.

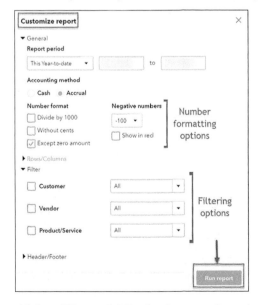

Figure 5.22

Options available in
customization sidebar

In the **Customize report** sidebar (Figure 5.22), the format of numbers can be changed and data included can be filtered.

Profit and Loss reports have similar modification and customization options. Keep in mind that financial statements may be distributed to:

* Owners
* Management
* Lenders
* Potential investors
* Regulatory agencies

They should be clear and professional in appearance. There are a few standard reporting conventions to consider:

* Assets are generally reported in descending order of liquidity (how quickly or easily they can be converted to cash).
* Liabilities are generally reported in descending order of their priority for payment.
* Revenue and expense sections of the income statement are generally reported in order of dollar amount (highest to lowest).
    * Categories are sorted first; then individual accounts within each category.

> **BEHIND THE SCENES** There are no absolute rules for presentation, particularly in the order of accounts on the profit and loss statement. For instance, there are some accounts that are frequently reported last (like depreciation expense and miscellaneous expense) regardless of the dollar amount. As the accountant, your responsibility is to organize the information in the clearest and most meaningful manner possible.

QBO doesn't have an easy way to change the account order. In your homework assignment, you'll be using account numbers. Account numbers can be changed to reorder the accounts. Another option for companies using QBO is to export the statements to Excel and reorder the accounts there. Exporting reports to Excel will be covered in Chapter 11.

PRACTICE
EXERCISE
5.4

Prepare year-end financial statements for Craig's Design and Landscaping.
(Craig's Design needs a balance sheet and profit and loss statement.)

1. If you didn't log out of QBO after the last practice exercise, you'll need to sign out now to clear your previous transactions. Log back in to continue.

2. Review balance sheet.
    a. Click **Reports** on the navigation bar.
    b. Click **Balance Sheet** in the **Favorites** section.
    c. Select **This Month-to-date** in the **Report period** dropdown menu.
    d. Click **Customize**.
    e. In the **General** tab, select **(100)** in the dropdown for **Negative numbers**.
    f. In the **Rows/Columns** tab, select **Non-zero** for both rows and columns in the **Show non-zero or active only** dropdown menu.
    g. Click **Run Report**.
    h. **Make a note** of the balance in **Accounts Receivable**.

(continued)

(continued from previous page)

  i.   Click **back to report list**. **TIP:** It's in blue right above the **Report period** field in the top left corner.

 3. Review the income statement.

  a.   Click **Profit and Loss** in the **Favorites** section.

  b.   Select **All Dates** in the report period dropdown menu.

  c.   Click **Run report**.

  d.   **Make a note** of the total for **NET INCOME**.

  e.   Select **Cash** as the **Accounting method**.

  f.   Click **Run report**.

  g.   **Make a note** of the total for **NET INCOME** on the cash basis.

  h.   Click **Dashboard** to close the report window.

CLOSING A PERIOD

There are really two types of period closings:

- Closing a period after financial statements are prepared and distributed (generally every month).

- Year-end closing (closing the books at the end of the company's legal year [fiscal year]).

Closing an Accounting Period

When we talk about closing an accounting period, we are usually simply talking about not making any additional entries to that accounting period. An additional small bill might come in that relates to the period or we might discover that we made a small error in a reconciliation affecting the closed period, but, once financial statements have been prepared and distributed, we generally don't want to go back and make changes. Instead, we simply record those transactions in the current period.

> **BEHIND THE SCENES** The constraint of **materiality** applies here. If the dollar amount of a potential adjustment is significant (would influence decisions made by users of the financial statements), the entry should be made and the statements reissued.

So what does all this have to do with QBO? QBO gives us a tool that's useful here.

 As I'm sure you've noticed by now, QBO will let you enter any date you want for transactions. Many of our students (and clients) have spent hours trying to reconcile their financial statements and it turns out they simply entered a wrong date on a transaction or two.

 QBO allows you to set a **Closing Date** in your company file. When a closing date is set, QBO will warn you if you try to enter a transaction dated prior to that date. You can override the warning but at least it's there.

 Closing dates are set in **Account and Settings**.

Materiality An accounting guideline that states that insignificant data that would not affect a financial statement user's decisions may be recorded in the most expedient manner.

Click the ⚙ on the icon bar and select **Account and Settings**.

Figure 5.23

Accounting settings
on Advanced tab of
Account and Settings

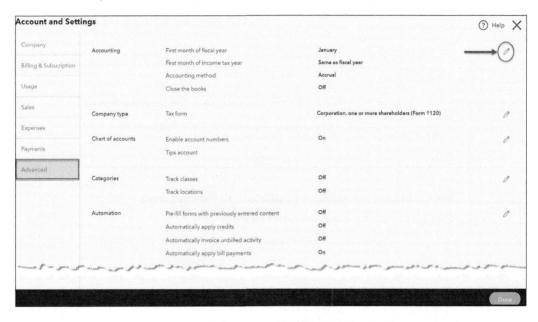

On the **Advanced** tab, click the **pencil** icon in the top right corner of the **Accounting** section.

Figure 5.24

Option to close books

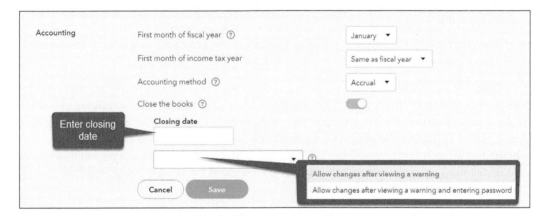

Toggle the **Close the books** button to activate the feature. Enter a **Closing date**. You then select one of two options.

- You can require a password to make changes.
  - Changes to transactions in the closed period could only be made after the correct password is entered.

- You can allow changes after viewing a warning.
  - Changes to transactions in the closed period could be made once the user clicks **Yes** on the warning screen.

PRACTICE

EXERCISE

5.5

Set a closing date for Craig's Design and Landscaping.

(Craig's Design sets a closing date in QBO.)

1. Click the ⚙ on the icon bar.

2. Click **Account and Settings**.

(continued)

(continued from previous page)

3. Click the Advanced tab.

4. Click the pencil icon to edit the Accounting section.

5. **Make a note** of the month displayed in the First month of fiscal year field.

6. Toggle the button next to Close the books.

7. Enter the last day of the current month as the Closing date.

8. Select Allow changes after viewing a warning in the dropdown menu.

9. Click Save.

10. Click Done.

11. Enter a transaction dated prior to the closing date to verify.

    a. Click **+ New** on the navigation bar.

    b. Click Check.

    c. Enter a date prior to the closing date (the date you set in Step 7) as the Payment date.

    d. Select Cal Telephone as the payee and Telephone as the CATEGORY.

    e. Enter $200 as the AMOUNT.

    f. Click Save and close.

    g. **Make a note** of the second sentence in the Double-check the transaction date message.

    h. Click No.

    i. Click Cancel.

12. Click Yes to close the window.

Year-end Closing

When a company file is originally set up, you must enter the first month of the fiscal (legal) year. QBO uses that date in reporting and budgeting. It also uses that date to automatically close (clear) all revenue and expense account types (Income, Cost of Goods Sold, Expense, Other Income, and Other Expense) to an equity account at the end of the year. The **closing process** is done automatically by QBO. QBO does **not** automatically close out any temporary equity accounts.

Closing process A step in the accounting cycle in which the balances of all temporary accounts are transferred to the Retained Earnings account, leaving the temporary accounts with zero balances.

> **BEHIND THE SCENES** To close revenue and expense accounts, QBO doesn't create an entry that's visible in the Journal. It does, however, change the reports. For example, let's say a company started business on 3/1/X1 and its year-end was 12/31/X1. For all reports dated between 3/1/X1 and 12/31/X1, revenues and expenses for the period would be reported on the profit and loss statement. A total for net income or loss would show as a single line item on the balance sheet in the equity section.
>
> On 1/1/X2, the reports would automatically change. None of the 20X1 revenue and expense activity would appear on the profit and loss statement. Unless there were already some entries posted on 1/1/X2, the profit and loss statement would show net income of $0.00. On the balance sheet, the net income (or loss) line (related to 20X1 transactions) would also no longer appear. Instead, Retained Earnings would have been credited (or debited) for the 20X1 operating results.

Although QBO appropriately closes out revenue and expense accounts at year-end, there may be some final housekeeping entries that need to be made to close out any temporary equity accounts. These entries vary depending on the type of entity.

- For proprietorships: Most proprietorships set up separate capital investment and draw accounts (equity accounts) so that activity for the year is visible on the balance sheet. If so, those accounts should be closed out to an Owner's Equity at the beginning of a new year. Retained Earnings should also be closed out to Owner's Equity. (Sole proprietorships would not normally maintain a retained earnings account.)
- For partnerships: Most small partnerships set up separate capital investment, draw, and capital balance accounts (equity accounts) for each partner. If so, the capital investment, draw, and Retained Earnings accounts should be closed out to each partner's capital balance account at the beginning of a new year.
- For corporations: Most corporations set up a dividends account (equity account) so that current-year distributions to shareholders are visible on the balance sheet. If so, the dividend account should be cleared out to Retained Earnings at the beginning of a new year.

ANSWER TO
QuickCheck
5-1

Credit Card Payable	XXX	
Accounts Payable		XXX

CHAPTER SHORTCUTS

Reconcile an account
1. Click ⚙ on the icon bar
2. Click **Reconcile**

Record adjusting journal entries
1. Click **+ New** on the navigation bar
2. Click **Journal Entry**

CHAPTER REVIEW

Matching

MBC
Assignments with the
MBC are available in
myBusinessCourse.

Match the term or phrase (as used in QuickBooks Online) to its definition.

1. journal entry
2. statement ending date
3. reconciled
4. charge

5. cleared
6. payment
7. fiscal year
8. closing date

_____ company's legal year

_____ status of a bank transaction marked as cleared **during** the reconciliation process

_____ date set by user; used to limit entry of transactions dated prior to that date

_____ date of statement received from bank

_____ title of column in the credit card reconciliation screen listing all debits to the account being reconciled

_____ status of bank transaction that has been marked as cleared as part of a completed reconciliation

_____ transaction type used for recording an adjusting entry

_____ title of column in the credit card reconciliation screen listing all credits to the account being reconciled

Multiple Choice

1. All transactions posted to an account being reconciled will appear on the bank reconciliation screen in QBO EXCEPT

    a. cleared transactions and uncleared transactions recorded through a general journal entry.

    b. cleared transactions.

    c. uncleared transactions.

    d. uncleared **bill payment** transactions.

2. Which of the following accounts **could** be reconciled using the reconciliation tool in QBO? (Select all that apply. Assume all of the accounts listed were in the company's chart of accounts.)

    a. Cash (Bank account type)

    b. Prepaid Expenses (Other Current Asset account type)

    c. Accounts Payable (Accounts Payable account type)

    d. Unearned Revenue (Other Current Liability account type)

3. The **Journal** report includes _____.

    a. all accounting transactions no matter where (how) they were recorded

    b. only those accounting transactions recorded in the **Journal Entry** form

    c. only accounting transactions recorded through certain forms

    d. only accounting transactions NOT recorded in the **Journal Entry** form

4. When a credit card statement is reconciled,

    a. the user can elect to create a **bill** for the statement balance.

    b. the user can elect to write a **check** for the statement balance.

    c. the user can elect to retain the balance in the credit card liability account.

    d. the user can elect any of the three options listed.

5. On the first day of a new fiscal year, QBO automatically closes

    a. all temporary accounts.

    b. all revenue and expense accounts.

    c. all revenue, expense, and equity accounts.

    d. all revenue, expense, and dividend accounts.

BEYOND THE CLICKS—THINKING LIKE A MANAGER

Accounting: A company issued inaccurate financial statements at the end of the year. There was no fraud involved and the accounting staff was competent. What might have caused the error(s)?

Information Systems: How do closing dates work in a computerized system? How does setting a closing date prevent or reduce errors in the company's records?

ASSIGNMENTS

Background information: Martin Smith, a college student and good friend of yours, has always wanted to be an entrepreneur. He is very good in math, so, to test his entrepreneurship skills, he has decided to set up a small math tutoring company serving local high school students who struggle in their math courses. He set up the company, Math Revealed!, as a corporation in 2021. Martin is the only owner. He has not taken any distributions from the company since it opened.

The business has been successful so far. In fact, it's been so successful he has decided to work in his business full time now that he's graduated from college with a degree in mathematics.

He has decided to start using QuickBooks Online to keep track of his business transactions. He likes the convenience of being able to access his information over the Internet. You have agreed to act as his accountant while you're finishing your own academic program.

Martin currently has a number of regular customers that he tutors in Pre-Algebra, Algebra, and Geometry. His customers pay his fees by cash or check after each tutoring session but he does give terms of Net 15 to some of his customers. He has developed the following fee schedule:

Name	Description	Rate
Refresher	One-hour session	$ 60 per hour
Persistence program	Two one-hour sessions per week	$100 per week
Crisis program	Five one-hour sessions per week	$225 per week

The tutoring sessions usually take place at his students' homes but he recently signed a two-year lease on a small office above a local coffee shop. The rent is only $750 per month starting in January 2022. A security deposit of $500 was paid in December 2021.

The following equipment is owned by the company:

Description	Date placed in service	Cost	Life	Salvage Value
Computer	7/1/21	$3,000	36 months	$300
Printer	7/1/21	$ 240	24 months	$ 0
Graphing Calculators (3)	7/1/21	$ 300	36 months	$ 30

All equipment is depreciated using the straight-line method.

As of 12/31/21, Martin owed $2,500 to his father (Richard Smith) who initially helped him get started. Richard is charging him interest at a 6% annual rate. Martin has been paying interest only on a monthly basis. His last payment of interest only was on 12/31/21.

Over the next month or so, he plans to expand his business by selling a few products he believes will help his students. He has already purchased a few items:

Category	Description	Vendor	Quantity on Hand	Cost per Unit	Sales Price
Books and Tools					
	Geometry in Sports	Books Galore	20	18	25
	Solving Puzzles: Fun with Algebra	Books Galore	20	15	22
	Getting Ready for Calculus	Books Galore	20	20	28
	Geometry Kit	Math Shack	10	12	18
	Handheld Dry-Erase Boards	Math Shack	25	10	15
	Notebooks (pack of 5)	Paper Bag Depot	10	8	12

1/31/22

✓ Martin asks you to give him a summary of the hours you worked in January. He agrees to pay you $30 per hour for the 10 hours you worked on his accounting. You are only doing this temporarily since you have some extra time so you set yourself up as a 1099 vendor and write yourself a check for the $300. The check number is 1111. You consider this a professional service expense.

- Use 333-44-5555 as your Business ID number and 2119 Abacus Drive as your address. Use your home city, state to complete the address. You select Net 10 in Terms.

✓ You reconcile the bank statement for January. You get the following information from the bank's website. **TIP:** Since this is the first time the checking account has been reconciled in QBO, the 12/31 balance will show as a deposit. Make sure you mark that deposit as cleared. Also, note that the dates showing on the bank statement are the dates checks and deposits were received by the bank. They will not always be the same as the dates transactions were recorded in your company file.

CITY BANK OF SACRAMENTO
51 Capital Avenue
Sacramento, CA 95822 (916) 585-2120

Student Name Math Revealed!
3835 Freeport Blvd
Sacramento, CA 95822
Account # 1616479   **January 31, 2022**

	CREDITS	CHARGES	BALANCE
Beginning Balance, January 1			$3,415.00
1/6, Check 1102—Pro Spaces		$ 750.00	2,665.00
1/10, Check 1101—Protector Insurance		360.00	2,305.00
1/12, Deposit	$ 445.00		2,750.00
1/14, Check 1103—Kathy's Coffee		25.00	2,725.00
1/17, Check 1104—Math Shack		441.07	2,283.93
1/19, Deposit	1,465.00		3,748.93
1/21, Check 1100—Gus Ranting		20.00	3,728.93
1/21, Check 1105—Paper Bag Depot		80.00	3,648.93
1/21, Deposit	320.00		3,968.93
1/24, Check 1106—Samantha Levin		125.00	3,843.93
1/28, Deposit	3,505.00		7,348.93
Ending Balance, January 31			**$7,348.93**

HINT: Your check numbers on bill payments may differ slightly from above. Pay attention to the payee and amount.

✓ You also receive the credit card statement in the mail. You reconcile the card and set up the balance for payment later to Prime Visa Company. Use JanCC as the Bill no. **TIP:** Make sure you click Enter a bill to pay later before you click Done.

PRIME VISA COMPANY
55 Wall Street
New York, NY 10005

Student Name Math Revealed!
3835 Freeport Blvd
Sacramento, CA 95822
Account # 212456770439   **January 31, 2022**

	PAYMENTS	CHARGES	BALANCE
Beginning Balance, January 1			$ 0.00
1/3—Paper Bag Depot		$1,701.00	1,701.00
1/7—Cardinal Gas & Snacks		30.00	1,731.00
1/10—Math Shack		28.61	1,759.61
1/25—Cardinal Gas & Snacks		30.00	1,789.61
1/28—Kathy's Coffee		8.75	1,798.36
Ending Balance, January 31			**$1,798.36**

Minimum Payment Due: $10   Payment Due Date: February 15

✓ You make adjusting journal entries for the month of January as needed. (Start with Journal no. Jan22.1.) You carefully consider the following:

- Math Revealed! used the straight-line method to determine depreciation expense for all office equipment.
  - Monthly depreciation expense for the equipment purchased prior to 12/31 is $92.50. (Computer $75; Printer $10; Calculators $7.50)
  - Math Revealed! purchased $726 of furniture on 1/3. You expect the furniture to last 4 years, with a $150 salvage value. You take a full month depreciation on the furniture.
  - Two computers ($1,260) and three calculators ($441) were also purchased on 1/3. You expect the computers to have a 3-year life (no salvage value) and the calculators to have a 3-year life ($63 salvage value). You take a full month depreciation on the equipment.
  - On 1/29, shelving was installed. The cost of the shelving was $820. You expect the shelving to last for the term of the lease (24 months). You estimate the salvage value at $100 at the end of the 2 years. You started using the shelving on February 1.
- You check the supplies on hand. You estimate that $120 of supplies were used during January.
  - You charge the amount to a new account (Tutoring supplies expense, a sub-account of Office and Tutoring Costs). You use 632 as the account number and Other Business Expenses as the detail type.
- The insurance policy premium paid in January was $360. The policy term is 1/1–12/31/22.
- You check to make sure that all the revenue recorded in January was earned during the month.
  - You realize that the $3,000 paid by Teacher's College on 1/27 was for a workshop to be held in February.
  - You also take a look at INV-1009 to Annie Wang. Half of the $400 billed on 1/14 was for February tutoring.
  - TIP: Consider whether you need a new account here. Choose an account number that fits with the account numbering scheme (assets are 100s; liabilities are 200s; revenues are 400s; expenses are 600s).
- Martin has agreed to pay his father interest on the $2,500 loan to help get the business started. The last payment was made on 12/31/21. The annual interest rate (simple interest) on the loan is 6%. You forgot to pay him in January. You call and let him know that the check will come in February.
  - TIP: Just because you didn't pay it in January doesn't mean you don't owe it in January. Consider whether you need a new account here.

Check numbers as of 1/31

Checking account balance:	**$ 4,002.93**
Total assets:	**$14,166.00**
Total current liabilities:	**$ 5,976.07**
Net income (January only):	**$ 1,579.93**

TIP: If you are having a hard time getting to these check numbers, try some of the hints for finding errors and getting it right in Appendix 5A.

Suggested reports for Chapter 5:

All reports should be in portrait orientation.

- Journal—1/31 transactions only
- Balance Sheet (as of 1/31)
- Profit and loss statement (January)

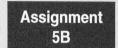

Assignment 5B

Salish Software Solutions

Background information: Sally Hanson, a good friend of yours, double majored in Computer Science and Accounting in college. She worked for several years for a software company in Silicon Valley but the long hours started to take a toll on her personal life.

Last year she decided to open up her own company, Salish Software Solutions. Sally currently advises clients looking for new accounting software and assists them with software installation. She also provides training to client employees and occasionally troubleshoots software issues.

She has decided to start using QuickBooks Online to keep track of her business transactions. She likes the convenience of being able to access financial information over the Internet. You have agreed to act as her accountant while you're working on your accounting degree.

Sally has a number of clients that she is currently working with. She gives 15-day payment terms to her corporate clients but she asks for cash at time of service if she does work for individuals. She has developed the following fee schedule:

Name	Description	Rate
Select	Software selection	$500 flat fee
Set Up	Software installation	$ 75 per hour
Train	Software training	$ 50 per hour
Fix	File repair	$ 60 per hour

Sally rents office space from Alki Property Management for $600 per month.

The following furniture and equipment are owned by Salish:

Description	Date placed in service	Cost	Life	Salvage Value
Office furniture	6/1/21	$1,400	60 months	$200
Computer	7/1/21	$4,620	36 months	$300
Printer.	7/1/21	$ 900	24 months	$ 0

All equipment is depreciated using the straight-line method.

As of 12/31/21, she owed $3,500 to Dell Finance. The monthly payment on that loan is $150 including interest at 5%. Sally's last payment to Dell was 12/31/21.

Over the next month or so, Sally plans to expand her business by selling some of her favorite accounting and personal software products directly to her clients. She has already purchased the following items.

Item Name	Description	Vendor	Quantity on Hand	Cost per Unit	Sales Price
Easy1	Easy Does It	Abacus Shop	15	$100	$ 200
Retailer	Simply Retail	Simply Accounting	2	$400	$ 800
Contractor.	Simply Construction	Simply Accounting	2	$500	$1,000
Organizer	Organizer	Personal Software	20	$ 25	$ 50
Tracker	Investment Tracker	Personal Software	20	$ 20	$ 40

1/31/22

✓ You talk to Sally about getting paid for the work you're doing. You suggest $25 an hour and she agrees. You are only doing this temporarily since you have some extra time so you set yourself up as a 1099 vendor and write yourself a check for the 12 hours you worked in January ($300). The check number is 1111. You consider this a professional fees expense.

- Use 999-88-7777 as your Business ID number and 3056 Abacus Drive as your address. Use your home city, state to complete the address. You select Net 10 in **Terms**.

✓ You decide to reconcile the bank statement for January. You get the following information from the bank's website:

- **TIP:** Since this is the first time the checking account has been reconciled, the beginning balance in QBO will be $0. That is ok. Once you start the reconciliation the opening balance per the bank statement will appear as a deposit. Select that as an amount that has cleared. Also, note that the dates showing on the bank statement are the dates checks and deposits were received by the bank. They will not always be the same as the dates transactions were recorded in your company file.

SACRAMENTO CITY BANK
1822 Capital Avenue
Sacramento, CA 95822 (916) 585-2120

Student Name Salish Software Solutions
3835 Freeport Blvd
Sacramento, CA 95822
Account # 855922   January 31, 2022

	CREDITS	CHARGES	BALANCE
Beginning Balance, January 1			$10,500.00
1/5, Check 1102—Albright Insurance		$720.00	9,780.00
1/7, Check 1101—Alki Property Management		600.00	9,180.00
1/10, Deposit	$ 630.00		9,810.00
1/14, Check 1103—Personal Software		135.00	9,675.00
1/15, Check 1104—Abacus Shop		200.00	9,475.00
1/15, Check 1105—Simply Accounting		900.00	8,575.00
1/20, Deposit	2,160.00		10,735.00
1/21, Deposit	1,450.00		12,185.00
1/21, Check 1108—Entrepreneur Magazine		120.00	12,065.00
1/28, Check 1106—Hacker Spaces		200.00	11,865.00
1/28, Deposit	$ 970.00		12,835.00
1/31, Bank service charge		$ 15.00	12,820.00
Ending Balance, January 31			$12,820.00

HINT: Your check numbers on **bill payments** may differ slightly from above. Pay attention to the payee and amount.

✓ You also receive the credit card statement in the mail. You reconcile the card and set up the balance for payment later. Use JanCC as the Bill no.

CAPITAL THREE
58 Wall Street
New York, NY 10005

Student Name Salish Software Solutions
3835 Freeport Blvd
Sacramento, CA 95822
Account # 646630813344   January 31, 2022

	PAYMENTS	CHARGES	BALANCE
Beginning Balance, January 1			$ 0.00
1/5—Paper Bag Depot		$500.00	500.00
1/14—Hacker Spaces		300.00	800.00
1/14—Hacker Spaces		300.00	1,100.00
1/25—The Blue Door		110.00	1,210.00
Ending Balance, 1/31			$1,210.00
Minimum Payment Due: $10.00		Payment Due Date: February 15	

✓ You make adjusting journal entries for the month of January as needed. (Start with Journal no. Jan22.1.) You carefully consider the following:

• Salish Software Solutions used the straight-line method to determine depreciation expense for all fixed assets.

   ○ None of the assets purchased prior to 12/31 were fully depreciated. **TIP:** Use the information provided in the table included in Background Information at the top of this assignment to determine the monthly amount.

Sally paid $960 for software on 1/7. She expected the software to last two years, with no salvage value. The software was not placed in service until 1/7 so you decide to take 75% of a full month's depreciation.

The storage cabinets were installed on 1/28. The cost was $1,500. Sally expects the cabinets to last for five years. You don't think the cabinets will have any resale value at the end of the five years. Sally started using the cabinets on February 1.

- You check the supplies on hand. You estimate that $175 of supplies were used during January.

- The insurance policy premium paid in January was $720. The policy term is 1/1–12/31/22.

- You check to make sure that all the revenue recorded in January was earned during the month.

You ask Sally about the Butter and Beans installation work. She says that she has completed about half the work (20 of the 40 hours billed on INV-1009 for $3,000).

You also take a look at INV-1011 to Albus Software. The workshop will be held in mid-February.

TIP: Consider whether you need to create a new account here. Choose an account number that fits with the account numbering scheme (assets are 100s; liabilities are 200s; revenues are 400s; expenses are 600s).

- Sally's last payment to Dell Finance was 12/31/21. That payment included interest through 12/31. The next payment of $150 is due on February 1. The annual interest rate (simple interest) on the loan is 5%.

TIP: Think about what that February 1st payment will cover. Does any of the amount relate to January activity? You may need to create a new account.

Check numbers as of 1/31

Checking account balance:. . . . .$ 9,365.00
Total assets:. $30,137.50
Total current liabilities: . . . .$ 6,928.53
Net income (January):. . . . .$ 3,488.97

TIP: If you are having a hard time getting to these check numbers, try some of the hints for finding errors and getting it right in Appendix 5A.

Suggested reports for Chapter 5:

All reports should be in portrait orientation; fit to one page wide

- Journal—1/31/22 transactions only

- Balance Sheet (as of 1/31)

- Profit and loss statement (January only)

APPENDIX 5A GETTING IT RIGHT

Most accountants work the hardest (use their brains the most!) at the end of an accounting period. They know the income statement for the period should accurately reflect the earnings (or loss) for the period. They know the balance sheet as of the period end should accurately reflect the assets owned and the liabilities owed by the company. The difficulty doesn't lie in knowing the basic concepts. The difficulty lies in knowing what the "accurate" amounts are.

Most students have the most difficulty with the assignments for Chapter 5 and Chapter 8. You have check numbers to refer to, which will hopefully help, but if your numbers don't match those numbers, how do you figure out where you went wrong?

Here are some suggestions for finding your mistakes:

- Start by checking dates.
  - Entering an incorrect date is the **single most common** cause of student errors (and student headaches!). QBO enters default dates when you first open a form. It defaults to the current date when you start entering transactions during a work session. If you change the date on the first invoice, it will default to that new date when you enter the second invoice. If you open a new form, however, it will default back to the current date. Accounting is date driven, so your financial statements won't match the check figures if you enter a transaction in the wrong month. First thing to do? Pull a report of transactions dated BEFORE the first transaction date in the assignment and then one of transactions dated AFTER the last transaction date of the assignment. Transaction List by Date is a great report for this. Make sure you're only checking for transactions that **you** entered. (There were some transactions entered in the initial setup of the company file you are using for your homework. Those should **not** be changed.)

- Really **LOOK** at the balance sheet.
  - The account balances will be positive if they reflect the normal balance for that type of account. Are any of the amounts on your balance sheet negative numbers? If so, should they be negative? If they are contra accounts, the answer would be yes. If there are no negative amounts on your balance sheet, should there be? Again, if you have any contra accounts, the answer would be yes. Accumulated depreciation is a contra account so, if entries were made correctly, it would show as a negative number on the balance sheet. If accumulated depreciation isn't negative, you might have mixed up your debits and credits when making an entry. That's easy to do. Double-click on the amount, then double-click on the underlying entry(ies) and make the necessary corrections.
  - Don't worry about errors in Cash, A/R, or A/P until you are comfortable with the other balances. This is double-entry bookkeeping so if one account is wrong, then at least one other account is also wrong. It's hard to find errors in Cash, A/R, and A/P due to the sheer volume of transactions that affect these accounts. SO: if you don't match the check figures, see if you can find the other account(s) that is (are) also off. If you can find and correct the other error(s), these accounts will, of course, fix themselves!
  - Pay particular attention to other current assets and to liabilities other than accounts payable. Are they adjusted properly? Does the supplies on hand account equal the check number given to you? Does the balance in prepaid insurance represent the cost of future (unused) insurance coverage? Should there be any interest accrued on debt? Keep asking questions.

- Really **LOOK** at the profit and loss statement.
  - Again, look for negative amounts that shouldn't be negative. There are some contra revenue and expenses accounts, of course. Sales discounts and purchase discount accounts are two examples of contra accounts that you'll be working with in future chapters.
  - Look at the detail for accounts that just look "odd." Is rent expense higher than income? That could happen, of course, but probably not in this class!

- If you're still off, you're going to have to do some detective work. Try to narrow down the possible errors first.
  - For example, let's say your A/R number is **higher** than the check figure given for A/R. You wouldn't start by looking for unrecorded invoices or cash sales.

Why? Because missing invoices or cash sales wouldn't overstate A/R. You **would** start by looking for unrecorded customer payments or customer credits. Look through the assignment (day by day) and agree any customer payments or credits described to the payment and credit memo transaction types listed in your journal.

- Another example—Let's say your cash number is **lower** than the check number given for cash. You might start by looking for undeposited checks by making sure there isn't a balance in the undeposited funds account. You might also look for duplicated customer payments. Then look through the assignment (day by day) and agree any payment transactions to check, expense, and bill payment transaction types listed in your journal.

- Don't give up. Keep checking transactions. You'll find the error.

- I have one other suggestion. It's listed last here only because students tend to waste a lot of time looking for a specific amount when the difference is often the sum of several errors. That being said, sometimes you just get lucky! So, determine the difference between the check figure and your total. Is the number divisible by 9? You may have a transposition error (for example, you entered 18 instead of 81). Is the difference equal to the amount of a transaction? Maybe you forgot to enter it (or entered it on the wrong date). Is the difference equal to twice one of your transactions? You may have entered a journal entry backwards (watch those debits and credits!).

APPENDIX 5B UNDERSTANDING THE RECONCILIATION REPORT

eLectures

The purpose of a bank reconciliation is to make sure the amount reported as cash in the balance sheet is accurate. Reconciliations are performed by comparing activity reported on statements received from the bank (an external source of information) to activity recorded internally in the cash general ledger account. Because internal information is being reconciled to external information, bank reconciliations are considered part of a company's internal control system.

There will be differences between what's recorded in the general ledger and what's reported on the bank statement.

Differences that represent **errors** are considered permanent differences. Permanent differences must be corrected before the reconciliation process is considered complete. If the error was made by the company, an adjusting entry would be made. If the error was made by the bank, the correction would be in the bank's records. Permanent differences are relatively uncommon.

Temporary differences, on the other hand, are very common. Temporary differences occur when a transaction is recorded by the company **before or after** that transaction is recorded by the bank.

Here are some examples:

- A check to a vendor is recorded by the company (cash is credited) when the check is issued. The check is sent to the vendor, the vendor records receipt of the check, and the vendor deposits the amount in its bank account. In the final step, the vendor's bank requests and receives the cash from the company's bank to cover the check. This process can occur over several days or even weeks.

- A check from a customer is received by the company. The customer payment is recorded (cash is debited) immediately but the checks are not deposited with the bank until a later date.

- The bank charges a monthly service fee to the company's account. The company isn't aware of the fee until the bank statement is received.

Most temporary (timing) differences are resolved before the bank statement is reconciled. As long as a transaction is recorded in the same accounting period (usually a month), any timing difference won't be an issue. Issues arise when the transactions are recorded by the bank and the company in two different accounting periods.

The two most common types of temporary differences are:

- Outstanding checks—Checks that were recorded by the company but had not been presented to the company's bank for payment as of the statement date.

- Deposits in transit—Deposits that were recorded by the company but had not yet been deposited at the bank as of the statement date.

The reconciliation report in QBO provides information about the differences that remain as of the statement date.

The top section of a reconciliation report looks something like this:

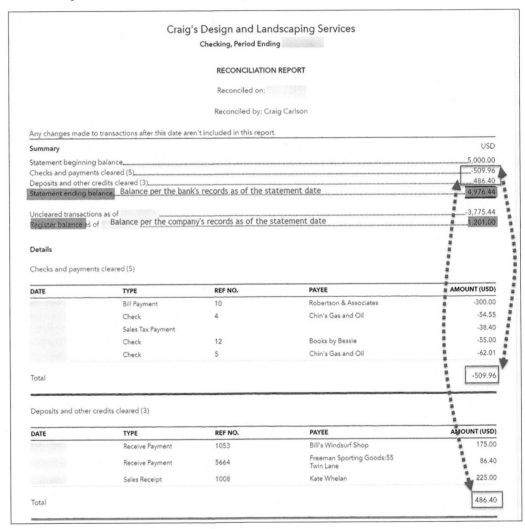

This section includes all of the transactions that were "matched" during the period. Although all of the transactions listed here were recorded in the bank's records during the current period, they could have been recorded in the company's records during the current period or in a prior period. If they were recorded in the company's books during a prior period, they would have been listed as outstanding checks in the prior reconciliation.

The balance in the company's cash account as of the statement date is also listed in this section.

The bottom section of a reconciliation report looks something like this:

Figure 5B.2

Outstanding checks and deposits in transit as of the statement date

Additional Information

Uncleared checks and payments as of

DATE	TYPE	REF NO.	PAYEE	AMOUNT (USD)
	Expense	12	Robertson & Associates	-250.00
	Sales Tax Payment			-38.50
	Expense	9	Tania's Nursery	-89.09
	Expense	15	Tania's Nursery	-108.09
	Bill Payment	7	Hicks Hardware	-250.00
	Expense	8	Hicks Hardware	-24.36
	Check		Tony Rondonuwu	-100.00
	Cash Expense		Bob's Burger Joint	-5.66
	Cash Expense		Squeaky Kleen Car Wash	-19.99
	Check	70	Chin's Gas and Oil	-185.00
	Cash Expense		Chin's Gas and Oil	-52.14
	Bill Payment	11	Hall Properties	-900.00
	Expense	13	Hicks Hardware	-215.66
	Check	2	Mahoney Mugs	-18.08
	Cash Expense		Bob's Burger Joint	-3.86
	Bill Payment	1	Brosnahan Insurance Agency	-2,000.00
	Bill Payment	3	Books by Bessie	-75.00
	Refund	1020	Pye's Cakes	-87.50
	Check	Debit	Squeaky Kleen Car Wash	-19.99
	Expense	108	Tania's Nursery	-46.98
	Bill Payment	45	Tim Philip Masonry	-666.00
	Bill Payment	6	PG&E	-114.09
	Cash Expense		Chin's Gas and Oil	-63.15
	Check	75	Hicks Hardware	-228.75
	Expense	76	Pam Seitz	-75.00
	Cash Expense		Tania's Nursery	-23.50
	Credit Card Credit			-900.00

Total			Outstanding checks	-6,560.39

Uncleared deposits and other credits as of

DATE	TYPE	REF NO.	PAYEE	AMOUNT (USD)
	Receive Payment		Amy's Bird Sanctuary	105.00
	Receive Payment	1886	Cool Cars	694.00
	Sales Receipt	10264	Dylan Sollfrank	337.50
	Receive Payment		Freeman Sporting Goods:55 Twin Lane	50.00
	Deposit			218.75
	Receive Payment	2064	Travis Waldron	103.55
	Deposit			408.00
	Deposit			868.15

Total			Deposits in transit	2,784.95

All of the timing differences are listed in this section—outstanding checks and deposits in transit. This list includes all the transactions that had been recorded in the company's books but had not been recorded by the bank as of the statement date. Some of the transactions were recorded by the company during the statement period. Others were recorded by the company during a prior period. These would have been timing differences in the prior reconciliation as well.

The final step is to reconcile the bank statement balance to the book balance.

Although QBO doesn't include this in the report, the reconciliation summary you learned in your introduction to financial accounting course can be created using the data in the reconciliation report. It would look something like this given the information in Figures 5B.1 and 5B.2.

Balance per bank as of the statement date	$4,976.44
Add: Deposits in Transit	2,784.95
Less: Outstanding Checks	6,560.39
Balance per book as of the statement date	$1,201.00

APPENDIX 5C FIXING RECONCILIATION ERRORS

Although the process is time-consuming, the safest way to fix reconciliation errors is to manually unreconcile all the transactions and then start over.

> ✳ **HINT:** Users with the QBO Accountant version of the software can **undo** a bank reconciliation. Check with your instructor to see if they might be able to use that feature.

- Print out the reconciliation report for the period that was reconciled incorrectly. This will give you a list of all transactions cleared during the period.
  - ▪ Click the ⚙ on the icon bar.
  - ▪ Click **Reconcile**.

Figure 5C.1

Access to reconciliation history

- ▪ Click **History by account**.

Figure 5C.2

Link to reconciliation report

- ▪ Click **View report**.
- ▪ Print or save a PDF of the report.
- Find and delete the reconciliation discrepancy entry, if any. This is the entry QBO would have made if you clicked **Finish Now** before the difference between the book balance and the bank balance was zero.
  - ▪ Click **Reports** on the navigation bar.
  - ▪ Click **Profit and Loss**.
  - ▪ Change the dates to include the bank statement ending date.
  - ▪ Click the Reconciliation Discrepancies account to open the account **Transaction Report**.
  - ▪ Click the entry amount to open the form.
  - ▪ Click **More** on the black bar at the bottom of the form and select **Delete**.
- Open the **check register** and sort the list by cleared status.
  - ▪ Click the ⚙ on the icon bar and select **Chart of Accounts**.

Figure 5C.3

Link to account register

■ Click **View Register** in the **ACTION** column for the account being corrected.

Figure 5C.4

Status column in account register

■ Change the order of transactions by clicking the checkmark at the top of the column between **DEPOSIT** and **BALANCE** (the status field). The list is now sorted by status.

> **BEHIND THE SCENES** The status field for every **bank** account transaction listed in a register will either be R, C, or blank.
> - **R** means that the transaction has been reconciled. The reconciliation has been closed.
> - **C** means that the transaction has been identified as 'cleared' but the reconciliation is still open.
> - Blank means that the transaction is outstanding.

● Unreconcile the transactions cleared as part of the inaccurate reconciliation.
   ■ Every transaction listed on the reconciliation report as cleared will have an **R** in the status field. Click in the box until the status field is blank.
      ○ You will get the following message each time you clear a status field.

Figure 5C.5

Warning message before changing status

      ○ Click **Yes**.

○   Depending on the closing date set in your company file, you may also get
      this message:

Figure 5C.6

Warning message
about making changes
to transactions in
closed periods

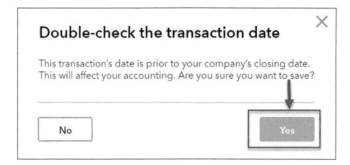

○   Click **Yes**.

▪   Do **not** change the status of any transaction that does not appear as 'cleared' in
      the reconciliation report you printed out in the first step of the process.

●   Re-reconcile the account.

▪   Click the ⚙ on the icon bar.

▪   Click **Reconcile**.

▪   Select the account to be re-reconciled.

▪   The **beginning balance** should now equal the ending balance from the prior
      month's reconciliation (the last correct reconciliation).

▪   Enter the ending date and the ending balance from the bank statement.

> **!   WARNING: An offer to "help you fix" the reconciliation will likely be avail-
> able in QBO. If you accept the offer, a Reconcilation Discrepancy Report
> window will be displayed. In the window you can change the status of any
> unreconciled transaction. This would not solve the problem of missing
> transactions or transaction errors. It's best to ignore the offer.**

▪   Proceed with the reconciliation.

QuickBooks

SECTION THREE

Merchandising Companies

In this section, we'll primarily be looking at how QuickBooks Online handles the unique needs of merchandising companies. However, some of the new processes and procedures you will learn can also be, and are, used by service companies.

Accounting in a merchandising company is a little more complex. For example, inventory purchases and sales need to be accounted for and sales tax may need to be collected and remitted.

Merchandising companies are also, generally, larger than service companies. That means more employees, including more employees involved in accounting functions. Although **internal controls** are important in **any** company, the complexity and size of merchandising companies make the review and development of internal control systems even more important.

Two of the primary purposes of a good internal control system are:

- To safeguard assets.

- To ensure the accuracy of financial records.

QBO has some features that can be part of a good internal control system.

CONTROLS IN QUICKBOOKS ONLINE

Managing Users

Many merchandising companies have multiple employees involved in the record-keeping functions. Those employees must, of course, have access to the accounting software. Allowing every employee **full** access to the software, however, presents opportunities for **fraud**.

QBO allows individual users to be limited in access to particular areas of the program and even to functions within those areas. QBO requires that at least one user, the administrator, have access to all functions. The administrator sets up the other users.

Internal controls Policies and procedures implemented by an organization to safeguard its assets, ensure integrity of its accounting records, ensure its compliance with laws and regulations, and monitor effectiveness and efficiency of its operations.

Fraud Any act by the management or employees of a business involving an intentional deception for personal gain.

6-1

To manage users, click the ⚙ on the icon bar.

Figure S3.1

Access to user management feature

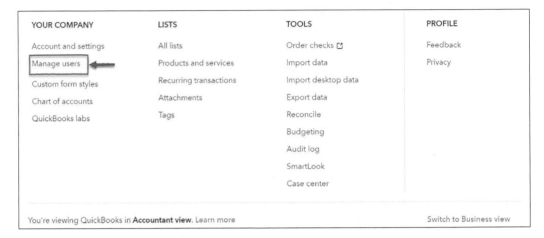

Click **Manage users**.

Figure S3.2

User Center

There are two tabs in the User Center. Owners and employees with accounting responsibilities are added on the **User** tab. In QuickBooks Online Plus (the version provided to you), a company can add up to 5 **Users**. (Employees with access only to reports or timesheets are not included in the **user** limit.)

External accountants are normally added on the **Accountants** tab. Up to 2 **Accountants** can be added.

Adding Users

Adding Standard Users With Full Access

Click the ⚙ on the icon bar and select **Manage Users** to open the User Center.

Figure S3.3

User Center

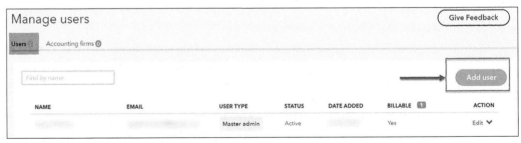

Click **Add user.**

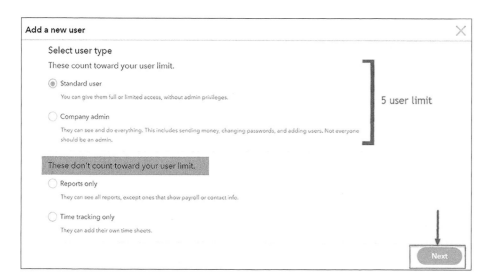

Figure S3.4

User type selection
screen

Employees with accounting responsibilities would normally be set up as **standard users**.

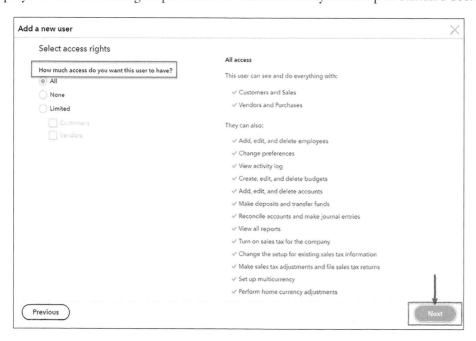

Figure S3.5

Access rights selection
screen

Users can be given access to all features or access can be limited. In a small company, for example, the accountant might be given access to all the accounting functions listed on the screen shown in Figure S3.5. Click **Next** to identify access rights to administrative functions.

Figure S3.6

Administrative access
selection screen

Administrative features include managing users and QBO subscriptions and editing information on the **Company** tab in **Account and Settings** (company contact details and tax structure).

Click **Next**.

Figure S3.7

New user contact information screen

In the final screen, the new **user's** name and email address are entered. The email address becomes their user name. Once the information is saved, an email is automatically sent to the new **user**. The setup is completed when the new user logs in and accepts the invitation.

Adding Standard Users With Limited Access

Click the ⚙ on the icon bar and select **Manage users** to open the User Center.

On the **Users** tab, click **Add user**.

Figure S3.8

Access rights selection screen

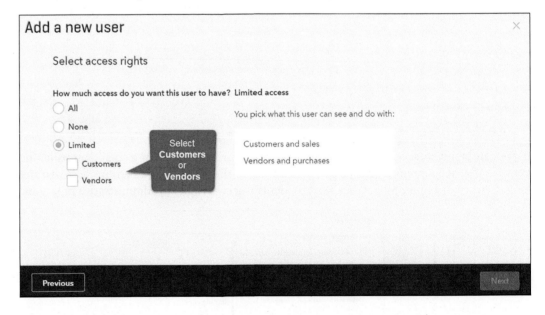

Users can be limited to sales cycle functions by clicking **Customers**. **Users** can be limited to purchase cycle functions by clicking **Vendors**. Click **Next** once the selection has been made.

The allowed (and disallowed) functions are displayed on the next screen. If **Customers** were selected, the screen would look like this:

Figure S3.9

Access rights for standard user with access to sales functions

The process is similar for setting up a **user** with access to purchasing cycle functions. The **Select access rights** screen looks something like this:

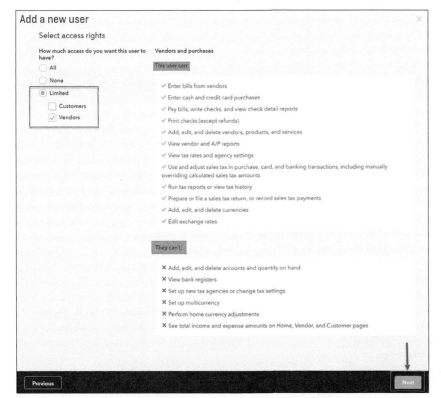

Figure S3.10

Access rights for standard user with access to purchasing functions

Click **Next**.

The final two screens for entering **users** with sales or purchase cycle responsibilities include setting administrative access rights (see Figure S3.6) and entering **user** contact information (see Figure S3.7). An invitation is automatically emailed to the employee once the information is saved.

If an employee only needs to enter their own time, select **Time tracking only** on the screen in Figure S3.4. Access to timesheets is given in the following screen:

Figure S3.11

Employee selection for time-tracking only

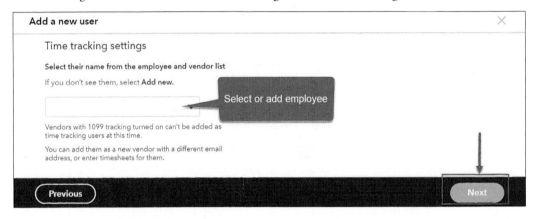

Select employee name and click **Next**.

Figure S3.12

Contact information screen

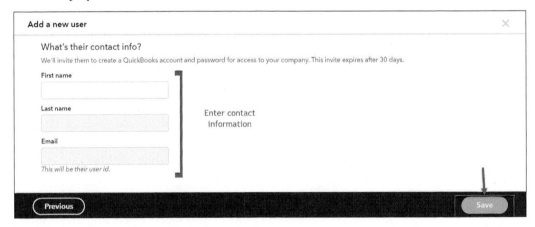

In the final screen, contact information is added.

Click **Save**. An email invitation to the employee is automatically generated.

Adding Accountant Users

Companies can give company file access to two external accountants by setting them up as **accountant users**. This allows the accountant(s) to easily make any necessary adjustments.

Click the ⚙ on the icon bar and select **Manage users**.

Figure S3.13

Accounting firms tab in user management screen

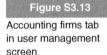

Click the **Accounting firms** tab.

Enter the external accountant's email address and click **Invite**.

An email to the accountant is automatically generated by QBO. Once the accountant accepts the invitation, the process is complete.

Figure S3.14
Accountant user setup screen

Users can resend an invitation if necessary. Accountant access can also be deleted by selecting **Delete** in the **ACTION** column dropdown menu.

> **BEHIND THE SCENES** There are no screens for limiting access and rights for **Accountants**. Accountant users will have administrator rights.

Editing, Monitoring, and Deleting Users

To edit, monitor, or delete a user, open the **Manage Users** screen. (Click the ⚙ icon to access the link.)

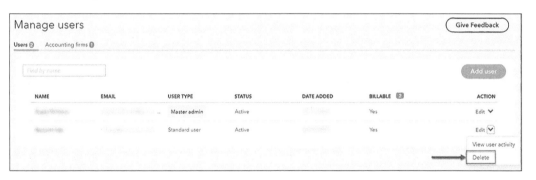

Figure S3.15
User Center actions

Select **Edit** in the **ACTION** dropdown menu to change access rights for a **user**. Select **Delete** to remove a **user**.

Clicking **View user activity** allows the administrator to view all user activity in chronological order. Activity would include logins, transactions added or edited, setting changes, etc. Activity can also be accessed using the reports introduced in the next section (**Reporting on Transaction History**).

Reporting on Transaction History

QBO tracks all significant changes to transactions including the name of the user entering or modifying the transaction. Several reports are available.

The **Audit Log** is accessed by clicking the ⚙ icon in the icon bar and selecting **Audit Log** in the **Tools** column.

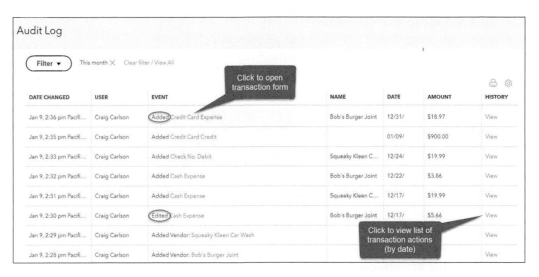

On the main page, transactions are listed in chronological order. Certain information is listed for every transaction (name of user initiating transaction, entry date, amounts, etc.). An initial entry is identified as **Added**. Any revisions are flagged as **Edited**. Links to the transactions are provided in the **Event** column. Further details about each transaction can be obtained by clicking the **View** link.

HINT: The **Audit Log** can be filtered by user, date, and activity type using the **Filter** menus.

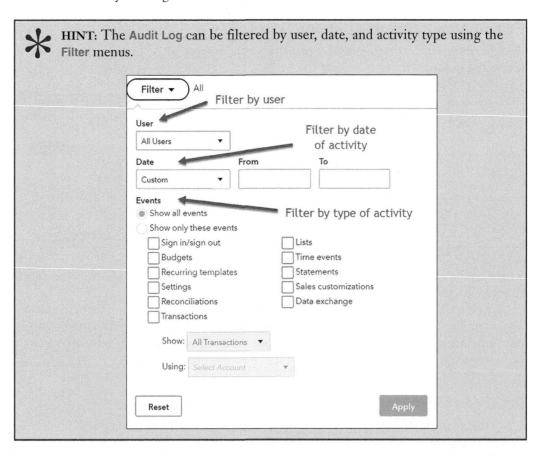

If a closing date has been set in a company file, an **Exceptions to Closing Date** report can be created. The report lists only those prior period transactions that were changed after the closing date and includes the name of the user making the change. The **Exceptions to Closing Date** report, if available, is located in the **For My Accountant** section of **Reports**.

Reports, obviously, can't prevent fraud. However, the fact that these reports are available acts as a fraud deterrent because employees know they are identified (by user name) with all transactions they enter (or change).

SECTION OVERVIEW

Chapter 6 will cover the sales cycle in a merchandising company.
Chapter 7 will cover the purchase cycle in a merchandising company.
Chapter 8 will cover end-of-period accounting in a merchandising company.

6

Sales Activity
(Merchandising Company)

After completing Chapter 6, you should be able to:

1. Set up sub-customers.

2. Set up sales taxes.

3. Manage customer shipping addresses.

4. Set up and edit inventory items.

5. Record various types of customer discounts.

6. Record pending sales transactions.

7. Write off uncollectible accounts.

8. Record customer credit card payments.

9. Record early payment discounts taken by customers.

10. Process customer checks returned by the bank due to insufficient funds in the customer's bank account.

11. Prepare reports of sales by product and service.

12. Create customer statements.

WHAT IS THE SALES CYCLE IN A MERCHANDISING COMPANY?

- Get orders.
- Fill orders.
- Bill for the products.
- Collect the sales price.

The sales cycle in a merchandising company is similar to that of a service company and many of the accounting functions are the same. There are some differences though. In this chapter, we'll cover those differences. We'll also cover some more advanced topics that apply to both service and merchandising companies.

MANAGING CUSTOMERS

The process for setting up and editing customers is covered in Chapter 3. This section covers:

- Setting up sub-customers.
- Entering sales tax information for customers.
- Entering shipping information for customers.

Setting Up Sub-Customers

Customers may have multiple locations or subsidiaries and they may want **invoices** to reflect the specific location or subsidiary being charged.

This can be accommodated by setting up a parent customer with **sub-customers** in QBO. The relationship is identified in the **sub-customer's** record.

Figure 6.1

Sub-customer setup

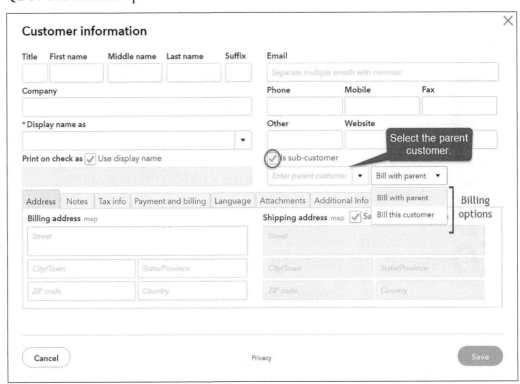

There are two billing options available when setting up **sub-customers** related to future billings.

- **Bill with parent**—If this option is selected, **invoices** created for the **sub-customer** will be included on **statements** created for the parent customer. In addition, when recording payments received directly from the parent, any outstanding invoices for the **sub-customer** will appear in the **receive payment** window.

- **Bill this customer**—If this option is selected, **invoices** created for the **sub-customer** will not be included on **statements** created for the parent customer. In addition, any outstanding invoices for the **sub-customer** would not appear in the **receive payment** window if the payment was received from the parent customer.

PRACTICE EXERCISE 6.1

Set up a sub-customer for Craig's Design and Landscaping.

(Craig gets a call from the owner of Pye's Cakes. She just opened a new location in California and wants Craig's Design to do some landscaping work in the future. She wants services for the new location billed on separate invoices, but she wants to pay for all services at the same time.)

1. Set up a sub-customer.
   a. Click **Sales** on the navigation bar.
   b. Select the **Customers** tab.
   c. Click **New customer**.
   d. Check the box next to **Is sub-customer**.
   e. Select **Pye's Cakes** in the **Enter parent customer** field.
   f. Select **Bill with parent** in the next dropdown menu.
   g. Enter "Pye's Cakes" in the **Company** field and "West Sac Pye's" in the **Display name as** field.
   h. Uncheck the **Same as billing address** box.
   i. Enter the **shipping address** as "2501 Capital Drive, West Sacramento, CA 95605."
   j. **Make a note** of the zip code in the **Billing address**.
   k. Click **Save**.

Shipping Addresses

Merchandising companies often ship products to locations with addresses different from the customer's billing address. Billing **and** shipping addresses can be maintained in QBO.

Both addresses are entered in the **Customer Information** window.

Figure 6.2

Address tab in customer record

If the billing and shipping addresses are the same, you can check the **Same as billing address** field in the **Shipping address** section of the window. (The shipping address fields will be grayed out if **Same as billing address** is checked.)

Uncheck the **Same as billing address** field to add a shipping address. The shipping address would then be available on sales transaction forms.

> **BEHIND THE SCENES** In the current version of QBO, a single customer can only have one shipping address. If a customer had multiple shipping addresses, sub-customers could be set up.

PRACTICE
EXERCISE
6.2

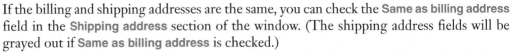

Manage shipping addresses for customers of Craig's Design and Landscaping.
(Craig's Design needs to enter a shipping address for Amy's Bird Sanctuary.)

1. Click **Sales** on the navigation bar.

2. Click the **Customers** tab.

3. Click **Amy's Bird Sanctuary**.

4. Click **Edit**.

5. Uncheck the **Same as billing address** box.

6. Enter the shipping address as:

   2580 Bluebird St.

   Bayshore, CA 94326

7. **Make a note** of the street name for Amy's billing address.

8. Click **Save**.

MANAGING SALES TAXES

Many states levy a tax on purchases of tangible products by consumers (users) of those products. The tax is called a "sales" tax because it is charged to the customer at the point of sale.

Unless a merchandising company is selling to a tax-exempt entity or to a reseller (a company that will, in turn, sell to consumers), the seller is responsible for collecting the tax from their customers and remitting the taxes to the taxing authorities.

The sales tax feature in QBO is highly automated. QBO updates rates and agency information for every sales tax authority as needed and automatically calculates sales taxes on all sales transactions.

Whether or not QBO calculates tax on a **particular** charge depends on the following:

- First, is the customer a consumer, a reseller, or a tax-exempt entity? If the customer is a reseller or tax-exempt entity, no sales tax is added.

    - QBO relies on the information included on the **Tax info** tab in the customer record.

- Second, if the customer is a consumer, does the charge represent a sale of a taxable item? If the item is taxable, sales tax is added to the sales transaction.

    - QBO relies on the information included in the **product** or **service** item record.

In most states, the **amount** of tax, if any, QBO charges on a taxable item is determined by either the company's address (address where sale was made or where the product was shipped from) or the customer's address (address where taxable goods or services were received).

> **BEHIND THE SCENES** Almost all states (currently 45 of them) impose a tax on sales. All sales of taxable products or services to non-exempt customers located in the same state as the company are subject to tax. Determining when a company must collect sales taxes on taxable sales to customers in **other** states can be difficult. The basic rule is this: If the company has a **presence** (called nexus) in the state (people, property, and/or significant sales), the company must collect sales taxes on sales to non-tax-exempt customers in that state. The actual rules about how many people, how much property, or how much in sales dollars is enough to establish nexus (and which products and services are taxable) vary from state to state. QBO users are responsible for knowing the rules.

eLectures

Setting Up Sales Taxes

Overall management of sales taxes is done through the Sales Tax Center.

Click Taxes on the navigation bar to get started. In your homework company, the screen will look something like this:

Let's set you up to collect and track sales tax.
Add sales tax to your invoices and receipts, plus track how much you owe
Set up sales tax

Figure 6.3

Access to sales tax activation screens

> ✳ **HINT:** In the test drive company, you have the option of using either the new or old sales tax feature.
>
>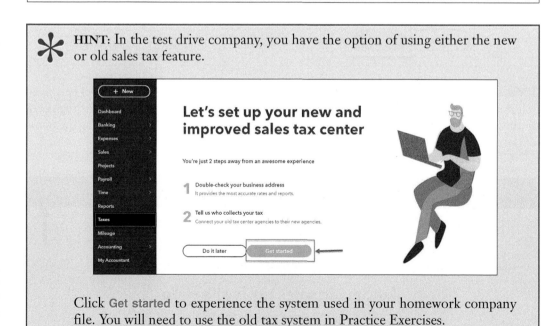
>
> Click Get started to experience the system used in your homework company file. You will need to use the old tax system in Practice Exercises.

Click Set up sales tax.

© 2022 Cambridge Business Publishers

Figure 6.4

Confirmation of company address screen

QBO autofills the address information using information from the **Company** tab in **Account and Settings**. Click the **pencil** icon if the information is incorrect.

Click **Next**.

Figure 6.5

Interstate sales information screen

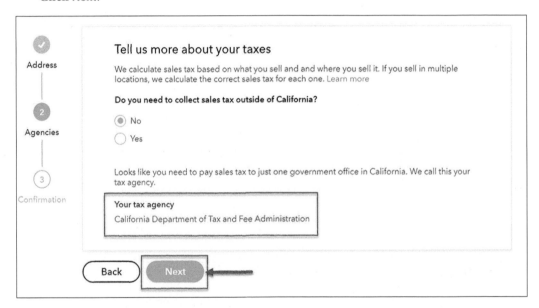

If **Yes** is selected as the answer to the question about out-of-state sales, the user will be able to select additional tax jurisdictions from a list of tax authorities. QBO updates the list regularly. In this course, you will only be selling in California, so select **No**. QBO will display the name of the appropriate sales tax agency based on the company address.

Click **Next**.

Figure 6.6

Successful sales tax activation message

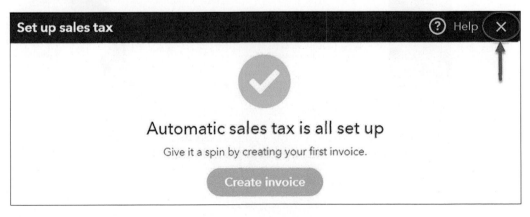

Since you are not entering invoices yet, click the **X** in the top right corner of the screen to escape.

The following screen (or the one in Figure 6.8) should appear. (You may see Figure 6.8 at the same time.)

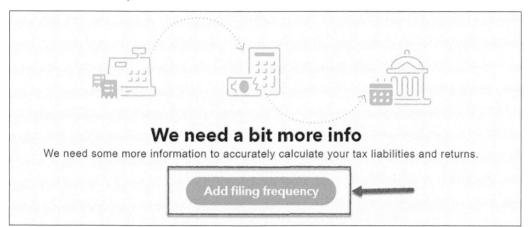

Figure 6.7

Access to sales tax settings

Click **Add filing frequency**.

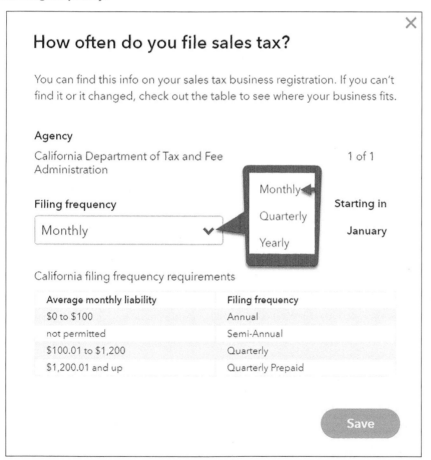

Figure 6.8

Filing frequency options

BEHIND THE SCENES Filing frequencies are set by the state. They are normally based either on the average tax amounts collected or the average sales revenues.

Select **Monthly**.

Figure 6.9

Assignment of default start month for sales tax collection

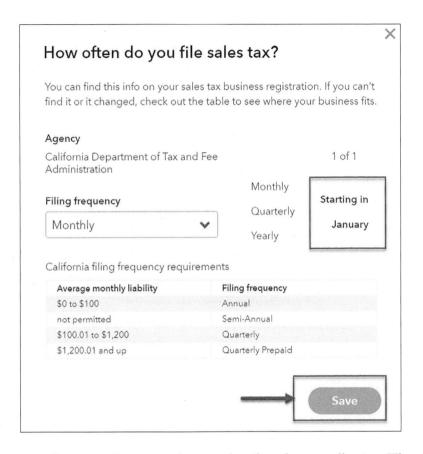

QBO automatically assigns January as the start date for sales tax collection. That date can be changed later. Click **Save** to move to the Sales Tax Center.

Figure 6.10

Access to sales tax settings

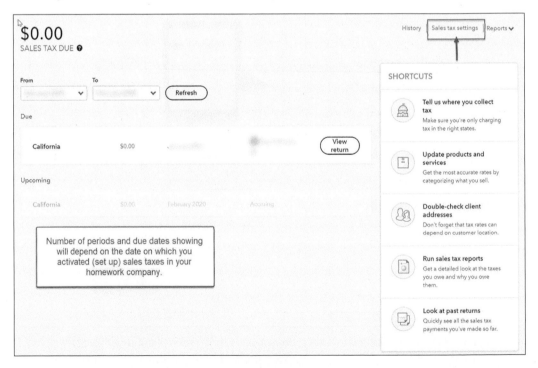

Depending on the date on which you are setting up sales taxes, the next screen may show a number of overdue filings! To correct this, QBO must be updated with the actual start date (the date the company began selling taxable items).

Click **Sales tax settings**.

Figure 6.11

Edit sales tax settings screen

Click **Edit**.

Figure 6.12

Sales tax filing information screen

> **! WARNING:** It's important to enter the correct starting date. QBO will not calculate tax on a sales form dated prior to the date entered here.

Enter the correct date in the sidebar and click **Save**. The correct date for your homework company will be given to you in your assignment.

> **BEHIND THE SCENES** QBO automatically sets up separate liability accounts (**Other current liability account type**) for all taxing authorities. When sales taxes are paid, QBO automatically debits the appropriate liability account. These accounts cannot be deleted.

Managing the Tax Status of Customers

When sales tax is activated in a company file, QBO will assume all new and existing customers are taxable.

Depending on state laws, QBO will either use the company location or the customer location in determining the appropriate tax rate. The shipping address entered in the customer record is considered the customer's physical location. If no shipping address is entered, QBO will use the billing address. If no address is entered in the customer record, QBO will use the **company's** physical address (the rate that would be charged on in-store sales). If necessary, a different sales location can be entered on sales transaction forms.

For nontaxable customers (for example resellers of products) the tax status must be set as tax exempt in the customer record.

Click **Sales** on the navigation bar and open the **Customers** tab.

Figure 6.13

Link to new customer
setup

Click **New customer**.

Figure 6.14

Tax status on customer
record

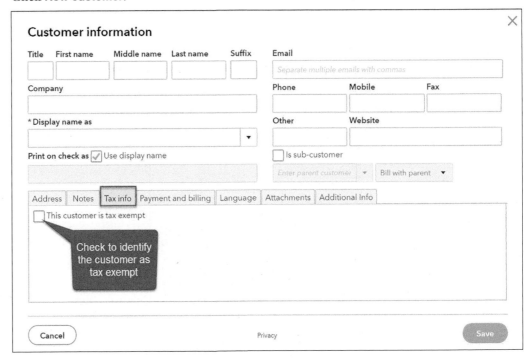

Check the **This customer is tax exempt** box on the **Tax info** tab.

Figure 6.15

Tax exempt status
options

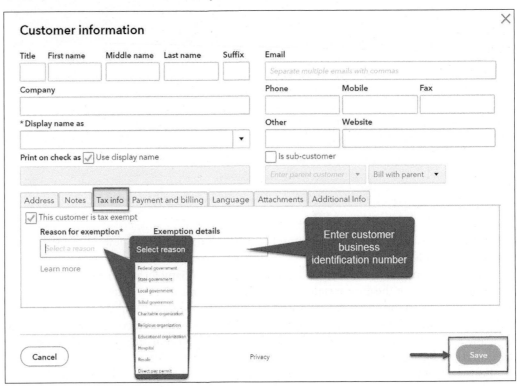

A reason for the tax exemption must be selected in the **Reason for exemption** dropdown menu. The customer's taxpayer identification number is entered in the **Exemption details** field.

> **BEHIND THE SCENES** Individual states set the rules for taxability of organizations and taxability of transactions with those organizations. Users would need to know those state rules in order to select an appropriate reason for not collecting sales tax.

PRACTICE
EXERCISE
6.3

MBC

Set up a tax-exempt customer for Craig's Design and Landscaping.
(Craig's Design wants to set up a new Sacramento customer.)

> NOTE: You will be using the old sales tax system. The steps in this Practice Exercise do not match the information on the prior pages.

1. Set up a new Sacramento customer, a reseller of concrete.

   a. Click **Sales** on the navigation bar.

   b. Click the **Customers** tab.

   c. Click **New Customer**.

   d. In the **Customer Information** window:

      i.   Enter "Sacramento Supplies" in the **company** and **display name as** fields.

      ii. Enter "1122 Main Street, Sacramento CA 95822" on the **Address** tab.

      iii. Uncheck **This customer is taxable** on the **Tax info** tab and enter "91-4444772". **TIP:** In your homework company, you would check **This customer is tax exempt** and would select the reason for the exemption in addition to entering the customer's taxpayer identification number.

   e. Click **Save**.

MANAGING ITEMS (MERCHANDISING COMPANY)

The single biggest difference between service and merchandising companies is, of course, inventory. There are several systems used by merchandising companies to track inventory (**periodic** and **perpetual**) and a number of acceptable methods used to value inventory (**FIFO, LIFO,** etc.).

Merchandising companies can use QBO whether they choose to use periodic or perpetual inventory systems. However, the program is most effectively used as a perpetual tracking system. QBO values inventory using the FIFO method.

A company will need to set up an item for each and every product that it sells. There are two **item types** that can be used for inventory:

- Inventory
  - Used for products that a company sells, maintains in inventory, **and** tracks using a perpetual inventory system.

- Non-inventory
  - Used for products that a company sells, maintains in inventory, but doesn't track.
    - Generally insignificant items.
    - More frequently used by manufacturing companies.
  - Used for products that a company purchases to order and doesn't maintain in inventory.
  - Used in a periodic tracking system.

Periodic inventory A system in which cost of goods sold is determined and recorded when a physical count of inventory is taken.

Perpetual inventory A system in which cost of goods sold is determined and recorded when products are sold.

First-in, first-out (FIFO) method An inventory costing method that assumes that the oldest (earliest purchased) goods are sold first.

Last-in, first-out (LIFO) method An inventory costing method that assumes that the newest (most recently purchased) goods are sold first.

> **BEHIND THE SCENES** There is a third **product/service type** called **Bundle** in QBO. **Bundles** are used when a company sells multiple products or services as a package. **Service**, **inventory**, and **non-inventory** items can be included in a **bundle**. You will not be working with **bundles** in this course.

Setting Up Inventory Items

The process for setting up **inventory** items is similar to the process for setting up **service** items. Click the ⚙ on the icon bar.

Figure 6.16

Link to Products and Services Center

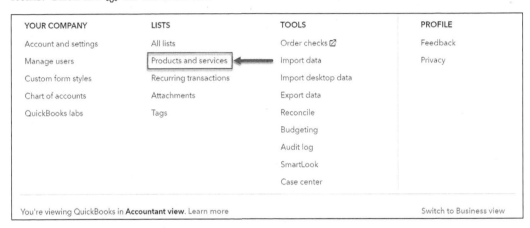

Click **Products and Services**.

Figure 6.17

Link to set up new item

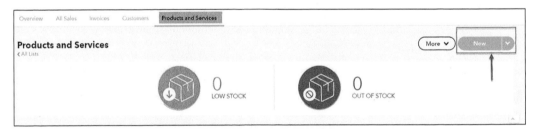

Click **New** to add an **inventory** item.

The initial window for adding items looks something like this:

Figure 6.18

New item sidebar

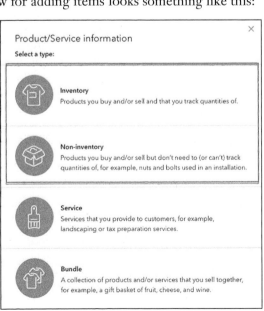

Setting Up Non-inventory Items

Click **Non-inventory**.

When a new item is set up as a **non-inventory** item, the screen initially looks like this:

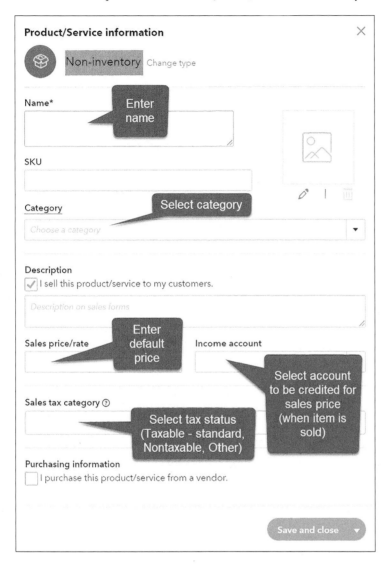

Figure 6.19

Non-inventory setup
screen

A **name** must be assigned. Items can be identified using names or numbers. SKUs (identifier codes) are optional.

Users can elect to attach **products** to a **category**. See Chapter 3 for help with **categories**.

If the **product** is sold to customers (the most likely scenario in service and merchandising companies), additional information is needed.

A check in the box next to **I sell this product/service to my customers** opens the necessary additional fields for entering:

- A description of the item to appear on sales forms

- A default sales price/rate

- The general ledger revenue account to be credited in a sales transaction (debited if a credit memo is issued)

If the sale of a specific **product** or **service** item is **ever** taxable, **Taxable—standard rate** should be selected in the **Sales tax category** field.

If a particular **customer** is nontaxable, the customer tax status will automatically override the item tax status when an **invoice** or **sales receipt** is created. You can also manually override the default item tax status, if needed, when preparing **invoices** or sales **receipts**.

In most merchandising companies, **non-inventory** items are purchased from vendors.

Check the box next to **I purchase this product/service from a vendor** to display additional fields related to purchase transactions.

A default cost and description can be entered when the item is set up. The amount in the **Cost** field will automatically appear when a **product** is added to a purchase transaction. The actual cost, if different, would be entered before saving the transaction.

The account selected in the **Expense account** field will be debited for the purchase price when **non-inventory** items are purchased (and credited if items are returned).

A **preferred vendor** can also be entered in the item record. The benefit of entering a **preferred vendor** will be covered in Chapter 7.

Setting Up Inventory Items

Inventory items are set up by clicking **New** in the **Products and Services** list and selecting **Inventory** as the type.

The screen looks like this:

Figure 6.21

Inventory item setup
screen

The **inventory** item name is entered in the top section along with the **category** (if used). Important, required information is included in the next section.

- **Initial quantity on hand**, required
  - When setting up a new **inventory** item, the **initial quantity on hand must** be set at 0. Inventory purchases are then recorded through **bills**, **checks**, or **expenses**.

> **!** **WARNING: If you do not set the starting quantity at 0, QBO will debit the inventory account for an amount equal to the quantity entered times the default cost listed.**

- **As of date**, required
  - When setting up a new **inventory** item, the **as of date** represents the first date the item would be available for sale. In your homework company, the **as of date** must be a date prior to 2/1/21.

> **BEHIND THE SCENES** When a company is converted to QBO from the desktop version or when inventory data is imported into QBO, the **as of date** would be the conversion date. The **initial quantity on hand** would represent the amount of inventory on hand as of the conversion date.

- **Inventory asset account**
  - The account selected here will be debited when **inventory** items are purchased or when a customer return is recorded. The account will be credited when **inventory** items are sold or when the company returns an item to the vendor. The account selected would be an asset account (**current asset account type**) because **inventory** items are tracked using a perpetual tracking system in QBO.

You can also set a reorder point for **inventory** items. A reorder point indicates the lowest level of inventory the company wants to have on hand at any point in time. Reorder points will be discussed further in Chapter 7.

The next three fields include information used in recording sales transactions.

- The standard (default) description to appear on sales forms is entered in the **Description** field.

- The standard price charged for the item is entered in the **Sales price/rate** field.

- The **revenue** account to be credited when the item is sold (or debited if the customer returns the item) is selected in the **Income account** field.

Taxable—standard rate should be selected in the **Sales tax category** field if the sale of the **inventory** item is **ever** taxable to a customer.

The **Purchasing information** section is identical to the purchasing section for **non-inventory** items. The description used in purchase transactions and the default **cost** is entered. The **Expense account** selected here, however, will be debited for the cost of the **inventory** item when it's sold, not when it's purchased. (The account selected would be credited if a customer return is recorded.)

> **BEHIND THE SCENES** The **Expense account** selected for **inventory** items would normally have a **cost of goods sold account type**. Most merchandising companies prepare multi-step income statements. QBO reports all **cost of goods sold** accounts directly below **income** accounts on the **profit and loss** report and appropriately includes a **gross profit** subtotal so the **account type** is important.
>
> QBO creates the following journal entry when an **inventory** item is purchased:
>
>   Inventory (using the asset account specified in item setup)
>   Accounts payable (or cash)
>
> QBO creates the following journal entry when an **inventory** item is sold:
>
>   Accounts Receivable (or Undeposited Funds if cash sale)
>
>   Cost of goods sold (using the **expense** account specified in **inventory** setup)
>   Revenue (using the **income** account specified in **inventory** setup)
>   Inventory (using the **inventory asset** account specified in **inventory** setup)
>   Sales tax payable (if sale was subject to sales tax)
>
> QBO uses FIFO as the inventory valuation method. The debit to Cost of Goods sold and the credit to Inventory in an **inventory** item sales transaction are at the FIFO cost, not the purchase or default cost.

A **preferred vendor** can also be entered in the inventory item record. The benefit of entering a **preferred vendor** will be covered in Chapter 7.

Click **Save and close** to complete the setup.

Add a new inventory item for Craig's Design and Landscaping.

(Craig's Design has decided to sell small sprinkler systems. It expects to purchase the systems from Glorious Growers for $75 and sell them for $140. The company will be selling the product to consumers.)

1. Click the ⚙ on the icon bar.

2. Click **Products and Services**.

3. Click **New**.

4. Click **Inventory**.

5. Enter "Sprinkler System" as item **name**.

6. Select **Add new** in the **Category** dropdown menu.

7. Enter "Garden products" as the **category name**.

8. Click **Save**.

9. Enter "0" as the **Initial quantity on hand** and the current date as the **As of Date**.

10. Select **Inventory Asset** as the **inventory asset account**, if necessary.

11. Enter "Small sprinkler system" in the **Sales information** field.

12. Enter "140" as **Sales price/rate**.

13. Select **Sales of Product Income** as the **income account**, if necessary.

14. Select **Taxable—standard rate** in the **Sales tax category** field.

15. Enter "Small sprinkler system" in the **Purchasing information** field.

16. Enter "75" as the **cost**.

17. Select **Cost of Goods Sold** as the **Expense account**, if necessary.

18. **Make a note** of the profit Craig's Design will make on each small sprinkler system it sells.

19. Click **Save and close**.

RECORDING SALES REVENUE

Merchandising companies, like service companies, make cash and credit sales. Recording **invoices** and **sales receipts** is covered in Chapter 3. In this chapter, we're going to cover:

- Customer discounts

- Delayed charges and credits

- Uncollectible accounts

None of the above are unique to merchandising companies. The processes outlined below would be used in service companies as well.

Customer Discounts

Companies often give discounts to customers. They might include:

- Price breaks for large orders
- Discounts for nonprofits, senior citizens, students

Customer-specific discounts can be entered directly on sales forms (**Invoices** and **sales receipts**) if the **Discount** feature is activated.

Activating Sales Discounts

Activating sales discounts is a two-step process. You have to turn on the feature and then identify what account to use to capture the discount.

To activate **discounts**, click the ⚙ on the icon bar and click **Account and Settings**.

Figure 6.22

Access to edit sales form content features

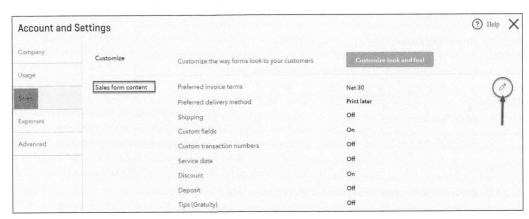

On the **Sales** tab, click the **pencil** icon in the **Sales form content** section.

Figure 6.23

Discount activation box

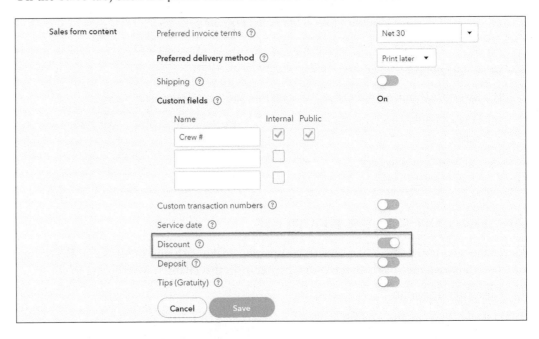

Use the toggle button next to **Discount** to turn the feature on and click **Save**. A discount field will now be available on all sales forms.

Users must then identify the account to be debited for the amount of the discount. This is done on the **Advanced** tab of **Account and Settings**.

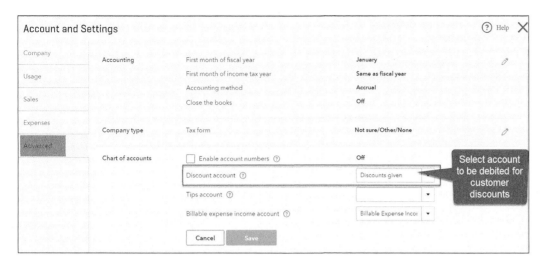

Selection of account for recording customer discounts

Click the **pencil** icon in the **Chart of accounts** section and change the **Discount account** as needed. (QBO uses a default account (**Discounts given**) in the test drive company.)

> **BEHIND THE SCENES** Sales discounts are normally reported as contra revenue accounts. For proper reporting, the account linked to **Discounts** should have an **Income account type**.

Recording Sales Discounts

> ✳ **HINT:** The instructions below use an **invoice** form as an example. The process would be the same for **sales receipts**.

To include a discount on an **invoice**, click ⊕**New** on the navigation bar and select **Invoice**.

Figure 6.25

Discount options

Either a discount percent or amount can be given to a customer. Use the dropdown menu to make the selection. In Figure 6.26, a customer was given a 10% discount. The discount is always calculated on the **Subtotal** amount ($150 in Figure 6.26) so the discount is 10% of $150.

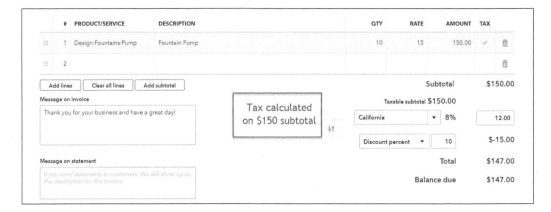

Since the tax rate field appears above the discount field in Figure 6.26, the tax is calculated before any discount. There were no nontaxable items in the Figure 6.26 transaction so the **Taxable subtotal** equals the **Subtotal** ($150) and the sales tax is calculated as 8% of $150.

If the discount should be applied first, click the **arrows** icon next to the discount field.

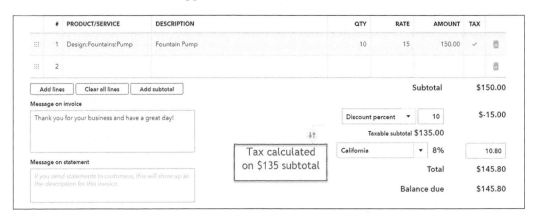

In Figure 6.27, the discount field appears above the tax field, so the discount is subtracted **before** sales tax is calculated. The **Taxable subtotal** is now $135 ($150 less the 10% discount) and the sales tax is 8% of $135.

**PRACTICE
EXERCISE
6.5**

Set up and give sales discounts in Craig's Design and Landscaping.
(Craig's Design has decided to give 10% sales discount on pumps sold to Dukes Basketball Camp.)
NOTE: For this practice exercise, you must use the old sales tax system. If you have activated the newer automated sales tax feature, log out and then log back in.

1. Activate sales discounts. (The feature should already be activated in your test drive company. Go through Steps 1*a* to 1*e* to make sure.)

   a. Click the ⚙ on the icon bar.

   b. Click **Account and Settings**.

   c. Open the **Sales** tab.

   d. Click the **pencil** icon in the **Sales form content** section.

(continued)

(continued from previous page)

    e. **Make a note** of the options available in the **Preferred delivery method** dropdown menu.

    f. Toggle the button next to **Discount** to activate the feature, if necessary.

    g. Click **Save**.

2. Link the discount to a general ledger account.

    a. Click the **Advanced** tab. (You should still be in the **Account and Settings** screen.)

    b. Click the **pencil** icon in the **Chart of accounts** section.

    c. Open the **Discount account** dropdown menu.

    d. Select **Add new**.

    e. Select **Income** as the **Account Type** and **Discounts/Refunds Given** as the **Detail Type**.

    f. Use "Sales Discounts" as the **Name**.

    g. Click **Save and close**.

    h. Click **Save**.

    i. Click **Done**.

3. Create an invoice for Dukes Basketball Camp (40 pumps with a 10% discount applied before tax).

    a. Click **+ New** on the navigation bar.

    b. Click **Invoice**.

    c. Select **Dukes Basketball Camp** as the customer.

    d. Select **Net 30** as the **Terms** and enter the current date as the **Invoice date**.

    e. Select **Pump** as the **PRODUCT/SERVICE** and enter "40" as the **QTY**.

    f. Leave the rate at 15.

    g. Enter "10" in the **Discount percent** field.

    h. **Make a note** of the balance due.

    i. Switch the order of the tax and discount fields so that the discount appears before the tax field.

    j. The balance due should be $583.20.

    k. Click **Save and close**.

Delayed Charges and Delayed Credits

There are times when a company wants to be able to track a sales transaction that is in process but not yet completed. Here are two examples:

- A customer places an order for some products. The order has not yet been shipped.

- A customer requests a credit for damaged or unwanted merchandise but the merchandise has not yet been returned.

Neither of these is an accounting transaction because the accounting equation hasn't changed yet. The customer order won't be an accounting transaction until the product is shipped or delivered. The customer credit won't be an accounting transaction until the company actually receives the damaged merchandise.

The company could, of course, track pending transactions outside of their accounting system but it's most efficient to be able to have information available in the system.

Delayed charges (for pending sales) and **delayed credits** (for pending customer returns or allowances) are options available in QBO for tracking these types of transactions. Both of these are **non-posting** transactions. A **non-posting** transaction does not create a journal entry and with pending transactions, we don't want a journal entry. The information is available in the system but account balances are not affected.

Delayed charge or **delayed credit** forms are accessed by clicking **+ New** on the navigation bar.

Figure 6.28

Access to delayed credit and delayed charge forms

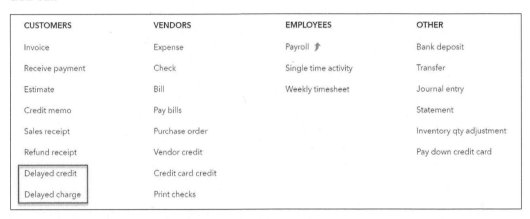

CUSTOMERS	VENDORS	EMPLOYEES	OTHER
Invoice	Expense	Payroll 🔥	Bank deposit
Receive payment	Check	Single time activity	Transfer
Estimate	Bill	Weekly timesheet	Journal entry
Credit memo	Pay bills		Statement
Sales receipt	Purchase order		Inventory qty adjustment
Refund receipt	Vendor credit		Pay down credit card
Delayed credit	Credit card credit		
Delayed charge	Print checks		

Recording and Processing Delayed Charges

When a customer places an order that will not be fulfilled immediately, a **delayed charge** can be created. A **delayed charge** might look something like this:

Figure 6.29

Delayed charge forms

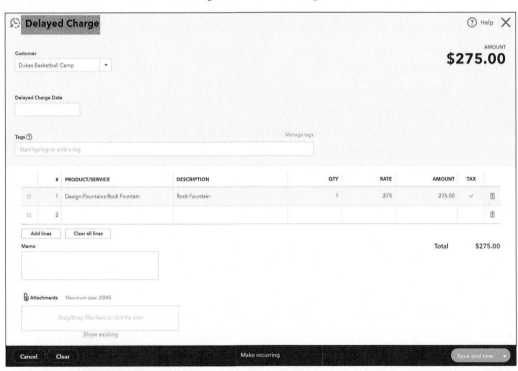

Remember, a **delayed charge** does not create a journal entry so it does not affect account balances. A **delayed charge** would show up as a transaction in the customer record but it would not be included in the customer balance. For example, Figure 6.30 shows the account balance for a customer with a **delayed charge**.

Figure 6.30

Example of customer balance with delayed charge

> **BEHIND THE SCENES** Sales tax and sales discount fields are not available on **delayed charge** forms although estimated taxes, if any, are included in the delayed charge balance showing in the customer record. Both fields are available when the **delayed charge** is converted to an **invoice**.

When the product is shipped or the work completed, the user clicks **Create invoice** to change the **delayed charge** to an **invoice**.

Recording and Processing Delayed Credits

A **delayed credit** is created if a user wants to track a credit that will be available to a customer at some future date. For example, if a company promised a customer a 10% discount on an **invoice** IF the customer provided two referrals within a two-week period, that could be set up as a **delayed credit**. If and when the customer provided the referrals, the credit would be applied.

A **delayed credit** might look something like this:

Figure 6.31

Delayed credit form

Delayed credits, like **delayed charges**, are **non-posting** transactions so account balances are not affected. The balance of a customer with a **delayed credit** would look something like this:

Figure 6.32

Example of customer balance with delayed credit

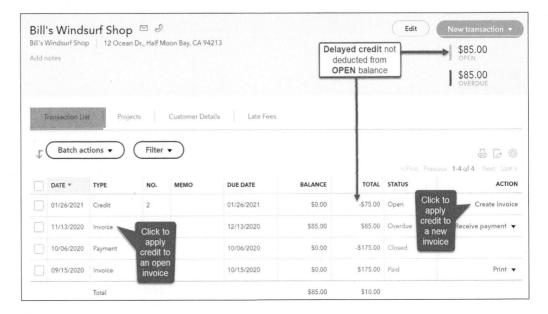

When the event that triggered the credit is completed, the **delayed credit** would be applied to a new or an open **invoice** by the user.

If a **delayed credit** is being applied to an open **invoice**, the unpaid **invoice** form is opened. To display the **delayed credit**, the small < icon in the top right corner of the **invoice** is clicked to open the sidebar. (The < changes to > when the sidebar is open.) It would look something like this:

Figure 6.33

Application of delayed credit to invoice

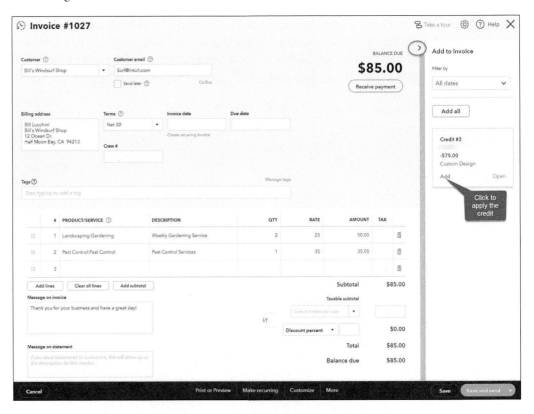

Clicking **Add** applies the credit to the **invoice**. After application, the **invoice** would look something like this:

Figure 6.34

Invoice with delayed credit added

Managing Non-posting Transactions

Non-posting transactions can be deleted by opening the form, clicking **More** at the bottom of the screen, and selecting **Delete**.

For a list of all **delayed credit** and **delayed charge** transactions, click **Reports** on the navigation bar.

Select **Transaction List by Date** in the **For My Accountant** section.

Click **Customize** and open the **Filter** section.

Put a checkmark by **Transaction Type** and select **non-posting**.

Click **Run report**.

Set up a delayed charge for Craig's Design and Landscaping.

(Craig's Design has agreed to a fee of $400 for some gardening work to be done next month and wants to get the invoice set up in QBO. The work will be invoiced when the work is performed.)

1. Create the **delayed charge**.

    a. Click **➕ New** on the navigation bar.

    b. Click **Delayed Charge**.

    c. Click **Wedding Planning by Whitney** as the **Customer**.

    d. Enter the current date as the **Invoice date**.

    e. Select **Trimming** as the **PRODUCT/SERVICE**.

(continued)

PRACTICE

EXERCISE

6.6

Homework

MBC

(continued from previous page)

    f.   Enter "12" as the **QTY**.

    g. **Make a note** of the **Total** amount.

    h. Click **Save and close**.

2. Create the **invoice** from the **delayed charge**.

    a. Click **Sales** on the navigation bar.

    b. Click the **Customers** tab.

    c. In the dropdown menu in the **ACTION** column for Wedding Planning by Whitney, click **Create Invoice**.

    d. Click **Add** in the **Charge** box in the sidebar.

    e. Leave the terms as **Net 30**.

    f. Enter the 1st day of next month as the **Invoice date**.

    g. Click **Save and close**.

Bad debt expense The expense stemming from the inability of a business to collect an amount previously recorded as receivable. It is normally classified as a selling or administrative expense.

Allowance method An accounting procedure whereby the amount of bad debts expense is estimated and recorded in the period in which the related credit sales occur.

Direct write-off method An accounting procedure whereby the amount of bad debts expense is not recorded until specific uncollectible customer accounts are identified.

Recording Uncollectible Accounts

Unfortunately, companies don't always collect the balances owed to them by their customers. Merchandisers will often try to get the product back when the customer defaults but, depending on the type and value of the products sold, that may not be feasible or even possible.

If the company has exhausted all reasonable collection methods, the invoice must be written off. Deleting or voiding the invoice in QBO would not be good accounting. The company did make the sale and should show the revenue. They should also report that uncollectible sales (recorded as **bad debt expenses**) are a real cost of selling on credit.

There are two methods for accounting for uncollectible accounts: the **allowance method** and the **direct write-off method**. Only the allowance method is acceptable under generally accepted accounting principles.

Allowance Method Refresher

Under the allowance method, an estimate of the amount of uncollectible receivables is made at the end of an accounting period. The initial entry to establish an allowance for those amounts is:

	Bad debt expense		
	Allowance for bad debts		

> **BEHIND THE SCENES** The allowance account is a contra asset account (contra to accounts receivable). Accounts receivable net of the allowance is referred to as the net realizable value of receivables (amount that the company actually expects to collect or "realize").

When a **specific** customer account is determined to be uncollectible, the account is written off. The entry is:

	Allowance for bad debts		
	Accounts receivable		

If a previously written off amount is subsequently received, the entry is:

	Cash		
	Allowance for bad debts		

At the end of each accounting period, the allowance account is adjusted to reflect the amount that is currently considered uncollectible. For example, if the end-of-period balance in the allowance account is estimated to be too low, the entry is:

	Bad debt expense		
	Allowance for bad debts		

Direct Write-off Method Refresher

Companies that historically do not have many uncollectible accounts often use the direct write-off method. Under this method, bad debt expense is only recognized when a specific customer account is determined to be uncollectible. This method violates generally accepted accounting principles but is sometimes used when the amount of bad debts is insignificant.

The entry is:

	Bad debt expense		
	Accounts receivable		

Which accounting principle is violated under the direct write-off method?

QuickCheck
6-1

Recording Bad Debts

Either the allowance or the direct write-off method can be used in QBO.

 HINT: There are several ways uncollectible accounts can be written off in QBO. The method described below uses **service** items to record write-offs and recoveries. Journal entries can also be used. However, using **service** items allows users to easily apply write-offs to specific invoices.

If the allowance method is used, the entry to set up or adjust the allowance account should be made as a general journal entry (**Journal entry transaction type**). See Chapter 5 if you need help with making adjusting journal entries.

The actual write-off of an invoice (under either the allowance or direct write-off method) can be done by creating a **credit memo** recognizing the bad debt and then applying the **credit memo** to the uncollectible **invoice**.

The first step is to set up the necessary accounts. Under either method, a Bad Debt Expense account is necessary. Under the allowance method, an Allowance for Bad Debts account is also necessary. Remember, the Allowance account is a contra asset account.

Click the ⚙ on the icon bar and select **Chart of Accounts**. Click **New** to add accounts.

- For the bad debt expense account, the **account type** would be **Expenses** and the **detail type** would be **Bad Debts**.

- For the Allowance account, the **account type** would be **Other Current Assets** and the **detail type** would be **Allowance for Bad Debts**.

The second step is to set up a new **service** item.

Click the ⚙ on the icon bar and select **Products and Services**.

Click **New** and select **Service**. (A **service** item is normally selected for any non-product related fee or charge.)

The item might be set up something like this if the company uses the direct write-off method of recording uncollectible accounts:

Figure 6.35

Bad debt write-off
setup screen

If the allowance method is used, the account selected in the **Income account** field should be Allowance for Doubtful Accounts. Bad debt expense would be the account selected if the direct method is used.

> **BEHIND THE SCENES** It might seem counterintuitive to select an asset or expense account in the **income** field of the **service** item setup. QBO automatically credits the account selected here when an **invoice** or **sales receipt** is created. QBO automatically debits the account selected here when a **credit memo** is created. Because write-offs are entered through **credit memos**, you're identifying the account to be debited when the **credit memo** is prepared. For uncollectible accounts, the debit account should be either bad debt expense or the allowance account, depending on the method used.

Whether sales tax should be recorded on the credit memo depends on the sale items included on the **invoice** being credited. That tax status, of course, is not known when the item is set up. It's most efficient, then, to select the most likely status. That can always be changed when the **credit memo** is created. If the sale items **were** taxable and sales tax was included on the **credit memo**, the sales tax liability account would be debited appropriately.

Once the **service** item is created and the appropriate general ledger accounts are set up, the user creates a **credit memo** to record the write-off. The **credit memo** is then applied to the uncollectible **invoice**. (The application is automatic if the **automation** feature is turned on in **Account and Settings**. The **credit memo** must be manually applied if **automation** is turned off.)

The process is demonstrated in the next practice exercise.

Record an uncollectible account at Craig's Design and Landscaping.

(Jeff's Jalopies has gone bankrupt. There is an $81 balance due on his account. The original charge was for taxable services. Craig's Design and Landscaping has very few uncollectible accounts and has elected to use the direct write-off method to account for bad debts.)

1. Set up the appropriate account.

   a. Click the ⚙ on the icon bar.

   b. Click **Chart of Accounts**.

   c. Click **See your Chart of Accounts**, if necessary.

   d. Click **New**.

   e. Select **Expenses** as the **account type** and **Bad Debts** as the **detail type**.

   f. Enter "Bad Debt Expense" as the **name**.

   g. Click **Save and close**.

2. Set up the new **service** item.

   a. Click the ⚙ on the icon bar.

   b. Click **Products and Services**.

   c. Click **New**.

   d. Select **Service**.

   e. Enter "Write off" as the **name**.

   f. Select **Add new** in the **Category** dropdown menu.

      i. Enter "Other Charges" as the **Name** and click **Save**. **Note:** If the add new category form does not appear then exit out of this setup and add this category in the **Product Categories** list. Return here to step 2 to set up your new service.

   g. Enter "Write off of uncollectible account" in the **description** field.

   h. Select **Bad Debt Expense** as the **Income Account**.

   i. Select **Taxable—Standard rate** in the **Sales tax category** dropdown menu. (We'll assume that most of Craig's revenue is subject to tax.)

   j. Click **Save and close**.

3. Change an automation setting.

   a. Click the ⚙ icon.

   b. Click **Account and Settings**.

   c. Click the **Advanced** tab.

   d. Click the **pencil** icon in the **Automation** section.

   e. Toggle the button next to **Automatically apply credits** to turn the feature off.

   f. Click **Save**.

   g. Click **Done**.

4. Create a credit memo.

   a. Click **+ New** on the navigation bar.

   b. Select **Credit Memo**.

   c. Select **Jeff's Jalopies** as the **name**.

   d. Use the current date.

(continued)

(continued from previous page)

    e.   Select **Write off** as the **PRODUCT/SERVICE** and enter "75" as the amount.

    f.   Select **California** in the **Select a sales tax rate** dropdown menu.

    g.   Click **Save and close**.

5. Apply the credit memo.

    a.   Click **Sales** on the navigation bar.

    b.   Click the **Customers** tab.

    c.   Click **Jeff's Jalopies**.

    d.   In the **ACTION** column for Invoice 1022, select **Receive payment**.

    e.   Check the box next to Invoice 1022 and the box next to the credit memo.

    f.   The **Amount received** should show as 0.00. The **Amount to apply** should show as $81.00.

    g.   Click **Save and close**.

RECORDING PAYMENTS FROM CUSTOMERS

Chapter 3 outlines the process for recording cash (or check) payments from customers. This chapter covers:

- Customer payments by credit card

- Customer checks returned by the bank due to insufficient funds (NSF checks)

- Early payment discounts

Customer Payments by Credit Card

Most retail stores accept credit cards as a form of payment. Credit card payments are considered **almost** the equivalent of cash. "Almost" because:

- The company pays a fee to the financial institution processing credit card receipts for the company (commonly called the merchant bank) on all credit card receipts.

- The merchant bank generally makes the deposits directly to the merchandiser's account (net of any fees) within a few days, in batches that correspond to the credit card type (VISA, MasterCard, etc.).

Credit card payments can be received at the time of sale or as payment on an account balance.

 HINT: Users can purchase a credit card processing service through QBO. Credit card receipts are processed automatically when entered. The processes described below assume that the company does **not** have that service.

Recording Receipt of Customer Credit Card Payment

Most companies receive credit card receipts from the merchant bank within a few days so sales paid by credit card, at point of sale, are normally recorded as **Sales Receipts** (cash sales). The type of credit card used (VISA, MasterCard, etc.) is selected as the payment method.

    When customers use credit cards to pay account balances, the payment is recorded through the **Receive Payment** window (similar to payments of account balances by cash or check). The type of credit card used (VISA, MasterCard, etc.) is selected as the payment method.

Record customer credit card transactions for Craig's Design and Landscaping.
(The merchant bank is America's Bank. The transaction fee is 3% of credit card receipts.)

1. Record cash sale using a credit card. (Cool Cars pays $108 to purchase some garden lights.)

   a. Click **+ New** on the navigation bar.

   b. Click **Sales Receipt**.

   c. Select **Cool Cars** as the customer.

   d. Use the current date.

   e. Select **Visa** as the **Payment method**.

   f. Make sure Undeposited Funds appears in the **Deposit to** field.

   g. Select **Lighting** as the **Product/Service**.

   h. Enter a **QTY** of "5" and a **RATE** of "20."

   i. Select **California** in the **Select a sales tax rate** dropdown menu.

   j. **Make a note** of the tax rate for California.

   k. Click **Save and close**.

2. Record customer payment of an account balance with a credit card. (Mark Cho pays his $314.28 invoice balance with a credit card.)

   a. Click **+ New** on the navigation bar.

   b. Click **Receive Payments**.

   c. Select **Mark Cho** as the customer.

   d. Use the current date.

   e. Select **Visa** as the **Payment method**.

   f. Make sure Undeposited Funds appears in the **Deposit to** field.

   g. Enter "314.28" as the **Amount received**.

   h. Click **Save and close**.

 WARNING: The next practice exercise uses the transactions just entered. You'll save yourself some time if you continue through to the next exercise.

"Depositing" Credit Card Receipts

As you learned in Chapter 3, unless the default preference is changed, QBO debits **Undeposited Funds** for all payments received from customers through **Sales Receipt** or **Payment** forms. The receipts are transferred, in batches that correspond to the actual deposit amounts, from the **Undeposited Funds** account to the cash account through the **Bank Deposit** form.

The same considerations must be made for credit card receipts. The merchant bank makes deposits to the merchandiser's bank account in batches (grouped by credit card type), net of any transaction fees charged. The deposit in QBO for credit card receipts should be made in corresponding batches, net of the fees. Checks and cash receipts should not be included on the same deposit form in QBO as credit card receipts because they would show as separate transactions on bank statements.

Recording a deposit of credit card receipts is done using the **Bank Deposit** form accessed by clicking **+ New** on the navigation bar.

The user should mark (check) all receipts of the same credit card type for deposit.

Credit card fees are entered in the **Add funds to this deposit** section. To record the fee, the merchant bank is entered in the **RECEIVED FROM** field. The account used to record merchant bank fees should be selected in the **ACCOUNT** field. The fee is entered as a negative number in the **AMOUNT** field.

The screen would look something like this:

Figure 6.36

Example of deposit of credit card receipts

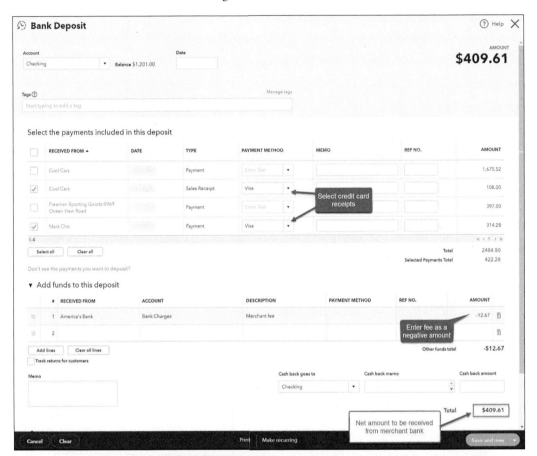

BEHIND THE SCENES Remember, the default journal entry underlying a deposit transaction includes a debit to the Bank account indicated for the total deposit amount and a credit to the Account(s) indicated on the deposit form. Credit card processing fees are expenses. Entering the amount as a negative tells QBO to debit, not credit, the **ACCOUNT** for the merchant fees.

HINT: QBO has a built-in calculator feature that can be useful here. The feature is activated by entering a number and then a mathematical operator (+, −, *, or /). Ignore the **This value is out of range** warning that appears when you enter the operator. The message will disappear when you enter the next number.

If the transaction fee amount is not known when the deposit is initially recorded in QBO, the deposit form can be edited later (fees added) so that the net amount agrees to the amount actually received from the merchant bank.

Merchant fees can also be entered as **journal entries**.

Make a deposit of credit card receipts for Craig's Design and Landscaping.
(Craig's Design processes its VISA credit card receipts.)

PRACTICE
EXERCISE
6.9

 WARNING: This practice exercise uses transactions entered in the last exercise. If you logged out or timed out after the last practice exercise, you'll need to complete that exercise again before moving forward.

1. Click **+ New** on the navigation bar.

2. Click **Bank Deposit**.

3. Select **Checking** as the bank account, if necessary.

4. Use the current date.

5. Check all VISA transactions displayed in the **Select Existing Payments** section.

   a. **Selected Payments Total** should be $422.28.

6. Enter the credit card fees in the **Add funds to this deposit** section.

   a. Enter "America's Bank" as a vendor in the **RECEIVED FROM** field.

      i. Add without additional detail.

   b. Select **Bank Charges** as the **ACCOUNT**.

   c. Enter "Credit card fees" in the **DESCRIPTION** field.

   d. Enter the 3% transaction fee ($12.67) as a negative in the **AMOUNT** field.

7. **Total** should be $409.61.

8. Click **Save and close**.

Early Payment Discounts

Companies often give customers discounts if credit sales are paid before the due date. Any available early payment discounts are included as part of the credit terms listed on the invoice.

Examples of credit terms with early payment discounts include:

- 2/10, Net 30

  - Discount of 2% of the invoice total if paid within 10 days of the due date. Balance is due in full 30 days from the invoice date.

- 1/15, Net 45

  - Discount of 1% of the invoice total if paid within 15 days of the due date. Balance is due in full 45 days from the invoice date.

In QBO, all credit terms used by the company (for customers OR vendors) are included in the **Terms** lists accessed by clicking the ⚙ on the icon bar and selecting **All Lists**. Setting up **terms** was covered in Chapter 3.

The credit terms granted to a **specific** customer are entered on the **Payment and billing** tab of the customer record. These credit terms are automatically included on invoices prepared for the customer. They can be changed on a specific invoice if necessary.

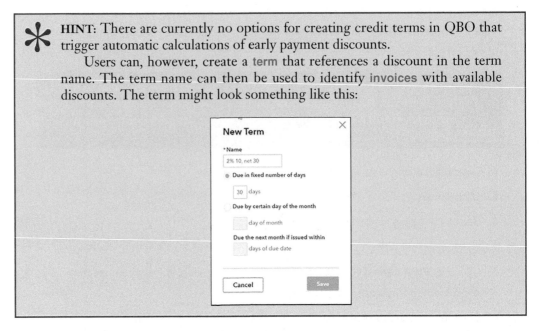

> **HINT:** There are currently no options for creating credit terms in QBO that trigger automatic calculations of early payment discounts.
>   Users can, however, create a **term** that references a discount in the term name. The term name can then be used to identify **invoices** with available discounts. The term might look something like this:

To record an early payment discount taken by a customer, a **credit memo** for the amount of the discount taken by the customer is created and applied when the customer's payment is recorded.

> **BEHIND THE SCENES** Because early payment discounts should not be recognized until the customer actually takes the discount, the user would not enter the discount that **might** be taken on the original invoice.
>   A user could possibly edit the original invoice when the payment is received. However, this would not be an acceptable choice if the original invoice was recognized in a prior period. (Editing the invoice would automatically change the prior period's financial statements.)

The first step is to create a new **service** item.

Click the ⚙ on the icon bar and select **Products and Services**. Click **New** and select **Service**.

The early payment discount item might be set up something like this:

Figure 6.37

Setup of early payment discount item

When a customer takes an early payment discount, the **credit memo** should be created for the discount amount before the payment is recorded. (This assumes the user is applying credit memos manually. If the **automation** feature is turned on, it shouldn't matter which step is done first.) Refer back to Chapter 3 for help with applying credits to customer **invoices**.

The credit memo is then applied to the **invoice** when the payment is recorded.

BEHIND THE SCENES States vary in how early payment discounts are treated for sales tax purposes. Many states allow taxpayers to deduct the amount of any early payment discounts taken on taxable sales when reporting revenues. The adjustment would normally be made when sales taxes are remitted.

Record an early payment discount taken by a customer of Craig's Design and Landscaping.

(Geeta Kalapatapu took a 2% early payment discount ($12.58) when she paid Invoice #1033 ($629.10).)

1. Turn off the **automation** feature to allow for manual application of credit memos.
   a. Click the ⚙ on the icon bar.
   b. Click **Account and Settings** screen.
   c. Click the **Advanced** tab.
   d. Click the **pencil** icon in the **Automation** section.
   e. Toggle the button next to **Automatically apply credits** to deactivate the feature.
   f. Click **Save**.
   g. Click **Done**.

2. Set up a **service** item for early payment discounts.
   a. Click the ⚙ on the icon bar.
   b. Select **Products and Services**.
   c. Click **New**.
   d. Select **Service**.
   e. Enter "Early Payment Discount" as the **Name**.
   f. Select **Add new** in the **Category** dropdown menu.
   g. Enter "Other Charges" as the **Name**. **Note:** If the add new category form does not appear then exit out of this setup and add this category in the **Product Categories** list. Return here to step 2 to set up your new service.
   h. Click **Save**.
   i. Enter "Early payment discount" as the **Description**.
   j. Select **Discounts given** as the **Income account**. **TIP:** If you haven't logged out since Practice Exercise 6.7, the account name will be Sales Discounts.
   k. Select **Nontaxable** in the **Sales tax category** dropdown menu.
   l. Click **Save and close**.

3. Create a **credit memo** for Geeta Kalapatapu in the amount of $12.58 for the early payment discount taken on Invoice 1033.
   a. Click **+ New** on the navigation bar.
   b. Select **Credit Memo**.
   c. Select **Geeta Kalapatapu** as the customer.
   d. Use the current date.

(continued)

PRACTICE
EXERCISE
6.10

(continued from previous page)

  e. Select **Early Payment Discount** as the **PRODUCT/SERVICE**.

  f. Enter "12.58" in the **AMOUNT** field.

  g. Click **Save and close**.

4. Record Geeta's check for $616.52.

  a. Click **+ New** on the navigation bar.

  b. Select **Receive Payment**.

  c. Select **Geeta Kalapatapu** as the customer.

  d. Use the current date as the **Payment date**.

  e. Enter "Check" as the **Payment method** and "10987" as the **Reference no.**

  f. Place checkmarks in the boxes next to **Invoice 1033** and the **credit memo** you created in Step 3.

  g. The **Amount received** should show as $616.52. Enter the amount if necessary.

  h. Make sure the **PAYMENT** fields show as 629.10 for the **invoice** and 12.58 for the **credit memo**.

  i. Click **Save and close**.

Customer Checks Returned by Bank Due to Insufficient Funds (NSF Checks)

Every company that accepts checks from customers accepts a risk that the customer does not have sufficient funds in the bank to cover the check.

When customer checks are returned NSF (non-sufficient funds), the companies will normally either:

- Attempt to redeposit the check OR
- Write off the invoice as a bad debt OR
- Re-invoice the customer (for the amount of the check plus processing fees).

Regardless of the choice made, an NSF check must be recorded in the accounting records along with any fees associated with the NSF check.

Remember, when the customer check was originally recorded in QBO, the entry was:

Undeposited Funds		
Accounts receivable (or income)		

When the check was deposited, the amount was transferred from Undeposited Funds to the Cash account.

Cash		
Undeposited Funds		

Cash is now overstated by the amount of the NSF check. The entry underlying the invoice created will need to reduce (credit) the Cash account, not an income account.

> **BEHIND THE SCENES** The process for handling NSF checks described below assumes that the company will attempt to collect the full amount. A new invoice is created for the amount of the NSF check and any processing fees the company might decide to charge the customer. If the company later decides that the amount is uncollectible, the following procedures should still be followed so that there is a record of the NSF check associated with the customer. The new invoice should then be written off as described earlier in the **Recording Uncollectible Accounts** section of this chapter.

Recording a Customer NSF (Bounced) Check and Associated Fees

The most efficient process in QBO is to set up two new **service** items that can be used to record an **invoice** charging the customer for the bounced check amount and any fees.

- **Bounced Check Amount**—used to invoice the customer for the check amount. The appropriate bank account would be selected as the income account associated with this item.

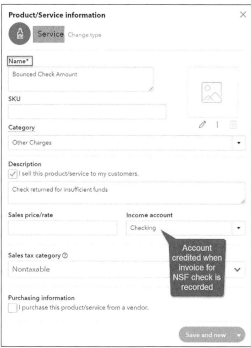

Figure 6.38

Setup of bounced check item

- **Processing Fee**—used to invoice the customer for any processing fees charged by the company. Most companies would select the Bank Service Charges expense account as the associated **income** account for this item to offset the fee charged to them by their bank.

Figure 6.39

Setup of processing fee item

BEHIND THE SCENES The underlying entry for the new **invoice** would then be:

	Accounts Receivable		
	Checking		
	Bank Service Charges		

The credit to cash offsets the original deposit amount—the amount that didn't clear the bank. The credit to Bank Service Charges offsets any fees charged by the company's bank. Fees charged by the bank would normally be entered through the bank reconciliation process or by journal entry.

**PRACTICE
EXERCISE
6.11**

Record a bounced check and related fees for Craig's Design and Landscaping.
(The check received from Travis Waldron for $81 was returned marked NSF. Craig's Design charges its customers $25 for processing bounced checks. Craig's Design intends to pursue collection of the $81.)

1. Set up the new **service** items.
   a. Click the ⚙ on the icon bar.
   b. Click **Products and Services**.
   c. Click **New**.
   d. Select **Service**.
   e. Enter "Bounced Check" as the **name**.
   f. Select **Other Charges** as the **category**.
      i. Set up the **Other Charges category** if needed. **Note:** If the add new category form does not appear then exit out of this setup and add this category in the **Product Categories** list. Return here to step 1 to set up your new service.
   g. Enter "Check returned for insufficient funds" in the **sales information** field.
   h. Select **Checking** as the **Income Account**.
   i. Select **Nontaxable** in the **Sales tax category** dropdown menu.
   j. Click **Save and new**.
   k. Enter "Processing Fee" as the **name**.
   l. Select **Other Charges** as the **category**.
   m. Enter "Fee for processing NSF check" in the **sales information** field.
   n. Select **Bank Charges** as the **Income Account**.
   o. Select **Nontaxable** in the **Sales tax category** dropdown menu.
   p. Click **Save and close**.

2. Create an **invoice**.
   a. Click **+New** on the navigation bar.
   b. Select **Invoice**.
   c. Select **Travis Waldron** as the **name**.
   d. Use the current date.
   e. Select **Bounced Check** as the **PRODUCT/SERVICE** and enter "81" as the **AMOUNT**.
   f. On the next line, select **Processing fee** as the **PRODUCT/SERVICE** and enter "25" as the **AMOUNT**.
   g. The **Balance due** should show as $106.
   h. Click **Save and close**.

CUSTOMER REPORTS

The sales and receivables reports in QBO used by merchandising companies are generally the same as those used by service companies (introduced in Chapter 3). However, the **Sales by Product/Service Summary** report used by a merchandising company would normally include cost of goods sold and gross margin (gross profit) fields for **inventory** items. A report of inventory item sales (included in the **Sales and Customers** section of **Reports** and customized to include **inventory** items only) would look something like this:

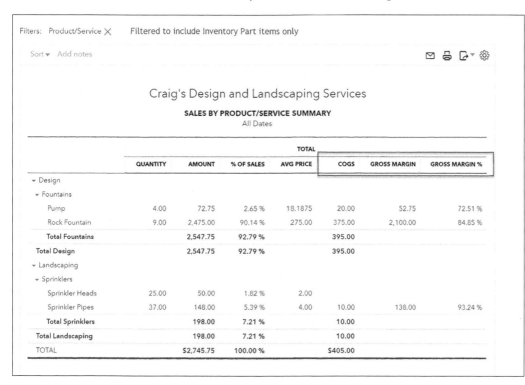

Figure 6.40

Report of sales of inventory items

Filters: Product/Service ✕   Filtered to include Inventory Part items only

Craig's Design and Landscaping Services

SALES BY PRODUCT/SERVICE SUMMARY
All Dates

	QUANTITY	AMOUNT	% OF SALES	TOTAL AVG PRICE	COGS	GROSS MARGIN	GROSS MARGIN %
▾ Design							
▾ Fountains							
Pump	4.00	72.75	2.65 %	18.1875	20.00	52.75	72.51 %
Rock Fountain	9.00	2,475.00	90.14 %	275.00	375.00	2,100.00	84.85 %
Total Fountains		2,547.75	92.79 %		395.00		
Total Design		2,547.75	92.79 %		395.00		
▾ Landscaping							
▾ Sprinklers							
Sprinkler Heads	25.00	50.00	1.82 %	2.00			
Sprinkler Pipes	37.00	148.00	5.39 %	4.00	10.00	138.00	93.24 %
Total Sprinklers		198.00	7.21 %		10.00		
Total Landscaping		198.00	7.21 %		10.00		
TOTAL		$2,745.75	100.00 %		$405.00		

 HINT: To recreate the report in Figure 6.40, click **Customize** on the **Sales by Product/Service Summary** report screen.

In the **General** section of the sidebar, select **All Dates** as the **Report period**.

Open the **Filter** section and check box next to **Product/Service**. Select **Pump, Rock Fountain, Sprinkler Heads**, and **Sprinkler Pipes** in the dropdown menu.

Click **Run report**.

One useful report that we haven't looked at yet is the **Collections Report**. The default report, available in the **Who Owes You** section of **Reports**, includes only those invoices that are at least one day past due. (The minimum number of days past due can be changed in the **Customize** sidebar.) The customer's phone number is included which comes in handy when making collection calls to tardy customers!

The report, customized to remove invoice and due dates, looks something like this:

Craig's Design and Landscaping Services

Collections Report

As of

TRANSACTION TYPE	NUM	PAST DUE	AMOUNT	OPEN BALANCE
▾ Amy's Bird Sanctuary (650) 555-3311				
Invoice	1021	18	459.00	239.00
Total for Amy's Bird Sanctuary			**$459.00**	**$239.00**
▾ Bill's Windsurf Shop (415) 444-6538				
Invoice	1027	44	85.00	85.00
Total for Bill's Windsurf Shop			**$85.00**	**$85.00**
▾ Freeman Sporting Goods:55 Twin Lane (650) 555-0987				
Invoice	1028	44	81.00	81.00
Invoice	1005	5	54.00	4.00
Total for Freeman Sporting Goods:55 Twin Lane			**$135.00**	**$85.00**
▾ Jeff's Jalopies (650) 555-8989				
Invoice	1022	18	81.00	81.00
Total for Jeff's Jalopies			**$81.00**	**$81.00**
▾ John Melton (650) 555-5879				
Invoice	1007	21	750.00	450.00
Total for John Melton			**$750.00**	**$450.00**
▾ Kookies by Kathy (650) 555-7896				
Invoice	1016	45	75.00	75.00
Total for Kookies by Kathy			**$75.00**	**$75.00**
▾ Red Rock Diner (650) 555-4973				
Invoice	1024	65	156.00	156.00
Total for Red Rock Diner			**$156.00**	**$156.00**
▾ Shara Barnett:Barnett Design (650) 557-1289				
Invoice	1012	10	274.50	274.50
Total for Shara Barnett:Barnett Design			**$274.50**	**$274.50**
▾ Sushi by Katsuyuki (505) 570-0147				
Invoice	1018	5	80.00	80.00
Total for Sushi by Katsuyuki			**$80.00**	**$80.00**
TOTAL			**$2,095.50**	**$1,525.50**

Prepare various sales and receivable reports for Craig's Design and Landscaping.
(Craig asks for information about sales over the last two months. He also wants to see which customers have unpaid balances.)

1. Click **Reports** on the navigation bar.

2. Click **Sales by Product/Service Summary** in the **Sales and Customers** section.

   a. Select **All Dates** in the **Report period** dropdown menu.

   b. Click **Run report**.

   c. **Make a note** of the **AVG PRICE** amount for **Concrete**.

   d. Click **Customize**.

(continued)

(continued from previous page)

    e. Open the **Filter** section.

    f. Check the box next to **Product/Service** and select **Pump** and **Rock Fountain**.

    g. Click **Run report**.

    h. Click **Back to report list**.

3. Click **Collections Report** in the **Who owes you** section.

    a. Select **All Dates** in the **Report period** dropdown menu.

    b. Click **Customize**.

    c. Open the **Filter** section.

    d. Check the box next to **Customer**.

    e. In the **Customer** dropdown menu, select Sushi by Katsuyuki and all Freeman Sporting Goods customers.

    f. Click **Run report**.

    g. **Make a note** of the **OPEN BALANCE** total.

4. Click **Dashboard** to close the window.

Customer Statements

Companies will often send statements to customers on a monthly basis. Statements, for the most part, are simply summaries of activity over some period of time. They generally include a beginning balance, a list of all invoices and payments during the period, and an ending balance. Statements can be an effective way of communicating with customers.

For internal control purposes, most companies will not pay from a statement. (Companies choose to only pay from original invoices to avoid the risk of making duplicate payments.) For that reason, statements rarely include new charges (amounts not previously billed using an invoice). The most common exception would be finance charges assessed on past-due balances.

Statements can be prepared in QBO and are easily accessed by clicking **+ New** on the navigation bar and selecting **Statement** in the **Other** column.

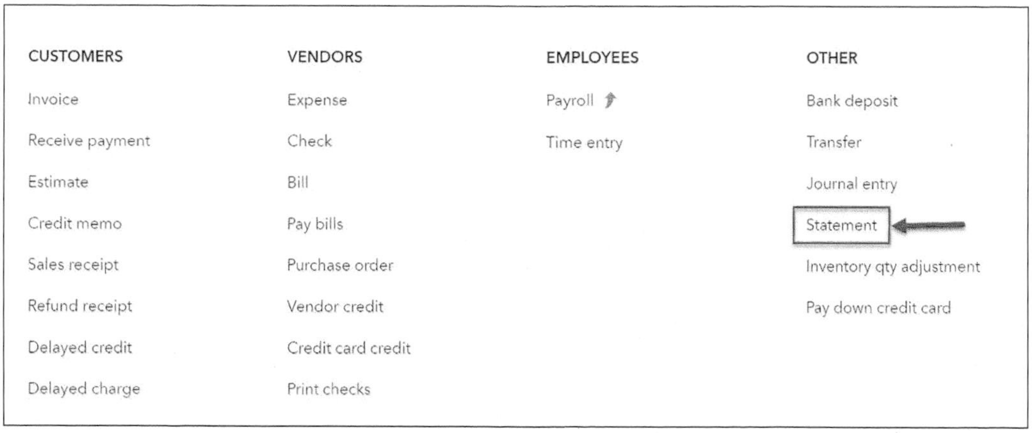

CUSTOMERS	VENDORS	EMPLOYEES	OTHER
Invoice	Expense	Payroll 🔒	Bank deposit
Receive payment	Check	Time entry	Transfer
Estimate	Bill		Journal entry
Credit memo	Pay bills		Statement ←
Sales receipt	Purchase order		Inventory qty adjustment
Refund receipt	Vendor credit		Pay down credit card
Delayed credit	Credit card credit		
Delayed charge	Print checks		

Figure 6.42

Access to statement feature

The screen looks something like this:

Figure 6.43

Statement options

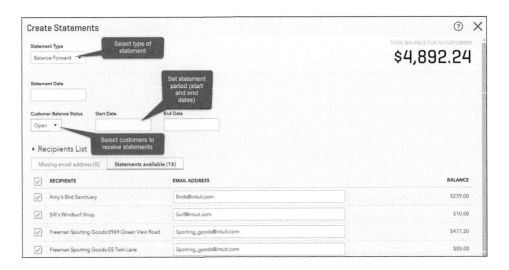

A statement date is entered. A company can choose the data that will appear on the statements by selecting one of the options in the **Statement Type** dropdown menu.

- **Balance forward**—The ending balance from the prior period and all current period transactions are displayed. An aging of the current balance is included at the bottom of the statement.

- **Open item (last 365 days)**—All open transactions are displayed. An aging of the current balance is included at the bottom of the statement.

- **Transaction Statement**—Transactions during the period are listed in two columns. The **Amount** column includes any **invoices**, **credit memos**, or **sales receipts**. The **Received** column includes payments received. No ending balance is included.

The company can also choose which customers will receive statements. In the **Customer Balance Status** dropdown menu, options are available to select only customers with balances, only customers with overdue balances, or all customers. Specific customers can be selected in the **Recipients List** section.

**PRACTICE
EXERCISE
6.13**

Prepare statements for Craig's Design and Landscaping.

(Craig's Design decides to send statements to all customers with unpaid balances.)

1. Click **+ New** on the navigation bar.

2. Click **Statement**.

3. Select **Balance Forward** as the **Statement type**.

4. Use the current date.

5. Select **Overdue** in the **Customer Balance Status** dropdown menu.

6. Leave default dates.

7. Click **Apply**.

8. Click **Print or Preview** at the bottom of the screen to view statements.

9. Click **Close** (bottom left corner).

10. Click **Cancel** (bottom left corner of the window).

| The matching (expense recognition) principle. | **ANSWER TO**
QuickCheck
6-1 |

CHAPTER SHORTCUTS

Activate sales tax
1. Click **Taxes** in the navigation bar
2. Click **Set up sales tax**

Add item (inventory, non-inventory, service)
1. Click the ⚙ on the icon bar
2. Click **Product and Services**
3. Click **New**

Create a delayed charge
1. Click **+ New** on the navigation bar
2. Click **Delayed Charge**

Create a delayed credit
1. Click **+ New** on the navigation bar
2. Click **Delayed Credit**

CHAPTER REVIEW

Matching
Match the term or phrase (as understood in QuickBooks Online) to its definition.

Assignments with the
MBC are available in
myBusinessCourse.

1. inventory item
2. statement
3. discount
4. delayed charge

5. bounced check
6. non-inventory item
7. delayed credit
8. nexus

_____ transaction type used for recording a pending sale

_____ product available for sale that is not being tracked in a perpetual tracking system

_____ sufficient presence used in determining seller sales tax requirements

_____ percentage or dollar amount reduction in charge to customer

_____ transaction type used for recording a pending customer credit

_____ report sent to customer to summarize activity for a period

_____ product available for sale that is being tracked in a perpetual tracking system

_____ customer check returned by bank due to insufficient funds in account

Multiple Choice

1. When a **customer** makes a purchase using his or her credit card, it would normally be recorded as a(n):

   a. invoice.
   b. bill.
   c. sales receipt.
   d. credit card charge.

2. When a bounced customer check is recorded, which account should QBO credit for the amount of the customer check?

   a. Cash (or Checking)
   b. Bad debt expense
   c. Accounts payable
   d. Unearned revenue
   e. Undeposited funds

3. The inventory valuation method used by QBO is:
   a. FIFO.
   b. LIFO.
   c. Specific identification.
   d. Weighted average.
   e. Any of the above can be selected by the user.

4. Which form might be used to record a customer order before the items are shipped?
   a. Delayed Charge
   b. Delayed Credit
   c. Invoice
   d. Sales Receipt

5. Credit card processing fees charged by merchant banks _____.
   a. can be recorded when the deposit is recorded
   b. can be recorded using a journal entry
   c. can be recorded when the fee is known by editing the deposit transaction
   d. All of the above are options for recording credit card fees.

BEYOND THE CLICKS—THINKING LIKE A MANAGER

Accounting: Identify and explain three things that a company should consider when determining the selling price of a new inventory item.

Information Systems: Review the steps used to process the bounced check received from a customer in your homework company. Why is this method preferable to simply creating a journal entry to record the bad check?

ASSIGNMENTS

Assignment 6A

Math Revealed!

Background information: Martin Smith, a college student and good friend of yours, has always wanted to be an entrepreneur. He is very good in math, so, to test his entrepreneurship skills, he has decided to set up a small math tutoring company serving local high school students who struggle in their math courses. He set up the company, Math Revealed!, as a corporation in 2021. Martin is the only owner. He has not taken any distributions from the company since it opened.

The business has been successful so far. In fact, it's been so successful he has decided to work in his business full time now that he's graduated from college with a degree in mathematics.

He has decided to start using QuickBooks Online to keep track of his business transactions. He likes the convenience of being able to access his information over the Internet. You have agreed to act as his accountant while you're finishing your own academic program.

Martin currently has a number of regular customers that he tutors in Pre-Algebra, Algebra, and Geometry. His customers pay his fees by cash or check after each tutoring session but he does give terms of Net 15 to some of his customers. He has developed the following fee schedule:

Name	Description	Rate
Refresher	One-hour session	$ 60 per hour
Persistence program	Two one-hour sessions per week	$100 per week
Crisis program	Five one-hour sessions per week	$225 per week

The tutoring sessions usually take place at his students' homes but he recently signed a two-year lease on a small office above a local coffee shop. The rent is only $750 per month starting in January 2022. A security deposit of $500 was paid in December 2021.

The following equipment is owned by the company:

Description	Date placed in service	Cost	Life	Salvage Value
Computer	7/1/21	$3,000	36 months	$300
Printer	7/1/21	$ 240	24 months	$ 0
Graphing Calculators (3)	7/1/21	$ 300	36 months	$ 30

All equipment is depreciated using the straight-line method.

As of 12/31/21, Martin owed $2,500 to his father (Richard Smith) who initially helped him get started. Richard is charging him interest at a 6% annual rate. Martin has been paying interest only on a monthly basis. His last payment of interest only was on 12/31/21.

Over the next month or so, he plans to expand his business by selling a few products he believes will help his students. He has already purchased a few items:

Category	Description	Vendor	Quantity on Hand	Cost per Unit	Sales Price
Books and Tools					
	Geometry in Sports	Books Galore	20	18	25
	Solving Puzzles: Fun with Algebra	Books Galore	20	15	22
	Getting Ready for Calculus	Books Galore	20	20	28
	Geometry Kit	Math Shack	10	12	18
	Handheld Dry-Erase Boards	Math Shack	25	10	15
	Notebooks (pack of 5)	Paper Bag Depot	10	8	12

2/1/22

✓ Now that Martin is selling more products, you know that Math Revealed! will need to start collecting sales taxes so you click **Taxes** on the navigation bar and set up the sales taxes feature.

- You use 3835 Freeport Blvd, Sacramento, CA 95822 as the address.

- You do not expect to sell any products to out-of-state customers.

- You confirm that the tax agency is the California Department of Tax and Fee Administration (CDTFA).

    TIP: Don't click the **Create invoice** link. Exit out of the screen. You should then see the final setup screen. If not, click **Taxes** on the navigation bar.

- You know that you will be required to file monthly.

- You change the tax collection start date to 2/1/22. **TIP:** You will need to edit the **sales tax settings** to enter the starting date. You must enter as 02/01/2022.

✓ You review the records of all items in the **Product and Services** list, making sure that all **inventory** items are identified as **Taxable-standard rate** and all **service** items as **Nontaxable**. **TIP:** Click **Edit** for **every item** to review the settings. You will need to **save and close** whether you change the tax status or not. To make sure every item's tax status is correct, run a **Product/Service List** report. Customize the report by adding the **Taxable** field.

✓ Martin comes in early with some great news. A new Center for High Academic Achievement has just opened in downtown Sacramento with a satellite campus in Elk Grove, CA. The space is supported and staffed by the local high schools. The director of the new program, Michelle Farman, has contacted Martin and asked him to provide materials that could be purchased by students enrolled in their program.

- You first set the Center up as a **customer**. **TIP:** This will be considered the **parent customer**.

> Center for High Academic Achievement
> 3635 Freeport Blvd
> Sacramento, CA 95822
> (916) 855-5558
> Terms are Net 30

- You check the **This customer is tax exempt** on the **Tax Info** tab. The Center is a re-seller of the materials and isn't subject to tax. You enter the Center's resale number (SRY-333-444444) in the **Exemption details** field.
- Next you set up both locations as **sub-customers** and select the **Bill with parent** option. You use the same company name, billing address, terms, and reseller number as the **parent customer** for both locations. You use "Downtown" and "Elk Grove" as the **display names**. **TIP:** If you check **sub-customer** first and select Center for High Academic Achievement as the **parent**, the address fields will be automatically filled. You will need to enter the **display** and **company names**. You will also need to check the **Terms** and complete the **Tax info** tab.
   - For the Downtown location, the shipping address is the same as the billing address.
   - For the Elk Grove location, the shipping address is 445 Forest Drive, Elk Grove, CA 95624.

2/4/22

✓ Martin delivers supplies as promised to both locations of the Center for High Academic Achievement. You prepare separate invoices for:
- Downtown shipment
   - 5 each of the following books:
      - Geometry in Sports (**Sports**)
      - Solving Puzzles: Fun with Algebra (**Puzzles**)
      - Getting Ready for Calculus (**Ready**)
   - INV-1013 totals $375.
- Elk Grove shipment
   - 3 each of the following books:
      - Geometry in Sports (**Sports**)
      - Solving Puzzles: Fun with Algebra (**Puzzles**)
   - INV-1014 totals $141.
- **TIP:** The Center is a reseller of books so there should be no sales tax.

✓ You receive a check in the mail from Jon Savidge for $1,000 in payment of INV-1010. (Check #3359, dated 2/4). Jon took the discount issued on the 1/27 credit memo. **TIP:** This can be tricky. Before you close the transaction, make sure that the **PAYMENT** field for the **Invoice** shows the full amount (the original amount of the invoice), the **Amount received** is accurate, and the **Credit memo** box is checked. Review the **Warning** on page 3-35 if you need help.

✓ You realize that Kim Kowalski still hasn't paid the remaining $100 due on INV-1002. You had called her a month ago and she had promised to pay the balance by the end of January. You give her a call. She apologizes and drives over with a check for $100. (Check #198, dated 2/4)

2/8/22

✓ Martin gives you the detail for the tutoring sessions scheduled during the first week of February.
- Two customers paid using their VISA card. You complete **sales receipts** (dated 2/8) for both (starting with SR-107).
   - Alonso Luna—5 **Refresher** sessions and one **Puzzles** book to help him with Algebra—$323.93 (tax included). **TIP:** You may need to click down to the second row before the tax field is updated.
   - Marcus Reymundo—2 **Refresher** sessions—$120
- You complete invoices (dated 2/8) for the following customers:

○ Paul Richard—3 weeks of the Crisis program starting 2/8—$675 (INV-1015)

○ Debbie Han—4 weeks of the Crisis program starting 2/1—$900 (INV-1016)

✓ You deposit the credit card receipts received today and the two checks received on 2/4. **TIP:** You'll be making one deposit for the credit card receipts and another for the checks.

- The check deposit totals $1,100.

- The bank charges a 2% fee on all credit card sales. You record the fee and charge it to the Bank Service Charges account. You select City Bank of Sacramento in the RECEIVED FROM field.

- The credit card deposit totals $435.05 (after the fee).

2/11/22

✓ Martin delivers another order to the Downtown location of the Center for High Academic Achievement.

- You prepare INV-1017 for $656.

  ○ 10 Geometry in Sports (Sports)

  ○ 8 Solving Puzzles: Fun with Algebra (Puzzles)

  ○ 5 Getting Ready for Calculus (Ready)

  ○ 5 Geometry Kits (Kit)

✓ You receive checks in the mail from:

- Center for High Academic Achievement—$516 in payment of INV-1013 and INV-1014. Check #9758844, dated 2/11. **TIP:** You only need to select the parent customer (Center for High Academic Achievement) when you receive the payment since the bill with parent option was selected in the customer setup for the locations.

- Marley Roberts—$100, Check #1731, dated 2/11, in payment of INV-1012

✓ You deposit the two checks received in the bank. Total deposit is $616.

2/14/22

✓ The Teacher's College workshop was a huge success. One of the teachers Martin met there asked him whether he'd be willing to put on a similar workshop this Friday (2/18). The teacher explains that this is for an independent group of educators and asks Martin if he'd consider discounting the Educator Workshop fee. Martin agrees to give the group a 10% discount on the $2,500 fee. (The fee is lower than the previous workshop because Martin will be making fewer speeches!)

- You set up a new account (Sales Discounts) to track discounts given to customers. You use #490 as the account number. **TIP:** Discounts are contra revenue accounts. Make sure you pick the correct account type.

- You turn on the Discount feature on the Sales tab of Account and Settings.

- You select the new sales discount account in the Chart of accounts section in the Advanced tab of Account and Settings.

- You don't want to forget to send the invoice next week so you create a Delayed Charge (DC-1000). **TIP:** You won't be able to add the discount directly on the Delayed Charge form. You'll do that when you convert it to an invoice.

  ○ The new customer is:

    Dynamic Teaching
    2121 Parallel Street
    Sacramento, CA 95822
    Dynamic Teaching is subject to sales taxes.
    Terms Net 30

2/16/22

✓ The Downtown location of the Center for High Academic Achievement returns two of the geometry kits (**Kit**). Both sets had broken compasses! Martin will be returning the compasses to Math Shack later.

- You create a $36 credit memo (CM-1017) for the **Downtown** location.

2/18/22

✓ You receive notice from the bank that the $100 check from Kim Kowalski that was recorded on 2/4 (deposited on 2/8) was returned for insufficient funds. You call Kim and she lets you know that she closed her bank account. She agrees to pay the $20 processing fee and the $100 owed to you with her VISA card.

- You set up two **service** items. Neither of the items is taxable. You classify them both in a new **category** called Other Charges.
  - For the first **service** item (Bounced Check) you use "Check returned for insufficient funds" as the **description**. You wouldn't need a default price here. **TIP:** Think about the account you want credited for the check amount.
  - For the second **service** item (Processing Fee), you use "Processing fee on NSF check" as the **description** and you select **Bank service charges** as the **income account**. You enter $20 as the default **sales price/rate** for the processing fee.
- You record her $120 payment using SR-109. **TIP:** The only items on the sales receipt will be the **Bounced check** and **Processing fee** items.

> **BEHIND THE SCENES** This transaction can seem complicated. It might help to remember that the journal entry underlying this **sales receipt** is DR Undeposited Funds; CR Cash; CR Bank Service Charges.

✓ You process the credit card receipt right away. The deposit amount (after the 2% fee) is $117.60.

✓ You create the invoice for the workshop Martin put on for the Dynamic Teaching group from the **delayed charge** you created on the 14th. You remember to give the customer the promised discount of 10%. INV-1018 totals $2,250. **TIP:** The **delayed charge** will show up in the sidebar when you start the **invoice**.

2/19/22

✓ Martin holds another Mathmagic Clinic. This time 50 students show up, almost double last month's attendance! Luckily, Samantha is able to help out with the tutoring clinic again. You tell Martin he might want to think about hiring an assistant on a regular basis. Martin says he might think about doing that in the fall.

- All the students pay in cash—$20 each for the tutoring.
- Some of the students also purchase some supplies, with cash. You sell:
  - 10 Handheld dry-erase boards (**Dry Erase**)
  - 5 Notebook packs (**Notebook**)
  - 3 Geometry Kits (**Kit**)
- You create one **sales receipt** (SR-110), using Drop-In as the customer.
  - The **sales receipt** total is $1,287.10 (including sales tax).

2/21/22

✓ One of the students from the Mathmagic Clinic on the 19th (Isla Parker) returns the **Kit** she purchased. The compass broke the first time she used it! You write her a check (#1112) for the full $19.58 cost of the set plus sales tax. **TIP:** Refunds are recorded on **refund receipts**. RR-101.

- Her address is 1164 Rosa Drive, Sacramento, CA 95822.
- Martin is definitely going to talk to Math Shack about the quality of the sets. If they can't find a better substitute, he may need to find another supplier.

✓ Martin gives you the details for tutoring sessions held in the past two weeks.

  • You create invoices (starting with INV-1019 and dated 2/21) for:

    ○ Navi Patel—Two weeks of **Crisis** starting 2/8—$450. Net 15

    ○ Eliot Williams—One week of **Persistence** starting 2/15—$100.

✓ You go to the bank and deposit the cash from Saturday's Mathmagic Clinic. The total deposit is $1,287.10

✓ Martin lets you know that he's going to take a few days off.

2/25/22

✓ You receive a check in the mail (# 9759115) from the Center for High Academic Achievement for $620 in payment of INV-1017. They took the credit for the returned Geometry Kits. **TIP:** This can be tricky. Before you close the transaction, make sure that the **PAYMENT** field for the **Invoice** shows the full amount (the original amount of the invoice), the **Amount received** is accurate, and the **Credit memo** box is checked. Review the **Warning** on page 3-35 if you need help.

✓ You deposit the check right away.

✓ You review the Collections Report. INV-1005 to Marcus Reymundo was due over a month ago. You try calling him but discover that his phone has been disconnected. You decide to write off the balance of $60 to bad debt expense. Math Revealed uses the direct write-off method because it has historically had very few uncollectible accounts. You consider bad debt expense to be a sub-account of **Marketing Costs**.

  • **TIP:** You'll need to set up a new account and then a new nontaxable **service** item. (You're writing off a nontaxable service (tutoring).) You set up the bad debt account as a **sub-account** of **Marketing Costs**. Use 648 as the account number. Include the new item in the **Other Charges category**. Use "Write-off of uncollectible account" as the **description**.

  • You create a **credit memo** (CM-1005) for the $60 write-off.

  • You apply the credit to INV-1005 through the **receive payment** form.

Check numbers 2/28

Checking account balance: $8,059.10
Accounts receivable: $4,775.00
Total cost of goods sold (February): . . . . . . $ 979.00
Net income (February) $6,168.72

Suggested reports for Chapter 6:

All reports should be in portrait orientation.

• Journal—February transactions only

• Sales by Product/Service Summary (February)

• A/R Aging Detail (2/28)

• Balance Sheet as of 2/28

• Profit and Loss (February)

  ▪ Add a **Year-to-date** column to the report

Background information: Sally Hanson, a good friend of yours, double majored in Computer Science and Accounting in college. She worked for several years for a software company in Silicon Valley but the long hours started to take a toll on her personal life.

Last year she decided to open up her own company, Salish Software Solutions. Sally currently advises clients looking for new accounting software and assists them with software installation. She also provides training to client employees and occasionally troubleshoots software issues.

Assignment 6B

Salish Software Solutions

She has decided to start using QuickBooks Online to keep track of her business transactions. She likes the convenience of being able to access financial information over the Internet. You have agreed to act as her accountant while you're working on your accounting degree.

Sally has a number of clients that she is currently working with. She gives 15-day payment terms to her corporate clients but she asks for cash at time of service if she does work for individuals. She has developed the following fee schedule:

Name	Description	Rate
Select	Software selection	$500 flat fee
Set Up	Software installation	$ 75 per hour
Train	Software training	$ 50 per hour
Fix	File repair	$ 60 per hour

Sally rents office space from Alki Property Management for $600 per month.

The following furniture and equipment are owned by Salish:

Description	Date placed in service	Cost	Life	Salvage Value
Office furniture	6/1/21	$1,400	60 months	$200
Computer	7/1/21	$4,620	36 months	$300
Printer.	7/1/21	$ 900	24 months	$ 0

All equipment is depreciated using the straight-line method.

As of 12/31/21, she owed $3,500 to Dell Finance. The monthly payment on that loan is $150 including interest at 5%. Sally's last payment to Dell was 12/31/21.

Over the next month or so, Sally plans to expand her business by selling some of her favorite accounting and personal software products directly to her clients. She has already purchased the following items.

Item Name	Description	Vendor	Quantity on Hand	Cost per Unit	Sales Price
Easy1	Easy Does It	Abacus Shop	15	$100	$ 200
Retailer	Simply Retail	Simply Accounting	2	$400	$ 800
Contractor.	Simply Construction	Simply Accounting	2	$500	$1,000
Organizer	Organizer	Personal Software	20	$ 25	$ 50
Tracker	Investment Tracker	Personal Software	20	$ 20	$ 40

2/1/22

✓ Now that Sally is ready to start selling products, you realize that you'll need to set up sales taxes in QBO so you click **Taxes** on the navigation bar to set up the sales tax feature.

- You use 3835 Freeport Blvd, Sacramento, CA 95822 as the company address.

- You do not expect to sell any products to out-of-state customers.

- You confirm that the tax agency is the California Department of Tax and Fee Administration (CDTFA).

  TIP: Don't click the **Create invoice** link. Exit out of the screen. You should then see the final setup screen. If not, click **Taxes** on the navigation bar.

- You contact the CDTFA and find out Salish Software will need to report monthly.

- You change the tax collection start date to 2/1/22. **TIP:** You will need to edit the **sales tax settings** to enter the starting date. You must enter as 02/01/2022.

✓ You review the records of all items in the **Product and Services** list, making sure that all **inventory** items are identified as **Taxable-standard rate** and all **service** items as **Nontaxable**. **TIP:** Click **Edit** for **every item** to review the settings. You will need to **save and close** whether you change the tax status or not. To make sure every item's tax status is correct, run a **Product/Service List** report. Customize the report by adding the **Taxable** field.

2/2/22

✓ A friend of Sally's, Rey Butler, has been doing very well in his financial management firm Reyelle Consulting. He has an office in Sacramento and a recently opened office in Davis. He gives Sally a call to ask about purchasing some electronic tools to sell to his customers. Sally suggests that he try the **Organizers** and **Investment Trackers**.

- You first set Reyelle up as a **customer**. This will be the **parent customer**.
  Reyelle Consulting
  3200 Bullish Lane
  Sacramento, CA 95822
  (916) 558-4499
  Terms are Net 30

- Don't forget to check the **This customer is tax exempt** field in the **Tax info** tab. Reyelle is a reseller of the materials and isn't subject to tax. You enter the company's resale number (SRY-424-424242) in the **Exemption details** field.

- You also set up both locations as **sub-customers** and select the **Bill with parent** option. You use the same company name, billing address, terms, and reseller number as the **parent customer** for both locations. You use "Sacramento" and "Davis" as the **display names**. **TIP:** If you check **sub-customer** and select Reyelle Consulting as the **parent**, the address fields will be automatically filled. You will need to enter the **display** and **company names**. You will also need to enter the **Terms** and complete the **Tax info** tab.

    For the Sacramento location, the shipping address is the same as the billing address.

    For the Davis location, the shipping address is 2911 Equity Street, Davis, CA 95616.

2/4/22

✓ Sally delivers the software CDs to both Reyelle locations. You prepare separate **invoices** for:
- Sacramento shipment
    6 each of the following:
    ☐ **Organizer**
    ☐ **Tracker**
    INV-1013 totals $540.
- Davis shipment
    3 each of the following:
    ☐ **Organizer**
    ☐ **Tracker**
    INV-1014 totals $270
- **TIP:** Reyelle Consulting is a reseller so there should be no sales tax on either invoice.

✓ You receive two checks in the mail. Both are dated 2/4.
- Check # 9210 from Butter and Beans for $3,000. (INV-1009).
- Check #86115 from Fabulous Fifties for $500. (INV-1010).

2/8/22

✓ Sally gives you her client work hours for the past week and you prepare the invoices as follows:
- Fabulous Fifties—10 hours of **Set Up**—$750. INV-1015
- Alki Deli—8 hours of **Set Up** and 4 hours of **Train**—$800. INV-1016

✓ One of the owners of mSquared Enterprises (a local general contractor) stops in to ask about construction accounting software. Sally gives her a demonstration of **Contractor** and she's impressed. She uses her VISA card to purchase the software.
- You complete a **sales receipt** (SR-106) to record the $1,087.50 purchase (tax included). **TIP:** You may need to click down to the second row before the tax field is updated.
- You set the company up with the following address:
    595 Newbuild Avenue
    Sacramento, CA 95822
    Net 30 terms

✓ You deposit the credit card receipts received today and the two checks received on 2/4. **TIP:** You'll be making one deposit for the credit card receipts and another for the checks.

- The check deposit totals $3,500.
- The credit card deposit totals $1,065.75 (after the fee).
  ○ The bank charges a 2% fee on all card sales. You charge the fee to the **Bank Service Charges** account. You select **Sacramento City Bank** in the **RECEIVED FROM** field.

2/11/22

✓ Sally delivers another order to the Davis location of Reyelle Consulting. The **Trackers** are selling quickly. Reyelle also decides to purchase a few of the **Easy Does It** programs for its Davis location. It has a few clients that own very small businesses and the **Easy Does It** program would be sufficient for their needs.

- You prepare the invoice (INV-1017) for $1,000.
  ○ 10 **Tracker**
  ○ 3 **Easy1**

✓ You receive a $300 check, dated 2/11, in the mail from Dew Drop Inn (Check 8160). (INV-1012)

- You call Harry over at Dew Drop to ask about the $200 balance. He says they've had some issues recently. A guest at the hotel got stuck in the elevator for 16 hours and is now suing for emotional distress. He'll try to get the balance to you by the end of February.
- You deposit the check right away.

✓ Sally tells you that she was talking to the staff at Fabulous Fifties. They mentioned that they knew some people who might be interested in getting some help picking out new accounting software. Sally offers them a $50 referral fee for any new software selection clients that they steer her way. You go ahead and set up a **delayed credit** (DCR-1000). You use **Select** as the **service** item. You enter 0 as the **QTY** so the quantity sold on reports isn't affected. **TIP:** You don't need to adjust the **RATE** field. Enter the $50 directly in the **AMOUNT** field.

2/16/22

✓ The Effective Troubleshooting (**TIPS**) workshop was a huge success. At the end of the workshop, Albus' CEO (Anatoly Deposit) tells Sally that he mentioned the workshop to James Gooden, a business acquaintance from Cezar Software who is very interested in presenting a similar workshop. Anatoly suggests giving James a call.

✓ Sally calls James Gooden right away. James would like to host the workshop at their facility this coming Monday (the 21st). James explains that Cezar Software creates software programs used by nonprofit organizations. He's hoping that there might be some kind of nonprofit discount available. Sally agrees to offer a 25% discount on the $2,500 fee.

- You set up a new account (Sales Discounts) to track discounts given to customers. You use #490 as the account number. **TIP:** Discounts are contra revenue accounts. Make sure you pick the correct **account type**.
- You turn on the **Discount** feature on the **Sales** tab of **Account and Settings**.
- You select the new **sales discount** account in the **Chart of accounts** section in the **Advanced** tab of **Account and Settings**.
- You don't want to forget to send the invoice for the **Tips** workshop so you create a **Delayed Charge** (DC-1000) for the full $2,500. **TIP:** You won't be able to add the discount directly on the **Delayed Charge** form. You'll do that when you convert it to an **invoice**.
  ○ The new customer is:
  Cezar Software
  8644 Technology Avenue
  Sacramento, CA 95822
  Terms Net 30

2/17/22

✓ The Sacramento location of Reyelle's returns one of the **Organizer** CDs because it was damaged. Sally finds another damaged disk in the storage cabinet. She'll return both to Personal Software sometime next week.

- You create a $50 credit memo (CM-1013) for the Sacramento location of Reyelle.

✓ You get a call from the bank. Dew Drop Inn's check for $300 was returned for insufficient funds. You call Harry. He apologizes and agrees to pay a $25 processing fee. He uses his credit card to cover the $325 total.

- You set up two **service** items. Neither of the items are taxable. You classify them both in a new **category** called Other Charges.

  - For the first **service** item (Bounced Check), you use "Check returned for insufficient funds" as the **description**. You don't need to set a sales price. **TIP:** Think about the account you want credited for the check amount.

  - For the second **service** item (Processing Fee) you use "Processing fee on NSF check" as the **description** and you select **Bank service charges** as the **Income account**. You enter $25 as the default **sales price/rate** for the processing fee.

- You record Dew Drop Inn's payment using **sales receipt** SR-107. **TIP:** The only items on the sales form will be the **Bounced Check** and **Processing Fee**.

> **BEHIND THE SCENES** This transaction can seem complicated. It might help to remember that the journal entry underlying this **sales receipt** is DR Undeposited Funds; CR Cash; CR Bank Service Charges.

✓ You process the credit card payment right away. The deposit amount (after the 2% fee) is $318.50.

2/21/22

✓ You receive checks in the mail from the following customers, all dated 2/21

- Albus Software—Check 755566, $2,500 for INV-1011
- Fabulous Fifties—Check 415161, $750 for INV-1015
- Alki Deli—Check 71144, $800 for INV-1016

✓ You record the checks and take them down to the bank. The deposit totals $4,050.

2/24/22

✓ Sally gives you her work schedule since 2/8. You create the following invoices using 2/24 as the date.

- You create invoices (starting with INV-1018) for:

  - Metro Market—**Select**—$500

    - Metro Market is a new client. It was referred to Salish by Fabulous Fifties.

      - Metro Market
        210 Admiral Way
        Sacramento, CA 95822
        Net 15

  - Alki Deli—5 hours of **Train**—$250

  - Butter and Beans—11 hours of **Train**—$550

  - Fabulous Fifties—6 hours of **Fix** and 4 hours of **Train**—$560

    - You remember to apply the $50 referral credit. The **Balance due** shows as $510.00. **TIP:** You may need to expand the sidebar on the right side of the window in order to see the **delayed credit**.

✓ Sally tells you she's taking a few days off (2/25 to 2/28) to visit family in Chicago.

2/25/22

✓ You create the **invoice** for the workshop Sally put on for Cezar Software from the **delayed charge** you created on the 16th. You remember to give the customer the promised discount of 25%. INV-1022 totals $1,875. **TIP:** The **delayed charge** will show up in the sidebar when you start the **invoice**.

✓ You receive a check (# 9759115) in the mail from Reyelle Consulting-Sacramento for $490 in payment of INV-1013. The check was dated 2/25. Reyelle took the credit for the returned **Tracker** disk. **TIP:** This can be tricky. Before you close the transaction, make sure that the **PAYMENT** field for the **Invoice** shows the full amount (the original amount of the invoice), the **Amount received** is accurate, and the **Credit memo** box is checked. Review the **Warning** on page 3-35 if you need help.

✓ You deposit the check right away.

✓ You get a call from Harry at Dew Drop Inn. The lawsuit has bankrupted his company. He apologizes but lets you know there are no assets remaining to cover the balance owed to Salish. You decide to write off the $200 to bad debt expense. Salish Software uses the direct write-off method because it has historically had very few uncollectible accounts.

  • You set up a bad debt expense account as a **sub-account** of Marketing Costs. You use account #638.

  • You create a new **service** item (Write off) and include it in the **Other Charges** category. You enter "Write off of uncollectible account" as the **description**. The new **service** item is not taxable. (You're writing off a nontaxable service (tutoring).)

  • You create a **credit memo** for the $200 write off. (You use WO-1012 as the **Credit Memo no.**)

> **BEHIND THE SCENES** This transaction can seem complicated. It might help to remember that the journal entry underlying the **credit memo** is DR Bad Debt Expense; CR Accounts Receivable.

  • You apply the credit to INV-1012 through the **receive payment** form.

Check numbers 2/28

Checking account balance: $18,789.25
Account receivable: . . . . $ 4,955.00
Total cost of goods sold (February): . . . . . . $ 1,380.00
Net income (February) . . . . $ 6,411.75

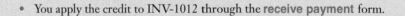

Suggested reports for Chapter 6:

All reports should be in portrait orientation

  • Journal—February transactions only

  • Sales by Product/Service Summary (February)

  • A/R Aging Detail (2/28)

  • Balance Sheet as of 2/28

  • Profit and Loss (February)

    ▪ Add a **Year-to-date** column to the report

7

Purchasing Activity
(Merchandising Company)

After completing Chapter 7, you should be able to:

1. Record the purchase of inventory by check.

2. Set up reorder points for inventory items.

3. Create and edit purchase orders.

4. Record the receipt of inventory with or without a vendor bill.

5. Enter and apply vendor credit memos.

6. Take early payment discounts on payments to vendors.

7. Prepare inventory and purchase order reports.

8. Use the **Inventory Valuation Detail** report to identify activity in FIFO layers (Appendix 7A).

WHAT IS THE PURCHASE CYCLE IN A MERCHANDISING COMPANY?

- Place an order for products.

- Receive the products.

- Receive a bill for the products.

- Pay the vendor.

The single biggest cost in service companies is usually labor. The single biggest cost in merchandising companies is usually inventory.

Proper inventory management is critical to the success of a merchandising company because:

- It costs money to store inventory.
  - Costs include warehouse rent, insurance, utilities, security, interest, etc.

- Inventory held too long can become obsolete.
  - It's hard to charge full price (or sometimes any price!) for last year's model.

- You can't sell what you don't have.
  - Customers who can't find what they want to buy are not happy customers!

To determine the optimal level of product inventory, management needs information about sales volume, accessibility of products, product returns, gross margins, etc. That information frequently comes from the accounting system.

In this chapter, we will cover transactions related to the purchase and management of inventory. We'll also add some purchase cycle topics that apply to both service and merchandising companies.

PURCHASING INVENTORY

In Chapter 3 and again in Chapter 6, we covered how the various QBO items (**service**, **inventory** and **non-inventory** items) are used in sales cycle transactions. In this chapter, we look at how inventory items are used in purchase cycle transactions.

In summary, every inventory item (**inventory** or **non-inventory** items) represents a product purchased and sold by the merchandising company.

> **BEHIND THE SCENES** Some companies record parts not sold individually to customers as **non-inventory** items. All inventory items in your homework represent products held for sale.

General information about each product is stored in the inventory part record. That information includes:

- The standard sales price

- The expected unit cost

- The asset account (normally the inventory account) that should be debited if the item is purchased for future sales

- The income account that should be credited if the item is sold

- The expense account (cost of goods sold account) that should be debited if the item is sold

In addition, information about inventory quantities and values is maintained by QBO for each **inventory** item including the quantity and value of units ordered, received, sold, and on hand.

Using items allows a company to maintain considerable detail without creating a gigantic chart of accounts. For example, a retail store might have only one income account called "Sales Revenue" but it can still generate a report that lists sales quantities and dollars for each and every product sold in the store. A retail store might also have only one inventory (asset) account but it can still track how many units are on hand at any point in time for each individual product.

In order to maintain that detail, of course, all transactions related to products must be recorded using items. That includes purchase and adjustment transactions as well as sales transactions.

> **!** **WARNING:** **Bill, Check, Expense Purchase Order, Vendor Credit and Credit Card Credit** forms all have two distribution sections. One section is labeled **Category details** and one is labeled **Item details.** In order to properly adjust the subsidiary ledgers, the **Item details** section must always be used when entering inventory transactions. Charging a purchase to the "Inventory" account on the **Category details** tab <u>will</u> result in a debit to the asset but will not properly adjust the inventory quantity in the subsidiary ledgers.

Paying at Time of Purchase

In most cases, merchandise inventory is **not** purchased by going directly to the supplier's location and paying at time of purchase BUT it could be. This might happen if the company needs to ship an order to a customer right away and it doesn't have sufficient products on hand to fill the order.

A company might pay for inventory at time of purchase using a check or credit card. The only difference between entering checks or credit card charges for inventory purchases and entering checks and credit charges for other purchases is the section used to identify the account distribution. We'll use a purchase by check to demonstrate using the appropriate section. (Refer to Chapter 4 for a refresher on entering credit card charges.)

If a company writes a check for the purchase, the **check** form is accessed by clicking **+ New** on the navigation bar and selecting **Check** in the **Vendors** column.

> **BEHIND THE SCENES**   Remember:
> - The vendor name, date, and amount of purchase are all used by QBO to credit the bank account and to prepare the check (if checks are printed directly from QBO).
> - The distribution section of the form is used to identify the debit account(s) in the underlying journal entry.

Purchases of inventory must be entered on the **Item details** section.

Figure 7.1

Check form

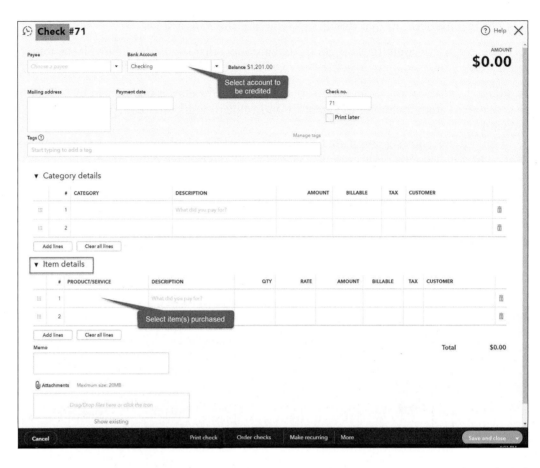

If an item is being purchased for a specific customer, the customer name can be included in the item row.

When distributions are entered on the **Item details** section (and the form is saved), QBO automatically:

- Debits the asset account specified in the item setup for the amount of the purchase.

- Updates the quantity records for the item purchased.

PRACTICE EXERCISE 7.1

Purchase inventory for Craig's Design and Landscaping with a check.
(Purchased five **Fountain Pumps** for $65 to have on hand.)

1. Click **+ New** on the navigation bar and select **Check**.

2. Select **Norton Lumber and Building Materials** as the vendor.

    a. You may have to close the sidebar to access the full form. Click the > on the top left edge of the sidebar to close it.

3. Enter "71" as the check number.

4. Use the current date as the **Payment date**.

5. Open the **Item details** section (lower half of the screen) by clicking the **triangle** next to **Item details**.

6. Select **Pump** as the **PRODUCT/SERVICE** and enter "5" as the **QTY**.

(continued)

(continued from previous page)

7. Enter "65" as the **AMOUNT**.

8. Make a note of the **RATE** calculated by QBO.

9. Click **Save and close**.

Ordering Inventory

Setting Reorder Points

At the beginning of this chapter, we reviewed some important considerations in inventory management.

- Inventory levels should be high enough that customer orders can be promptly filled.

- Inventory levels should be low enough that costs and the risks of obsolescence are minimized.

Management generally puts considerable effort into determining what inventory level is appropriate for each product. As part of that process, they determine the **minimum** amount of product they should have on hand at any point in time to safely meet customer demand. When the quantity on hand reaches that minimum level, an order for more inventory is placed with the vendor. The minimum level is called the reorder point.

A reorder point can be set for every **inventory** item in QBO. Reports can then be generated that list products that should be ordered based on current inventory levels.

The reorder point is set in the **inventory** item record. (As a reminder, the item records are accessed by clicking the ⚙ on the icon bar and selecting **Products and Services**.) The screen looks something like this:

Figure 7.2

Inventory item record

The reorder point is entered in the **Reorder Point** field in the middle of the screen.

> **BEHIND THE SCENES** Reorder points are used by management to determine **when** to place orders. Setting a **reorder point** in QBO does not generate a transaction. QBO does not automatically generate a purchase order when the reorder point is reached.

Inventory items that have quantities on hand less than the reorder point (or have quantities of 0) are highlighted at the top of the Products and Services Center.

Figure 7.3

Stock status indicator

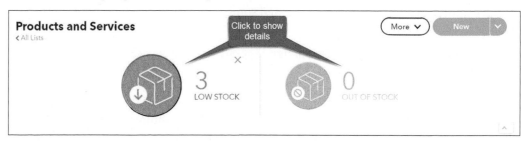

Click the quantity of low stock or out of stock items to display the item details.

Figure 7.4

List of items with quantity on hand lower than reorder point

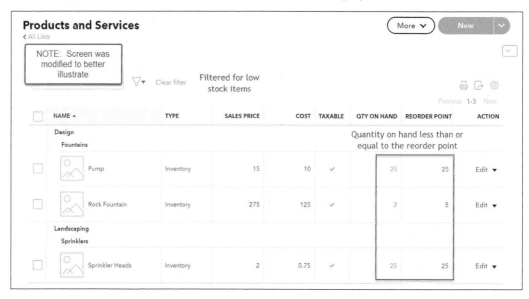

> **BEHIND THE SCENES** The words "stock" and "inventory" are often used interchangeably. In manufacturing companies, the word "stock" is sometimes used to refer specifically to finished goods held for sale. The word "inventory" is generally used to refer either to finished goods held for sale or any of the materials used to manufacture those goods. QBO uses stock and inventory interchangeably.

Reports can be created to assist employees responsible for ordering inventory.

To create a stock status report, select **Run report** in the **More** dropdown menu on the Products and Services Center screen. Customize the report by adding **Reorder Point** as a **Rows/Columns** field and removing **Price** as a **Rows/Columns** field. **Filter** the report by including only **inventory** items (**Fountains** and **Sprinklers**).

The customized report will look something like this after you complete the practice exercise:

Figure 7.5

Customized Product/
Service list report

Craig's Design and Landscaping Services
Stock Status

PRODUCT/SERVICE	TYPE	DESCRIPTION	COST	QTY ON HAND	REORDER POINT
Design:Fountains:Pump	Inventory	Fountain Pump	10.00	25.00	25.00
Design:Fountains:Rock Fountain	Inventory	Rock Fountain	125.00	2.00	5.00
Landscaping:Sprinklers:Sprinkler ...	Inventory	Sprinkler Heads	0.75	25.00	25.00
Landscaping:Sprinklers:Sprinkler ...	Inventory	Sprinkler Pipes	2.50		25.00

Adding **Preferred Vendor** and **Qty On PO** fields to the report would further improve the usefulness of the report.

Edit inventory items to include reorder points for Craig's Design and Landscaping.
(Craig's Design wants to set reorder points for pumps and rock fountains.)

1. Edit inventory items.
   a. Click the ⚙ on the icon bar.
   b. Select **Products and Services**.
   c. In the **Pump** row, click **Edit** in the **ACTION** column.
      i. Enter "50" as the **Reorder point**.
      ii. Click **Save and close**.
   d. In the **Rock Fountain** row, click **Edit** in the **ACTION** column.
      i. Enter "8" as the **Reorder point**.
      ii. Click **Save and close**.
   e. In the **Sprinkler Heads** and **Sprinkler Pipes** rows, click **Edit** in the **ACTION** column.
      i. Enter "25" as the **reorder point** for both.
      ii. Click **Save and close**.
2. Prepare a custom Stock Status report.
   a. Click **Run report** in the **More** dropdown menu on the **Products and Services** screen.
   b. Click **Customize**.
   c. Open the **Rows/Columns** section.
      i. Click **Change Columns**.
      ii. Check the **Reorder Point** field and uncheck the **Price** field.
   d. Open the **Filter** section.
      i. Check **Product/Service**.
      ii. In the **Product/Service** dropdown menu, check:
         1. **Design:Fountains:Pump**
         2. **Design:Fountains:Rock Fountain**
         3. **Landscaping:Sprinklers:Sprinkler Heads**
         4. **Landscaping:Sprinklers:Sprinkler Pipes**
   e. Open the **Header/Footer** section.
      i. Change the **Report title** to "Stock Status Report."
   f. Click **Run Report**.
   g. **Make a note** of the **QTY ON HAND** for **Sprinkler Heads**.
3. Click **Dashboard** on the navigation bar to exit the screen.

PRACTICE
EXERCISE
7.2

Homework
MBC

---

eLectures

Creating Purchase Orders

Once the company decides how many of each item need to be purchased, the suppliers are contacted. Many suppliers will not fill an order without written documentation (a purchase order) from their customer. Even when the supplier doesn't require written documentation, most companies create purchase orders as part of their internal control system.

Although ordering inventory is not an accounting transaction, a good accounting software program will include a purchase order tracking system so that management knows, at all times, how many units are on their way.

> **BEHIND THE SCENES** Purchase orders are tracked in QBO for informational purposes only. No journal entry is recorded in QBO when a purchase order is created.

QuickCheck
7-1

> Why isn't ordering inventory an accounting transaction?

The use of purchase orders is a **setting** (preference) in QBO. In the test drive company, the setting is turned on. To verify, click the ⚙ on the icon bar and select **Account and Settings**. Open the **Expenses** tab. **Use purchase orders** must be set to **On** for the feature to be available to use.

The **purchase order** form is accessed by clicking ⊕ New on the navigation bar and selecting **Purchase Order** in the **Vendors** column.

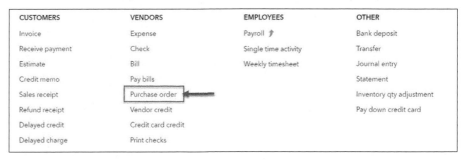

CUSTOMERS	VENDORS	EMPLOYEES	OTHER
Invoice	Expense	Payroll 🖋	Bank deposit
Receive payment	Check	Single time activity	Transfer
Estimate	Bill	Weekly timesheet	Journal entry
Credit memo	Pay bills		Statement
Sales receipt	Purchase order		Inventory qty adjustment
Refund receipt	Vendor credit		Pay down credit card
Delayed credit	Credit card credit		
Delayed charge	Print checks		

The form looks like this:

You need to enter the vendor name, the date, and the **products** being ordered to complete the form.

> **BEHIND THE SCENES** QBO will automatically enter the default cost when an **inventory** item is selected. The unit cost can be changed at this point, if appropriate. The cost can also be changed later when the vendor bill is received.

If a **product** is being purchased for a specific customer, the customer name can be included in the product row. If a product will be shipped directly to the customer, the customer name should also be selected in the **Ship to** field.

> **BEHIND THE SCENES** Once a **purchase order** has been created, **product** records are automatically updated to show the number of items on open orders.

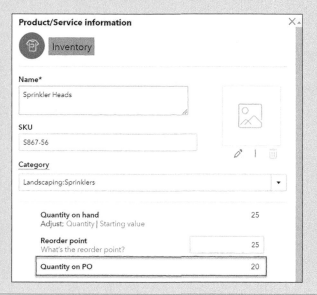

Create purchase orders for Craig's Design and Landscaping.
(Management decides to order 20 **Sprinkler Heads** and 10 **Sprinkler Pipes**.)

1. Click **+ New** on the navigation bar and select **Purchase Order**.

2. Select **Tania's Nursery** as the vendor.

3. Use the current date as the **Purchase Order** date.

4. In the **Item details** section:

   a.   Select **Sprinkler Heads** as the **PRODUCT/SERVICE** and enter "20" as the **QTY**.

      i.   Use the default **Rate**.

   b.   In the next row, select **Sprinkler Pipes** as the **PRODUCT/SERVICE** and enter "10" as the **QTY**.

      i.   Use the default **Rate**.

5. **Make a note** of the **Total** for the order as calculated by QBO.

6. Click **Save and close**.

PRACTICE
EXERCISE
7.3

Homework
MBC

Using Preferred Vendors To Create Purchase Orders

If items are always (or almost always) ordered from the same vendor, identifying a **preferred vendor** in the item record can streamline the ordering process.

To add a **preferred vendor** to an existing item record, click the ⚙ on the icon bar and click **Products and Services**.

Figure 7.8

Access to item record

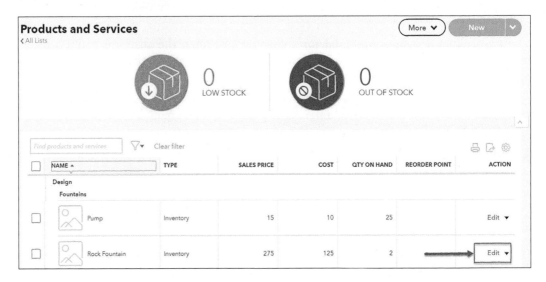

Click **Edit** in the **ACTION** column of the item.

Figure 7.9

Preferred vendor field in inventory item record

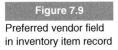

Select the **Preferred Vendor** and click **Save and close** to exit the item record and return to the **Products and Services** list.

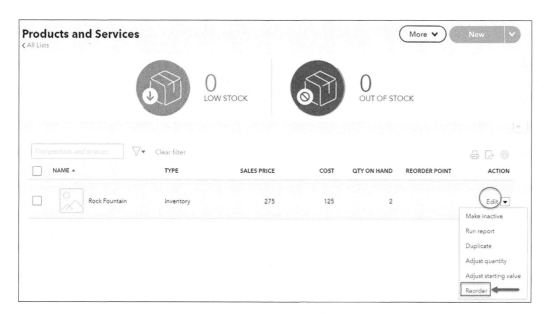

Figure 7.10

Link to purchase order form from Products and Services Center

To create a **purchase order** for an item with a preferred vendor, select **reorder** in the drop-down menu (**ACTION** column).

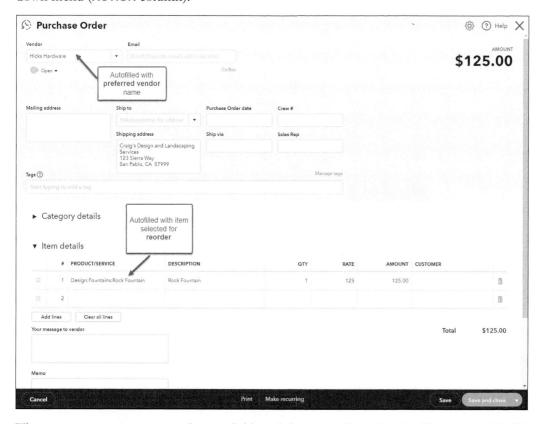

Figure 7.11

Purchase order form autofilled with preferred vendor information

The **Preferred Vendor** name and terms fields and the item to be ordered will automatically fill. Quantities and rates can be edited; additional items can be added.

Receiving Ordered Inventory

Receiving Ordered Inventory with a Bill

When a vendor bill is received with the inventory shipment, click **+ New** on the navigation bar and select **Bill**.

eLectures

Select the vendor name.

The screen will look something like this when a **bill** is entered for a vendor with an open purchase order:

In the sidebar on the right side of the screen, click **Add** to transfer the information from the **purchase order** to the **bill**.

 HINT: The **purchase order** can be opened by clicking **Open** in the sidebar to make changes before the information is transferred.

The **bill** will look something like this after the information is transferred over:

The **Bill no.**, **Bill date**, and **Terms** should be added. **RATE** or **AMOUNT** fields can be changed. Additional charges can also be added. The final **bill** should match the vendor invoice.

To view or remove the **purchase order**, click **linked transaction** in the top left corner of the **bill**.

Figure 7.14

Options to open or remove a linked purchase order in a bill

Click **Purchase Order** to view the original form.
To remove the purchase order (unlink it) from the **bill**, click **Remove**.

> **HINT:** A **purchase order** can be **removed** after the **bill** is saved. However, there must be some purchase information remaining or the form can't be **saved**. (QBO will not **save** blank transactions.) If there is no other purchase information, the best practice is to delete the **bill**. The status of **purchase orders** will change to **open** if the **linked bill** is deleted.

Receive ordered inventory with a bill for Craig's Design and Landscaping.
(Items ordered on PO #1002 from Tim Philip Masonry received in full with a bill (#5011-33) for $130.00—slightly higher than expected.)

1. Click **Expenses** on the navigation bar.

2. Click the **Vendors** tab to open the Vendor Center.

3. In the **ACTION** column in the row for **Tim Philip Masonry**, select **Create Bill**.

4. Click **Add** in the sidebar on the right side of the screen to transfer the **purchase order** information to the **bill** form.

5. **Make a note** of the **product** (description) transferred to the **bill**.

6. In the **Item details** section, change the **AMOUNT** to "130."

7. Select **Net 30** in the **Terms** field.

8. Use the current date as the **Bill date**.

9. Enter "5011-33" as the **Bill no.**

10. Click **Save and close**.

PRACTICE

EXERCISE
7.4

Homework
MBC

Receiving Partial Shipments

It's not unusual for a vendor to fill an order in multiple shipments. This would happen when:

- Ordered materials are coming from different locations.

- Vendors are out of stock of a particular item when the first shipment is sent but are able to send the backordered items at a later date.

QBO will track partially filled orders so that users can properly record inventory purchases as they're received.

To record a partial shipment, click **+ New** on the navigation bar and select **Bill**.

Select the vendor's name and click **Add** in the sidebar to transfer information from the **purchase order** to the **bill**.

Enter the actual quantity received in the **QTY** field and save the **purchase order**.

To view the automatic changes to the **purchase order**, open the form. (To find the form, use the **Advanced Search** feature and filter the search to **Purchase Orders**. The search can be further filtered by entering the vendor name.)

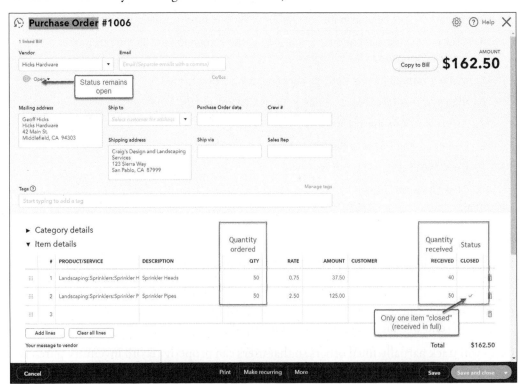

The purchase order will now display a RECEIVED quantity column and the purchase order will remain open.

When the remaining items are received, a new bill would be created from the updated purchase order.

Receive a partial shipment of ordered inventory for Craig's Design and Landscaping.
(Five of the eight fountain pumps ordered on PO #1005 from Norton Lumber and Building Materials received with a bill (#46464).)

PRACTICE
EXERCISE
7.5

1. Create a purchase order for eight fountain pumps and three rock fountains.

   a. Click ➕ New on the navigation bar.

   b. Click Purchase order.

   c. Select Norton Lumber and Building Materials as the Vendor.

   d. Use the current date as the Purchase Order date.

      i. QBO may have automatically added items and quantities based on previous transactions with the vendor. (This happens when automation is not turned off in Account and Settings.) Click the trash icon in the far right of each row to remove them.

   e. Select Pump as the PRODUCT/SERVICE and enter "8" as the QTY.

   f. On the next line, select Rock Fountain as the PRODUCT/SERVICE and enter "3" as the QTY.

   g. Click Save and close.

2. Enter the bill for the items received:

   a. Click ➕ New on the navigation bar.

   b. Click Bill.

   c. Select Norton Lumber and Building Materials as the Vendor.

   d. Click the trash icon in the far right column for any rows automatically added by QBO.

   e. Click Add in the sidebar on the right side of the screen to transfer the purchase order information to the bill form.

   f. Select Net 30 in the Terms field.

   g. Use the current date as the Bill date.

   h. Enter "46464" as the Bill no.

   i. In the Item details section, change the QTY for Fountain Pumps from 8 to 5.

   j. Change the QTY for Rock Fountains from 3 to 0.

   k. **Make a note** of the new Total.

   l. Click Save and close.

3. Receive the backordered items.

   a. Click ➕ New on the navigation bar.

   b. Click Bill.

   c. Select Norton Lumber and Building Materials as the Vendor.

      i. Select Net 30 in the Terms field.

      ii. Use the current date as the Bill date.

      iii. Enter "46468" as the Bill no.

   d. Click the trash icon in the far right column for any rows automatically added by QBO.

(continued)

(continued from previous page)

   e. Click **Add** in the sidebar on the right side of the screen to transfer the remaining items to the **bill**.

   f. **Make a note** of the **Total** amount.

   g. Click **Save**.

   h. Click **1 linked Purchase Order**.

   i. Click **Purchase Order**.

   j. Each item should have a checkmark in the **Closed** column.

   k. Click **Save and close**.

Receiving Ordered Inventory without a Bill

Merchandising companies need to update their inventory records as soon as purchased goods arrive so that their inventory on hand quantities are accurate. However, many suppliers include a packing slip (detailing the products and quantities included in the carton) with their shipments but no bill. The vendor's invoice (detailing costs) frequently arrives after the shipment. This might be done:

- As part of a supplier's internal control system.
- Because a supplier's warehouse or store is physically separate from the supplier's accounting office.

QBO does not currently have a feature that allows the company to record an increase in inventory and the creation of a related liability in the accounting records without a **bill** being created.

To keep inventory quantities updated, the company would normally create a **bill** using the anticipated costs. The **bill** would then be updated (with actual costs and vendor reference numbers) when the vendor invoice was finally received.

It would be good practice to make a note of the packing slip number in the **Memo** box of the **bill**. This should make it easier to match the final bill to the draft bill created in QBO from the packing slip.

Managing Purchase Orders

QBO automatically "closes" purchase orders when all of the items have been received.

Sometimes a company might need to manually close a purchase order (or a single item on a purchase order). This might happen when:

- The supplier is unable to ship the item(s).
- The company decides to order from a different supplier.

Closing a purchase order is a housekeeping task. There are no underlying journal entries!

To manually close a purchase order, the **Purchase Order** form must be open. **Purchase orders** can be found by selecting **Open Purchase Orders Detail** report in the **Expenses and Vendors** section of **Reports**.

Click the purchase order number of the **purchase order** you want to manually close to open the form.

Figure 7.18

Option to manually close purchase order

Select **Closed** on the purchase order status dropdown menu to close the entire order. (The purchase order status menu is directly below the vendor name field.)

Figure 7.19

Option to close a purchase order line item

To close a single item on a purchase order, check the box in the **Closed** column.

Manually close a purchase order for Craig's Design and Landscaping.
(Craig's Design decides it doesn't need the Rock Fountain ordered from Tim Philip Masonry on PO #1002.)

1. **TIP:** If you didn't log out of the test drive company after the last practice exercise, log out to clear out previous transactions. Log back in to continue.

2. Click **Reports** on the navigation bar.

3. Click **Open Purchase Order List** in the **Expenses and Vendors** section.

4. Click PO #1002.

(continued)

PRACTICE
EXERCISE
7.6

(continued from previous page)

5. Click **Open** (directly under the vendor name field) to access the **Purchase Order status** dropdown menu.

6. Select **Closed**.

7. Click **Save and close**.

Ordering Inventory Without Using the Purchase Order System

Given the importance of maintaining proper inventory levels, most companies want to track the status of orders they've placed with suppliers (purchase orders) and choose to use the purchase order system outlined above.

Companies that do not use purchase orders can still, of course, use QBO!

VENDOR CREDITS

Vendors issue credit memos for a variety of reasons. Those reasons might include the following:

- Goods were returned.

- There was an error on a previously issued bill.

- To give a "good faith" allowance when a customer isn't satisfied with goods or service.

Vendor credits aren't unique to merchandising companies. Service and manufacturing companies would also use the procedures outlined here.

Entering Credits from Vendors

Credit memos from vendors are recorded in QBO as **transaction type Vendor Credit**. (Remember: a credit issued to a customer is **transaction type Credit Memo**.)

To access the vendor credit form, click **+ New** on the navigation bar and select **Vendor Credit** in the **Vendors** column.

Figure 7.20

Vendor credit form

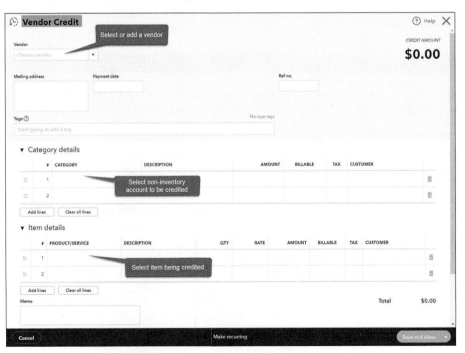

You'll need to enter the vendor name, date of the credit memo (identified as **Payment date** in QBO), vendor reference number, and the account (or items) that should be credited. The form includes some familiar sections (**Category details** and **Item details**).

Vendor credits received for returned inventory items or overbillings on inventory items would be entered in the **Item details** section. All other vendor credits would be entered in the **Category details** section.

Vendor credits are tracked in the vendor subsidiary ledger. All available credits are displayed on the **transaction list** tab in the vendor record.

Applying Credits from Vendors

To apply a **vendor credit**, click **Expenses** on the navigation bar.

Click the **Vendors** tab to open the Vendor Center. Click the **vendor** to be paid to open the vendor record.

The **transaction list** tab will look something like this in your practice exercise:

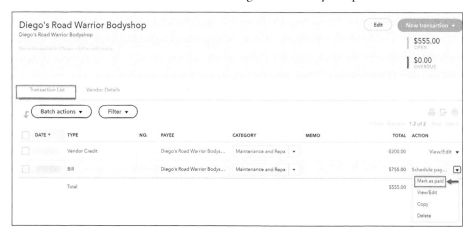

Figure 7.21

Access to vendor payment

Click **Mark as paid** in the **ACTION** column of an open **bill**.

Figure 7.22

Example of credit applied on payment to a vendor

If there are available credits, QBO will automatically apply them. The **credit** can be deselected if the user elects to retain the credit for future use.

Vendor credits can also be applied through the **pay bills** screen.

Click **+ New** on the navigation bar.

Select **Pay bills**.

Figure 7.23

Example of credit applied in pay bills screen

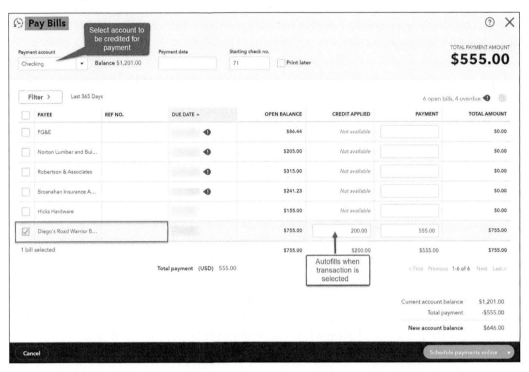

Available credits will be displayed for all vendors selected (checked).

If any of the available credit amount is manually entered in the **CREDIT APPLIED** field, the **PAYMENT** amount will automatically adjust.

PRACTICE
EXERCISE
7.7

Enter a vendor credit for Craig's Design and Landscaping.

(Craig's Design receives a credit memo from Diego's Road Warrior Bodyshop. They had been overcharged for some repair work done by Diego's.)

1. Record the **vendor credit**.

   a. Click **+ New** on the navigation bar and select **Vendor Credit**.

   b. Select **Diego's Road Warrior Bodyshop** as the **Vendor**.

   c. Use the current date as the **Payment date**.

   d. On the **Category details** section, select **Equipment Repairs** as the **ACCOUNT**.

   e. Enter "Overcharge" in the **DESCRIPTION** field.

   f. Enter "200" as the **AMOUNT**.

   g. Click **Save and close**.

2. Apply the **vendor credit**.

   a. Click **Expenses** on the navigation bar.

   b. Click the **Vendors** tab to open the Vendor Center.

(continued)

(continued from previous page)

    c.   Click **Make Payment** in the **ACTION** column of **Diego's Road Warrior Bodyshop**.

    d.   Select **Checking** as the payment method in the **Bank/Credit account** field.

    e.   Use the current date as the **payment date**.

    f.   Use "71" as the check number in the **Ref no.** field.

    g.   Make sure that both the **credit** and the **bill** are checked.

    h.   **Make a note** of the check amount.

    i.   Click **Save and close**.

Special Considerations for Returns of Inventory

QBO uses the FIFO method for valuing inventory. When an item is returned (through a **vendor credit**), QBO credits the inventory account for the cost in the oldest FIFO layer. That may or may not agree to the amount on the vendor credit. If it doesn't agree, QBO will automatically debit (or credit) the difference to the **Expense account** identified in the item record (normally a cost of goods sold account).

To illustrate, let's assume we return one Fountain Pump to Norton Lumber and Building Material. The pumps had cost us $10 each to purchase. The **vendor credit** would look like this if Norton only gave us a $9 credit for the return.

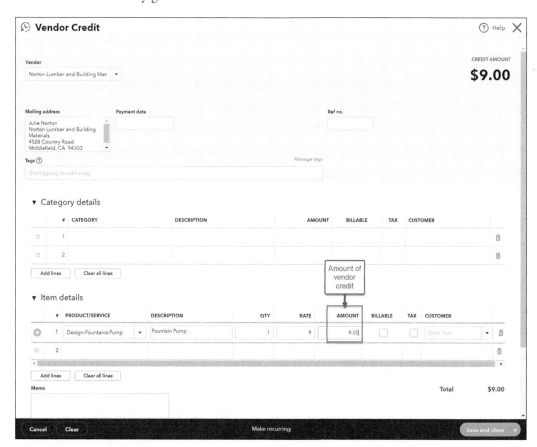

Figure 7.24

Example vendor credit for inventory item

To see how the inventory valuation is impacted, click **Reports** on the navigation bar. Select **Inventory Valuation Detail** in the **Sales and Customers** section. Change the dates to see transactions over the last thirty days. Click **Run report**.

The **Inventory Valuation Detail** report should look something like this:

Figure 7.25

Illustration of inventory account detail

Two lines appear for the transaction. The first line shows a reduction of 1 unit at a FIFO cost of $9 (the amount of the credit). The second line shows an adjustment to the FIFO cost of an additional $1. This represents the difference between the credit of $9 and the oldest FIFO layer cost of $10 per unit.

To see the underlying journal entry, click the **Vendor Credit** transaction in the report.

Figure 7.26

Access to journal entry underlying form

Click **More** and select **Transaction Journal**.

Figure 7.27

Example of a journal entry underlying vendor credit

In the entry (Figure 7.27), Inventory Asset has been credited for $10, Accounts Payable has been debited for $9, and the $1 difference has been debited to Cost of Goods Sold.

Enter a vendor credit for return of inventory for Craig's Design and Landscaping.
(One damaged Fountain Pump was returned to Norton Lumber.)

PRACTICE
EXERCISE
7.8

1. Record the vendor credit for return of inventory.

   a. Click **+ New** on the navigation bar and select **Vendor Credit**.

   b. Select **Norton Lumber and Building Materials** as the **Vendor**.

   c. Use the current date as the **Payment date**.

   d. In the **Item details** section, select **Pump** as the **PRODUCT/SERVICE**. **TIP:** You may need to click the triangle next to **Item details** to open the section.

   e. Enter "1" as the **QTY** and "9" as the **AMOUNT**.

   f. Click **Save**.

2. Review the underlying entry for the **vendor credit**.

   a. Select **Transaction journal** in the **More** dropdown menu (bottom of page).

   b. **Make a note** of the account debited for $1.

PAYING VENDOR BALANCES

We covered the basics of paying vendor account balances in Chapter 4.

In this chapter, we'll look at reducing payments to vendors by taking available early payment discounts.

Although early payment discounts can be small in dollar amount, the return is quite high. For example, a common payment term is 2%/10, net 30. The customer gets a reduction of 2% off the bill just for paying 20 days early. The effective interest rate earned on that discount is almost 37%! Most companies want to take those discounts whenever possible.

Although vendor payment terms are set in the vendor record, QBO does not currently have a feature that allows users to track **bills** by discount date or to automatically apply any allowable early payment discounts when a **bill** is paid. There are some tools that can be used, though, as a substitute for automatic tracking.

Early Payment Discounts

Setting Up Early Payment Discount Terms

Before we start, let's review the process for setting up payment terms initially covered in Chapter 3.

Click the ⚙ on the icon bar and select **All Lists**.

eLectures

Lists

Chart of Accounts	**Payment Methods**
Displays your accounts. Balance sheet accounts track your assets and liabilities, and income and expense accounts categorize your transactions. From here, you can add or edit accounts.	Displays Cash, Check, and any other ways you categorize payments you receive from customers. That way, you can print deposit slips when you deposit the payments you have received.
Recurring Transactions	Terms ⟵
Displays a list of transactions that have been saved for reuse. From here, you can schedule transactions to occur either automatically or with reminders. You can also save unscheduled transactions to use at any time.	Displays the list of terms that determine the due dates for payments from customers, or payments to vendors. Terms can also specify discounts for early payment. From here, you can add or edit terms.
Products and Services	**Attachments**
Displays the products and services you sell. From here, you can edit information about a product or service, such as its description, or the rate you charge.	Displays the list of all attachments uploaded. From here you can add, edit, download, and export your attachments. You can also see all transactions linked to a particular attachment.
Product Categories	
A means of classifying items that you sell to customers. Provide a way for you to quickly organize what you sell, and save you time when completing sales transaction forms.	**Tags**
	Displays the list of all tags created. You can add, edit, and delete your tags here.
Custom Form Styles	
Customize your sales form designs, set defaults, and manage multiple templates.	

Figure 7.28

Access to credit terms list

Click **Terms** and click **New**.

Although QBO currently doesn't include automatic early payment discount feature options, you can create a **term** that identifies the available discount in the **name**. This would then appear on vendor **bills** and on customer **invoices**.

Credit term setup screen

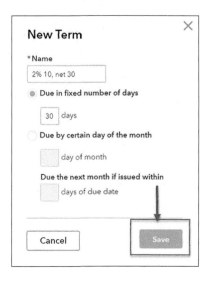

A payment term of 2% 10, net 30 means that the bill is due in full in 30 days. However, if you pay within 10 days you get a discount of 2%. Figure 7.29 shows how that payment term would be set up in QBO.

Tracking Bills with Early Payment Discounts

For tracking early payment discounts, it's fairly easy to create a custom report that can be used to identify discount opportunities.

Click **Reports** on the navigation bar. Select **Unpaid Bills** in the **What You Owe** section.

Click **Customize**. Open **Rows/Columns** and click **Change columns**. Check **Terms** to add that column to the report. **Past Due** and **Due Date** columns could be removed. The order of the columns could also be rearranged. The changes might look something like this:

Illustration of customization for report of available early payment discounts

Open **Filter** on the **Customization** sidebar.

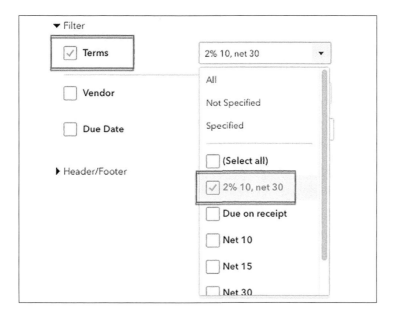

Figure 7.31

Illustration of filters for report of available early payment discounts

Check **Terms** and select all terms that include early payment discounts. The report title could be changed in **Header/Footer**.

Click **Run Report**. The report might look something like this:

Figure 7.32

Example of customized unpaid bills report

Craig's Design and Landscaping Services

POSSIBLE EARLY PAYMENT DISCOUNTS

DATE	NUM	AMOUNT	TERMS		OPEN BALANCE
▾ Robertson & Associates					
(650) 557-1111					
		315.00	2% 10, net 30		315.00
Total for Robertson & Associ...		$315.00			$315.00
TOTAL		$315.00			$315.00

The report can then be scanned for available discounts.

Taking Available Early Payment Discounts

As noted earlier, QBO does not currently have a feature that allows users to automatically apply available early payment discounts when a **bill** is paid.

> **BEHIND THE SCENES** Although it would be possible to enter the amount of the early payment discount as a line item in the **bill**, early payment discounts should not be recognized until it is certain that payment will be made within the payment terms.

What users can do is create a **vendor credit** in the amount of the discount just before the payment is processed.

The **vendor credit** would then be applied to the **bill** when the payment is recorded.

BEHIND THE SCENES Under GAAP, discounts related to the purchase of inventory are properly accounted for as a reduction of the cost in inventory. QBO does not have the capacity to handle that level of complexity. As long as the error in inventory values (due to these discounts) is not material (not significant), crediting cost of goods sold for early payment discounts on inventory items is acceptable.

PRACTICE
EXERCISE
7.9

Record payment of a bill with an early payment discount for Craig's Design and Landscaping.

(Robertson & Associates has changed its credit terms to 2%/10, net 30. Craig's intends to take the discount as allowed on the $315 bill currently due to Robertson.)

1. Set up the new terms.
    a. Click the ⚙ icon on the icon page.
    b. Click **All Lists**.
    c. Click **Terms**.
    d. Click **New**.
    e. Enter "2% 10, net 30" as the **Name**.
    f. Toggle **Due in Fixed number of days**.
    g. Enter "30" in the **days** field.
    h. Click **Save**.

2. Add the new terms to Robertson & Associates' vendor record.
    a. Click **Expenses** on the navigation bar.
    b. Click the **Vendors** tab to open the Vendor Center.
    c. Click **Robertson & Associates**.
    d. Click **Edit**.
    e. Under **Terms**, select **2% 10, net 30**.
    f. **Make a note** of the **Account no.**
    g. Click **Save**.
    h. Click the **Transaction List** tab. (You should still be in the vendor record.)
    i. Click the $315 open bill.
    j. Select **2% 10, net 30** in the **Terms** field.
    k. Click **Save and close**.

3. Create a **vendor credit** to record the early payment discount.
    a. Click **+ New** on the navigation bar and select **Vendor Credit**.
    b. Select **Robertson & Associates** as the **Vendor**.
    c. Use the current date as the **Payment date**.
    d. On the **Category details** section, select **Miscellaneous** as the **ACCOUNT**.
        i. If the discount is related to a purchase of inventory, a cost of goods sold account would be more appropriate.
    e. Enter "2% early payment discount on $315 bill" in the **DESCRIPTION** field.
    f. Enter "6.30" as the **AMOUNT**.

(continued)

(continued from previous page)

    g. Click **Save and close.**

4. Pay the discounted bill.

    a. Click **Expenses** on the navigation bar.

    b. Click the **Vendors** tab to open the Vendor Center.

    c. Click **Make Payment** in the **ACTION** column for **Robertson & Associates.**

    d. Select **Checking** as the payment method.

    e. Use the current date as the **payment date.**

        i. In this example, it is possible that the payment date is more than 10 days past the invoice date. Since the test drive company dates are constantly changing, we'll have to accept some departures from reality!

    f. Use "72" as the check number in the **Ref no.** field.

    g. Make sure that both the **credit** and the **bill** are checked.

    h. **Make a note** of the amount of the check.

    i. Click **Save and close.**

VENDOR REPORTS

We reviewed some of the standard vendor and payables reports in Chapter 4. For this chapter, we're most interested in inventory and purchase reports.

    Inventory valuation reports are accessed through the **Sales and Customers** section of **Reports.** A commonly used inventory report is:

- **Inventory Valuation Summary**
  - A report of quantity, average cost, and total cost of units on hand, by item.

Inventory purchase reports are accessed through the **Expenses and Vendors** section of **Reports.** Commonly used reports include:

- **Open Purchase Order List**
  - List of all unfilled purchase orders.

- **Purchases by Product/Service Detail**
  - A report of purchases, by item, including information about quantity, unit cost, and vendor.

- **Purchases by Vendor Detail**
  - A report of purchases, by vendor, including information about items, quantity, and unit cost.

Prepare reports on inventory for Craig's Design and Landscaping.
(Craig's Design wants an inventory valuation report.)

1. Click **Reports** on the navigation bar.

    a. Click **Inventory Valuation Summary** in the **Sales and Customers** section.

    b. **Make a note** of the four columns included in the report.

    c. Click **Dashboard** to close the report screen.

PRACTICE
EXERCISE
7.10

ANSWER TO
QuickCheck
7-1

> Because there is no change in the accounting equation when an order is placed.

CHAPTER SHORTCUTS

Record vendor credit memos
1. Click **+ New** on the navigation bar
2. Click **Vendor Credit**

Record purchase orders
1. Click **+ New** on the navigation bar
2. Click **Purchase Order**

CHAPTER REVIEW

Assignments with the
MBC **are available in**
myBusinessCourse.

Matching

Match the term or phrase (as used in QuickBooks Online) to its definition.

1. vendor credit
2. item details
3. make payment
4. open purchase orders list

5. reorder point
6. purchase order
7. stock
8. Inventory Valuation Summary

_____   inventory
_____   dropdown option in vendor center used to open a bill payment form
_____   section of a form used to identify distribution of inventory charges or credits
_____   transaction type used to record credit memos received from vendors
_____   report summarizing the quantity and value of inventory items
_____   report of all unfilled purchase orders
_____   order for goods sent to vendor
_____   minimum desired quantity of inventory to have on hand

Multiple Choice

1. A liability is recorded in QBO when:
   a. inventory is ordered from the supplier.
   b. a vendor bill for inventory is paid.
   c. inventory is received with a bill from the supplier.
   d. inventory purchases are made by check.

2. Vendor credits _____.
   a. must be manually applied to specific bills by the user
   b. are automatically included in the **CREDIT APPLIED** field when bill is selected for payment
   c. are automatically applied by QBO when vendor credit is entered

3. If some but not all of the items on a purchase order have been received, and the **bill** has been created,
   a. the purchase order is automatically marked as "closed" by QBO.
   b. the purchase order must be manually updated by checking the **CLOSED** column for each item received.
   c. the purchase order remains open until the bill has been paid.
   d. the purchase order remains open until all items have been received or the user manually closes the purchase order.

4. QBO uses the _____ method of valuating inventory.

    a. FIFO

    b. LIFO

    c. weighted average

    d. Any of the above methods can be used in QBO.

5. To take an early payment discount on a vendor bill, _____.

    a. a vendor credit can be created for the amount of the discount and applied to the bill when paid

    b. the potential discount can be included on the bill (in Terms)

    c. Both a and b are possible in QBO.

BEYOND THE CLICKS—THINKING LIKE A MANAGER

Accounting: You opened an office supply store several years ago. Business is picking up and you realize you're going to need to delegate some of your duties in order to continue growing. You will continue to decide which products to sell but you want one of your managers to take on the responsibility for deciding when and how much of each item to order. Do you choose the accounting manager, the sales manager, or the warehouse manager on staff? Explain your choice.

Information Systems: The owner of the company has asked you to create a detailed report of vendor activity over the last 60 days. Look through the standard QBO reports. Which QBO report do you think would be the most useful to the owner? What modifications (customizations), if any, would you make to the report?

ASSIGNMENTS

Background information: Martin Smith, a college student and good friend of yours, has always wanted to be an entrepreneur. He is very good in math, so, to test his entrepreneurship skills, he has decided to set up a small math tutoring company serving local high school students who struggle in their math courses. He set up the company, Math Revealed!, as a corporation in 2021. Martin is the only owner. He has not taken any distributions from the company since it opened.

The business has been successful so far. In fact, it's been so successful he has decided to work in his business full time now that he's graduated from college with a degree in mathematics.

He has decided to start using QuickBooks Online to keep track of his business transactions. He likes the convenience of being able to access his information over the Internet. You have agreed to act as his accountant while you're finishing your own academic program.

Martin currently has a number of regular customers that he tutors in Pre-Algebra, Algebra, and Geometry. His customers pay his fees by cash or check after each tutoring session but he does give terms of Net 15 to some of his customers. He has developed the following fee schedule:

Name	Description	Rate
Refresher	One-hour session	$ 60 per hour
Persistence program	Two one-hour sessions per week	$100 per week
Crisis program	Five one-hour sessions per week	$225 per week

The tutoring sessions usually take place at his students' homes but he recently signed a two-year lease on a small office above a local coffee shop. The rent is only $750 per month starting in January 2022. A security deposit of $500 was paid in December 2021.

The following equipment is owned by the company:

Description	Date placed in service	Cost	Life	Salvage Value
Computer	7/1/21	$3,000	36 months	$300
Printer	7/1/21	$ 240	24 months	$ 0
Graphing Calculators (3)	7/1/21	$ 300	36 months	$ 30

All equipment is depreciated using the straight-line method.

As of 12/31/21, Martin owed $2,500 to his father (Richard Smith) who initially helped him get started. Richard is charging him interest at a 6% annual rate. Martin has been paying interest only on a monthly basis. His last payment of interest only was on 12/31/21.

Over the next month or so, he plans to expand his business by selling a few products he believes will help his students. He has already purchased a few items:

Category	Description	Vendor	Quantity on Hand	Cost per Unit	Sales Price
Books and Tools					
	Geometry in Sports	Books Galore	20	18	25
	Solving Puzzles: Fun with Algebra	Books Galore	20	15	22
	Getting Ready for Calculus	Books Galore	20	20	28
	Geometry Kit	Math Shack	10	12	18
	Handheld Dry-Erase Boards	Math Shack	25	10	15
	Notebooks (pack of 5)	Paper Bag Depot	10	8	12

2/1/22

✓ You pay the February rent to your landlord, Pro Spaces, (Check #1113 $750).

✓ You also mail a check to Martin's dad (Richard Smith) for the interest owed to him for January (Check #1114). **TIP:** Look at the balance sheet if you've forgotten the interest amount due.

  • You write the check to Richard Smith (Martin's dad). The address is 5406 Hawthorne Ave, Seattle, WA 98107. The terms are Net 30.

2/8/22

✓ Martin went to a Math Educators Conference in Los Angeles last weekend (2/5). You charge all his expenses to 624 Professional development expense in QBO, a new sub-account of 620 Labor Costs. You use **Office/General Administrative Expenses** as the **Detail Type**. He used the VISA credit card to pay for the following:

  • Gas for the trip $45 (LA Gasoline Stop)

  • Hotel room (2 nights) $380 (Good Sleep Inn)

  • Meals $150 (Good Sleep Inn)

  • **TIP:** You **must** create a **separate** Expense transaction for each charge. The reason will become clear in the homework for Chapter 8. Use 2/8/22 as the date of the transactions.

2/10/22

✓ Since Martin has started selling products, you decide to enter reorder points for the items currently in QBO. You enter reorder points of 15 for the books (**Puzzles**, **Sports**, and **Ready**), 15 for the geometry kits and dry-erase boards (**Kit** and **Dry-Erase**), and 8 for the notebooks (**Notebook**).

✓ You want to keep track of any orders you place so you turn on the purchase order feature in the **Expense** tab of **Account and Settings**. You also check the **Custom transaction numbers** box.

✓ You look at the inventory items on hand and see that many of the items are below the reorder point.

✓ You prepare a **purchase order** (PO-100) and order the following from Books Galore:

- 15 each of **Puzzles** and **Sports**
- 10 **Ready**
- The PO total is $695.

✓ You also place an order with Math Shack (PO-101 for $120) for 10 of the geometry kits (**Kit**). You decide to wait and order more **Notebooks** later.

2/11/22

✓ You pay all bills due on or before 2/20.

- There are two bills to be paid. The total amount is $1,943.57. The first check number is 1115.

2/14/22

✓ Martin learned about a new product at the Math Educators Conference he attended in Los Angeles. It's a low-cost handheld game console that can be loaded with a variety of educational math games. His plan is to sell the consoles and the software packs to local math tutoring centers for elementary school children. He has found the following supplier:

- Cartables, Inc.
  1390 Freestone Road
  San Diego, CA 92104
  Main Phone: (619) 378-5432

- You see that Cartables allows a 2% discount if the payment is made within 10 days. You set up a new term in the **All Lists** menu of the ⚙ window. You name it "2% 10, net 30." **TIP:** Since the bill is due in 30 days if you do not pay it early, you use 30 as the **fixed number of days** in the term.

- You decide to set up a new category called "Math Games" for the new product line. **TIP:** Select **Manage categories** in the **More** dropdown menu in the **Products and Services** center to create a new **category**.

- You talk with Martin and decide that each new **inventory** item:
  - Will have a reorder point of 3.
  - Will be recorded in the **130 Inventory Asset** account.
  - Will use account **420 Sales of Product Income** and **500 Cost of Goods Sold** as the **Income** and **Expense** accounts, respectively.
  - Is taxable.
  - Has Cartables as the **preferred vendor**.
  - **TIP:** Enter 0 as the **initial quantity on hand** and 02/01/2022 as the **As of date**. You'll be entering purchases of the items when they are received.

- You set up all the new **inventory** items **TIP:** Once you create one new item, you can select **Duplicate** the item on the **ACTION** menu for that item and edit the copy for each additional item.
  - Console (Description—Game Console)—Expected cost $225; Selling price $350
  - Fractions (Description—Parts of a Whole)—Expected cost $35; Selling price $50
  - Equations (Description—Equal or Not?)—Expected cost $35; Selling price $50
  - Ratios (Description—Ratios and Proportions)—Expected cost $35; Selling price $50

- You prepare PO-102 for the first Cartables order—5 consoles and 5 each of the three game packs. The PO totals $1,650.00.

✓ You receive the 10 **Kits** from Math Shack ordered on PO-101. There was no bill included in the shipment. You go ahead and enter a **bill** dated 2/14 using the expected costs and terms (Net 15). The total is $120.

2/15/22

✓ You receive the following bills in the mail:

- Sacramento Utilities February bill (for heat and light) #01-77135 for $202.75 dated 2/15. The terms are Net 30.

- Horizon Phone February bill #121–775 for $62.44 dated 2/15. You charge the amount to the Utilities Expense account. The terms are Net 30.

2/17/22

✓ You receive the books ordered from Books Galore on PO-100. All items were received except for the 15 **Puzzles** books. Bill # 2117 for $470 was included. The terms are Net 30.

2/18/22

✓ The order from Cartables (PO-102) comes in today. All items are received. A bill (#949444-55) for $1,650.00 is included with the shipment. You make a note to yourself to remember to pay the amount by 2/28 so that you can take advantage of the 2% discount.

✓ You receive a bill dated 2/18 from Math Shack for the 10 **Kits** received on 2/14. The bill (#M58822) is for $140, which is a little higher than expected. You call Math Shack and they let you know that they had to find a new supplier for the **Kits** and the price went up to $14 per kit. You adjust the bill you already recorded in QBO accordingly (date and amount). The terms are Net 15. **TIP:** Consider using the search feature to find the Math Shack bill. You can ignore any message about linked transaction.

✓ You edit the **Kit** item in **Products and Services** to reflect the new default cost ($14). You also raise the default sales price to $20 to offset the increase in cost.

> **BEHIND THE SCENES** Most users prefer to enter the bill date, rather than the receive date, when recording vendor invoices so that the payable records are more accurate. (Due dates are generally based on the invoice date.) The difference in dates may affect the FIFO layer(s). However, this would normally be an insignificant amount.

2/22/22

✓ Martin sees a great new book when he stops by Books Galore. The book is called "Making Sense with Statistics." He purchases 10 of them to hold for resale, using check #1117. The total cost is $170.00.

- You set up the new **inventory** item using "Statistics" as the item name and "Making Sense with Statistics" as the description. The cost is $17 each. You set the sales price at $30 after discussing it with Martin and the reorder point at 5. **TIP:** Make sure you link the new item to a **category** and set the item as taxable.

✓ Samantha Levin stops by. She worked at the Mathmagic clinic for 5 hours last Saturday so you write her a check (#1118) for $125. **TIP:** Use the same labor cost account you did in the Chapter 4 payment to Samantha.

2/24/22

✓ Martin returns the 3 broken **Kits** to Math Shack. They prepare a credit memo, which he brings back to the office. You record the credit (#R2525-8) for $36. **TIP:** The rate on the returned **kits** is $12.

✓ You and Martin meet at Dick's Diner for lunch and a short meeting. You decide to bring him an $1,800 dividend check (Check # 1119). It's less than last month because you're a bit concerned about the big bill from Cartables. You want to take advantage of the discount, and plan to pay the bill tomorrow.

✓ The lunch at Dick's Diner comes to $19.50. You use the VISA card to pay the bill.

- You charge the lunch to **628 Staff Relations**.

✓ Martin reviews the inventory on hand when he gets back from the meeting.

- He places an order with Books Galore (PO-103) for the following:

    10 each **Sports** and **Ready**

    ○   He decides not to order **Puzzles** yet. He's still waiting for the backordered shipment from PO-100.

  • He places an order with Math Shack (PO-104) for 8 **Kits**. You use the new $14 unit price.

✓ You enter both purchase orders in QBO. The total for PO-103 is $380. The total for PO-104 is $112.

2/25/22

✓ You receive a bill (#3330) for $750 in the mail from a consulting firm, Les & Schmidt, LLC. Martin had hired the company to create a business plan for him. Les & Schmidt completed the work in February. The bill is dated 2/25. The bill is due in 30 days. **TIP:** This is a consulting service.

  • The address for Les & Schmidt is 25 Norton Way, Sacramento, CA 95822.

✓ You pay the Cartables bill, taking advantage of the early payment discount.

  • You start by creating a **vendor credit** to record the early payment discount you will be taking on the Cartables bill. The discount is 2% of the total $1,650 due. You use "DISC" as the **Ref no.**

    ○   Since the early payment discount applies to inventory purchases, you charge the amount to a new **Cost of Goods Sold** account—"Purchase discounts." You use 510 as the account number and **Supplies & Materials—COGS** as the **detail type**.

  • You then pay the Cartables bill with check #1120. The check totals $1,617. **TIP:** Available credits are displayed when you check the box next to the **bill**. The check total shows up in the **PAYMENT** column.

✓ You write a check (#1121) to Martin's father (Richard Smith) for February interest. Martin also asks you to include a $100 principal payment in the check. He wants to start paying his father back. **TIP:** Interest was paid through 1/31 on 2/1. Ignore the number of days in February. Apply the 6% annual rate to the principal balance and calculate one month's interest.

✓ You plan to take a few days off so you prepare and mail the $750 March rent check (#1122) to your landlord (Pro Spaces).

  • **TIP:** The matching (expense recognition) principle applies here.

Check numbers 2/28

    Checking account balance:.....$ 778.53
    Inventory: $2,927.00
    Accounts Payable: $2,409.19
    Net income (February): $3,706.53

Suggested reports for Chapter 7:

All reports should be in portrait orientation.

• Journal—2/01 through 2/28.

    ▪ Transaction types: Check, Bill, Vendor Credit, Bill Payment (check), Expense

• Inventory Valuation Summary as of 2/28

• Open Purchase Order Detail

    ▪ Change **Report period** to **All Dates**

• A/P Aging Summary as of 2/28

• Balance sheet as of 2/28

• Profit and Loss for February

    ▪ Add a **Year-to-date** column to the report

Background information: Sally Hanson, a good friend of yours, double majored in Computer Science and Accounting in college. She worked for several years for a software company in Silicon Valley but the long hours started to take a toll on her personal life.

Last year she decided to open up her own company, Salish Software Solutions. Sally currently advises clients looking for new accounting software and assists them with software installation. She also provides training to client employees and occasionally troubleshoots software issues.

She has decided to start using QuickBooks Online to keep track of her business transactions. She likes the convenience of being able to access financial information over the Internet. You have agreed to act as her accountant while you're working on your accounting degree.

Sally has a number of clients that she is currently working with. She gives 15-day payment terms to her corporate clients but she asks for cash at time of service if she does work for individuals. She has developed the following fee schedule:

Name	Description	Rate
Select	Software selection	$500 flat fee
Set Up	Software installation	$ 75 per hour
Train	Software training	$ 50 per hour
Fix	File repair	$ 60 per hour

Sally rents office space from Alki Property Management for $600 per month.

The following furniture and equipment are owned by Salish:

Description	Date placed in service	Cost	Life	Salvage Value
Office furniture	6/1/21	$1,400	60 months	$200
Computer	7/1/21	$4,620	36 months	$300
Printer.	7/1/21	$ 900	24 months	$ 0

All equipment is depreciated using the straight-line method.

As of 12/31/21, she owed $3,500 to Dell Finance. The monthly payment on that loan is $150 including interest at 5%. Sally's last payment to Dell was 12/31/21.

Over the next month or so, Sally plans to expand her business by selling some of her favorite accounting and personal software products directly to her clients. She has already purchased the following items.

Item Name	Description	Vendor	Quantity on Hand	Cost per Unit	Sales Price
Easy1	Easy Does It	Abacus Shop	15	$100	$ 200
Retailer	Simply Retail	Simply Accounting	2	$400	$ 800
Contractor.	Simply Construction	Simply Accounting	2	$500	$1,000
Organizer	Organizer	Personal Software	20	$ 25	$ 50
Tracker	Investment Tracker	Personal Software	20	$ 20	$ 40

2/1/22

✓ You pay the February rent ($600) to your landlord, Alki Property Management (Check #1112).

✓ You review unpaid bills and pay all bills that are due on or before February 10th. You pay two bills totaling $203.95 starting with check number 1113.

✓ You also write a check (Check # 1115) for the $150 monthly loan payment to Dell Finance. **TIP:** Think about what the payment is covering.

2/3/22

✓ Sally has decided to go to a seminar on new accounting software being held in San Francisco on Friday and Saturday of this week. She asks you to use the credit card to pay the $175 registration fee to the AAASP (American Association of Accounting Software Providers). You enter the credit card expense in QBO. **TIP:** This is a type of professional development.

✓ Now that Sally has started selling products, you decide to enter reorder points for the items currently in QBO. You enter reorder points of 20 for Tracker and Organizer; 15 for Easy1; and 2 for Contractor and Retailer. (Contractor and Retailer are expensive so Sally doesn't want too many of those on the shelf!)

✓ You want to keep track of any orders you place so you turn on the purchase order feature in the Expense tab of Account and Settings. You check the Custom transaction numbers box.

2/4/22

✓ You receive the following bills in the mail:
- Sacramento Light and Power's February bill (for heat and light) #01-84443—$99.00 dated 2/4. The terms are Net 30.
- Western Phone February bill #8911-64 for $105.75 dated 2/4. The terms are Net 30.

2/8/22

✓ You look at the inventory on hand and see that some of the items are below the reorder point.

✓ You prepare PO-100 and order 10 Organizers and 20 Trackers from Personal Software. The PO total is $650.

✓ You see that there are a few other items you might need to order but you want to talk with Sally first.

2/9/22

✓ You pay the balance due to Capital Three ($1,210) with check #1116.

✓ Sally had a great time at the software seminar last weekend. You record the credit card receipts she brings in for her travel expenses using 2/5 as the date:
- Hotel and Saturday breakfast—The Franciscan—$235.85
- Gas—Bell Gas—$35
- Friday Dinner—Top Of The Hill—$42.66
- You consider all the travel costs to be part of the cost of attending the seminar.
- **TIP:** You **must** create a **separate** Expense transaction for each charge. The reason will become clear in the homework for Chapter 8.

✓ Sally places an order for two Contractor packages and one Retailer package from Simply Accounting. You create PO-101 for the $1,400 purchase.
- You decide to give the vendor a call about their payment terms. The item costs are high and you're hoping to get some kind of early payment discount. Simply Accounting agrees to give Salish terms of 2% 10, net 30. You add a new Term to the Terms list in QBO. You change the payment terms in the vendor record. **TIP:** Since the bill is due in 30 days if you do not pay it early, you use 30 as the fixed number of days in the term.

2/11/22

✓ Sally was very impressed with a couple of the new products demonstrated by Abacus Shop at the AAASP Conference in San Francisco. The company has created appointment and client management systems for various types of professional firms. Sally decides to offer the products to her Sacramento clients.
- Since the product line is expanding, you decide to reorganize the product categories a bit.
  - You decide to set up a category called "Management Products." You also change the name of the Products category to "Accounting Products."
  - You edit the Organizer and Tracker items to include them in the new Management Products category.

- You talk with Sally and decide that each new **inventory** item:
  - Will be included in the Management Products **category**.
  - Will have a reorder point of 1.
  - Will be recorded in the **130 Inventory Asset** account.
  - Will use account **420 Sales of Product Income** and **500 Cost of Goods Sold** as the **Income** and **Expense** accounts, respectively.
  - Will be taxable at the standard rate.
  - Will use Abacus Shop as the preferred vendor.
  - **TIP:** You **must** enter 0 as the **initial quantity on hand** and 02/11/2022 as the **As of date**. You'll be entering purchases of the items when they are received.
- The new **inventory products** are:
  - Legal (Description—Manage Your Law Firm)—Expected cost $350; Selling price $500
  - Medical (Description—Manage Your Medical Practice)—Expected cost $350; Selling price $500
  - Engineering (Description—Manage Your Engineering Firm)—Expected cost $350; Selling price $500
  - **TIP:** Once you create one new item, you can **Duplicate** the item from the **ACTION** menu and edit the copy for each additional item.

✓ You prepare a purchase order (PO-102) to Abacus to buy 2 of each of the new items. The PO totals $2,100.

2/15/22

✓ You receive the shipment from Personal Software for items ordered on PO-100. All items were received except for 2 of the **Trackers**. No bill was included with the shipment. You go ahead and create a **bill** using the expected costs and terms. The total is $610. **TIP:** Don't forget to **Add** the purchase order information from the sidebar of the **bill**.

2/17/22

✓ The order from Simply Accounting (PO-101) comes in today. All items are received. A bill (#65411-8) for $1,400 is included with the shipment. You make a note to yourself to remember to pay the amount within the discount period so that you can take advantage of the 2% discount.

✓ You receive the bill from Personal Software for the **Organizers** and **Trackers** received on 2/15. The bill (#744466) for $619.00 is dated 2/15/22 (the date the shipment was received). The terms are Net 30. The **Trackers** were slightly more than expected ($20.50 per unit instead of $20). You call Personal Software and they apologize for not letting you know about the price and term changes sooner. You open the **bill** to make the edits. **TIP:** Consider using the Find feature to locate the bill.

2/22/22

✓ You receive the shipment from Abacus Shop for all items ordered on PO-102. The bill (TAS 25344) for $2,100 has terms of Net 15.

✓ You ask Sally whether she wants you to follow up on the 2 **Trackers** that weren't received in the Personal Software shipment on 2/15. She says she'll go ahead and call Personal Software to cancel the backorder. You close PO-100 in QBO.

2/24/22

✓ Sally returns the two damaged **Organizer** CDs to Personal Software and picks up a credit memo (RR744466) for $50, which you record. **TIP:** This is a vendor credit. Make sure you enter the items in the correct **details** section.

✓ You and Sally meet at Roscoe's for lunch and a short meeting before she takes off for Chicago. You decide to bring her a $2,500 dividend check (Check # 1117).

✓ The lunch at Roscoe's comes to $28.50. You use the credit card to pay the bill.

- You decide to set up a new account, **Staff meetings expense**, a subaccount of **600 Labor Costs** to track the cost of staff meetings. You use **Office/General Administrative Expenses** as the **Detail Type** and 608 as the account number.

✓ Sally takes a few minutes to review the inventory on hand when she gets back from lunch.

- She places an order with Abacus Shop for 5 **Easy1s**. You record the PO-103 for $500.

2/25/22

✓ You receive a bill (#3330) for $575 in the mail from an accounting firm, Dovalina & Diamond, LLC. Sally hired the company to do a two-year financial projection. The work was completed in February. She thinks she may need to either borrow some money from a bank or attract investors in order to grow as quickly as she'd like. The bill is dated 2/25. The bill is due in 30 days. **TIP:** This is a type of professional service.

- The address for Dovalina & Diamond is 419 Upstart Drive, Sacramento, CA 95822.

✓ You decide to pay all bills due on or before 3/7 PLUS any bills with early payment discounts expiring before 3/7.

- You start by creating a **vendor credit** to record the early payment discount you will be taking on the Simply Accounting bill. You use 65411-8D as the **ref no**. The discount is 2% of the total $1,400 due.

    Since the early payment discount applies to inventory purchases, you charge the amount to a new **Cost of Goods Sold** account—"Purchase discounts." You use 510 as the account number and **Other Costs of Services—COS** as the **Detail Type**.

- You pay four bills. The first check number is 1118. You apply a credit on one of them. The total of the three checks is $3,076.75. **TIP:** The check total shows up in the **PAYMENT** column.

✓ You plan to take a few days off so you prepare and mail the $600 March rent check (#1122) to your landlord (Alki Property Management).

- **TIP:** The matching (expense recognition) principle applies here.

Check numbers 2/28

Checking account balance: $10,448.55
Inventory: .... $ 6,889.00
Account payable: .... $ 3,244.00
Net income (February): ...... $ 4,542.99

Suggested reports for Chapter 7:

All reports should be in portrait orientation.

- Journal (2/1-2/28)
    - Transaction types: Check, Bill, Vendor Credit, Bill Payment (check), Expense
- Inventory Valuation Summary as of 2/28
- Open Purchase Orders List
    - Remove **Memo/Description** and **Ship Via** columns
- A/P Aging Summary as of 2/28
- Balance sheet as of 2/28
- Profit and Loss for February
    - Add a Year-to-date column

APPENDIX 7A FIFO LAYERS IN QBO

An important concept in many inventory valuation methods is that of **inventory layers**. Layers represent the quantity and unit cost of any addition to the inventory account. A separate layer is created:

- every time inventory items are received from vendors.
- every time inventory items are returned by customers.

Layers are reduced:

- whenever inventory items are sold.
- whenever inventory items are returned to vendors.

Under FIFO, the oldest layer is reduced first. In a sales transaction, the unit cost in the oldest layer is what is used to calculate the debit to Cost of Goods Sold and the credit to inventory. In a return of items to vendors, the unit cost in the oldest layer is what is used to calculate the credit to inventory. The debit would most likely either go to accounts payable (to reduce any balance owing to the vendor) or accounts receivable (to record the amount due from the vendor).

Here's an example of how FIFO layers work using the test drive company and a new product (Wheelbarrows):

1. On 1/15, Craig purchases 3 new Wheelbarrow products ($50 per unit).
2. On 1/18, Craig sells 2 of the Wheelbarrows for $75 each.
3. On 1/20, the customer returns one of the Wheelbarrows they purchased on 9/22. Craig reduces the customer's account balance by $75.
4. On 1/22, Craig returns a Wheelbarrow to the vendor for a $50 refund.
5. On 1/23, Craig purchases 4 more Wheelbarrows ($55 per unit).
6. On 1/26, Craig sells 3 Wheelbarrows for $75 each.

Here's how the inventory cost layers work given those transactions:

Transactions	Layer 1	Layer 2	Layer 3	Quantity on Hand
1/15 purchase	3 @ $50 each			3
1/18 sale	(2 @ $50 each)			1
1/20 customer return		1 @ $50		2
1/22 return to vendor	(1 @ $50)			1
1/23 purchase			4 @ $55 each	5
1/26 sale		(1 @ $50)	(2 @ $55)	2
Balance	0	0	2 @ $55	

At 1/26, Inventory equals $110 (2 @ $55 each).

In QBO, the FIFO layer activity can be seen in the **Inventory Valuation Detail** report:

Figure 7A.1

Inventory valuation
detail report

Craig's Design and Landscaping Services

Inventory Valuation Detail

DATE		TRANSACTION TYPE		NUM	NAME	QTY	RATE	FIFO COST	QTY ON HAND	ASSET VALUE
▼ Landscaping										
▼ Wheelbarrow										
01/01		Inventory Starting Value		START		0.00	50.00	0.00	0.00	0.00
01/15	Layer 1	Bill		456-7	Hicks Hardware	3.00	50.00	150.00	3.00	150.00
01/18		Invoice	From Layer 1	1038	Amy's Bird Sanctuary	(2.00)	50.00	(100.00)	1.00	50.00
01/20	Layer 2	Credit Memo		CM1038	Amy's Bird Sanctuary	1.00	50.00	50.00	2.00	100.00
01/22		Vendor Credit	From Layer 1	CM456-7	Hicks Hardware	(1.00)	50.00	(50.00)	1.00	50.00
01/23	Layer 3	Bill		567-8	Hicks Hardware	4.00	55.00	220.00	5.00	270.00
01/26		Invoice	From Layer 2	1039	Diego Rodriguez	(1.00)	50.00	(50.00)	4.00	220.00
01/26		Invoice	From Layer 3	1039	Diego Rodriguez	(2.00)	55.00	(110.00)	2.00	110.00
Total for Wheelbarrow						2.00		$110.00	2.00	$110.00
Total for Landscaping						2.00		$110.00	2.00	$110.00

The valuations of the inventory layers in QBO correspond to our table.

 HINT: Check your dates if your inventory values are incorrect. QBO uses a perpetual inventory tracking system. If layers are created in the wrong order (incorrect dates are entered) and purchase costs are increasing or decreasing, unit costs used for reducing inventory balances and calculating cost of goods sold can be affected. You may need to delete and reenter transactions. Changing the date on a recorded transaction may not correct your error.

End-of-Period and Other Activity
(Merchandising Company)

Objectives

After completing Chapter 8, you should be able to:

1. Adjust inventory quantities.

2. Pay sales taxes.

3. Record non-customer cash receipts.

4. Record transfers between bank accounts.

5. Upload credit card transactions into QBO.

6. Inactivate and merge accounts.

7. Add comments to reports.

8. Download bank transactions directly into QBO (Appendix 8A).

All of the "end-of-period" procedures we covered in Chapter 5 apply to merchandising companies as well as service companies. Bank accounts must be reconciled. Adjusting journal entries must be made. Remember: end-of-period procedures are focused on making sure the financial records are as accurate as possible. The financial statements should give internal and external users a fair picture of:

- The operations of the company for the period (profit and loss statement).
- The financial position of the company at the end of the period (balance sheet).

There are a few additional procedures unique to merchandising companies that we'll cover in this chapter.

- Inventory adjustments
- Managing sales taxes

We'll also look at a few procedures and QBO features not covered in previous chapters:

- Recording non-customer cash receipts
- Recording bank transfers
- Inactivating and merging accounts
- Adding comments to reports

ADJUSTING INVENTORY

As you know, QBO features a perpetual inventory tracking system for **inventory** items so quantities are automatically updated when goods are received, sold, or returned.

If life were perfect, the inventory quantities in QBO would **always** equal inventory quantities on hand (physically in the store or warehouse). Unfortunately, we know that that isn't always the case. Differences can occur because of:

- Theft
- Unrecorded transactions (sales, item receipts, returns by customers, or returns to vendors)
- Damaged goods

In addition to needing to know the quantity on hand for valuing inventory, companies must have an accurate record of how many of each of their products they have available to sell. That's part of a good inventory management system. A few of you have probably asked a clerk about a book you can't find on the shelf at your favorite bookstore. The clerk looks the book up in the store's computer system and it says that they should have two in stock. You go back to the shelves with the clerk and neither of you can find the book. It may just be misplaced or it may have been stolen but both you and the clerk have wasted time looking for it and you're a disappointed customer. The more accurate the inventory records, the smoother the operation and the more accurate the financial statements. So, periodically, the inventory on hand is physically counted and the inventory records are adjusted as necessary.

Counts can be taken at any point during a year but are usually taken, at a minimum, at the end of the year. (Companies that need audited financial statements **must** take a count, with auditors present, at the end of the year.) Counts are frequently taken more often (quarterly, for example). It's usually a big job to take a physical inventory count so many companies don't count inventory monthly. If there hasn't been a history of significant inventory adjustments, taking an annual physical inventory count is probably sufficient. (If you're in the bookstore business and you have lots of books on shelves, you might want to consider more frequent counts!)

To get a good inventory count, it's usually best to take the count when products aren't moving (aren't being sold or received). Many companies take inventory counts after closing or on weekends. Counters are given a list of products and the unit of measure that should be used to count the products (units, cartons, pounds, etc.). As a control, the count sheets should not list the expected quantity. Why? For one thing, it's just too easy to see what you think you **should** see (i.e., what the count sheet says)!

Once the physical inventory count is taken, the count sheets are compared to the accounting records. Significant variations should be investigated. Documentation (particularly packing slips) related to transactions occurring close to the count date can often provide useful information. Goods might have been received or shipped out earlier or later than the customer invoice or vendor bill dates used in the accounting system. In practice, physical inventory counts usually involve a lot of recounts.

Once the company is confident that it has gotten a good count and all known transactions have been recorded, the accounting records are adjusted to the count.

In QBO, count sheets are available in the **Sales and Customers** section of **Reports**.

Figure 8.1

Access to inventory count sheet

The **Physical Inventory Worksheet** looks something like this:

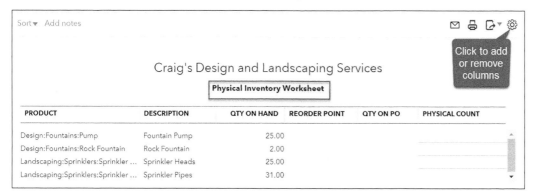

Figure 8.2

Physical inventory count sheet

The worksheet can easily be modified by clicking **Customize**. For example, a company that uses SKU numbers would likely want those included on the count sheet. The **QTY ON HAND** column should be removed. **REORDER POINT** and **QTY ON PO** information isn't necessary for a count and could be removed.

> **HINT:** You might have noticed that the date for the worksheet can't be changed. The count sheets must be printed on the day the count is taken.

After the count sheets are completed, the listed counts are compared to the inventory quantities in QBO. As noted earlier, recounts are normally requested if the counts vary significantly from the perpetual records.

Once the company determines that the count is accurate, any necessary inventory adjustments are recorded through the **Inventory Qty Adjustment** form accessed by clicking **+ New** in the navigation bar.

Figure 8.3

Access to inventory quantity adjustment

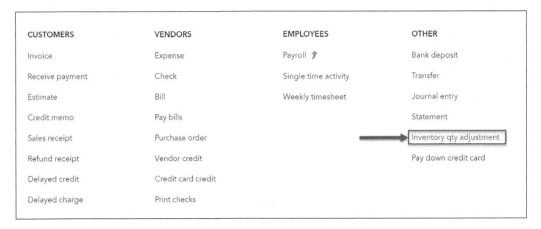

The form looks like this:

Figure 8.4

Inventory adjustment form

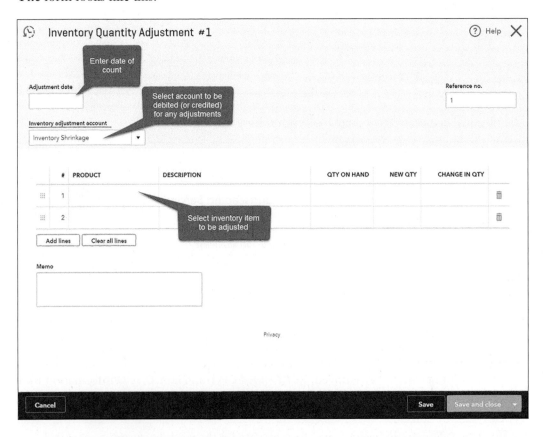

The **Adjustment date** would be the date of the inventory count. The **Inventory adjustment account** is the choice of management. Most companies debit or credit inventory adjustments to an account with a **cost of goods sold account type**. The offset account is, of course, the inventory (asset) account.

The **inventory** items to be adjusted are selected in the **PRODUCT** column.

> **!** **WARNING: Occasionally, QBO will not allow users to select a product in the Inventory Quantity Adjustment screen. In that case, use the following workaround:**
>
> 1. **Exit out of the Inventory Quantity Adjustment screen.**
> 2. **Click the ⚙ on the icon bar.**
> 3. **Click Products and Services.**
> 4. **In the far left column, check the box next to the items to be adjusted.**
> 5. **Select Adjust Quantity in the Batch actions dropdown menu. (The menu is on the right side of the list near the top.)**

The form will look something like this when items have been selected:

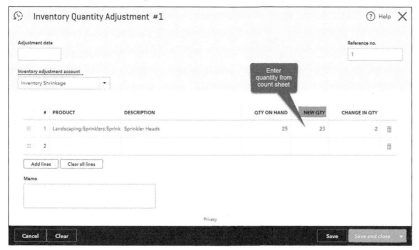

Figure 8.5

Example of inventory item adjustment

QBO automatically updates the **QTY ON HAND** with the current quantity in the item record. Users enter the quantity from the count sheet as the **NEW QTY**.

Once the **Inventory Qty Adjustment** form is saved, QBO adjusts both the quantity and the value of items selected in the form. The oldest FIFO layer is used to determine the amount of the value adjustment.

An **Inventory Valuation Detail** report customized to show only the items adjusted in the next Practice Exercise would look something like this:

Figure 8.6

Inventory transaction report after quantity adjustment

Craig's Design and Landscaping Services
Inventory Valuation Detail
All Dates

TRANSACTION TYPE	NUM	NAME	QTY	RATE	FIFO COST	QTY ON HAND	ASSET VALUE
▾ Design							
▾ Fountains							
▾ Pump							
Inventory Qty Adjust	START		16.00	10.00	160.00	16.00	160.00
Check	75	Hicks Hardware	3.00	10.00	30.00	19.00	190.00
Bill		Norton Lumber and Building Ma...	8.00	10.00	80.00	27.00	270.00
Invoice	1036	Freeman Sporting Goods:0969 ...	-1.00	10.00	-10.00	26.00	260.00
Invoice	1037	Sonnenschein Family Store	-1.00	10.00	-10.00	25.00	250.00
Inventory Qty Adjust	YE Adj		-2.00	10.00	-20.00	23.00	230.00
Total for Pump			**23.00**		**$230.00**	**23.00**	**$230.00**
Total for Fountains			**23.00**		**$230.00**	**23.00**	**$230.00**
Total for Design			**23.00**		**$230.00**	**23.00**	**$230.00**
▾ Landscaping							
▾ Sprinklers							
▾ Sprinkler Heads							
Inventory Qty Adjust	START		10.00	0.75	7.50	10.00	7.50
Check	75	Hicks Hardware	15.00	0.75	11.25	25.00	18.75
Inventory Qty Adjust	YE Adj		-1.00	0.75	-0.75	24.00	18.00
Total for Sprinkler Heads			**24.00**		**$18.00**	**24.00**	**$18.00**
Total for Sprinklers			**24.00**		**$18.00**	**24.00**	**$18.00**
Total for Landscaping			**24.00**		**$18.00**	**24.00**	**$18.00**

> **BEHIND THE SCENES** Under GAAP, FIFO inventory values must be adjusted when the reported cost is less than the estimated selling price (net of any reasonably predictable selling costs). This is known as the "lower of cost or net realizable value" rule. Currently, QBO does not have a feature allowing users to change values for inventory to comply with the rule. As an alternative, companies could create a contra asset account and record an allowance to cover any difference.
>
> Inventory starting values (values entered when an existing company is initially set up in QBO) **can** be adjusted with or without changing quantities. This is done by selecting **Adjust starting value** in the **ACTION** column for the specific item in the **Products and Services** list.

PRACTICE
EXERCISE
8.1

Adjust inventory for Craig's Design and Landscaping.

(Inventory was counted today. All of the counts agreed to the QBO records except for Fountain Pumps (there were only 23 pumps) and Sprinkler Heads (there were only 24).)

1. Click **+ New** on the navigation bar.

2. Click **Inventory Qty Adjustment**.

3. Enter the current date as the **Adjustment date**.

4. Select **Add new** in the **Inventory adjustment account** field.

    a. Select **Cost of Goods Sold** as the **Account Type**.

    b. Select **Supplies & Materials—COGS** as the **Detail Type**.

    c. Enter "Inventory adjustments" as the **Name**.

    d. Click **Save and close**.

5. Enter "YE Adj" as the **Reference no.**

6. In the first row, select **Pump** in the **PRODUCT** field and enter "23" as the **NEW QTY**.

    a. **TIP:** If you are unable to select a product in the field, use the workaround described in the WARNING box in this section.

7. In the second row, select **Sprinkler Heads** in the **PRODUCT** field and enter "24" as the **NEW QTY**.

8. Click **Save and close**.

9. Click **Reports** on the navigation bar.

10. Click **Physical Inventory Worksheet** in the **Sales and Customers** section.

11. **Make a note** of the **QTY ON HAND** for **Rock Fountains** and **Sprinkler Pipes**.

MANAGING SALES TAXES

Sales taxes are remitted to taxing authorities on a periodic basis—generally annually, quarterly, or monthly, depending on the size of the company. Remember, the responsibility to pay the tax is on the consumer but the responsibility to collect and remit the tax is on the seller. In most states, sellers are responsible for remitting to the tax authorities the amount they **should** have charged (which hopefully agrees with the amount they actually **did** charge!).

BEHIND THE SCENES In most cases, a company is required to report and remit sales taxes when the tax is **charged** to the customer (accrual method). Some states allow a company to remit the tax when it's **collected** from the customer (cash method). The default in QBO is the "charged" date (the date of the invoice or sales receipt). In the example below, and in the homework assignments, the default (charged) date will be used.

At the end of a tax-reporting period, a report should be prepared detailing sales and sales taxes charged, by taxing jurisdiction, and reviewed.

The **Sales Tax Liability**, **Taxable Sales Summary**, and **Taxable Sales Detail** reports are accessible in the **Sales tax** section of **Reports**.

Figure 8.7

Available sales tax reports

The **Sales Tax Liability** report will look something like this if **All Dates** is selected in the **Report period** field:

Figure 8.8

Report of total taxable sales and tax charged to customers by jurisdiction

Craig's Design and Landscaping Services
Sales Tax Liability Report
All Dates

	GROSS AMOUNT	NON TAXABLE AMOUNT	TAXABLE AMOUNT	TAX AMOUNT
▼ Arizona Department of Revenue				
AZ State tax	422.00	0.00	422.00	29.96
Tucson City	422.00	0.00	422.00	8.44
TOTAL				38.40
▼ California Department of Tax a…				
California	5,323.00	205.00	5,118.00	409.44
TOTAL				409.44

This report lists taxable sales by jurisdiction. This report would be used to prepare the various tax reports that are filed with the state and local tax agencies.

BEHIND THE SCENES For control purposes, the company should carefully review its tax reports. Remember, QBO is reporting what **did** happen, not what **should** have happened.

The **Taxable Sales Summary** report lists taxable sales by product. Drilling down on any of the items listed allows you to see the specific sales included in the total. The report would look something like this if **All dates** was selected as the **Report period**.

In the **Taxable Sales Detail** report, taxable sales are listed by sales transaction, grouped by customer.

Remitting Sales Tax Liabilities

> **WARNING: Your homework company includes the current, fully auto-mated sales tax feature covered in Chapter 6. Although the automated system can be activated in Craig's Design and Landscaping Service (the test drive company), students have experienced a number of technical issues when using that system. As a result, there will be no Practice Exercise for this section. To help you with your homework, the processes and procedures described below are from the automated version.**

Sales tax functions (like tax payments and adjustments) are accessed through the Sales Tax Center.

Click **Taxes** on the navigation bar in your homework company to open the Sales Tax Center.

If you're working on your homework prior to February 1, 2022, the screen should look something like this:

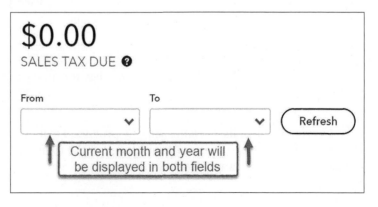

If you're completing the homework in February 2022, the screen should look something like this:

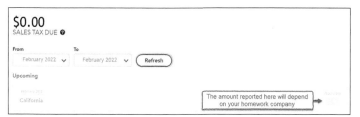

Figure 8.11

Alternative Sales Tax Center display

If you're completing the homework after February 2022, you will see sections for **Due**, **Upcoming**, and possibly **Overdue**. You will also see a **View return** link next to the amounts in the **Overdue** and **Due** sections.

The difference in screen displays is related to sales tax filing periods. In QBO, no amounts are displayed in the Sales Tax Center if the sales tax **start date** is in a period (month) subsequent to the date QBO is accessed. (The **start date** was identified as the date sales taxes were first collected by the company as part of the sales tax feature activation process.) Since sales taxes were activated in your homework company as of 2/1/22, you would not see tax information displayed if you opened the Sales Tax Center prior to that date.

Depending on timing, then, the Sales Tax Center can expand to include up to three sections:

- **Due This Month**
  - List of taxes that are currently due for the reporting period just ended, by tax authority
  - The amount, tax period, and tax due date would be displayed.

- **Upcoming**
  - List of taxes being accrued in the current tax period, by tax authority
  - The amount of tax charged to date will be displayed. The word **Accruing** appears above the amount.

- **Overdue**
  - List of unpaid, past due taxes, by tax authority and by tax period

> **! WARNING: If you're completing your homework prior to March 2022, you will not be able to complete the remittance process in your homework company. (Tax on February 2022 sales would not be due until March 2022.) Directions for recording the payment are included in the assignments.**

To illustrate the material covered in the remaining sales tax sections, screenshots from a demonstration company (Abacus Text) are used. The Sales Tax Center for Abacus Text looks like this in February 2021.

Figure 8.12

Sales Tax Center in demonstration company for this section

Click **View Return** to start the tax payment (remittance) process for any tax amounts included in the **Due this month** or **Overdue** sections.

Sales tax review screen

Users have a chance to review or adjust the return on this screen. Users can also click the link in the **File your sales tax now** section (Step 1 in Figure 8.13) to access the appropriate form.
        Click **Record payment**.

 HINT: You may see **Select filing method** instead of **Record payment**. If you do, click **File manually.** Your next screen will look similar to Figure 8.14.

Sales tax filing method option screen

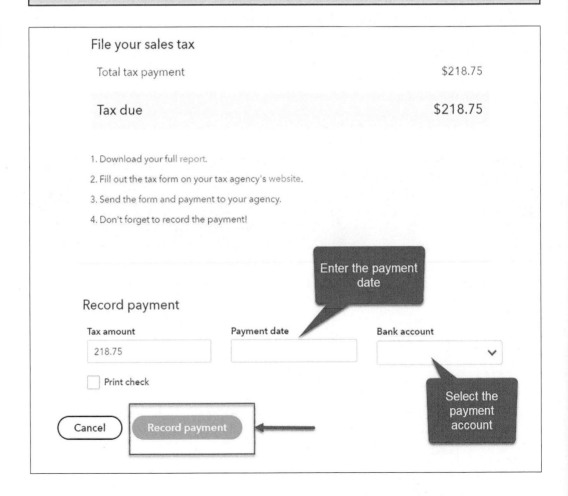

Enter the date and bank account to be charged. Click **Record payment** to enter the transaction. (The **transaction type** for sales tax remittances is **Sales Tax Payment**.)

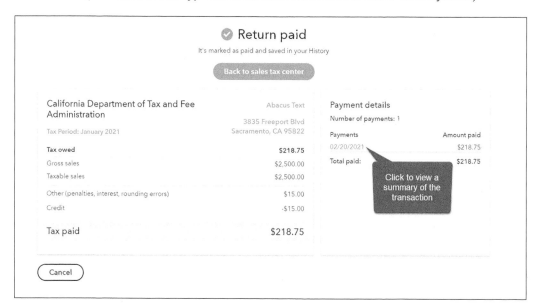

Figure 8.15
Tax payment review screen

Click the payment date to see a summary of the transaction.

Once a **Sales Tax Payment** has been recorded, it can be deleted but not adjusted.

> **BEHIND THE SCENES** QBO automatically sets up a separate liability account (**Other currently liability account type**) for each sales tax agency. When sales taxes are paid, QBO automatically debits the appropriate liability account. These accounts cannot be changed in any way or deleted.

Adjusting Sales Tax Liabilities

The liability might need to be adjusted because:

- QBO wasn't yet updated for a recent rate change.

- A specific customer was inadvertently overcharged or undercharged for sales tax.

- The company is located in a state that levies an additional tax (called an excise tax) on the **seller**.

> **BEHIND THE SCENES** Excise taxes are generally based on gross sales revenue. Excise taxes cannot be entered as a sales tax item because they are not charged to the customer. They are an expense of the seller.

Although sales tax payments can't be adjusted after they are recorded, adjustments **can** be made on the **Review your sales tax** screen before the payment is processed.

Figure 8.16

Access to sales tax adjustment screen

Click ✚ **Add an adjustment**

Figure 8.17

Sales tax adjustment screen

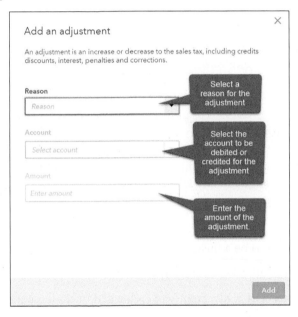

A reason for the adjustment must be selected from one of the following options.

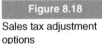

Figure 8.18

Sales tax adjustment options

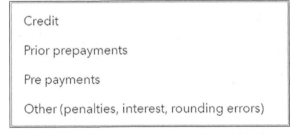

The account to be charged for the amount of the adjustment is entered in the **Account** field.

Adjustments due to corrections of errors would normally be charged to a miscellaneous expense or income account. Rounding errors and adjustments for excise taxes would normally be charged to a business tax expense account.

The **Amount** is entered as a positive number if the user wants to increase the tax payment. If the payment amount should be decreased, the **Amount** is entered as a negative number.

An adjustment to increase the amount to be paid by $15.00 (penalty) would look something like this:

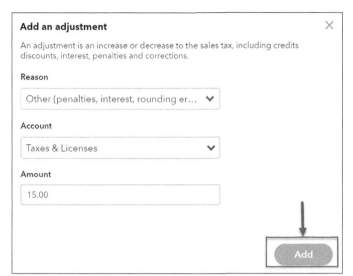

Figure 8.19
Example of sales tax adjustment

Click **Add** to adjust the tax amount to be paid.

Users have a chance to review the payment amount on the next screen.

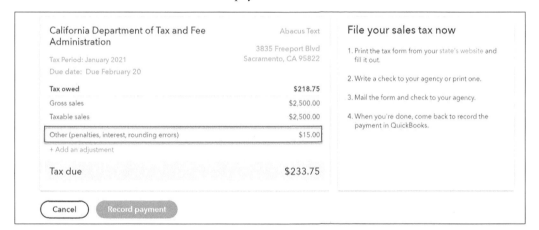

Figure 8.20
Example of sales tax review screen with tax adjustment

Click **Record payment.** Enter the payment date and select the bank account on the next screen (Figure 8.14) and click **Record payment.**

> **BEHIND THE SCENES** If a customer was overcharged, the company would generally want to reimburse the customer, if possible, by issuing a check or credit memo. If a customer was undercharged, the company might choose to invoice the customer for the tax. In that case, the company would need to set up a **service** item for uncollected tax. That item would, of course, be non-taxable.

Deleting Sales Tax Payments

Although **sales tax payments** can't be edited once they've been recorded, they can be deleted.

 HINT: The sales tax liability is automatically restored when **sales tax payments** are deleted. The user can then record the correct payment.

To delete the payment, click **Taxes** on the Navigation bar.

Figure 8.21

Access to sales tax
history from Sales Tax
Center

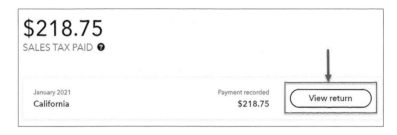

Click **History**.

Figure 8.22

Access to prior
sales tax payment
information

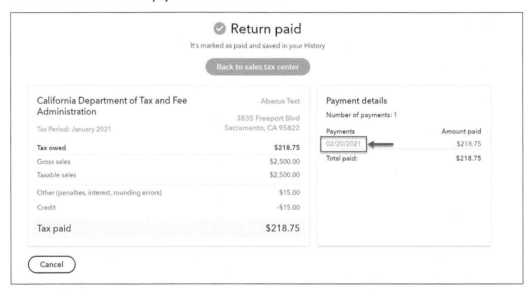

Click **View return** for the payment to be deleted.

Figure 8.23

Access to sales tax
payment screen

Click the payment date.

Figure 8.24

Sales tax payment
screen

Click **Delete**.

QBO automatically reopens the **Review your sales tax** screen (Figure 8.16) so that the tax remittance can be reprocessed.

Sales Tax Payment transactions can also be deleted by drilling down (clicking) on the transaction in journal reports to open the **View payment** screen (Figure 8.24).

ENTERING CASH RECEIPTS FROM NON-CUSTOMERS

In companies, most cash receipts come from customers. (At least we hope they do!) There are other sources of cash though:

- Borrowings
- Sales of company stock
- Sales of property or equipment
- Etc.

In previous chapters, all cash receipts were entered through one of the following forms:

- Sales Receipts
  - Used for cash or credit card sales to customers
- Payments
  - Used for cash or credit card payments by customers on account receivable balances

As you know, the default debit account in the underlying entry for both **sales receipt** and **payment** transactions is **Undeposited Funds**, an asset account. Receipts are later transferred from **Undeposited Funds** to the appropriate **Bank** account through the **Deposit** form.

When cash is received from **non-customers**, the amounts are entered **directly** into the **Deposit** form.

The **Deposit** form is opened by clicking **+ New** on the navigation bar and selecting **Bank Deposit**.

If there are pending undeposited funds, the initial screen will look like this:

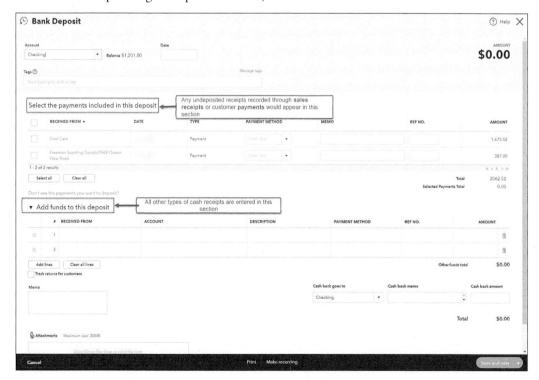

Figure 8.25

Example of deposit form with undeposited funds from customer receipts

If there are no undeposited funds, the **Deposit** form will look something like this:

Figure 8.26

Example of deposit
form with no pending
deposits

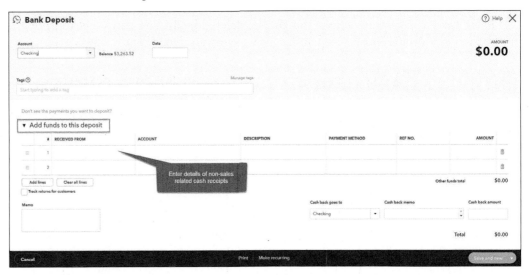

The appropriate bank account should be selected and the deposit **Date** entered.

Non-customer receipts would be added in the **Add funds to this deposit** section of the form. The payer's name should be selected in the **RECEIVED FROM** field, although this field is optional, and the account to be credited should be selected in the **ACCOUNT** field.

 HINT: Deposits should be grouped to correspond to the actual bank deposits. If a non-customer receipt is being deposited with customer receipts, both types should be recorded in the same deposit form.

PRACTICE EXERCISE 8.2

Record a non-customer cash receipt for Craig's Design and Landscaping.

(Craig's Design received a $100 rebate check from one of its vendors (Norton Lumber). Craig's deposited it along with a few checks from customers.)

1. Click **+ New** on the navigation bar.

2. Click **Bank Deposit**.

3. Check the boxes next to the two payments listed in the **Select the payments included in the deposit** section.

   a. **Make a note** of the customer names appearing in the **RECEIVED FROM** column.

4. In the **Add funds to this deposit** section:

   a. Select **Norton Lumber and Building Materials** in the **RECEIVED FROM** column (first line).

   b. Select **Decks and Patios** as the **ACCOUNT**.

   c. Enter "Rebate" as the **DESCRIPTION**.

   d. Select **Check** as the **PAYMENT METHOD**.

   e. Enter "1007" as the **REF NO.**

   f. Enter "100" as the **AMOUNT**.

5. The **Total** should be $2,162.52.

6. Click **Save and close**.

RECORDING BANK TRANSFERS

Many companies maintain more than one bank account. Other than the general checking account, a company will frequently have a separate checking account for payroll. They might also open a savings or a money market account to earn some interest on funds not needed for immediate operations.

If the accounts are with the same bank, transfers between accounts can generally be made either electronically (through the bank's website) or by phone.

In QBO, electronic or phone transfers are recorded using the **Transfer** form. The **Transfer** form is accessed by clicking **+ New** on the navigation bar and selecting **Transfer** in the **Other** column. The screen looks like this:

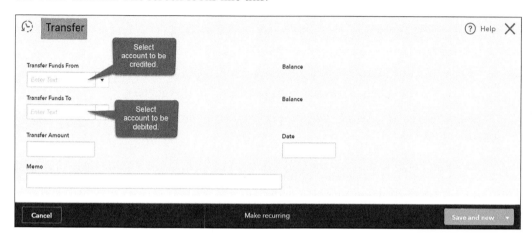

Figure 8.27

Transfer form

The account selected in the **Transfer Funds From** field represents the account to be credited. The account selected in the **Transfer Funds To** field represents the account to be debited. QBO will display the current balances in each account once they are selected.

The amount to be transferred is recorded in the **Transfer Amount** field. The **date** must also be entered.

Transfer funds between accounts for Craig's Design and Landscaping.

(Craig's Design decides to open a money market account with a $500 transfer from checking.)

1. Click **+ New** on the navigation bar.
2. Click **Transfer**.
3. Select **Checking** in the **Transfer Funds From** dropdown menu.
   a. **Make a note** of how many accounts in the dropdown menu have the **account type Bank**.
4. Select **Add new** in the **Transfer Funds To** dropdown menu.
   a. Select **Bank** as the **Account Type**.
   b. Select **Money Market** as the **Detail Type**.
   c. Leave the **Name** as **Money Market**.
   d. Click **Save and Close**.
5. Enter "500" as the **Transfer Amount**.
6. Enter the current date in the **Date** field.
7. In the **Memo** field, enter "Opened new money market account."
8. Click **Save and close**.

PRACTICE EXERCISE 8.3

Homework
MBC

UPLOADING CREDIT CARD TRANSACTIONS INTO QBO

 HINT: There is no Practice Exercise for this section. (Transactions cannot be uploaded to the practice company because of frequent date changes.) The steps outlined can be used when completing your homework assignment.

Companies that provide credit cards to employees need to make sure that all transactions are properly recorded in QBO. In most cases, the credit card holders supply a report (with credit card receipts attached) to the accounting department. The transactions can then be entered from that report.

Companies can also download transactions into QBO from the credit card company. There are two ways to do that:

- Download transactions directly from the credit card company.
  - To do that, the user must add (link) the credit card account to QBO.
  - Direct downloading is covered in Appendix 8A of this chapter.
- Download transactions from the credit card company into a CSV file and then upload them into QBO.

To ensure that all transactions are recorded and to simplify the reconciliation process, credit card transactions can be entered manually AND uploaded into the company file. This does not result in duplicate entries. Instead, the transactions are matched, and any necessary changes are added to the company file. This is what you'll be doing in your homework company.

Click **Banking** in the navigation bar.

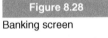

Figure 8.28

Banking screen

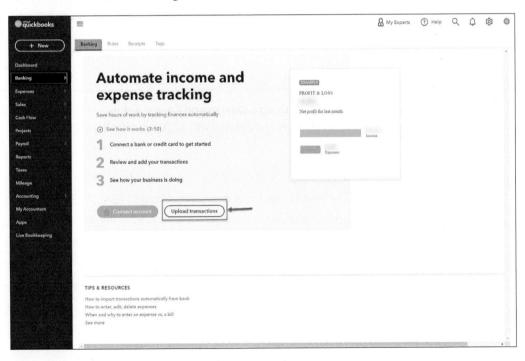

Click **Upload transactions**.

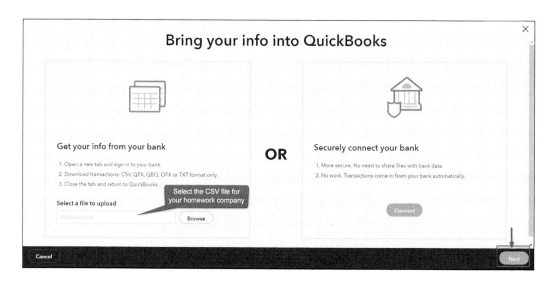

Figure 8.29

Upload selection screen

Browse to select the CSV file of downloaded transactions. (A CSV file for your homework company can be found at https://cambridgepub.com/book/qbo2021#ancillaries.)
    Click **Next**.

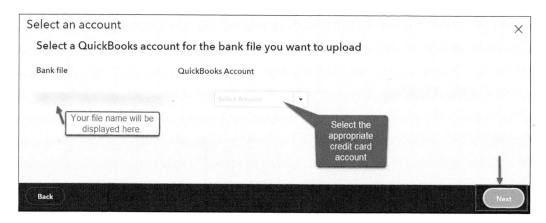

Figure 8.30

Selection of credit card account

Use the dropdown menu under **QuickBooks Account** and select the appropriate credit card liability account.

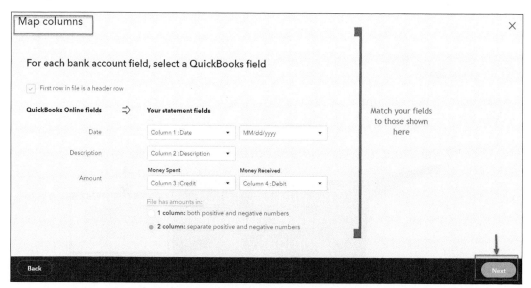

Figure 8.31

Mapping options

In the next screen, the fields in the uploaded spreadsheet are mapped to QBO. Complete the **Map columns** window as follows:

● Check the **First row in file is a header row** box.

● In the **Date** row, select **Column 1 :Date** in the first (left) dropdown menu and **MM/dd/yyyy** in the right dropdown menu.

● In the **Description** row, select **Column 2 :Description** in the dropdown menu.

   ▪ The **description** field is usually the payee name.

● Toggle the **2 column: separate positive and negative numbers** option.

● In the **Amount** row, select **Column 3 :Credit** in the **Money Spent** dropdown menu and **Column 4 :Debit** in the **Money Received** dropdown menu.

> **BEHIND THE SCENES** Both credit card charges and payments are uploaded into QBO. Credit card charges (**Money Spent**) are credited to the credit card liability account. Credit card payments (**Money received**) are debited to the credit card liability account. The columns in those fields indicate the appropriate column in the worksheet.

Click **Next**.

Figure 8.32

Transaction selection for import screen

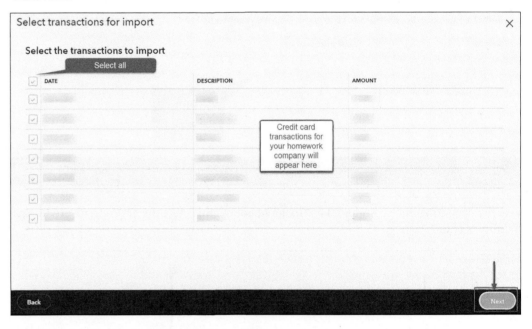

Select transactions to be imported into QBO.
    Click **Next**.

Figure 8.33

Acceptance of transactions for import screen

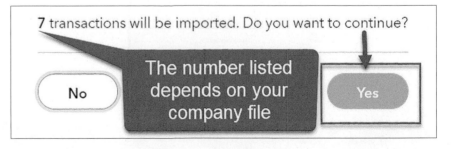

Click **Yes**.

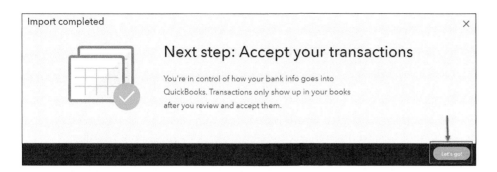

Figure 8.34

Final acceptance screen

Once the import has been completed, you will need to match the uploaded transactions to the **Expense** transactions in QBO. Click **Let's go!** to start the process

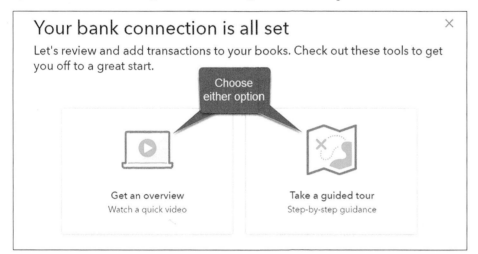

Figure 8.35

Intuit tools for managing banking transactions

You'll need to pick an option before you can move forward.

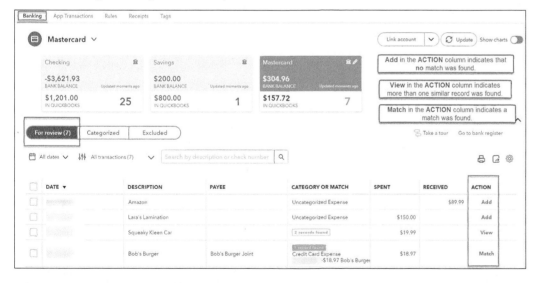

Figure 8.36

Imported transaction review screen

There are three tabs on the next screen.

Uploaded transactions first appear on the **For Review** tab.

If **Match** appears in the **ACTION** column, QBO has matched that transaction to one previously recorded in QBO. Click **Match** to move the transaction to the **Categorized** tab.

> ✳ **HINT:** Transactions in the **For Review** tab can be edited (date or account changed) by clicking anywhere in the transaction row.

If **View** appears in the **ACTION** column, QBO has found more than one record that is similar to the uploaded transaction. Click **View** to open an edit screen. You will be able to select one of the listed records to match the transaction, enter an account (or accounts) to categorize the transaction, or record the transaction as a transfer to another account.

If **Add** appears in the **ACTION** column, QBO has not found a matching transaction. Click anywhere in the transaction row (other than **Add**) to open the transaction.

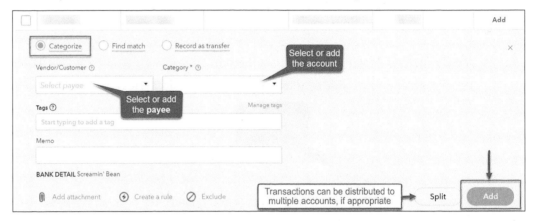

Figure 8.37

Banking transaction edit screen

If you click **Find match** at the top of the screen, QBO searches for and displays similar transactions, if any. If you click **Record as transfer**, the offset account is identified. In most cases, **Categorize** would be selected and the **payee** and **category** (account) identified.

Click **Add**. The transaction will then be recorded in QBO.

> **BEHIND THE SCENES** You may see an account listed in the **CATEGORY** field of unmatched transactions. QBO uses natural language processing (a cognitive technology) to "guess" the appropriate classifications of uploaded transactions based on any text included in the CSV file. Cognitive technologies in QBO are covered in Chapter 13.

Once a transaction has been accepted (**Added**), it is moved to the **Categorized** tab.

If there is an error in the upload, a transaction can be moved to the **Excluded** tab by checking the box in the left column of the incorrect transaction and clicking **Exclude** in the popup menu bar that automatically appears above the list of transactions.

Once the review has been completed, all transactions should have been **matched**, **added** or **excluded**.

When the credit card is later reconciled, all transactions listed on the **Categorized** tab will be marked as cleared.

> **BEHIND THE SCENES** The general process outlined above can be used with banking transactions as well as credit card transactions. The process for downloading transactions is directly from financial institutions covered in Appendix 8A.

INACTIVATING AND MERGING GENERAL LEDGER ACCOUNTS

Companies generally set up their initial chart of accounts based on expected activities and informational needs. As companies grow and change, the chart of accounts usually expands.

Often it expands substantially! An effective chart of accounts, though, contains only those accounts that provide useful detail for owners and managers.

Periodically, a company should take a look at the structure of its chart of accounts to make sure it still meets the needs of the company. We already know how to group accounts. Accounts can be moved from one group to another (within the same **account type**) and parent accounts can be added or deleted. But what do we do with accounts that are no longer needed or useful?

Accounts cannot be permanently deleted but QBO does provide two tools for managing unused accounts:

- Temporarily deleting accounts ("inactivating" the account)
- Merging accounts

Inactivating an Account

Inactivating an account is an option when a company needs to maintain detail about past transactions. Let's use an example. Let's say five years ago, a barbershop sold shampoo in addition to cutting hair. It has since discontinued selling products because of the high cost of maintaining inventory. The barbershop no longer needs the inventory account or the cost of goods sold account. It might, however, need that information in the future. That might be the case if it is ever audited or if it decides to reconsider merchandise sales.

Once an account is inactivated, it will not be available for searching, for filtering, or for use in future transactions.

Inactivated accounts **will**, however, appear on reports if the accounts had balances in the report period. The phrase "(deleted)" will appear after the account name.

Inactivating an Account with a Zero Balance

Inactivating an account with a zero balance is a relatively simple process.

To inactivate the account in QBO, click the ⚙ on the icon bar and select **Chart of Accounts**.

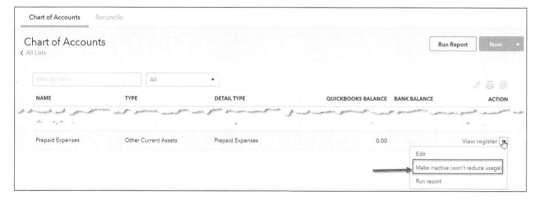

Figure 8.38

Tool for inactivating account

In the **ACTION** column of the account you want to inactivate, select **Make inactive**. QBO will ask you to confirm your decision. Once an account has been made inactive, it is no longer visible on the default **Chart of Accounts** screen.

Reactivating Accounts

Accounts can be reactivated. The first step is to make the account visible in the chart of accounts. The simplest process is to click the ⚙ icon just above the **ACTION** column in the **Chart of Accounts**.

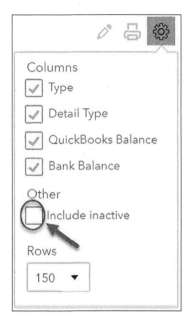

Check the **Include inactive** box and refresh the screen.

Click **Make active**. The account will now be available to use in transactions, filters, or searches.

Inactivating an Account with a Non-zero Balance

QBO allows users to inactivate accounts with balances. This would not normally be something done by an accountant but sometimes accounts are inactivated in error and it's important to understand what happens to those account balances.

If the account being inactivated is a permanent (balance sheet) account, QBO will display the following message:

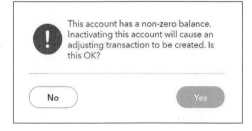

If **Yes** is selected, QBO will automatically make a journal entry to clear the account (bring it to zero). The offset account used is **Opening Balance Equity** (an **equity account type**). For example, if a user deleted Prepaid Insurance and that account had a $200 debit balance, QBO would make the following entry:

	Opening Balance Equity	200	
	Prepaid Insurance		200

If the account to be inactivated is a temporary (revenue or expense) account, no journal entry will be made. The account (identified as a deleted account) would still appear on applicable profit and loss reports with the balance at the point it was inactivated. For example, if Rent Expense with a balance of $500 was deleted, it would continue to appear on profit and loss reports as Rent Expense (deleted) through the end of the year.

If accounts with balances at the time of inactivation are reactivated, the transaction detail prior to the inactivation will be visible. The entry made by QBO to zero out **permanent** accounts, however, will NOT be reversed. The reactivated account will show a zero balance.

Merging Accounts

Merging an account would be the best option when an account does not (and maybe never did) provide useful detail. Let's use another example. Let's say the accountant for a barbershop set up separate general ledger accounts for every service item. There was an account for shampoos, another for haircuts, another for beard trims, etc. Those accounts were unnecessary because the revenue detail is already available in Sales by Item reports. It would make sense, then, to merge some or all of those accounts.

Merging an account really means transferring activity out of the account you no longer wish to use INTO an appropriate existing account. There needs to be two accounts: the "transferor account" (the account you want to eliminate) and the "transferee account" (the account that you intend to keep). The account types and detail types of the two accounts must be the same.

To merge an account, the Chart of Accounts list must be open. In the ACTION column of the "transferor account" (the account you want to eliminate), select Edit.

Change the Name of the account to the name of the "transferee account" (the account you intend to keep). The name must be **identical** or you'll create a new account.

When you click Save and close, QBO will give you the following message:

Figure 8.42

Message displayed when accounts are merged

Clicking Yes will **permanently** delete the transferor account. All transactions posted to the account will now appear in the transaction detail of the remaining account.

Manage the chart of accounts in Craig's Design and Landscaping.
(The Promotional expense account is inactivated and the Bookkeeper and Accounting expense accounts are merged.)

1. Click the ⚙ on the icon bar.

2. Click **Chart of Accounts**.

3. Click **See your Chart of Accounts**, if necessary.

4. Inactivate an account.

    a. In the ACTION column for Promotional expense, click the arrow next to Run Report and select Make inactive.

    b. Click Yes.

(continued)

PRACTICE

EXERCISE

8.4

(continued from previous page)

5. Merge an account.

   a. In the **ACTION** column for **Bookkeeper** (an **expense** account), click **Run Report**.

   b. **Make a note** of the amount of the check to **Books by Bessie**.

   c. Click **Accounting** in the navigation bar.

   d. Open the **Chart of Accounts** tab.

   e. In the **ACTION** column for **Bookkeeper** expense, click the arrow next to **Run Report** and select **Edit**.

   f. Change the **Name** to "Accounting."

      i. Make sure you enter the name exactly as noted. If you have any differences, QBO will not merge the accounts.

   g. Click **Save and close**.

   h. Click **Yes** at the prompt to merge.

      i. If this prompt doesn't appear, you most likely made a spelling error when you entered the account name. Log out of the test-drive. Open the test-drive again and go back to Step 5a.

   i. Verify that the **Bookkeeper** account is no longer listed in the **Chart of Accounts** list.

   j. In the **ACTION** column for **Accounting** expense, click **Run Report**.

   k. Select **All Dates** in the **Report period** dropdown menu.

   l. Verify that the check to **Books by Bessie** is included in the account balance.

      i. **Make a note** of the balance in the account.

6. Click **Dashboard** to exit out of the **Chart of Accounts** window.

ADDING NOTES TO REPORTS

At the end of an accounting period, after all adjustments have been made, the accountant should be comfortable with the balances in each of the accounts on the financial statements. For many accounts, there are subsidiary ledgers or worksheets that provide documentation. For example, agings (by customer or by vendor) support accounts receivable and accounts payable account balances. Bank reconciliations support cash balances. **Sales by Item** reports provide support for revenue and cost of goods sold amounts.

For other accounts (such as prepaid or unearned revenue accounts), there may not be any standard, formal documentation. For control purposes (and in case of memory lapses!), the accountant would want to document the balances in those accounts as well.

There is a feature in QBO reports that allows the user to add notes to reports. This feature can be very useful to accountants as part of the end-of-period process. For example, instead of preparing an offline worksheet detailing the components of Prepaid Expenses, the accountant can simply include that detail in the balance sheet for the period by adding a note to the report.

Other uses of this feature might include:

- Adding a note to an **inventory valuation summary** report, reminding the reader that a particular item is nearing obsolescence.

- Adding a note to an **open purchase order** report, reminding the reader to contact the vendor and determine the status of a backorder.

A report must be open before notes can be added.

Figure 8.43

Tool to open note box in report

Clicking **Add notes** on the report menu bar adds a new field at the bottom of the report.

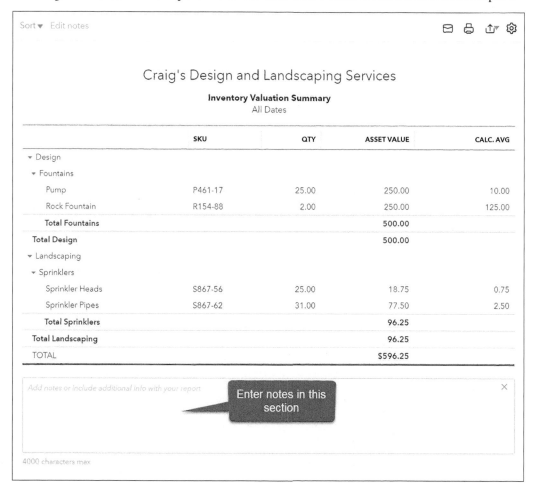

Figure 8.44

Example of note box in report

Note boxes can include up to 4,000 characters.

Reports that contain notes can be printed, emailed, or saved as a PDF file. The notes will appear at the bottom of the report.

Reports with notes can also be saved for future reference by clicking **Save customization** at the top of the report window.

Figure 8.45

Options when saving reports

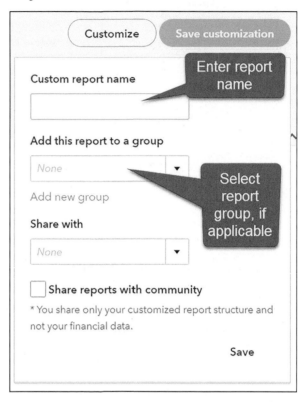

A unique name should be given to the saved report. Customized reports can be saved in groups and can also be restricted to certain users.

For example, an **inventory valuation summary** report might be saved in a group of inventory reports accessible to all users. Customization would look something like this:

Figure 8.46

Example of options selected on saved report with notes

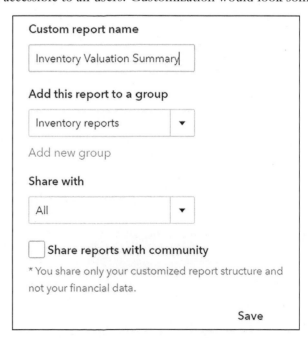

BEHIND THE SCENES Checking the box next to Share reports with community allows other QBO users to see your report structure (no amounts are displayed). Most users would choose not to share reports.

Saved reports are accessed by clicking Reports on the navigation bar and selecting the Custom Reports tab.

NAME	CREATED	DATE RANGE	EMAIL	ACTION
Inventory Valuation Summary	Craig Carlson	All Dates	Unscheduled	Edit ⌄

Figure 8.47

Access to saved, customized reports

All saved reports will be displayed by group on the **My Custom Reports** tab.
Saved reports can be edited and modified.

Add a comment to a report.

(Craig's Design adds a note to the balance sheet related to the cost of its truck.)

1. Click Reports on the navigation bar.

2. Click Balance Sheet in the Favorites section.

3. **Make a note** of the balance in Accounts Payable (A/P).

4. Click Add notes.

5. In the notes field, type "Cost to refit the truck is not yet included in the Truck account balance."

6. Click Save customization.

7. Enter "Balance Sheet with Notes" as the Custom report name.

8. Click Add new group.

9. Enter "Month End Reports" as the New group name.

10. Click Add.

11. Click Save.

12. Click the printer icon to open a preview of the customized report.

13. **Make a note** of where, in the report, the comment appears.

14. Click Close.

15. Click Dashboard to exit out of reports.

PRACTICE

EXERCISE

8.5

CHAPTER SHORTCUTS

Adjust inventory quantities

1. Click **+ New** on the navigation bar

2. Click Inventory Qty Adjustment

Record payment of sales tax

1. Click Sales tax on the navigation bar

2. Click Review return

Record non-customer cash receipt

1. Click ➕ New on the navigation bar
2. Click Bank Deposit

Record bank transfer

1. Click ➕ New on the navigation bar
2. Click Transfer

Inactivate an account

1. Click ⚙ on the icon bar
2. Click Chart of Accounts

3. Select Make inactive in the ACTION column of the account to be inactivated

Merge two accounts

1. Click ⚙ on the icon bar
2. Click Chart of Accounts
3. Select Edit in the ACTION column of the account to be merged
4. Change the name of the account

CHAPTER REVIEW

Matching

Assignments with the MBC are available in myBusinessCourse.

Match the term or phrase (as used in QuickBooks Online) to its definition.

1. quantity on hand
2. inventory quantity adjustment
3. custom report
4. transfer

5. merging
6. add other funds to this deposit
7. inactive account
8. sales tax liability report

_____   number of inventory items available

_____   transaction type used to record cash transfers between bank accounts

_____   section of the bank deposit form used to record non-customer cash receipts

_____   tool used to transfer all activity from one account into another account

_____   transaction type used to record quantity corrections to inventory items

_____   account that is unavailable for posting or searching

_____   saved report that may include manually entered user comments

_____   report of taxable sales revenue and related tax amount by jurisdiction

Multiple Choice

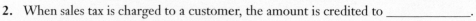

1. Adjustments to inventory can be made in QBO:
   a. to the current quantity of inventory on hand only.
   b. to the current value of inventory on hand only.
   c. to both the current value and current quantity of inventory on hand.

2. When sales tax is charged to a customer, the amount is credited to _____.
   a. an accounts payable account type
   b. an income account type
   c. an other current liability account type
   d. a sales tax payable account type

3. It is possible, in QBO, to:
   a. delete an account by merging the account with another.
   b. permanently delete an account that has been used in a transaction.
   c. inactivate a permanent account with a balance without creating an adjusting entry.
   d. separate two accounts that have been merged.

4. An inactive account in QBO:
   a. can be used in transactions.
   b. can be used to filter reports.
   c. can be used in the search function.
   d. None of the above statements are true.

5. Recording proceeds from a bank loan could be done:
   a. through a general journal entry.
   b. by entering a deposit.
   c. either by creating a general journal entry or by entering the transaction as a deposit.

BEYOND THE CLICKS—THINKING LIKE A MANAGER

Accounting: Physically counting inventory is normally done at least annually in retail companies. The physical count is then compared to the quantity on hand in the accounting system (QBO, for example). List two events that would make the physical count of a specific item less than the quantity reported in the accounting system. List two events that would make the physical count greater than the reported quantity.

Information Systems: Part A: How would you use (filter) the Audit Log if you needed to look at all cash transactions recorded by a specific employee? The Audit Log tool in QBO was introduced in the introduction to Section Three. Part B: Find and **View** an **Edited event** in Craig's Landscaping and Design. How many times has the transaction been changed? What changes were made to the transaction?

ASSIGNMENTS

Background information: Martin Smith, a college student and good friend of yours, has always wanted to be an entrepreneur. He is very good in math, so, to test his entrepreneurship skills, he has decided to set up a small math tutoring company serving local high school students who struggle in their math courses. He set up the company, Math Revealed!, as a corporation in 2021. Martin is the only owner. He has not taken any distributions from the company since it opened.

The business has been successful so far. In fact, it's been so successful he has decided to work in his business full time now that he's graduated from college with a degree in mathematics.

He has decided to start using QuickBooks Online to keep track of his business transactions. He likes the convenience of being able to access his information over the Internet. You have agreed to act as his accountant while you're finishing your own academic program.

Martin currently has a number of regular customers that he tutors in Pre-Algebra, Algebra, and Geometry. His customers pay his fees by cash or check after each tutoring session but he does give terms of Net 15 to some of his customers. He has developed the following fee schedule:

Name	Description	Rate
Refresher	One-hour session	$ 60 per hour
Persistence program	Two one-hour sessions per week	$100 per week
Crisis program	Five one-hour sessions per week	$225 per week

The tutoring sessions usually take place at his students' homes but he recently signed a two-year lease on a small office above a local coffee shop. The rent is only $750 per month starting in January 2022. A security deposit of $500 was paid in December 2021.

The following equipment is owned by the company:

Assignment 8A

Math Revealed!

Description	Date placed in service	Cost	Life	Salvage Value
Computer	7/1/21	$3,000	36 months	$300
Printer	7/1/21	$ 240	24 months	$ 0
Graphing Calculators (3)	7/1/21	$ 300	36 months	$ 30

All equipment is depreciated using the straight-line method.

As of 12/31/21, Martin owed $2,500 to his father (Richard Smith) who initially helped him get started. Richard is charging him interest at a 6% annual rate. Martin has been paying interest only on a monthly basis. His last payment of interest only was on 12/31/21.

Over the next month or so, he plans to expand his business by selling a few products he believes will help his students. He has already purchased a few items:

Category	Description	Vendor	Quantity on Hand	Cost per Unit	Sales Price
Books and Tools					
	Geometry in Sports	Books Galore	20	18	25
	Solving Puzzles: Fun with Algebra	Books Galore	20	15	22
	Getting Ready for Calculus	Books Galore	20	20	28
	Geometry Kit	Math Shack	10	12	18
	Handheld Dry-Erase Boards	Math Shack	25	10	15
	Notebooks (pack of 5)	Paper Bag Depot	10	8	12

2/28/22

✓ You call Martin at home and tell him that the bank balance is quite low. He meets with his banker at City Bank of Sacramento and explains the situation. The bank agrees to provide a $2,500 loan at 6% based on Martin's personal credit. The loan is set up to be repaid over a 12-month period ($215.17 per month including interest). You record the deposit of $2,500 into the company's checking account. **TIP:** You're going to need to set up a new account for this loan. Think carefully when choosing the **account type**.

✓ Your friend, Samantha Levin, agrees to come in to help Martin count the inventory on hand.

• She counts the inventory at the end of the day and gives you this list:

Taken by Samantha Levin	Inventory Count Sheet—2/28	Unit of Measure	Quantity on Hand
Books and Tools			
	Dry erase boards	Units	13
	Kit	Units	12
	Statistics	Units	10
	Notebooks	Packages of 5	3
	Puzzles	Units	3
	Ready	Units	20
	Sports	Units	16
Math Games			
	Console	Units	5
	Equations	Units	5
	Fractions	Units	5
	Ratios	Units	5

✓ You do a few rechecks to make sure the count is correct, which it is.

• You talk to Martin about the shortages. He believes that some of the items were probably used by the tutors during the Mathmagic Clinic. You decide to charge the inventory adjustment to the Tutoring supplies expense account.

- You adjust the inventory quantities in QBO to agree to the count using 2/28 as the transaction date. **TIP:** You can either add all products to the inventory adjustment window and change only those items that differ from the count, or you can compare the count sheet provided above to the Product/Service List in QBO first and then add only those items that need adjustment to the window.

- You use FebInvAdj as the reference no.

- **TIP:** To check your accuracy, click Save. Click More and select Transaction journal. The total adjustment should be $54.

✓ Because Samantha is willing to stay a bit longer, you ask her to count the supplies on hand. She tells you that there is $41.50 worth of tutoring supplies on hand. You adjust the accounts appropriately. You use Feb22.1 as the Journal no.

✓ It took Samantha only two hours to count the inventory and supplies. You write her a check (#1123) for $50 ($25 per hour) and charge the amount to the Contract labor account.

✓ You get ready to pay your sales tax liability.

- You review your Sales Tax Liability report. The total tax liability for February sales is $23.45. (Most of your product sales were made to the Center for Academic Excellence, a reseller of the products.)

- You remit your taxes using Check #1124, dated 2/28.

  TIP: QBO will not allow you to use the normal process for remitting sales tax payments (as outlined in the chapter) if you're completing this assignment before March 2022. If that's the case, create a check to the CDTFA (California Dept of Tax and Fee Admin) instead and charge the California Department of Tax and Fee Administration Payable account for the $23.45.

After month end:

✓ You receive the February bank statement. You see that the bank charged a $20 processing fee for the NSF check from Kim Kowalski. You enter the charge when you reconcile the statement to your records using 2/28 (the reconciliation date) as the transaction date.

CITY BANK OF SACRAMENTO
51 Capital Avenue
Sacramento, CA 95822 (916) 585-2120

Student Name Math Revealed!
3835 Freeport Blvd
Sacramento, CA 95822
Account # 1616479   **February 28, 2022**

	CREDITS	CHARGES	BALANCE
Beginning Balance, February 1			$7,348.93
2/1, Check 1107, 24 Hour Quick Stitch Clinic		$ 220.00	7,128.93
2/2, Check 1109, Frank's Furniture		726.00	6,402.93
2/2, Check 1108, Parent's Survival Weekly		100.00	6,302.93
2/3, Check 1114, Richard Smith		12.50	6,290.43
2/4, Check 1111, Student		300.00	5,990.43
2/4, Check 1113, Pro Spaces		750.00	5,240.43
2/8, Deposit	$ 435.05		5,675.48
2/8, Deposit	1,100.00		6,775.48
2/11, Check 1110, Martin Smith		2,000.00	4,775.48
2/11, Deposit	616.00		5,391.48
2/17, Check 1115, Prime Visa Company		1,798.36	3,593.12
2/19, Deposit	117.60		3,710.72
2/18, SR-109 Chargeback for NSF check		100.00	3,610.72
2/18, Processing fee, NSF check		20.00	3,590.72
2/21, Deposit	1,287.10		4,877.82
2/24, Check 1117, Books Galore		170.00	4,707.82

(continued)

(continued from previous page)

CITY BANK OF SACRAMENTO
51 Capital Avenue
Sacramento, CA 95822 (916) 585-2120

Student Name Math Revealed!
3835 Freeport Blvd
Sacramento, CA 95822
Account # 1616479

February 28, 2022

	CREDITS	CHARGES	BALANCE
2/25, Check 1119, Martin Smith		1,800.00	2,907.82
2/25, Deposit	620.00		3,527.82
2/23, Check 1112, Isla Parker		19.58	3,508.24
2/24, Check 1118, Samantha Levin		125.00	3,383.24
2/28, Loan proceeds	2,500.00		5,883.24
Ending Balance, February 28			**$5,883.24**

✓ Martin has downloaded the credit card transactions for you from the credit card company's website. He gives you the file so that you can upload these transactions into QBO. You have been entering all of the receipts Martin has given you but you want to be sure all the transactions match and that he didn't miss a receipt.

- You upload the credit card transactions using the CSV file. **TIP:** To obtain this file, open the ancillary page for this textbook on the publisher's website (cambridgepub.com) and download: **MR Credit Card Upload Ch8.csv**. To upload the file, click **Banking** on the navigation bar and click **Upload transactions** on the **Banking** tab.

- You select **220 Prime Visa Payable** as the **QuickBooks Account** to use for the upload.

- In the **Map Columns** screen, you check the **First row in file is a header row** box and indicate that your file has two columns. You update the following fields:

QuickBooks Online fields	Your statement fields
Date	Column 1: Date (MM/dd/yyyy)
Description	Column 2: Description
Amount	
Money Spent	Column 3 : Credit
Money Received	Column 4 : Debit

- You import all transactions and accept transactions.

- For all items with **Match** in the **ACTION** column on the review tab, you click **Match**.

- You see one transaction that QBO was unable to match. **TIP: Add** appears in the **ACTION** column for unmatched transactions.

  ○ You ask Martin about this. He searches through his desk and finds the receipt for 2/21. He purchased gas at Cardinal Gas & Snacks. You verify the **Payee** and update the **category** to the appropriate account, if necessary. You **add** the transaction.

 HINT: If you have more than one unmatched transaction, you may have missed entering a transaction in an earlier chapter or you may have entered multiple transactions with the same vendor on a single **Expense** form. If you missed a transaction, verify the vendor (payee) name, select the appropriate account, and click **Add**. If you incorrectly entered multiple transactions with the same vendor, you can **Add** the charges here but then you'll need to delete the earlier entries.

✓ You receive the credit card statement in the mail and prepare the credit card reconciliation. **TIP:** All of the transactions you imported that were matched or added should already be marked as reconciled.

✓ When you finish the reconciliation, you set up the balance for payment later. You use FEB-VISA as the Bill no.

PRIME VISA COMPANY
55 Wall Street
New York, NY 10005

Student Name Math Revealed!
3835 Freeport Blvd
Sacramento, CA 95822
Account # 212456770439

	PAYMENTS	CHARGES	February 28, 2022 BALANCE
Beginning Balance, February 1			$1,798.35
2/8-LA Gasoline Stop		$ 45.00	1,843.35
2/8-Good Sleep Inn		380.00	2,223.35
2/8-Good Sleep Inn		150.00	2,373.35
2/15-Prime Visa	$1,798.35		575.00
2/24-Dick's Diner		19.50	594.50
2/24-Cardinal Gas & Snacks		21.00	615.50
Ending Balance, February 28			**$615.50**

Minimum Payment Due: $10.00   Payment Due Date: March 15

✓ You realize you forgot to pay yourself for work done in February. You create an account called "Accrued Expenses" (Account #221) and record the $300 due you for your accounting work. You use Feb22.2 as the entry number. (**TIP:** Use other current liabilities as the detail type.)

✓ You review the account balances and make additional adjusting journal entries for February (dated 2/28) as needed, carefully considering the following:

- Your last loan payment to Martin's father was made on 2/26 and covered interest for the month of February.

- Martin borrowed the $2,500 from the bank on 2/28. Interest will start accruing on 3/1.

- You review your revenue and unearned revenue accounts to make sure all earned revenue (and only earned revenue) is recognized.

  ○ All the income billed in February was earned in February so you don't need to defer any revenue.

  ○ For Unearned revenue, you review the entries made in January. The unearned revenue for Annie Wang at the end of January was for sessions held in February. The unearned revenue for Teacher's College was for a workshop held in February. You make the appropriate entry to properly recognize any February revenue.

- You record depreciation for the shelving placed in service on 2/1. The cost was $820. You think the shelving will have a $100 salvage value. You depreciate it over the lease term (24 months). **TIP:** Don't forget to depreciate all the fixed assets purchased in prior months. The depreciation amount for those items will be the same as the entry in January.

- You make other adjusting journal entries, dated 2/28, as needed.

  ○ **TIP:** Look at all the current asset and liability accounts on the balance sheet. Should any of them be adjusted? Look at the profit and loss statement. Are there expenses recorded that shouldn't be recognized in February? Are there expenses that should have been recorded but haven't been? It's often very helpful to be able to compare months when doing month-end work. Consider customizing the profit and loss report by changing the dates to 1/1 to 2/28 and selecting Months in the Display columns by dropdown menu.

✓   You review your chart of accounts.

- You aren't using the Inventory Shrinkage account (a **Cost of Goods Sold** account) so you make it inactive.

- You decide to move the $750 paid to Les & Schmidt for the marketing study out of Accounting and consulting fees and into a new Marketing expenses account. You use account #642. **TIP:** Consider whether it should be a sub-account.

Check numbers 2/28

Checking account balance:	$ 3,185.08
Total assets:	$18,326.58
Total liabilities:	$ 8,224.69
Net income for the two months ending 2/28:	$ 7,791.89

Suggested reports for Chapter 8:

All reports should be in portrait orientation.

- Journal (2/28 entries only)

- Balance Sheet as of 2/28

- Profit and Loss for February (with year to date column included)

- Inventory Valuation Summary as of 2/28

- Bank Reconciliation Summary 2/28

Assignment 8B

Salish Software Solutions

Background information: Sally Hanson, a good friend of yours, double majored in Computer Science and Accounting in college. She worked for several years for a software company in Silicon Valley but the long hours started to take a toll on her personal life.

Last year she decided to open up her own company, Salish Software Solutions. Sally currently advises clients looking for new accounting software and assists them with software installation. She also provides training to client employees and occasionally troubleshoots software issues.

She has decided to start using QuickBooks Online to keep track of her business transactions. She likes the convenience of being able to access financial information over the Internet. You have agreed to act as her accountant while you're working on your accounting degree.

Sally has a number of clients that she is currently working with. She gives 15-day payment terms to her corporate clients but she asks for cash at time of service if she does work for individuals. She has developed the following fee schedule:

Name	Description	Rate
Select	Software selection	$500 flat fee
Set Up	Software installation	$ 75 per hour
Train	Software training	$ 50 per hour
Fix	File repair	$ 60 per hour

Sally rents office space from Alki Property Management for $600 per month.

The following furniture and equipment are owned by Salish:

Description	Date placed in service	Cost	Life	Salvage Value
Office furniture	6/1/21	$1,400	60 months	$200
Computer	7/1/21	$4,620	36 months	$300
Printer	7/1/21	$ 900	24 months	$ 0

All equipment is depreciated using the straight-line method.

As of 12/31/21, she owed $3,500 to Dell Finance. The monthly payment on that loan is $150 including interest at 5%. Sally's last payment to Dell was 12/31/21.

Over the next month or so, Sally plans to expand her business by selling some of her favorite accounting and personal software products directly to her clients. She has already purchased the following items.

Item Name	Description	Vendor	Quantity on Hand	Cost per Unit	Sales Price
Easy1	Easy Does It	Abacus Shop	15	$100	$ 200
Retailer	Simply Retail	Simply Accounting	2	$400	$ 800
Contractor	Simply Construction	Simply Accounting	2	$500	$1,000
Organizer	Organizer	Personal Software	20	$ 25	$ 50
Tracker	Investment Tracker	Personal Software	20	$ 20	$ 40

2/28/22

✓ Sally meets with her banker at Sacramento City Bank. She wants to have easy access to funds in case a good opportunity comes along. The banker explains that with a line of credit, Sally can borrow as much as she needs up to the credit line maximum. Only interest (on any unpaid balance) will be due on a monthly basis although Sally can make principal payments at any time. The bank agrees to provide Sally with a $5,000 line. Interest will be set at 6%. Interest payments will be due on the last day of the month. The line will have a term of one year. Sally doesn't borrow on the line today but you set up the account so it's ready for the future. **TIP:** Think carefully when choosing the **account type**.

✓ Oscar Torres agrees to come in to count the inventory on hand.

   • He counts the inventory at the end of the day and gives you this list:

Taken by Oscar Torres	Inventory Count Sheet—2/28	Unit of Measure	Quantity on Hand
Accounting Products			
	Contractor	Units	3
	Easy1	Units	12
	Retailer	Units	3
Management Products			
	Engineering	Units	2
	Legal	Units	2
	Medical	Units	2
	Organizer	Units	15
	Tracker	Units	18

   • You do a few rechecks to make sure the count is correct, which it is.

   • You're a little surprised that so many **Organizers** are missing. You discuss it with Sally but neither of you can come up with an explanation. You decide to keep a closer eye on the storage cabinet in the future.

   • You make an adjustment for the inventory count, charging the differences to a new **cost of goods sold type** account called Inventory Adjustments (#509). You use detail type: **Supplies & Materials—COGS** and use FebInvAdj as the **reference no.** You use 2/28 (the last day of the month) as the transaction date. **TIP:** You can either add all products to the **inventory adjustment** window and change only those items that differ from the count or you can compare the count sheet provided above to the Product/Service List in QBO first and then add only those items that need adjustment to the window.

   • **TIP:** To check your accuracy, click **Save**. Click **More** and select **Transaction journal**. The total adjustment should be $145.

✓ It took Oscar an hour to count the inventory. You write him a check (#1123) for $30 and charge the amount to a new Contract labor expense account (#609). You set it up as a sub-account of Labor Costs.

✓ You go ahead and look at the amount of office supplies there are on hand. You estimate the cost at $225. You make the adjustment using Feb22.1 as the entry number and 2/28 as the date.

✓ You get ready to pay your sales tax liability.

- You review your **Sales Tax Liability** report. The total tax liability for February sales is $87.50.

- You remit your taxes using Check # 1124, dated 2/28.

    ○ **TIP:** QBO will not allow you to use the normal process for remitting sales tax payments (as outlined in the chapter) if you're completing this assignment before March 2022. If that's the case, create a check to the CDTFA (California Dept of Tax and Fee Admin) instead and charge the California Department of Tax and Fee Administration Payable account for the $87.50.

After month end:

✓ Sally has downloaded the credit card transactions for you from the credit card company's website. She gives you the file so that you can upload these transactions into QBO. You know you have been entering all of the receipts Sally has given you but you want to be sure all the transactions match and that she didn't miss a receipt.

- You upload the credit card transactions to QBO using the CSV file. **TIP:** To obtain this file, open the ancillary page for your textbook and download: **SS Credit Card Upload Ch8.csv.** To upload the file, click **Banking** on the navigation bar and click **Upload transactions** on the **Banking** tab.

- You select 220 Capital Three Visa Payable as the **QuickBooks Account** to use for the upload.

- In the **Map Columns** screen, you check the **First row in file is a header row** box and indicate that your file has two columns. You update the following fields:

QuickBooks Online fields	Your statement fields
Date	Column 1: Date (MM/dd/yyyy)
Description	Column 2: Description
Amount	
Money Spent	Column 3 : Credit
Money Received	Column 4 : Debit

- You import all transactions and accept transactions.

- For all items with **Match** in the **ACTION** column on the review tab, you click **Match**.

- You see one transaction that QBO was unable to match. **TIP: Add** appears in the **ACTION** column for unmatched transactions.

    ○ You ask Sally about this. She searches through her desk and finds the receipt for 2/16. She had taken a couple of people from Butter and Beans out to lunch at Screamin' Bean. (Good client relations!) You enter the **Payee** and update the **category** to the appropriate account, if necessary. You **add** the transaction.

 HINT: If you have more than one unmatched transaction, you may have missed entering a transaction in an earlier chapter or you may have entered multiple transactions with the same vendor on a single **Expense** form. If you missed a transaction, verify the vendor (payee) name, select the appropriate account, and click **Add**. If you incorrectly entered multiple transactions with the same vendor, you can **Add** the charges here but then you'll need to delete the earlier entries.

✓ You receive the credit card statement in the mail and prepare the credit card reconciliation. **TIP:** All of the transactions you imported that were matched or added should already be marked as reconciled.

✓ You finish the reconciliation and set up the balance for payment later. You use Feb22 as the Bill no.

CAPITAL THREE
55 Wall Street
New York, NY 10005

Student Name Salish Software Solutions
3835 Freeport Blvd
Sacramento, CA 95822
Account # 646630813344   **February 28, 2022**

	PAYMENTS	CHARGES	BALANCE
Beginning Balance			$1,210.00
2/3, American Association of Accounting Software Providers		$175.00	1,385.00
2/5, Top Of The Hill		42.66	1,427.66
2/5, Bell Gas		35.00	1,462.66
2/5, The Franciscan		235.85	1,698.51
2/9, Payment	$1,210.00		488.51
2/16, Screamin' Beans		21.85	510.36
2/24, Roscoe's		28.50	538.86
Ending Balance, 2/28			**$ 538.86**

Minimum Payment Due: $10.00   **Payment Due Date: March 15**

✓ You receive the February bank statement. You see that the bank charged a $25 processing fee for the NSF check from Dew Drop Inn. You enter the charge when you reconcile the statement to your records, using 2/28 as the transaction date.

SACRAMENTO CITY BANK
1822 Capital Avenue
Sacramento, CA 95822 (916) 585-2120

Student Name Salish Software Solutions
3835 Freeport Blvd
Sacramento, CA 95822
Account # 855922   **February 28, 2022**

	CREDITS	CHARGES	BALANCE
Beginning Balance, February 1			$12,820.00
2/1, Check 1109, Oscar Torres		$ 120.00	12,700.00
2/2, Check 1107, Abacus Shop		960.00	11,740.00
2/3, Check 1100, Marie Elle		75.00	11,665.00
2/3, Check 1111, Student Name		300.00	11,365.00
2/4, Check 1112, Alki Property Management		600.00	10,765.00
2/6, Check 1115, Dell Finance		150.00	10,615.00
2/6, Check 1110, Sally Hanson		2,000.00	8,615.00
2/8, Deposit	$3,500.00		12,115.00
2/8, Deposit	1,065.75		13,180.75
2/11, Deposit	300.00		13,371.80
2/12, Check 1114, Western Phone Company		108.95	13,071.80
2/14, Check 1113, Sacramento Light & Power		95.00	13,276.80
2/17, Check returned for insufficient funds		300.00	12,976.80
2/17, Fee for NSF check		25.00	12,951.80
2/17, Deposit	318.50		13,270.30
2/18, Check 1116, Capital Three		1,210.00	12,060.30
2/21, Deposit	4,050.00		16,110.30
2/25, Deposit	490.00		16,600.30
Ending Balance, 2/28/22			**$16,600.30**

✓ You realize you forgot to pay yourself for work done in February. You create an account called "Accrued Expenses" (Account # 221) and record the $350 due you for your accounting work. You use Feb22.2 as the entry number.

✓ You review your revenue and unearned revenue accounts to make sure all earned revenue (and only earned revenue) is recognized.

- For the revenue accounts, you check with Sally to make sure that all the hours and fees billed in February were completed in February. All the income billed in February was earned in February so you don't need to defer any of that revenue.

- For Unearned revenue, you review the entries made in January. The unearned revenue for Butter and Beans at the end of January was for the remaining 20 hours of work billed on INV-1009. Sally lets you know that all that work has now been completed. The unearned revenue for Albus Software was for a workshop held in February. You make the appropriate entry to properly recognize February revenue.

✓ You record depreciation for the month of February for all fixed assets, including depreciation on the $1,500 cabinets placed in service on February 1st. You depreciate the cabinets over 5 years. Sally doesn't think there will be any resale value at the end of the service life. **TIP:** Make sure the computer software is depreciated for a full month in February. Only a partial month was taken in January.

✓ You made the last payment to Dell Finance on 2/1. The $150 payment covered January interest ($14.58) and reduced the loan balance by $135.42. **TIP:** The annual interest rate is 5%. Round to two decimals.

✓ You make other adjusting journal entries, dated 2/28 as needed.

- **TIP:** Look at all the current asset and liability accounts on the balance sheet. Should any of them be adjusted? Look at the profit and loss statement. Are there expenses recorded that shouldn't be recognized in February? Are there any expenses that weren't recorded that should be? It's often very helpful to be able to compare months when doing month-end work. Consider customizing the **profit and loss** report by changing the dates to 1/1 to 2/28 and selecting **Months** in the **Display columns by** dropdown menu.

✓ You review your chart of accounts.

- You see that QBO has created a new **Cost of Goods Sold** account (Inventory Shrinkage). You realize this was created by default when you made your inventory adjustment entry. You decide to use the default account set up by QBO so you merge 509 Inventory Adjustments into the Inventory Shrinkage account. You want to keep the account number.

  ○ **TIP:** You will need to edit the Inventory Adjustment account by changing the name to Inventory Shrinkage and removing the account number. Then you can go back in and change the name and account number.

Check numbers 2/28

Checking account balance:. $10,306.05
Net income for the two months ending 2/28:. $11,043.59
Total assets: $32,275.05
Total liabilities: . . . .$ 7,511.46

Suggested reports for Chapter 8:

- Journal (2/28 entries only)

- Balance Sheet as of 2/28

- Profit and Loss for February (with year to date column included)

- Inventory Valuation Summary as of 2/28

- Bank Reconciliation Report 2/28

- Credit Card Reconciliation Report 2/28

APPENDIX 8A DIRECT DOWNLOADING OF BANK TRANSACTIONS INTO QBO AND SETTING BANK RULES

One of the most time-saving features of QBO is the ability to download banking and credit card transactions directly into the company file.

Although you will not be able to use the direct download feature in the homework file, you can get a feel for the process in the test drive company.

There are three fictitious accounts connected to the test drive company (Mastercard, Checking, and Savings).

Click **Banking** on the navigation bar. The screen will look something like this:

Figure 8A.1

Banking screen

Transactions are automatically downloaded nightly from most financial institutions although some institutions limit the number of downloads.

Click **Checking**. There are three tabs: **For Review**, **Categorized**, and **Excluded**.

Figure 8A.2

For Review tab of Banking screen

For each connected account, downloaded transactions first appear on the **For Review** tab.

For each downloaded transaction on the **All** tab, there will be one of three options available in the **ACTION** column. Users can click anywhere in a downloaded transaction other than in the **ACTION** column to expand the details.

- **Match**
  - QBO has found a match for the transaction in the company file. QBO uses the following logic for determining matches:
    - Transaction downloaded from the bank matches a transaction manually entered in QBO.
    - Downloaded transaction matches an open balance on an **invoice/bill**.

Figure 8A.3

Expanded Match transaction

- User can
  - ○ accept QBO's categorization by clicking **Match** in the **ACTION** column.
  - ○ click anywhere in the transaction line to manually change the **category**.

- **View**
  - ▪ QBO found multiple possible matches for the transaction.
  - ▪ User can see the possible matching records by clicking **View** in the **ACTION** column.

Figure 8A.4

Expanded View transaction

- ○ If one of the possible matching records is acceptable, user would click **Match**.
- ○ If none of the possible matching records is acceptable, user could click **Categorize** to manually select the **category** (account).
- ○ If the transaction represents a transfer, user would click **Record transfer** and identify the offset account.

- **Add**
  - ▪ QBO was unable to find a match for the transaction.

Figure 8A.5

Expanded Add transaction

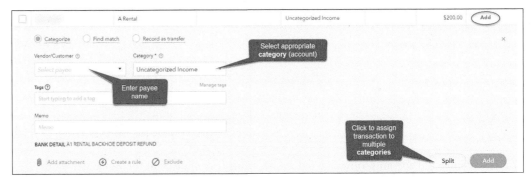

- ○ **Uncategorized income** is displayed in the **CATEGORY** field if the transaction represents a cash receipt; **Uncategorized expense** is displayed in the **CATEGORY** field if the transaction represents a cash disbursement.
- ▪ Users would click **Add** after manually selecting the appropriate **category** (account).

> **!** **WARNING: Sometimes the Vendor/Payee field is not completed when a transaction is downloaded. (The payee name may, instead, be listed in the Memo field.) Although not required, it's best practice to select (or add) the payee's name. Only transactions with a vendor name in the Vendor/Payee field will be included in the Vendor Center and accessible in searches by Payee or Vendor.**

Users can change a transaction to a **Transfer** (movement of cash from one account to another) in any of the expanded transaction screens.

Users are able to distribute a transaction to multiple accounts by clicking **Split** in the **Add** screen.

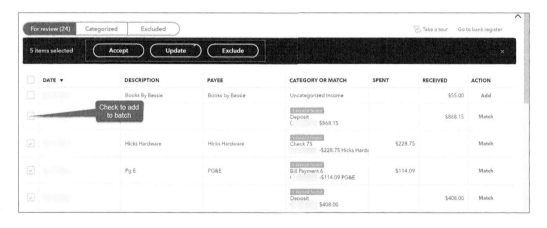

Figure 8A.6

Split transaction screen

Once the user reviews the transaction and selects either **Match** or **Add**, the transaction will be recorded and moved to the **Categorized** tab.

Figure 8A.7

Option to undo banking transaction added to QBO

If a user incorrectly added or matched a transaction, clicking **Undo** on the **Categorized** tab will return the transaction to the **For Review** tab.

Reviewed transactions can also be added to QBO in batches.

Figure 8A.8

Batch processing options

A check is placed in each reviewed row, and **Accept** is selected. Transactions can also be excluded in batches.

Occasionally, duplicate transactions will be downloaded into QBO. Using the **Exclude Selected** batch option will move the transactions to the **Excluded** tab. **Excluded** transactions can be deleted.

Setting Banking Rules

Users can set **rules** to guide QBO in managing downloaded transactions. To set rules, click **Banking** on the navigation bar and select the **Rules** tab.

Figure 8A.9
Bank rules tab

Click **New rule**.

Figure 8A.10
Setup of bank rules

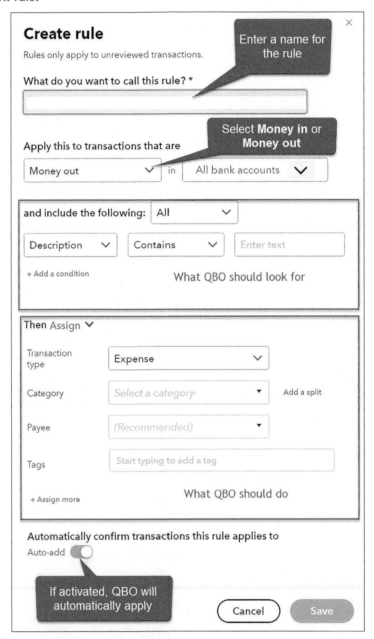

Rules can be created for bank deposit transactions (**Money in**) and bank withdrawal transactions (**Money out**).

Each rule can have up to five conditions. The user defines whether a single transaction must meet all of the conditions or if only one condition must be met. Each condition relates to either **bank text**, **description**, or **amount**. The filtering options depend on which of the three conditions are selected. For example, if **amount** is selected, the user can choose between **Equals**, **Is greater than**, **Is less than**, or **Doesn't equal**.

The treatment for any transaction meeting the conditions is defined in the **Then Assign** section. The dropdown menu options available will change depending on whether the rule applies to **Money in** transactions or **Money out** transactions but **transaction type**, **payee** (name), and **category** (account) are always the primary fields.

For each downloaded transaction, only one rule will be applied. The order in which the rules are listed in the **Rules** list determines the priority of application.

QuickBooks

SECTION FOUR

Beyond the Basics

So far, we've covered how basic transactions in the sales, purchase, and end-of-period cycles of service and merchandising companies are recorded and managed in QuickBooks Online.

Although recording transactions is a very important part of accounting, reporting accounting activity in a way that is useful to management is just as important. In this section, a number of tools and features that can be very useful in managing a business will be introduced.

We'll also look at more detailed ways of tracking revenues and costs in QBO. Construction companies, law firms, accounting firms, architectural firms, and custom shops are just a few examples of the types of companies that normally need the ability to track worker time and direct costs (costs specific to a customer). The information is useful in managing the business and, in many cases, is needed for billing purposes. We'll look at features in QBO that allow users to track projects and to identify time and costs as billable.

Chapter 9 covers segment reporting (using classes and locations) and budgeting, two important management tools in QBO. Managing recurring entries and creating reversing entries will also be covered

Chapter 10 covers project costing and billing for time and expenses.

Chapter 11 covers a variety of other tools in QBO including customizing forms and reports, managing attachments, and exporting reports to Excel.

9 Management Tools

After completing Chapter 9, you should be able to:

1. Use class and location tracking.

2. Prepare reports by class and location.

3. Set up budgets.

4. Prepare budget and budget variance reports.

5. Create reversing entries.

6. Create recurring transactions.

7. Create and use tags (Appendix 9A).

In your first financial accounting course, you might have heard or read a definition of accounting that went something like this:

Accounting is a system in which an organization's economic events are identified, recorded, summarized, analyzed, and reported. From this system comes financial information that can be used by management, creditors, and investors to plan and evaluate.

In this course, we focus on **recording and reporting** transactions in an electronic environment but it's also important to look at ways accounting software might be helpful in the planning and evaluation functions of an organization.

In this chapter, we're going to cover a few of the tools in QBO that can be used to provide useful information to management.

- Tracking operating results by class and by location

- Preparing budgets

We're also going to cover a few time-saving tools (recurring and reversing transactions). Tagging (a new reporting tool first introduced in early 2020) will be covered in Appendix 9A.

TRACKING BY CLASS AND LOCATION

One of the main advantages of computerized accounting systems is the incredible amount of detail that can effectively AND efficiently be maintained. The use of inventory items in QBO is a good example of that. A company can easily track revenues and costs for every model of every product sold by a company and still have a one-page income statement!

Class and location are additional tools in QBO available for tracking detail. Both are used to represent specific reporting **segments**. Examples of business segments include:

Segment A subdivision of an entity for which supplemental financial information is disclosed.

- Departments

- Divisions

- Sales regions

- Product lines

- Service types

- Stores

> **BEHIND THE SCENES** Classes and locations are not linked in any way to general ledger accounts. They are simply tools for identifying the segment of the business that a particular transaction is related to.

Users can use class tracking or location tracking or both. Using class or location tracking is not mandatory in QBO. It is a preference.

Users can have up to five levels of tracking for classes and locations in QBO Plus. Levels 2–5 are known as sub-classes or sub-locations.

Although the two features are similar, there is one important distinction between the two. If class tracking is used, a preference can be set allowing users to link each line item within each transaction (each form) to a specific class. If location tracking is used, the entire transaction is linked to one specific location on forms other than timesheets and journal entries. (On timesheets and journal entries, it is possible to assign location by line item.)

Because of that difference, it generally makes the most sense to use **location** tracking for business units like stores or departments or divisions and to use **class** tracking for focus areas, like product lines or service types that cross a number of business units.

Both types are available for filtering in reports. For example, if you had a Consulting Services **class**, you could filter a sales report or a profit and loss report so that only transactions classified as Consulting Services would be included in your report. If you had a Portland **location**, you could filter a report of expenses so that only Portland expenses would be included. If you were using both **classes** and **locations**, you could filter a report so that only Consulting Services transactions in the Portland office were included.

Segment tracking requires additional work so it should only be used if an organization CAN be separated into segments AND there are meaningful differences between the segments that make them worth tracking.

As an example, let's look at three retail companies selling jewelry. Company A has one store and one manager and only sells diamond rings. Company B has five stores and five managers and only sells diamond rings. Company C has three stores and three managers and sells diamond rings and also provides cleaning and repair services related to diamond rings.

Company A **could** set up a **class** for every type of diamond ring sold but that information is already available in **product** reports. The company could also set up a **class** for every day of the week but that probably wouldn't give management much meaningful information and would require a LOT of allocation! Company A has only one store so **location** tracking is unnecessary. Company A doesn't appear to have any meaningful segments.

Company B, on the other hand, might use **locations** to track sales and costs for each of their five stores. Management could then use that information to evaluate product mix at the various stores, to evaluate the performance of store managers or in planning for new stores. Because the only product is diamond rings, it would be unlikely that using **classes** would be helpful.

Company C, like Company B, might use **locations** to track operations for the three stores. **Classes** might be used to track information about sales from rings separate from information about the cleaning and repair services they provide.

Here are two tips for using segment tracking:

- Set up **classes** or **locations** for the segments that provide the most useful information.
  - Segment information is useful if it can help a company evaluate or plan OR if segment detail is necessary for reporting to regulatory authorities.

- Make sure all transactions are assigned to a segment.
  - Most companies set up a separate **class** and **location** to be used to track activities that don't fit in one of the other identified business segments.
    - If, for example, a company sets up a **class** for each product line, owners' salaries or corporate legal fees might be examples of transactions that would be assigned to an "Other" or "Administration" **class**.

 HINT: Intuit introduced a new tracking tool, called **tagging**, in early 2020. **Tags**, like **classes** and **locations**, can be used to report on various activities. Appendix A of this chapter provides additional information.

Turning on Class Tracking

Setting up **class** tracking is done in **Account and Settings**. (Use the ⚙ on the icon bar to open **Account and Settings**.)

Open the **Advanced** tab.

Figure 9.1

Access to class and location tracking

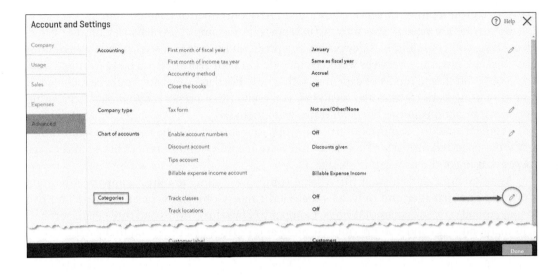

Click the **pencil** icon in the **Categories** section.

Figure 9.2

Class tracking setting and options

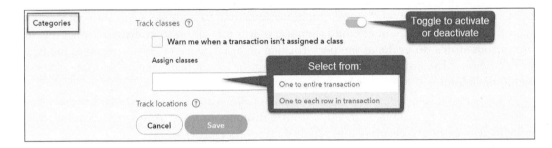

Toggle the **Track classes** button to activate the tool.

Using the **Warn me when a transaction isn't assigned a class** feature is an optional (but very useful!) tool.

There are two options available under **Assign classes**.

Selecting **One to each row in transaction** provides more flexibility because it allows you to easily enter transactions that include activities for more than one **class**. Selecting **One to entire transaction** would save time in companies that would not have multiple **class** activities in the same transaction. Click **Save** and then **Done** to complete the setup and exit **Account and Settings**.

Once **class** tracking is turned on, fields will be available on most forms for designating the appropriate classification. Here's an example of an **invoice** form after **class** tracking is activated with assignment by row.

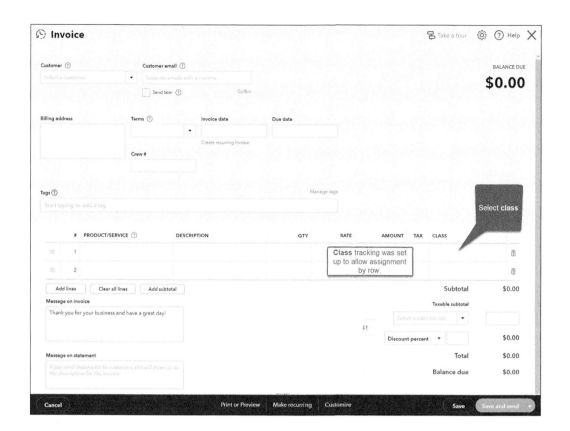

Figure 9.3

Class field on invoice form

If **class** tracking had been activated with assignment by transaction, a **Class** field would appear to the right of the **Due date** field.

> **BEHIND THE SCENES:** **Transfer** and **Payment** forms (**transaction types**) do not include boxes for tracking **location** or **class**. On **payment** transactions, the segments would already have been identified on the related **invoice** or **sales receipt** forms so that information would not be necessary.

Turning on Location Tracking

Setting up **location** tracking is also done on the **Advanced** tab of **Account and Settings**. Click the **pencil** icon in the **Categories** section to turn **location** tracking on.

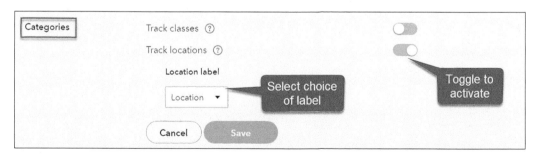

Figure 9.4

Location tracking setting

QBO uses "location" as the default title for this type of segment but users can change the title to one of the following:

Label options for location tracking

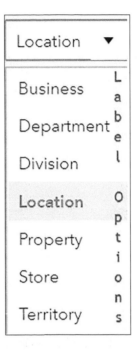

Click **Save** and then **Done** to complete the setup and exit **Account and Settings**.

Once **location** tracking is turned on, fields will be available on most forms for designating the appropriate classification. Here's an example of a **bill** form after **location** tracking was activated and **Store** was selected as the **location label**.

Location field on bill form

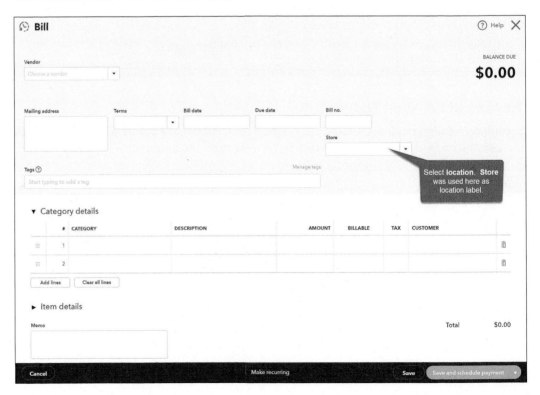

PRACTICE
EXERCISE
9.1

! **WARNING: The settings changed in this practice exercise will be used in Practice 9.2 through 9.4. You'll save yourself some time if you continue through to the end.**

Turn on class tracking for Craig's Design and Landscaping.
(Craig's Design decides to track revenues and costs related to their primary sources of revenue.)

1. Click the ⚙ on the icon bar.

2. Click **Account and Settings**.

3. Click **Advanced**.

4. Click the **pencil** icon in the **Categories** section.

5. Toggle the button next to **Track Classes** to activate the feature. Check the box next to **Warn me when a transaction isn't assigned a class**.

6. Select **one to each row in transaction** in the **Assign classes** dropdown menu.

7. Toggle the button next to **Track Locations** to activate the feature.

    a.   **Make a note** of the label options available in the dropdown menu.

8. Select **Territory** in the **Location label** dropdown menu.

9. Click **Save**.

10. Click **Done**.

Setting Up Classes and Locations

Once you've activated segment reporting in QBO and identified the segments you want to track, creating specific **classes** and **locations** is a simple process.

Click the ⚙ on the icon bar.

YOUR COMPANY	LISTS	TOOLS	PROFILE
Account and settings	All lists	Order checks ⧉	Feedback
Manage users	Products and services	Import data	Privacy
Custom form styles	Recurring transactions	Import desktop data	
Chart of accounts	Attachments	Export data	
QuickBooks labs	Tags	Reconcile	
		Budgeting	
		Audit log	
		SmartLook	
		Case center	

You're viewing QuickBooks in **Accountant view**. Learn more   Switch to Business view

Figure 9.7

Access to Class and Location lists

Click **All Lists** under the **Lists** column.

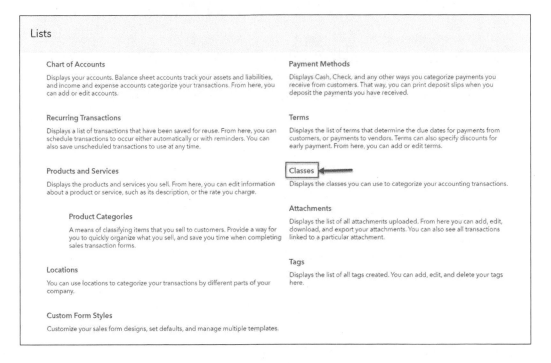

Click **Classes**.

Click **New**.

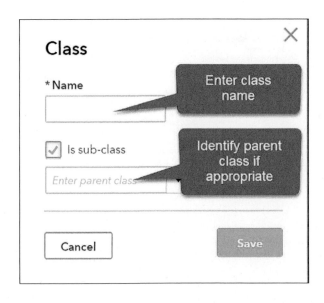

Enter a **Name** for the **class**. Check **Is sub-class** and select the appropriate **parent class** if multiple **class** levels are used.

 HINT: You can't rearrange the order of the **classes** on the **Class List**. The order listed is the order that will be displayed on reports. If it's important to have the **classes** in a particular order, companies might consider using numbers as part of the **class** names. The names could then be edited later to change the order. Reports can also be downloaded into Excel and reordered there. (Exporting to Excel is covered in Chapter 11.)

Clicking **Save** completes the setup of a new **class**.

The process for setting up **locations** is similar to the process for **class** setup.

Click the ⚙ on the icon bar and select **All Lists** to open the following window.

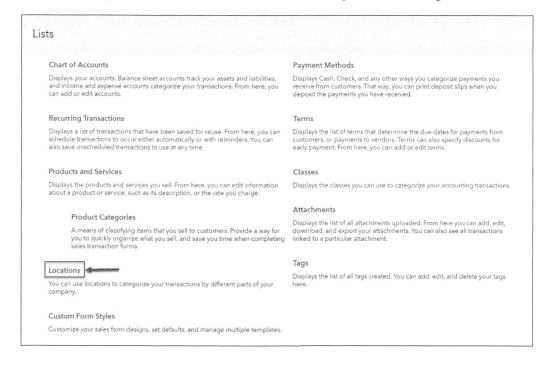

Figure 9.11

Access to Locations list

Click **Locations**.

Figure 9.12

Access to new location setup

Click **New**.

New location service record

There are a variety of options available when setting up **locations**. If **Is sub-location** is checked, a field for selecting a parent location would be displayed.

In the remaining options, QBO allows users to customize titles of forms and contact information for various locations. For example, if a user wanted to use a different company name and phone number for each store on **invoices**, **sales receipts**, and other forms sent to customers, a setup might look something like this:

Location options

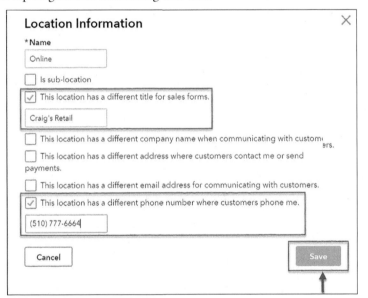

Clicking **Save** completes the setup of a new **location**.

Classes and **locations** can be edited or deleted by selecting **Edit** or **Delete** on the drop-down menu in the **ACTION** column of the appropriate list.

PRACTICE
EXERCISE
9.2

Set up classes and locations for Craig's Design and Landscaping.
(Craig's Design has decided to track operations by type of service and by territory. One class, labeled Design and Installation, will be used to report on landscape design services. A class labeled Gardening will be used to track all gardening services. A class labeled General will be used for all shared costs. Two territories will be used (Midtown and Uptown).)

(continued)

(continued from previous page)

1. If you have logged out since the last practice exercise, you'll need to activate **class** and **location** tracking by following the instructions in Practice Exercise 9.1.

2. Click the ⚙ on the icon bar.

3. Click **All Lists**.

4. Click **Classes**.

   a. Click **New**.

   b. Enter "Design and Installation" as the **Name**.

   c. Click **Save**.

   d. Click **New**.

   e. Enter "Gardening" as the **Name**.

   f. Click **Save**.

   g. Click **New**.

   h. Enter "General" as the **Name**.

   i. Click **Save**.

5. Click the ⚙ on the icon bar.

6. Click **All Lists**.

7. Click **Territories**.

   a. Click **New**.

   b. Enter "Midtown" as the **Name**.

   c. Leave the other boxes unchecked.

   d. Click **Save**.

   e. Click **New**.

   f. Enter "Uptown" as the **Name**.

   g. Leave the other boxes unchecked.

   h. Click **Save**.

8. Click **Dashboard** to exit out of the window.

 WARNING: Practice Exercises 9.3 and 9.4 use the classes set up in this exercise. You'll save yourself some time if you continue through to the end.

Adding Class to Item Records

To minimize data entry and standardize reporting, **classes** can be directly linked to **products** and **services** in the item record if you selected the option to assign classes to each row in a transaction. This option is not available if you selected the option to assign a class to the entire transaction. (**Locations** cannot be linked to other records.)

Click ⚙ on the icon bar and select **Products and Services**.

Select **New** to create a new item or **Edit** to revise an existing item.

Class field in service
item record

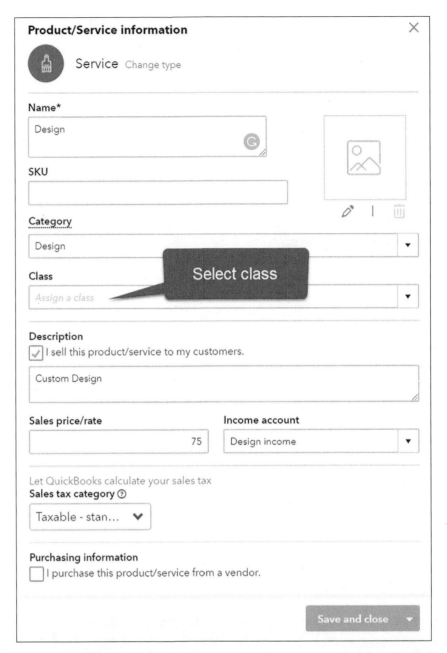

Select the appropriate segment in the **Class** field.

Once a **class** is linked to a **product** or **service**, **class** fields on sales or purchase transactions that include those items will be automatically updated. **Class** can be changed on specific transactions if necessary.

PRACTICE EXERCISE 9.3

Assign classes to products.

(Craig's Design decides to link some services to the Gardening class.)

1. If you have logged out since the last practice exercise, you'll need to redo Practice Exercises 9.1 and 9.2.

(continued)

(continued from previous page)

2. Open the Products and Services list.

    a.   Click the on the icon bar.

    b.   Click Products and Services.

3. Link two Services to the Gardening class.

    a.   Click Edit in the ACTION column of the Trimming row.

    b.   Select Gardening in the Class dropdown menu.

    c.   Click Save and Close.

    d.   Click Edit in the ACTION column of the Pest Control row.

    e.   Select Gardening in the Class dropdown menu.

    f.   Click Save and Close.

4. Click Dashboard to exit Products and Services.

> **! WARNING: The next practice exercise uses the work just completed. You'll save yourself some time if you continue without logging or timing out.**

Adding Class and Location to Transactions

Assigning classes and locations is done within forms (invoices, bills, journal entries, timesheets, etc.). The assignment can be changed at any time by simply editing the form.

> **HINT:** Although class can be assigned to transactions affecting balance sheet accounts, segment reporting is most commonly used for operating reports like profit and loss statements, wage summaries, sales summaries, etc. QBO does not require that every transaction (or every line item in a transaction) be linked to a class. If the user selected Warn me when a transaction isn't assigned a class when turning the feature on, a prompt similar to the screenshot below will appear if a transaction without a class on one or more lines is saved.
>
>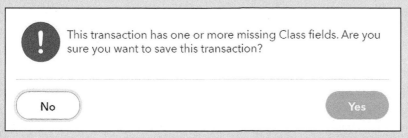
>
> No warning message appears when the location field is left blank.

Since only one location can be assigned to a single form in most cases, the location field is usually located in the top right section of the form.

If the preference for adding class to line items is selected, fields for entering class are normally entered in one of the final columns for each row. If the preference is set to one class per transaction, the class field is normally displayed directly below the location field.

Here's an example of a bill when both class and location tracking are turned on and the preference is to assign class by line item.

Figure 9.16

Location and Class
fields on a bill form

Figure 9.16

Location and Class
fields on a bill form

BEHIND THE SCENES If you take a minute to think about it, you'll realize that there's quite a bit of information included in the **bill** shown in Figure 9.16. In this one form, the user would have:

- Increased inventory
- Expensed some supply costs
- Set up a liability

PRACTICE

EXERCISE

9.4

Assign classes to a few transactions for Craig's Design and Landscaping.
(Craig's Design invoices Rondonuwu Fruit and Vegi for some gardening work and records a check for a consultation with an advertising agency about promoting the design services in the Uptown neighborhood.)

1. If you have logged out since the last practice exercise, you'll need to redo Practice Exercises 9.1 through 9.3.

(continued)

(continued from previous page)

2. Click **+ New** on the navigation bar.

3. Click **Invoice.**

   a.   Select **Rondonuwu Fruit and Vegi** as the customer.

   b.   Use the current date as the **Invoice date**.

   c.   Select **Midtown** as the **Territory**.

   d.   Select **Trimming** as the **PRODUCT/SERVICE**.

   e.   Leave the **QTY** and **RATE** as is.

   f.   Check the **TAX** box.

   g.   The **Class** field should have auto-filled with **Gardening**.

   h.   Select **California** in the **select a sales tax rate** dropdown menu.

   i.   **Make a note** of the total amount due.

   j.   Click **Save and close.**

4. Click **+ New** on the navigation bar.

5. Click **Check.**

   a.   Select **Lee Advertising** as the vendor.

   b.   Use the current date as the **Payment date**.

   c.   Leave the check number as is.

   d.   **Make a note** of the check number.

   e.   Select **Uptown** as the **Territory**.

   f.   Select **Advertising** as the **CATEGORY**.

   g.   Enter "Consultation" as the **DESCRIPTION**.

   h.   Enter "500" as the **AMOUNT**.

   i.   Select **Design and Installation** as the **Class**.

   j.   Click **Save and close.**

Reporting by Class or Location

There are several reports that are frequently used to report segment information but most reports can be filtered by **class** or **location**.

The **Profit & Loss by Class** and **Profit & Loss by Location** reports are probably the ones most commonly used. Both reports can be accessed in the **Business Overview** section of **Reports**. Each **class** or **location** will be shown in a separate column. Any transactions that have NOT been classified will appear in a **Not Specified** column.

 HINT: Users can drill down on transactions appearing in the **Not Specified** column. The transactions can then be edited so that they are properly classified.

Here's an example of what a **Profit and Loss by Class** might look like:

Figure 9.17

Example of Class
report

Craig's Design and Landscaping Services
Profit and Loss by Class

Classes created and assigned by authors

	ADMINISTRATION	DESIGN AND INSTALLATION	GARDENING	TOTAL
▾ Income				
Design income		937.50		$937.50
Discounts given		(59.00)		$ (59.00)
Landscaping Services		1,117.50	297.50	$1,415.00
Pest Control Services			70.00	$70.00
Sales of Product Income		868.75		$868.75
Total Income	$0.00	$2,864.75	$367.50	$3,232.25
▾ Cost of Goods Sold				
Cost of Goods Sold	.	405.00		$405.00
Total Cost of Goods Sold	$0.00	$405.00	$0.00	$405.00
GROSS PROFIT	$0.00	$2,459.75	$367.50	$2,827.25
▾ Expenses				
Advertising	74.86			$74.86
Automobile	19.99	63.15	52.56	$135.70
Equipment Rental		112.00		$112.00
Job Expenses		46.98		$46.98
Legal & Professional Fees	390.00			$390.00
Maintenance and Repair		755.00		$755.00
Total Expenses	$484.85	$977.13	$52.56	$1,514.54
NET OPERATING INCOME	$ (484.85)	$1,482.62	$314.94	$1,312.71
NET INCOME	$ (484.85)	$1,482.62	$314.94	$1,312.71

Here's an example of what a **Profit and Loss by Location** might look like:

Figure 9.18

Example of Location
report

Craig's Design and Landscaping Services
Profit and Loss by Location

Locations created and assigned by authors

	GENERAL	MENLO PARK	PALO ALTO	TOTAL
▾ Income				
Design income		375.00	562.50	$937.50
Discounts given		(8.75)	(50.25)	$ (59.00)
Landscaping Services		155.00	1,260.00	$1,415.00
Pest Control Services		70.00		$70.00
Sales of Product Income		291.00	577.75	$868.75
Total Income	$0.00	$882.25	$2,350.00	$3,232.25
▾ Cost of Goods Sold				
Cost of Goods Sold		135.00	270.00	$405.00
Total Cost of Goods Sold	$0.00	$135.00	$270.00	$405.00
GROSS PROFIT	$0.00	$747.25	$2,080.00	$2,827.25
▾ Expenses				
Advertising	74.86			$74.86
Automobile	135.70			$135.70
Equipment Rental			112.00	$112.00
Job Expenses		46.98		$46.98
Legal & Professional Fees	390.00			$390.00
Maintenance and Repair	755.00			$755.00
Total Expenses	$1,355.56	$46.98	$112.00	$1,514.54
NET OPERATING INCOME	$ (1,355.56)	$700.27	$1,968.00	$1,312.71
NET INCOME	$ (1,355.56)	$700.27	$1,968.00	$1,312.71

The **Sales and Customers** and **Expenses and Vendors** sections in **Reports** include a number of segmented reports preset by QBO.

CREATING AND USING BUDGETS

"The general who wins the battle makes many calculations in his temple before the battle is fought. The general who loses makes but few calculations beforehand."—Sun Tzu

Managing a business is certainly not like going to war but having a plan and being able to evaluate actual results against that plan can definitely help a business succeed.

A financial plan for a business is commonly called a "budget." In a simple budget, revenues and costs are generally estimated by month. Estimates might be based on:

- Past experience

- Projections of sales growth (or contraction)

- Industry statistics

- Combinations of the above

There are a number of tools in QBO for creating and using profit and loss budgets.

Creating Budgets

Companies can create multiple budgets in QBO.

Profit and loss budgets can be prepared for a company overall, by **Customer**, by **Class**, or by **Location**. In this course, we'll cover creating a budget for a company overall.

All of the planning tools in QBO are accessed by first clicking the ⚙ on the icon bar.

Figure 9.19

Access to budgeting feature

Select **Budgeting** in the **Tools** column.

Figure 9.20

Link to budget screen

Click **Add budget**.

Figure 9.21

Initial budget setup screen

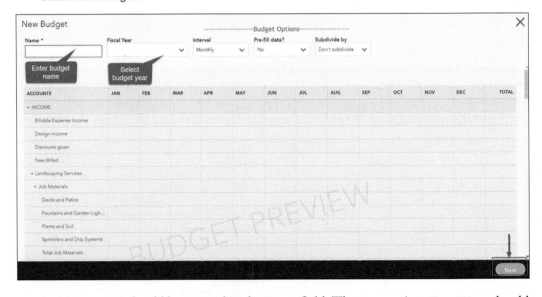

A unique name should be entered in the **Name** field. The appropriate **Fiscal Year** should also be selected.

Users can create monthly, quarterly, or yearly budgets. (The choice is selected in the **Interval** field.) For the most flexibility in reporting, most companies would create monthly budgets. Users have two choices for entering data in a budget.

Figure 9.22

Options for setting budget amounts

- Budgets can be started from scratch. (**No** selected in **Pre-fill data?** field.)
- Budgets can be filled with actual data from one of the two prior fiscal years. (The appropriate year selected in **Pre-fill data?** field.)
  - Edits can be made to budgets created using prior period data.

All budgets must be set up by account and by period (month, quarter, or year). You can expand the budget by adding **location**, **class**, or **customer**. This is called **subdividing** in QBO.

For each fiscal year then, a company could have an overall budget, budgets for each **class**, budgets for each **location**, AND budgets for each **customer** (project). Each one would be created separately and each would include amounts by account and by period.

Subdivisions are selected in the final field. The dropdown menu looks like this:

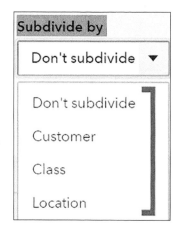

Figure 9.23

Options for budget detail level

Click **Next** in the bottom right corner of the budget screen (Figure 9.21) after all options are selected.

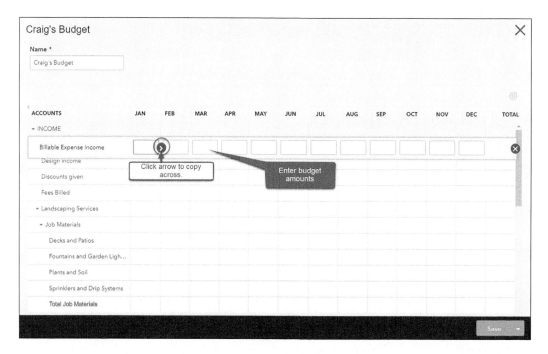

Figure 9.24

Budget screen

Enter the budget amounts in the appropriate month fields. It is not necessary to enter an amount for every month. There are some income and expense accounts that may have activity only in the first half of the year or only in every other month. Budget amounts should represent the best estimates of the expected activity. If it's expected that an account will have the same activity in successive periods, enter the amount in the first month and click the right arrow next to the amount to copy across the row. You can copy across from any field in the budget form.

Click **Save and close** when all budget amounts have been entered.

To see the final budget, click **Reports** on the navigation bar. Select **Budget Overview** in the **Business overview** section. A final budget might look something like this:

Figure 9.25

Budget report

Craig's Design and Landscaping Services ✏
Budget Overview: Craig's Budget - FY22 P&L
January - December 2022

	JAN 2022	FEB 2022	MAR 2022	APR 2022	MAY 2022	JUN 2022	JUL 2022	AUG 2022	SEP 2022	OCT 2022	NOV 2022	DEC 2022	TOTAL
▾ Income													
Design Income	15,000.00	15,000.00	15,000.00	15,000.00	15,000.00	15,000.00	15,000.00	15,000.00	15,000.00	15,000.00	15,000.00	15,000.00	$180,000.00
▾ Landscaping Services													$0.00
Job Materials	2,000.00	2,000.00	2,000.00	2,000.00	2,000.00	2,000.00	2,000.00	2,000.00	2,000.00	2,000.00	2,000.00	2,000.00	$24,000.00
Labor	1,500.00	1,500.00	1,500.00	1,500.00	1,500.00	1,500.00	1,500.00	1,500.00	1,500.00	1,500.00	1,500.00	1,500.00	$18,000.00
Total Landscaping Services	3,500.00	3,500.00	3,500.00	3,500.00	3,500.00	3,500.00	3,500.00	3,500.00	3,500.00	3,500.00	3,500.00	3,500.00	$42,000.00
Total Income	$18,500.00	$18,500.00	$18,500.00	$18,500.00	$18,500.00	$18,500.00	$18,500.00	$18,500.00	$18,500.00	$18,500.00	$18,500.00	$18,500.00	$222,000.00
▾ Cost of Goods Sold													
Cost of Goods Sold	1,500.00	1,500.00	1,500.00	1,500.00	1,500.00	1,500.00	1,500.00	1,500.00	1,500.00	1,500.00	1,500.00	1,500.00	$18,000.00
Total Cost of Goods Sold	$1,500.00	$1,500.00	$1,500.00	$1,500.00	$1,500.00	$1,500.00	$1,500.00	$1,500.00	$1,500.00	$1,500.00	$1,500.00	$1,500.00	$18,000.00
GROSS PROFIT	$17,000.00	$17,000.00	$17,000.00	$17,000.00	$17,000.00	$17,000.00	$17,000.00	$17,000.00	$17,000.00	$17,000.00	$17,000.00	$17,000.00	$204,000.00
▾ Expenses													
Advertising	100.00	100.00	100.00	100.00	100.00	100.00	100.00	100.00	100.00	100.00	100.00	100.00	$1,200.00
Equipment Rental	0.00	0.00	300.00	0.00	0.00	300.00	0.00	0.00	300.00	0.00	0.00	300.00	$1,200.00
▾ Job Expenses													$0.00
Cost of Labor	6,000.00	6,000.00	6,000.00	6,000.00	6,000.00	6,000.00	6,000.00	6,000.00	6,000.00	6,000.00	6,000.00	6,000.00	$72,000.00
Job Materials	800.00	800.00	800.00	800.00	800.00	800.00	800.00	800.00	800.00	800.00	800.00	800.00	$9,600.00
Total Job Expenses	6,800.00	6,800.00	6,800.00	6,800.00	6,800.00	6,800.00	6,800.00	6,800.00	6,800.00	6,800.00	6,800.00	6,800.00	$81,600.00
Office Expenses	300.00	300.00	300.00	300.00	300.00	300.00	300.00	300.00	300.00	300.00	300.00	300.00	$3,600.00
Rent or Lease	1,200.00	1,200.00	1,200.00	1,200.00	1,200.00	1,200.00	1,200.00	1,200.00	1,200.00	1,200.00	1,200.00	1,200.00	$14,400.00
Taxes & Licenses	0.00	0.00	50.00	0.00	0.00	0.00	0.00	0.00	0.00	50.00	0.00	0.00	$100.00
Total Expenses	$8,400.00	$8,400.00	$8,750.00	$8,400.00	$8,400.00	$8,700.00	$8,400.00	$8,400.00	$8,700.00	$8,450.00	$8,400.00	$8,700.00	$102,100.00
NET OPERATING INCOME	$8,600.00	$8,600.00	$8,250.00	$8,600.00	$8,600.00	$8,300.00	$8,600.00	$8,600.00	$8,300.00	$8,550.00	$8,600.00	$8,300.00	$101,900.00
NET INCOME	$8,600.00	$8,600.00	$8,250.00	$8,600.00	$8,600.00	$8,300.00	$8,600.00	$8,600.00	$8,300.00	$8,550.00	$8,600.00	$8,300.00	$101,900.00

PRACTICE
EXERCISE 9.5

WARNING: **Practice Exercise 9.6 is based on the work you will perform in this Practice Exercise. To save yourself time, complete Practice Exercises 9.5 and 9.6 before you log out.**

Set up a budget for Craig's Design and Landscaping.
(Craig's Design decides to create a simple budget for 2022.)

1. Click the ⚙ on the icon bar.

2. Click **Budgeting** in the **Tools** column.

3. Click **Add budget**.

4. Enter "Craig's Budget" as the **Name**.

5. Select **FY2022(Jan 2022–Dec 2022)**.

6. Select **Monthly** as the **Interval**.

7. Select **No** in **Pre-fill data?**.

8. Select **Don't subdivide** in **Subdivide by**.

9. Click **Next**.

10. In the **INCOME** section,
    a. Click in the **Jan** field of **Design income**.
       i. Enter "2,000" and click the **right arrow**.

(continued)

(continued from previous page)

     b. Click in the **Jan** field of **Fountains and Garden Lighting**.

         i. Enter "500" and click the **right arrow**.

     c. Click in the **Jan** field of **Installation**.

         i. Enter "4,000" and click the **right arrow**.

11. In the **COST OF GOODS SOLD** section,

     a. Click in the **Jan** field of **Cost of Goods Sold**.

         i. Enter "200" and click the **right arrow**.

12. In the **EXPENSES** section,

     a. Click in the **Jan** field of **Advertising**.

         i. Enter "200" and click the **right arrow**.

     b. Click in the **Jan** field of **Equipment Rental**.

         i. Enter "300" in the **Mar, Jun, Sep,** and **Dec** fields.

     c. Click in the **Jan** field of **Job Materials**.

         i. Enter "400" and click the **right arrow**.

     d. Click in the **Jan** field of **Office Expenses**.

         i. Enter "300" and click the **right arrow**.

     e. Click in the **Jan** field of **Rent or Lease**.

         i. Enter "1,200" and click the **right arrow**.

     f. Click in the **Jan** field of **Taxes and Licenses**.

         i. Enter "50" in the **Mar** and **Oct** fields.

13. Click **Save and close**.

14. Click **Dashboard** to exit out of the budget window.

15. Complete the next practice exercise before logging out.

Creating Budget Reports

There are a variety of budget reports in QBO. All of them can be accessed in the **Business overview** section of **Reports**.

- The **Budget Overview** report presents budget figures only.

- The **Budget vs. Actuals** report presents actual and budget figures by month. The dollar difference (actual less budget) and the percentage relationship of actual to budget (actual divided by budget) are also displayed for each account.

 HINT: There are many options for customizing this report. In the **Rows/Columns** section of the **Customize Report** sidebar, users can elect to summarize data by quarter instead of by month. Comparison fields can be added or deleted as well. For example, if the report is being created for a manager during the budget period, **$ Remaining** or **% Remaining** columns can be very helpful.

PRACTICE
EXERCISE
9.6

Prepare budget report for Craig's Design and Landscaping.

(Craig's Design wants to review the budget just created.)

1. If you logged or timed out after the last practice exercise, go back and set up the budget again using the directions in Practice Exercise 9.5.

2. Click Reports on the navigation bar.

3. Click Budget Overview in the Business overview section.

4. **Make a note** of the budgeted GROSS PROFIT for 2022.

5. **Make a note** of the budgeted NET INCOME for 2022.

6. Click Dashboard to close the window.

REVERSING ENTRIES

We're sure it's clear by now that accountants typically make a lot of adjusting journal entries when financial statements are prepared!

Many (if not most) of the adjusting entries are made to properly recognize (or defer) revenues or expenses for the reporting period. These adjusting entries must be made because physical transactions (sending out invoices to customers, receiving bills from vendors, preparing paychecks for employees, etc.) don't always occur in the month that the related activities should be recognized in the financial statements.

> **BEHIND THE SCENES** This book is written assuming the accrual method of accounting is used. (The accrual method is required under GAAP.) Companies that use the cash method of accounting recognize revenue when collected and expenses when paid. Entries to defer revenues or expenses would not be required.

For example, many companies receive bills from vendors in the month **after** costs are incurred. A bill received from the company's attorney for work performed in January might be received (and dated) in February. Since the work was performed in January, the expense should be recognized in January.

If the accountant enters the bill using the bill date, the expense will be recognized (reported on the income statement) in February. January's legal expense will be understated (too low) and February's legal expense will be overstated (too high). The accountant **could** enter the bill using a January date so that January's income statement is correct, but then the accounts payable subsidiary ledger wouldn't be accurate.

Most accountants solve the problem by entering an adjusting journal entry in January to recognize the expense. The bill received from the vendor in February is entered using the bill date. The expense and the liability, of course, now appear in TWO months; in January through the adjusting journal entry and in February through the bill. The accountant, then, makes an adjusting journal entry in February to offset the duplicate charge.

Reversing entries in QBO are a tool for minimizing the possibility of duplicate transactions not being cleared. When an adjusting entry is dated the month **before** the standard entry (form) is recorded, the accountant can flag the journal entry as a reversing entry. QBO will then automatically create a new entry (dated the first day of the subsequent month) to completely reverse the original entry. That way, when the appropriate form is created, it will **not** result in a double recognition of the same transaction. Reversing entries are very easy to create.

As an example, let's say a company hired an attorney to look over some employment contracts. The attorney estimated the fee would be about $1,000. The attorney did the work in November and sent a bill, dated December 15, to the company for the $1,000. The expense needs to be recognized in November (since the work was performed in November) so the company would make an adjusting entry dated November 30.

Figure 9.26
Journal entry example

Once the entry is saved (click **Save**, not **Save and new**), the option to reverse the entry becomes available.

> **BEHIND THE SCENES** When accruing expenses, a separate liability account (accrued expenses in Figure 9.26) is normally used. This avoids multiple entries to the vendor subsidiary ledger. Similarly, a separate asset account is used when income is accrued (when income has been earned but has not yet been invoiced to the customer).

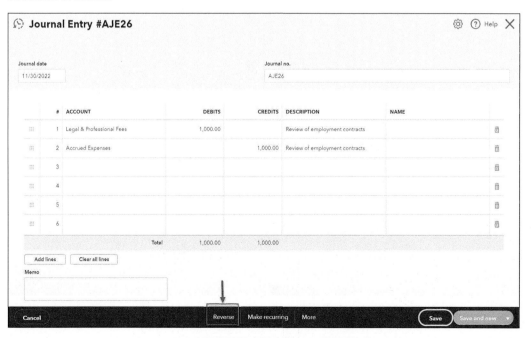

Figure 9.27
Access to reversing entry feature

Clicking **Reverse** automatically creates a new entry.

Figure 9.28

Reversing entry

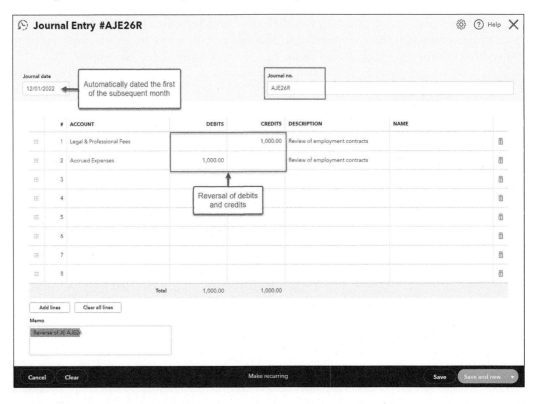

Reversing entries are always dated the first day of the subsequent month. The date can be changed later if appropriate.

When the attorney's bill is received in December, it would be entered as a **bill** using December 15 as the **bill date**. The debit to Legal & Professional Fees will be offset by the credit to Legal & Professional Fees from the reversing entry shown above. The expense is now properly reported in November's profit and loss statement and the **bill** will have the correct December 15 date.

The activity in the expense account would look like this:

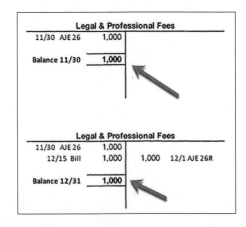

> **!** **WARNING:** Once created, reversing entries are not linked to the original entry. Deleting or modifying the original entry will not change the reversing entry. Changes to the reversing entry will not affect the original entry.

Prepare a reversing entry for Craig's Design and Landscaping.
(Craig's Design receives a $500 bill for legal services performed in the prior month. The bill is dated in the current month.)

PRACTICE
EXERCISE
9.7

Homework
MBC

1. Click ➕ **New** on the navigation bar.

2. Select **Journal Entry**.

3. Enter the last day of **last** month in the **Journal Date** field.

4. In the first row, select **Lawyer** in the **ACCOUNT** field.

    a. **Make a note** of the parent account for **Lawyer**.

5. Enter "500" in the **DEBITS** column.

6. In the second row select **Add new** in the **ACCOUNT** column.

7. Select **Other Current Liabilities** as the **account type**.

8. Select **Other Current Liabilities** as the **Detail Type**.

9. Enter "Accrued Expenses" in the **Name** field.

10. Enter "500" in the **CREDITS** field.

11. Click **Save**.

    a. Click **Yes** if you get a message about missing **classes**.

12. Click **Reverse**.

13. The reversing entry will be displayed.

    a. **Make a note** of the journal entry date for the reversing entry.

14. Click **Save and close**.

RECURRING TRANSACTIONS

eLectures 📹

Some companies have transactions that occur every month, in the same amount. For example, office cleaning service companies often bill customers a set fee for a particular monthly cleaning service. The entry for straight-line depreciation is another possible example.

QBO allows users to set up these recurring transactions so that they are easily recreated on a set schedule.

To set up a recurring transaction, click the ⚙ on the icon bar.

YOUR COMPANY	LISTS	TOOLS	PROFILE
Account and settings	All lists	Order checks ↗	Feedback
Manage users	Products and services	Import data	Privacy
Custom form styles	Recurring transactions	Import desktop data	
Chart of accounts	Attachments	Export data	
QuickBooks labs	Tags	Reconcile	
		Budgeting	
		Audit log	
		SmartLook	
		Case center	

You're viewing QuickBooks in **Accountant view**. Learn more   Switch to Business view

Figure 9.29

Access to recurring transaction center

 HINT: Recurring transactions can also be created within most forms.

Click **Recurring Transactions**.

Figure 9.30

Access to recurring
transaction form

HINT: The transactions you see in Figure 9.30 were automatically set up by Intuit in the test drive company.

Click **New** to enter a new transaction.

Figure 9.31

Options for recurring
transactions

The type of transaction to be entered is selected first.

The options available in the **recurring transaction** setup form would depend on the type of transaction selected. For example, if **Invoice** was selected, the form would look something like this:

Figure 9.32

Setup form for a
recurring invoice

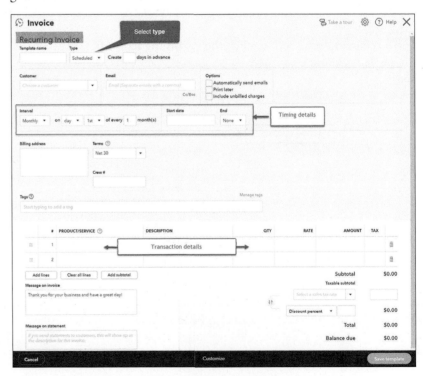

A name for the recurring entry must be entered in the **Template name** field. The name should clearly identify the purpose of the recurring entry. For example, "Weekly-Melton" would be a reasonable name for an entry to bill John Melton for weekly gardening services.

There are a number of options for recurring entries:

- In the **Type** field, transactions can be set as:
  - **Scheduled**
    - Transactions will be automatically created.
  - **Reminder**
    - Transactions will be added to a reminder list but will not be created until the user chooses to create them. (The user would then have the option of not recording the entry in a particular period.)
  - **Unscheduled**
    - Transaction is saved in the **Recurring Transactions** list but would not appear on the reminder list and would not be automatically created.
    - **Unscheduled** would be the **type** selected when users don't have all the necessary information for the transaction yet.
    - The **type** could also be used to set up a template for a complex transaction that the user wants to have available when needed.

If **scheduled** or **reminder** transaction templates are created:

- The frequency of the transaction would be set in the **Interval** fields.
- The date of the next entry would be identified in the **Start date** field.
- The user can specify how far into the future the transaction should be entered by entering a date or number of occurrences in the **End** field.

Special options available when **recurring invoices** are set up include automatically emailing invoices to customers, batching **invoices** to be printed later, and automatically adding any unbilled time or costs to the **invoice**. (Billable time and costs are covered in Chapter 10.)

A **recurring invoice** for Craig's Design and Landscaping might be set up something like this:

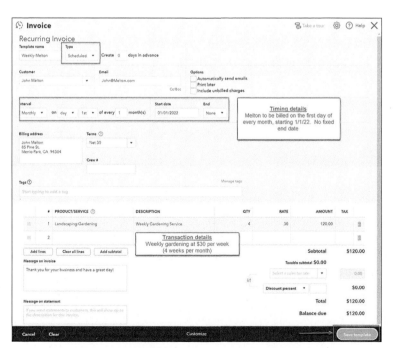

Figure 9.33

Example of recurring invoice setup form

Click **Save template** to complete the setup.

All **recurring** transactions can be accessed in the **Recurring Transactions** list (accessed by clicking the ⚙ on the icon bar and selecting **recurring transactions**).

Figure 9.34
Recurring transaction list

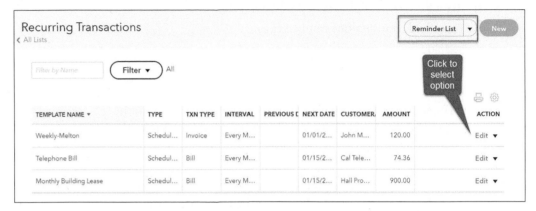

Figure 9.34

Recurring transaction list

The options available in the **ACTION** column depend on the type of **recurring transaction**. For the Weekly-Melton **invoice**, the options in addition to **Edit** would be:

Figure 9.35

Options for editing recurring invoices

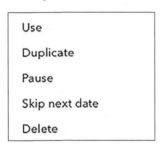

If **Use** is selected, a transaction would be created using the details from the **recurring** transaction. The form can be edited before saving.

If **Duplicate** is selected, an **invoice** would be created that includes the same terms, etc. This is a useful feature for a company that has a number of similar fixed monthly fee customers. Changes to customer name, etc. could be made on the duplicated form. A new **template name** would be entered to save the duplicated transaction.

The **Pause** and **Skip next date** options are used to delay recording **scheduled** transactions.

The **ACTION** options for recurring **journal entries** are the same as those for **invoices**. For **bills**, **ACTION** options include **Edit**, **Use**, **Duplicate**, and **Delete**.

The **recurring transaction** details are included on the **Reminder List** (identified on Figure 9.34).

> **!** **WARNING:** **Recurring transactions** can be very useful but they must be monitored, especially if they are set up as automatic entries.

PRACTICE
EXERCISE
9.8

Prepare a recurring entry for Craig's Design and Landscaping.
(Craig's Design has decided to try placing a small ad ($20 per month) in a local magazine, Trees for Sacramento. The advertising fee will be charged to the company credit card. Craig decides to place the ad over the next six-month period.)

1. Click **+ New** on the navigation bar.

(continued)

(continued from previous page)

2. Select **Expense**.

3. Select **Add new** in the **Choose a payee** field.

4. Enter "Trees for Sacramento" as the **Name**.

5. Select **Vendor** as the **Type** and click **Save**.

6. Select **Visa** as the **Payment account**.

7. Enter the current date as the **Payment date**.

8. Select **Visa** as the **Payment method**.

9. **Make a note** of the number of methods (other than **Add new**) appearing in the **Payment method** dropdown menu.

10. In the first row of the **Category details** section, select **Advertising** in the **CATEGORY** field.

11. Enter "20" in the **AMOUNT** column.

12. Click **Make recurring**.

13. Change the **Template name** to "Magazine ad."

14. Select **Scheduled** in the **Type** field.

15. Leave **Trees for Sacramento** as the **Payee**.

16. Select **Visa** as the **Account**.

17. Select **Monthly**, **last** and **Friday** in the **Interval** fields.

18. Enter the current date as the **Start date**.

19. Select **After** in the **End** field.

20. Enter "6" in the **occurrences** field.

21. Click **Save template**.

CHAPTER SHORTCUTS

Set up class and location tracking
1. Click the ⚙ on the icon bar
2. Click **Account and Settings**
3. Click **Advanced**
4. Click the **pencil** icon in **Categories** section
5. Toggle the buttons next to **Track classes** and **Track locations**

Set up classes or location
1. Click the ⚙ on the icon bar
2. Click **All Lists**
3. Click **Classes** or **Locations**
4. Click **New**

Create a budget
1. Click the ⚙ on the icon bar
2. Click **Budgeting**

CHAPTER REVIEW

Matching

Match the term or phrase (as used in QBO) to its definition.

1.	budget subdividing	**5.**	budget
2.	class tracking	**6.**	budget overview
3.	budget v actuals report	**7.**	location tracking
4.	reversing entry	**8.**	profit and loss by class report

_____   report that displays revenue and expenses by class for a specified period of time

_____   tool most likely to be used to classify revenues and expenses by product line

_____   report that shows variances between actual and budgeted results for a period of time

_____   tool most likely to be used to classify revenues and expenses by store

_____   estimate of future operating results

_____   tool used to add class, location, or customer when creating a budget

_____   an entry created by a user that is the exact opposite of an entry in a prior period

_____   report that shows budgeted account balances for a period of time

Multiple Choice

1. In QBO, a **class** might represent a specific _____.
   a. department in a company
   b. customer type
   c. product line
   d. any of the above could be used

2. Which of the following statements is true?
   a. **Class** tracking is done automatically by QBO.
   b. A **class** must be assigned to every entry in a transaction.
   c. Users can track by **class** or **location** but not both.
   d. Only one **location** can be set per vendor bill.

3. Budgets can be created for:
   a. the company overall.
   b. a specific customer (project).
   c. a specific **class**.
   d. a specific **location**.
   e. any of the above.

4. When creating a budget for a company with a 12/31 year end, you enter $300 in March for one of the rows and click the blue arrow next to the field. The amount that will appear as the **total** for that row will be:
   a. $3,000.
   b. $2,700.
   c. $600.
   d. $300.

5. If a recurring transaction is set as **unscheduled**, _____.

    a. you will receive a reminder to record the transaction after two weeks

    b. it will be entered once and only once

    c. it will be available for posting but QBO will not automatically create the transaction

    d. None of the above answers are correct. There is no such thing as an unscheduled recurring transaction.

BEYOND THE CLICKS—THINKING LIKE A MANAGER

Accounting: Who should be responsible for creating budgets? Explain your answer. How might managers use budget information? (Think about department managers as well as corporate managers.)

Information Systems: Aki's Accounting provides bookkeeping services for multiple clients for a monthly fee of $500, billed in advance. Aki and his staff also provide other services periodically (tax return preparation, financial planning, etc.). Additional services are billed, in arrears, on an hourly basis. Aki asks you to set up **recurring invoices** for his clients. What type would you use? Which settings and options would you select? What concerns, if any, would you have with Aki's use of **recurring invoices**?

ASSIGNMENTS

Background information: Martin Smith, a college student and good friend of yours, has always wanted to be an entrepreneur. He is very good in math, so, to test his entrepreneurship skills, he has decided to set up a small math tutoring company serving local high school students who struggle in their math courses. He set up the company, Math Revealed!, as a corporation in 2021. Martin is the only owner. He has not taken any distributions from the company since it opened.

    The business has been successful so far. In fact, it's been so successful he has decided to work in his business full time now that he's graduated from college with a degree in mathematics.

    He has decided to start using QuickBooks Online to keep track of his business transactions. He likes the convenience of being able to access his information over the Internet. You have agreed to act as his accountant while you're finishing your own academic program.

    Martin currently has a number of regular customers that he tutors in Pre-Algebra, Algebra, and Geometry. His customers pay his fees by cash or check after each tutoring session but he does give terms of Net 15 to some of his customers. He has developed the following fee schedule:

Name	Description	Rate
Refresher	One-hour session	$ 60 per hour
Persistence program	Two one-hour sessions per week	$100 per week
Crisis program	Five one-hour sessions per week	$225 per week

The tutoring sessions usually take place at his students' homes but he recently signed a two-year lease on a small office above a local coffee shop. The rent is only $750 per month starting in January 2022. A security deposit of $500 was paid in December 2021.

    The following equipment is owned by the company:

Description	Date placed in service	Cost	Life	Salvage Value
Computer	7/1/21	$3,000	36 months	$300
Printer	7/1/21	$ 240	24 months	$ 0
Graphing Calculators (3)	7/1/21	$ 300	36 months	$ 30

Assignment 9A

Math Revealed!

All equipment is depreciated using the straight-line method.

As of 12/31/21, Martin owed $2,500 to his father (Richard Smith) who initially helped him get started. Richard is charging him interest at a 6% annual rate. Martin has been paying interest only on a monthly basis. His last payment of interest only was on 12/31/21.

Over the next month or so, he plans to expand his business by selling a few products he believes will help his students. He has already purchased a few items:

Category	Description	Vendor	Quantity on Hand	Cost per Unit	Sales Price
Books and Tools					
	Geometry in Sports	Books Galore	20	18	25
	Solving Puzzles: Fun with Algebra	Books Galore	20	15	22
	Getting Ready for Calculus	Books Galore	20	20	28
	Geometry Kit	Math Shack	10	12	18
	Handheld Dry-Erase Boards	Math Shack	25	10	15
	Notebooks (pack of 5)	Paper Bag Depot	10	8	12

3/1/22

✓ You talk to Martin today about the need for more management tools to help him run his business effectively. You both decide that using **class** tracking would be helpful.

✓ You turn on **class** tracking in the **Advanced** tab of **Account and Settings**.

- You want to be able to assign a class to individual line items in transaction forms.
- You also turn on the "warning" feature. You don't want to have to go back and fix issues later.

✓ You decide to set up four **classes**.

- Products
  - To be used for tracking revenues and costs related to sales of products and product training revenues.
- Workshops
  - To be used for tracking revenues and costs related to workshop presentations.
- Tutoring
  - To be used for tracking revenues and costs related to all tutoring services.
- Administrative
  - To be used for tracking general business costs.

✓ You realize that it will save you time in the long-run to go ahead and assign a **class** to each of the products and services that you sell. You open the **Products and Services** list and assign the **classes** as follows:

- You assign the Workshops **class** to the Educator Workshop service.
- You assign the Tutoring **class** to the Crisis, Mathmagic, Persistence and Refresher services.
- You assign the Products **class** to all the **Inventory** type products.
- You don't assign a **class** for items in the **Other Charges category**. You'll determine the **class** when you record transactions that include these items.

✓ You also decide you want to use the budgeting tool in QBO.

✓ You create a monthly profit and loss budget for 2022 from scratch (no subdividing). (You use "2022 Budget" for the name.) You use the following estimates:

- Tutoring ($3,500 for January to June; $4,000 per month for July through December)
- Workshops ($5,500 for February; $4,000 for March through December)
- Sales of Product Income ($1,500 for February and March; $2,500 from April through December)
- Cost of Goods Sold ($1,000 for February and March; $1,650 for April through December)

- Facility Costs
  - Rent ($750 every month)
  - Utilities ($250 every month)
- Office and Tutoring Costs
  - Office supplies ($25 every month)
  - Tutoring supplies ($100 every month)
  - Depreciation ($150 every month)
- Labor costs
  - Professional development ($200 per month)
  - Contract labor ($125 for January through March; $700 for April through May; $900 for September through December)
- Marketing Costs
  - Advertising ($100 per month)
- Taxes, Insurance, and Professional Services
  - Accounting and consulting fees ($300 for January and February, $500 for March through December)
  - Insurance ($30 every month)
- Other Costs
  - Gasoline ($40 every month)
  - Bank service charges ($10 every month)
- Interest expense ($15 every month)

✓ You let Martin know that the budget shows $68,135 in profit for the year. **TIP:** You might need to click **Save** to see the totals.

3/3/22

✓ You write yourself a check (# 1125) for the work you did in **February**. **TIP:** Use **Administrative** as the **class** if a cost isn't directly related to tutoring, workshops, or product sales.

✓ You look at the collections report and notice that you have quite a few past due bills. You make calls to Debbie Han, Paul Richard, and Annie Wang.

- Debbie and Annie apologize and agree to send their checks in a few days.
- Paul explains that he's been waiting to receive a credit for the two missed sessions in February. You tell him that you'll talk to Martin and get that credit memo to him as soon as possible.

✓ You ask Martin about Paul's missed sessions. He explains that he forgot to tell you about that. You create a credit memo for $90 (CM-1015) in QBO and send it off to Paul. You charge the $90 to the **Crisis** item since that was the package Paul had purchased. The amount is small so you decide to recognize the credit memo in March. **TIP:** Leave the **QTY** at 1. Update the **RATE** field. You enter "Credit for missed sessions. Sorry for the delay!" in the **Message displayed on credit memo** box. **TIP:** The **CLASS** field should automatically fill with Tutoring. If it doesn't, go back to the **Product/Service** list and make sure you've assigned a **class** to each item.

✓ Martin lets you know that he will be putting on another **Educator Workshop** for Dynamic Teaching later this month. Based on the content and the expected attendance, Martin plans to charge $2,475. You decide **not** to create a **delayed charge**. You'll wait to create the **invoice** when you have all the details.

✓ You look at your unpaid bills and realize you forgot to pay Frank's Furniture last month. You call and apologize. You pay all bills due on or before 3/15, net of available credits. The total of the three checks is $1,539.50. The first check number is 1126.

3/4/22

✓ You receive two checks in the mail and record them in QBO:

- $400 from Annie Wang for INV-1009. Check #2895, dated 3/4.
- $900 from Debbie Han for INV-1016. Check #4555, dated 3/4.

✓ You deposit both checks in the bank. The total deposit is $1,300.

✓ You receive the remaining products ordered from Books Galore on PO-100 and PO-103. In addition to the books, Books Galore charged $230.41 for some supplies Martin had called them about. ($202.16 for tutoring supplies; $28.25 for office supplies) You charge the cost of the tutoring supplies to the Supplies on Hand account. You expense the office supplies. The total amount on the invoice (#2244) is $835.41. (The terms are Net 30.) **TIP:** Because the POs were created before **class** was added to **inventory** items, you will have to complete the **class** fields.

✓ Martin gives you the detail for the tutoring sessions he had this week. He also sold a few products to these customers.

  • You create invoices (starting with INV-1021and dated 3/4) for:
    ○ Navi Patel—One week of **Crisis** starting 3/1 plus one Geometry in Sports Book (**Sports**) and one Geometry Kit (**Kit**). The total invoice after sales tax is $273.94 and terms are Net 15.
    ○ Debbie Han—Two weeks of **Persistence** starting 3/1 and one Getting Ready for Calculus (**Ready**) book. Net 15. The total invoice after sales tax is $230.45.

3/7/22

✓ Martin gets a call from Harold at Mad Math, a tutoring center for elementary school age children. He heard about the math games from the Center for High Academic Achievement (Elk Grove) and places an order for two **consoles** and one of each game (**Equations**, **Fractions**, and **Ratios**). Martin ships out the order and you prepare INV-1023 for $ 924.38 (tax included).

  • Mad Math's address is 1388 Taller Drive, Sacramento, CA 95822. Terms are Net 30. The games will be used at the center so the sale is taxable.

✓ Martin calls the director at the Elk Grove location to thank her for the referral. He asks you to give Elk Grove a $100 credit on its next workshop. You prepare a **delayed credit** (DC-1001), charging the $100 to **Educator Workshop**. **TIP: Delayed credits** were introduced in Chapter 6.

✓ Martin had gotten so many requests from students and parents for more tutoring time, he decided to offer two Mathmagic clinics this month. The first one was last Saturday. 45 students showed up. They all paid cash ($900). You record the revenue on SR-111.

3/11/22

✓ Martin delivers another order to the Downtown location of the Center for High Academic Achievement. You prepare INV-1024 for $710.
  • 10 Geometry in Sports (**Sports**)
  • 10 Solving Puzzles: Fun with Algebra (**Puzzles**)
  • 5 Getting Ready for Calculus (**Ready**)
  • 5 Geometry Kits (**Kit**)

✓ There is a MathMagic clinic coming up soon and Martin wants you to make sure there are enough products on hand. You review the inventory and create two **purchase orders**.
  • PO-105 ($225) is for 9 **Puzzles** and 5 **Sports** from Books Galore.
  • PO-106 ($130) is for 5 **Dry-Erase** and 10 **Notebooks** from Math Shack.

✓ Parent's Survival Weekly calls and asks if Martin wants to run another ad for his workshops. They are getting ready to print their next edition. You check with Martin and he decides to run a slightly larger ad for the Mathmagic clinic coming up later this month. You pay the $115 advertising fee with the VISA credit card. Since this is related to tutoring, you assign this to the Tutoring **class**.

✓ Martin gets a call from Books Galore. The company president has started a new program called "Thanks for being a great customer." Every month one customer receives a $50 credit against any outstanding invoices. This month Math Revealed! was the lucky recipient. Martin has decided to use it to offset the advertising fee from Parent's Survival Weekly so you record the credit (BG-101) and charge it to Advertising expense. You assign it to the **Tutoring class**.

3/14/22

✓ You receive two utility bills in the mail. Both are dated 3/14.

* Sacramento Utilities for March services, #01-88112, $206.85. The terms are Net 30.
* Horizon Phone for March service, #121-1000, $65.45. The terms are Net 30.

✓ You receive a check from the Center for High Academic Achievement for INV-1024. The check (#9759819) was for $710.00.

3/15/22

✓ Martin gives you the information on his tutoring sessions for last week. You record them using 3/15 as the sales date. Everyone wanted to pay with their Mastercard. Fortunately, Math Revealed is set up to accept both VISA and Mastercard. **TIP:** You'll need to set up a new **payment method**. VISA and Mastercard receipts would need to be deposited separately.

* Alonso Luna—8 **Refresher** sessions $480 (SR-112)
* Marley Roberts—2 **Persistence** $200 (SR-113)

✓ You prepare deposits for the credit card receipts and for the cash and check received last week. The total on the credit card deposit (after the 2% merchant fee) is $666.40. Since the credit cards were used to pay tutoring fees, you assign the merchant fee to the Tutoring **class**. The cash and check deposit totals $1,610.

✓ The **Educator Workshop** at Dynamic Teaching last weekend went well. More people attended than were expected so Martin was glad he increased the fee. You create an invoice (INV-1025) for $2,475.

✓ You pay all bills due on or before the 31st of March. You take all available credits. The first check # is 1129. **TIP:** The four bills paid total $1,435.19.

3/18/22

✓ You receive the following checks in the mail.

* $585 from Paul Richard for INV-1015. Check # 45777, dated 3/18. **TIP:** Go back and read the hint on page 3-35 if you're having trouble applying the credit.
* $723.94 from Navi Patel for INV-1019 and INV-1021. Check #4555, dated 3/18.

✓ All the items ordered from Books Galore on PO-105 arrive. The shipment includes a bill (#2298) for $225.00. The payment terms are Net 30.

✓ The Elk Grove Location of the Center for High Academic Achievement asked Martin to come out Monday night and do a one day **Educator Workshop** for a fee of $1,500. He asks you to prepare the invoice so he can take it with him. They also asked him to bring 5 each of the **Ready** and **Statistics** books. You prepare INV-1026 dated 3/18. The invoice totals $1,690 after the **delayed credit** is applied.

✓ The order from Math Shack (PO-106) arrives just in time for the Saturday clinic. A bill (#M61142) for $130 is included. The terms are Net 15.

* The **Kits** backordered from PO-104 are not included. You call Math Shack. They promise to look into the order.

3/21/22

✓ Mathmagic was almost standing room only on Saturday. 55 students attended. You record the cash sale (SR-114 for $1,494.76). **TIP:** Use Drop-in as the customer.

* Total tutoring income collected was $1,100.
* Product sales (all taxable):
  ○ 5 **Notebooks**
  ○ 4 **Dry Erase**
  ○ 6 **Ready**
  ○ 3 **Sports**

✓ You deposit the checks received on the 18th with the cash from Saturday's Mathmagic clinic. The total is $2,803.70.

3/23/22

✓ Martin let you know that Samantha Levin had helped out for 8 hours at the two Mathmagic clinics this month. You write her a check (# 1133) for $200 ($25 per hour) and charge it to contract labor. You select the **class** based on the type of work Samantha helped with.

✓ You call Cartables and place an order for 3 of every Math Games product. PO-107 totals $990.

3/25/22

✓ Gus Ranting is back again! He's sure that his son is wasting his time at the Mathmagic Clinic. Martin lets him know that his son is a great kid who obviously believes the tutoring is helping him. He shows Gus his son's work and encourages him to follow up with the math teachers at the school. He gives Gus a partial refund of $10 (Check #1134) but says this will be the last time for any refunds (RR-102).

✓ Mad Math calls and lets Martin know that the math games are really helping the students. They order another **console** and one of each game (**Fractions**, **Equations**, and **Ratios**). Martin delivers the products and you prepare INV-1027 for $543.75.

✓ Martin hands you two gas receipts for March. One, dated 3/14 for $29 and one dated 3/25 for $26. He used the Visa card each time to pay for the gas he purchased at Cardinal Gas & Snacks. You enter the charges in QBO using the credit card receipt dates. You use the Administrative **class**.

3/30/22

✓ Math Shack calls and says there's a shipping delay with the **Kits** ordered on PO #104. The **Kits** should arrive in May. You check and see that only six geometry kits were sold in March and you still have some in stock so you're not concerned. You leave the purchase order open.

✓ You receive the following checks in the mail.
  • Dynamic Teaching $2,250 for INV-1018. (Check # 5235)
  • Eliot Williams $100 (Check #8166)

✓ Martin gives you the information on his tutoring sessions for the last half of March. You record them using 3/30 as the sales date. This time everyone paid with cash! All sessions were completed by 3/30. Martin has no sessions scheduled for tomorrow.
  • Annie Wang—2 **Crisis** $450 (SR-115)
  • Kim Kowalski—2 **Crisis** $450 (SR-116)

✓ You deposit the checks and cash in the bank. The deposit total is $3,250.

✓ You write Martin a dividend check for $2,500. (Check #1135) **TIP:** Use the Administrative **class**.

✓ You write Martin's father (Richard Smith) a check (#1136) for March's interest plus a principal payment of $200. **TIP:** Calculate the interest on the unpaid balance of the note.

✓ You know Les & Schmidt did some marketing work for Martin in March but you haven't received an invoice from them. You ask Martin and he says the agreed-upon fee was $350. You go ahead and create a journal entry (Mar22.1) to record the expense in the proper period. The marketing plan is related to growing the Workshop business. You create a **reversing entry** so that you can enter the bill when it's received without duplicating the expense. **TIP:** You need to click **Save** on entry Mar21.1 before you can create the reversing entry. Use Accrued Expenses as the liability account and 642 Marketing expense as the expense account.

✓ Parent's Survival Weekly calls and offers Martin a reduced price of $75 per ad if he agrees to run a monthly ad for a six month period. The ad would appear in the first issue each month. The $75 will be automatically charged to the VISA card on the 1st of each month. Martin agrees but does not want to start this until May. Since this will automatically be charged to the VISA credit card you set up a new **scheduled Recurring Transaction**. You select **Expense** as the transaction type, use Parent's **Ad** as the **Template name**, and set the **interval** to be the

1st day of each month beginning on 5/1/22 and ending after 6 occurrences. You assign this to the tutoring class.

3/31/22

✓ You talk to Martin about your increasing workload. He is very appreciative of your work and agrees to pay you $500 (accounting fees) starting in March. You enter a bill (ACCT22, dated 3/31) for accounting fees with Net 15 terms. You decide to set this up as a scheduled recurring transaction (bill). **TIP:** Click Save before you move forward.

  • You click Make recurring on the black bar at the bottom of the form and complete the template. You enter Accounting as the template name. Future bills are scheduled for the last day of each month with 4/30/22 as the Start date. You don't identify an end date.

✓ You spend the rest of the day making the final adjustments for March. **TIP:** Remember, if an expense isn't directly related to sales of products, workshops, or tutoring, it should be charged to the administrative class.

✓ You don't have your bank statement yet but you go online and see that the balance is $9,540.49 at 3/31. All deposits for March have cleared. All checks written prior to 3/20/22 cleared the bank. There were no service charges during March. You reconcile the books to the $9,540.49 balance. **TIP:** Checks include check, refund, and bill payment transaction types.

✓ You also reconcile the Prime Visa credit card statement as of 3/31. The balance is $170. All recorded charges and payments are included on the statement. You enter the bill for payment later. You use MARCC as the bill no. **TIP:** Use Administrative as the class.

✓ You compare the inventory on hand to the inventory report in QBO. All amounts agree.

✓ You make the necessary adjustments, dated 3/31, after considering the following:

  • Tutoring supplies on hand at 3/31 equal $125.

  • No new equipment was purchased in March.

  • You decide to track all facilities and equipment expenses in the Administrative class.

  • The annual interest rate on both loans is 6%. No payments were made on the bank loan in March.

  • You look carefully at the profit and loss statement and make sure that all March expenses are properly recorded. (**TIP:** Include the YTD column on your profit and loss report. Compare the March expenses with the year-to-date expenses. Are there any of the common operating expenses missing? Do any of the expenses appear unusually high?)

  • You look carefully at the balance sheet paying particular attention to Other Current Assets and Other Current Liabilities. Many of the common month-end adjustments affect accounts in those categories. **TIP:** Look at the journal entries you made at the end of last month.

Check numbers 3/31

Checking account balance:. . . . .$ 6,618.49
Other current assets: . . . .$ 2,354.00
Total assets: $21,058.07
Total liabilities: . . . .$ 7,351.49
Gross profit (March). . . . .$ 8,692.00
Net income for March:. . . . .$ 6,104.69

Suggested reports for Chapter 9:

All reports should be in portrait orientation.

• Balance Sheet as of 3/31

• Profit and Loss (March)

    Include a year-to-date column in the report

- Profit and Loss by Class (March)

- A/R Aging Summary as of 3/31

- A/P Aging Summary as of 3/31

- Sales by Product/Service Summary (March)

- Inventory Valuation Summary (March 31)

- Recurring Template List

- Budget Overview Report 2022 (by Quarter)
  - To display quarters, click **Customize**, click **Rows/Columns**, select **Accounts vs Qtrs** on **Show Grid** dropdown menu.

- Budget vs Actual report (January 1 through March 31)
  - Click **Customize** and click **Rows/Columns**. In the **Show Grid** dropdown menu, select **Accounts vs Total**.

- Journal report (March)

Assignment 9B

Salish Software Solutions

Background information: Sally Hanson, a good friend of yours, double majored in Computer Science and Accounting in college. She worked for several years for a software company in Silicon Valley but the long hours started to take a toll on her personal life.

Last year she decided to open up her own company, Salish Software Solutions. Sally currently advises clients looking for new accounting software and assists them with software installation. She also provides training to client employees and occasionally troubleshoots software issues.

She has decided to start using QuickBooks Online to keep track of her business transactions. She likes the convenience of being able to access financial information over the Internet. You have agreed to act as her accountant while you're working on your accounting degree.

Sally has a number of clients that she is currently working with. She gives 15-day payment terms to her corporate clients but she asks for cash at time of service if she does work for individuals. She has developed the following fee schedule:

Name	Description	Rate
Select	Software selection	$500 flat fee
Set Up	Software installation	$ 75 per hour
Train	Software training	$ 50 per hour
Fix	File repair	$ 60 per hour

Sally rents office space from Alki Property Management for $600 per month.

The following furniture and equipment are owned by Salish:

Description	Date placed in service	Cost	Life	Salvage Value
Office furniture	6/1/21	$1,400	60 months	$200
Computer	7/1/21	$4,620	36 months	$300
Printer.	7/1/21	$ 900	24 months	$ 0

All equipment is depreciated using the straight-line method.

As of 12/31/21, she owed $3,500 to Dell Finance. The monthly payment on that loan is $150 including interest at 5%. Sally's last payment to Dell was 12/31/21.

Over the next month or so, Sally plans to expand her business by selling some of her favorite accounting and personal software products directly to her clients. She has already purchased the following items.

Item Name	Description	Vendor	Quantity on Hand	Cost per Unit	Sales Price
Easy1	Easy Does It	Abacus Shop	15	$100	$ 200
Retailer	Simply Retail	Simply Accounting	2	$400	$ 800
Contractor.	Simply Construction	Simply Accounting	2	$500	$1,000
Organizer	Organizer	Personal Software	20	$ 25	$ 50
Tracker	Investment Tracker	Personal Software	20	$ 20	$ 40

 HINT: If you didn't turn off Automation in Chapter 2, you might want to consider doing that now. It's easy to get confused when QBO automatically adds accounts to your transactions. Click the ⚙ on the icon bar and select **Account and Settings**. In the **Automation** section of the **Advanced** tab, turn **Pre-fill forms with previously entered content** to **Off**.

3/1/22

✓ Business is going well for Sally. She has a number of different revenue streams and new opportunities keep coming her way. You talk to her about the need to understand how each segment of her company is doing. She's open to your suggestions.

✓ You turn on **class** tracking in the **Advanced** tab of **Account and Settings**.

- You want to be able to assign a **class** to individual line items in transaction forms.
- You also turn on the "warning" feature. You don't want to have to go back and fix issues later.

✓ You decide to set up four **classes**.

- Products
  - To be used for tracking revenues and costs related to sales of products.
- Workshops
  - To be used for tracking revenues and costs related to Workshop presentations.
- Consulting
  - To be used for tracking revenues and costs related to all software consulting services.
    - e.g., Installation, Setup, Training
- Administrative
  - To be used for tracking general business costs.

✓ You realize that it will save you time in the long-run to go ahead and assign a **class** to each of the products and services that you sell. You open the **Products and Services** list and assign the **classes** as follows:

- You assign the Workshop **class** to both the Tips and Picks workshop services.
- You assign the Consulting **class** to the Fix, Select, Set Up and Train services.
- You assign the Products **class** to all the **Inventory** type products.
- You don't assign a **class** for items in the **Other Charges category**. You'll determine the **class** when you record transactions that include these items.

✓ You also decide you want to use the budgeting tool in QBO.

✓ You create a monthly profit and loss budget for 2022 from scratch (no subdividing). (You use "2022 Budget" for the name.) Sally gives you some projections that she put together when she was first starting out. You use her numbers as a starting place:

- Software Selection and Installation—$4,000 January through February; $5,000 March through December
- Troubleshooting Revenue—$250 every month
- Workshop Revenues—$2,000 January; $4,500 February through December

- Sales of Product Income—$2,500 February; $3,000 March to June; $4,000 July to December
- Cost of Goods Sold—$1,250 February; $1,750 March through June; $2,000 July through December
- Labor Costs
  ○ Contract Labor—$2,000 every month, starting in April
- Professional Development Costs
  ○ Technical reading materials—$100 every month
  ○ Software Seminar—$500 in February and June
- Facility Costs
  ○ Rent—$600 every month
  ○ Telephone—$100 every month
  ○ Utilities—$100 every month
- Marketing Costs
  ○ Advertising—$100 every month
  ○ Client relations—$100 every month
- Office Costs
  ○ Office supplies—$100 every month
  ○ Depreciation—$200 January; $250 February through December
- Taxes, Insurance, and Professional Services
  ○ Accounting and consulting—$300 January; $350 February and March; $500 April through December
  ○ Insurance—$60 every month
- Workshop Costs
  ○ Space rental $500 every other month starting in January
- Other Costs
  ○ Bank service charges—$15 every month
- Interest—$15 every month
- You let Sally know that the budget shows $84,820 in profit for the year. **TIP:** You might need to click **Save** to see the totals.

3/2/22

✓ You spent a lot of time working on the budget yesterday and got a bit behind on your work.

✓ You make the $150 monthly debt payment to Dell Finance. (Check #1125.) **TIP:** You're paying interest through 2/28 plus some principal.

✓ You write yourself a check (Check #1126) for the work you did in **February**.

✓ Sally places an order for 4 copies of **Retailer** from Simply Accounting. You record the $1,600 order on PO-104.

✓ Sally brings you a VISA credit card receipt for her $1,200 purchase of an **annual** subscription to Advances in Software Design, a well-respected magazine. The magazine is published monthly. She received the March issue already. This is a professional development type of cost (technical reading materials). You use the adminstrative class.

✓ Metro Market calls and talks to Sally about scheduling an **Effective Troubleshooting (Tips)** workshop next week for some of the company's IT staff. It's short notice but Sally agrees to do it next Wednesday (the 10th). Sally quotes them a fee of $2,500. You decide not to create a **delayed charge**. You'll create the invoice when you know all the details.

3/4/22

✓ You receive three checks in the mail and record them in QBO. All were dated 3/4.

- $510 from Fabulous Fifties for INV-1021. Check # 86910

- • $550 from Butter and Beans for INV-1020. Check # 9299
- • $270 from Reyelle Consulting for INV-1014. Check # 9759201

✓ You deposit the checks in the bank. The total deposit is $1,330.

✓ You receive 4 of the 5 **Easy1** products ordered from Abacus Shop on PO-103. In addition to the software, Abacus shipped one laptop Sally had ordered for use in the field. The total cost of the laptop was $1,200 (including tax). The total amount on the invoice (#8944-50) is $1,600. **TIP:** Because the PO was created before **class** was added to **inventory** items, you will have to complete the **class** field.

✓ You write a $400 check to Hacker Spaces to pay for the rental space for the Metro Market workshop next week. You record the payment (Check #1127). **TIP:** Assign this to a **class** that matches the type of service Sally is providing to Metro Market.

3/8/22

✓ Sally decides to do some advertising of her new management products. She places an ad in the Sacramento Journal. The ad will run in the March online issue, out 3/11. She uses the credit card to pay the $250 fee. Since the ad promotes the company's products, you assign this expense to the **Products class**.

✓ The software ordered from Simply Accounting on PO-104 arrives, along with a bill for $1,600 (65501-9) dated 3/8. Simply Accounting's payment terms are 2% 10, Net 30.

3/9/22

✓ You receive two bills in the mail. Both are dated 3/9.
- • Sacramento Light and Power's March bill (for heat and light) #01-94442—$90.18. The terms are Net 30.
- • Western Phone March bill #9144-64 for $122.45. The terms are Net 30.

✓ You also receive 2 checks in the mail, both dated 3/9.
- • Check #77066 from Alki Deli for $250, in payment of INV-1019.
- • Check #989899 from Metro Market for $500, in payment of INV-1018.

✓ You deposit the checks in the bank. ($750 total).

3/11/22

✓ Although it looks like there will be enough cash to pay bills, Sally decides to draw the full $5,000 on the line. She wants to have a bit of a cushion in case a really good deal comes along. You record the deposit into your account by Sacramento City Bank. **TIP:** You already have an account set up for the credit line.

✓ You pay all bills due on or before 3/20. There are four bills (three checks). The total amount paid is $4,807.86 and the first check number is #1128.

✓ The Effective Troubleshooting (**Tips**) workshop for Metro Market was a success. Sally says she even got some leads on other companies that might be interested in her services. You record the invoice (INV-1023), dated 3/11, to Metro with terms of Net 15. The total amount billed is $2,500. **TIP:** The **CLASS** field should automatically fill with Workshops. If it doesn't, go back to the **Product/Service** list and make sure you've assigned a **class** to each item.

3/15/22

✓ Sally can't believe the response she's getting from her ad in the *Sacramento Journal*. She has already gotten calls from 5 different companies. Two of them stopped by to pick up the software. Both paid with a credit card (VISA). You make sure that the office address (3835 Freeport Blvd) shows as the **Location of sale** so that the appropriate amount of tax is charged.
- • Delightful Dental purchased Managing Your Medical Practice (**Medical**) for $543.75 (SR-108).

- Westside Engineers purchased Managing Your Engineering Firm (**Engineering**) for $543.75 (SR-109).

✓ Sally places an order with Abacus Shop. You record the order on PO-105. The total is $1,750.
  - 2 **Medical**
  - 2 **Engineering**
  - 1 **Legal**

3/17/22

✓ You receive a check in the mail from Reyelle Consulting in full payment of INV-1017. The check (9759301) is for $1,000.

✓ You deposit the credit card receipts received Tuesday and the check received today. The credit card deposit totals $1,065.75 (after the 2% fee). The check deposit totals $1,000. You assign the credit card fee to the administrative **class**.

✓ You realize that the early payment discount on Simply Accounting's bill #65501-9 expires tomorrow. You create a **vendor credit** for the discount of $32 (2% of $1,600). You use DISC-SA as the **ref no.** and select **Products** as the **class**. You pay the bill with check #1131.

3/18/22

✓ Reyelle Consulting calls and asks Sally to deliver more software. Sally delivers the software CDs to both Reyelle locations. You prepare separate **invoices** with terms of Net 30 for:
  - Sacramento shipment
    - 6 each of the following books:
      - **Organizer**
      - **Tracker**
    - INV-1024 totals $540.
  - Davis shipment
    - 4 each of the following books:
      - **Organizer**
      - **Tracker**
    - INV-1025 totals $360.

✓ Sally lets you know that she needs to order 20 **Organizers** and 15 **Trackers** from Personal Software. You prepare PO-106. The purchase order total is $800.

3/21/22

✓ Sally continues to receive calls about the management products so she decides to put on a workshop in the office next week. She decides to charge $75 per attendee. She sends out an email to all the people who have contacted her for information.

✓ Cezar Software pays INV-1022 with a $1,875 check (#740062) dated 3/21.

✓ You deposit the check from Cezar into the bank. The deposit totals $1,875.

3/22/22

✓ Sally gives you the information on her client work through March 15th. You invoice the customers using 3/22 as the sales date.
  - Fabulous Fifties—20 **Train** hours $1,000 (INV-1026). The terms are Net 15.
  - mSquared Enterprises—16 **Set Up** hours $1,200 (INV-1027). The terms are Net 30.

✓ All products ordered from Abacus Shop (PO-105) are received today. You record the bill (#8944-55) for $1,750. Terms are Net 15.

✓ You notice that the 5th copy of **Easy1** you ordered from Abacus on PO-103 still hasn't arrived. Sally gives them a call. They explain that they're having trouble getting that product from their supplier. She decides to go ahead and cancel the PO for now. You change the PO status to **closed** in QBO. **TIP:** Consider using the search feature to find the purchase order. You can ignore the warning about the missing **class**.

3/23/22

✓ Reyelle Consulting (Davis) returned another **Organizer**. Sally asks you to create a credit memo. You create CM-1025 for $50 and mail it to Reyelle.

✓ Sally calls Personal Software to complain about the quality of the **Organizers**. They apologize and give you a credit for $25 when they stop by to pick up the **Organizer**. (#4494CM)

✓ You receive a check for $2,500 from Metro Market in the mail. The check (#989950) is payment in full for INV-1023.

3/28/22

✓ Twenty-five people showed up for the demonstration on Saturday. A few of the attendees also purchased software. Everyone wanted to pay with their Mastercard. Fortunately, Salish is set up to accept both VISA and Mastercard. **TIP:** You'll need to set up a new payment method. VISA and Mastercard receipts would need to be deposited separately.

  • You record the income using a **sales receipt** (SR-110 dated 3/26), and Cash Customer as the **customer**. You use **Picks** as the **service** item.

  • The total including the sale of one each of **Medical**, **Engineering**, and **Legal** was $3,506.25. **TIP:** Tax would only be charged on the product sales.

✓ Sally lets you know that Oscar Torres helped with the workshop. He worked for 2 hours. You write Oscar a check (Check #1132) for $60 and charge it to the Workshop helper account.

✓ You deposit the Metro Market check from 3/23 and the credit card receipts from Saturday into the bank. **TIP:** You create two **deposits**. One for the checks and one for the credit card payments.

  • The check deposit totals $2,500.

  • The credit card deposit , less the 2% fee, totals $3,436.12.

✓ You pay the Dovalina & Diamond and Abacus Shop bills. The total is $2,325. The first check is #1133.

✓ You receive a partial shipment of the software you ordered from Personal Software on PO-106. Three of the **organizers** were not included. The bill, dated 3/28 (#792114), totals $725. The terms are Net 30. You contact Personal Software. The customer service representative apologizes and lets you know the remaining items will be sent out next week.

3/30/22

✓ Sally gives you the information on her client work since March 15th. You record the invoices using 3/30 as the invoice date.

  • Fabulous Fifties—4 **Train** hours and 10 **Fix** hours $800. INV-1028

  • Lou's Barber Shop—8 **Fix** hours $480. INV-1029

  • mSquared Enterprises—6 **Set Up** hours and 10 **Train** hours $950. INV-1030

  • Champion Law—20 **Set Up** hours $1,500. INV-1031

✓ The Sacramento Journal calls and offers Sally a reduced price of $200 per ad if she agrees to run a monthly ad for a six month period. Sally agrees but does not want to start this until May. The $200 will be automatically charged to the VISA card on the 1st of each month, so you set up a new **scheduled Recurring Transaction**. You select **Expense** as the transaction type and you set the interval to be the 1st day of each month beginning on 5/1/22 and ending after 6 occurrences. You name the template Sacramento Ad and assign this to the Products **class**.

✓ You write a check (#1135) for $2,500 to Sally for March dividends.

✓ Before you leave for the day, you talk to Sally about the credit line. You have a healthy cash balance now and you suggest that Sally pay down the line a bit. She can always borrow again if needed. Sally agrees. You pay Sacramento City Bank $2,500 **plus** interest with check #1136. **TIP:** The simple annual interest rate charged by the bank is 6%. Sally borrowed $5,000 on 3/11. Use ½ month for the interest payment.

✓ You also talk to Sally about setting a fixed fee of $375 per month for your services starting in March. She is very happy with your work and agrees to the amount. You enter a **bill**

(ACCT22) for accounting fees dated 3/30 with Net 15 terms. You decide to set this up as a **scheduled recurring transaction (bill)**. **TIP:** Click **Save** before you move forward.

- You click **Make recurring** on the black bar at the bottom of the form and complete the template. You enter Accounting as the **template name**. Future bills are scheduled for the last day of each month with 4/30/22 as the **Start date**. You don't identify an end date.

3/31/22

✓ You spend the day making the final adjustments for March.

✓ You don't have your bank statement yet but you go online and see that the balance is $19,987.06 at 3/31. All deposits made in March cleared the bank. All checks written prior to 3/24 cleared the bank. There were no service charges. You reconcile to the $19,987.06 balance. **TIP:** Checks include **check** and **bill payment transaction types**.

✓ You also reconcile the credit card statement dated 3/31. The balance is $1,450.00. All recorded charges and payments are included on the statement. You enter the bill for payment later. You use MARCC as the **bill no**.

✓ You remember that Dovalina & Diamond came in for a follow-up meeting with Sally. You haven't received their bill yet. Sally says that the bill will be for $150. You go ahead and create a journal entry (Mar22.1) to record the consulting fees expense in the proper period. You create a **reversing entry** so that you can enter the bill when it's received without duplicating the expense. **TIP:** You need to click **Save** on entry Mar22.1 before you can create the reversing entry. Use the Accrued Expenses account to record the liability.

✓ You compare the inventory on hand to the inventory report in QBO. All amounts agree.

✓ You make the necessary adjustments, dated 3/31, after considering the following:

- Supplies on hand at 3/31 equal $150.
- The last payment to Dell Finance was 3/1. **TIP:** The annual, simple interest rate on the loan is 5%.
- You purchased a laptop on 3/4 for $1,200. It was placed in service right away. You go ahead and take a full month's depreciation on the computer. Sally thinks it will last 2 years, with no salvage value. **TIP:** There's no change on depreciation expense for the assets purchased prior to March 1.
- You look carefully at the profit and loss statement and make sure that all March expenses are properly recorded. (**TIP:** Include the **Prior Period** column on your profit and loss report. Compare the March expenses with the February expenses. Are there any of the common operating expenses missing? Do any of the expenses appear unusually high?)
- You look carefully at the balance sheet paying particular attention to Other Current Assets and Other Current Liabilities. Many of the common month-end adjustments affect accounts in those categories. **TIP:** Look at the journal entries you made on February 28th. There will likely be similar entries for March.

Check numbers 3/31

Checking account balance:. $12,589.56
Other current assets: $10,804.00
Total assets: $39,926.06
Total liabilities:. . . . .$ 8,848.43
Gross profit (March): $11,507.00
Net income for March:. . . . .$ 8,814.04

Suggested reports for Chapter 9:

All reports should be in portrait orientation.

- Balance Sheet as of March 31
- Profit and Loss (March)
  - Include a year-to-date column in the report
- Profit and Loss by Class (March)

- Sales by Product/Service Summary (March)
- Inventory Valuation Summary (March 31)
- Recurring Template List
- Budget Overview Report 2022 (by Quarter)
  - To display quarters, click Customize, click Rows/Columns, select Accounts vs Qtrs on Show Grid dropdown menu.
- Accounts Receivable Aging Summary (March 31)
- Accounts Payable Aging Summary (March 31)
- Budget vs Actual report (January 1 through March 31)
  - Click Customize and click Rows/Columns. In the Show Grid dropdown menu, select Accounts vs Total.
- Journal Report (March)

APPENDIX 9A CREATING AND MANAGING TAGS

In early 2020, Intuit rolled out a new tracking feature called Tags.

Most of you are familiar with the idea of tagging from various web services (e.g., social networks and blogs). Tagging is simply a convenient way to organize and find information.

Tagging in QBO works in much the same way as it does in other web services. In QBO:

- A tag is a keyword or phrase.
- One or more tags can be added to most sales and purchase transactions.
  - Tags currently cannot be added to deposits, journal entries, or transfers.
- Tags can be grouped.
- You can add an unlimited number of tags to a transaction, but each tag must come from a different group.

Creating Tag Groups

To create a tag group, click ⚙ on the icon bar.

YOUR COMPANY	LISTS	TOOLS	PROFILE
Account and settings	All lists	Order checks ☐	Feedback
Manage users	Products and services	Import data	Refer a friend
Custom form styles	Recurring transactions	Import desktop data	Privacy
Chart of accounts	Attachments	Export data	Switch company
QuickBooks labs	Tags	Reconcile	
		Budgeting	
		Audit log	
		SmartLook	
		Case center	

Figure 9A.1

Access to tag management

Click Tags.

Figure 9A.2

Link to new tag group setup

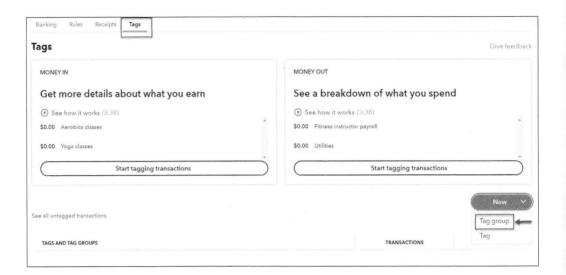

> ✳ **HINT: Tags** can also be accessed by clicking **Banking** on the navigation bar and selecting the **Tabs** tab.

Select **Tag group** in the **New** dropdown menu.

Figure 9A.3

Tag group setup screen

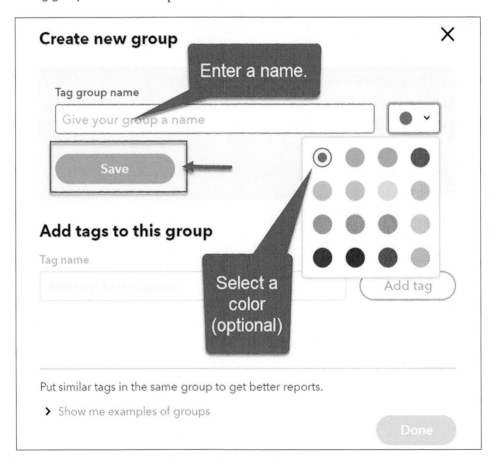

Enter the name for your **tag group**. You can also use a different color for each group as a highlighter.

Click **Save**. The screen should look something like this:

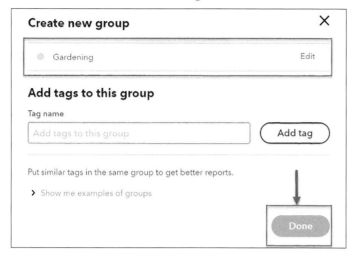

Figure 9A.4

Example of new tag group

Click **Done**.

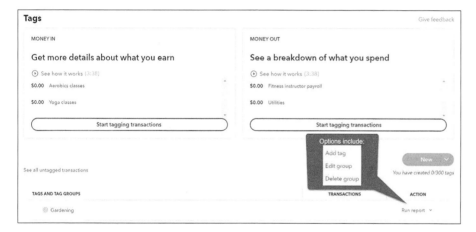

Figure 9A.5

Options for tag groups

In the Tags Center, **tag groups** can be edited (name and color) or deleted.

Creating Tags

Tags can be set up in the Tags Center or directly on a specific transaction form.

To set up a **tag** in the Tags Center, click ⚙ on the icon bar and select **Tags** or click **Banking** on the navigation bar and select the **Tags** tab.

Figure 9A.6

Tags Center

Select **Tag** in the **New** dropdown menu.

Figure 9A.7

Tag setup screen

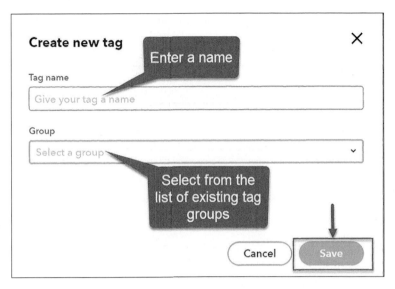

Enter a name and select a **Tag group** if appropriate.
     Click **Save**.

Adding Tags to Transactions

Tags can be added to most transactions. The process is independent of the transaction form used.

     As an example, when the **tag** feature is activated, the top half of a **bill** form would look something like this:

Figure 9A.8

Tag field on form

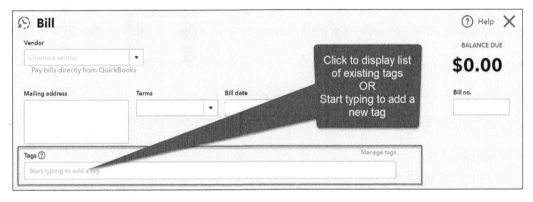

Click inside the **Tags** field.

Figure 9A.9

Example of tags available to add to form

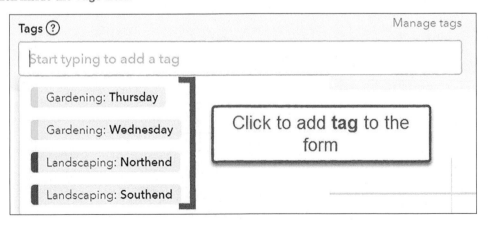

A list of existing **tags** will be displayed. Clicking one or more of the **tags** adds them to the form.

You can also create a new **tag** to add.

Figure 9A.10

Options for creating a new tag within a form

To create a new **tag**, you can type a new name in the field and click **+ Add**, or you can click **Manage tags** and select **Create new tag**. New **tags** can be linked to an existing **group** under either option. You cannot create a new **tag group** within a transaction form.

Reporting on Tagged Transactions

A summary of activity is available in the Tags Center.

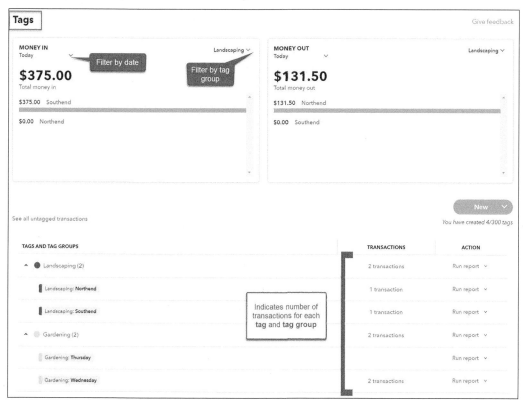

Figure 9A.11

Tags Center

The page can be filtered by date or by **tag group**. Additional reports will be available by clicking **Run report** in the **ACTION** column.

How Do Tags Differ From Classes and Locations?

In general, **tags** are a bit more flexible.

	TAGS	CLASSES	LOCATIONS
Number per transaction	Unlimited	$\leq$ the number of line items	1 (for most)
Number per specific line item	None	1	None (for most)

Project Tracking and Billing for Time and Expenses

Objectives

After completing Chapter 10, you should be able to:

1. Set up project tracking.

2. Set up independent contractors.

3. Track time by customer and by service using timesheets.

4. Create invoices from tracked time.

5. Add billable expenses to invoices.

6. Work with estimates. (Appendix 10A)

In this chapter, we're going to cover billing for time and expenses.

Most of the time, companies don't need to track employee time by customer or by project. In a retail store, for example, management generally doesn't track how much profit the store makes on a specific customer during the month. Instead, management might track how much gross profit the store makes on sales of a specific product or how much profit it makes in a specific store. Management may need to track which store an employee works in but it doesn't generally need to track how much time a specific employee spent helping a specific customer. Restaurants, banks, manufacturing companies, and gas stations are examples of other companies that don't normally need to track time by customer. This chapter will not apply to those types of companies. (We covered tracking profit by department or location in Chapter 9.)

However, there are many companies that **do** need to track time by customer and/or project.

For example, let's look at two construction companies. One bills its customers under "time and materials" contracts. The other bills its customers under "fixed fee" contracts. The time and materials contractor is billing for labor and materials plus some kind of markup. Payroll records **must** include the hours for each customer, by project **and** by type of work if billing rates differ, because those hours will be used to invoice customers. If those hours are tracked in QBO (which they can be), the invoicing process is more efficient.

The fixed fee contractor generally bills a percentage of the agreed-upon price (the fixed fee) as the work progresses. The number of hours worked aren't needed to prepare the invoice. However, in order to evaluate project profitability, fixed fee contractors need to be able to compare the revenue earned on a specific project to the specific costs of that project. That information helps them evaluate the company's overall performance and the specific performance of project managers and improves their ability to bid on future projects.

Tracking revenues and costs by job is commonly known as project costing (or job costing).

BEFORE WE BEGIN

Understanding a few basic concepts will help when working with projects in QBO:

- Multiple projects can be tracked for a single customer.
  - Time and expenses can be charged to **customers** as well so be careful to identify the specific **project** when recording transactions.

- Multiple **projects** for a **customer** cannot be billed on the same invoice. A separate invoice is created for each project.

- Hours worked and any external costs incurred on a project must be defined as billable if you intend to later charge the customer for those hours or costs. A **billable** field is included on all appropriate forms (**timesheets, bills, checks,** etc.).
  - External costs that are not defined as **billable** will be included in project reports but will not be accessible when preparing invoices or sales receipts.

WORKING WITH PROJECTS

Setting Up Projects

Project tracking is a preference in QBO. The default setting in most new company files is **On**. If **Projects** appears on the navigation bar, the feature has been activated.

If **Project** tracking has not been activated, click the ⚙ on the icon bar and select **Account and Settings.**

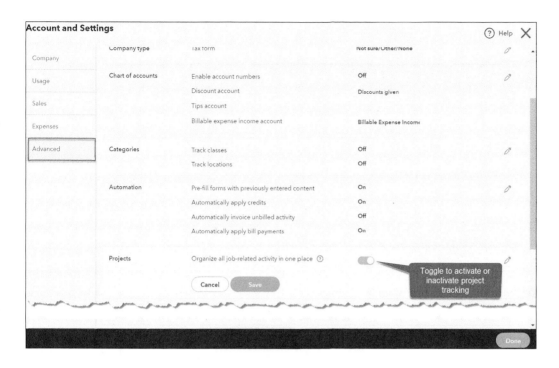

Figure 10.1

Project activation tool

On the **Advanced** tab, click the **pencil** icon in **Projects**.

The toggle switch next to **Organize all job-related activity in one place** is used to activate or inactivate the feature.

Click **Save** to activate **projects** and **Done** to exit the **Account and Settings** window.

Once **project** tracking is activated, a link will appear in the navigation bar.

Figure 10.2

Navigation bar with Projects activated

To set up a project, click **Projects** on the navigation bar.

The first time you access **projects**, the screen will look something like this:

Figure 10.3

Initial project screen

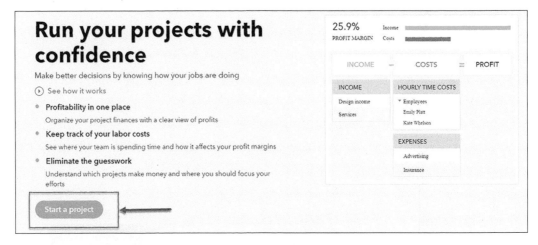

Click **Start a project** to open a sidebar.

Figure 10.4

Project setup screen

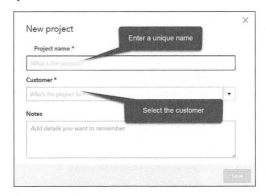

On the sidebar, enter a **project name** and select the **customer**. You can also enter notes here. Some companies might want to add information about the scope of the project or the names of customer personnel in charge of the project.

Click **Save**.

✳ **HINT:** It may take some time, usually less than five minutes, for a new **project** to be accessible in transaction forms. Try refreshing your browser. You may need to log out and log back into your homework company if it's been more than five minutes.

PRACTICE

EXERCISE

10.1

Add jobs for Craig's Design and Landscaping.

(Craig's Design has just gotten a request from Jeff's Jalopies for some landscaping work. Jeff has other projects in mind for the future so Craig's Design wants to set up a project for tracking hours spent on the landscaping job.)

1. Turn on project tracking. (If project tracking is already activated, skip to Step 2.)

    a. Click the on the icon bar.

    b. Click **Account and Settings**.

    c. Click **Advanced**.

    d. Click **Projects**.

    e. Check the box next to **Organize all job-related activity in one place**.

(continued)

(continued from previous page)

  f. Click **Save** and **Done**.

 2. Set up job.

  a. Click **Projects** on the navigation bar.

  b. Click **Start a project**.

  c. Enter **Jalopies' Landscaping** as the **project name**.

  d. Select **Jeff's Jalopies** as the **Customer**.

  e. Click **Save**.

  f. Click **Dashboard** to exit the Project Center.

Managing Projects

Click **Projects** on the navigation bar to access the Project Center. The Project Center looks like this if the list is filtered to show **All statuses**.

Figure 10.5

Project Center

Summary information including **PROFIT MARGIN** to date and **STATUS** is displayed on the main page for all **projects**.

Using the **OPTIONS** dropdown menu in the **ACTIONS** column, **projects** can be marked as completed or canceled. Notes can be added to the **project** and the **project** name can be changed by selecting **Edit this project**.

Click a specific **project** to see additional details.

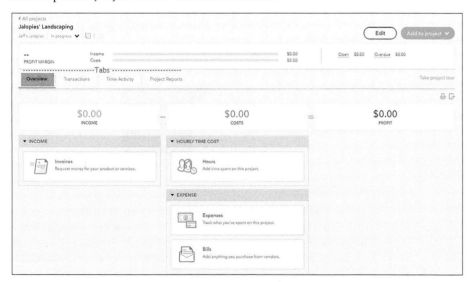

Figure 10.6

Project screen

HINT: You can also access a specific project record by opening the **Customers drawer** on the **Sales** link in the navigation bar and clicking a customer name.

| Transaction List | Projects | Customer Details |

Clicking **Projects** takes you to the screen displayed in Figure 10.6.

There are four tabs on a **project** screen.

- **Overview**
  - Summary of profit to date is displayed.
  - Includes links to transaction forms (**invoices**, **bills**, **expenses**, or **timesheets**).

- **Transactions**
  - All transactions related to project are displayed.
  - Includes links to transaction forms (**invoices**, **estimates**, **bills**, or **expenses**).

- **Time activity**
  - Hours by date are displayed.
  - Includes link to **timesheet**.

- **Project reports**
  - Includes links to **Project Profitability**, **Time cost by employee or vendor**, and **Unbilled time and expenses** reports.

BEHIND THE SCENES For companies that don't want to link actual labor costs to **projects** in QBO, **cost rates** can be set up. These rates are used for project reporting purposes **only**. There are no journal entries created.

Click **Hourly cost rate** in the top right corner of the Project Center (Figure 10.5). Click **Add** in the **COST RATE** column for Emily Platt.

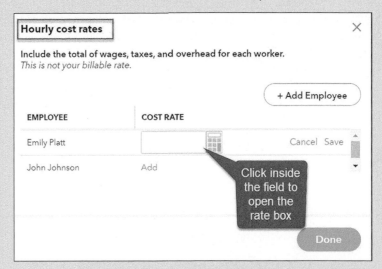

The rate entered might include wages, payroll taxes, and company overhead. These costs would be included in the summary profit amounts displayed in the Project Center. The costs would **not** be included in project profitability reports.

SETTING UP INDEPENDENT CONTRACTORS

In Chapter 4, we covered setting up 1099 vendors (landlords, attorneys, independent contractors, etc.) in QBO. In this chapter, we're going to look specifically at independent contractors.

Independent contractors are often used by companies to work on projects. This works especially well when a company is growing. As new customers come in, there might be too much work for existing employees to manage but not quite enough new work to justify hiring another permanent employee.

BEHIND THE SCENES The difference between an **independent contractor** and an employee is not clear-cut. In fact, there are 57 questions on the form the Internal Revenue Services uses (SS-8) in making the determination! In general, though, a person would be considered an independent contractor if they are in control of how the work is done, if they provide much of the equipment and supplies needed to complete the work, and if they provide similar services to others.

To set up an independent contractor, open the **Contractors** drawer of **Payroll** on the navigation bar.

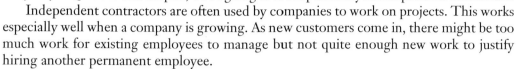

Figure 10.7

Access to contractor setup screen

Click **Add a contractor**.

 HINT: Any vendors previously set up as 1099 vendors will appear on this screen. If there were no 1099 vendors in a company file, an **Add your first contractor** screen would be displayed.

Figure 10.8

Contractor setup screen

The contractor's name is entered here. If the user elects to have the contractor enter the tax information online, an email address must be entered as well.

Figure 10.9

Link to vendor setup screens

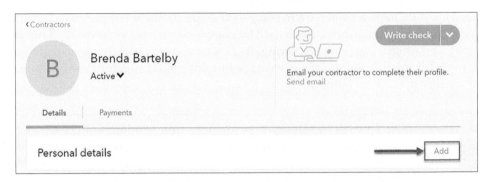

If the user does not invite the contractor to enter personal information online, the user must click **Add** to complete the setup.

Figure 10.10

Options for contractor type

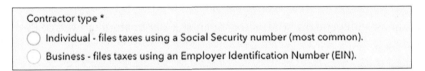

The contractor type (individual or business) is selected first.

If **Individual** is selected, the sidebar will expand to allow for entry of additional details.

Figure 10.11

Contractor setup screen

A tax ID number and address information are required. (The screen for **Business** has similar fields.)

Click **Save** to complete the setup.

A new **vendor** is automatically created (added to the Vendor List). Similarly, independent contractors initially set up through the **Vendors** tab of **Expenses** (and identified as 1099 vendors) are automatically added to the **Contractor** list. Additional information about the vendor (terms, billing rates, phone number, etc.) is entered in the vendor's record.

Add an independent contractor for Craig's Design and Landscaping.

(Craig has a large installation project coming up soon and expects to need some additional help. One of Craig's employees has a friend (Sue Stevens) who has landscaping experience and is looking for work. Craig brings her on as an independent contractor.)

1. Set up Sue Stevens as a **Contractor**.

   a. Click **Payroll** on the navigation bar.

   b. Click **Contractors**.

   c. Click **Add a contractor**.

   d. Enter "Sue Stevens" as the **Name**.

   e. Remove the checkmark in the box next to **Email this contractor to complete their profile**.

   f. Click **Add** to input Personal details.

   g. Check **Individual**.

   h. Enter the following information:

      i. Sue Stevens

      ii. 444-54-4474 as the social security number.

      iii. 2111 Riversedge Drive
         Sacramento, CA 95822

      iv. **Make a note** of the fields in the contractor setup sidebar that are not required.

   i. Click **Save**.

2. Edit Sue's vendor record.

   a. Click **Expenses** on the navigation bar.

   b. Click **Vendors**.

   c. Click **Sue Stevens**.

   d. Click **Edit**.

   e. Select **Due on receipt** as the **Terms**.

   f. Click **Save**.

   g. Click **Dashboard** to exit the vendor screen.

USING TIMESHEETS TO TRACK HOURS

The timesheet feature in QBO is available to track hours worked by both hourly and salaried employees in a company and by independent contractors. Timesheet data can be used to do one or more of the following:

- If the user subscribes to a payroll plan in QBO, timesheets can be used to:

  - Track labor costs by project for all employees.

  - Track paid time off for all employees.

- Create a paycheck based on hours worked for hourly employees.
- Users with or without payroll activation can use timesheets to:
    - Track billable hours for invoicing customers.
    - Track billable and non-billable hours for management purposes.

Payroll activity will be covered in Chapter 12. In this chapter, timesheets will only be used to track independent contractor hours for billing purposes.

Setting Up Time Tracking

Tracking hours for payroll processing purposes is automatically available to QBO users. To track hours by customer or project or to identify billable hours, certain features must be activated. Click the ⚙ on the icon bar and select **Account and Settings**.

Click the **Advanced** tab and open the **Time tracking** section.

Figure 10.12

Contractor setup screen

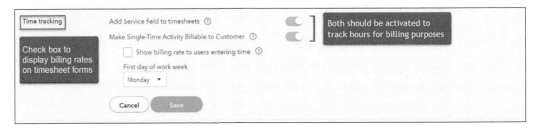

One or both options in the **Time tracking** section can be activated.

Adding **service fields** to timesheets allows users to track the type of work performed by employees or contractors. Turning on **Make Single-Time Activity Billable to Customer** allows the user to bill customers for work performed.

When billable time tracking is turned **On**, users have the option of displaying (or not displaying) the billing rate on the form. The first day of the work week must be selected.

Entering Timesheet Data

Intuit released a new time tracking feature in early 2021. The new feature allows employees to enter their own time directly into QBO. Those hours are then available for payroll processing and for billing customers. In this class, timesheets will be entered manually.

Figure 10.13

Time Center

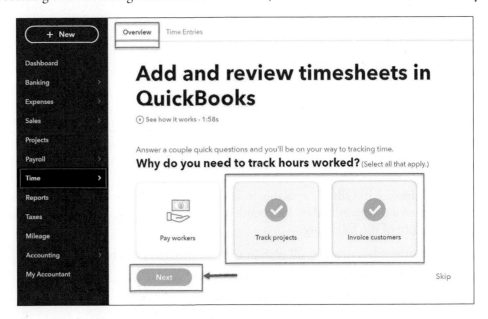

Click **Time** on the navigation bar and select **Track projects** and **Invoice customers**.
Click **Next**.

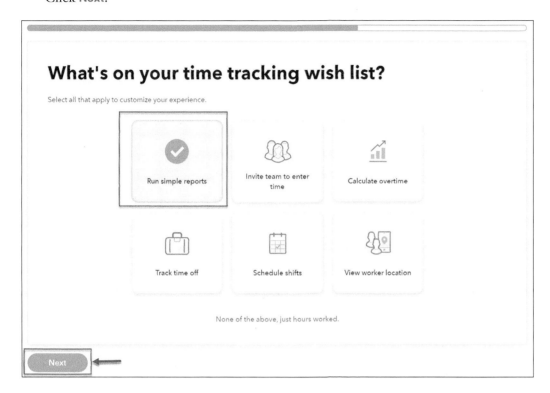

Figure 10.14

Time options

Select **Run simple reports** and click **Next**.

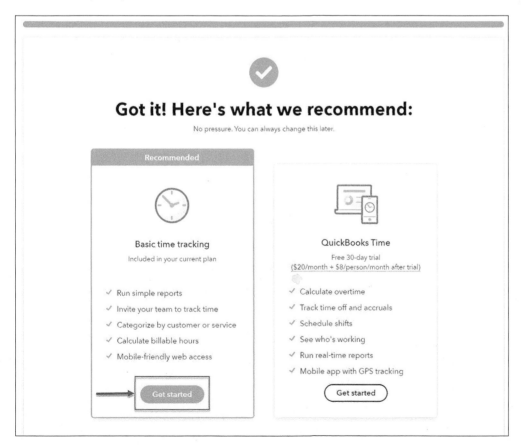

Figure 10.15

Time plan selection

Click **Get started** in the **Basic time tracking** option.

Time Center

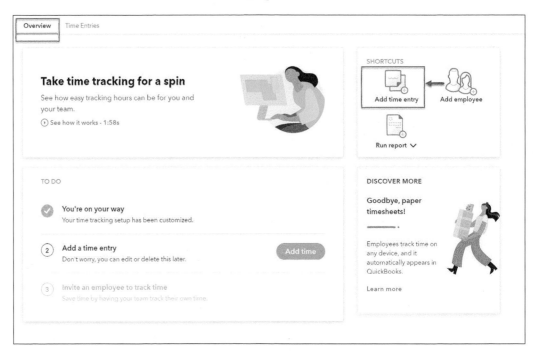

There are two tabs in the Time Center. Adding employees and entering time can be done using links on the **Overview** tab.

> **BEHIND THE SCENES** Companies who subscribe to a QBO payroll plan would need to set up employees through the Payroll Center accessed by clicking **Payroll** on the navigation bar. Compensation amounts, withholding information, and other required employee details cannot be entered through the Time Center. Payroll is covered in Chapter 12.

To enter time, click **Add time entry** in the **SHORTCUTS** section.

List of individuals

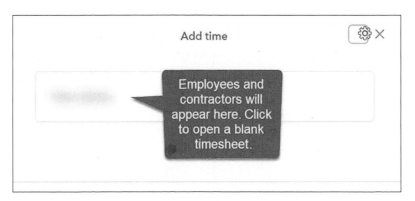

Select an employee (or contractor) name to open a new timesheet.

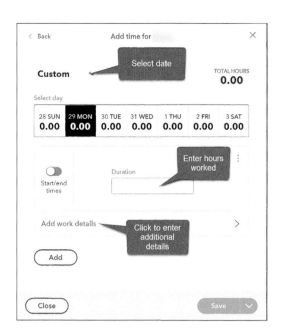

Figure 10.18

Timesheet

Select the week and highlight a day. Enter hours worked in the **Duration** field. Multiple entries can be created for a single day. This would be necessary for companies whose employees work on multiple projects in a single day.

If the hours should be tracked or billed, click **Add work details**.

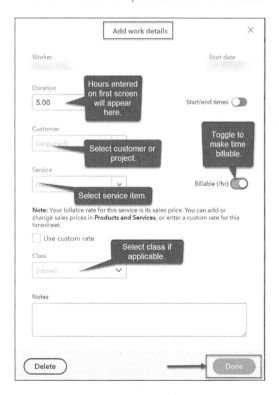

Figure 10.19

Additional details
related to hours worked

A customer (or project) must be selected if hours are being tracked. If the customer is being billed for the hours, **Billable (/hr)** should be toggled on.

QBO automatically uses the rate associated with the item selected in the **Service** field for billing purposes. That rate can be changed by checking the **Use custom rate** box and entering a new rate. A **Class** field will appear if **class** tracking has been activated.

Click **Done**.

Hours are entered in the same fashion for each day of the week.

Figure 10.20

Completed timesheet

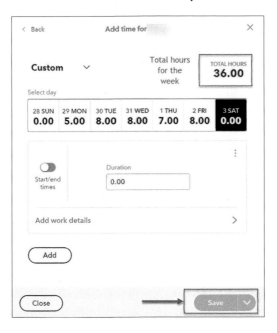

When all hours for the week have been entered, the total hours worked by the worker are displayed on the timesheet screen.

Click **Save**.

BEHIND THE SCENES If independent contractors perform billable services, the account to be debited when the contractor bill is entered (or a check is created) must be identified in the **service** item record.

(continued)

(continued from previous page)

> Check the box next to **I purchase this product/service from a vendor** to open the **Purchasing information** section of the item record. Enter the description to be displayed on purchase forms and the account to be debited when entering contractor charges. A default cost and preferred vendor can also be identified.

Editing Timesheets

The customer or project name, the number of hours worked, the billable status, and the **class** can be changed by opening the timesheet and clicking the day to be changed.

> **HINT:** Timesheets can be opened by clicking **Add time entry** in the Time Center, selecting the employee, and then selecting the appropriate week. To correct a single time entry, open the **Time Activities by Employee Detail** report in the **Employees** section of **Standard Reports** and select the appropriate day.

As of the date the book was written, **service** item selected in a timesheet entry cannot be changed. Entries can, however, be deleted. Click the day in the timesheet. Click the customer (or project) name to open the **Add work details** screen. Click **Delete**. You can then re-enter time for that date.

There is no practice exercise for this section. As of the date this book was written, timesheets could not be created in the test drive company.

TRACKING COSTS OTHER THAN LABOR BY PROJECT

There are usually costs other than labor that a company incurs when working on customer jobs. If a company is going to get a clear picture of profits earned on a project, these costs (usually referred to as direct costs or direct expenses) need to be linked to the **project** in QBO.

In addition, many companies that work with projects (jobs) bill some or even all direct expenses to their customers. For example, construction companies would likely bill their customers for appliances purchased for their home. Law firms would likely bill their clients for work performed by outside investigators.

If certain features are turned on in QBO, users can flag purchases as billable to specific customers when **bills**, **checks**, and **expenses** are entered. Those charges are then available when **invoices** are created.

Turning on Features for Tracking and Billing Direct Expenses

Features needed to track and bill expenses are activated by clicking the ⚙ on the icon bar and selecting the **Expenses** tab in **Account and Settings**.

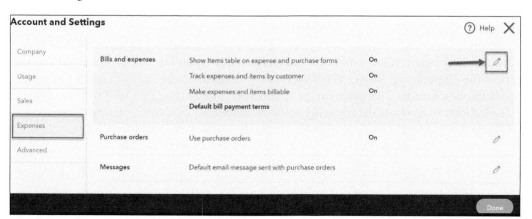

Figure 10.21

Access to settings for billing costs to customers

Click the **pencil** icon in the **Bills and expenses** section.

Figure 10.22

Options available for
tracking and billing
direct costs

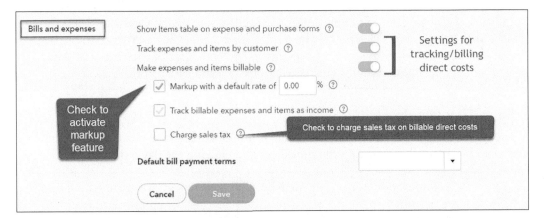

Track expenses and items by customer must be turned on if a company tracks project costs. **Make expenses and items billable** must also be turned **On** if a company intends to bill customers for some or all direct costs.

There are two initial questions that must be answered if a company bills customers for direct costs:

- Does the company expect to earn a profit on costs it incurs on behalf of customers?

- Are billable direct costs subject to sales tax?

Generating profits on direct costs

The simplest way to generate a profit on a direct cost is to "mark up" the cost charged to the customer. This is normally done using a percentage. For example, an accounting firm might incur a cost of $500 on software purchased for a client's use. If the company decides to mark up the cost by 10%, the client would be billed $550. (The $500 cost plus the 10% ($50) markup.) The firm's profit would be $50 (the $550 billed to the client less the $500 cost of the software).

To record markups in QBO, the box next to **Markup with a default rate of** must be checked (Figure 10.22). If the company has a standard markup rate that is applied to direct costs, the rate can be entered as a default. (The rate can later be changed on specific transactions.)

The markup rates for items on a sales transaction are identified when the billable, direct costs are recorded (on **bill**, **expense**, or **check** forms) in QBO. The rate is entered in a field automatically added to purchase transaction forms when the markup feature is activated. Entering billable costs is discussed in the **Identifying Costs as Billable** section of this chapter.

Taxability of direct costs billed to a customer

Taxability of customer charges is dictated by state laws. However, in general, direct costs (plus markup) billed to customers are subject to sales tax unless the company paid tax as part of the original purchase or the direct cost isn't taxable.

If the box next to **Charge sales tax** is checked (Figure 10.22), QBO will, by default, include direct costs when determining sales tax amounts. This can be changed on specific sales transactions.

Companies would check the box if most billable costs were taxable.

> **BEHIND THE SCENES** If taxes are paid by the company on the original purchase, the full amount (tax included) should be billed to the customer. No additional tax would, of course, be added to that amount.

Accounting for Direct Costs Billed to Customers

When direct costs are billed to customers on an **invoice** or **sales receipt**, QBO creates a journal entry for:

- the amount the customer owes
- the amount of any markup
- the amount of the direct expense

The amount the customer owes is debited to Accounts Receivable if the customer is billed on an **invoice** or Undeposited Funds (or Checking) if the customer is billed on a **sales receipt**.

The account credited for the markup amount, if any, must be identified in the **Chart of accounts** section of the **Advanced** tab of **Account and Settings**.

The section looks something like this:

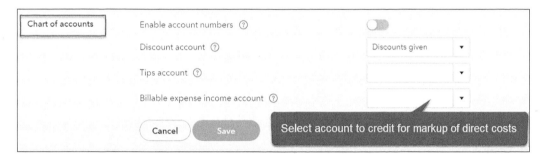

Figure 10.23

Account selection field for markup income

> **HINT:** The **Markup income account** field only appears if the markup feature has been activated on the **Expenses** tab of **Account and Settings**.

The account credited for the direct cost (the amount incurred on behalf of the customer, not the markup amount) is a little more complicated. Let's go back to the **Expense** window in **Account and Settings** again.

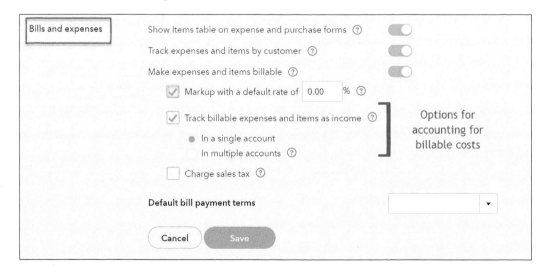

Figure 10.24

Options for accounting for billable costs

If **Track billable expenses and items as income** is NOT checked, then the amount charged to the customer for the direct cost will be credited to the account that was debited when the original cost was entered. For example, let's say a company incurred $320 in travel costs billable to a customer. When the bill for the travel costs is entered, the company might debit a Travel and Entertainment Expense account and flag the cost as billable. The journal entry underlying the **bill** would be:

	Travel and Entertainment Expense	320	
	Accounts Payable		320

The company adds a 10% markup to all direct costs. When the invoice is later created to bill the customer for the travel, QBO would automatically debit the $352 to Accounts receivable and credit $320 to the Travel and Entertainment Expense account and $32 to the markup account identified in the **Advanced** tab of **Account and Settings**. The journal entry underlying the **invoice** would be:

	Accounts receivable	352	
	Travel and Entertainment Expense		320
	Markup on billable direct costs		32

The balance in the Travel and Entertainment Expense account, related to this transaction, would be zero. The general ledger activity would look like this:

A/R (Asset)	A/P (Liability)	Markup on billable costs (Income)	Travel & Entertainment Expense
352	320	32	320 320
			0

If **Track billable expenses and items as income** IS checked, the company must decide whether to track the transactions in a single account or in multiple accounts. If the transactions are tracked in a single account, then the account to be credited must be identified in the **Advanced** tab of **Account and Settings**.

The screen would look something like this if an income account called Reimbursed job costs was set up.

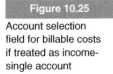
Figure 10.25

Account selection field for billable costs if treated as income-single account

Using the travel cost example again, the journal entry underlying the **invoice** would now look like this:

	Accounts receivable	352	
	Reimbursed job costs		320
	Markup on billable costs		32

The general ledger activity would look like this:

A/R (Asset)		A/P (Liability)		Markup on billable costs (Income)		Reimbursed Job costs (Income)		Travel & Entertainment Expense	
352			320		32		320	320	

If **Track billable expenses and items as income** is checked and **in multiple accounts** is also selected, any **expense** or **cost of goods sold** account that might include billable costs must be associated with an income account. QBO will automatically add a field to the account record just for this purpose. The screen looks like this:

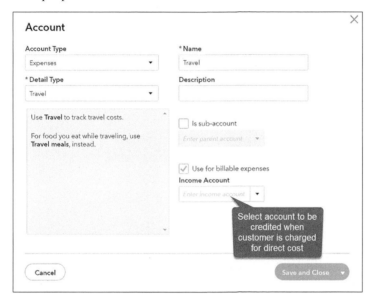

Figure 10.26

Account selection field for billable costs if treated as income-multiple accounts

This can be done when the account is originally set up or by editing the account. It cannot be done through **Account and Settings**.

Going back once more to the example we were using, let's say that in addition to travel costs, the company purchased $700 in job materials billable to the customer. If the **income** associated with Job Materials was Landscaping Services and the **income account** identified in the Travel account was Reimbursed job costs, the journal entry underlying the **invoice** would now look like this assuming no sales taxes were charged to customer:

Accounts receivable	1,122	
Landscaping Services		700
Reimbursed job costs		320
Markup on billable costs		102

The general ledger activity would look like this:

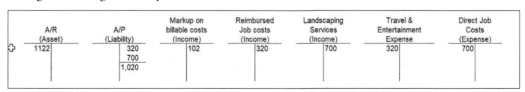

A/R (Asset)		A/P (Liability)		Markup on billable costs (Income)		Reimbursed Job costs (Income)		Landscaping Services (Income)		Travel & Entertainment Expense		Direct Job Costs (Expense)	
1122			320 700 1,020		102		320		700	320		700	

PRACTICE
EXERCISE
10.3

Turn on features for billing direct costs to customers.
(Craig's Design decides to bill customers a 5% markup on costs incurred specifically for the project. The markup amount will be tracked in an income account. Billable costs will not be tracked in income accounts.)

1. Click the ⚙ on the icon bar.
2. Click **Account and Settings**.
3. Click the **Expenses** tab.
   a. Click the **pencil** icon in the **Bills and expenses** section.
   b. Make sure **Track expenses and items by customer** and **Make expenses and items billable** are both activated.
   c. Check the box next to **Markup with a default rate of**.
   d. Enter "5" in the percent field.
   e. Uncheck **Track billable expenses and items as income**.
   f. Click **Save**.
4. Click the **Advanced** tab.
   a. Click the **pencil** icon in the **Chart of accounts** section.
   b. Select **Add new** in the dropdown menu for **Markup income account**.
   c. Select **Income** as the **Account Type**.
   d. Select **Other Primary Income** as the **Detail Type**.
   e. Enter "Markup on billable direct costs" as the **Name**.
   f. Click **Save and close**.
   g. Click **Save**.
5. Click **Done**.

Identifying Costs as Billable

Any costs (including costs of **products** and **services**) can be identified as **billable** on **Expense**, **Check**, or **Bill** forms. Although customers can be identified on **Purchase Orders**, costs cannot be marked as billable until the related **bill** is entered.

The necessary fields are automatically added to the forms when the option of tracking and billing customers for direct costs is turned on in **Account and Settings**. Tracking and billing options are explained in the **Turning on Features for Tracking and Billing Direct Expenses** section of this chapter.

For example, the form for entering a **Check** looks something like this after the tracking feature is turned on.

Figure 10.27

Fields related to tracking/billing direct costs

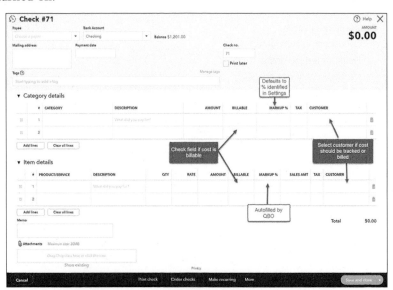

The **BILLABLE** field must be checked. The **CUSTOMER** must also be selected. This would be the **project** name if projects existed for the customer.

In the **Category details** section, the default markup % identified on the **Expenses** tab of **Account and Settings** will automatically display in the **MARKUP %** field if the line is marked as **billable**. The percent can be changed.

The **MARKUP %** field calculations are more complicated in the **Item details** section.

- If there is no default cost listed in the **product** or **service** item record, the default markup rate set in **Account and Settings** will display and will be used to determine the **SALES AMT**.

- If there is a default cost listed in the **product** or **service** item record, QBO autofills the **AMOUNT** and **SALES AMT** fields with the default **cost** and default **sales price/ rate** amounts identified in the **product** or **service** item record when the item is initially selected in the **PRODUCT/SERVICE** field and the line is marked as billable. The **MARKUP %** field autofills with the percentage difference between the two fields. For example, let's say wheelbarrows were sold by Craig's. If the default **cost** is $31.25 and the default **sales price/rate** is $68.75, the **MARKUP %** would show as 120% ($68.75 – $31.25 = $37.50. $37.50/$31.25 = 1.2 (120%)).

  - Technically, QBO is using a gross margin calculation, not a markup calculation here. If markup was used, the sales amount for an item with a cost of $31.25 and a markup of 120% would be $37.50. ($31.25*1.2=$37.50)

  - If the **AMOUNT** field (the cost) is changed, the **SALES AMT** field will automatically change to provide the same margin. For example, let's say the **AMOUNT** field in our wheelbarrow example was changed from $31.25 to $50. The **SALES AMT** field would automatically change to $120 ($120 – $50 = $70; $70/$50 = 1.2 (120%)).

    - $120 would be the amount used when the cost was later billed to the customer on an **invoice**.

    - The item record defaults are not changed.

  - If the **MARKUP %** field was changed, the **SALES AMT** would again automatically change. Back to that wheelbarrow: If the **AMOUNT** was $50 and the **MARKUP %** was changed from 120% to 90%, the **SALES AMT** would change to $95 ($95.00 – $50.00 = $45.00. $45.00/50.00 = .9 (90%)).

> **! WARNING: When an independent contractor performs services for a company's clients and the company bills those hours at a marked up rate, the billable hours are normally entered through timesheets. Those hours are then available to add to the customer invoice using the rate set in the service item record. To avoid duplication, users must be careful not to mark those same hours as billable when the contractor's bill is recorded in QBO. For tracking purposes, only the service item and customer or project name should be identified on the bill.**

Enter a billable cost for Craig's Design and Landscaping.

(Craig's Design staff work overtime on the Cool Cars job at the client's request. Craig stops at Bob's Burger Joint to pick up dinner for the crew and pays with a check. He decides to bill the client for the meal but not charge them a markup.)

1. Click **+ New** on the navigation bar.
2. Select **Check** in the **Vendors** column.

(continued)

PRACTICE
EXERCISE
10.4

(continued from previous page)

3. Select **Bob's Burger Joint** in the **Choose a payee** field.

   a.   Ignore any **Bills** displayed in the sidebar.

4. Leave **Checking** as the bank account.

5. **Make a note** of the **balance** (dollar balance) displayed next to Checking.

6. Use the current date as the **Payment date**.

7. Enter "83" as the **Check no.**

8. Select Meals and Entertainment as the **CATEGORY** in the **Category details** section.

9. Enter "43" as the **AMOUNT**.

10. Check the **BILLABLE** box.

11. Delete any **MARKUP %**. **TIP:** A markup field would only appear if you didn't log out after the last practice exercise.

12. Select **Cool Cars** as the **CUSTOMER**.

13. Click **Save and close**.

    a.   If you are not allowed to save the transaction, close the browser window and log back in to clear all settings.

BILLING FOR TIME AND COSTS

If there are pending billable hours or costs for a specific customer, the details will appear in a sidebar when an **invoice** is opened. At the time this book was written, billable hours and direct costs were not available when entering a **sales receipt**.

The sidebar will look something like this for customers with billable hours and billable costs:

If there are multiple charges for hours, the hours can be grouped by service by selecting **Group time by service** in the dropdown menu above **Add all**. The sidebar would look like this:

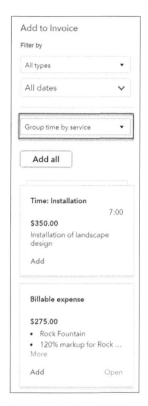

Billable charges can be added to the invoice by clicking **Add** in the sidebar for individual charges. Clicking **Add all** transfers all billable charges to the **invoice**. If all charges were added and hours were grouped by service, an **invoice** would look something like this:

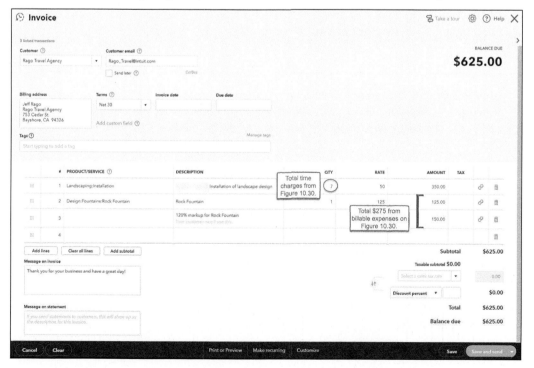

Most fields (**RATES, QTY, DESCRIPTION**, etc.) can be changed before the form is saved.

BEHIND THE SCENES The **rate** used on an **invoice** for labor hours will be the rate specified in the **service** item record, **not** the wage rate.

The markup is shown on a separate line for internal purposes only. This allows the user to change the tax status for either the item or the markup if necessary. In some states, markup amounts are subject to sales tax even if the cost itself is not.

The final **invoice** might look something like this:

Figure 10.31

Example of invoice for billed time and costs

Craig's Design and Landscaping Services
123 Sierra Way
San Pablo, CA 87999
noreply@quickbooks.com

INVOICE

BILL TO				**INVOICE #** 1038
Jeff Rago				**DATE**
Rago Travel Agency				**DUE DATE**
753 Cedar St.				**TERMS** Net 30
Bayshore, CA 94326				

SERVICE	DESCRIPTION	QTY	RATE	AMOUNT
Installation	Installation of landscape design	7:00	50.00	350.00
Rock Fountain	Rock Fountain	1	275.00	275.00

| Thank you for your business and have a great day! | BALANCE DUE | **$625.00** |

BEHIND THE SCENES If an **invoice** is later deleted, the status of any included billable hours or costs automatically changes back to "billable."

PRACTICE
EXERCISE
10.5

Homework
MBC

Charge a Craig's Design and Landscaping client for time.
(Craig's Design decides to use project tracking. Direct costs are incurred on a patio job for Mark Cho. The time and costs are recorded and Mark Cho is billed.)

1. Change some settings for billable costs in Craig's Design.
   a. Click the ⚙ on the icon bar.
   b. Click **Account and Settings**.
   c. Click the **Expenses** tab and click the pencil icon in the **Bills and expenses** section.
   d. Check the box next to **Markup with a default rate of** and enter 40 as the %.
       TIP: Track expenses and items by customer and **Make expenses and items billable** should be on. **Track billable expenses and items as income** should also be on. **In a single account** should be selected.
   e. Click **Save**.
   f. Click the **Advanced** tab.

(continued)

(continued from previous page)

g. Select **Billable Expense Income** as the **Markup income account**. (The same account will be used for both the cost and the markup.)

h. Click **Save**.

i. Click **Done**.

2. Change a **service** item setup to allow for recording work done by subcontractors.

   a. Click the ⚙ on the icon bar.

   b. Click **Products and Services**.

   c. For **Installation**, select **Edit** in the **ACTION** column dropdown menu.

   d. Check the box next to **I purchase this product/service from a vendor**.

   e. Select **Cost of Labor** as the **Expense account**.

   f. Click **Save and close**.

3. Set up the new project using the default settings in Craig's Design.

   a. Click **Projects** on the navigation bar.

   b. Click **Start a project**.

   c. Enter "Cho Patio" as the project name.

   d. Select **Mark Cho** as the **Customer**.

   e. Click **Save**.

4. Enter a bill from Pam Seitz (a Craig's Design subcontractor) for the 36 hours she spent on the Cho project. **TIP:** Since timesheets are currently not available in the test-drive company, hours will be identified as billable using the **bill** form.

   a. Click **+ New** on the navigation bar.

   b. Click **Bill**.

   c. Select **Pam Seitz** in the name field.

   d. Use the current date as the **Bill date** and **Net 30** as the **Terms**.

   e. Enter "PS-142" as the **Bill no.**

   f. Select **Installation** as the **Product/Service** in the first row of the **Item details** section.

   g. Enter "36" as the **QTY** and "40" as the **RATE**.

   h. Check the **BILLABLE** box.

   i. Leave the **MARKUP%** at 40.

      i. **Make a note** of the **SALES AMT**.

   j. Select Cho patio as the **CUSTOMER/PROJECT**.

   k. Click **Save and new**.

5. Enter a $250 billable charge for rental of equipment used on the Cho job.

   a. Select **Hicks Hardware** as the **Vendor**.

   b. Select **Net 30** as the **Terms**.

   c. Use the current date as the **Bill date**.

   d. Enter "1234" as the **Bill no.**

   e. Select **Equipment Rental** (a subaccount of **Job Expenses**) as the **CATEGORY** in the **Category details** section.

(continued)

(continued from previous page)

      f. Enter "$250" as the amount.

      g. Check the **BILLABLE** box.

      h. Leave the **MARKUP%** at 40.

      i. Select Cho Patio as the **CUSTOMER/PROJECT**.

      j. Click **Save and close**.

6. Bill Mark Cho for time and costs.

      a. Click **+ New** on the navigation bar.

      b. Click **Invoice**.

      c. Select Cho Patio as the **Customer**.

      d. Select **Net 30** as the **Terms**.

      e. Use the current date as the **Invoice date**.

      f. On the sidebar, click **Add all**.

           i. **Make a note** of the **Balance due**.

      g. Click **Save and close**.

> **BEHIND THE SCENES** If a timesheet had been used to enter Pam Seitz's time, the billing rate used on the Mark Cho **invoice** would have been the rate identified in the **Installation** item record, not the billable amount calculated from the **bill** entered for Seitz's time.

7. Look at a Cho Patio profit report.

      a. Click **Projects** on the navigation bar.

      b. Click Cho Patio.

      c. Click the **Project Reports** tab.

      d. Click **Project Profitability**.

           i. **Make a note** of the profit on the Cho Patio job.

8. Click **Dashboard** on the navigation bar to exit the Project Center.

QuickCheck
10-1

> Employees at Davis Industries work for four hours on the Selma project. Their billing rate is $100 per hour. Their wage rate is $40 per hour. A special tool costing $35 was needed for the job. This cost of the tool plus a markup of 10% was charged to the client. How much profit did Davis make on the Selma project?

PREPARING PROJECT REPORTS

There are a variety of reports that can be used to review and evaluate projects. Four of the most commonly used reports are:

- Profit and Loss by Customer
    - Shows revenues and direct costs for each **customer**, **project**, or **sub-customer**, by general ledger account, for a specified accounting period.
    - Accessed in the **Business Overview** section of **Reports**.

- Project Profitability
  - Shows revenues and direct costs for a specific **project**.
  - Accessed by clicking **Projects** on the navigation bar and clicking the **project** name.
- Unbilled Time and Expenses
  - Shows all unbilled direct costs and hours for a specific **project**.
  - Accessed by clicking **Projects** on the navigation bar and clicking the **project** name.

Prepare project reports for Craig's Design and Landscaping.
NOTE: Make sure you log out of QBO before beginning this Practice Exercise. Since no projects have been set up in the test-drive file, a report of profits on sub-customers is looked at in this Practice Exercise.

1. Click **Reports**.

2. Click **Profit and Loss by Customer** in the **Business Overview** section.
   a. In the **Report period** dropdown menu, select **All Dates**.
   b. In the **Display columns by** dropdown menu, select **Customers**.
   c. Click **Customize**.
   d. Click **Filter**.
   e. Check the **Customer** box.
   f. Select **0969 Ocean View Road** and **55 Twin Lane** in the dropdown menu for **Customer**. (Both are sub-customers of **Freeman Sporting Goods**. The same report could be used for **projects**.)
   g. Click **Run Report**.
   h. **Make a note** of the net income amount for each sub-customer.

3. Click **Dashboard** to close the report window.

PRACTICE
EXERCISE
10.6

Homework
MBC

Davis earned a profit of $243.50. Total revenue related to hours was $400 (4 × $100 per hour). Total billed to Selma for the tool was $38.50 ($35 plus a 10% ($3.50) markup). Total cost to Davis was $160 for labor (4 × $40 per hour) and $35 for the tool.

ANSWER TO
QuickCheck
10-1

CHAPTER SHORTCUTS

Add a project
1. Click **Projects** on the navigation bar
2. Click **New project**

Enter a timesheet
1. Click **+New** on the navigation bar
2. Click **Weekly Timesheet**

Charge customers for billable time and expenses
1. Click **+New** on the navigation bar
2. Click **Invoice**
3. Choose the **customer** or **project**
4. Add billable hours or costs appearing in the sidebar

CHAPTER REVIEW

Assignments with the MBC are available in myBusinessCourse.

Matching

Match the term or phrase (as used in QuickBooks Online) to its definition.

1. project
2. unbilled charges report
3. account and settings
4. Project Profitability report

5. billable
6. add all
7. parent customer
8. markup %

_____   customer with multiple separately tracked projects

_____   command included in the sidebar of an invoice form

_____   name of window used to select features and set preferences

_____   identifiable job tracked for a specific customer

_____   report that summarizes revenues and expenses by job

_____   status of hours or direct costs to be charged to customers

_____   list of all pending employee hours and direct costs identified as billable

_____   default rate used to increase direct cost billable to customer

Multiple Choice

1. An engineering company enters into "fixed fee" and "time and materials" contracts with their clients. The company _____.
   a. would have no reason for tracking labor hours for "fixed fee" jobs
   b. would have no reason for tracking labor hours for "time and materials" jobs
   c. would normally track labor hours for both "fixed fee" and "time and materials" jobs
   d. must track hours for "time and materials" jobs but should never track hours for "fixed fee" jobs

2. A **service** item must be selected for timesheet entries _____.
   a. only if time will be billed to a client
   b. only if the user tracks time by job but doesn't bill time to clients
   c. if the user tracks time by client (whether time is billed or not)
   d. None of the above. **Service** items must be identified for all timesheet entries.

3. The rates used to bill clients for employee or independent contractor hours are _____.
   a. found in the **products and services** list
   b. found in the employee record
   c. always set when the **invoice** or **sales receipt** is created
   d. found in either the **products and services** list or employee record, depending on preferences selected

4. Which of the following statements is not true?
   a. Both **expenses** and **product** or **service** items can be identified as **billable** as part of the entry of a vendor bill.
   b. Changes to billable hours and rates can be made in the **invoice** form.
   c. Changes to the **markup %** field can be made when billable items are entered on a **bill**.
   d. Changes to the **sales amt** field can be made when billable items are entered on a **bill**.

5. The **Profit and Loss by Customer** report is found in the _____ section of **Reports**.

   a. **Sales and Customers**

   b. **Projects**

   c. **Business Overview**

   d. **For my accountant**

BEYOND THE CLICKS—THINKING LIKE A MANAGER

Accounting: Home remodeling contractors normally enter into either fixed-fee or time-and-material contracts with clients. From a management point of view, what are the advantages and disadvantages of both types of contracts?

Information Systems: List five types of sensitive business or personal client information that might be stored on law firm networks. For each type of information, give an example of an outside party that might be interested in obtaining that information.

ASSIGNMENTS

Background information: Martin Smith, a college student and good friend of yours, has always wanted to be an entrepreneur. He is very good in math, so, to test his entrepreneurship skills, he has decided to set up a small math tutoring company serving local high school students who struggle in their math courses. He set up the company, Math Revealed!, as a corporation in 2021. Martin is the only owner. He has not taken any distributions from the company since it opened.

 The business has been successful so far. In fact, it's been so successful he has decided to work in his business full time now that he's graduated from college with a degree in mathematics.

 He has decided to start using QuickBooks Online to keep track of his business transactions. He likes the convenience of being able to access his information over the Internet. You have agreed to act as his accountant while you're finishing your own academic program.

 Martin currently has a number of regular customers that he tutors in Pre-Algebra, Algebra, and Geometry. His customers pay his fees by cash or check after each tutoring session but he does give terms of Net 15 to some of his customers. He has developed the following fee schedule:

Assignment 10A

Math Revealed!

Name	Description	Rate
Refresher	One-hour session	$ 60 per hour
Persistence program	Two one-hour sessions per week	$100 per week
Crisis program	Five one-hour sessions per week	$225 per week

The tutoring sessions usually take place at his students' homes but he recently signed a two-year lease on a small office above a local coffee shop. The rent is only $750 per month starting in January 2022. A security deposit of $500 was paid in December 2021.

 The following equipment is owned by the company:

Description	Date placed in service	Cost	Life	Salvage Value
Computer	7/1/21	$3,000	36 months	$300
Printer	7/1/21	$ 240	24 months	$ 0
Graphing Calculators (3)	7/1/21	$ 300	36 months	$ 30

All equipment is depreciated using the straight-line method.

 As of 12/31/21, Martin owed $2,500 to his father (Richard Smith) who initially helped him get started. Richard is charging him interest at a 6% annual rate. Martin has been paying interest only on a monthly basis. His last payment of interest only was on 12/31/21.

Over the next month or so, he plans to expand his business by selling a few products he believes will help his students. He has already purchased a few items:

Category	Description	Vendor	Quantity on Hand	Cost per Unit	Sales Price
Books and Tools					
	Geometry in Sports	Books Galore	20	18	25
	Solving Puzzles: Fun with Algebra	Books Galore	20	15	22
	Getting Ready for Calculus	Books Galore	20	20	28
	Geometry Kit	Math Shack	10	12	18
	Handheld Dry-Erase Boards	Math Shack	25	10	15
	Notebooks (pack of 5)	Paper Bag Depot	10	8	12

4/1/22

✓ Martin gets a phone call from Jan Sprint, Assistant Director of Instruction for Sacramento Public Schools. Many of Sacramento's middle schools have purchased the math games that Math Revealed! is selling. For the most part, the games have been great, but some of the students are struggling. Jan is hoping that Martin can provide some game training/tutoring assistance. Martin explains that he can't take on the tutoring work himself, but he'd be willing to find and supervise a tutor. The tutor would work with groups of 4-5 students for a fee of $50 per hour. Jan wants to give this a try at two of Sacramento's schools (American River and Capitol Hill).

✓ Martin talks with one of his former classmates (Kenny Chen). Kenny is interested in in the opportunity and agrees to start next Monday.

- Kenny will submit timesheets to you weekly.

- Martin agrees to pay him $30 per hour.

✓ Martin's not sure how much work he'll have for him and Kenny will continue to offer his services to other companies, so you plan to treat him as a **contractor** in QBO at least for the next couple of months. You set Kenny up through the **Contractors** tab in **Payroll**.

Name	Kenny Chen
Street address	259 Rosa Court
City, State	Sacramento, CA
Zip code	95822
SSN	999-88-7777
Terms	Net 15

TIP: After you set Kenny up as a **contractor**, you'll need to enter the **terms** in the vendor record.

✓ You turn on **Time tracking** in the **Advanced** tab of **Account and Settings**.

- You check **Add service field to timesheets** and **Make Single-Time Activity Billable to Customer** fields.

- You check **Show billing rate to users entering time**.

- You set Monday as the **first day of work week**.

✓ You set up Sacramento Public Schools as a new customer.

- 2566 Central Avenue
Sacramento, CA 95822
Terms are Net 30.

✓ School administrators want information about the training hours by school so you decide to use the project feature in QBO. You add the two schools as **projects**. Both of them have Sacramento Public Schools as the **Customer**. **TIP:** If **Projects** doesn't show up on the navigation bar, you'll need to activate the **projects** feature on the **Advanced** tab of **Account and Settings**.

- American River
- Capitol Hill

✓ You also set up a new **service** item. **TIP:** The **service** item is not taxable.

- Item name: Game tutoring
- Category: Tutoring
- Class: Tutoring
- Description: Tutoring with Math Games
- Sales price/rate: $50 (per hour)
- Income account: 400 Tutoring Revenue
- Cost: $30 **TIP:** To see the purchase section, check the **I purchase this product/service from a vendor** box.
- Expense account: 621 Contract labor
- Preferred Vendor: Kenny Chen

✓ You write checks for the following:

- Rent $750 (Check 1137 to Pro Spaces)
- Monthly loan payment to the City Bank of Sacramento ($215.17—Check #1138) **TIP:** Some of that payment covers March interest.

4/4/22

✓ You pay the six bills due on or before the 15th of April starting with check #1139. The total paid is $1,907.71.

✓ Martin is putting on several workshops this month. For the first one at Teacher's College next week, he needs to have a projector and screen. The College agrees to cover the cost.

- You turn on the features related to tracking and billing expenses and items by customer in the **Expenses** tab of **Account and Settings**.
  - You make sure **Track expenses and items by customer** and **Make expenses and items billable** are both turned on.
  - Martin has agreed on a markup of 5% with the Center. He thinks he'll use the same markup on other costs incurred for customers.
  - You decide **not** to track the billable expenses and items as income.
  - You do **not** check the **Charge sales tax** box.
  - On the **Advanced** tab of **Account and Settings**, you click **Add new** in the **Markup income account** field. You set up a new account (480 Markup Income) as the **markup income account**. You use **Service/Fee Income** as the **detail type**.

✓ You decide to track reimbursable costs in a separate account. You set up a "Reimbursable costs" account as an **Expense** and an **Other Miscellaneous Service Costs detail type**. You make it a **sub-account** of **Other Costs** and use "698" as the account number.

4/5/22

✓ Martin goes to Paper Bag Depot and picks up a projector and a screen. The total, including tax, is $426.55. He uses the VISA to make the purchase. You make it billable to Teacher's College. You enter "Projector" in the description field. **TIP:** This is a non-taxable reimbursable cost for the Teacher's College workshop.

✓ You receive the $350 bill from Les & Schmidt for March's marketing services. The bill (#3358) is due in 30 days. **TIP:** This entry will offset the reversing entry you made to 642 Marketing expense in Chapter 9. The **class** was Workshops.

✓ Martin brings back some supplies he purchased from Paper Bag Depot. He bought them on account. (Invoice #8009, $124.58, Terms of Net 15) Tutoring supplies totaled $109.25. You charge those to the Supplies on Hand account. You expense the $15.33 in office supplies.

- You notice that the vendor changed the terms from Net 30 to Net 15. You use the Net 15 but intend to give them a call next week to follow up.

✓ Mad Math has developed a new online tutoring program using a video conferencing platform. The sales manager has decided to try selling some of the math games to their customers as part of the new online program, and he orders 5 consoles and 4 of each game (**Fractions**, **Equations**, and **Ratios**).

- You set up a new **project** for Mad Math (Online Program), so you can track this business separately.
- You decide to wait until you know the products have shipped before you create Mad Math's **invoice**.

✓ Since there is not enough inventory on hand to fill the order, Martin calls Cartables and asks them to ship the consoles and games (the entire order) directly to Mad Math. They agree and fax you a bill for $1,545 (#956224-53). The terms are 2% 10, Net 30. You do **not** mark the items as **billable**. (You will be billing them using the regular sales price.) You do identify the **project** though. **TIP:** This bill is not related to PO-107.

4/6/22

✓ The Center for High Academic Achievement (Downtown) places an order for books. You ship them out and bill the Center for the following:

- **4 Statistics**
- **10 Puzzles**
- **10 Ready**
- **5 Sports**
- The invoice (INV-1028) totals $745. The terms are Net 30.

✓ You realize inventory is getting low on books so you create PO-108 to Books Galore for $795 for the following books:

- **15 Statistics**
- **10 Puzzles**
- **15 Ready**
- **5 Sports**

✓ All the products ordered from Cartables on PO-107 arrive this afternoon. Bill #956225-64 for $990 is included. Terms are 2% 10, Net 30.

✓ Now that Martin knows the math games are being used in schools, he plans to contact some of the middle schools in neighboring towns. He also hopes to convince Sacramento Public Schools to order from Math Revealed. He'll wait before placing another order but he has great hopes for the products.

4/7/22

✓ Martin lets you know that the workshop for the Teacher's College was a success. You create an invoice (INV-1029) for the agreed-upon fee of $3,400 for the **Educator Workshop** plus the charge for the projector/screen setup and the related markup on the invoice. The workshop fee was a little higher than last time because Martin added some additional training sessions. The total invoice amount is $3,847.88. The terms are Net 30. "Projector" should appear in the **DESCRIPTION** field for the $426.55 amount. If not, type it in.) **TIP:** Since Martin already paid sales tax on the projector and screen, tax is not charged to Teacher's College.

✓ You also hear that Cartables shipped the order to Mad Math so you prepare INV-1030 for the 5 **Consoles** and 12 games (4 of each of the three games). Since Mad Math is a reseller of these products, you uncheck the **TAX** box. You'll wait until to see how much reselling Mad Math will do before you change the tax status in the customer record. The invoice totals $2,350. **TIP:** Make sure you select the **project** in the **Customer** field.

4/8/22

✓ You receive the following checks in the mail:

- Dynamic Teaching—$2,475 in payment of INV-1025, check #743255
- Debbie Han—$230.45 in payment of INV-1022, check #4576
- Mad Math—$1,468.13 in payment of INV-1023 and INV-1027, check #88421

✓ You deposit the checks in the bank. The deposit totals $4,173.58.

✓ Kenny turns in his timesheet for the week.

Date	Day of the Week	Project	# of hours	Billable?
4/4	Monday	American River	5	Y
4/5	Tuesday	Capitol Hill	6	Y
4/6	Wednesday	Capitol Hill	5	Y
4/7	Thursday	American River	6	Y
4/8	Friday			
		Total Hours	22	

- You enter Kenny's timesheet data using **Game Tutoring** as the **service** item, the **project** as the **customer**, and **Tutoring** as the **class**. All hours are billable. **TIP:** If you don't see Kenny's name when you click **Add time entry**, you'll need to set him up as an employee. Click **Add employee** on the **Overview** tab of the Time Center. In the **Display name as** field, enter "Kenny Chen (E)." (QBO won't allow you to use a name identical to the vendor you set up previously (Kenny Chen).) Use the information from the 4/1 transaction to complete the record (address and social security number). Enter 4/1/22 as the **Hire date**. Save the record. Kenny's name should now appear on the **Add time entry** screen.

 HINT: Remember, Kenny Chen is an independent contractor (a vendor). Setting him up as an employee is only necessary if independent contractors can not be selected in the Time Center.

- You also enter a **bill** for the amount Martin owes Kenny ($660—KC408). You use **Game Tutoring** for the **service** item. Since you will be creating the invoice for Sacramento Public Schools using the timesheet hours, you don't make the charges billable here. **TIP:** Don't forget to charge the hours to the correct **project** though. Kenny spent 11 hours at Capitol Hill and 11 hours at American River.

✓ You create invoices for Kenny's work at Sacramento Public Schools. The invoices are dated 4/8 with terms of Net 30.

- American River (INV-1031) $550
- Capitol Hill (INV-1032) $550

4/11/22

✓ Martin created a new workshop he's calling "Making Math Come Alive." He's hosting the first workshop at Dynamic Teaching tomorrow.

- You set up the new **service** item (**Alive**). You use **Workshops** as the **category** and **Workshops** as the **class**. You select 405 Workshop Revenue as the **income account**. You leave the **salesprice/rate** blank. Workshops are not taxable.

✓ All items arrive for PO-108. The shipment from Books Galore includes invoice #2315 for $795, with Net 30 terms.

✓ Martin needs some handheld calculators for his tutoring sessions. You purchase 5 of them at Math Shack for $24.75, using the credit card. Martin doesn't think these will last for more than a few months so you charge them to Supplies on Hand.

✓ 50 students showed up at the Mathmagic clinic on Saturday. All paid cash. No products were sold this time. You create SR-117 to record the $1,000 in revenue.

4/12/22

✓ Martin gave the **Alive** workshop at Dynamic Teaching today and he brought along a math instructor to help. Dynamic Teaching agreed to pay a fee of $1,200 for Martin's services and agrees to pay for the additional help including Martin's customary 5% markup. The instructor is charging $300.

- The instructor is:

    Olen Petrov
    2 Granite Way
    Sacramento, CA 95822

- You set him up as a **contractor**. Olen is an individual so you enter his social security number (191-99-9911). His terms are Net 15.

✓ You enter Olen's bill for the $300 service (#04-13 with terms of Net 15) and make it billable to Dynamic Teaching. Since Dynamic Teaching had agreed to cover Olen's fee plus the 5% markup, you charge it to the Reimbursable costs account. You enter "Fee for Olen Petrov" in the **DESCRIPTION** field. The instructor's fee is not taxable.

✓ You create an invoice for Dynamic Teaching. (INV-1033) for $1,515. **TIP:** The **Alive** workshop fee was $1,200 before adding in Olen's fee plus the markup.

4/14/22

✓ You decide to pay all bills due on or before 4/30 plus the Cartables bill dated 4/5 (#956224-53). You create a **vendor credit** (DISC) to record the 2% early payment discount on the $1,545 bill from Cartables. This is a purchase discount. You assign **Products** as the **class**.

- There are five bills. Total amount paid is $2,823.68. The first check number is #1145.

✓ Martin gives you the information on his tutoring sessions for the first half of the month. He's been doing less individual tutoring lately. He's considering hiring some college students to grow that side of the business while he concentrates on workshops and product sales. All sessions were completed as of 4/14. You prepare invoices, dated 4/14, for the following.

- Alonso Luna—2 **Persistence** $200 (INV-1034, Net 15)
- Paul Richard—1 **Crisis** $225 (INV-1035, Net 15)
- Jon Savidge – 1 **Crisis** $225 (INV-1036, Net 15)

✓ You receive a $1,690 check (#97788212) from the Center for High Academic Achievement in payment of INV-1026. You deposit the check and the cash from the Mathmagic clinic in the bank at the end of the day. The total deposit is $2,690.

✓ You receive two utilities bills in the mail. Both are dated 4/14.

- Sacramento Utilities for April services, #01-88991, $235.40. The terms are Net 30.
- Horizon Phone for April service, #121-1180, $49.35. The terms are Net 30.

4/15/22

✓ Kenny turns in his timesheet for the second week of April.

Date	Day of the Week	Project	# of hours	Billable?
4/11	Monday	American River	5	Y
4/12	Tuesday	American River	5	Y
4/13	Wednesday	Capitol Hill	6	Y
4/14	Thursday	Capitol Hill	5	Y
4/15	Friday			
		Total Hours	21	

- You enter Kenny's timesheet data using **Game Tutoring** as the **service** item, **project** as the **customer**, and **Tutoring** as the **class** for all billable hours.

- You also enter a **bill** for the amount Martin owes Kenny ($630—KC415). You use **Game Tutoring** for the **service** item. Since you will be creating the invoice for Sacramento Public Schools using the timesheet hours, you don't make the charges billable here. **TIP:** Don't forget to charge the hours to the correct project. Kenny worked 10 hours at American River and 11 hours at Capitol Hill.

✓ You create invoices for Kenny's work. The invoices are dated 4/15 with terms of Net 30.
   - Capitol Hill (INV-1037) $550
   - American River (INV-1038) $500

✓ You remember that the March sales taxes are due. You write a check (#1150) to remit sales taxes of $156.28. **TIP:** Use a **check** form if you can't pay the tax through the Sales Tax Center. The vendor is CDTFA (California Dept of Tax and Fee Admin). The **class** is Products.

✓ Martin brings you the receipt for lunch at Kathy's Coffee ($29.45) with Kenny. They met today to go over the school tutoring program. Kenny says it's going very well. The games are really helping the students and the teachers are pleased. He hopes to be able to expand the service to all Sacramento middle schools. Martin pays for their lunch with the VISA card. You consider this a staff relations cost and use the same **class** you use for Kenny's time.

✓ You and Martin are going to meet soon to go over the first 3 ½ months of the year. You want to give Martin a clear picture of operations so you make some adjusting journal entries, dated 4/15, related to activity in the first half of the month.
   - You check the inventory. All counts agree to the quantities in QBO.
     - You notice some low stock items (**Dry-Erase**, **Kit**, and **Notebooks**). You're still waiting for the **Kits** to come in from PO-104. Martin says he'll put in an order before the next **Mathmagic** clinic for **Notebooks** and **Dry-Erase**.
   - Tutoring supplies on Hand at 4/15 equal $202.35. There were no office supplies on hand. Martin is planning to restock tomorrow. You use Apr22.1 as the entry number.
   - You adjust the following expense accounts so that they represent about one-half of April's expenses.
     - Rent expense should be $375
     - Utilities expense should be $142.35
     - Insurance expense should be $15
     - Depreciation expense should be $90
     - Interest expense should be $11.25
     - Accounting expense should be $250
     - **TIP:** In some of the above entries you'll be debiting expenses; in some you'll be crediting expenses. Consider using Other Prepaid Expenses and Accrued expenses in some of the adjustment entries.
   - You ask Martin whether he has used the credit card to purchase gasoline in April. He says he hasn't needed to fill the tank.

Check numbers 4/15

Checking account balance:........$ 7,629.23
Other current assets: ....$ 4,210.75
Total assets: $29,229.86
Total liabilities: ....$ 8,289.08
Net income for April 1–15:........$ 7,234.20

Suggested reports for Chapter 10:

- Balance Sheet as of 4/15
- Profit and Loss (April 1–15)
  - Include a year-to-date column

- Profit and Loss by customer (4/1–4/15)
- Accounts Receivable Aging Summary as of 4/15
- Accounts Payable Aging Summary as of 4/15
- Inventory Valuation Summary as of 4/15
- Journal Report (4/1–4/15)
- Profit and Loss by Class (April 1–15)
- Sales by Product/Service Summary (April 1-15)

Assignment 10B

Salish Software Solutions

Background information: Sally Hanson, a good friend of yours, double majored in Computer Science and Accounting in college. She worked for several years for a software company in Silicon Valley but the long hours started to take a toll on her personal life.

Last year she decided to open up her own company, Salish Software Solutions. Sally currently advises clients looking for new accounting software and assists them with software installation. She also provides training to client employees and occasionally troubleshoots software issues.

She has decided to start using QuickBooks Online to keep track of her business transactions. She likes the convenience of being able to access financial information over the Internet. You have agreed to act as her accountant while you're working on your accounting degree.

Sally has a number of clients that she is currently working with. She gives 15-day payment terms to her corporate clients but she asks for cash at time of service if she does work for individuals. She has developed the following fee schedule:

Name	Description	Rate
Select	Software selection	$500 flat fee
Set Up	Software installation	$ 75 per hour
Train	Software training	$ 50 per hour
Fix	File repair	$ 60 per hour

Sally rents office space from Alki Property Management for $600 per month.

The following furniture and equipment are owned by Salish:

Description	Date placed in service	Cost	Life	Salvage Value
Office furniture	6/1/21	$1,400	60 months	$200
Computer	7/1/21	$4,620	36 months	$300
Printer.	7/1/21	$ 900	24 months	$ 0

All equipment is depreciated using the straight-line method.

As of 12/31/21, she owed $3,500 to Dell Finance. The monthly payment on that loan is $150 including interest at 5%. Sally's last payment to Dell was 12/31/21.

Over the next month or so, Sally plans to expand her business by selling some of her favorite accounting and personal software products directly to her clients. She has already purchased the following items.

Item Name	Description	Vendor	Quantity on Hand	Cost per Unit	Sales Price
Easy1	Easy Does It	Abacus Shop	15	$100	$ 200
Retailer	Simply Retail	Simply Accounting	2	$400	$ 800
Contractor	Simply Construction	Simply Accounting	2	$500	$1,000
Organizer	Organizer	Personal Software	20	$ 25	$ 50
Tracker	Investment Tracker	Personal Software	20	$ 20	$ 40

4/1/22

✓ Sally just got a call from Hiroshi Tanaka, the IT director at Delucca Deli, a Northern California deli chain. He had gotten Sally's name from the IT Director at Metro Market. They've decided to start expanding their operations and would like to hire Sally to make sure all their new stores are properly set up to use their in-house technology. They also want her to train all the new store managers. She is excited about the opportunity but explains that she wouldn't be able to do work herself. Hiroshi is fine with using assistants as long as Sally is available if needed. They agree on a rate of $75 per hour for the work.

✓ Sally gives Olivia Patel a call. Sally successfully worked with Olivia a few years ago on a large project and they've stayed in touch ever since. Olivia agrees to work with Sally on the Delucca project and will start next Monday.

- Sally agrees to pay Olivia $50 per hour.
- Olivia will submit timesheets to you weekly.

✓ Sally's not sure how much work she'll have for Olivia and Olivia will continue to offer her services to other companies, so you plan to treat her as a **contractor**. You set Olivia up in QBO through the **Contractors** tab in **Payroll** (on the navigation bar).

Name	Olivia Patel
Street address	3667 Admiral Avenue
City, State	Sacramento, CA
Zip code	95822
SSN	455-22-9874
Terms	Net 15

TIP: After you set up Olivia as a contractor, you will need to enter the **terms** in the vendor record.

✓ You turn some features on in the **Time tracking** section of the **Advanced** tab of **Account and Settings**.

- You check **Add service field to timesheets** and **Make Single-Time Activity Billable to Customer**.
- You check **Show billing rate to users entering time**.
- You set Monday as the **first day of work week**.

✓ You set up Delucca Deli as a new customer.

- 3582 Expansion Drive
  Sacramento, CA 95822
  Terms are Net 15.

✓ Since the rates are higher for this type of work, you decide to set up a new **service** item. The service is not taxable.

- Item name: Group Train
- Description: Group software training at corporate location
- Category: Consulting and Installation
- Class: Consulting
- Sales price/rate: $75 (per hour)
- Income accounting: 400 Software Selection and Installation
- Cost: $50 **TIP:** To see the purchase section, check the **I purchase this product/service from a vendor** box.
- Expense account: 609 Contract labor
- Preferred vendor: Olivia Patel

✓ Although all **invoices** will be paid by Delucca Deli, management does want information about the hours by location so you decide to use the project feature in QBO. You verify that projects are activated by reviewing the **Advanced** tab of **Account and Settings** to be sure projects are turned on. You add the first two locations as **projects**. All of them have Delucca Deli as the **parent customer**.

- Mendocino
- Sausalito

✓ Metro Market has asked Sally to put on another **Tips** workshop this month. Some of its IT employees were unable to attend the one in March. Sally agrees to host the workshop at Hackers next Thursday but this time she asks Metro Market to cover the rental space cost (plus a 10% markup). The company agrees and Sally finalizes arrangements with Hacker Spaces.

✓ You realize you're going to have to activate some features in QBO to handle billable costs.

- You decide to track reimbursable costs in a separate account. You set up a "Reimbursable costs" account as an **Expense account type** and an **Other Miscellaneous Service Costs detail type**. You make it a sub-account of **Other Costs** and use "698" as the account number.

- You turn on the features related to tracking and billing expenses and items by customer in the **Expenses** tab of **Account and Settings**. **TIP:** You may need to open **Make expenses and items billable** to see the options.

  ○ You decide **not** to track the billable expense as income.
  ○ Sally will be charging a 10% markup on Metro Markets direct costs. She expects to use the same rate for other customers.

- You do want to track the markup amounts separately. On the **Advanced** tab of **Account and Settings**, you add a new account in the **Markup income account** dropdown menu (480 Markup Income). You use **Service/Fee income** as the **detail type**.

4/4/22

✓ You write checks for the following:

- Rent $600 (#1137) to Alki Property Management
- Monthly Dell Finance payment $150 (#1138) **TIP:** This includes March interest.
- Hacker Spaces $400 (#1139) to pay for the rental space for the Metro Market workshop. You make it billable with a 10% markup. This will not be taxable. **TIP:** If you're going to bill the cost to Metro Market, it's a reimbursable expense.

✓ You receive a $1,000 check in the mail from Fabulous Fifties in payment of INV-1026. Check #87101 was dated 4/4.

✓ You deposit the check into the bank.

4/5/22

✓ Sally is putting on a workshop next week for Albus Software. It's a newly developed workshop she's calling "Getting to the Source of the Problem." You set up a new **service** item. You name it "Source." You leave the **Sales price** blank for now. Workshops aren't taxable. In case Sally asks Oscar or Olivia to help with the workshop, you select account 665 (Workshop helpers) as the **Expense** account.

✓ You pay all bills that are due before April 14th. You pay three bills, starting with check #1140, totaling $587.63.

4/6/22

✓ Both locations of Reyelle Consulting place an order for more **trackers** and for some of the management software products. They have quite a few professional services clients and they think they might be able to sell the product to them. They're going to start with a small order and see how it goes.

	Davis:	Sacramento:
Tracker	5	3
Engineering	1	0
Legal	0	1
Medical	1	0

- You create INV-1032 for the Davis location and INV-1033 for the Sacramento location. The invoice totals are $1,200 and $620 respectively. The terms are Net 30. Sally ships the order to Reyelle.

✓ Sally let you know that inventory of the management products is getting low and asks you to place the following orders:

- PO-107; Personal Software, 10 **Trackers**, Total $200

- PO-108; Abacus Shop; 3 each of **Engineering**, **Legal**, and **Medical**. Total $3,150

✓ You receive the following bills in the mail today. Both are dated 4/6.

- Sacramento Light and Power's April bill (for heat and light) #01-988811—$98.45. The terms are Net 30.

- Western Phone Company's April bill #9299-64 for $182.45. The terms are Net 30.

4/7/22

✓ The **Tips** workshop for Metro Market was a success. You record the invoice (INV-1034) to Metro with terms of Net 15. The total amount billed (including the space rental cost and the $2,500 workshop fee) is $2,940.

✓ mSquared Enterprises has referred a new customer to Sally. After talking with Sally, the new customer decides to hire Sally to do some work for them. You set up the new customer:

- Green Design
254 Indiana St
Sacramento, CA 95822
Terms are Net 15.

✓ You realize that PO-106 (Personal Software) is still open. Since you just placed a new order yesterday for the same product, you call and tell Personal Software to cancel the remaining items on PO-106. You close the purchase order in QBO.

✓ You receive the $150 bill from Dovalina & Diamond for March's accounting services. The bill (#3425) is due in 30 days. **TIP:** This entry will offset the reversing entry you made to 651 Accounting and Consulting fees in Chapter 9.

4/8/22

✓ Olivia turns in her timesheet for the week.

Date	Day of the Week	Project	# of hours	Billable?
4/4	Monday	Sausalito	4	Y
4/5	Tuesday	Sausalito	4	Y
4/6	Wednesday	Mendocino	6	Y
4/7	Thursday	Mendocino	6	Y
4/8	Friday			
		Total Hours	20	

- You enter Olivia's timesheet data using **Group Train** as the **service** item, the **project** as the **customer**, and **Consulting** as the **class**. All hours are billable. **TIP:** If you don't see Olivia's name when you click **Add time entry**, you'll need to set her up as an employee. Click **Add employee** on the **Overview** tab of the Time Center. In the **Display name as** field, enter "Olivia Patel (E)." (QBO won't allow you to use a name identical to the vendor you set up previously (Olivia Patel).) Use the information from the 4/1 transaction to complete the record (address and social security number). Enter 4/1/22 as the **Hire date**. Save the record. Olivia's name should now appear on the **Add time entry** screen.

 HINT: Remember, Olivia Patel is an independent contractor (a vendor). Setting her up as an employee is only necessary if independent contractors can not be selected in the Time Center.

- You also enter a **bill** for the amount Sally owes Olivia ($1,000—OP408). You use **Group Train** for the **service** item. Since you will be creating the invoice for Delucca using the timesheet hours, you don't make the charges billable here. **TIP:** Don't forget to charge the hours to the correct **project** though. Olivia spent 8 hours at Sausalito and 12 hours at Mendocino.
- ✓ You create invoices for Olivia's work for Delucca Deli. The invoices are dated 4/8 with terms of Net 15.
  - Sausalito $600 (INV-1035)
  - Mendocino $900 (INV-1036)
- ✓ You receive the following checks in the mail:
  - mSquared Enterprises—$1,200 in payment of INV-1027. Check # 8811
  - Fabulous Fifties—$800 in payment of INV-1028. Check #88244
- ✓ You deposit the checks in the bank. The deposit totals $2,000.
- ✓ Sally called in very sick. She's got a terrible case of the flu and won't be able to be at the **Source** workshop. She has already called Olivia who is more than willing to help out.

4/12/22

- ✓ The **Source** workshop at Albus was a success. Olivia did a great job. She even was able to convince the company to purchase, for resale, some of Salish's accounting software products. You enter Olivia's bill for $500 (#OP412). You select **Source** as the item. You identify Albus Software as the **customer** but you don't make the amount billable. This is not a reimbursable cost so you charge it to the Workshop helper account.
- ✓ You also prepare the **invoice** for Albus (INV-1037). The total fee set by Sally was $2,500 for the **Source** workshop. The company also purchased two **Retailer** products.
  - Since Albus is reselling the products, you first identify them as tax exempt in the customer record. The tax id number is SRY-789-4456-2.
  - The invoice (INV-1037) totals $4,100. Terms are Net 30.
- ✓ You received the products ordered from Personal Software on PO-107 today. All the ordered items were included. The bill (#778922) totaled $200. Terms are Net 30.
- ✓ You pay all bills due on or before 4/30.
  - There are three checks, starting with check #1143. The amount paid totaled $3,650. (You take the $25 credit from Personal Software.)
- ✓ You remember that the sales taxes are due. You write a check (#1146) to remit sales taxes of $218.75 for March sales tax collected. **TIP:** Use a **check** form if you can't pay the tax through the Sales Tax Center. The vendor is CDTFA (California Dept of Tax and Fee Admin). The **class** is **Products**.

4/13/22

- ✓ You receive the following checks in the mail, all dated 4/13:
  - Champion Law $1,500 in payment of INV-1031, Check #2045
  - Lou's Barber Shop $480 in payment of INV-1029, Check #3811
  - Reyelle Consulting $850 in payment of INV-1024 and INV-1025, Check #9759412. Reyelle takes the $50 available credit. **TIP:** Go back and read the hint on page 3-35 if you're having trouble applying the credit.

✓ Sally lets you know that she spent 4 hours on an urgent file repair for Leah Rasual. Leah paid the $240 with her VISA. You create a **Sales Receipt** (SR-111) for 4 hours of **File Repair (Fix)**.

✓ You deposit the checks received today into the bank account. The deposit totals $2,830.

✓ You record a second deposit for the credit card transaction less the 2% credit card fee. You assign the fee to the **Administrative class**. The deposit totals $235.20

4/14/22

✓ Sally emails you details of her client work for the last week. You prepare invoices, dated 4/14, for the following.

- Green Design 7 hours of **Set Up** ($525—INV-1038)
- mSquared Enterprises—5 hours of **Train** and 10 hours of **Fix** ($850—INV-1039)

✓ Sally gives you a receipt from Paper Bag Depot for $45.00. They were having a sale and she wanted to replenish a few of the office supplies to use over the next few months. She used the VISA card. You record the purchase and assign the transaction to the **Administrative class**.

✓ You received the products ordered from Abacus Shop on PO-108 today. All the ordered items were included. The bill (#8944-65) totaled $3,150.

✓ Sally meets with Olivia at The Blue Door to discuss progress on Delucca Deli. Olivia thinks everything's going well so far and is wondering if more projects will be coming later in the month. Sally agrees to check with Hiroshi and Delucca and will let her know. Sally uses the VISA to pay for the $105.82 lunch. She doesn't want to charge Delucca so you expense the amount to 608 Staff meetings expense. You don't charge the cost to any of the projects. You assign this to the **Administrative class**.

✓ Olivia turns in her timesheet for the second week of April. She didn't work on Friday. She completed the training for each Delucca location.

Date	Day of the Week	Project	# of hours	Billable?
4/11	Monday			
4/12	Tuesday	Sausalito	6	Y
4/13	Wednesday	Mendocino	4	Y
4/14	Thursday			
4/15	Friday			
		Total Hours	10	

- You enter Olivia's timesheet data using **Group Train** as the **service** item and the **project** as the **customer**. The **class** is **Consulting**. All hours are billable.
- You also enter a **bill** for the amount Sally owes Olivia for her work at Delucca ($500—OP415). You use **Group Train** for the **service** item. Since you will be creating the invoice for Delucca using the timesheet hours, you don't make the charges billable here. **TIP:** Don't forget to charge the hours to the correct **project** though.

✓ You create invoices for Olivia's work for Delucca Deli. The invoices are dated 4/14 with terms of Net 15.

- Sausalito $450 INV-1040
- Mendocino $300 INV-1041

✓ You suggest that Sally pay down the line of credit again. She agrees and you cut a check (#1147) for $1,500. **TIP:** Apply the full $1,500 to the loan balance. Sally would be paying interest to the bank at the **end** of the month. You will accrue interest for the $1,500 (plus the unpaid balance on the line of credit) as part of your 4/15 journal entries.

4/15/22

✓ You and Sally are going to meet soon to go over the first 3 ½ months of the year. You want to give her a clear picture of operations so you make some adjusting journal entries related to activity in the first half of the month. You number the first entry Apr22.1.

- Supplies on Hand at 4/15 equal $150.
- You check the inventory. All counts agree to the quantities in QBO.
- You adjust the following expense accounts so that they represent approximately one-half of April's expenses.
  - Rent expense should be $300
  - Utilities expense should be $49.25
  - Telephone expense should be $91.25
  - Insurance expense should be $30
  - Depreciation expense should be $146.25
  - Interest expense should be $14
  - Accounting and consulting fee $185
  - Technical reading materials should be $50 (half month of the subscription to Advances in Software Design)
- **TIP:** In some of the above entries you'll be debiting expenses; in some you'll be crediting expenses. Use Other Prepaid Expenses and Accrued Expenses as needed. Costs not attributable to a specific type of service or customer would be included in the **Administrative class**.

Check numbers 4/15

Checking account balance:. $11,548.38
Other current assets: $12,500.40
Total assets: $47,090.03
Total liabilities: . . . .$ 8,722.77
Net income for April 1–15:. . . . .$ 7,289.63

Suggested reports for Chapter 10:

- Balance Sheet as of 4/15
- Profit and Loss (April 1–15)
  - Include a year-to-date column
- Profit and Loss by Class (April 1–15)
- Profit and Loss by customer (4/1–4/15)
- Accounts Receivable Aging Summary as of 4/15
- Accounts Payable Aging Summary as of 4/15
- Inventory Valuation Summary as of 4/15
- Journal Report (4/1–4/15)
- Sales by Product/Service Summary (April 1–15)

APPENDIX 10A WORKING WITH ESTIMATES

Construction contractors and other companies that enter into large, long-term contracts often provide up-front estimates of the total expected cost of the project to their clients. The estimates will normally list, in some detail, the various components of the job. As the work is performed, the company bills the client for the work completed.

An important benefit of estimates is that they define what is being included in the scope of the project. Clients that request changes to the original scope would be given an estimate related to the change. (These are often called "change orders.") In a time and materials job, well-constructed estimates help reduce misunderstandings between the client and the company.

Estimates can be used even when the company is charging a fixed fee for the job. In a fixed fee job, an estimate is used simply to define what work is included in the fee. The fixed fee amount would be changed only if the client requested additional work not specified in the original agreement.

Companies can create estimates in QBO and can use those estimates when billing for work performed.

If a company only invoices the client when the project is complete, an estimate is created and then used to prepare a single invoice. Quantities and prices can be changed when the invoice is prepared, but any changes are not saved to the original estimate.

If a company invoices the client as work is completed (the more typical arrangement), the progress invoicing feature must be activated.

Activating Progress Invoicing

Progress invoicing is activated on the **Sales** tab of **Account and Settings**.

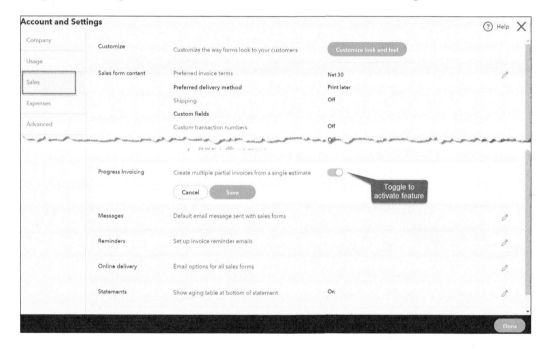

Figure 10A.1

Progress invoicing activation window

Use the toggle button next to **Create multiple partial invoices from a single estimate** to turn the feature **On**.

Creating Estimates

To create an **estimate**, click **+ New** on the navigation bar.

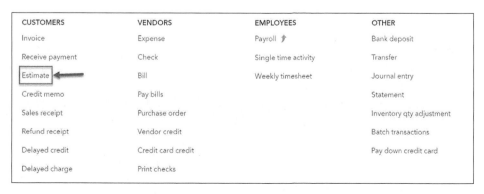

Figure 10A.2

Access to estimate form

Click **Estimate**. The form will look something like this:

Figure 10A.3

Estimate form

A client would normally be expected to either accept or reject an estimate in a reasonable period of time. If a client waits too long, costs to the company may have changed considerably. The date by which an estimate must be accepted is entered in the **Expiration date** field.

A completed **estimate** might look something like this:

Figure 10A.4

Completed estimate form

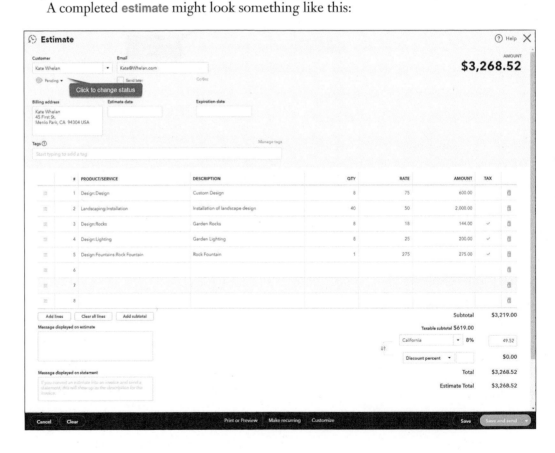

Once the client has reviewed and either accepted or rejected the estimate, the status can be changed by clicking the arrow next to **Pending**. The status options are:

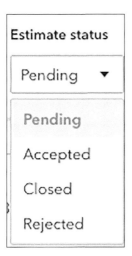

Figure 10A.5

Estimate status options

Creating Invoices from Estimates

To bill for some or all of the **estimate**, click **+ New** on the navigation bar and click **Invoice**. (As of now, estimates cannot be billed through **sales receipts** in QBO.)

Select the client's name in the **Customer** field.

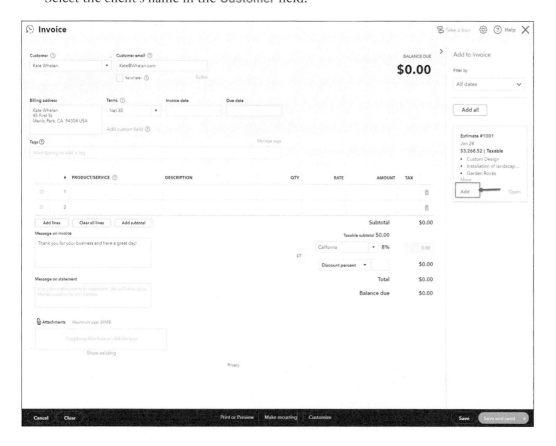

Figure 10A.6

Option to add estimate data to invoice

Click **Add** on the sidebar to transfer the information from the **estimate** to the **invoice**.

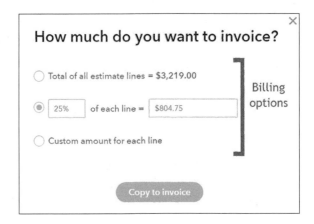

When **progress billing** is activated, the next screen displays billing options.

- The estimate can be billed in full.

- A percentage of each line can be billed.

- An amount for each line can be billed.

If a percentage was selected, the initial **invoice** would look something like this:

The process is repeated for all subsequent billings.
    Click **+ New** on the navigation bar and select **invoice**.
    Select the client's name in the **Customer** field.

Figure 10A.9

Option to add
remaining estimate
data to invoice

The **estimate** is not changed to reflect prior billings so the total on the sidebar will always show the original total.

Click **Add** to transfer the information from the **estimate** to the **invoice**.

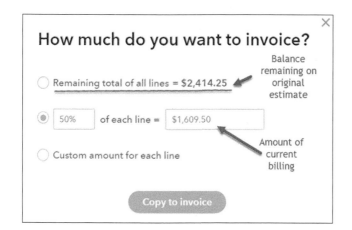

Figure 10A.10

Billing options in
progress invoicing—
second billing

The billing option screen will always show the balance remaining on the **estimate** (the **estimate** total less amounts billed on any previous **invoices**). Users can choose to invoice the balance, invoice a percentage of the **original estimate** (not a percentage of the current balance), or invoice specific dollar amounts (by line item).

Summaries of billing activity will be updated on each **invoice** form linked to the **estimate**. The summary on the final **invoice** might look something like this:

Figure 10A.11

Summary of billing activity added to invoices linked to estimates

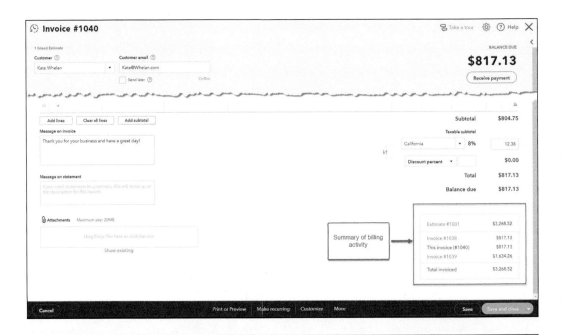

HINT: To display billing activity summaries on invoices prepared for clients, a custom **invoice** form must be created. Customizing forms is covered in Chapter 11.

Once all amounts have been billed, the **estimate** will be automatically marked as **closed**.

Creating Change Orders

Clients may request additional work during the project. To document those changes, a change order is often created. In QBO, change orders can be created by using a copy of the original estimate.

Figure 10A.12

Option to duplicate estimate

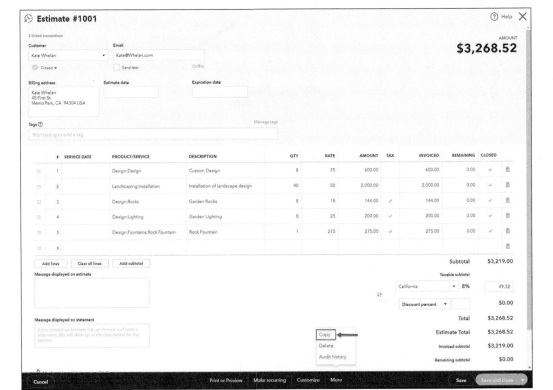

Click **Copy** in the **More** menu of the original **estimate**. A change order might look something like this:

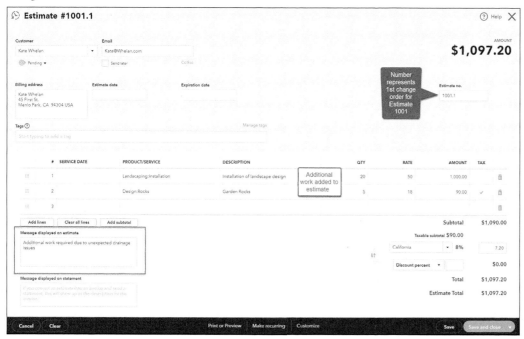

Creating Purchase Orders from Estimates

If **estimates** include **inventory** or **non-inventory** items that must be purchased specifically for the project, a company can create a purchase order directly from the **estimate** if the **purchase order** feature is activated.

HINT: **Purchase orders** must be created before the **estimate** is closed.

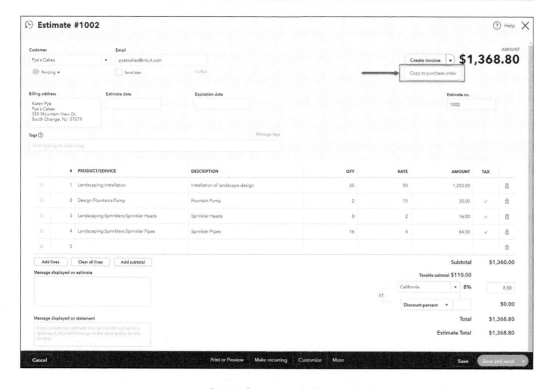

Click **Copy to purchase order** in the top right section of the estimate.
    The following message will appear:

Figure 10A.15

Estimate warning
message

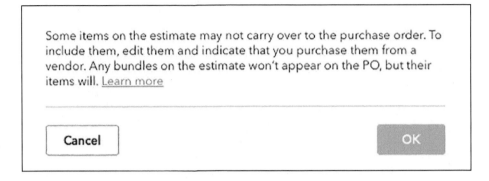

Click **OK**.
    A **purchase order** will be created for all **inventory** or **non-inventory** items.

Figure 10A.16

Purchase order created
from estimate

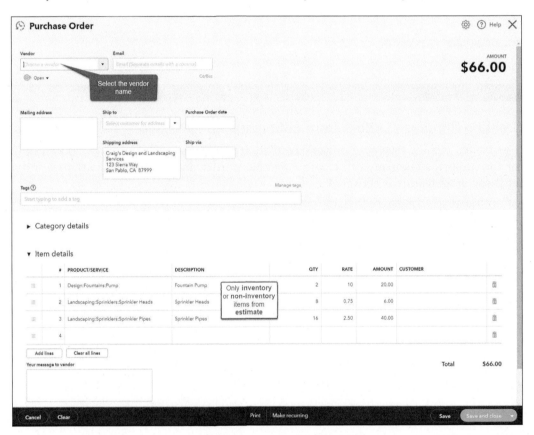

The **purchase order** is completed by adding a **vendor** and making any necessary changes. If the items included are purchased from multiple vendors, the **purchase order** would need to be copied.

11

Additional Tools

Objectives

After completing Chapter 11, you should be able to:

1. Save a customized report.

2. Create a management report.

3. Create custom fields.

4. Customize forms.

5. Export reports to Excel.

6. Manage attachments.

7. Upload receipts.

In this chapter, we will cover a few additional tools in QBO that can be very useful in practice.

SAVING CUSTOMIZED REPORTS

The reports most commonly used by companies are automatically included in QBO. In addition, QBO makes it relatively easy to customize reports to meet the specific needs of a company.

For example, Craig's Design and Landscaping might create a **Journal** report in QBO that includes only sales transactions.

Craig's Design and Landscaping Services
Sales Journal
January 2021

DATE	NUM	ACCOUNT	DEBIT	CREDIT
01/01/2021	1035	Accounts Receivable (A/R)	$314.28	
		Sales of Product Income		$275.00
		Cost of Goods Sold	$125.00	
		Inventory Asset		$125.00
		Cost of Goods Sold	$10.00	
		Sales of Product Income		$16.00
		Inventory Asset		$10.00
		Board of Equalization Payable		$23.28
			$449.28	$449.28
01/01/2021	1036	Accounts Receivable (A/R)	$477.50	
		Landscaping Services:Job Materials...		$50.00
		Landscaping Services:Job Materials...		$50.00
		Landscaping Services		$87.50
		Inventory Asset		$125.00
		Sales of Product Income		$275.00
		Cost of Goods Sold	$125.00	
		Inventory Asset		$10.00
		Cost of Goods Sold	$10.00	
		Sales of Product Income		$15.00
			$612.50	$612.50
01/01/2021	1037	Accounts Receivable (A/R)	$362.07	
		Sales of Product Income		$275.00
		Cost of Goods Sold	$125.00	
		Inventory Asset		$125.00
		Cost of Goods Sold	$10.00	
		Inventory Asset		$10.00
		Sales of Product Income		$12.75
		Landscaping Services:Job Materials...		$47.50
		Board of Equalization Payable		$26.82
			$497.07	$497.07
01/27/2021	1038	Accounts Receivable (A/R)	$375.00	
		Design income		$375.00
			$375.00	$375.00
01/27/2021	1039	Accounts Receivable (A/R)	$120.00	
		Landscaping Services		$120.00
			$120.00	$120.00
TOTAL			$2,053.85	$2,053.85

The above report was customized from the standard **Journal** report as follows:

● The date range was changed at the top of the screen.

- In the **Customize** sidebar:
  - Transaction types were filtered to include only **invoices**, **sales receipts**, and **credit memos**. (**Filter** section)
  - The **Name**, **transaction type**, and **Memo/Description** columns were removed. The **Customer** column was added. The columns were also slightly reordered. (**Rows/Columns** section)
  - The title of the report was changed. (**Header/Footer** section)

 HINT: Detailed instructions for customizing reports are included in the **REPORTING** section of Chapter 1.

Once the customized report is created, the report is saved by clicking **Save Customization** on the toolbar at the top of the report to open a final dialog box.

Figure 11.2

Setup fields for saving reports

In the dialog box, the user enters a name for the saved report. Users can also add it to a **report group**. In **Share with**, the creator of the report can select **All**, which allows all users to access the report, or **None**, which limits access exclusively to the creator.

 WARNING: If specific dates are listed in the date range fields of a saved report, those dates will be retained when the report is later accessed (i.e., the report dates will not automatically update). If a period is selected in the *Report period* dropdown menu (This Month-to-date, Last year, etc.), the report will be updated appropriately.

Saved reports can be accessed by clicking **Reports** on the navigation bar and opening the **Custom Reports** tab.

Figure 11.3

Custom report list

All reports in a **report group** can be scheduled for delivery by email on a scheduled basis. Click **Edit** in the **ACTION** column of the report group to set up the email schedule:

Access to set up
custom report email
schedule

Turn **Set email schedule** to **On**.

Custom report email
options

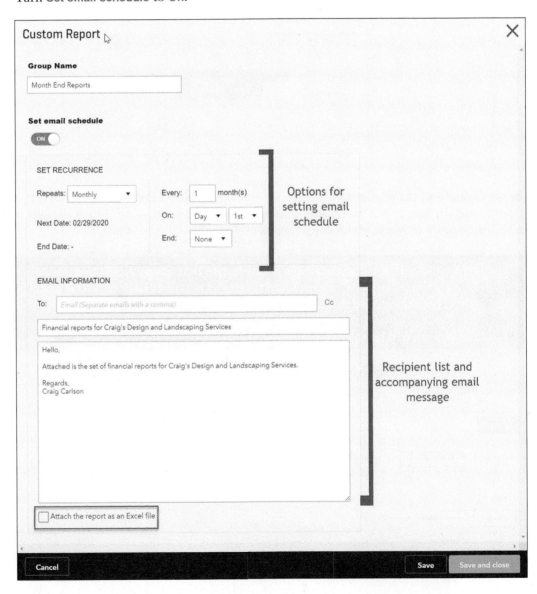

Users can set when reports are sent in the SET RECURRENCE section. Reports are sent as PDF files unless **Attach the report as an Excel file** is selected.

PRACTICE
EXERCISE
11.1

Customize and save a report for Craig's Design and Landscaping.
(Craig wants to review a monthly report of sales invoices.)

1. Click **Reports** in the navigation bar and select the **Standard** tab.

2. Click **Transaction List by Customer** in the **Sales and Customers** section.

3. Select **This Month-to-date** as the **Report period** and click **Run report**.

   a. If no data appears in the report, select **Last Month** as the **Report period** and click **Run report**.

4. Click **Customize**.

5. Open the **Rows/Columns** section.

   a. Select **None** in the **Group by** dropdown menu.

   b. Click **Change columns**.

   c. Uncheck **Posting**.

   d. Click the **keypad** icon next to **Num** and drag it to the top of the column.

   e. Close the **Rows/Columns** section.

      i. **TIP:** Sections are closed by clicking the triangle to the left of the section name.

6. Open the **Filter** section.

   a. Check the **Transaction type** box.

   b. Select **Invoice** in the dropdown menu.

   c. Close the **Filter** section.

7. Open the **Header/Footer** section.

   a. Enter "Current Month Invoices" in the **Report title** field.

8. Click **Run report**.

9. **Make a note** of the **AMOUNT** for Invoice #1037.

10. **Make a note** of the **ACCOUNT** for #1034.

11. Click **Save Customization**.

12. Leave **Current Month Invoices** as the **Custom report name**.

13. Click **Add new group**.

14. Enter "Sales Reports" as the **New group name**.

15. Click **Add**.

16. Select **None** in the **Share with** dropdown menu.

17. Click **Save**.

CREATING MANAGEMENT REPORTS

There are certain reports that are commonly shared with management every month. The financial statement group is one example. One method for sharing reports was described in the **SAVING CUSTOMIZED REPORTS** section of this chapter.

QBO has also set up a number of more formal management report packets that can be edited to fit the needs of the company.

To access management reports, click **Reports** on the navigation bar and select the **Management Reports** tab.

Figure 11.6

Management report list

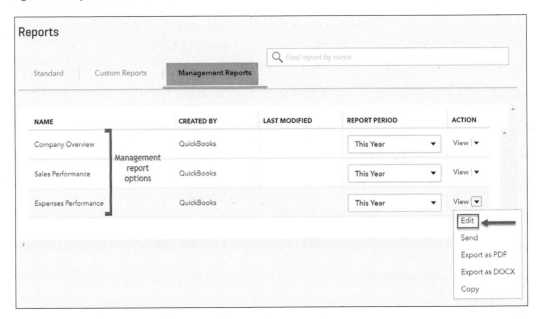

There are three management report options (packages):

- **Company Overview**
    - The default package includes a balance sheet and a profit and loss report.

- **Sales Performance**
    - The default package includes an A/R Aging Detail, a Sales by Customer Summary, and a Profit and loss report.

- **Expenses Performance**
    - The default package includes an A/P Aging Detail, an Expenses by Vendor Summary, and a Profit and loss report.

Each report package includes a title page, table of contents, and default group of reports. The reports included and other features can be edited by selecting **Edit** in the **ACTION** column dropdown menu.

If the **Company Overview** management report was selected for edit, the initial screen would look something like this:

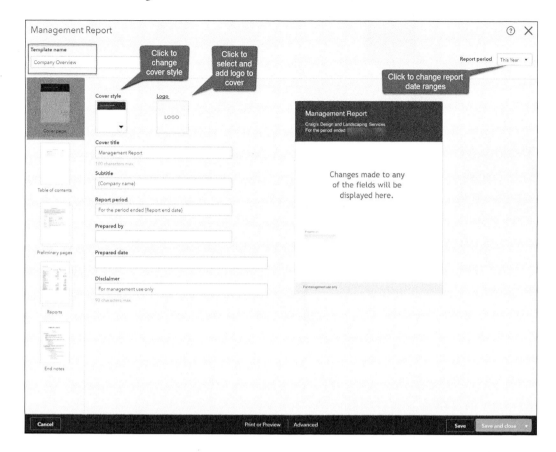

Figure 11.7

Cover page screen for Company Overview management report

Changes to the **cover page** of the report are made on the first screen. (The **template name** can also be changed here.) The **Report period** is selected in this screen and users can select from a number of different **cover styles**. The company logo can also be added to the cover. (Logos are uploaded to QBO in the **Company name** section on the **Company** tab of **Account and Settings**.)

Click the **Table of contents** tab.

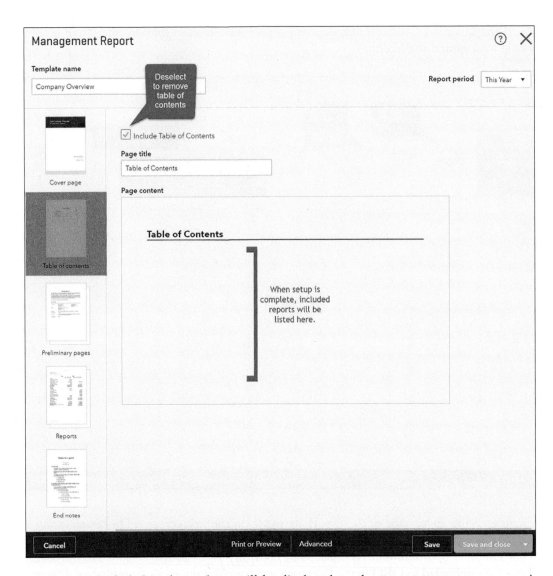

Figure 11.8

Table of contents screen for Company Overview management report

Reports included in the package will be displayed on the **Table of Contents** screen. A **Balance Sheet** and **Profit and Loss** are automatically included. Both can be removed and other reports can be added on the **Reports** screen.

Click **Preliminary pages**.

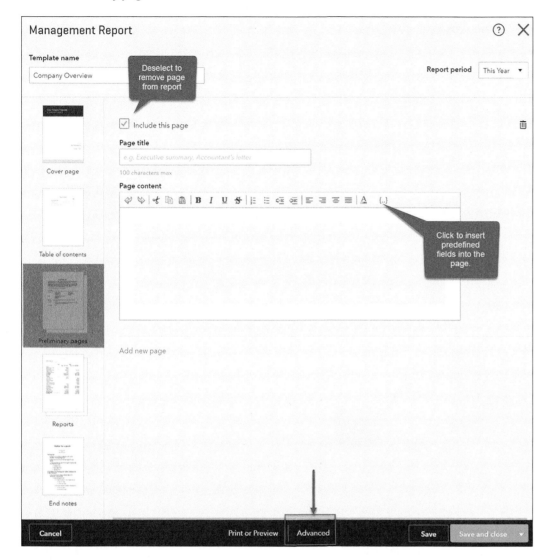

Figure 11.9

Preliminary pages screen for Company Overview management report

The purpose of **preliminary pages** is to give users a place to add introductory or explanatory information. There is certain information (predetermined fields) that can be automatically inserted into the page by clicking the {..} link on the toolbar. The predetermined fields can be accessed through the **Advanced** link in the black bar at the bottom of the screen. They include the company name and the report date. **Preliminary pages** do not need to be included in the management report.

Click the **Reports** tab.

Figure 11.10

Report selection screen
for Company Overview
management report

Financial reports to be included are identified on the **Reports** tab. Reports can be added or deleted. In addition, basic editing can be done on some of the reports by clicking the **pencil** icon. For example, on the Profit and Loss and Balance Sheet report, the title and period covered can be edited. Comparative information (previous year or previous period) can also be added.

Click the **End notes** tab.

Figure 11.11

End notes screen for
Company Overview
management report

End notes, like **preliminary pages**, are optional. Final conclusions about financial operations
or information about future plans could be included here.

If changes have been made to the defaults provided by QBO, a field for entering a new
report name would appear after clicking **Save and close**.

Create a management report for Craig's Design and Landscaping.
(Craig wants a full sales management report.)

1. Click **Reports** in the navigation bar.

2. Click the **Management reports** tab.

3. Select **Edit** in the **ACTION** column dropdown menu of the **Sales Performance** row.

4. Click **Cover Page**.

    a.   Select a different **Cover style**.

        i.   **Make a note** of the number of available styles.

(continued)

**PRACTICE
EXERCISE
11.2**

(continued from previous page)

    b.   Enter "Sales Report" as the **Cover title**.

    c.   Enter your name in the **Prepared by** field.

    d.   Enter the current date in the **Prepared date** field.

5. Click **Table of contents**.

    a.   Make sure **Include Table of Contents** is checked.

6. Click **Preliminary pages**.

    a.   Enter "Summary" as the **Page title**.

    b.   Enter "A/R clerk will follow up, by phone, on all past due accounts by Monday."

7. Click **Reports**.

    a.   Click the **pencil** icon in the **Profit and loss** section.

    b.   Click the **trash** icon.

    c.   Click **Add new report**.

    d.   Select **Collections Report** in the **Select a report** dropdown menu.

    e.   Leave the **Title** and **Period** as is.

8. Click **End notes**.

    a.   Uncheck **Include this page**.

9. In the top right corner of the screen, select **This Month-to-date** as the **Report period**.

10. Click **Save and close**.

11. Enter "Sales and Customer Accounts."

12. Click **Save**.

13. Click **Save and close**.

14. Your new report should now appear on the **Management Report** screen. If it doesn't, refresh your browser.

15. Select **This Month** in the **Report Period** in the **Sales and Customer Accounts** row.

16. Click **View** in the **ACTION** column.

    a.   **Make a note** of the amount owed by **Mark Cho** on Invoice #1035. **TIP:** This invoice will show up on the **A/R Aging Detail** report.

17. Click **Close**.

CREATING CUSTOM FIELDS

Although QBO provides many fields for tracking information, companies may need additional fields not currently built in to QBO.

For example, a sales representative field on sales forms would be very useful for companies that pay commissions to their sales staff. A purchasing agent field on purchase orders might be useful for companies that want to track purchases made by various employees.

QBO allows users to add up to three custom fields for use in sales transactions and up to three custom fields for use in purchase orders. Custom fields are currently not available for use in **bills**, **timesheets**, or other **transaction types**.

Custom fields are added in **Account and Settings** (accessed through the ⚙ on the icon bar).

To add custom fields for sales transactions, click the **Sales** tab.

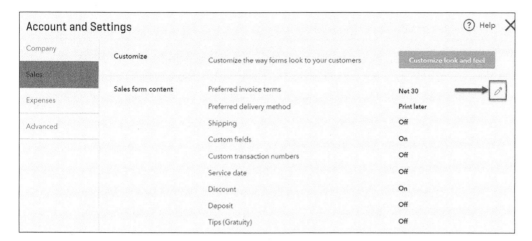

Figure 11.12

Access to custom field setup

Click the **pencil** icon in the **Sales form content** section.

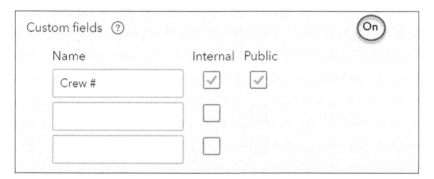

Figure 11.13

Custom field setup for sales forms

Labels for the custom fields are entered in the **Name** field. Users can elect to have the field visible only to those creating transactions (**Internal**) or to have the fields also visible on the forms provided to customers (**Public**).

Custom fields for purchase orders are set up on the **Expenses** tab of **Account and Settings**.

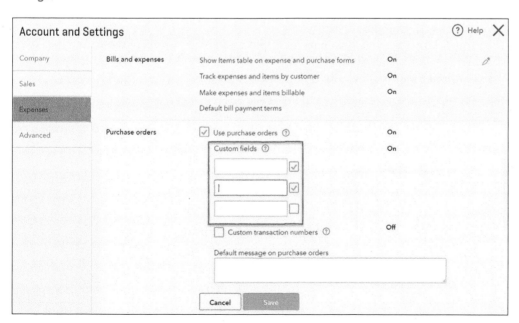

Figure 11.14

Custom field setup for purchase orders

Custom fields for purchase orders will be visible to internal users and on forms provided to vendors.

Add some custom fields for Craig's Design and Landscaping.
(Craig wants to include the project manager initials as a custom field on invoices and the project manager and the purchasing agent initials as a custom field on purchase orders.)

1. Click the ⚙ in the icon bar.

2. Click **Account and Settings**.

3. Click the **Sales** tab.

4. **Make a note** of the default **Preferred delivery method** in the **Sales form content** section.

5. Click **Custom fields** in the **Sales form content** section.

6. Change **Crew #** to "Project Manager."

7. Click **Save**.

8. Click **Expenses** tab.

9. Click **Purchase orders**.

10. Change **Crew #** to "Project Manager."

11. Change **Sales Rep** to "Purchase Agent."

12. Click **Save**.

13. Click **Done**.

CUSTOMIZING FORMS

eLectures

QBO has designed the basic forms needed in a business (**invoices**, **credit memos**, **sales receipts**, etc.). Most likely, however, a company will want to customize these forms by adding the company logo, changing descriptions, or by adding or deleting information included in the form. Companies can even have multiple customized forms of the same type. We're only limited by our imagination!

To customize a form, click the ⚙ on the icon bar.

Figure 11.15

Access to custom forms

YOUR COMPANY	LISTS	TOOLS	PROFILE
Account and settings	All lists	Order checks ⤤	Feedback
Manage users	Products and services	Import data	Privacy
Custom form styles	Recurring transactions	Import desktop data	
Chart of accounts	Attachments	Export data	
QuickBooks labs	Tags	Reconcile	
		Budgeting	
		Audit log	
		SmartLook	
		Case center	

Click **Custom Form Styles**.

Figure 11.16

Custom form options

Click **New style**.

Invoices, **Estimates**, or **Sales Receipts** can be customized. If **Invoice** is selected, the next screen looks something like this:

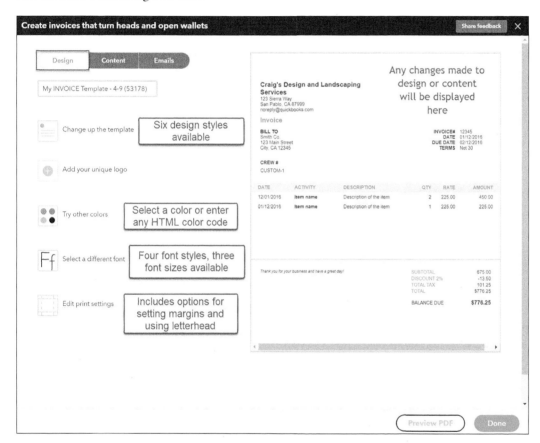

Figure 11.17

Design tab of custom form window

On the **Design** tab, the style of the form is set up. Clicking **Change up the template** displays six different invoice styles. The style differences include colors, font, and basic layout.

Users can further change colors and fonts on the selected style by clicking **Try other colors** and **Get choosy with your font**. A company logo can also be added to the form.

Figure 11.18

Content tab of custom form window (header section open for editing)

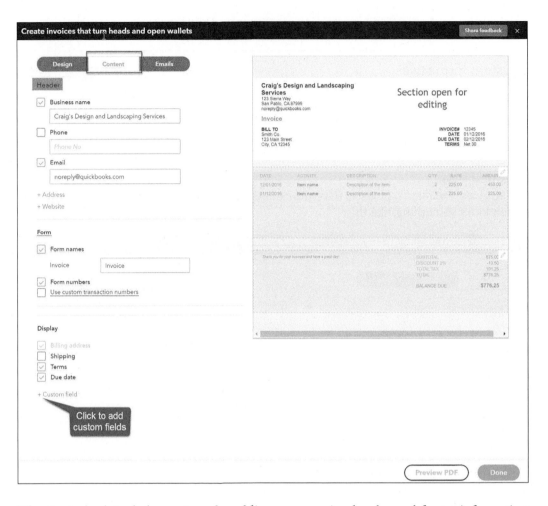

The **Content** tab includes options for adding or removing header and footer information and options for including various columns in the body of the form. Clicking the **pencil** icon in a section of the form opens it for editing. The options displayed on the left side of the screen depend on the section open for editing. The header section of the invoice form is open for editing in Figure 11.18. Fields displayed (including custom fields) can be added or removed.

Figure 11.19

Content tab of custom form window (body section open for editing)

The body of the form is open for editing in Figure 11.19. Columns (including custom fields) can be added or removed. Label and column widths can be changed as well.

Click the **Emails** tab.

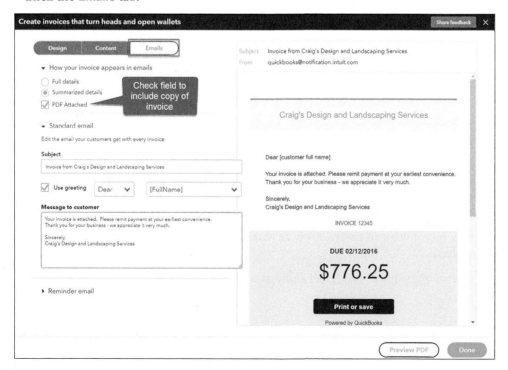

Figure 11.20

Emails tab of custom form window

Users can create a custom email message on the **Emails** tab. The message would be included on every sent form.

Using Customized Forms

Customized form templates can be selected when a new transaction is entered.

Figure 11.21

Access to template selection

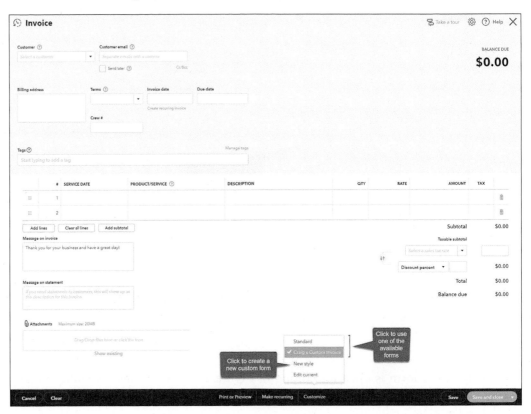

On an **invoice** form, the selection is made by clicking **Customize** on the black bar at the bottom of the screen.

Users can also start a new custom form template by clicking **New style**.

There is no practice exercise for this section. You will be creating a custom form as part of the Chapter 11 assignment so use the directions above to help you.

EXPORTING REPORTS TO EXCEL

There are a number of reasons that a user might want to export a QBO report to Excel:

- The report format cannot be modified sufficiently in QBO to meet the needs of the users.

- A user might want to create a report that includes QBO data with data maintained elsewhere.

- A user might want to use Excel analysis tools on QBO data.

QBO reports can be exported to new or existing Excel workbooks.
To export a report, the report window must be open.

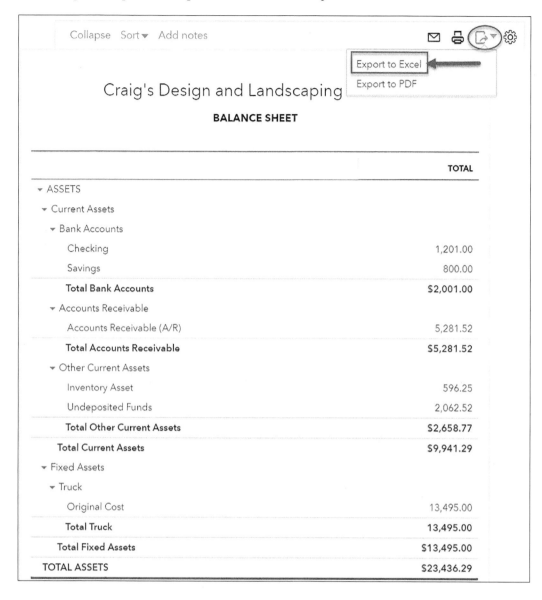

Figure 11.22

Tool for exporting
report to Excel

On the dropdown menu next to the **export** icon, click **Export to Excel**. A balance sheet exported to Excel for Craig's Design and Landscaping Services would look something like this:

Figure 11.23

Example of report exported to Excel

	A	B
1	**Craig's Design and Landscaping Services**	
2	**Balance Sheet**	
4		
5		Total
6	ASSETS	
7	Current Assets	
8	Bank Accounts	
9	Checking	1,201.00
10	Savings	800.00
11	Total Bank Accounts	$ 2,001.00
12	Accounts Receivable	
13	Accounts Receivable (A/R)	5,281.52
14	Total Accounts Receivable	$ 5,281.52
15	Other Current Assets	
16	Inventory Asset	596.25
17	Undeposited Funds	2,062.52
18	Total Other Current Assets	$ 2,658.77
19	Total Current Assets	$ 9,941.29
20	Fixed Assets	
21	Truck	
22	Original Cost	13,495.00
23	Total Truck	$ 13,495.00
24	Total Fixed Assets	$ 13,495.00
25	TOTAL ASSETS	$ 23,436.29

Formatting in Excel will be consistent with the formatting in QBO. Formulas for subtotals and totals will be retained in Excel as can be seen in Figure 11.24:

Figure 11.24

Formulas in report exported to Excel

	A	B
1	**Craig's Design and Landscaping Services**	
2	**Balance Sheet**	
4		
5		Total
6	ASSETS	
7	Current Assets	
8	Bank Accounts	
9	Checking	=1201
10	Savings	=800
11	Total Bank Accounts	=(B9)+(B10)
12	Accounts Receivable	
13	Accounts Receivable (A/R)	=5281.52
14	Total Accounts Receivable	=B13
15	Other Current Assets	
16	Inventory Asset	=596.25
17	Undeposited Funds	=2062.52
18	Total Other Current Assets	=(B16)+(B17)
19	Total Current Assets	=((B11)+(B14))+(B18)
20	Fixed Assets	
21	Truck	
22	Original Cost	=13495
23	Total Truck	=(B21)+(B22)
24	Total Fixed Assets	=B23
25	TOTAL ASSETS	=(B19)+(B24)

There is no practice exercise for this section. You may be exporting a report to Excel as part of your Chapter 11 assignment. If so, use the directions above to help you.

UPLOADING AND MANAGING ATTACHMENTS

Companies generally have a variety of documents specific to their customers and vendors. Examples include:

- Contracts with customers or vendors

- Sales orders from customers

- Lease agreements related to equipment or facilities

- Correspondence with customers or vendors

These documents can be uploaded to QBO and linked to customer or vendor records or to specific transactions. Having ready access to those documents and being able to attach them to customer/vendor records in QBO or to QBO forms can save a significant amount of time for users.

Documents can be uploaded in a variety of file formats (PDF, Word, Excel, JPG, etc.). At this time, there is no limit to the number of attachments that can be uploaded to a company file but there is a 20MB file size limit to a single attachment.

Adding Attachments to Customer or Vendor Records

Customer- or vendor-specific documents would generally be added to the appropriate vendor record. For example a completed 1099 Form for an independent contractor could be added to the contractor's vendor record.

Click **Expenses** on the navigation bar.

Click the **Vendors** tab and click the appropriate vendor name to open the vendor record.

Figure 11.25

Attachments section of vendor record

On the **Vendor Details** tab, click the **paperclip** icon and locate and click the document to be added to the record or drag and drop the document into the **Attachments** box.

The **Attachments** box would look something like this after uploading a file.

Figure 11.26

Example of file uploaded to vendor record as an attachment

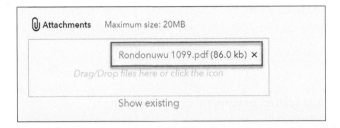

WARNING: Clicking the X next to the attachment will permanently delete it. Users should make sure another version of the document is retained outside of QBO.

Adding Attachments to Transactions

Documents can also be added to any QBO transaction form. For example, a landscaping contractor (like Craig's) could add a picture of a completed project to a customer **invoice**. Click **+ New** on the navigation bar and select **Invoice**.

Figure 11.27

Attachments section of an invoice form

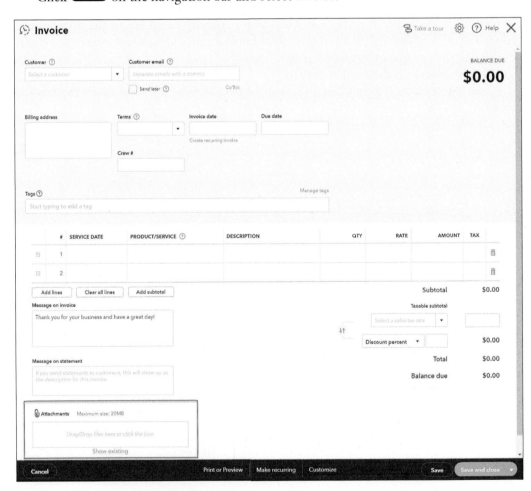

In the **Attachments** box, click the **paperclip** icon to locate the document to be added to the form or drag and drop the document into the box.

The **Attachments** box would look something like this after uploading an image.

Figure 11.28

Example of file uploaded to invoice as an attachment

If the **Attach to email** box is checked, the file will be emailed to the customer with the invoice.

Adding Attachments Directly to the Attachment Lists

All attachments are maintained in the **Attachments** list in QBO.

The list can be accessed by clicking the ⚙ on the icon bar.

Figure 11.29

Access to Attachments list

Click **Attachments** in the **Lists** column.

The **Attachments** list looks something like this:

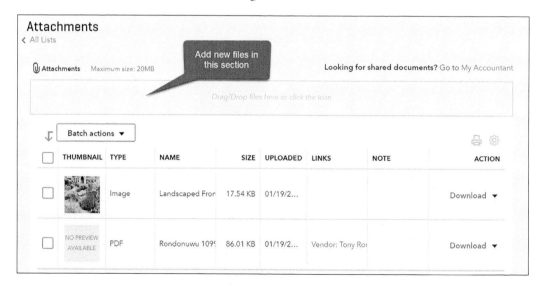

Figure 11.30

Attachments list

Attachments can be uploaded directly into the **Attachments** list by clicking the **paperclip** icon (upper left corner of the screen displayed in Figure 11.30) to browse for the document to be added to the list or by dragging and dropping the document into the **Attachments** box.

All documents in the list are available for attachment to customer or vendor records or to a transaction form.

For example, a company might upload a standard contract terms document to a customer's record in QBO.

Figure 11.31

Access to available attachments

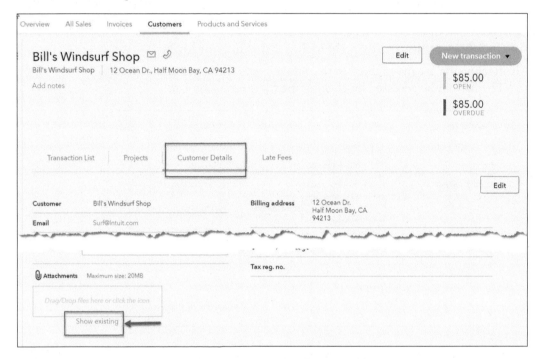

Click **Show existing** on the **Customer Details** tab.

Figure 11.32

Available attachments screen

A sidebar opens that displays **attachments**. To see all **attachments**, select **All** on the drop-down menu under **Add to Customer**. To display only those attachments not linked to other customers or vendors, select **Unlinked**.

Click **Add** to attach the file to the record.

There is no practice exercise for this section.

UPLOADING RECEIPTS

It's not unusual for companies to provide credit cards to employees. Having a company credit card allows employees to make purchases on the company's behalf, for travel, client entertainment, parking fees, etc., without using personal credit cards or cash. Employee credit cards are assigned to specific employees but are tied to the primary business card account. Most company cards carry the company's name as well as the name of the employee.

For control purposes and for determining the appropriate distribution of credit card charges, companies will usually require employees to submit original receipts. Unfortunately, paper credit card receipts are easily lost. And sometimes, employees fail to organize and hand in the receipts on a timely basis. A tool in QBO minimizes these issues.

- The employee makes a purchase and obtains a receipt.
  - Notes can be made on the receipt to help accounting determine the appropriate account distribution.
- The employee takes a picture of the receipt or scans the receipt to create a PDF file.
- Periodically, the employee emails the images (jpeg, jpg, gif, or png) or the PDFs to accounting.
- The files are then uploaded into the system as **attachments** and added to the company file as **expense** transactions.

Click **Banking** on the navigation bar and click **Receipts**.

Figure 11.33

Receipt upload screen

Browse for the file or drag and drop the file into the **Receipts** box.

Figure 11.34

Uploaded receipt before review

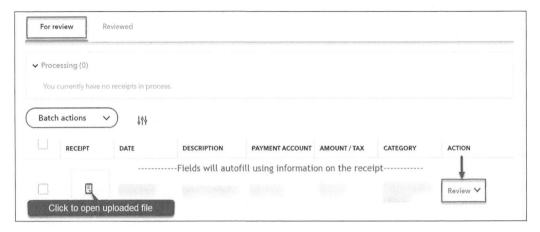

QBO will autofill all of the fields in the **For review** tab based on information included in the uploaded file.

Extraction of the information from the image takes some time. Try refreshing your browser after a few minutes if you don't see the uploaded file in QBO in the **For review** section of the screen.

Once you see the transaction in the **For review** tab, click **Review**.

Figure 11.35

Screen for verifying and adding details of uploaded receipt

For uploaded credit card receipts, **Receipt** should be selected as the **Document Type**.

Most of the fields, other than the **Bank/Credit account**, will be autofilled by QBO. For uploaded credit card receipts, the **Bank/Credit account** would normally be a credit card liability account.

The accuracy of the other fields should be verified. The fields can be changed if necessary.

Click **Save and close**.

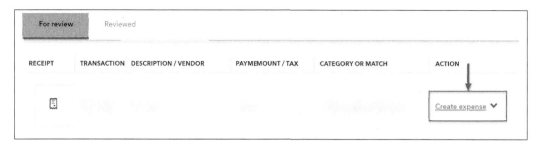

Click **Create expense** to add the transaction to the company file. The transaction is recorded as an **expense transaction type** and will be available on the credit card account reconciliation screen.

All uploaded receipts will be available in the **Attachments** list accessible through the ⚙ menu.

> **BEHIND THE SCENES** Receipts can also be emailed directly to the company file. Images will appear automatically in the **For review** tab. Emailing receipts is not covered in this course.

Credit card receipts are not the only charges that can be uploaded directly into QBO. Users can also upload vendor invoices. The process is the same except that users must select **Bill** in the **Document type** field on the **Receipt details** screen (Figure 11.35). **Bill document types** are entered as **bill** transactions in QBO with a corresponding credit to the accounts payable account. Uploaded vendor invoices are then available to pay through the **pay bills** form.

Receipt uploading is not available in the test drive company, so there is no practice exercise for this section. You will be uploading a receipt (in PDF format) as part of the Chapter 11 assignment. The PDFs for both homework companies are available in Student Ancillaries accessed through myBusinessCourse or from the publisher's website (https://cambridgepub.com/book/qbo2021#ancillaries).

CHAPTER SHORTCUTS

Save a customized report
1. Click **Reports** on the navigation bar
2. Open the report to be customized
3. Customize the report
4. Click **Save customization**

Create a management report
1. Click **Reports** on the navigation bar
2. Click **Management Reports**
3. Click **Edit** on the **ACTION** dropdown menu for the report to be adjusted

Create a custom field
1. Click the ⚙ on the icon bar
2. Click **Account and Settings**
3. On the **Sales** or the **Expenses (Purchase orders** section) tab, check a **Custom Fields** box and enter a name

Customize a form
1. Click the ⚙ on the icon bar
2. Click **Custom Form Styles**
3. Click **New**
4. Select the form to be customized

Export a report to Excel
1. Click **Reports** on the navigation bar
2. Select report to be exported
3. Click **Export to Excel** on the dropdown menu next to the **export** icon

Upload a receipt
1. Click **Banking**
2. Click **Receipts** tab
3. Upload receipt

Upload attachments
1. Click the ⚙ on the icon bar
2. Click **Attachments**

3. Drag and drop the document into the **Attachments** box OR click the **paperclip** icon in the **Attachments** box and locate and click the document to be uploaded

CHAPTER REVIEW

Matching

Assignments with the **are available in myBusinessCourse.**

Match the term or phrase (as used in QuickBooks Online) to its definition.

1. custom field
2. management report
3. paperclip icon
4. design

5. form template
6. custom reports
7. attachment
8. end notes

_____ a specific form style for customization

_____ tab in the **Reports** screen to locate reports that have been modified and saved for future use

_____ document that has been uploaded to QBO

_____ page in a management report that includes user comments

_____ name of tab in custom form template window

_____ link to browse for documents to upload as attachments

_____ a formal set of reports included in QBO

_____ a user-created field on sales and purchase order forms

Multiple Choice

1. If a receipt is uploaded with a **document type receipt**, the transaction
   a. will be recorded as an **Expense.**
   b. will be recorded as a **Bill.**
   c. will be recorded as a **Check.**
   d. will be recorded as a **Receipt.**

2. On April 15, you customize and save a job profitability report. The specified dates in the report are January 1 to March 31. On April 15, you run the saved report. The report will show the job profitability for:
   a. the period February 1 to April 30.
   b. the period January 1 to April 30.
   c. the period January 1 to March 31.
   d. the period April 1 to April 15.

3. Up to _____ **custom fields** can be created for use in sales transactions.
   a. two
   b. three
   c. six
   d. ten

4. A user-created customized form can be created for all the following except _____.

    a. Invoice

    b. Estimate

    c. Sales Receipt

    d. Purchase Order

5. The list of saved customized reports is found on the _____.

    a. **Custom reports** tab of the **Reports** screen

    b. **Standard** tab of the **Reports** screen

    c. **Management reports** tab of the **Reports** screen

    d. navigation bar

BEYOND THE CLICKS—THINKING LIKE A MANAGER

Accounting: Prepare a Management Report for the company Sales Manager at Craig's Design and Landscaping. Include two comments on either the Preliminary page or in End notes. Both comments should highlight a significant sales-related balance, transaction, or trend that you believe would be of interest to the Sales Manager. Which QBO reports did you include in the packet? Explain your two comments.

Information systems: Design three sales transaction custom fields for your homework company. Explain why the information in the fields would be useful to company management. Would the fields be visible on forms provided to customers? Why or why not?

ASSIGNMENTS

Background information: Martin Smith, a college student and good friend of yours, has always wanted to be an entrepreneur. He is very good in math, so, to test his entrepreneurship skills, he has decided to set up a small math tutoring company serving local high school students who struggle in their math courses. He set up the company, Math Revealed!, as a corporation in 2021. Martin is the only owner. He has not taken any distributions from the company since it opened.

The business has been successful so far. In fact, it's been so successful he has decided to work in his business full time now that he's graduated from college with a degree in mathematics.

He has decided to start using QuickBooks Online to keep track of his business transactions. He likes the convenience of being able to access his information over the Internet. You have agreed to act as his accountant while you're finishing your own academic program.

Martin currently has a number of regular customers that he tutors in Pre-Algebra, Algebra, and Geometry. His customers pay his fees by cash or check after each tutoring session but he does give terms of Net 15 to some of his customers. He has developed the following fee schedule:

Assignment 11A

Math Revealed!

Name	Description	Rate
Refresher	One-hour session	$ 60 per hour
Persistence program	Two one-hour sessions per week	$100 per week
Crisis program	Five one-hour sessions per week	$225 per week

The tutoring sessions usually take place at his students' homes but he recently signed a two-year lease on a small office above a local coffee shop. The rent is only $750 per month starting in January 2022. A security deposit of $500 was paid in December 2021.

The following equipment is owned by the company:

Description	Date placed in service	Cost	Life	Salvage Value
Computer	7/1/21	$3,000	36 months	$300
Printer	7/1/21	$ 240	24 months	$ 0
Graphing Calculators (3)	7/1/21	$ 300	36 months	$ 30

All equipment is depreciated using the straight-line method.

As of 12/31/21, Martin owed $2,500 to his father (Richard Smith) who initially helped him get started. Richard is charging him interest at a 6% annual rate. Martin has been paying interest only on a monthly basis. His last payment of interest only was on 12/31/21.

Over the next month or so, he plans to expand his business by selling a few products he believes will help his students. He has already purchased a few items:

Category	Description	Vendor	Quantity on Hand	Cost per Unit	Sales Price
Books and Tools					
	Geometry in Sports	Books Galore	20	18	25
	Solving Puzzles: Fun with Algebra	Books Galore	20	15	22
	Getting Ready for Calculus	Books Galore	20	20	28
	Geometry Kit	Math Shack	10	12	18
	Handheld Dry-Erase Boards	Math Shack	25	10	15
	Notebooks (pack of 5)	Paper Bag Depot	10	8	12

4/18/22

✓ You're meeting with Martin next week to go over the company's operating results. You decide to create a **Company Overview** management report for him.

✓ You customize (and save) the following reports to include in the package:

- Balance Sheet as of 3/31
  - negative numbers in parentheses
  - non-zero rows and columns only
- Profit and Loss 1/1–3/31
  - by month with a total column
  - negative numbers in parentheses
  - non-zero rows and columns only
- Profit and Loss 4/1–4/15
  - negative numbers in parentheses
  - non-zero rows and columns only
  - no YTD column
- Budget vs Actual report 1/1–3/31
  - total only (not by month)
  - columns for dollar difference and percentage of budget column
  - negative numbers in parentheses
  - non-zero rows and columns only

✓ You create the Company Overview management report.

- You add an appropriate logo to the **cover page** and make one other style change.
  - **TIP:** You'll need to find or create a logo and upload it in the **Company name** section on the **Company** tab of **Account and Settings** first.
- You include a **Table of Contents**.
- On **Preliminary pages**, you include comments about the first quarter operating results.

○ **TIP:** You'll need to review the reports before you can add the comments. You can create the management report, view it, and then go back in and edit the report to add your comments. You can include comments about differences between months, trends, or overall results.

- You leave out the End notes page.
- You save the report so you can use it again next quarter.

✓ You're a little surprised at QBO's formatting of the balance sheet. You download the customized 3/31 balance sheet report you created for the **management report** to Excel and change the formatting to better comply with what you learned in your financial accounting course. **TIP:** There are normally far fewer subtotals and dollar signs! Go ahead and leave the accounts in account number order.

5/2/22

✓ Martin is considering hiring some college students to provide tutoring services to Sacramento Public Schools. He is also considering adding some new salespeople to sell the math games line. He wants to be able to identify the person responsible for the revenue on sales forms. You create a custom field for that purpose and call it "Representative." You want the name to show on the forms sent to customers.

✓ Martin asks if you can change the **invoice** form a bit. He'd like to see the following:
- The logo added to the form.
- The representative's name on the form.
- A different design style.

✓ You use the new form on an invoice (INV-1075) for Alonso Luna for 3 **Persistence** sessions dated 5/2.
- Martin was Alonso's representative.
- **TIP:** To access your customized form, click **Customize** on the black bar at the bottom of the **invoice**.

✓ Martin has provided you a copy of a receipt for the purchase of supplies using the VISA card. You want to test the **Receipt** feature in QBO to see how it works and to be able to link supporting documents with transactions.
- **TIP:** Go to https://cambridgepub.com/book/qbo2021#ancillaries and download the *Math Revealed Chapter11 Receipt.pdf* file.
- You click **Banking** on the navigation bar and select the **Receipt** tab.
- You upload the receipt to the file area. **TIP:** You may have to refresh your browser or change tabs and then return to the **Receipt** tab before you see your uploaded file.
- You select **Review** from the **ACTION** column and enter the **Receipt details**. The supplies will be used over the next few months for tutoring. **TIP:** Martin used the VISA card.
- You finish by selecting **Create expense** in the final screen.

Suggested reports for Chapter 11:

- Management Report as described above.
- Balance Sheet as of 3/31 in Excel with formatting changes described in the assignment.
- Invoice for Alonso Luna dated 5/2 using your customized form.
  - **TIP:** To save the form as a PDF, click **Print or Preview** at the bottom of the form. Click **Print or Preview** again. Click **download** and save the file.
- **Journal** report for the **Expense** created from the uploaded Paper Bag Depot receipt.
  - **TIP:** Find the transaction and select **Transaction Journal** in the **More** menu (bottom of page).

Assignment 11B

Salish Software Solutions

Background information: Sally Hanson, a good friend of yours, double majored in Computer Science and Accounting in college. She worked for several years for a software company in Silicon Valley but the long hours started to take a toll on her personal life.

Last year she decided to open up her own company, Salish Software Solutions. Sally currently advises clients looking for new accounting software and assists them with software installation. She also provides training to client employees and occasionally troubleshoots software issues.

She has decided to start using QuickBooks Online to keep track of her business transactions. She likes the convenience of being able to access financial information over the Internet. You have agreed to act as her accountant while you're working on your accounting degree.

Sally has a number of clients that she is currently working with. She gives 15-day payment terms to her corporate clients but she asks for cash at time of service if she does work for individuals. She has developed the following fee schedule:

Name	Description	Rate
Select	Software selection	$500 flat fee
Set Up	Software installation	$ 75 per hour
Train	Software training	$ 50 per hour
Fix	File repair	$ 60 per hour

Sally rents office space from Alki Property Management for $600 per month.

The following furniture and equipment are owned by Salish:

Description	Date placed in service	Cost	Life	Salvage Value
Office furniture	6/1/21	$1,400	60 months	$200
Computer	7/1/21	$4,620	36 months	$300
Printer.	7/1/21	$ 900	24 months	$ 0

All equipment is depreciated using the straight-line method.

As of 12/31/21, she owed $3,500 to Dell Finance. The monthly payment on that loan is $150 including interest at 5%. Sally's last payment to Dell was 12/31/21.

Over the next month or so, Sally plans to expand her business by selling some of her favorite accounting and personal software products directly to her clients. She has already purchased the following items.

Item Name	Description	Vendor	Quantity on Hand	Cost per Unit	Sales Price
Easy1	Easy Does It	Abacus Shop	15	$100	$ 200
Retailer	Simply Retail	Simply Accounting	2	$400	$ 800
Contractor.	Simply Construction	Simply Accounting	2	$500	$1,000
Organizer	Organizer	Personal Software	20	$ 25	$ 50
Tracker	Investment Tracker	Personal Software	20	$ 20	$ 40

4/15/22

✓ You and Sally agree to meet on Monday to go over the first quarter's results. You decide you want to put together a **Company Overview** management report for her.

✓ You customize (and save) the following reports to include in the package:

- Balance Sheet as of 3/31
  - negative numbers in parentheses
  - non-zero rows and columns only
- Profit and Loss 1/1–3/31
  - by month (include a total column)
  - negative numbers in parentheses
  - non-zero rows and columns only

- Profit and Loss 4/1–4/15
    - negative numbers in parentheses
    - non-zero rows and columns only
    - no YTD column
- Budget vs Actual report 1/1–3/31
    - total only (not by month)
    - columns for dollar difference and percentage of budget column
    - negative numbers in parentheses
    - non-zero rows and columns only

✓ You create the Company Overview management report.
- You add an appropriate logo to the **cover page** and make one other style change.
    TIP: You'll need to find or create a logo and upload it in the **Company name** section on the **Company** tab of **Account and Settings** first.
- On **Preliminary pages**, you include comments about the first quarter operating results.
    TIP: You'll need to review the reports before you can add the comments. You can create the management report, view it, and then go back in and edit the report to add your comments. You can include comments about differences between months, trends, or your overall results.
- You leave out the **End notes** page.
- You save the report so you can use it again next quarter.

✓ You're a little surprised at QBO's formatting of the balance sheet. You download the customized 3/31 balance sheet report you created for the **management report** to Excel and change the formatting to better comply with what you learned in your financial accounting course. **TIP:** There are normally far fewer subtotals and dollar signs! Go ahead and leave the accounts in account number order.

4/18/22

✓ You review the management report with Sally. She thanks you for putting together a professional package and you discuss future plans for the company.

5/2/22

✓ Sally is in negotiation with several regional companies to offer setup and training services. She knows she's going to need to hire some help. She wants to be able to identify the person responsible for specific projects on sales forms. You create a custom field (called Representative). You want the name to show on the forms sent to customers.

✓ Sally asks if you can change the **invoice** form a bit. She'd like to see the following:
- The logo you chose for the management report added to the form.
- The sales representative's name on the form.
- A different design style.

✓ You use the new form on an invoice (INV-1075) for mSquared Enterprises for 15 hours of **Train** time and 1 **Organizer** dated 5/2.
- Sally was the sales representative.
- **TIP:** To access your customized form, click **Customize** on the black bar at the bottom of the **invoice**.

✓ Sally has provided you a copy of a receipt for the purchase of supplies. You want to test the **Receipt** feature in QBO to see how it works and to be able to link supporting documents with transactions.

- **TIP:** Go to https://cambridgepub.com/book/qbo2021#ancillaries and download the *Salish Software Chapter11 Receipt.pdf* file.
- You click **Banking** on the navigation bar and select the **Receipt** tab. You upload the receipt to the file area. **TIP:** You may have to refresh your browser or change tabs and then return to the **Receipt** tab before you see your uploaded file.
- You select **Review** from the **ACTION** column and enter the **Receipt details**. The supplies will be used over the next few months for tutoring. **TIP:** Martin used the VISA card.
- You finish by selecting **Create expense** in the final screen.

Suggested reports for Chapter 11:

- Management Report as described above
- Balance Sheet as of 3/31 in Excel
  - With formatting changes described in the assignment
- Invoice for mSquared Enterprises dated 5/2 using customized form.
  - **TIP:** To save the form as a PDF, click **Print or Preview** at the bottom of the form. Click **Print or Preview** again. Click **Download** and save the file.
- Journal report for the **Expense** created from the uploaded Paper Bag Depot receipt.
  - **TIP:** Find the transaction and select **Transaction Journal** in the **More** menu (bottom of page).

QuickBooks

SECTION FIVE

Paying Employees

Employee-related functions (hiring, managing, paying, evaluating, terminating, etc.) are some of the most complex functions in business. They are also some of the most important. There aren't many businesses that can be successful over the long term if they don't have a strong employee base.

In accounting for payroll, the primary focus is on:

- Calculating, processing, and recording employee compensation.
- Recording, reporting, and remitting payroll taxes and employee benefits.

Those two processes may look straightforward but, as anyone who has worked in payroll could tell you, they can be very complex.

BEFORE WE MOVE FORWARD

The payroll system in QBO is highly automated. Employer and employee payroll taxes are all directly calculated by QBO based on the federal, state, and local laws applicable to the company. Payroll tax reporting and tax remittances are automatically processed by QBO.

The high level of automation makes it impossible for payroll to be active in the test-drive company. Intuit does give users the option to try the payroll system on a 30-day free trial. You will be setting up a new company file and activating the payroll system in Chapter 12.

Payroll Activity

Objectives

After completing Chapter 12, you should be able to:

1. Activate payroll.

2. Add and edit salaried and hourly employees.

3. Add and edit payroll policies and settings.

4. Create paychecks and review payroll tax liabilities.

5. Create and modify payroll and payroll tax reports.

WHAT IS THE PAYROLL CYCLE?

- Hire employees and obtain their tax information.
- Track employee time if appropriate.
- Calculate compensation and withholdings for each employee for the pay period.
- Distribute paychecks to employees with information about current and year-to-date payroll information.
- Calculate employer taxes.
- Remit employee withholdings and employer taxes.
- File required tax reports with federal and state taxing authorities.

In a manual system, managing employees and processing payroll are very labor intensive. If any employees are paid on an hourly basis, employees must submit timesheets used in calculating compensation. Withholdings and deductions must be determined for each employee before paychecks can be prepared. Employer taxes must be calculated and tax forms must be completed. And, of course, payroll transactions must be journalized and entered into the general ledger. These functions are done in all types of companies (service, merchandising, and manufacturing).

PROCESSING PAYROLL IN QBO

Payroll is not a standard feature in QBO (i.e., not automatically available in all QBO products). To record payroll transactions, users can choose to:

- Activate a QBO payroll service.
  - All payroll transactions are completed in QBO.
  - Employee information and tax reports are maintained in QBO.
- Add a payroll app from an external payroll provider to QBO.
  - Payroll transactions are directly downloaded to QBO.
  - Employee information and tax reports are maintained in the payroll provider's system.

 HINT: Apps from several well-known payroll providers (ADP and Paychex, for example) are available in QBO.

- Manually enter payroll transactions into QBO using **journal entry** or **check transaction types** and maintain employee information and tax reports outside of QBO.
  - Payroll management would either be done internally (by company employees) or through an external payroll provider not directly linked to QBO.

Federal and state payroll tax rates and wage thresholds change fairly regularly, and labor laws can be complicated. Unless a company has a strong human resources department, it can be challenging for company staff to stay current. Most small to medium-sized companies use an external payroll service provider (QBO, for example).

PAYROLL PLANS AVAILABLE IN QBO

For an additional monthly fee, users can subscribe to one of QBO's payroll plans.

- **Core**
  - Withholding taxes and other deductions are automatically calculated as part of creating employee paychecks.

- Federal and state payroll taxes are calculated, reported to tax agencies, and paid automatically. (This includes year-end filings.)
  - QBO does not automatically report and remit local payroll taxes.
- Next-day direct deposit is available for employees.
- Users can track paid time off, contributions to retirement plans, and other types of employee deductions.
- **Premium** includes all features of **Core**. In addition:
  - Same-day direct deposit is available.
  - Employees can report time on any device. Hours can be reviewed, edited, and approved in QBO.
- **Elite** includes all features of **Premium**. In addition:
  - Payroll setup is done by Intuit specialists.
  - Clock in and out reminders can be sent to employees in the field.
  - Intuit covers any tax penalty fees and interest assessed by the IRS up to $25,000 per year.

CHAPTER 12 STRUCTURE

Because payroll is not available in the test-drive or homework company files, the structure of Chapter 12 will be unique.

The **PAYROLL PRIMER** section will include:

- A review of payroll basics (compensation, payroll taxes, etc.)
- General information about payroll in QBO's **Core** payroll plan.

In the **PAYROLL SYSTEM WALKTHROUGH** section, you will start by creating a new QBO company file. You will then follow a series of steps to edit payroll settings, add employees, and process payroll in that company file. Completion of the steps in this section constitutes the homework for Chapter 12. Additional information about general payroll options is included in BEHIND THE SCENES boxes.

PAYROLL PRIMER

Becoming an Employer

Before a company can hire or pay employees, it must obtain a federal identification number (EIN number) and a state employer identification number. In some states, separate numbers related to state unemployment taxes and workers' compensation must be obtained. Federal and state identification numbers are entered as part of the payroll activation process in QBO. They can also be added or edited by clicking the ⚙ in the icon bar.

Employers are responsible for complying with all federal and state labor laws. Labor laws prescribe standards for wages, hours, working conditions, etc. Information about federal labor laws can be found at the U.S. Department of Labor's website (https://www.dol.gov/). Links to state labor departments can be found on https://www.dol.gov/agencies/whd/state.

Hiring Employees

An employee must complete the following documents before he or she starts working:

- Federal I-9 (Federal Eligibility Verification) form
  - Employee must identify a reason for employment eligibility (citizen, lawful permanent resident, etc.) and sign form.
  - Employer reviews documents supporting employment eligibility and signs form.

- Federal W-4 (Employee's Withholding Certificate) form
  - Employee must identify his/her address, social security number, and filing status and sign form.
  - Used to determine amount for federal income tax to withhold on employee paychecks.
  - Input into QBO as part of the employee setup.
- State withholding form (in states with personal income taxes)
  - Same purpose as the Federal W-4.

BEHIND THE SCENES Starting in 2020, IRS Form W-4 was changed to reflect changes to federal payroll taxes. IRS Form W-4 looks like this for 2021:

Form **W-4**
(Rev. December 2020)
Department of the Treasury
Internal Revenue Service

Employee's Withholding Certificate

▶ Complete Form W-4 so that your employer can withhold the correct federal income tax from your pay.
▶ Give Form W-4 to your employer.
▶ Your withholding is subject to review by the IRS.

OMB No. 1545-0074

2021

Step 1:

Enter Personal Information

(a) First name and middle initial   Last name

(b) Social security number

Address

City or town, state, and ZIP code

▶ Does your name match the name on your social security card? If not, to ensure you get credit for your earnings, contact SSA at 800-772-1213 or go to www.ssa.gov.

(c) ☐ Single or Married filing separately
☐ Married filing jointly or Qualifying widow(er)
☐ Head of household (Check only if you're unmarried and pay more than half the costs of keeping up a home for yourself and a qualifying individual.)

Complete Steps 2–4 ONLY if they apply to you; otherwise, skip to Step 5. See page 2 for more information on each step, who can claim exemption from withholding, when to use the estimator at www.irs.gov/W4App, and privacy.

Step 2:

Multiple Jobs or Spouse Works

Complete this step if you (1) hold more than one job at a time, or (2) are married filing jointly and your spouse also works. The correct amount of withholding depends on income earned from all of these jobs.

Do **only one** of the following.

(a) Use the estimator at www.irs.gov/W4App for most accurate withholding for this step (and Steps 3–4); **or**

(b) Use the Multiple Jobs Worksheet on page 3 and enter the result in Step 4(c) below for roughly accurate withholding; **or**

(c) If there are only two jobs total, you may check this box. Do the same on Form W-4 for the other job. This option is accurate for jobs with similar pay; otherwise, more tax than necessary may be withheld . . . . . ▶ ☐

TIP: To be accurate, submit a 2021 Form W-4 for all other jobs. If you (or your spouse) have self-employment income, including as an independent contractor, use the estimator.

Complete Steps 3–4(b) on Form W-4 for only ONE of these jobs. Leave those steps blank for the other jobs. (Your withholding will be most accurate if you complete Steps 3–4(b) on the Form W-4 for the highest paying job.)

Step 3:

Claim Dependents

If your total income will be $200,000 or less ($400,000 or less if married filing jointly):

Multiply the number of qualifying children under age 17 by $2,000 ▶ $ _____

Multiply the number of other dependents by $500 . . . . ▶ $ _____

Add the amounts above and enter the total here . . . .   3 $ _____

Step 4 (optional):

Other Adjustments

(a) **Other income (not from jobs).** If you want tax withheld for other income you expect this year that won't have withholding, enter the amount of other income here. This may include interest, dividends, and retirement income . . . .   4(a) $ _____

(b) **Deductions.** If you expect to claim deductions other than the standard deduction and want to reduce your withholding, use the Deductions Worksheet on page 3 and enter the result here . . . .   4(b) $ _____

(c) **Extra withholding.** Enter any additional tax you want withheld each **pay period** .   4(c) $ _____

Step 5:

Sign Here

Under penalties of perjury, I declare that this certificate, to the best of my knowledge and belief, is true, correct, and complete.

▶ _____   ▶ _____
Employee's signature (This form is not valid unless you sign it.)   Date

Employers Only

Employer's name and address

First date of employment

Employer identification number (EIN)

(continued)

(continued from previous page)

In the past, employees identified the number of withholding allowances they were claiming on their W-4. Withholding allowances acted to reduce the amount of federal income tax withheld. In most cases, individuals would claim allowances for themselves and any dependents. The amount of federal income tax withheld was based on the employee's filing status and the number of withholding allowances claimed.

Withholding amounts are now based on the following:

- For employees without dependents, with only one job, and without additional withholding requirements, the amount of federal income taxes withheld is calculated based on their federal filing status (Step 1c on Form W-4).

  - If an individual's filing status is Married, Filing Jointly, and their spouse works, they would be considered to have more than one job.

  - Directions for determining tax withholdings for employees with multiple jobs are available on Form W-4. (See Step 2 on the W-4.)

- For employees with dependents or with additional withholding requirements, the amount of federal income taxes withheld is based on their federal filing status PLUS information included in Steps 3 and 4 of Form W-4.

  - The adjustment for dependents is calculated in Step 3. This only applies to taxpayers making less than $200,000 (or less than $400,000 if married, filing jointly).

  - Other adjustments (increases or decreases) are reported in Step 4. Directions for determining those amounts are included on Form W-4 available at irs.gov.

Compensation

Employees are normally paid in the form of a salary (usually stated as an annual or monthly amount) or an hourly wage. In addition, they might be paid:

- Bonuses

  - Bonus (additional) pay is often given to salaried or hourly employees as a reward for the achievement of a specific, individual goal.

  - Sometimes bonuses are paid to employees when the company itself meets certain financial goals.

- Commissions

  - Commission pay is typically based on sales volume (units or dollars). For example, a salesperson might be paid 5% of each sales dollar generated from their customer.

- Overtime premiums

  - When certain employees work more than a prescribed number of hours in a day or in a week, most states require employers to pay them a premium for those hours. State laws mandate the standard hour limits and the type of employees eligible for overtime pay.

- Paid time off (also known as sick pay and vacation pay)

  - Most employers allow their employees to be paid for a certain number of hours at their standard rate, even when absent due to illness or vacation.

Gross pay The amount an employee earns before any withholdings or deductions.

Net pay The amount of an employee's paycheck, after subtracting withheld amounts.

The total amount earned by an employee during a pay period is called the employee's **gross pay**. The amount of the paycheck (gross pay less taxes and other withholdings) is called the employee's **net pay**.

In QBO Payroll, compensation options are known as **pay types**. Each employee must be set up initially as an **Hourly**, **Salary**, or **Commission Only** employee. Additional **pay types** (e.g., **overtime**, **paid time off**, **bonus**, or **commission**) can be added to hourly or salaried employees.

Payroll Taxes—Reporting and Remitting

There are federal, state, and local payroll taxes. Some are the responsibility of the employer, some are the responsibility of the employee, and some are a shared responsibility of both employer and employee. Payroll taxes that are the responsibility of the employee are automatically withheld from employee paychecks in QBO Payroll.

Most payroll taxes are calculated as a percentage of a base amount. The percentage and the base will depend on the specific payroll tax. Tax rates and base amounts can (and do!) change periodically.

Federal payroll taxes include:

- Federal income (FIT)—Employee only tax
  - The base amount of FIT withheld is determined by the employee's filing status. See the BEHIND THE SCENES insert on page 12-6 for more information.

- FICA (Social Security and Medicare)—Shared tax
  - Both employer and employee pay a social security tax of 6.2% of wages up to a maximum wage threshold.
    - Maximum wage thresholds change. $142,800 was the threshold in 2021.
  - Both employer and employee pay a Medicare tax of 1.45% of all wages. In addition, employees pay an additional 0.9% of wages over a threshold based on their filing status. The threshold for a single individual was $200,000 in 2021.

- Federal unemployment (FUTA)—Employer only tax
  - Employers pay a 6% FUTA tax on wages up to a threshold of $7,000 for each employee. Employers are eligible for a credit of up to 5.4% of wages for any state unemployment taxes paid.
    - The tax rate, threshold amount, and credit rate have not changed since 1983.

State payroll taxes may include personal income tax, unemployment taxes, disability insurance, and others. In California, the state payroll taxes include:

- Personal income (PIT)—Employee only tax

- State unemployment (UI)—Employer tax

- Employment training (ETT)—Employer tax

- State disability (SDI)—Employee tax

BEHIND THE SCENES Employers are also required to maintain workers' compensation insurance in most states. Workers' compensation provides benefits for workers who are injured or contract an illness due to their work. In some states, employers pay into a state government program. Other states allow employers to purchase the coverage from private insurance carriers or self-fund their workers' compensation plan.

In QBO Payroll, all payroll taxes are automatically calculated based on the employer's location(s) and information provided by employees and federal and state taxing authorities.

Schedules for reporting and remitting federal payroll taxes (employer and employee shares) depend on the size of a company's payroll.

- Federal income tax and FICA taxes are reported quarterly on Form 941. Remittance timing varies based on the size of the payroll tax liability.
  - Small companies (generally those with payroll tax liabilities of less than $2,500 per quarter) can deposit 941 taxes with the quarterly return.
  - Companies with payroll tax liabilities greater than $50,000 during the 12 months ending June 30 of the **prior** year must deposit 941 taxes semi-weekly. (For 2021, the prior year would end June 30, 2020.) Deposits must be remitted electronically.
  - All other companies must deposit 941 taxes monthly. Deposits must be remitted electronically.
- Federal unemployment taxes are reported on Form 943. Remittance timing varies based on the size of the payroll tax liability.
  - The FUTA tax deposit requirement is based on the company's FUTA tax liability **year-to-date**. A deposit is due once the year-to-date tax liability exceeds $500 (calculated quarterly).

Schedules for reporting and remitting state and local payroll taxes (employee and employee shares) are set by the various tax authorities. Some states adopt the federal remittance and filing schedules.

Other Payroll Deductions and Costs

Employers often provide benefits to employees. These might include:

- Medical insurance
  - Can be fully or partially paid by the employer
- Retirement plans
  - Can be fully or partially paid by the employer

Employee and employer contributions related to health or retirement plans are set up as part of the employee record in QBO. Employee contributions are automatically withheld from employee paychecks.

Employers may also withhold funds from employee paychecks related to garnishments (child support, tax levies, etc.), union dues, repayment of cash advances, etc. These deductions are also set up in the employee record in QBO.

PAYROLL SYSTEM WALKTHROUGH

The Chapter 12 homework assignment for either *Math Revealed!* or *Salish Software Solutions* consists of following the steps outlined in this section. When you have completed the steps, you will have worked through the full QBO Payroll process for two employees.

In Step 1, you'll start by setting up a new company file and activating the 30-day payroll trial option. Follow the instructions for this step carefully.

Step 1—Set Up a New Company File

The process for setting up your payroll company file is similar to the one you followed in Chapter 2. This time, however, you'll only be importing your chart of accounts.

Your instructor will send you an invitation for the new file.

HINT: If your instructor is unable to send a second license to you, you can still obtain a free 30-day trial company. Instructions are included at https://cambridgepub.com/book/qbo2021#ancillaries.

Figure 12.1

New company setup

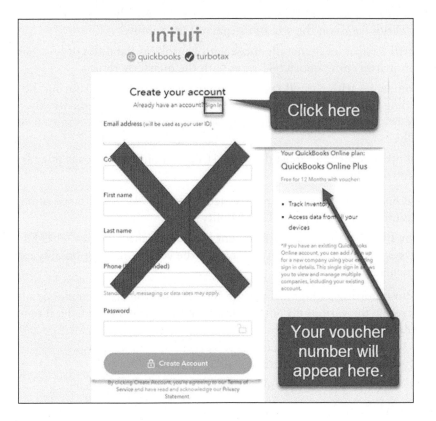

Accept the invitation and sign in using your homework company email address and password.

 HINT: Registering with the same email address allows you to access multiple companies using the same login. When you log in at qbo.intuit.com, all companies associated with the same email address/password are displayed.

Figure 12.2

Welcome screen

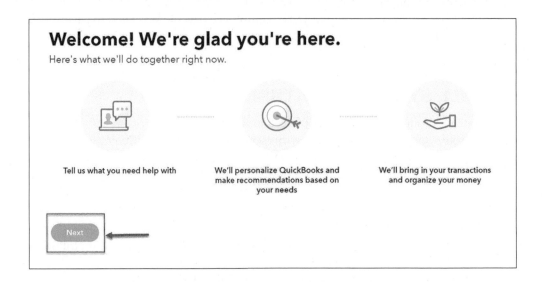

Click **Next** in the Welcome screen to start the setup process.

Use the following table to guide you through the screens. You may not see all of these questions in your setup. You may also see the questions in a different order and with slightly different wording, but the basic information requested is the same.

Screen Heading	Answers
What's your business name?	Enter a name that is distinct from your homework company name. For example, you could use your homework company file name followed by the word Payroll. Do not check the box next to **I use QuickBooks Desktop and want to bring in my data**. **TIP:** Check to make sure your instructor doesn't have special instructions for your company name.
What's your role at the company?	Select the option that includes the word **Accountant**.
Who helps run this business? or Who works at this business?	Select **Employees**.
Link your accounts	Select **Skip for now** or **Manually add transactions**.
What kind of business is this?	**Corporation** or **C-Corp**
What does your business do? or What's your industry?	Enter *Professional services* in the field. From the displayed options, select **All other professional, scientific, and technical services**.
How does your business make money?	Select **I sell services** and **I sell products**.
What is everything you want to set up?	Select all options other than those related to accepting online payments, and purchasing insurance.
Ready for a free trial of QuickBooks Payroll?	Select **Yes**.

Table 12.1

Company setup questions

Once you finish answering the setup questions, you will be on the **Dashboard**.

You will need to change a few settings before moving forward. Click the ⚙ on the icon bar.

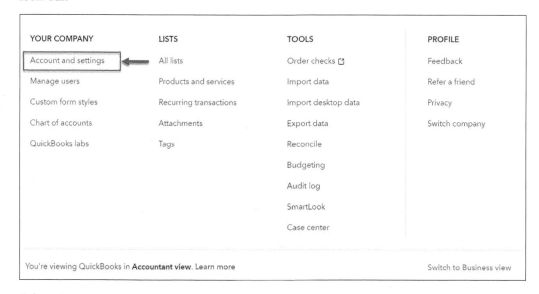

YOUR COMPANY	LISTS	TOOLS	PROFILE
Account and settings	All lists	Order checks ⧉	Feedback
Manage users	Products and services	Import data	Refer a friend
Custom form styles	Recurring transactions	Import desktop data	Privacy
Chart of accounts	Attachments	Export data	Switch company
QuickBooks labs	Tags	Reconcile	
		Budgeting	
		Audit log	
		SmartLook	
		Case center	

You're viewing QuickBooks in **Accountant view**. Learn more   Switch to Business view

Figure 12.3

Link to file settings

Select **Account and Settings**.

Figure 12.4

Sales settings selection screen

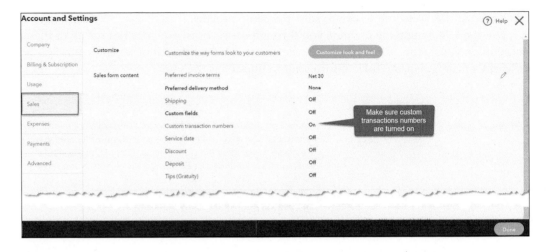

On the **Sales** tab, make sure **Custom transaction numbers** is **On**.

Click **Save**.

Figure 12.5

Advanced settings selection screen

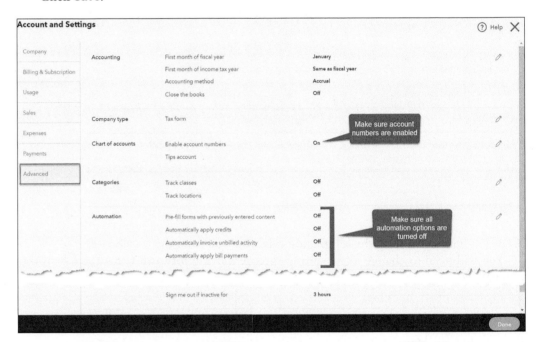

On the **Advanced** tab, turn **Enable account numbers** to **On** and check the box next to **Show account numbers**.

Toggle all **Automation** settings to **Off**. You may also want to extend the time before QBO automatically logs you out to 3 hours on the **Advanced** tab.

Click **Save** in each modified section.

Click **Done** to exit **Account and Settings**.

You will now need to purge the default chart of accounts and import the same chart of accounts you used in your homework company file.

Change the URL address to read https://qbo.intuit.com/app/purgecompany. (Leave any C number that appears after https://.)

Press **Enter**.

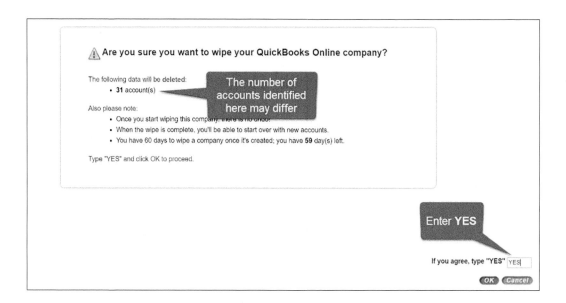

Figure 12.6

Warning before file purge

Enter YES in the box at the bottom right of the screen and click OK.

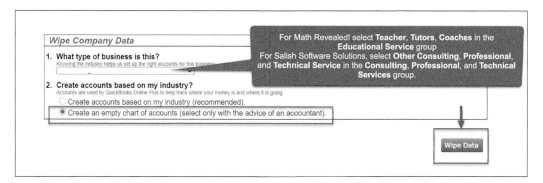

Figure 12.7

Options for account setup

Complete the purge by answering the two questions on the screen using the instructions in Figure 12.7. Click Wipe Data.

Click the ⚙ on the icon bar.

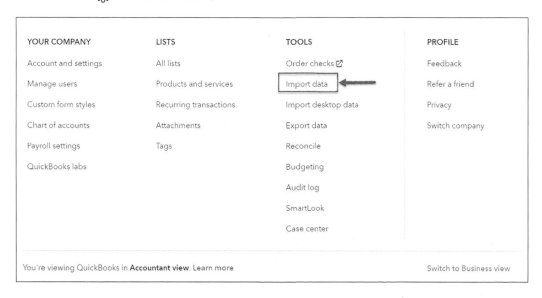

Figure 12.8

Link to import file data

Click Import Data.

Figure 12.9

Selection of data to be imported

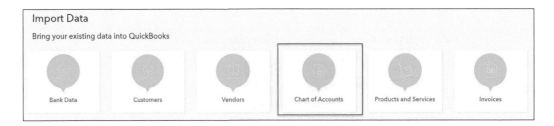

Select **Chart of Accounts**.

Figure 12.10

Selection of import file

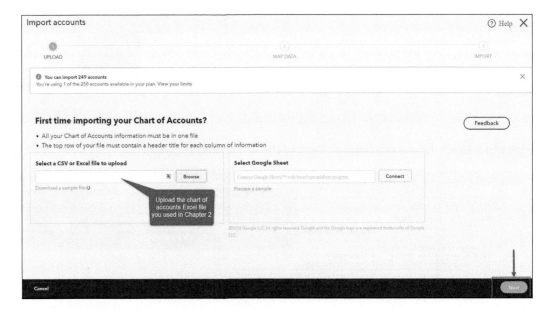

Click **Browse** and select the Chart of Accounts Excel file that you used to set up your homework company file in Chapter 2. You will be selecting **one** of the following:

- QBO 2021 Math Revealed Chart of Accounts for Importing.xlsx

- QBO 2021 Salish Software Chart of Accounts for Importing.xlsx

Select **Next**.

Figure 12.11

Mapped fields for account import

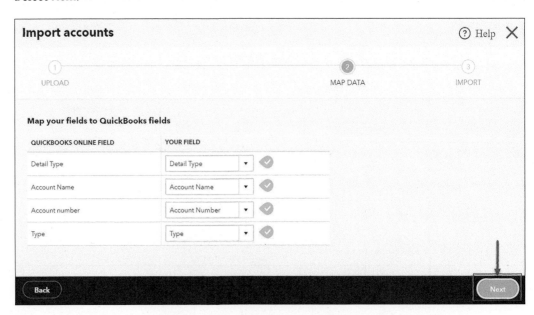

Ensure the fields in the Excel file match the QBO fields and select **Next**.

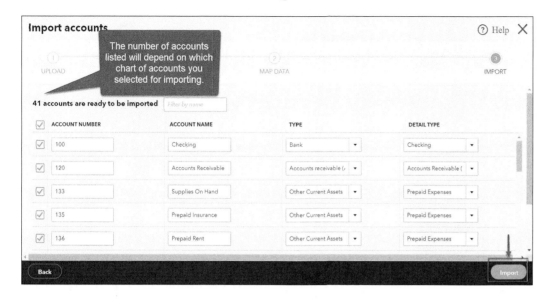

Figure 12.12

Accounts to be imported

Review the accounts in the list and correct any errors.
    Click **Import**.

Step 2—Activate Payroll

Before activating payroll, increase the cash balance to cover the payroll transactions you will be recording. (You wouldn't want to bounce a payroll check!) You can record a **deposit**, or you can create the following **journal entry**. The transaction date (either method) should be the first day of the **current** month (the month in which you're doing the assignment).

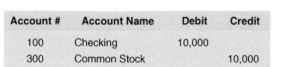

Account #	Account Name	Debit	Credit
100	Checking	10,000	
300	Common Stock		10,000

If you use a **deposit** form, you can leave the **RECEIVED FROM** and **PAYMENT METHOD** fields blank. **Common Stock** should be selected in the **ACCOUNT** field.
    To activate payroll, click **Payroll** on the navigation bar.

HINT: Payroll is a QBO feature that changes regularly. The order of setup may change and you may see additional questions or different screens. Use your best judgment when confronted with slight differences. If the differences are significant, check for updates at https://cambridgepub.com/book/qbo2021#ancillaries or check with your instructor.

Link to payroll
activation

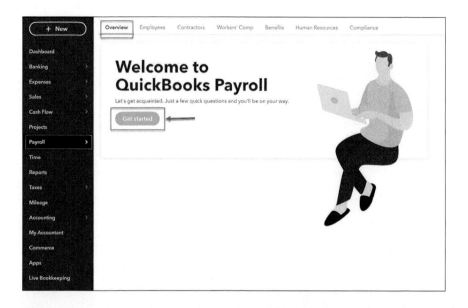

 HINT: If you see a screen asking you to select a specfic payroll plan, pick **Core**.

Click **Get started** on the **Overview** tab.

Question about prior
payroll in calendar year

Select **No** to answer the **Have you paid employees in 2021?** question. (If you're doing your homework in 2022, the question will ask about 2022!)

Click **Next**.

Identification of initial
pay date

Select the 15th of the current month when asked **When is your next payday?**. (Use the 15th even if it falls on a weekend.)

   Click **Next**.

Figure 12.16
Identification of
business location

Enter 3835 Freeport Blvd, Sacramento, CA, 95822 as the address for your payroll company.

   Click **Next**.

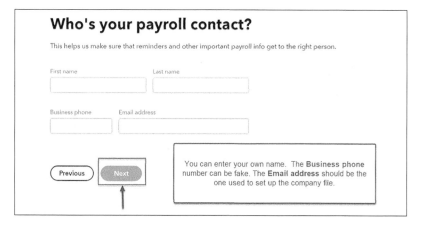

Figure 12.17
Identification of payroll
contact

The **Email address** field in the **Who's your payroll contact?** screen should be the one used to set up the company file. The other fields can be fake.

   Click **Next**.

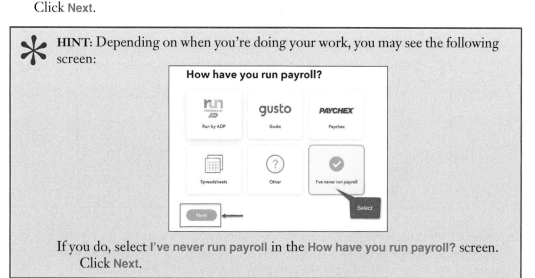

Figure 12.18

Add employee screen

Step 3—Add Employees

You will be adding two employees: Shaniya Montero and Abe Martin.

Click **Add employee**.

> ✳ **HINT:** QBO Payroll changes regularly. The order and wording of the employee setup questions may be different in your company file. Keep in mind that QBO is asking for the basic employee information needed to process payroll (compensation, hire date, withholdings, time off policies, etc). Use your best judgment with confronted with slight differences. If the differences are significant, check for updates at https://cambridgepub.com/book/qbo2021#ancillaries or check with your instructor.

There are eight sections to be completed for each employee. In QBO, all the sections will appear on the same screen. To simplify the instructions, each section will be shown separately over the next pages.

Figure 12.19

Employee name screen

In Section 1, the employee's name is entered. For your first employee, enter Shaniya Montero as the employee name.

Figure 12.20

Employee hire date screen

In Section 2, the employee's hire data and work location are entered. Enter the first day of the **current month** as the **Hire date**. (The current month is the month in which you're completing the homework.) Leave the company address as the **Work Location**.

BEHIND THE SCENES QBO uses the hire date in determining whether a paycheck should be created for an employee during a particular payroll period.

In Section 3, the pay frequency is identified. Most companies will issue paychecks weekly, bi-weekly (every two weeks), or semi-monthly (twice a month).

Because Shaniya is the first employee, you'll need to create a company **pay schedule** first. Click **Create pay schedule**.

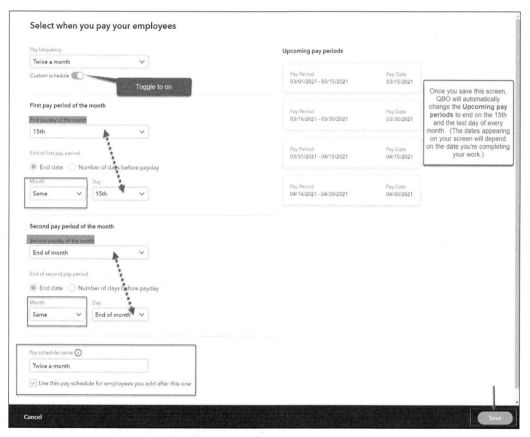

Select **Twice a Month** in the **Pay frequency** dropdown menu.

Toggle **Custom schedule** to on.

Select **15th** as the **First payday of the month** and **End of month** as the **Second payday of the month**. The **End dates** of the first and second pay periods are the 15th and the last day of the same month.

Enter "Twice a Month" as the **Pay schedule name** and check the **Use this pay schedule for employees you add after this one** box.

BEHIND THE SCENES Companies might pay groups of employees on different schedules (e.g., weekly for hourly employees, semi-monthly for salaried employees). Multiple **pay schedules** can be created in a QBO company file.

Click **Save**.

In Section 4, the types of compensation paid to the employee are identified.

Employee
compensation screen

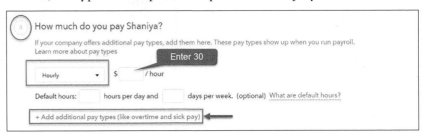

Shaniya is paid $30 per hour, so select **Hourly** in the compensation dropdown menu and enter "30" in the **/hour** box.

> **BEHIND THE SCENES** If an hourly employee normally works a set schedule (same hours and days per week), defaults can be entered in the employee record. Default hours will automatically be included in payroll processing. The hours can be changed before paychecks are created.

Click **+ Add additional pay types (like overtime and sick pay)**.

Identification of
additional types
of employee
compensation

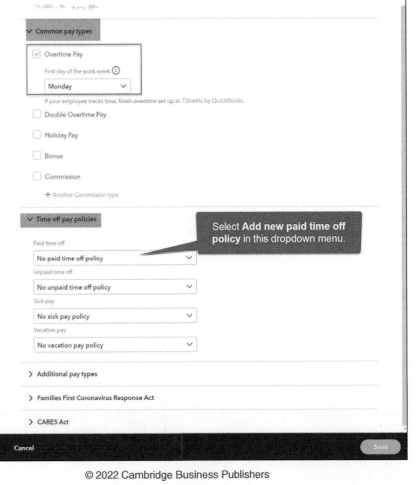

✳ **HINT:** Your screen may look like this:

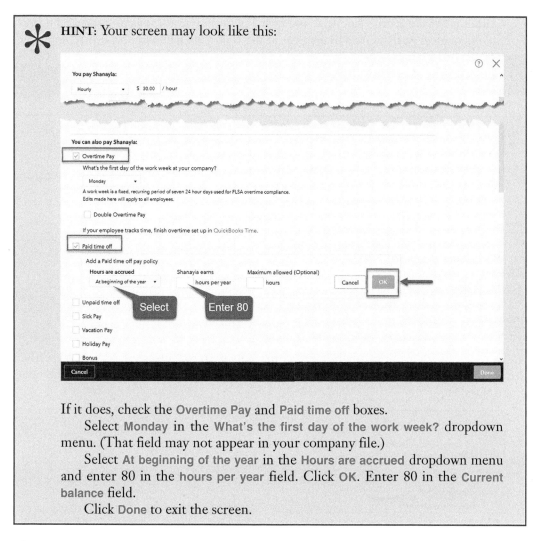

If it does, check the **Overtime Pay** and **Paid time off** boxes.

Select **Monday** in the **What's the first day of the work week?** dropdown menu. (That field may not appear in your company file.)

Select **At beginning of the year** in the **Hours are accrued** dropdown menu and enter 80 in the **hours per year** field. Click **OK**. Enter 80 in the **Current balance** field.

Click **Done** to exit the screen.

Check the **Overtime Pay** box. (QBO will automatically calculate **overtime pay** using 1.5 times the hourly rate.) Select **Monday** in the **First day of the work week** dropdown menu.

Select **Add new paid time off policy** in the **Paid time off** dropdown menu.

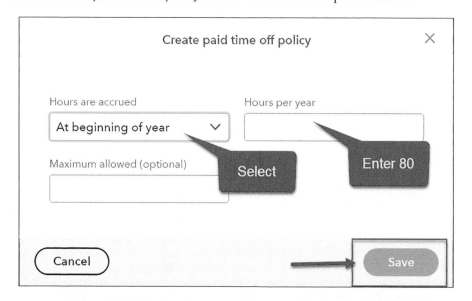

Figure 12.25

Paid time off options

Companies normally accrue paid time off each pay period or at the beginning of the year. For Shaniya, select **At beginning of the year** in the **Hours are accrued** dropdown menu and enter 80 as the **Hours per year**.

Click **Save**. Make sure 80 shows as in the **Current balance** field. Enter the amount if necessary.

> ✳ **HINT:** Depending on when you are doing your assignment, you may see additional options for employees/companies affected by COVID-19. You can ignore those.

Click **Save** to exit the **Add pay types** window.

> **BEHIND THE SCENES** Instead of a paid-time off (PTO) policy, some companies may separate sick and vacation pay. Under any of those policies, companies may elect to accrue hours at the beginning of the year, per pay period, per hour worked, or on the employee's anniversary date (date of hire). Companies may have different leave policies for different employees. QBO will track available leave time based on the pay policy identified in the employee's record.

In Section 5, withholdings (deductions) other than payroll taxes are identified. Other deductions might include medical insurance premiums, retirement plans, garnishments, union dues, etc.

Figure 12.26

Employee deductions screen

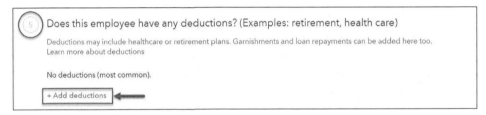

Click **+ Add deductions**.

Figure 12.27

Employee deduction options

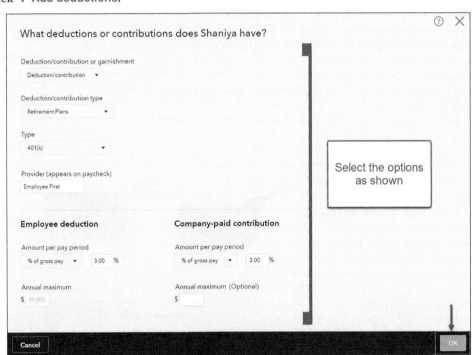

The only deductions (other than payroll taxes) in your payroll company will be a 401(k) plan administered by "Employee First" (the **provider**). Both the employee and the company will contribute 3% of gross pay per pay period to the plan.

Use Figure 12.27 as a guide when completing the deduction page.

Click **OK**.

BEHIND THE SCENES 401(k) plans can be solely funded by employees, solely funded by employers, or jointly funded. Contributions may be calculated as a percentage of wages or as a fixed amount per pay period. Employer contribution amounts are often capped by the company at a certain annual amount. The maximum annual contribution amount for employees is set by law. In 2021, the maximum was set at $19,500 ($26,000 for employees over age 50). If you're doing your work in 2022, the 2022 maximum will be displayed.

In Section 6, information from the W-4 completed by the employee is entered.

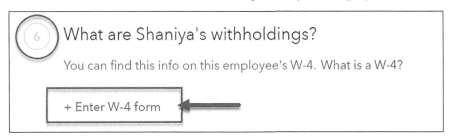

Figure 12.28

Employee withholdings screen

Click **+ Enter W-4 form**.

 HINT: You may get a message about changes in Form W-4. Information about the new W-4 and calculations of federal income tax withholding are included in the Hiring Employees section of this chapter.

Click **Got it** to move forward.

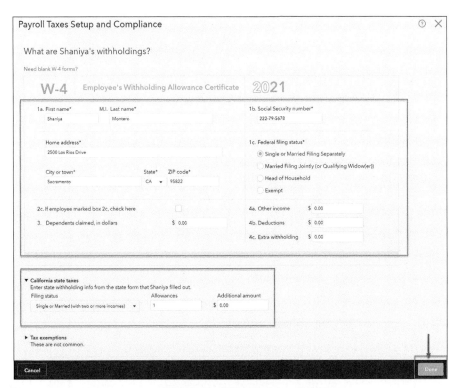

Figure 12.29

Required information for employee withholdings

The information entered in the **Payroll Taxes Setup and Compliance** screen is taken from the employee-completed W-4 form and, if applicable, the employee-completed state withholding form.

Shaniya provided the following information:

- Social security number: 222-79-5678.

- Address: 2500 Los Rios Drive, Sacramento, CA 95822.

- Federal filing status: **Single or Married Filing Separately**.

  - Shaniya has no dependents and does not want any additional monies withheld.

- California filing status: **Single or Married (with two or more incomes)**, 1 allowance, no additional monies withheld.

Click **Done**.

Birth date information is entered in Section 7.

Enter 08/21/1986 as Shaniya's birth date.

In Section 8, the compensation payment method is identified. QBO can be set up to handle direct deposit of employee checks. Employees can also be paid by paper check, which is the method used for this assignment.

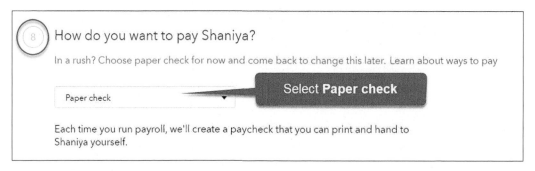

Select **Paper check** in the dropdown menu.

All sections for Shaniya are now completed.

Click **Done** (in the bottom right corner of the employee setup screen).

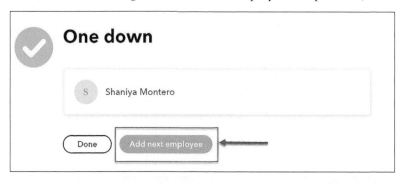

To add the second employee, click **Add next employee**.

  HINT: If Figure 12.32 does not appear, you will be in the Employee Center. Click **Add an employee** to move forward.

You will now go through the same sections for Abe Martin. This time, however, you will be able to use certain options (like **pay schedules**) that you created in the setup for Shaniya.

Use the following information to complete the eight sections:

Section 1	The second employee's name is Abe Martin. No email address is needed. Uncheck the employee invitation box.
Section 2	His hire date is the first day of the current month. His work location is the company address.
Section 3	Abe has the same twice-a-month pay schedule as Shaniya. NOTE: Depending on when you do the assignment, you may see the last day of the month identified in the screen, instead of the 15th. You will be able to change that when you process payroll.
Section 4	Abe is paid a salary of $55,000 per year and works 8 hours per day, 5 days per week. He's not eligible for overtime. He is eligible for paid time off. (This is an additional pay type.) Select **80 hours/year (accrued at start of year)**. His current paid time off balance should be 80 hours. Enter 80 if necessary.
Section 5	Add a deduction. In the first screen, select **Deduction/Contribution** in the first field, **Employee First - 401(k)** in the second field. The provider should default to Employee First. The contribution is 3% of gross pay for both Abe (the employee) and the company.
Section 6	Abe's social security number is 222-79-8765. His address is 1856 K Street, Sacramento, CA 95822. His federal filing status is: **Single or Married Filing Separately**. Abe has no dependents. His California status is: **Single or Married (with two or more incomes)**. California allowances are: 1 No additional monies are to be withheld for federal or state income taxes.
Section 7	Abe's birth date is 07/23/1991.
Section 8	Abe will be paid with a paper check.

Click **Done** in the bottom right corner of the screen.

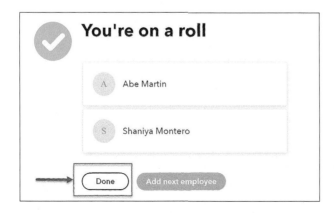

Click **Done**.

Figure 12.34

Continue setup screen

Click **Continue setup**.

Figure 12.35

Workers' Comp screen

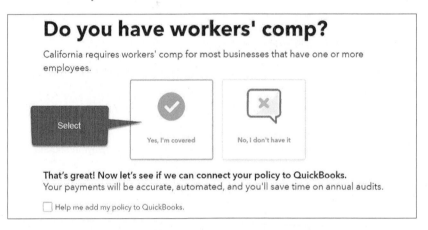

Additional questions may appear depending on the address of the employer. In California, a workers' compensation plan is required. You won't be working with workers' compensation in this assignment.

Click **Yes, I'm covered** to move forward.

Click **Next**. You should now be in the Employee Center.

Figure 12.36

Payroll Center

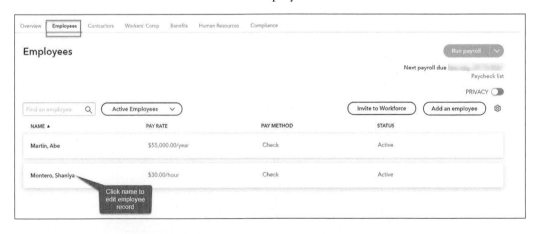

Employees are managed on the Employees tab of the Employee Center.

Editing and terminating employees

To edit an employee, click his/her name in the **Employees** tab of the Employee Center.

If no paychecks have been issued for the employee, you will be returned to the eight-step employee entry screen shown in Figures 12.19 to 12.31. Edits can be made in any of the sections.

If a paycheck has been issued for the employee, Figures 12.37 through 12.39 will be displayed.

Figure 12.37

Employee details
screen example

There are three sections: **Pay**, **Profile**, and **Employment**.

If you click the pencil icon at the top of the **Pay** section, you will be returned to the eight-step entry screen (Figure 12.19).

If you click the pencil icon at the top of the **Profile** section, you can edit the employee's contact information, birth date, and gender.

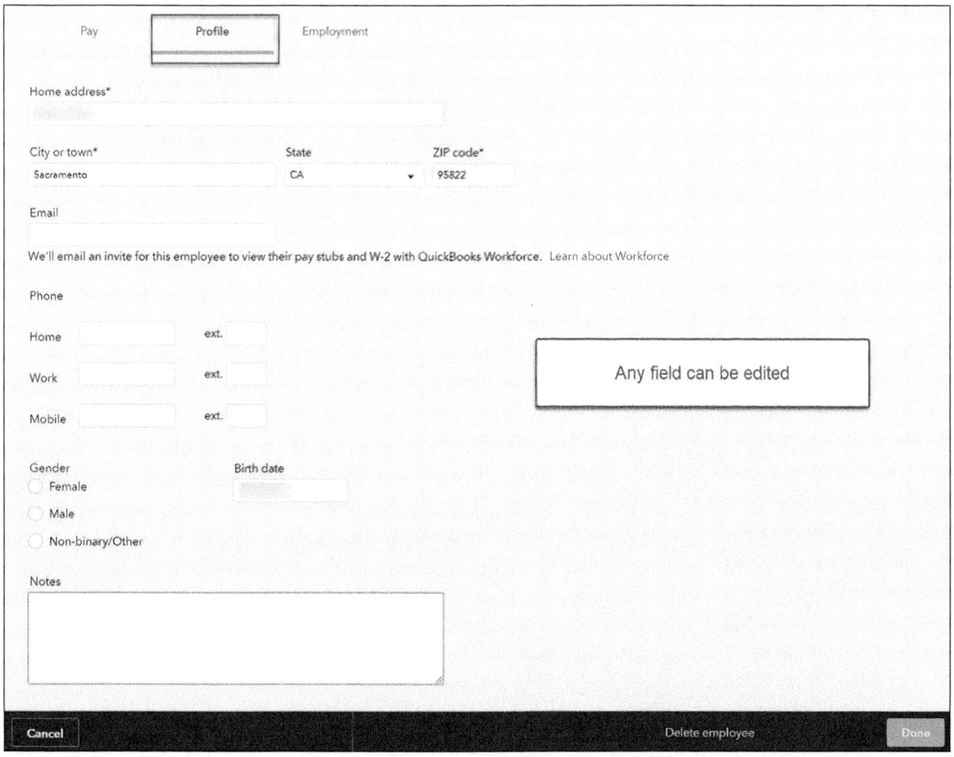

Figure 12.38

Employee profile
screen

Click the pencil icon at the top of the **Employment** section to edit the employee's status or work location or to enter or change the employee's title, hire date, identification number, or workers' compensation class.

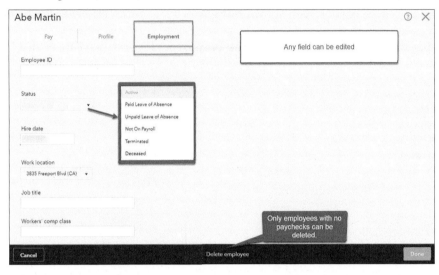

If an employee leaves the company (voluntarily or involuntarily), **Terminated** should be selected in the Status dropdown menu. A new **Termination date** field would automatically be added to the screen. Employees with a status of **Terminated**, **Deceased**, or **Not on payroll** would not be available for payroll processing.

Step 4—Finish the Payroll Setup

Entering federal and state payroll tax information and identifying the accounts to be debited and credited in payroll transactions is done next.

Click **Payroll** on the navigation bar and open the **Overview** tab of the Employee Center.

eLectures

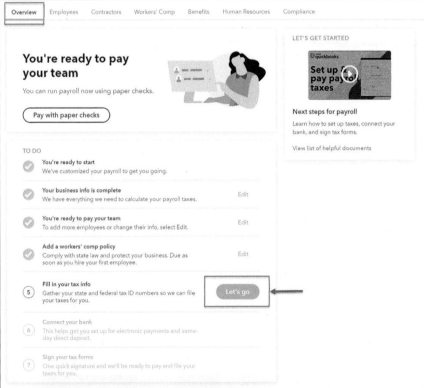

Click **Let's go** next to **Fill in your tax info**.
There are three tabs in the tax setup window.

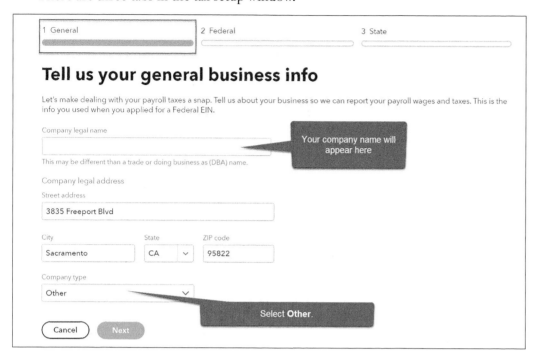

Figure 12.41

General tab of payroll
taxes setup screen

The company name and address fields on the **General** tab will autofill. **Other** should
be selected as the **Company type**. (Your company is not a sole proprietorship or nonprofit
corporation, the only other options in the dropdown menu.)

Click **Next**.

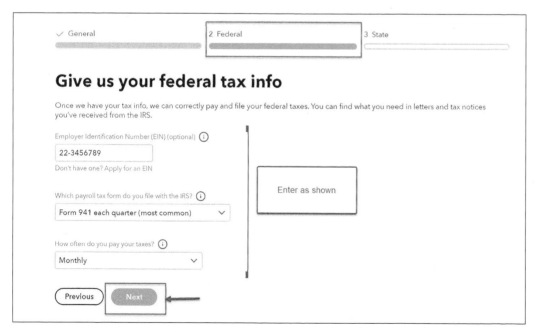

Figure 12.42

Federal tab of payroll
taxes setup screen

Federal payroll tax information is entered next. Your company's employer identification number is 22-3456789.

You file Form 941 quarterly. Payroll taxes are deposited monthly.

Click **Next** to enter state payroll tax information.

Figure 12.43

State tab of payroll
taxes setup screen

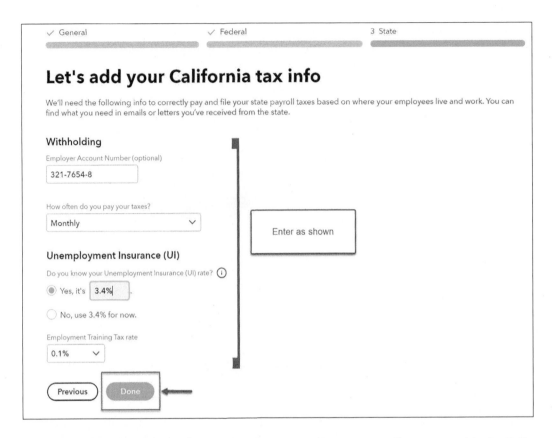

Figure 12.44

Link to payroll settings
screen

Your state employer number is 321-7654-8. You deposit payroll taxes monthly. In California, employers pay for unemployment insurance. Your company's UI rate is 3.4%. The Employment Training Tax rate is 0.1%.

Click **Done**.

The final setup steps, including identifying the accounts to be debited and credited in payroll transactions, are done in **Payroll Settings**.

Click the ⚙ on the icon bar.

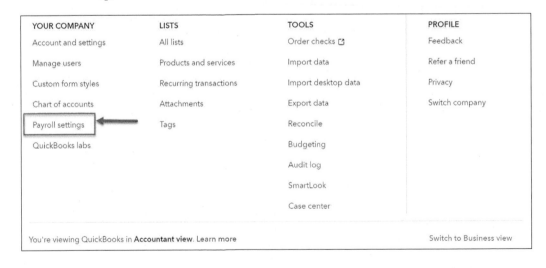

Click **Payroll Settings**.

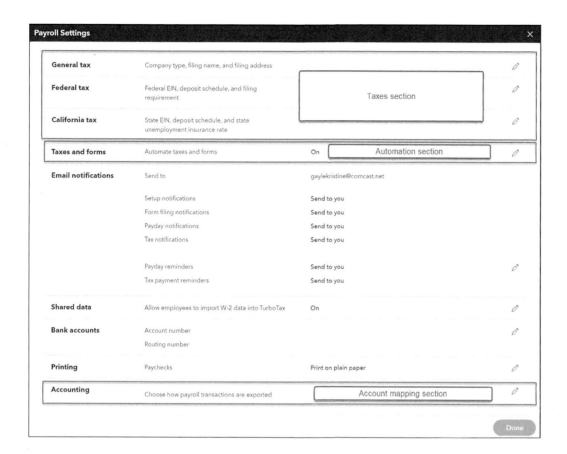

Figure 12.45

Payroll Setting screen

Open the **Taxes and forms** section to turn off automation in QBO payroll processing.

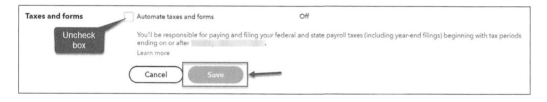

Figure 12.46

Payroll automation option

Uncheck the box next to **Automate taxes and forms**. A message letting you know that you won't be able to use QBO to file payroll taxes will pop up. You can ignore that.

Click **Save**.

Open the **Accounting** section.

Figure 12.47

Accounting preferences
screen

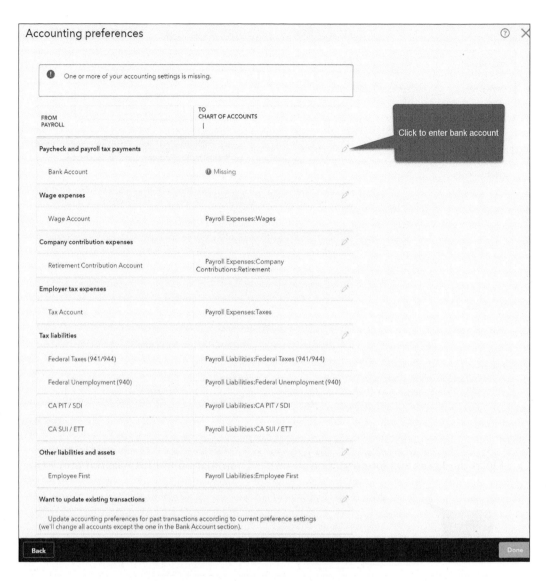

Click the pencil icon in the **Paycheck and payroll tax payments** section to select the account
QBO should credit in recording payroll and payroll tax payment transactions.

Figure 12.48

Checking account
selection

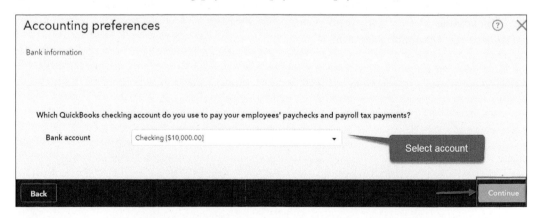

Select the checking account in the **Bank account** dropdown menu.

HINT: You should see the $10,000 balance figure on your screen. If you don't, check to make sure you made the deposit described at the beginning of Step 2 before moving on to Step 5.

In the remaining sections, you will be identifying the general ledger accounts that should be debited or credited in payroll transactions. For payroll expenses (wages, employer payroll taxes, and employer-paid benefits), users have the option of setting up separate accounts for individual employees, for different types of labor, different groups of taxes, etc. In your homework, you will be posting all payroll-related expenses to one of three accounts: Salaries & wages expense, Payroll tax expense, or Employee benefits expense.

Click the pencil icon in the **Wages expenses** section.

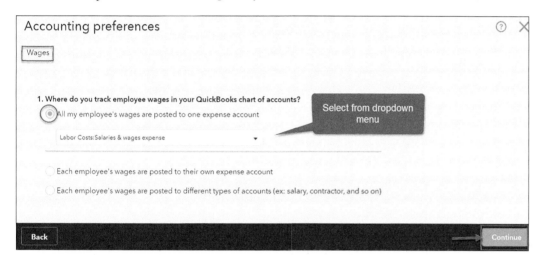

Figure 12.49

Wage distribution account

Select **Salaries & wages expense** (a subaccount of **Labor Costs**) as the account to be debited for compensation.

Click **Continue**.

Click the pencil icon in the **Company contribution expenses** section.

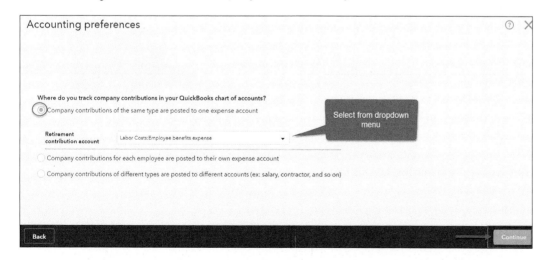

Figure 12.50

Employer-paid benefits distribution account

Select **Employee benefits expense** (a subaccount of **Labor Costs**) as the account to be debited for the company's 401(k) contributions.

Click **Continue**.

Click the pencil icon in the **Employer tax expenses** section.

Figure 12.51

Payroll tax distribution accounts

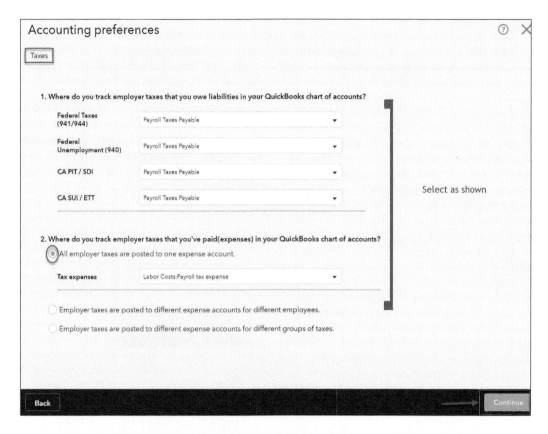

All payroll taxes (expense and liabilities) will be displayed.

Select the **Payroll Taxes Payable** account for all tax liability accounts. Select the **Payroll tax expense** (a subaccount of **Labor Costs**) account for employer payroll tax expenses.

Click **Continue**.

Click the pencil icon in the **Other liabilities and assets** section.

Figure 12.52

Other payroll-related distribution accounts

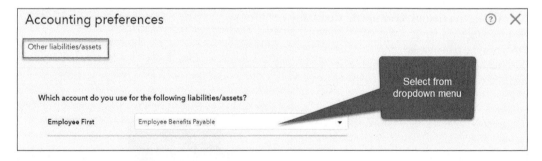

Select **Employee Benefits Payable** as the account to be credited for employee and employer retirement contribution liabilities.

Click **Continue**.

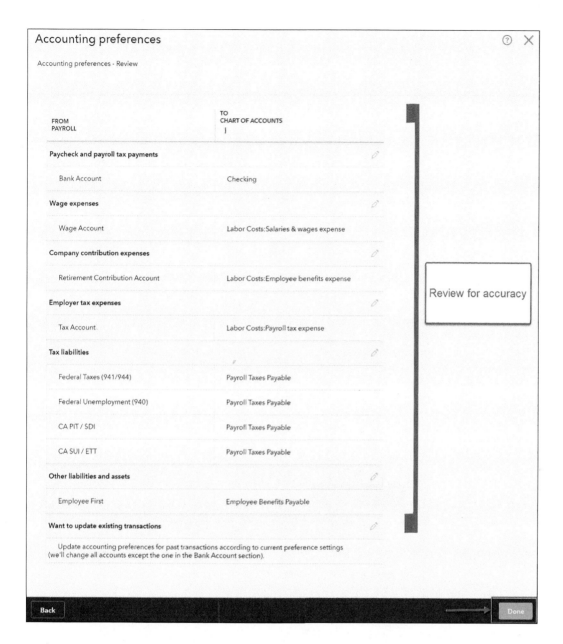

Figure 12.53

Completed accounting preferences

Make sure your accounts match those in Figure 12.53. Edit if necessary.
    Click **Done**.
    Click **Done** again to exit the **Payroll Settings** window.

Step 5—Process Payroll

Click **Payroll** on the navigation bar and open the **Employees** tab.

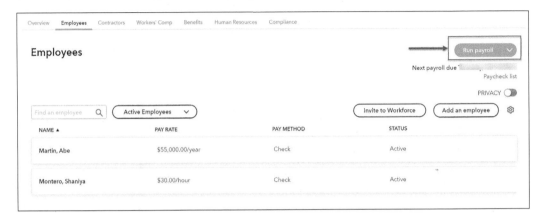

> ✱ **HINT:** You may get a message about E-sign legal authorization forms. If so, click the link and click **Cancel**, not **Verify**, on the next screen. Click **Done** if necessary.

Click **Run payroll**.

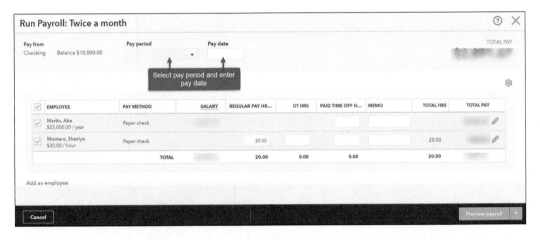

Select the first through the 15th of the **current** month in the **Pay period** field.

If you are completing your assignment before the 15th of the month, enter the 15th in the **Pay date** field. If you are completing your assignment after the 15th, enter the current date as the **Pay date**. (QBO will not allow you to use a paycheck date earlier than the current date. The pay period covered is not affected by a difference in the pay date.)

Enter 20 in the **REGULAR PAY HRS** box for Shaniya. (Abe's salary will autofill.)

Click **Preview payroll**.

Figure 12.56

Review screen for
payroll

A summary of the payroll (wages, payroll taxes, and other deductions) will appear on the next screen.

   Paychecks can be edited. To edit a **paycheck** (before it's processed), click the pencil icon in the **NET PAY** column. Users cannot edit payroll tax amounts, but hours and certain other deductions can be changed. You will not be editing any **paychecks**.

   Click **Submit payroll**.

Figure 12.57

Identification of payroll
check numbers

The final step is to enter the numbers of the paper checks. Use 2001 for Abe Martin and 2002 for Shaniya Montero.

   Click **Finish payroll**.

   To process payroll for the second half of the month, click **Payroll** on the navigation bar and select the **Employees** tab.

Figure 12.58

Link to run payroll
through Employee
Center

Click **Run payroll** and repeat the process used in recording payroll for the first half of the month.

In the first screen, select the second half of the current month in the **Pay period** drop-down menu and enter the last day of the current month in the **Pay date** field.

Enter 32 regular hours and 2 overtime hours for Shaniya. Abe's salary will autofill.

Click **Preview payroll**.

Verify that total hours for Shaniya are 34 and click **Submit payroll**.

In the final screen, enter 2003 as the paycheck number for Abe and 2004 as the paycheck number for Shaniya.

Click **Finish payroll**.

Step 6—Remit Payroll Taxes

Click **Taxes** on the navigation bar and open the **Payroll Tax** tab.

Figure 12.59

Payroll tax center

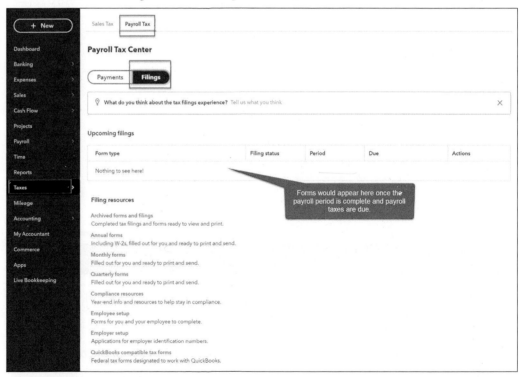

The Payroll Tax Center includes two tabs: **Filings** and **Payments**.

On the **Filings** tab, there are links to a variety of resources, including information about filing requirements and COVID-19 payroll programs. There are also links to standard employee and employer federal and state compliance forms and links to completed, ready-for-filing tax forms.

Because you are processing payroll in the current month, you should not see any tax forms listed in the **Upcoming filings** section. Forms appear once a payroll period is completed and payroll taxes are due.

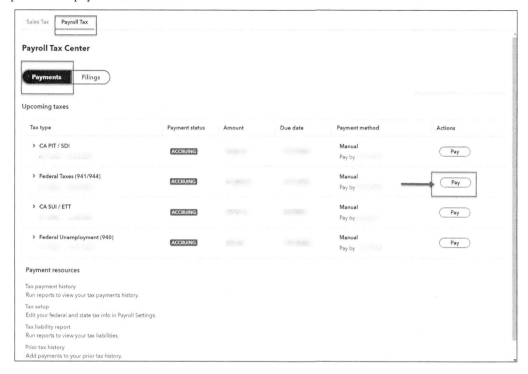

Figure 12.60

Payment tab in Payroll Tax Center

On the **Payments** tab, liabilities to date and future payment dates are displayed. QBO does allow users to pay accrued payroll taxes in advance.

Click **Pay** on the **Federal Taxes (941/944)** row.

You will receive a message warning you against paying payroll taxes before the tax period has ended. Click **Continue**.

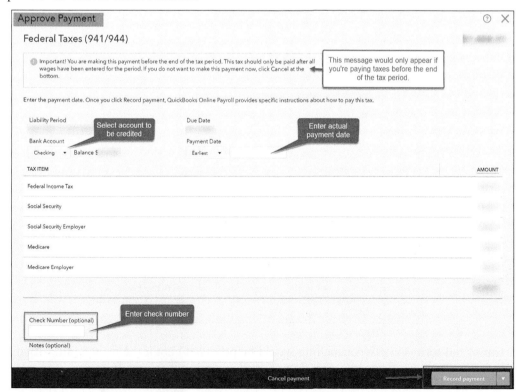

Figure 12.61

Payroll tax payment screen

The calculated tax amounts (employer and employee totals) will be listed on the **Approve Payment** screen.

Select Checking in the **Bank Account** dropdown menu and select **Other** in the **Payment Date** dropdown menu. Enter the last day of the current month in the date field. Enter 1001 as the **Check Number**.

Click **Record payment**.

Figure 12.62

Payroll tax payment confirmation

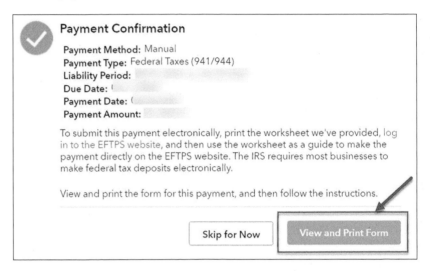

Payment details are included on the confirmation screen. Users can also print a form from this screen that can be used when submitting electronic payments to the taxing authority.

Figure 12.63

Federal tax deposit worksheet

A completed form suitable for mailing would be provided here if the taxing authority did not accept electronic payments. You do not need to print out the worksheet.

Step 7—Access Payroll Reports

To view available payroll reports, click **Reports** on the navigation bar.

Payroll reports are included in the **Payroll** section on the **Standard** reports tab.

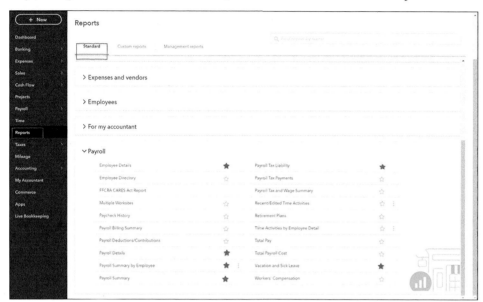

Figure 12.64

Payroll section of reports menu

Commonly used payroll reports are starred in Figure 12.64.

 HINT: On some payroll reports, the options to print or save to PDF are included in the **Share** dropdown menu in the top right corner of the report.

CHAPTER SHORTCUTS

Add an employee

1. Click **Payroll**
2. Open **Employees** tab
3. Click **Add an employee**

Edit an employee

1. Click **Payroll**
2. Open **Employees** tab
3. Click the name of employee to change
4. Click the pencil icon in the section to be edited

Pay an employee

1. Click **+ New** on the navigation bar
2. Click **Payroll**

Edit a paycheck

1. Click **Employees**
2. Click employee name to open employee record
3. Click **Paycheck list**
4. Click paycheck to be changed
5. Click **Edit**

CHAPTER REVIEW

Matching

Match the term or phrase (as used in QuickBooks Online) to its definition.

1. employee status
2. payroll settings
3. pay type
4. pay frequency

5. paycheck
6. pay policies
7. pay schedule
8. profile

Homework
MBC

Assignments with the MBC are available in myBusinessCourse.

_____   a category of compensation

_____   transaction type used to record wage payments to employees

_____   tool available to pay employees in specific cycles

_____   how often employee wages are paid

_____   section in employee record where contact information and birth date are recorded

_____   place where preferences for tax, pay policies, and payroll accounts are identified

_____   indicator of employee's current standing as an employee

_____   available paid time off benefits offered by a company

Multiple Choice

1. W-4 information for new employees is entered in which section of the new employee setup?
   a. Does employee have any deductions?
   b. What are the employee's withholdings?
   c. What are the employee's personal details?
   d. Personal info.

2. Which of the following statements is true?
   a. Employees are limited to one **pay type**.
   b. An employee must be identified as either a salaried, hourly, or commission only employee.
   c. Salaried employees would never be eligible for overtime pay.
   d. Hourly employees can be assigned only one hourly pay rate.

3. Which of the following taxes are paid by both the employee and the employer?
   a. Federal withholding
   b. Federal unemployment
   c. FICA
   d. State withholding (if applicable)

4. Taxes withheld from employees are:
   a. remitted on or before the tax report due date, depending on the size of the employer.
   b. always remitted monthly.
   c. always remitted within three days of issuing paychecks.
   d. always remitted with the tax report.

5. Which of the following is not an expense of the employer?
   a. State unemployment
   b. Federal unemployment
   c. FICA
   d. All of the above are expenses of the employer.

BEYOND THE CLICKS—THINKING LIKE A MANAGER

Accounting: The sales manager is deciding between two possible compensation structures for sales staff. Under one plan, salespeople would receive a base compensation of $80,000 per year plus a 1% commission on all sales to their customers. Under the other plan, the base compensation would drop to $40,000 per year, but the commission rate would increase to 5%. What are the advantages and disadvantages, to the **company**, of both plans? As the accounting manager, would you have a preference? Why or why not?

Information Systems: Payroll functions in QBO include: adding and editing employee information (pay rates, leave policies, etc.), processing payroll, and managing payroll settings. Currently, users either have full access or no access to payroll functions. Name two ways an employee with full access to the payroll functions could commit fraud. What could a company do to prevent or detect the fraud examples you identified? (Assume you can't reprogram QBO!)

ASSIGNMENT

Suggested reports for Chapter 12 after completing the PAYROLL SYSTEM WALK-THROUGH section of this chapter

Assignment 12

TIP: Click Share in the top right corner of the report and select Export to Excel or Printer Friendly to save or print your report. PDFs can be created by clicking Printer Friendly and selecting Save as PDF in the dropdown menu at the top of the print screen. (Click Print to open the menu.)

- Payroll Details
  - For the pay period ending on the 15th
  - For the pay period ending on the last day of the month

- Employee Details

- Payroll Tax Liability
  - For the 1st through the last day of the payroll month

- Payroll Summary by Employee
  - For the 1st through the last day of the payroll month
  - Check the **Hour** and **Rate** boxes next to **Run Report**.

QuickBooks

SECTION SIX

Cognitive Technologies, Data Analysis, and QBO

Ever since humans first started engaging in trade and barter activities that involved shipping goods or selling/purchasing on account, some sort of recordkeeping has been required. Archaeologists have found evidence of trading records, dating back thousands of years, in Egyptian and Mesopotamian civilizations. Once there were records, the data from those records started to be used to highlight operating results and financial positions.

As commerce grew and transactions became more complex, accounting systems became more sophisticated. The first accounting "textbook," written by Luca Pacioli and published in 1494, explained the double-entry bookkeeping system you learned in your introductory financial accounting course. Pacioli didn't just give the rules, though; he also explained the purpose of the system. He wrote, "If you are in business and do not know all about it, your money will go like flies, that is, you will lose it." Sage advice!

Fast-forward 525+ years. If Pacioli were alive today, he might be overwhelmed by how much company owners can "know" about their business.

This section looks at new types and sources of information and new tools for analyzing that information.

Chapter 13 covers the growth in data available for analysis, new technologies, and how Intuit uses these technologies in QBO to increase automation and provide additional management tools.

Chapter 14 covers various types and tools of data analysis and when they might be used. Best practices for communicating insights to management are also covered.

Big Data, Cognitive Technologies, and QBO

Objectives

After completing Chapter 13, you should be able to:

1. Explain what constitutes Big Data, identify types and sources of data, and describe how that data is processed.

2. Describe the types and uses of artificial intelligence.

3. Identify examples of cognitive technologies in QBO software.

4. Describe privacy and ethical issues related to Big Data and cognitive technologies.

WHAT IS BIG DATA?

Data is defined in the Merriam-Webster dictionary as "factual information . . . used as a basis for reasoning, discussion, or calculation." Data can be quantitative (numerical) or qualitative (non-numerical). Quantitative information is used to measure or count. Qualitative data is used to classify or categorize.

There is no standard, agreed-upon definition of **Big Data**. However, big data is generally understood to mean a set of high-volume, high-variety, and high-velocity information. Gartner, a leading research and advisory company, defined big data as "data that contains great variety, arriving in increasing volumes, with ever-higher velocity." Some data scientists and researchers add "unknown veracity" as another characteristic of big data.

> **BEHIND THE SCENES** If you want a visual of high-volume, high-velocity, and high-variety data, go to internetlivestats.com. Internet Live Stats, an international team of researchers and analysts, collects data from several different sources and uses statistical analysis tools to make real-time estimates of the total amounts of various types of data. For example, on January 5, 2021, at 10:00 am, it was estimated that more than 111 billion emails had been sent, and more than 37 million photos had been uploaded to Instagram **so far that day**. In the next three hours, another 36 billion emails were sent, and another 12 million images were uploaded.

In big data, **volume** refers to the amount of data. According to **IDC** (a global provider of research and advisory information)[1], there were 33 available zettabytes of data globally in 2018. IDC predicted that the amount of data would increase to 175 zettabytes by 2025. (Just so you know, there are 21 zeros in one zettabyte.) Massive amounts of data cannot be managed on a single machine. They must be stored in clusters over multiple physical or virtual machines.

Variety refers to the type and source of data. Data can include numbers, symbols, words, sounds, or video—any information that can be stored in digital form. Data might be generated from business software applications, posts on social media, phone calls, smartwatches, industrial machines, employee suggestion boxes, and so on. Big data would typically include different types of data coming from a number of different sources.

Velocity refers to the speed at which the data is being produced. The amount of data is not only growing; it's growing exponentially as more people gain internet access, and more technology is created that connects humans to machines and machines to machines. Collecting and processing data is complicated by the speed at which that data is generated.

Veracity refers to the quality (accuracy) of the data. Data quality can be negatively affected by untrustworthy data sources, inconsistent or missing data, statistical biases, and human error.

In summary, a collection of data, a dataset, would be considered "big data" if:

- The dataset is too large to be managed by traditional methods.
- The dataset includes a variety of data types from a variety of sources.
- The amount of data in the dataset is expanding rapidly.
- The accuracy and reliability of the data may be uncertain.

More about Types and Sources of Big Data

There are three basic types of data:
- Structured data
  - Highly organized, resides in a tabular format (rows and columns)
  - Easy to search, sort, or combine

---

[1] Reinsel, Gantz, Rydning, *The Digitization of the World From Edge to Core*, IDC, November 2018.

- Unstructured data
  - No pre-defined structure
  - Difficult to search, sort, or combine
- Semi-structured data
  - Doesn't reside in a tabular format but contains tags or markers that can be used in search functions
  - Moderately difficult to search, sort, or combine

Examples of Data Types		
Structured	**Unstructured**	**Semi-structured**
Accounting data	Images	Dates and sender/recipient information in emails
Customer/Vendor data	Social media posts	Tags used to identify location or dates of videos/images
Employee data	Videos	Tabs in webpages (Home, Contact, etc.)
Inventory/Shipping data	Audio files	
	Content portion of emails	
	Text portion of webpages	

IDC estimates that 80 to 90 percent of worldwide data is unstructured. Although big data can include all three types of data, unstructured data is the most high-volume, high-variety, and high-velocity.

Data can be:

- derived from a company's IT systems (accounting, human resources, production, etc.).
- streamed from smart devices (medical devices, industrial equipment, wearables, etc.).
- obtained from customers through their activities in web applications.
  - Spotify, Amazon, and Uber are examples of companies that use data from customer search and purchase activity.
- obtained from other companies through application programming interfaces (APIs). APIs act as intermediaries between two companies (the company application or server requesting specific information and the company application or server providing the requested information).
  - QBO has an API that is used by third parties to develop and manage software that can be integrated with QBO.
- accessed through open data sources like the US government's data.gov (https://www.data.gov/).
  - There are over 215,000 datasets on Data.gov. One dataset included information from consumer complaints made to the Federal Communications Commission (FCC) since 2014. Complaints about telemarketing calls were some of the most common!

Processing Big Data (Extracting, Transforming, and Loading)

Combining and then organizing structured, semi-structured, and unstructured data results in a powerful source of information for organizations.

There are many different data processing tools and systems. Most of them involve three steps.

- Data is copied or exported from the various data sources.
  - Sources could include accounting software systems, sensors from factory equipment, survey data, etc.
  - Known as **extracting** data
- Inconsistent, inaccurate, or duplicated data is corrected or removed.
  - Known as **transforming** data
- Data is stored in a centralized repository.
  - Known as **loading** data

The first step is to **extract** useable data from the data source(s). Structured data is already in a row/column format, but unstructured or semi-structured data is not. The extraction process for non-structured data requires some translation work.

Let's say a company wants to look at customer satisfaction data for its various products or services. Customer comments posted to its website might be a great source of information. Artificial intelligence algorithms (discussed in the next section) could be used to analyze the words in the comments and translate the text into one of three categories (satisfied, unsatisfied, neutral). The extracted data might now show comment ID numbers in rows; product and satisfaction levels in columns. (Company employees could also read all the comments and manually create a dataset, but that might take a lot of time!)

In many data processing systems, **transforming** the data is the second step. An essential part of the data transformation process is **data cleaning** (removing duplicates and empty (null) rows and columns and identifying and correcting inconsistencies). Changes to the data itself might also be necessary. For example, single columns might be split into multiple columns, or data values might be reformatted. For example, a field defining sales regions using a numeric code might be changed to a text field using the region name. Mapping data from multiple sources might also be part of the transformation process.

Data warehouse
Large repository of processed data collected from different sources.

Data lake Large repository of raw data collected from different sources.

If the extracting and transforming steps are done first, the data is typically loaded into a **data warehouse**. This approach is known as ETL (extract, transform, load). Various users within the organization can access the data warehouse to create smaller databases for internal use.

Some companies reverse the order of the last two steps. Data is loaded **before** it's transformed (ELT instead of ETL), and the extracted data is often loaded into a **data lake** instead of a data warehouse. Data lakes can hold both structured and unstructured data, so with ELT, much of the translation of unstructured data is done as part of the transformation process.

IBM, Microsoft, and Oracle are three companies that offer data processing platforms.

To make sense of the data, companies often use business analytics solutions like Tableau or Power BI. Excel can also be used. These software applications allow companies to turn datasets into interactive visualizations (in graphic and pictorial formats) that can be shared across organizations. Visualizations are discussed in Chapter 14.

WHAT IS ARTIFICIAL INTELLIGENCE AND HOW IS IT USED?

Artificial intelligence (AI) is the simulated capacity for abstract, creative, and deductive thought (human capabilities) in computer systems (machines). Although there are researchers involved in developing computers that can do **any** task a human can do (the theme of many science fiction movies and books!), most data science progress is in the area of Applied AI. In Applied AI, the focus is on developing computer systems that can carry out specific tasks (drive a car, take an order, classify a transaction, etc.) that humans would typically do.

AI is developed using machine learning and deep learning. Machine learning is a type of artificial intelligence based on the idea that systems can learn from data and can identify patterns. With machine learning, algorithms (sets of rules) are generated by the programmer. Training data is then fed into the computer, which uses the algorithms to classify the data. The computer's correct application of those rules improves as more data is examined. Algorithms can be changed but only by the programmer. **Amazon** uses machine learning to train systems to provide product recommendations to consumers based on their preferences. It's also used in assessing the veracity (quality) of big data and extracting structure from unstructured data.

Deep learning is a subset of machine learning. The difference is that with deep learning, the computer "learns" to modify the algorithms, to improve results, **without** programmer assistance.

Technologies that incorporate artificial intelligence are known as **cognitive technologies**. There are many different cognitive technologies (and the list is growing!), but here are some examples:

- Natural language processing (NLP)—enables computer systems to analyze and understand human language
  - Examples of usage: Voice text messaging, Siri, spell check
  - Developed using machine learning
- Object detection—enables computer systems to locate and classify objects
  - Examples of usage: video surveillance, self-driving vehicles
  - Developed using machine learning or deep learning
- Robotic process automation (RPA)—enables computer systems to perform repetitive, rules-based tasks (no "thinking" involved)
  - Examples of usage: Recurring entries, sending out monthly past due notices to customers
  - RPA itself is not an "intelligent" technology but can be combined with machine learning to expand the functionality

ARTIFICIAL INTELLIGENCE IN QBO

Intuit continues to develop QBO, and artificial intelligence plays a significant part in that development.

You have already worked with a variety of QBO processes that use cognitive technologies:

- Banking transaction downloads (Appendix 8A)
  - QBO first looks to match the downloaded transaction to an existing transaction
    - NLP (natural language processing) and RPA (robotic process automation) technologies would be involved
  - If no matching transaction is found, QBO "guesses" an appropriate general account
    - NLP and machine learning would be involved
- Scheduled recurring transactions (Chapter 9)
  - The rules are initially set by the user (frequency, account distributions, etc.). QBO automatically creates the transaction.
  - RPA would be involved
- Receipt capture (Chapter 11)
  - QBO first looks to match the receipt to an existing transaction
    - NLP and RPA technologies would be involved

> ▪ If no matching transaction is found, QBO identifies an appropriate general account based on the similarities in text or amounts to historical transactions.
>> ○ NLP and RPA technologies would be involved

Intuit started offering short-term loans to qualified customers several years ago. After customers complete the application process, cognitive technologies are used to analyze their creditworthiness.

PRIVACY AND ETHICAL ISSUES WITH BIG DATA

Big data and artificial intelligence are exciting topics, but with new technologies come new issues, not all of them positive.

Privacy (or lack of privacy) is of paramount concern. Think of the amount of information you're likely giving to an online retailer. Once you sign up, the company can track your purchases, use of coupons, returns, calls to customer support, address changes, when and how many times you visited the website, and what you looked at when you were on the site. Assumptions about your age, marital status, income, and whether or not you have children can be inferred from your purchasing history. You may or may not be aware of the information the retailer has collected. Even if you are aware, you may not realize how that information is being used or whom it's being shared with.

And that's just information provided to online retailers. The information many of us regularly post on social media sites can reveal much more about our lives. If in the wrong hands, that information can even be dangerous.

Data breach Release of confidential, sensitive, or protected information to unauthorized entities.

Companies have privacy concerns, as well. According to a study by IBM and Ponemon[2], the average global cost of a **data breach** in 2020 was $3.86 million. The industry with the highest average cost ($7.13 million) was healthcare. The country with the highest average cost ($8.64 million) was the United States. (The study was geographically limited. For example, it did not include data from China, Russia, and African countries other than South Africa.) The study found that the root cause of over 50 percent of the data breaches was a **malicious attack**. About 25 percent was due to system glitches, and the balance was due to human error.

Malicious attack Attempt to cripple or take over a computer system.

Breaches of company computer systems aren't the only privacy concern for businesses. Information intentionally or unintentionally leaked by employees or bad reviews posted by customers on social media or company websites can negatively affect future business.

There are also ethical concerns with AI.

With deep learning, algorithms can be changed without human intervention or awareness. That can lead to users being affected without any understanding of how or why the changes were made. Explainable AI (XAI) is a new field in deep learning. In XAI, data scientists are working on tracking the source and reasons behind algorithmic changes.

Built-in bias is another concern. AI systems "learn" from the datasets used in the training process. If a dataset reflects assumptions or preferences, the applications powered by that AI may result in suboptimal or discriminatory practices. That's of particular concern in applications used in recruiting, credit scoring, and judicial sentencing. In 2015, Amazon learned that its new recruiting software was not promoting women applicants. Why? It turns out that the dataset used to train the system consisted of resumes submitted to the company over the prior 20-year period. The vast majority of applicants during that period were men. Amazon's system had "learned" from the data that male candidates were preferable and proceeded to penalize resumes that included the word "women's" or were from candidates who attended all-women's colleges.

---

[2] IBM Security and Ponemon Institute LLC, *Cost of a Data Breach Report 2020*, July 2020.

Accountability for failures of AI will also need to be determined. If a patient dies after being misdiagnosed by medical software powered by AI, who is responsible? The doctor, the hospital, the data scientist? Or what if a self-driving car doesn't stop at a red light and damages another vehicle? Who should pay for that damage? The driver, the insurance company, the data scientist?

Finally, companies should consider the impact on employees as they automate more tasks using AI and terminate the employees who formerly did those tasks. Retraining is a possibility considered by many companies. Severance pay, job search assistance, and extended health benefits are other possible solutions.

CHAPTER REVIEW

Matching

Match the term or phrase (as used in this chapter) to its definition.

1.	volume	5.	cognitive technologies
2.	structured data	6.	veracity
3.	variety	7.	load
4.	extract	8.	data breach

_____   amount of data

_____   sources and types of data

_____   move data to a data warehouse

_____   tools that incorporate artificial intelligence

_____   accuracy of data

_____   copy or export data

_____   clearly formatted data

_____   unauthorized release of information

Homework
MBC

Assignments with the MBC are available in myBusinessCourse.

Multiple Choice

1. Which of the following might include both structured and unstructured data?
   a. Chart of accounts
   b. Email
   c. Report of sales by region
   d. Balance sheet

   Homework MBC

2. Which of the following is not a characteristic of big data?
   a. High-Volume
   b. High-Velocity
   c. High-Variety
   d. High-Veracity
   e. All of the above are characteristics of big data.

   Homework MBC

3. Removing duplicates in a dataset is often done as part of the _____ step.
   a. extract
   b. transform
   c. load
   d. Duplicates would never be included in a dataset.

   Homework MBC

4. Which of the following statements is true?
   a. Every transaction recorded in QBO involves some form of artificial intelligence.
   b. Machine learning was used in programming recurring journal entries in QBO.
   c. Object detection is used when receipts are uploaded to QBO.
   d. Natural language processing is used as part of the receipt capture in QBO.

5. Which of the following might result in a data breach?
   a. An employee checks their personal email on a company computer and opens an attachment.
   b. An external party hacks into a company computer using a stolen password.
   c. An employee sends a transaction file to the wrong person.
   d. Any of the above might result in a data breach.

BEYOND THE CLICKS—THINKING LIKE A MANAGER

Accounting: Your company has just announced its decision to significantly increase the number of AI-based technology tools used in the business within the next year. Your accounts receivable, accounts payable, and payroll clerks have expressed deep concerns to you about losing their jobs. What could the company do to alleviate their fears? Should they?

Information systems: Your company has just announced its decision to significantly increase the number of AI-based technology tools used in the business within the next year. You were not included in the group that made that decision, but the company president has asked you to take over from here and manage the transition. What is the first thing you might do?

ASSIGNMENT

All 2023 sales transactions for your company (Math Revealed! or Salish Software Solutions) are included in an Excel file.

1. Extract the appropriate Excel file from the Cambridge Business Publishers website (https://cambridgepub.com/book/qbo2021#ancillaries).

2. Transform the data. **TIP:** Detailed instructions for completing this step are included on the Cambridge website (https://cambridgepub.com/book/qbo2021#ancillaries).
   a. Remove the address from the Customer field. (Only the customer name is needed.)
   b. Remove any duplicate transactions.
   c. Resolve inconsistencies in the Product Name column.
   d. Complete any missing fields.

3. Load the sales transactions into QBO using the Import process. **TIP:** Importing invoices was done in Chapter 2.

4. Determine the following using the cleaned data:
   a. Total revenue for the year
   b. Average unit price
   c. Number of customers

Data Analytics and Data Visualization

Objectives

After completing Chapter 14, you should be able to:

1. Identify and define the four types of data analytics.

2. Compare various data analysis tools.

3. Describe best practices in data visualizations.

4. Explain the impact of new technologies on careers in accounting.

Data analysis went on long before anyone had heard of "big data" and long before artificial intelligence existed anywhere outside of science fiction. For example, Henry Ford used analytics in measuring the speed of automobile assembly lines in the early 1900s.

The first data analysis projects, of course, were done manually (with pencil and paper!) using an organization's data and data found in books and periodicals. Once productivity software like Excel became available, accountants could key in financial information from the internal accounting records and from outside sources and then quickly categorize and summarize that data.

New technologies like those discussed in Chapter 13 now make it possible for us to include financial and non-financial data from various sources in the analysis process.

WHAT IS DATA ANALYTICS?

Data analytics involves examining data to draw conclusions and insights from that data. There are four primary types of data analytics.

- **Descriptive analytics**
  - Used to answer the question: "What happened?"

- **Diagnostic analytics**
  - Used to answer the question: "Why did it happen?"

- **Predictive analytics**
  - Used to answer the question: "What is likely to happen in the future?"

- **Prescriptive analytics**
  - Used to answer the question: "What is the best course of action?"

Descriptive analytics address what, how many, where, and when type questions. Historical accounting reports are the basis for much of the descriptive analytics in a business. In QBO, you're using descriptive analytics when you:

- prepare a profit and loss report

- prepare an inventory valuation detail report

Diagnostic analytics involves drilling down on information to determine **why** something occurred. In QBO, a budget variance report can be used to identify why the company's net income was lower than expected. Maybe a particular revenue source was down, or a specific expense category was up. In Excel, PivotTables can be used for this purpose. For example, suppose a dataset included information about sales dollars by location and the location store manager's years of experience. A PivotTable might illustrate that sales dollars are lower at locations where the store manager is new. Similar analytic tools are available in other types of software.

Predictive analytics is all about identifying trends and relationships. Predictive analytics often uses statistical modeling techniques. For example, suppose a dataset included information from the past two years about sales dollars by product, month, and store. Statistical modeling techniques could be used to determine how closely the month and the store location correlates to (tracks with) sales of specific products. If a strong correlation exists, the store manager could use that information to estimate revenues for the next quarter.

Prescriptive analytics uses information from descriptive, diagnostic, and predictive analytics to suggest the best course of action in a specific scenario. For example, a retail company could use prescriptive analytics to determine the most appropriate product mix to place on the shelves at each of their stores. As part of the process, modern prescriptive analytics uses multiple types of artificial intelligence systems. Self-driving cars are examples of prescriptive analytics in action. The car's computer might use video data, audio data, GPS, and LiDAR in determining when to turn, when to go straight, and when to stop.

> **BEHIND THE SCENES** LiDAR (light detection and ranging) is a tool for measuring distance. In self-driving cars, LiDAR works by sending out laser pulses (light waves) from a sensor on the vehicle. The light waves collide with objects in the surrounding area (other cars, pedestrians, curbs, signs, etc.) and return to the sensor. The LiDAR system then determines how long it took the light waves to reach the object and return to the vehicle sensor and calculates the distance between the vehicle and the object using the speed of light. Uber and Toyota are currently using LiDAR and cameras to map out the surrounding area. Tesla currently uses radar and cameras. (Radar uses radio waves instead of light waves.)

TOOLS FOR DATA ANALYSIS

Analysis Tools in QBO

As noted in **WHAT IS DATA ANALYTICS?**, there are many reports in QBO Plus that can be used for descriptive and diagnostic analytics.

In QBO Advanced, a version of QBO, users have access to Fathom, an interactive business analytics tool capable of descriptive, diagnostic, and predictive data analytics. Fathom also allows users to develop benchmarks (standards) that can be used to review overall operations and to compare performance between locations or even customers.

Fathom is also available in QBO Accountant, a version of QBO used by accountants and bookkeepers with multiple clients. QBO Accountant is probably also used by your instructor.

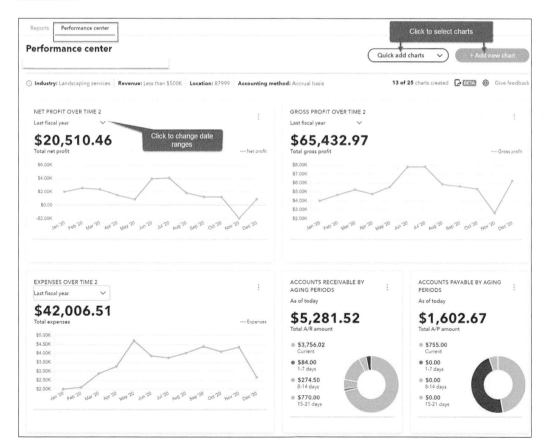

Figure 14.1

Business Performance screen in QBO Accountant

Figure 14.1 gives you a partial view of the **Performance center** screen in QBO Accountant. In addition to revenue, expense, and profitability graphs, users can view standard financial ratios (gross profit margin, current ratio, days in accounts receivable, etc.) over time. Industry data is also available for comparative purposes.

Although Fathom is not available in QBO Plus, several different analytics apps can be purchased as add-ons. To review the options, click **Apps** on the navigation bar and type "analytics" in the search field or select **Perform Analytics** in the **Browse category** dropdown menu.

Analysis Tools in Spreadsheet Programs

There are many different analysis tools in spreadsheet programs like Microsoft Excel and Google Sheets. In this section, we'll be looking at a **few** Excel tools available in Microsoft 365. Many of these are also available in older versions of Excel. Similar tools would be available in other spreadsheet programs.

PivotTables

Many of you are already familiar with **PivotTables**. PivotTables are interactive summaries of data found in a spreadsheet. Using PivotTable tools, data can be grouped, filtered, and rearranged in nearly endless ways.

Figure 14.2

PivotTable tool

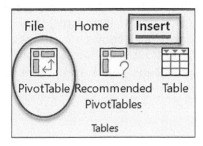

To create a PivotTable, highlight (select) the data to be analyzed on the spreadsheet. Open the **Insert** tab on the **Ribbon** (main menu bar in Excel) and select **PivotTable** in the **Tables** group.

A simple PivotTable for a company with multiple locations and sales representatives might look something like this:

Figure 14.3

Example of a PivotTable in Excel

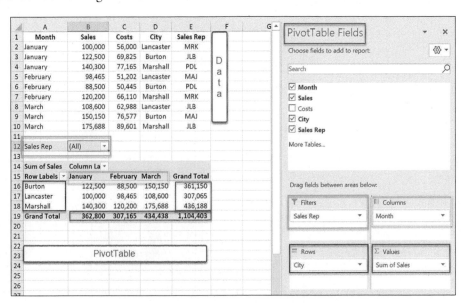

PivotTables are most useful in answering "why" type questions (performing diagnostic analytics). For example, in Figure 14.3, company management can quickly answer questions about why sales totaled over $1 million. They can see that the Marshall location had the most sales overall, that sales dropped in all cities in February, and that sales almost doubled in Burton between February and March. The filter field could be used to see the sales by month and city for individual sales reps. The PivotTable could also be modified to show cities in columns with month and sales reps in rows. Charts (known as PivotCharts) can be directly created from PivotTables. Changes in the dataset automatically update related PivotTables and PivotCharts.

Correlation and Regression Functions

Two commonly used predictive analytics tools in Excel are correlation and regression.

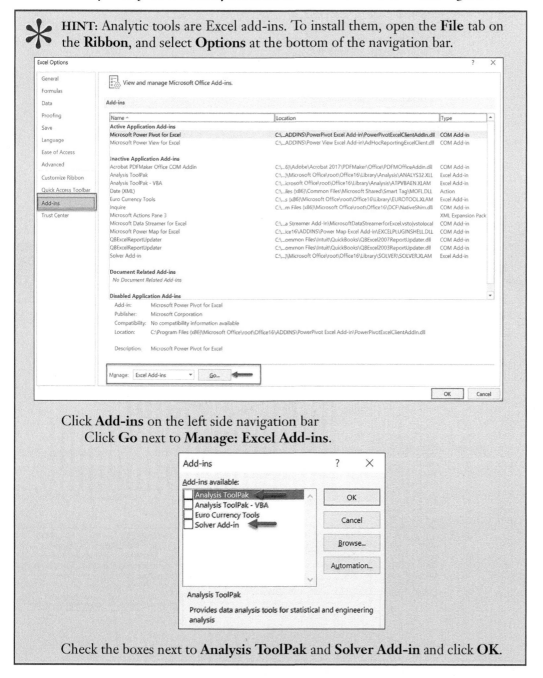

✳ HINT: Analytic tools are Excel add-ins. To install them, open the **File** tab on the **Ribbon**, and select **Options** at the bottom of the navigation bar.

Click **Add-ins** on the left side navigation bar
Click **Go** next to **Manage: Excel Add-ins**.

Check the boxes next to **Analysis ToolPak** and **Solver Add-in** and click **OK.**

Figure 14.4

Access to data analysis functions

Open the **Data** tab on the **Ribbon**. Both **Correlation** and **Regression** are found in the **Data Analysis** dropdown menu in the **Analyze** group.

Figure 14.5

Data Analysis menu

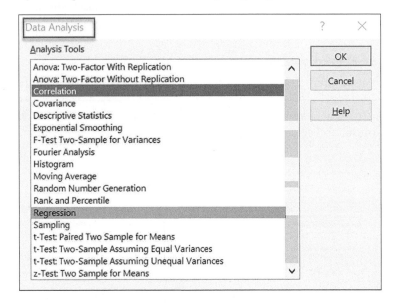

The **Correlation** function (**CORREL**) determines if two measurements vary together (increase or decrease in a similar pattern) and can be used in predictive analytics. Measures are grouped in columns or rows in an Excel worksheet. Excel will calculate the correlation percentage for every two-variable combination.

Figure 14.6

Correlation example

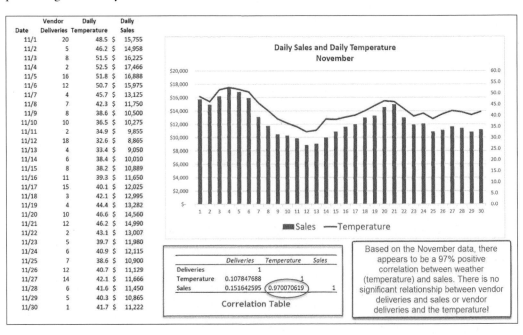

If, for example, sales revenue is found to increase when temperatures rise and decrease when temperatures fall (see Figure 14.6), a retail manager could predict changes in sales volume by paying close attention to weather forecasts!

The **Regression** function (**LINEST**) is also used to determine relationships. However, the end product of regression analysis is an equation that can be used to estimate a result. In accounting, regression analysis is often used to estimate total costs given changes in volume.

Figure 14.7

Regression example

Month	Machine Hours	Factory Utilities
January	3,050	$ 14,100
February	3,480	$ 15,750
March	3,980	$ 16,480
April	3,180	$ 14,925
May	5,010	$ 19,205
June	4,580	$ 17,725
July	4,790	$ 18,410
August	5,055	$ 19,085
September	4,695	$ 18,361
October	3,482	$ 15,280
November	3,062	$ 14,140
December	2,801	$ 13,475

Equation for estimating total factory utilities cost:
# of machine-hours X $2.43 + $6,854

SUMMARY OUTPUT

REGRESSION STATISTICS

Regression Statistics	
Multiple R	0.99454431
R Square	0.98911839
Adjusted R Squar	0.98803023
Standard Error	227.418811
Observations	12

Tells us that about 99% of the change in total utilities cost is related to changes in machine-hours

ANOVA

	df	SS	MS	F	Significance F
Regression	1	47011911.51	47011911.5	908.9817	3.7718E-11
Residual	10	517193.1543	51719.3154		
Total	11	47529104.67			

	Coefficients	Standard Error	t Stat	P-value	Lower 95%	Upper 95%	Lower 95.0%	Upper 95.0%
Intercept	6853.52051	323.7421505	21.1696886	1.23E-09	6132.17804	7574.863	6132.178	7574.86297
Machine Hours	2.43175562	0.080657054	30.1493235	3.772E-11	2.25204051	2.6114707	2.2520405	2.61147074

In Figure 14.7, regression analysis was used to estimate total monthly factory utilities costs given estimated machine-hours. The analysis found that there is a base monthly utility cost of approximately $6,854. (The base cost represents the minimum cost just to maintain services.) The total cost of utilities is expected to increase by roughly $2.43 for every machine-hour.

BEHIND THE SCENES Reviewing all the different regression statistics displayed in Figure 14.7 is beyond the scope of this book. For more information about the regression analysis, you might want to check out https://openstax.org/details/books/introductory-statistics, a free textbook published through OpenStax.

Forecasting Tool

Forecasting, another form of predictive analytics, can also be done in Excel. Forecasting uses historical data to estimate future results. In accounting, that data might be sales volume, sales dollars, profit, salaries, etc.

Forecasting can be done in Excel by adding **Trendlines** to line charts or by using the **Forecast Sheet** tool.

Figure 14.8

Chart menu

To add **trendlines** to line charts, highlight the historical data in the worksheet. Open the **Insert** tab on the **Ribbon** and click the line chart icon in the **Charts** group. Excel will automatically create a chart showing the historical data.

Figure 14.9

Trendline chart element

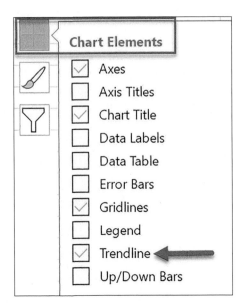

A **trendline** is added by checking the **Trendline** box on the **Chart Elements** menu. The number of forecasted periods is entered, and the type of trendline (linear, exponential, polynomial, etc.) is selected.

Figure 14.10

Example of a forecast using Trendline

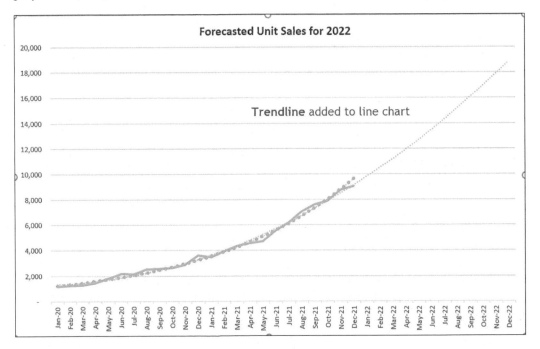

In Figure 14.10, a polynomial trendline was added to a chart created using monthly unit sales data from two prior years. The chart shows a sales forecast for December 2022 of approximately 19,000 units.

The second forecasting tool, the **Forecast Sheet**, is accessed by opening the **Data** tab on the **Ribbon** and clicking **Forecast Sheet** in the **Forecast** group.

Figure 14.11

Link to Forecast Sheet tool

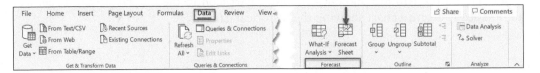

Forecast sheets present a range of forecasted results in chart form.

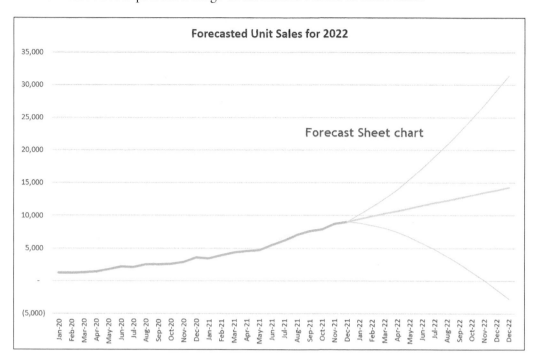

Figure 14.12

Example of a forecast
using Forecast Sheet

The data used to create the chart in Figure 14.10 was also used in Figure 14.12. It is not possible to change the type of trend line (linear, exponential, polynomial, etc.) in forecast sheets.

> **BEHIND THE SCENES** Both forecasts and budgets are tools used by management in planning for the future. Although they are often used together, there are distinct differences. A budget represents a plan for the future based on estimates of prices, costs, and volumes. A forecast represents likely results given past performance. Budgets are goals; forecasts are predictions.

Solver Tool

The **Solver** function is a prescriptive analytics tool in Excel. It's used to determine the best course of action given an objective and one or more constraints.

Figure 14.13

Access to Solver tool

Solver is accessed in the **Analyze** group on the **Data** tab in Excel.

Let's say a hardware store sells a number of different products. The physical size and the per-unit profit differ between products. The manager knows that it would take 44,343,925 cubic inches to store enough products to meet the monthly demand. Unfortunately, there's only 40,000,000 cubic inches of shelf space available! **Solver** can be used to determine the mix of products that maximizes profits.

Figure 14.14

Example of Solver

Products	Expected Demand per month	Profit Per Unit	Cubic Inches Per Unit	Solver Production Quantities	Total Cubic Inches	Total Profit	Prod < Demand
A1590	1,250	$ 37.70	1,680	1,250	2,100,000	$ 47,125.00	-
A1590S	1,375	$ 36.45	1,800	1,375	2,475,000	$ 50,118.75	-
A2000	1,550	$ 38.50	1,200	1,550	1,860,000	$ 59,675.00	-
A2000S	1,410	$ 38.90	1,400	1,410	1,974,000	$ 54,849.00	-
JK369	625	$ 36.50	2,045	-	-	$ -	625
JK745	750	$ 41.00	2,025	750	1,518,750	$ 30,750.00	-
LWW7891	3,125	$ 20.75	1,080	286	309,200	$ 5,940.65	2,839
LWW8025	3,250	$ 21.70	1,065	3,250	3,461,250	$ 70,525.00	-
LWW9338	3,000	$ 22.70	982	3,000	2,946,000	$ 68,100.00	-
LWW9799	3,400	$ 26.65	1,125	3,400	3,825,000	$ 90,610.00	-
R25	3,250	$ 9.35	280	3,250	910,000	$ 30,387.50	-
R28	7,500	$ 11.80	300	7,500	2,250,000	$ 88,500.00	-
R30	3,875	$ 15.25	310	3,875	1,201,250	$ 59,093.75	-
R25-D	7,500	$ 10.80	475	7,500	3,562,500	$ 81,000.00	-
R28-D	9,375	$ 13.25	490	9,375	4,593,750	$ 124,218.75	-
R30-D	6,250	$ 16.20	524	6,250	3,275,000	$ 101,250.00	-
TWZ225	1,560	$ 25.30	1,055	1,560	1,645,800	$ 39,468.00	-
TWZ399	1,875	$ 27.75	1,116	1,875	2,092,500	$ 52,031.25	-
					40,000,000	$ 1,053,642.65	

Objective: Maximize total profit
Constraints:
   1. Production for any specific product cannot exceed demand.
   2. Total cubic inches cannot exceed 40,000,000.

The objectives and the constraints were entered into the **Solver** dialog box. Excel's solution is displayed in Figure 14.14. To maximize profit, Excel suggests eliminating Product JK369 and carrying less than 300 LWW7891 units in stock.

 HINT: A store would not normally need to maintain a full month of stock on the shelf at any one point in time and would likely carry more than eighteen products! We've ignored reality a bit to provide you with a simple illustration of the **Solver** tool.

Analyze Data Tool

Excel added a new analytics tool a few years ago.

Figure 14.15

Analyze Data tool

Click anywhere in a set of data and click **Analyze Data** in the **Analysis** group on the **Home** tab. (It might also be called IDEAS or Data Analysis.)

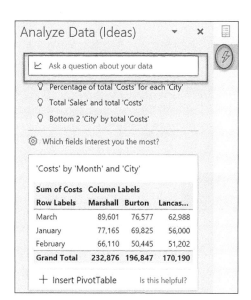

Figure 14.16

Analyze Data dialog box

Type a question into the **Ask a question about your data** field. Excel uses artificial intelligence (specifically natural language processing) to answer the question using charts and tables; no formulas are required! Excel will create charts and tables based on the data even if you don't enter a question! Sometimes the tables created automatically will highlight a relationship or trend you hadn't thought of; sometimes, the suggested tables or graphs are less useful.

There are many other analytics tools in Excel and other spreadsheet programs.

BEHIND THE SCENES The ETL process (Extract, Transform, and Load) discussed in Chapter 13 is done using the **Get & Transform Data** tool in Excel. (Get & Transform is also known as **Power Query**.)

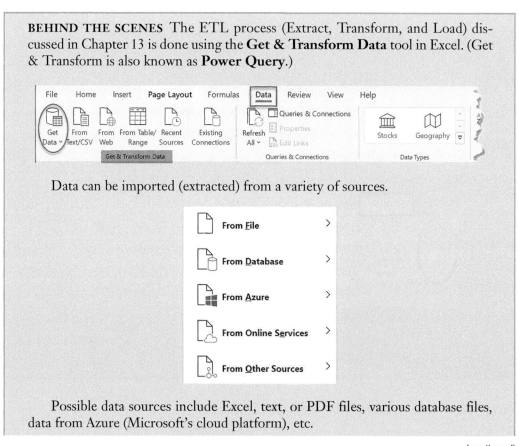

Data can be imported (extracted) from a variety of sources.

Possible data sources include Excel, text, or PDF files, various database files, data from Azure (Microsoft's cloud platform), etc.

(continued)

(continued from previous page)

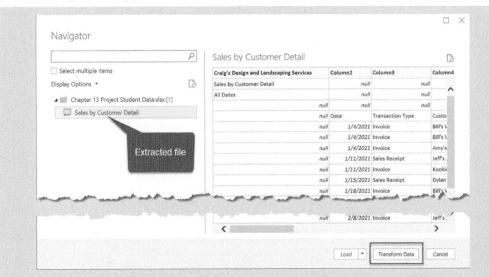

Once the data is extracted, data cleaning can be done by clicking **Transform Data.** Transforming the data is done in a dedicated window (Power Query Editor).

Using the Power Query Editor:

- data types can be changed

- columns can be added, split, or reformatted

- null rows can be deleted

- etc.

Each step is tracked.

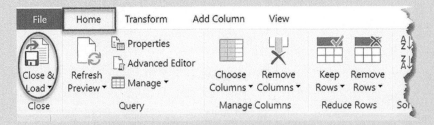

Once the data transformation is complete, Power Query takes a picture of the dataset and loads it into a new or existing Excel workbook for further analysis (creating PivotTables, using analysis functions, etc.).

Analysis Tools in Data Visualization Software

When it comes to data analysis, data visualization software is a tool for communicating results. It is not a replacement for spreadsheet software. Spreadsheet software like Excel includes built-in statistical and analytic functions like Solver, Correlation, and Regression described in the **Analysis Tools in Spreadsheet Programs** section of this chapter. Those types of functions don't exist in data visualization software (at least not yet!).

What data visualization software systems do very well is allow users to explore data interactively. That interaction can increase users' understanding of the data and result in insights that can be used in managing an organization.

A **visualization** is a visual representation of data. That might be a graph, a table, a chart, or even a map. Although visualizations can be created in spreadsheets, the process is faster and easier using data visualization software like Tableau or Microsoft's Power BI. (Figure 14.17 and Figure 14.18 are from Tableau.)

Visualization Graphical representation of data.

In both Tableau and Power BI:

- Large amounts of data from a variety of sources can be imported into files.

  - Data can come from Excel workbooks, PDFs, databases, websites, etc.

- Visualizations are created by dragging and dropping fields.

- Calculated fields can be created.

- Chart types and elements can be changed with a single click.

- Filters can be tied to single visualizations or multiple visualizations within the file.

- Multiple visualizations can be combined to create **dashboards**.

Dashboard Interactive set of related visualizations.

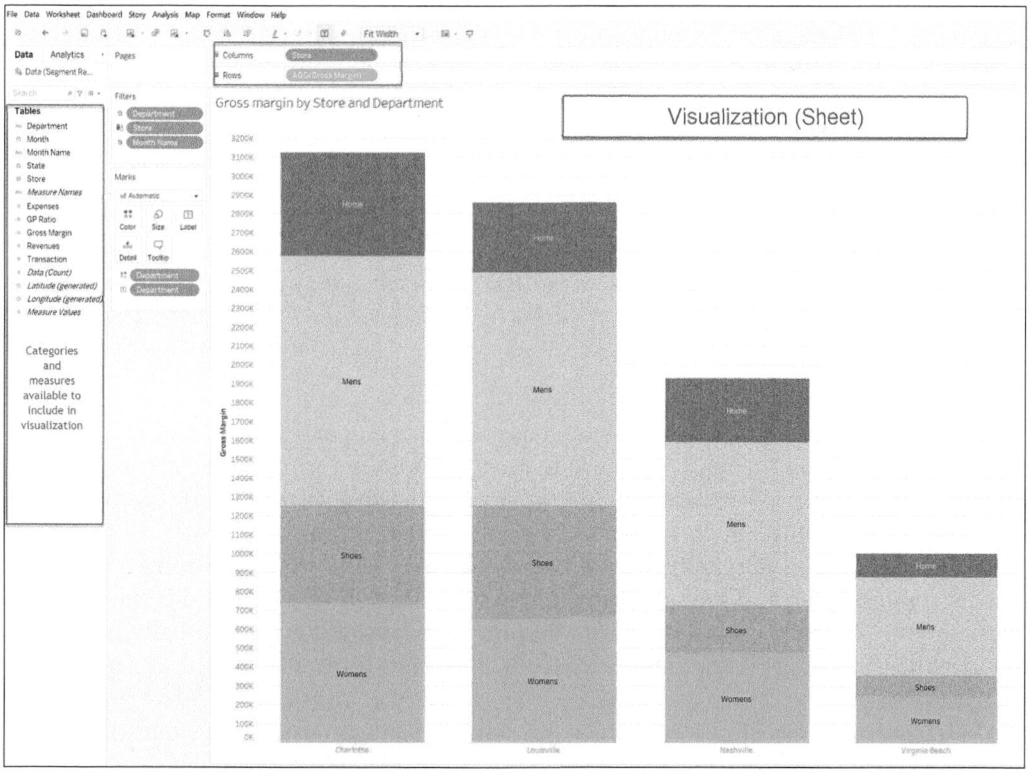

- Dashboards can be shared and used without affecting the underlying data.

- Security can be added to dashboards. For example, a store manager might be limited to data for a specific store; a regional manager might be limited to data for all stores in his or her region.

- Text can be added to a single visualization or a series of visualizations to create a data story.

Figure 14.17

Visualization worksheet

Using data visualization software is similar to creating a PivotTable in Excel and then turning it into a PivotChart.

- Fields are added to rows and columns.
- The chart type is selected.
  - Charts can be customized using labels, changing fonts and colors, etc.
- Filters can be selected.

Figure 14.18

Example of a Tableau Dashboard

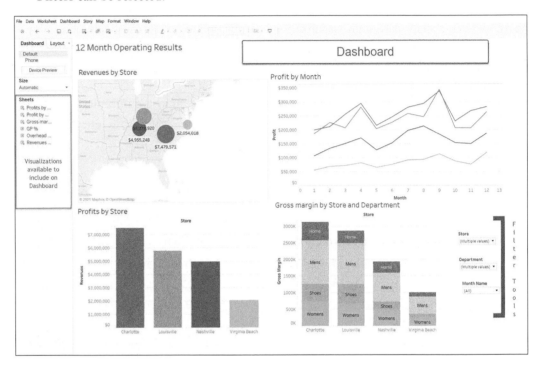

Dashboards consist of multiple visualizations. In Tableau, visualizations are created on separate pages (sheets). All or some are then selected to create the dashboard. The Performance Center in QBO Advanced is a dashboard.

BEST PRACTICES IN DATA VISUALIZATION

***Data analysis** is an exploratory process that often starts with specific questions. It requires curiosity, the desire to find answers, and a good level of tenacity because those answers aren't always easy to come by. **Data visualization** involves the visual representation of data, ranging from single charts to comprehensive dashboards. Effective visualizations significantly reduce the amount of time it takes for your audience to process information and access valuable insights.* [1]

Data visualization is all about making data accessible and understandable. You're probably familiar with the saying, "A picture is worth a thousand words." We could probably modify that to "Data visualizations are worth a thousand words." Better yet—"Well-designed visualizations and dashboards are worth at least a thousand words."

There are two basic types of visualizations. **Explanatory visualizations** are created to educate and inform. They can be a single visualization or a series of visualizations (sometimes referred to as a **datastory**). **Exploratory visualizations** (usually combined in a dashboard) are tools for further analysis. Filtering tools are critical in exploratory visualizations.

When creating visualizations, it helps to start by asking yourself a few questions.

---

[1] Murray, Eva, *What Is The Difference Between Data Analysis and Data Visualization?*, Forbes, March 29, 2019. (Eva Murray is one of thirty-four global Tableau Zen Masters.)

1. What is the purpose of the visualization? Will it be used to answer a question, explain a situation, or provide information that might generate new insights?

2. Who will be using the visualizations? Do they already have a solid understanding of the data that will be included? Will they need to be able to drill down on information? Should all users have access to all the data? Will the data need to be regularly updated?

Once you have the answers to those questions, you should be able to determine:

- the data that will be needed
- where to find that data (sources)
- whether a single visualization will suffice or whether you need to create a dashboard.

Select an Appropriate Chart Type

The next step is to select the appropriate visualizations. There are many different types of charts and graphs available in spreadsheet or data visualization software. The most common types are:

- Bar (horizontal) and column (vertical) charts
  - Often used to compare categories of data
- Line charts
  - Often used to show changes in data over time
- Pie charts
  - Often used to show data elements
- Scatter plots and bubble charts
  - Often used to show relationships between variables
- Map charts
  - Often used to illustrate differences in data volumes between geographic locations

Use Color to Highlight the Data

Color choices can help in highlighting important data.

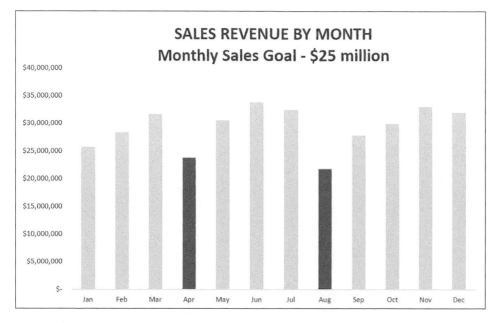

Figure 14.19

Color as highlighter

For example, in Figure 14.19, color is used to highlight the two months that did not meet the $25 million monthly sales goal.

Figure 14.20

Color as unifier

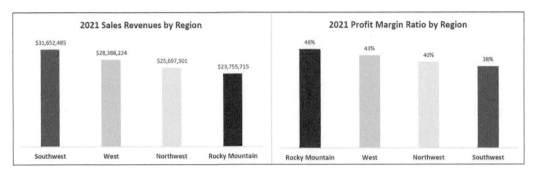

In dashboards, using the same color scheme in related visualizations can reduce the amount of effort needed to identify trends and anomalies. The dashboard in Figure 14.20 uses the same color for each sales region. Although the Southwest region generated the most sales dollars, it's easy to see that it had the lowest profit margin ratio. The opposite is true for the Rocky Mountain region.

Add Text to Explain and Add Context

Text is often added to visualizations, especially explanatory visualizations. Text can help prevent misinterpretation by clearly describing what's happening with the data. It can also summarize or highlight critical points, which can save user time. In exploratory visualizations, text can add context to the numbers. Dynamic texts (text that changes with the data) are particularly useful. Dynamic text boxes can be created in Excel, Tableau, and Power BI.

Remove Unnecessary Elements

The purpose of data visualization is to bring order to chaos, to allow a user to quickly read and understand multiple attributes of a particular issue, topic or data point.[2]

In visualizations, "less is more." Remove gridlines, axes titles, and legends if the message is clear without them. Effects like **3D format**, **shadow**, and **glow** can be distracting and are generally discouraged.

Make Sure the Visualizations are Objective and Balanced

Visualizations are powerful. They can provide clarity and stimulate discussion. They can also confuse or mislead, either intentionally or unintentionally.

Here are some examples of confusing or misleading visualizations:

Figure 14.21

Effect of changing axis range

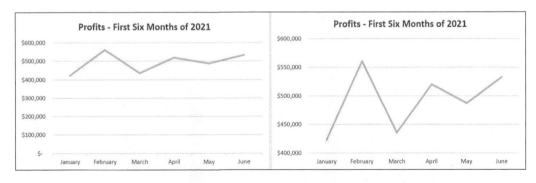

---

[2] Natoli, Joe, https://givegoodux.com/simplify-ui-data-visualizations-7-simple-steps/. (Joe Natoli is a UX (User experience) consultant, author, and speaker.)

In Figure 14.21, the vertical axis range in the chart on the right was shortened, starting at $400,000 instead of $0. That design choice overemphasized the volatility of month-to-month profit results.

Figure 14.22

Misuse of pie chart type

Pie charts can be an effective way to show relative elements of a whole. They can be less useful if the sum of the categories exceeds 100%! Figure 14.22 shows the results of a customer satisfaction survey. Forty thousand customers were asked to identify which customer services were important to them. They could choose more than one. It's clear from the chart that over 75% of the respondents chose online shopping as a preferred service. Still, it's not clear how many of those same respondents selected one or more other options, how many customers picked one option only, or whether there was a strong relationship between the size of the product line and either in-store or online shopping options.

BEYOND THE NUMBERS AND INTO THE FUTURE

By the time the school year is over (and even by the time this book is in print), technology will have changed and advanced even further. It is an exciting time as these advancements will open new opportunities for accounting students ready to merge their knowledge of accounting systems and processes with their understanding of technologies and innovations.

Newly developed software applications will bring more unstructured data into accounting systems, and businesses will be looking for accountants who can assist management with the analysis and interpretation of that data. Public accounting firms are increasing their use of analytics in their audits of financial statements and in the consulting services they provide and will need employees who are well versed in information technology.

In Robert Half's 2021 Accounting & Finance Salary Guide, the key technology skills listed were data analytics, protection and privacy (#2), advanced Excel (#5), financial modeling and forecasting (#6), and QuickBooks (#7). (Cloud-based payroll and human resource information systems was #1.) This should tell you something about the direction of the accounting profession! If possible, try to add some technology courses to your class schedule.

As you look forward to your future, think beyond the debits and credits. Start exploring the many new opportunities available to accountants and look for ways to develop and expand your technology skills.

CHAPTER REVIEW

Matching

Assignments with the MBC are available in myBusinessCourse.

Match the term or phrase (as used in this chapter) to its definition.

1. visualization
2. Fathom
3. predictive analytics
4. diagnostic analytics
5. dashboard
6. descriptive analytics
7. PivotTable
8. prescriptive analytics

_____ set of related visualizations in a single platform

_____ analysis focused on the identification of past trends

_____ analysis focused on determining the best course of action

_____ graphical representation of data

_____ analysis focused on forecasting results

_____ interactive summary of data

_____ analysis focused on identifying the reasons behind data results

_____ interactive analytics tool in QBO Advanced

Multiple Choice

1. The Correlation function in Excel _____.
   a. measures how closely one variable tracks another over time
   b. calculates the difference between two variables
   c. determines whether changes in one variable cause changes in another variable
   d. is used to forecast results in a future period

2. In QBO, a Budget vs Actuals report is an example of _____.
   a. Predictive analytics
   b. Prescriptive analytics
   c. Diagnostic analytics
   d. Descriptive analytics

3. Which type of chart would be the least useful in comparing sales revenue by product?
   a. Line chart
   b. Column chart
   c. Bar chart
   d. Pie chart

4. Your business is growing, and you want to apply for a bank loan for your growing business. What type of analytics would you most likely use to convince the lender that your company will be able to repay the loan?

   a. Descriptive

   b. Diagnostic

   c. Predictive

   d. Prescriptive

5. Which of the following cannot be done in the Transform function in Excel?

   a. Change the data type in a column

   b. Split data in a column

   c. Create a graph

   d. Remove columns or rows

BEYOND THE CLICKS—THINKING LIKE A MANAGER

Accounting: Clear Sights (an eyeglass manufacturer) has decided to develop a new commission structure for its sales representatives. What type(s) of data analytic(s) would be useful in this situation? What type of data would you need to include to perform that analysis?

Information Systems: Management has asked for a dashboard it can use to review and analyze operating results. You have information (by date and product) for units, revenues, and costs. Identify four visualizations that you think would be useful. What chart type would you choose for each?

ASSIGNMENT

This assignment has been created for students who have a strong understanding of Excel. If you are new to Excel, check with your instructor.

Assignment 14

   You are the accountant for Craig's Design and Landscaping. In May 2022, Craig lets you know that he is thinking about opening a new location as a way to expand his business. You offer to put together some information for him.

   Craig has been doing design work for customers outside of the San Francisco area where Craig's Design and Landscaping is located, so you decide to start by looking at recent sales data by geographic location.

- You export a sales activity report for the first four months of the year from QBO to Excel. You add the customer address to the file. **TIP:** Your export file is in Student Ancillaries on the Cambridge website (https://cambridgepub.com/book/qbo2021#ancillaries). The file includes transactions from the test-drive company (modified slightly) and transactions added for this project.

   TIP: Consider making a copy of the file before you start your assignment.

- You review the available data and decide that the following will be the most useful elements in your analysis:

  - Month

  - State and Zip Code of Customers

  - Sales amounts for each service and product sold

- You think you might be able to use transaction type, customer name, quantity, and sales price as well.

- You format the information in the dataset.
    - You delete unnecessary rows. (**TIP:** You'll need to keep a header row.)
    - You create a column for Month (spelled out) next to the Date column.
    - You only need the state and zip code for your analysis, so you parse the customer address field. **TIP:** State and zip code are in the nine digits on the far right of each cell. Excel's **Get & Transform** tool works well in this step as well as the next one.
        - You put state and zip code in separate columns. To properly sort, you format zip codes as text (5 digit minimum). You add leading 0s to any zip codes with less than 5 digits. **TIP:** Make sure you clear any white space in the new column fields.
    - You also parse the Product/Service column so you can easily sort information by product/service type.
        - **TIP:** Names in the Product/Service column include parent names. You are only interested in the item itself. For example, Rock Fountain is the item name in the field name Design:Fountains:Rock Fountain.

- **TIP:** If you used **Get & Transform** in the steps above, you may want to *unlink* the data (**Table Design** tab) after you **Close and load** the data to the new workbook. Check to make sure your fields are formatted correctly before moving on. (Text for state and zip code fields; number for quantity, sales price, and amount fields. Use two decimals for Sales price and amount fields.)

- You check for errors and inconsistencies in cells in the State and Sales Price columns and make the necessary corrections.
    - You assume blank State fields represent in-store sales. You use CA 94803 for those transactions.
    - You're not interested in discounts given to customers, so you remove any rows that include data related to those discounts in the Sales Price column. **TIP:** Percentages are used in determining discount amounts at Craig's (either 5% or 10%). If you used **Get & Transform** as a tool, the percentage cells in the original dataset would have been converted to decimals.

- You review the column titles and formats and modify them as needed. **TIP:** You'll be using the titles in reports, so you want them to be descriptive. **TIP:** If you used **Get & Transform**, cell formats might have changed to General when the file was closed and loaded. Date should be Short Date fields. state and zip code should be Text fields. Qty, Sales price, and Amount should be Number fields. (No decimals for quantity.)

- You delete any unnecessary columns. **TIP:** You previously identified Date, Month, Transaction type, Customer State, Zip Code, Product/Service, Qty, Sales price, and Amount as potentially useful elements for your analysis.

- **TIP:** You may want to consider saving a copy of your workbook at this point.

Analysis—Part 1

You decide to start by creating a **PivotTable** to look at sales amounts by state over the last four months organized greatest to least. You're interested in the type of services offered in each state as well. You display amounts with $ signs, no decimals.

1. Use the **PivotTable** to determine:
    a   Total Gardening sales in March, in dollars
    b   Total sales of Rock Fountains during the full four months, in dollars
    c   Percentage of overall sales from gardening services during the full four months

2. Use the **PivotTable** to answer the following questions:
    a Is there a location that could be eliminated from consideration? Why?
    b Do you have any concerns about Arizona as a possible location?

You realize that the report you just created doesn't provide information about the relative closeness of customers. Craig's Design and Landscaping offices are located near San Francisco. He could always open another location in the same general area, but you've already seen that Arizona may be a possibility, and you realize a location in Southern California may be an option as well. You decide to create another **PivotTable** to look at sales by Product/Service and by Zip Code.

3. Use the **PivotTable** to determine:
    a. The California zip code with the highest total Pest Control sales
    b. The zip code with the highest overall sales
    c. The zip code with the highest sales of sod in April

4. Should any analysis of potential locations focus on specific services or products? For example, until a new location is opened, gardening (lawn mowing, weeding, etc.) can only be done in northern California or through independent contractors. From experience, Craig knows that Design work often leads to ongoing gardening work.

You see that there are several California zip codes. You're looking for a location outside of the San Francisco area, so you decide to group all the zip codes by general location inside the table (Northern California, Southern California, Arizona, and New Jersey). **TIP:** All zip codes starting with 93 are in Southern California, all zip codes starting with 94 are in Northern California, all zip codes starting with 85 are in the Tucson area of Arizona.

5. Use the **PivotTable** to determine:
    a. The area with the highest Design revenue.
    b. Average gardening revenue in Northern California in March

6. Use the **PivotTable** to answer the following questions:
    a. Which area appears to be the most promising site for a new location? Why? Use the data to support your opinion.
    b. If Craig decided to open his new location in that area, where (which zip code) might make the most sense (based strictly on your analysis)? What other factors might be considered?

Analysis—Part 2

If you have access to Office 365 (Windows or Mac), you can access the **Analyze Data** feature. (It might also be called **Ideas** or **Data Analysis**.) This feature uses artificial intelligence to:

● Automatically analyze data and provide insights into possible trends or relationships.

● Answer user questions about the data without the need to create formulas. (Natural Language processing tools are used in the **Analyze Data** tool.)

All columns of data are initially used in suggesting reports or providing insights.

● Open the data worksheet. Click **Analyze Data** on the **Home** tab.

1. What suggested report or insight is an example of:
    a. descriptive analytics?
    b. diagnostic analytics?

You can also direct the **Analyze Data** tool to look at specific elements.

- Click **Which fields interest you the most?** near the top of the sidebar. Select Customer, State, Zip Code, and Amount. Change Amount to Average in the **Summarize value by** dropdown menu.

2. Using the reports suggested in **Analyze Data**, what was the state with the highest **average** amount of sales?

- Reselect all fields.

The **Ask a question about your data** field allows you to get a quick answer without creating much effort!

- Enter the following question in the **Ask a question about your data** field: "Which customer has the highest total amount during the period?"

3. What was the answer provided in the displayed report(s)?

NOTE: The usefulness of the **Ask a question about your data** tool depends, in part, on how carefully you word the question.

- Enter the following question in the **Ask a question about your data** field: "What percentage of total sales is generated by the sale of Rock Fountains?"

4. What was the answer provided in the displayed report(s)? (Note the percentage and field used in determining the percentage.)

- Change the question to "What percentage of the total amount is generated from Rock Fountains?"

5. What was the answer provided in the displayed report(s)? (Note the percentage and field used in determining the percentage.)

6. Which of Excel's answers was correct (gave you the answer you were looking for)?

APPENDIX

Is Computerized Accounting Really the Same as Manual Accounting?

Accounting equation An expression of the equivalency of the economic resources and the claims upon those resources of a business, often stated as Assets = Liabilities + Stockholders' Equity.

Journal entries An entry of accounting information into a journal.

Debits An entry on the left side (or in the debit column) of an account.

Credits An entry on the right side (or in the credit column) of an account.

Before we compare the two, let's briefly review the basics of accounting.

Accounting is an information system. The primary purposes of the system are:

- To identify and record accounting transactions
- To analyze, summarize, and report information about business activities

We identify accounting transactions by considering the impact, if any, of an economic event on the **accounting equation** (Assets = Liabilities + Equity). If any of the elements in the equation (assets, liabilities, or equity) change as the result of the event, it's an accounting transaction and must be recorded.

> **BEHIND THE SCENES** Assets are resources with future benefit that the entity owns or has a right to. Liabilities are obligations of the entity payable with money, product, or service. Equity represents owner claims on the assets of the entity. Equity includes owner investments in the company plus any undistributed earnings. The components of earnings are revenues and expenses.

We record accounting transactions using the double-entry bookkeeping system. Accounting transactions are expressed as **journal entries**. Each journal entry includes the date of the transaction, the names of the accounts to be debited and credited, and the amounts. Every journal entry must balance (the sum of the debit amounts must equal the sum of the credit amounts) so that the accounting equation stays in balance. **Debits** increase the left side of the equation; **credits** increase the right side of the equation. Debits decrease the right side of the equation; credits decrease the left side of the equation.

The entries are then recorded in (posted to) the appropriate accounts. All the accounts and all the activity in the accounts are collectively known as the general ledger. Accounts are often depicted like this (referred to as T-accounts):

A-1

Account Name

Debit	Credit

Accrual basis of accounting Accounting method whereby sales revenue is recorded when earned and realized and expenses are recorded in the period in which they help to generate the sales revenue.

Cash basis of accounting Accounting method whereby sales revenue is recorded when cash is received from operating activities and expenses are recorded when cash payments related to operating activities are made.

To understand when and how journal entries are made, you need to know the method of accounting being used by the entity. The two primary methods are the **accrual basis of accounting** and the **cash basis of accounting**.

There are a few basic accounting principles that are fundamental to understanding when to record revenue and expenses under the accrual method of accounting. These are part of the body of generally accepted accounting principles (GAAP) that guide accountants.

- **Revenue recognition principle**—Revenue should be recognized when the earnings process is complete and collectibility of the revenue is reasonably certain.

- **Expense recognition (matching) principle**—Expenses should be recognized in the same period as the related revenue. In other words, expenses incurred to generate revenue should be recognized with the revenue generated.

Under the cash basis of accounting, revenue is recognized when collected and expenses are recognized when paid. The cash basis of accounting is not allowed under GAAP but cash-based reports can provide useful information to management so some companies prepare both accrual and cash-based reports.

The primary way we summarize and report information about business activities is through the preparation of four basic financial statements. These statements are issued at the end of an accounting period (generally a month, quarter, or year).

- The balance sheet presents the financial condition of the entity at a point in time.
  - All asset, liability, and equity accounts appear on the balance sheet.
  - The balance sheet is also known as the statement of financial position.

- The income statement presents the operating results of the entity for a period of time.
  - All revenue and expense accounts appear on the income statement.
  - The income statement is also known as the profit and loss statement or statement of operations.

- The statement of cash flows presents the cash inflows and outflows over a period of time.
  - The cash flows are grouped into three categories: operating activities, investing activities, and financing activities.

- The statement of stockholders' (or owner's) equity presents the changes in equity during a period of time.
  - The changes would include any additional investments from owners, any distributions to owners, and operating earnings (or losses) during the period.

ACCRUAL AND CASH BASIS ACCOUNTING IN QUICKBOOKS ONLINE

Most companies use the accrual basis of accounting.

You can choose, however, to use the cash basis for reporting transactions in QBO. This is done on the **Advanced** tab of **Account and Settings** (accessed by clicking the ⚙ on the icon bar).

Click **Accounting method**.

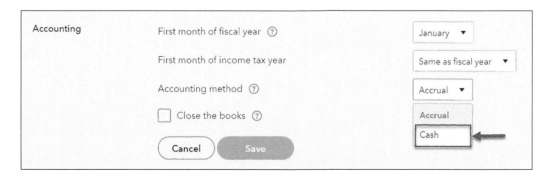

Select **Cash** in the dropdown menu next to **Accounting method**.

Click **Save** to complete the change of method.

Although most reports will now default to the cash basis, there are some reports that automatically default to the accrual method even when the user has selected cash as the preferred method. Taxable sales summary and detail reports are examples of reports that always default to the accrual method.

Users can also convert an accrual basis report to the cash basis by customizing the report. A condensed **Profit and Loss** report converted to the cash basis might look something like this:

Figure AppA.3

Example of collapsed profit and loss report on Cash basis.

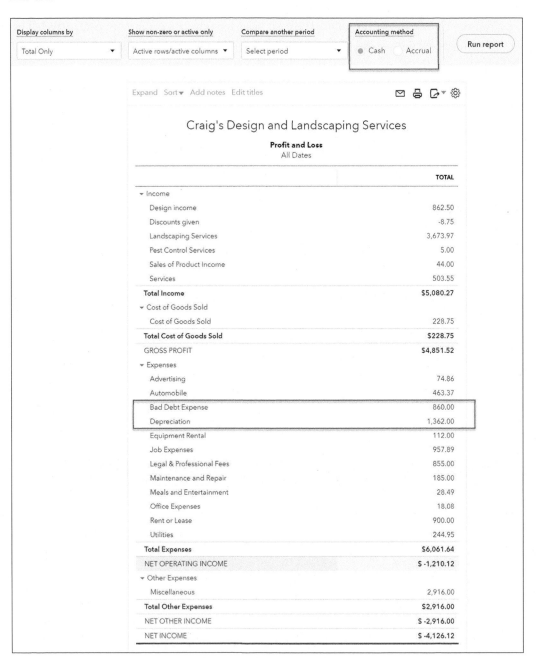

Display columns by	Show non-zero or active only	Compare another period	Accounting method	
Total Only ▼	Active rows/active columns ▼	Select period ▼	● Cash ○ Accrual	Run report

Expand Sort ▼ Add notes Edit titles

Craig's Design and Landscaping Services

Profit and Loss
All Dates

	TOTAL
▾ Income	
Design income	862.50
Discounts given	-8.75
Landscaping Services	3,673.97
Pest Control Services	5.00
Sales of Product Income	44.00
Services	503.55
Total Income	**$5,080.27**
▾ Cost of Goods Sold	
Cost of Goods Sold	228.75
Total Cost of Goods Sold	**$228.75**
GROSS PROFIT	**$4,851.52**
▾ Expenses	
Advertising	74.86
Automobile	463.37
Bad Debt Expense	860.00
Depreciation	1,362.00
Equipment Rental	112.00
Job Expenses	957.89
Legal & Professional Fees	855.00
Maintenance and Repair	185.00
Meals and Entertainment	28.49
Office Expenses	18.08
Rent or Lease	900.00
Utilities	244.95
Total Expenses	**$6,061.64**
NET OPERATING INCOME	**$ -1,210.12**
▾ Other Expenses	
Miscellaneous	2,916.00
Total Other Expenses	**$2,916.00**
NET OTHER INCOME	**$ -2,916.00**
NET INCOME	**$ -4,126.12**

There are some issues with converting accrual reports to cash basis reports. As you can see in Figure AppA.3, certain non-cash accounts like Depreciation and Bad Debt expense appear on the cash-basis **Profit and Loss** report. Also, if prepaid or accrued expenses had been recorded on the accrual basis, QBO would not adjust them in the conversion process. These issues result in inaccurate reports.

The best solution is to create the accrual basis reports in QBO, export them to Excel, and then make any additional adjustments necessary to fully convert from accrual to cash.

COMPARISON OF COMPUTERIZED AND MANUAL ACCOUNTING SYSTEMS

As stated in Chapter 1, a computerized accounting system is **fundamentally** the same as a manual accounting system. If that's true, we should be able to find the same journal entries, journals, general ledger accounts (T-accounts), and trial balances in QBO that you would find in a manual system, right? They might look a little different but they should be there.

Journal Entries

As you've learned, QBO creates a journal entry for almost every *form* completed by the user. Let's take a look at the entry underlying Invoice #1036.

Figure AppA.4

Search tool on icon bar

Click the magnifying glass on the icon bar.

Figure AppA.5

Simple search example

Enter "1036" in the search field and press Enter.

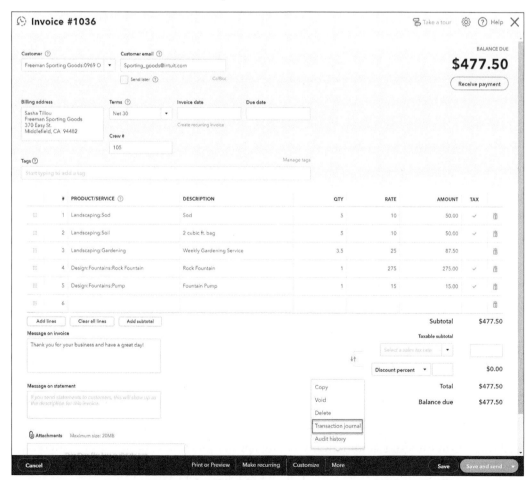

Figure AppA.6

Link to underlying journal entry

Click **More** and select **Transaction journal**.

Craig's Design and Landscaping Services
Journal
All Dates

TRANSACTION TYPE	NUM	NAME	MEMO/DESCRIPTION	ACCOUNT	DEBIT	CREDIT
Invoice	1036	Freeman Sporting Goods:0969 …		Accounts Receivable (A/R)	$477.50	
			Sod	Landscaping Services:Job Mater...		$50.00
			2 cubic ft. bag	Landscaping Services:Job Mater...		$50.00
			Weekly Gardening Service	Landscaping Services		$87.50
			Rock Fountain	Cost of Goods Sold	$125.00	
			Rock Fountain	Inventory Asset		$125.00
			Rock Fountain	Sales of Product Income		$275.00
			Fountain Pump	Inventory Asset		$10.00
			Fountain Pump	Cost of Goods Sold	$10.00	
			Fountain Pump	Sales of Product Income		$15.00
					$612.50	$612.50
TOTAL					$612.50	$612.50

This is the journal entry that was created when Invoice #1036 was entered.

Journals

In manual systems, separate journals (sometimes called special journals) are maintained for different types of transactions (sales, purchases, etc.). This simply makes it easier for the user when entering transactions. Special journals are used so that transactions for the period (usually a month) can be posted in summary (instead of in detail) to the general ledger. In QBO, each transaction (in detail) is automatically posted to the general ledger so special journals aren't needed to simplify posting.

As an example, the Sales Journal might look something like this in a manual system:

Date	Customer	Invoice #	A/R (DR)	Design income (CR)	Landscaping Services (CR)	Job Materials (CR)	Sales Tax Payable (CR)
	John Melton	1007	750.00	750.00			
	Amy's Bird Sanctuary	1021	459.00			425.00	34.00
	Jeff's Jalopies	1022	81.00		75.00		6.00
	TOTALS		1,290.00	750.00	75.00	425.00	40.00

Each transaction is recorded, in full, on a separate line instead of in journal entry form. In journal entry form, the first line (Invoice #1007) would be:

	Accounts receivable	750.00	
	Design Income		750.00

At the end of the period, the columns are totaled and all the sales transactions are recorded in one single journal entry as follows:

	Accounts Receivable	1,290.00	
	Design Income		750.00
	Landscaping Services		75.00
	Job Materials		425.00
	Sales Tax Payable		34.00

Although QBO doesn't automatically create special journal reports, a user can create a similar report fairly easily. These reports can be saved so they can be easily accessed every month. (Saving customized reports is covered in Chapter 11.)

A **Transaction Detail By Account** report customized to show specific **Invoice** transactions for a period of time and with Debit and Credit columns added would look something like this:

Craig's Design and Landscaping Services
Sales Journal

DATE	TRANSACTION TYPE	NUM	NAME	DEBIT	CREDIT
▾ Accounts Receivable (A/R)					
01/12/2021	Invoice	1019	Sushi by Katsuyuki	$80.00	
01/12/2021	Invoice	1010	Weiskopf Consulting	$375.00	
01/12/2021	Invoice	1023	Red Rock Diner	$70.00	
Total for Accounts Receivable (A/R)				$525.00	
▾ Design income					
01/12/2021	Invoice	1010	Weiskopf Consulting		$375.00
Total for Design income					$375.00
▸ Landscaping Services					$80.00
▾ Pest Control Services					
01/12/2021	Invoice	1023	Red Rock Diner		$70.00
Total for Pest Control Services					$70.00

The accounts are listed in rows instead of columns in the QBO Sales Journal but the basic information is the same.

General Ledger and T-Accounts

There is, of course, a general ledger in QBO. You can easily create a report to see the individual activity in a specific account in QBO. It doesn't look exactly like a T-account but it is close.

Click **Reports** on the navigation bar.

Click **General Ledger** in the **For my accountant** section. A report customized to show the Checking account for a period of time and to include Debit and Credit columns (other columns removed) would look something like this:

Craig's Design and Landscaping Services
General Ledger

DATE	TRANSACTION TYPE	NUM	NAME	DEBIT	CREDIT	BALANCE
▾ Checking						
Beginning Balance						3,752.61
01/08/2021	Expense	13	Hicks Hardware		$215.66	3,536.95
01/08/2021	Check	2	Mahoney Mugs		$18.08	3,518.87
01/09/2021	Sales Receipt	1003	Dylan Sollfrank	$337.50		3,856.37
01/10/2021	Cash Expense		Bob's Burger Joint		$3.86	3,852.51
01/11/2021	Bill Payment (Check)	1	Brosnahan Insurance Agency		$2,000.00	1,852.51
01/12/2021	Refund	1020	Pye's Cakes		$87.50	1,765.01
01/12/2021	Deposit			$218.75		1,983.76
01/12/2021	Bill Payment (Check)	3	Books by Bessie		$75.00	1,908.76
01/12/2021	Payment	2064	Travis Waldron	$103.55		2,012.31
01/12/2021	Check	Debit	Squeaky Kleen Car Wash		$19.99	1,992.32
01/12/2021	Payment		Freeman Sporting Goods:55 Twi...	$50.00		2,042.32
01/13/2021	Cash Expense		Chin's Gas and Oil		$63.15	1,979.17
01/13/2021	Bill Payment (Check)	45	Tim Philip Masonry		$666.00	1,313.17
01/13/2021	Bill Payment (Check)	6	PG&E		$114.09	1,199.08
01/13/2021	Deposit			$408.00		1,607.08
01/13/2021	Expense	108	Tania's Nursery		$46.98	1,560.10
01/14/2021	Expense	76	Pam Seitz		$75.00	1,485.10
01/14/2021	Check	75	Hicks Hardware		$228.75	1,256.35
01/14/2021	Deposit			$868.15		2,124.50
01/17/2021	Cash Expense		Tania's Nursery		$23.50	2,101.00
Total for Checking				$1,985.95	$3,637.56	

As you can see in Figure AppA.9, the balances of the T-accounts are shown in a separate column in QBO instead of at the bottom of each T-account. That might be a slightly different format than the T-accounts you're familiar with from your financial accounting courses but the information is the same.

Trial Balances

A trial balance is a report listing all the accounts and their balances at a point in time. In a manual system, trial balances are prepared for two primary reasons:

- To make sure the debits equal the credits in the general ledger.

- To use as a worksheet for preparing the financial statements.

In a computerized system like QBO, users don't need a trial balance for those reasons. Why? First, the program will not allow the user to create an unbalanced entry. (Unless, of course, the system malfunctions!) Second, QBO prepares the financial statements automatically.

Trial balance reports are available in QBO, however, and can be useful for other reasons.

Trial Balance reports are accessed in the **For my accountant** section of **Reports**. The report looks something like this:

Figure AppA.10

Example of a trial balance report

Craig's Design and Landscaping Services		
Trial Balance		
	DEBIT	CREDIT
Checking	4,195.75	
Accounts Receivable (A/R)	5,013.02	
Undeposited Funds	687.15	
Truck:Original Cost	13,495.00	
Accounts Payable (A/P)		1,972.39
Mastercard		366.09
Board of Equalization Payable		231.92
Opening Balance Equity		18,495.00
Retained Earnings		195.18
Landscaping Services		205.00
Landscaping Services:Job Materials:Plants and ...		1,695.08
Sales of Product Income		44.00
Services		400.00
Automobile	19.99	
Job Expenses:Job Materials:Decks and Patios	88.09	
Legal & Professional Fees:Lawyer	100.00	
Meals and Entertainment	5.66	
TOTAL	$23,604.66	$23,604.66

BEHIND THE SCENES It's really only the ending date that determines the amounts on a trial balance report. If you entered 12/31/21 to 12/31/21, you would get the same amounts as you got entering 6/30/21 to 12/31/21. Remember, a trial balance shows us the account balances at a point in time (not period of time). However, entering a specific period does give you the option of clicking on an amount and seeing the transactions that occurred during the identified period.

APPENDIX

B

Account Types and Common Transaction Types Used in QBO

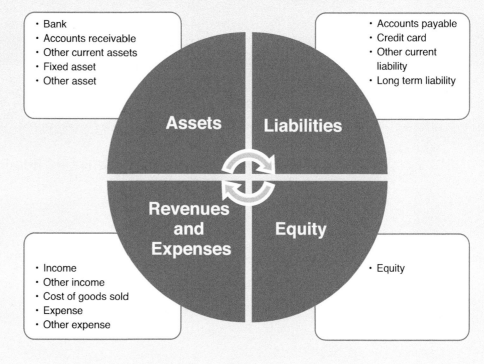

QuickBooks Account Types Grouped by Accounting Element

- Bank
- Accounts receivable
- Other current assets
- Fixed asset
- Other asset

- Accounts payable
- Credit card
- Other current liability
- Long term liability

Assets

Liabilities

Revenues and Expenses

Equity

- Income
- Other income
- Cost of goods sold
- Expense
- Other expense

- Equity

Common Transaction Types	Description
Bill	Bill received from vendor for purchase on account
Bill payment	Payment on vendor balance by cash/check/credit card
Charge	Pending customer charge
Check	Direct payment (not including payroll checks, payments on vendor balances, payments of payroll or sales taxes)
Credit	Pending customer credit
Credit card credit	Credit from vendor on credit card purchase
Credit memo	Credit given to customer (cash or credit sales)
Deposit	Bank deposit
Estimate	Estimate of fees
Expense	Direct payment generally made using a credit card
Inventory qty adjust	Adjustment to inventory quantity
Invoice	Sale on account
Journal entry	General journal entry
Liability payment	Payment of payroll liability
Paycheck	Employee payroll check
Payment	Customer payment on account balance
Purchase order	Order to vendor
Refund	Refund to customer
Sales receipt	Cash sale
Sales tax payment	Remittance of state sales taxes
Statement	Direct charge to customer account balance
Transfer	Transfers between cash accounts
Vendor credit	Credit received from vendor

Note: There are a few other transaction types in QBO that are not listed here.

APPENDIX

Common Options Available on Various Forms

🕐—Allows you to view recent transactions of the same type

✖—Allows you to exit out of the form

Audit history (on **More** dropdown menu)—Allows you to view the history of the transaction (date entered/modified, user name, etc.)

Cancel– Allows you to "erase" all the data entered on the form. This would only be used in the initial creation of the form.

Copy (on **More** dropdown menu)—Allows you to make a duplicate of the form

Delete (on **More** dropdown menu)—Allows you to delete the transaction

Make recurring—Allows you to memorize the form for later use

Mark as paid—Allows you to access a **bill payment** form directly from a saved **bill** form

Print or Preview—Allows you to print or view the form (Available on all sales forms. Print option is available on Purchase order and Check forms.)

Revert—Allows you to return to the original saved form. This is only available when you open a saved form, make changes, and want to undo those changes. This would not be available if you had already saved the new version.

Save—Allows you to save the current form without exiting

Save and close—Allows you to save the current form and exit

Save and new—Allows you to save the current form and open a new form of the same type

Save and schedule payment—Allows you to schedule a payment date for **bills**. Only available for users with a bank connection set up in QBO

Save and send—Allows you to save the current form and forward it to the customer via email (Also available on Purchase order forms.)

Transaction journal (on **More** dropdown menu)—Allows you to view the journal entry underlying the form

Void (on **More** dropdown menu)—Allows you to erase the amounts on the form but keep the remaining data

Quick Reference Guide To Accounting Terms

A

Account A record of the additions, deductions, and balances of individual assets, liabilities, equities, revenues, and expenses.

Accounting The process of measuring the economic activity of a business in money terms and communicating those financial results to interested parties. The purpose of accounting is to provide financial information that is useful in economic decision making.

Accounting equation An expression of the equivalency of the economic resources and the claims upon those resources of a business, often stated as Assets = Liabilities + Stockholders' Equity.

Accounting period The time period, usually one year or less, to which periodic accounting reports are related.

Accounting transaction An economic event that requires accounting recognition; an event that affects any of the elements of the accounting equation—assets, liabilities, or stockholders' equity.

Accounts receivable A current asset that is created by a sale of merchandise or the provision of a service on a credit basis. It represents the amount owed the seller by a customer.

Accrual basis of accounting Accounting method where revenue is recognized when earned and expenses are recognized when incurred or used.

Accrual entries Adjustments made to recognize revenues earned but not recorded and expenses incurred but not recorded.

Allowance for doubtful accounts A contra-asset account with a normal credit balance shown on the balance sheet as a deduction from accounts receivable to reflect the expected uncollectible amount of accounts receivable.

Allowance method An accounting procedure whereby the amount of bad debts expense is estimated and recorded in the period in which the related credit sales occur.

Assets The economic resources of a business that can be expressed in money terms.

B

Bad debt expense The expense stemming from the inability of a business to collect an amount previously recorded as receivable. It is normally classified as a selling or administrative expense.

Balance sheet A financial statement showing a business's assets, liabilities, and equity as of a specific date.

C

Cash basis of accounting Accounting method where revenue is recognized when payment is received and expenses are recognized when paid.

Classified balance sheet A balance sheet in which items are classified into subgroups to facilitate financial analysis and management decision making.

Closing process A step in the accounting cycle in which the balances of all temporary accounts are transferred to the Retained Earnings account, leaving the temporary accounts with zero balances.

Contra account An account with the opposite normal balance as other accounts of the same type.

Corporation A legal entity created under the laws of a state or the federal government. The owners of a corporation receive shares of stock as evidence of their ownership interest in the company.

Credit (entry) An entry on the right side (or in the credit column) of an account.

Credit memo A document prepared by a seller to inform the purchaser the seller has reduced the amount owed by the purchaser due to a return or an allowance.

D

Debit (entry) An entry on the left side (or in the debit column) of an account.

Deferral entries Adjustments made to postpone recognition of revenue received but not yet earned and recognition of expenses paid but not yet incurred.

Direct write-off method An accounting procedure whereby the amount of bad debts expense is not recorded until specific uncollectible customer accounts are identified.

Double-entry accounting A method of accounting that results in the recording of equal amounts of debits and credits.

E

Equity The residual interest in the assets of a business after all liabilities have been paid off; it is equal to a firm's net assets, or total assets less total liabilities.

F

First-in, first-out (FIFO) method An inventory costing method that assumes that the oldest (earliest purchased) goods are sold first.

Fiscal year The annual accounting period used by a business.

Fraud Any act by the management or employees of a business involving an intentional deception for personal gain.

G

General ledger A grouping of all of a business's accounts that are used to prepare the basic financial statements.

Gross pay The amount an employee earns before any withholdings or deductions.

I

Income statement A financial statement reporting a business's sales revenue and expenses for a given period of time.

Internal controls The measures undertaken by a company to ensure the reliability of its accounting data, protect its assets from theft or unauthorized use, insure that employees follow the company's policies and procedures, and evaluate the performance of employees, departments, divisions, and the company as a whole.

J

Journal A tabular record in which business transactions are analyzed in debit and credit terms and recorded in chronological order.

Journal entry An entry of accounting information into a journal.

L

Last-in, first-out (LIFO) method An inventory costing method that assumes that the newest (most recently purchased) goods are sold first.

Liabilities The obligations or debts that a business must pay in money or services at some time in the future as a consequence of past transactions or events.

Lower of cost or net realizable value A measurement method that, when applied to inventory, provides for ending inventory to be valued on the balance sheet at the lower of its cost (calculated under FIFO, weighted average, or specific identification methods) or its estimated selling price (net of any expected direct selling costs).

M

Materiality An accounting guideline that states that insignificant data that would not affect a financial statement user's decisions may be recorded in the most expedient manner.

Multi-step income statement An income statement in which one or more intermediate performance measures, such as gross profit on sales, are derived before the continuing income is reported.

N

Net pay The amount of an employee's paycheck, after subtracting withheld amounts.

Normal balance The side (debit or credit) on which increases to the account are recorded.

P

Partnership A voluntary association of two or more persons for the purpose of conducting a business.

Periodic inventory A system that records inventory purchase transactions; the Inventory account and the cost of goods sold account are not updated until the end of the period when a physical count of the inventory is taken.

Permanent account An account that is not closed at the end of each fiscal year. Permanent accounts include all asset and liability accounts. All equity accounts other than drawing (dividend) accounts are also permanent accounts.

Perpetual inventory A system that records the cost of merchandise inventory in the Inventory account at the time of purchase and updates the Inventory account for subsequent purchases and sales of merchandise as they occur.

R

Reorder point The minimum level of inventory on hand that can safely meet demand until a new inventory order is received.

S

Sale on account A sale of merchandise or the provision of a service made on a credit basis.

Segment A subdivision of an entity for which supplemental financial information is disclosed.

Sole proprietorship A form of business organization in which one person owns the business.

Statement of cash flows A financial statement showing a firm's cash inflows and cash outflows for a specific period, classified into operating, investing, and financing activity categories.

Statement of stockholders' equity A financial statement presenting information regarding the events that cause a change in stockholders' equity during a period. The statement presents the beginning balance, additions to, deductions from, and the ending balance of stockholders' equity for the period.

Stock Inventory on hand.

Subsidiary ledger A ledger that provides detailed information about an account balance.

T

Temporary account Account that is closed to a capital account at the end of each fiscal year. Temporary accounts include revenue, expense, and drawing (dividend) accounts.

Trial balance A list of the account titles in the general ledger, their respective debit or credit balances, and the totals of the debit and credit balances.

INDEX

A

B

C

F

Q

W

Y